ESOTERIC PSYCHOLOGY

VOLUME TWO

BOOKS BY ALICE A. BAILEY

ESOTERIC PSYCHOLOGY

VOLUME II

A TREATISE ON THE SEVEN RAYS

by

ALICE A. BAILEY

LUCIS PUBLISHING COMPANY
New York

LUCIS PRESS, LTD.
London

First Printing, 1942
Fifth Printing, 1970 (First Paperback Edition)
Eleventh Printing, 1995

ISBN No. 0-85330-119-0
Library of Congress Catalog Card Number: 53-019914

The publication of this book is financed by the Tibetan Book Fund which is established for the perpetuation of the teachings of the Tibetan and Alice A. Bailey.

This Fund is controlled by the Lucis Trust, a tax-exempt, religious, educational corporation.

The Lucis Publishing Company is a non-profit organisation owned by the Lucis Trust. No royalties are paid on this book.

This title is also available in a clothbound edition.

It has been translated into Danish, Dutch, French, German, Italian, Portuguese, Spanish, and Swedish. Translation into other languages is proceeding.

LUCIS PUBLISHING COMPANY
120 Wall Street
New York, NY 10005

LUCIS PRESS, LTD.
Suite 54
3 Whitehall Court
London SW1A 2EF

MANUFACTURED IN THE UNITED STATES OF AMERICA
By FORT ORANGE PRESS, INC., Albany, NY

SYNOPSIS OF
A TREATISE ON THE SEVEN RAYS

EXTRACT FROM A STATEMENT BY
THE TIBETAN

Suffice it to say, that I am a Tibetan disciple of a certain degree, and this tells you but little, for all are disciples from the humblest aspirant up to, and beyond, the Christ Himself. I live in a physical body like other men, on the borders of Tibet, and at times (from the exoteric standpoint) preside over a large group of Tibetan lamas, when my other duties permit. It is this fact that has caused it to be reported that I am an abbot of this particular lamasery. Those associated with me in the work of the Hierarchy (and all true disciples are associated in this work) know me by still another name and office. A.A.B. knows who I am and recognises me by two of my names.

I am a brother of yours, who has travelled a little longer upon the Path than has the average student, and has therefore incurred greater responsibilities. I am one who has wrestled and fought his way into a greater measure of light than has the aspirant who will read this article, and I must therefore act as a transmitter of the light, no matter what the cost. I am not an old man, as age counts among the teachers, yet I am not young or inexperienced. My work is to teach and spread the knowledge of the Ageless Wisdom wherever I can find a response, and I have been doing this for many years. I seek also to help the Master M. and the Master K.H. whenever opportunity offers, for I have been long connected with Them and with Their work. In all the above, I have told you much; yet at the same time I have told you nothing which would lead you to offer me that blind obedience and the foolish devotion which the emotional aspirant offers to the Guru and Master Whom he is as yet unable to contact. Nor will he make that desired contact until he has transmuted emotional devotion into unselfish service to humanity, — not to the Master.

The books that I have written are sent out with no claim for their acceptance. They may, or may not, be correct, true and useful. It is for you to ascertain their truth by right practice and by the exercise of the intuition. Neither I nor A.A.B. is the least interested in having them acclaimed as inspired writings, or in having anyone speak of them (with bated breath) as being the work of one of the Masters. If they present truth in such a way that it follows sequentially upon that already offered in the world teachings, if the information given raises the aspiration and the will-to-serve from the plane of the emotions to that of the mind (the plane whereon the Masters *can* be found) then they will have served their purpose. If the teaching conveyed calls forth a response from the illumined mind of the worker in the world, and brings a flashing forth of his intuition, then let that teaching be accepted. But not otherwise. If the statements meet with eventual corroboration, or are deemed true under the test of the Law of Correspondences, then that is well and good. But should this not be so, let not the student accept what is said.

AUGUST 1934.

THE GREAT INVOCATION

From the point of Light within the Mind of God
  Let light stream forth into the minds of men.
  Let Light descend on Earth.

From the point of Love within the Heart of God
  Let love stream forth into the hearts of men.
  May Christ return to Earth.

From the centre where the Will of God is known
  Let purpose guide the little wills of men —
  The purpose which the Masters know and serve.

From the centre which we call the race of men
  Let the Plan of Love and Light work out
  And may it seal the door where evil dwells.

Let Light and Love and Power restore the Plan on Earth.

"The above Invocation or Prayer does not belong to any person or group but to all humanity. The beauty and the strength of this Invocation lies in its simplicity, and in its expression of certain central truths which all men, innately and normally, accept — the truth of the existence of a basic Intelligence to Whom we vaguely give the name of God; the truth that behind all outer seeming, the motivating power of the universe is Love; the truth that a great Individuality came to earth, called by Christians, the Christ, and embodied that love so that we could understand; the truth that both love and intelligence are effects of what is called the Will of God; and finally the self-evident truth that only through *humanity* itself can the Divine Plan work out."

ALICE A. BAILEY

TABLE OF CONTENTS

Contents

I. *The Egoic Ray*

CHAPTER I

The Egoic Ray

I. The Growth of Soul Influence

BEFORE taking up our subject as outlined at the close of the previous volume, I would like to speak a word as to the symbolism we will employ in discussing egoic and personality control. All that is said in this connection is in an attempt to define and consider that which is really undefinable and which is so elusive and subtle that though we may call it energy or force, those words ill convey the true idea. We must, therefore, bear in mind that, as we read and consider this treatise on psychology, we are talking in symbols. This is necessarily so, for we are dealing with the expression of divinity in time and space, and until man is *consciously* aware of his divinity and demonstrating it, it is not possible to do more than speak in parable and metaphor with symbolic intent—to be ascertained through the medium of the mystical perception and the wisdom of the enlightened man. As is often glibly said with little real understanding of the significance of the words used, we are dealing with forces and energies. These, as they cyclically run their course and play upon and intermingle with other energies and potencies, produce those forms in matter and substance, which constitute the appearance and express the quality of the great all-enfolding Lives and of the Life in which all "lives and moves and has its being."

The unfoldment of the human consciousness is signalised sequentially by the recognition of life after life, of being after being, and the realisation that these lives are in themselves the sum total of all the potencies and energies whose will is to create and to manifest. In dealing, however, with these energies and forces, it is impossible to express their appearance, quality and purpose except in symbolic form, and the following points should therefore be remembered:

1. The personality consciousness is that of the third aspect of divinity, the creator aspect. This works in matter and substance in order to create forms through which the quality may express itself and so demonstrate the nature of divinity on the plane of appearances.

2. The egoic consciousness is that of the second aspect of divinity, that of the soul, expressing itself as quality and as the determining subjective "colour" of the appearances. This naturally varies, according to the ability of the soul in any form to master its vehicle, matter, and to express innate quality through the outer form.

3. The monadic consciousness is that of the first aspect of divinity, that which *embodies* divine life-purpose and intent, and which uses the soul in order to demonstrate through that soul the inherent purpose of God. It is this that determines the quality. The soul embodies that purpose and will of God as it expresses itself in seven aspects. The monad expresses the same purpose as it exists, unified in the Mind of God Himself. This is a form of words conveying practically nothing to the average thinker.

As these three expressions of the One Great Life are realised by man on the physical plane, he begins to tune in consciously on the emerging Plan of Deity, and *the whole story of the creative process becomes the story of God's realised purpose.*

In the first place, as the third aspect is consciously developed, man arrives at a knowledge of matter, of substance and of outer creative activity. Then he passes on to a realisation of the underlying qualities which the form is intended to reveal, and identifies himself with the ego, the soul or solar angel. This he comes to know as his true self, the real spiritual man. Later, he arrives at the realisation of the purpose which is working out through the qualities, as they express themselves through the form. The above paragraphs are only a summation of what has been earlier said, but it is necessary that there should be real clarity of thought on these matters. It is apparent as we study, how this entire sequential process of realisation pivots around *form manifestation*, and has relation to the quality and purpose of the divine Mind. This will inevitably be clear to the man who has studied the theme of *A Treatise on Cosmic Fire*, which deals specifically with the creative process and with manifestation. It deals therefore with the outer personality expression of that great all-encompassing *Life*, which we call God, for lack of a better term. We need to bear in mind that our universe (as far as the highest human consciousness can as yet conceive of it) is to be found on the seven subplanes of the cosmic physical plane, and that our highest type of energy, embodying for us the purest expression of Spirit, is but the force manifestation of the first subplane of the cosmic physical plane. We are dealing, therefore, as far as consciousness is concerned, with what might be regarded symbolically as the brain reaction and response to cosmic purpose,—the brain reaction of God Himself.

In man, the microcosm, the objective of the evolutionary purpose for the fourth kingdom in nature is to enable man to manifest as a soul in time and space and to tune in on the soul purpose and the plan of the Creator, as it is known and expressed by the seven Spirits before the Throne, the seven planetary Logoi. But at this point we can only hint at a great mystery, which is that all that the highest of the Sons of God on our manifested planetary world can grasp is a partial realisation of the purpose and plan of the Solar Logos, as it is grasped, apprehended and expressed by one of the planetary Logoi Who is (in His place and term of office) conditioned and limited by His own peculiar point in evolution. A seventh part of the unfolding Plan is being expressed by our particular planetary Life, and because this great Being is not one of the seven sacred Lives and is therefore not expressing Himself through one of the seven sacred planets, the Plan as unfolded upon the Earth is a part of a dual expression of purpose, and only as another non-sacred planet reaches its consummation can the whole plan for the Earth be realised. This may not be easily understood, for, it has been said, only those who are initiate can grasp some of the significance of the statement that "The twain shall be one and together shall express divinity."

All that concerns humanity at this time is the necessity for a steadily unfolding conscious response to the evolutionary revelation and a gradual apprehension of the Plan which will enable man to

   a. Work consciously and intelligently,
   b. Realise the relation of form and quality to life,
   c. Produce that inner transmutation which will bring

into manifestation the fifth kingdom in nature, the Kingdom of Souls.

All this has to be accomplished in the realm of conscious awareness or response, through the medium of steadily improving vehicles **or res**ponse mechanisms, and with the aid of spiritual understanding and interpretation.

With the bigger questions we will not deal. With the consciousness of the life of God as it expresses itself in the three subhuman kingdoms, we need not concern ourselves. We shall deal entirely with the following three points:

1. With the strictly human consciousness as it begins with the process of individualisation and consummates in the dominant personality.
2. With the egoic consciousness, which is that of the solar angel as it begins with the preparation for initiation on the Path of Discipleship and consummates in the perfected Master.
3. With the monadic realisation. This is a phrase that means absolutely nothing to us, for it concerns the consciousness of the planetary Logos. This begins to be realised at the third initiation, dominating the soul and working out through the personality.

Man, the average human being, is a sum total of separative tendencies, of uncontrolled forces and of disunited energies, which slowly and gradually become coordinated, fused, and blended in the separative personality.

Man, the Solar Angel, is the sum total of those energies and forces which are unified, blended and controlled by that "tendency to harmony" which is the effect of love and the outstanding quality of divinity.

Man, the living Monad, is the veiled reality, and that which the Angel of the Presence hides. He is the synthetic expression of the purpose of God, symbolised through revealed, divine quality and manifested through the form. Appearance, quality, life—again this ancient triplicity confronts us. Symbolically speaking, this triplicity can be studied as:

1. Man ....the Angel ....The Presence.
2. The root ....the lotus ....the fragrance.
3. The bush ....the fire ....the flame.

The work of evolution, being part of the determination of Deity to express divinity through form, is necessarily, therefore, the task of *revelation*, and as far as man is concerned, this revelation works out as the growth of soul evolution and falls into three stages:

1. Individualisation ....Personality.
2. Initiation ....Ego.
3. Identification ....Monad.

1. *The Three Stages of Egoic Growth*

We must hold the following statements firmly in our minds. The personality is a triple combination of forces, impressing and absolutely controlling the fourth aspect of the personality, which is the dense physical body. The three personality types of energy are the etheric body, which is the vehicle of vital energy, the astral body which is the vehicle of the feeling energy or sentient force, and the mental body which is the vehicle of the intelligent energy of will that is destined to be the dominant creative aspect. It is upon this truth that Christian Science has laid the emphasis. These forces constitute the lower man. The solar angel is a dual combination of energies—the energy of love, and the energy of will or purpose—and these are the qualities of the life thread. These two, when dominating the third energy of mind, produce the perfect man. They explain the human problem; they indicate the objective before man; they account for and explain the energy of illusion; and they point out the way of psychological unfoldment, which leads man (from the triangle of triplicity and differentiation) through duality to unity.

These truths are practical and hence we find today such dominant emphasis laid upon the understanding of the Plan amongst esotericists; hence likewise the work of the psychologists as they seek to interpret man and hence also their differentiations as to the human apparatus, so that man is seen—as it were—dissected into his component parts. The recognition is emerging that it is man's quality which outwardly determines his place on the ladder of evolution, but modern psychology of the extreme materialistic school erroneously supposes that man's quality is determined by his mechanism, whereas the reverse condition is the determining factor.

Disciples have the problem of expressing the duality of love and will through the personality. This statement is a true enunciation of the goal for the disciple. The initiate has the objective of expressing the Will of God through developed love and a wise use of the intelligence. The above preamble lays the ground for the definition of the three stages of egoic growth.

What, therefore, is *individualisation* from the standpoint of the psychological unfoldment of man? It is the focussing of the lowest aspect of the soul, which is that of the creative intelligence, so that it can express itself through the form nature. It will eventually be the first aspect of divinity thus to express itself. It is the emergence into manifestation of the specific quality of the solar angel through the appropriation, by that angel, of a sheath or sheaths, which thus constitute its appearance. It is the initial imposition of an applied directed energy upon that triple force aggregation which we call the form nature of man. The individual, on the way to full coordination and expression, appears upon the stage of life. The self-aware entity comes forth into physical incarnation. The actor appears in process of learning his part; he makes his debut and prepares for the day of full personality emphasis. The soul comes forth into dense form and on the lowest plane. The self begins the part of its career which is expressed through selfishness, leading finally to an ultimate unselfishness. The separative entity begins his preparation for group realisation. A God walks on earth, veiled by the fleshly form, the desire nature and the fluidic mind. He is a prey temporarily to the illusion of the senses, and dowered with a mentality which primarily hinders and imprisons but which finally releases and liberates.

There has been much written in *The Secret Doctrine* and *A Treatise on Cosmic Fire* on the subject of individualisation. It can be simply defined as the process whereby forms of life in the fourth kingdom in nature arrive at:

1. Conscious individuality, through experiencing the life of the senses.
2. The assertion of individuality through the use of the discriminating mind.
3. The ultimate sacrifice of that individuality to the group.

Today, the masses are occupied with the task of becoming conscious of themselves, and are developing that spirit or sense of personal integrity or wholeness which will eventuate in an increased self-assertiveness—that first gesture of divinity. This is well and good, in spite of the immediate complications and consequences in the world consciousness and state of being. Hence also the need for the immediate guidance of the disciples in every nation and their training in the life of *correct* aspiration, with their subsequent preparation for initiation. The task of the intelligent parent today and of the wise teacher of the young should be that of turning out, into world activity, those conscious individuals who will undertake the work of self-assertion in the affairs of today. The mass psychology of accepting information indiscriminately, of giving prompt mass obedience to imposed limitations of personal liberty, without due understanding of the underlying reasons, and the consequent blind following of leaders, will only come to an end through the intelligent fostering of individual recognition of selfhood and the assertions of the individual as he seeks to express his own ideas. One of the basic ideas underlying all human and individual conduct, is the necessity for peace and harmony in order that man may specifically work out his destiny. This is the deep foundational belief of humanity. The first developed evidence of the emerging self-assertion of the massed individuals must therefore be turned in this direction, for it will constitute the line of least resistance. There will follow then the eradication of war and the establishing of those conditions of peace which will bring about the opportunity for trained and carefully cultured growth. The dictator is the individual who has, under the process, flowered forth into knowledge and power, and is an example of the effectiveness of the divine character, when permitted scope and as the product of the evolutionary process. He expresses many of the divine potentialities of man. But the dictator will some day be an anachronism, for when the many are at the stage of individual self-awareness and potency and seeking the full expression of their powers, he will be lost from sight in the assertion of the many. He, today, indicates the goal for the lower self, for the personality.

Before, however, the many men can be safely self-assertive, there must be an increased appearance of those who have passed beyond that stage, and of those who know, teach and demonstrate, so that the many constituting the intelligent group, composed of the self-aware individuals, can then identify themselves discriminatingly with group purpose, and submerge their separative identities in organised group activity and synthesis. This is the predominant task of the New Group of World Servers. It should be the aspiration of the world disciples today. This work of training the individuals in group purpose must be accomplished in three ways:—

1. By personal, imposed identification with the group, through the experience of understanding, service and sacrifice. This can well constitute a useful self-imposed experiment.
2. By the education of the masses in the principles underlying group work, and the training of an enlightened public opinion in these concepts.
3. By the preparation of many in the New Group of World Servers for that great transition in consciousness which we call initiation.

What, therefore, is Initiation? Initiation might be defined in two ways. It is first of all the entering into a new and wider dimensional world by the expansion of a man's consciousness so that he can include and encompass that which he now excludes, and from which he normally separates himself in his thinking and acts. It is, secondly, the entering into man of those energies which are distinctive of the soul and of the soul alone,—the forces of intelligent love and of spiritual will. These are dynamic energies, and they actuate all who are liberated souls. This process of entering into and of being entered into should be a simultaneous and synthetic process, an event of the first importance. Where it is sequential or alternating, it indicates an uneven unfoldment and an unbalanced condition. There is frequently the theory of unfoldment, and a mental grasp anent the facts of the initiatory process before they are practiced experimentally in the daily life and thus psychologically integrated into the practical expression of the living process on the physical plane. Herein lies much danger and difficulty, and also much loss of time. The mental grasp of the individual is ofttimes much greater than his power to express the knowledge, and we have consequently those outstanding failures and those difficult situations which have brought the whole question of initiation into disrepute. Many people are regarded as initiates who are only endeavoring to be initiate. They are not, however, real initiates. They are those well meaning people whose mental understanding outruns the power of their personalities to practice. They are those who are in touch with forces which they are not yet able to handle and control. They have done a great deal of the needed work of inner contact, but have not yet whipped the lower nature into shape. They are, therefore, unable to express that which they inwardly understand and somewhat realise. They are those disciples who talk too much and too soon and too self-centeredly, and who present to the world an ideal toward which they are indeed working, but which they are as yet unable to materialise, owing to the inadequacy of their equipment. They affirm their belief in terms of accomplished fact and cause much stumbling among the little ones. But at the same time, they are working towards the goal. They are mentally in touch with the ideal and with the Plan. They are aware of forces and energies utterly unknown to the majority. Their only mistake is in the realm of time, for they affirm prematurely that which some day they will be.

When initiation becomes possible, it indicates that two great groups of energies (those of the triple integrated personality and those of the soul or solar angel) are beginning to fuse and blend. The energy of the soul is beginning to dominate and to control the lower types of force, and—according to the ray of the soul—so will be the body in which that control will begin to make its presence felt. This will be elaborated later in the section dealing with the rays as they govern the various bodies,—mental, emotional and physical. It should be remembered that very little egoic control need be evidenced when the first initiation is taken. That initiation indicates simply that the germ of soul life has vitalised and brought into functioning existence the inner spiritual body, the sheath of the inner spiritual man, which will eventually enable the man at the third initiation to manifest forth as "a full-grown man in Christ", and present at that time the opportunity to the Monad for that full expression of life which can take place when the initiate is identified consciously with the One Life. Between the first and second initiations, as has been frequently stated, much time can elapse and much change must be wrought during the many stages of discipleship. Upon this we will later dwell as we study the seven laws of egoic unfoldment.

Individualisation, carried to its full, consummates as the integrated personality, expressing itself as a unity through three aspects. This expression of personality involves:—

1. The free use of the mind so that focussed attention can be paid to all that concerns the personal self and its aims. This spells personality success and prosperity.
2. The power to control the emotions and yet have the full use of the sensory apparatus to sense conditions, to feel reactions, and to bring about contact with the emotional aspects of other personalities.
3. The capacity to touch the plane of ideas and to bring

them through into consciousness. Even if these are later subordinated to selfish purpose and interpretation, the man can, however, be in touch with that which can be spiritually cognised. The free use of the mind pre-supposes its growing sensitivity to intuitional impression.

4. The demonstration of many talents, powers and the working out of genius, and the emphatic bending of the whole personality to the expression of some one of these powers. There is often an extreme versatility and an ability to do many outstanding things noticeably well.

5. The physical man is frequently a wonderfully sensitive instrument of the inner, emotional and mental selves, and gifted with great magnetic power; there is often resilient, though never robust, bodily health, and great charm and personal outer gifts.

A study of the outstanding individuals in all fields of world expression today, when entirely divorced from the higher group concepts and the constant spiritual aspiration to serve humanity, will indicate the nature of the consummated individuality and the success of this part of the divine plan. It should be carefully noted that the successful demonstration of the dominant individual is just as much a divine success in its proper place and time as is the case with the great Sons of God. One success, however, is the expression of the third aspect of divinity as it veils and hides the soul, and the other is the expression of two aspects of divinity (the second and the third) as they veil and hide the life aspect of the Monad. When this is grasped, our evaluation of world achievement will undergo change, and we will see life more truly and divorced from the glamour which distorts our vision and the vision of the great Personalities as well. It should also be borne in mind that individual separative success is in itself an evidence of soul activity, for every individual is a living soul, actuating the lower sheaths of bodies, and proceeding to

1. Build sheath after sheath, life after life, that will be increasingly adequate to its own expression.
2. Produce that sensitivity in the sheaths—sequentially and finally simultaneously—which will enable them to respond to an ever increasing sphere or measure of divine influence.
3. Integrate the three sheaths into a unity which for three and sometimes seven lives (occasionally eleven lives) will function as a dominant personality in some field of wide expression, using the energy of ambition to bring this about.
4. Re-orient the lower individual self so that the realm of its desires and the satisfaction of personality achievement will eventually be relegated to their rightful place.
5. Galvanise the self-assertive man into that realisation of new achievements which will direct his steps on to the Path of Discipleship and eventually on to the Path of Initiation.
6. Substitute for past, necessarily self-interested and personal ambition, the needs of the group and the goal of world service.

Is not the above sufficiently practical?

Initiation carried to its consummation, as far as humanity is concerned, produces the liberated Master of the Wisdom, free from the limitations of the individual, garnering the fruits of the individualisation process and functioning increasingly as the solar angel, because focussed primarily in the inner spiritual body. Awareness of the Presence is thus steadily developed. This fact merits the deep study and meditation of all disciples. As the three rays which govern the lower triplicity blend and synthesise and produce the vital personality, and as they in their turn dominate the ray of the dense physical body, the lower man enters into a prolonged condition of conflict. Gradually and increasingly, the soul ray, "the ray of persistent and magnetic grasp", as it is occultly called, begins to become more active; in the brain of the man who is a developed personality, an increased awareness of vibration is set up. There are many degrees and stages in this experience, and they cover many lives. The personality ray and the egoic ray at first seem to clash, and then later a steady warfare is set up with the disciple as the onlooker— and dramatic participator. Arjuna emerges into the arena of the battlefield. Midway between the two forces he stands, a conscious tiny point of sentient awareness and of light. Around him and in him and through him the energies of the two rays pour and conflict. Gradually, as the battle continues to rage, he becomes a more active factor, and drops the attitude of the detached and uninterested onlooker. When he is definitely aware of the issues involved, and definitely throws the weight of his influence, desires, and mind on to the side of the soul, he can take the first initiation. When the ray of the soul focusses itself fully through him, and all his centres are controlled by that focussed soul ray, then he becomes the transfigured Initiate, and takes the third initiation. The ray of the personality is occultly "extinguished" or absorbed by the ray of the soul, and all the potencies and attributes of the lower rays become subsidiary to and coloured by the soul ray. The disciple becomes a "man of God",—a person whose powers are controlled by the dominant vibration of the soul ray and whose inner, sensitive mechanism is vibrating to the measure of that soul ray which—in its turn—is being itself reoriented to, and controlled by, the monadic ray. The process then repeats itself:—

1. The many rays which constitute the lower separative man are fused and blended into the three personality rays.
2. These are, in their turn, fused and blended into a synthetic expression of the dominant self-assertive man, the personal self.
3. The personality rays then become one ray and in their turn become subservient to the dual ray of the soul. Again, therefore, three rays are blended and fused.
4. The soul rays dominate the personality and the three become again the one, as the dual ray of the soul and the blended ray of the personality vibrate to the measure of the highest of the soul rays—the ray of the soul's group, which is ever regarded as the true egoic ray.
5. Then, in time, the soul ray begins (at the third initiation) to blend with the ray of the Monad, the life ray. The higher initiate is therefore a dual and not a triple expression.
6. In time, however, this realised duality gives place to the mysterious, indescribable process called *identification* which is the final stage of soul unfoldment. It is useless to say more for what might be said could only be comprehended by those preparing for the fourth initiation, and this treatise is written for disciples and initiates of the first degree.

In these successive stages we can glimpse the vision of what we are and may be. Steadily the unfolding purpose of our own souls (those "angels of persistent and undying love") should gain fuller and deeper control over each of us, and this, at any personal cost and sacrifice, should be our steadfast aim. For this, in truth and sincerity, we should strive.

We have thus touched upon the three great divisions which mark the soul's progress towards its goal. Through the process of *Individualisation*, the soul arrives at a true self-consciousness and awareness in the three worlds of its experience. The actor in the drama of life masters his part. Through the process of *Initiation*, the soul becomes aware of the essential nature of divinity. Participation in full consciousness with the group and the absorption of the personal and individual into the Whole, characterise this stage on the path of evolution. Finally comes that mysterious process wherein the soul becomes so absorbed into that supreme Reality and Synthesis through *Identification* that even the consciousness of the group fades out (except when deliberately recovered in the work of service). Naught is then known save Deity,—no separation of any part, no lesser syntheses, and no divisions or differentiations. During these processes it might be stated that three streams of energy play upon the consciousness of the awakening man:—

a. The energy of matter itself, as it affects the consciousness of the inner spiritual man, who is using the form as a medium of expression.

b. The energy of the soul itself, or of the solar angel, as that energy pours forth upon the vehicles and produces reciprocal energy in the solar form.

c. The energy of life itself, a meaningless phrase, and one that only initiates of the third initiation can grasp, for even the discoveries of modern science give no real idea as to the true nature of life.

Life or essential energy is more than the activity of the atom, or of that living principle which produces self-perpetuation, reproduction, motion, growth, and that peculiar something which we call "livingness". It may be possible to "create" or produce the lowest or third aspect of life in the scientific laboratories so-called, but to reproduce or create the other and more essential aspects which work out as the conscious response, the intelligent embryonic purpose which seems to animate all substances, that is not possible. When the third initiation is reached, man will understand why this impossibility exists. More cannot be said, for until that initiation is experienced it would not be understood.

To bring more light upon this question of the triple expansion of consciousness (for all these crises are aspects of one great unfolding purpose or process) which we call individualisation, initiation, and identification, it should be borne in mind that these words connote something to us today—from the angle of our present point in evolution, from our inherited teaching and thought habits, and from the standpoint of modern knowledge and terminologies. Later they may appear in a totally different light when we know more and the race has advanced further into the light. But from the light which streams forth from that larger synthesis, and from the angle of vision of Those Whose consciousness is higher and greater and more inclusive than the human, the significance of these words may appear totally different. Definition is simply the expression of the immediate understanding of a human mind. But a definition may later be seen to be imperfect and even false, from the angle of a wider knowledge and a more inclusive grasp of *wholes*, (just as is the case with a so-called fact). Hence all definition, and eventually all facts, will be known to be temporary; all exegesis is but passing in its usefulness. The basic truths of today may be seen later as simply aspects of still greater truths, and when the greater truth is grasped, the significance and the interpretation of its formerly important part is seen to be widely different to what was supposed. This must never be forgotten by any who may read this *Treatise on the Seven Rays*. An initiate, reading the three words we have been considering, has a very different idea about them than has a disciple or a person who has never thought or studied along these lines, and to whom our vocabulary is novel and strange, conveying little meaning, and that usually quite incorrect.

In individualisation, the life of God which has been subjected to the processes of growth, stimulation and development in the three lower kingdoms, becomes focussed in the fourth kingdom in nature, the human, through the agency of a "cycle of crisis", and becomes subjected to the influence of soul energy in one of the seven ray aspects. The quality of the form aspect, as embodied in the personality and expressed by the phrase, "the ray of the personality", becomes subject to the *quality* of the egoic ray. Those two great influences play upon and affect each other, interacting all the time, producing modifications and changes until, slowly and gradually, the ray of the personality becomes less dominant, and the ray of the soul steadily assumes prominence. Eventually it will be the soul ray that will be expressed, and not the form ray. This personality or form ray then becomes simply the medium of expression through which the quality of the soul can make its presence felt in full power. Something of this idea is conveyed in the ancient occult phrase "the lesser fire must be put out by the greater light". A symbol of this can be seen in the power of the sun apparently to put out a little fire when it can pour its heat right into it.

It was earlier pointed out that we can profitably use the words,—Life, Quality, Appearance—in lieu of Spirit, Soul and Body, for they express the same truth. The quality of matter, built up into human form and indwelt by the soul or solar angel, is that which normally colours the appearance. Later, this inherent quality of the appearance changes, and it is the *quality* nature of Deity (as expressed in the soul) which obliterates the quality of the forms. During the stage wherein it is the quality of matter which is the paramount influence, that material radiance makes itself felt in a triple form. These—from the angle of the entire sweep of the evolutionary process, and as far as the human personality is concerned—appear sequentially, and qualify the matter aspect with its three major presentations:

1. *The quality of physical substance.* During this stage of development, the man is almost entirely physical in his reactions and completely under the ray of his physical body. This is the correspondence in man to the Lemurian epoch and to the period of pure infancy.
2. *The quality of the astral body.* This governs the individual for a very long period, and still governs, more or less, the masses of men. It corresponds to the Atlantean period and to the stage of adolescence. The ray of the astral body is of very great power.
3. *The quality of the mental body.* This, as far as the race is concerned, is just beginning to wax in power in this Aryan race to which this era belongs. It corresponds to the stage of maturity in the individual. The ray of the mind has a very close relation to the solar angel, and there is a peculiar affiliation between the Angel of the Presence and the mental man. It is this deep-seated, though oft unrecognised, interplay and cultivated intercourse, which produces the at-one-ment between the soul and its mechanism, man in the three worlds.

From the angle of these three ray influences, we have (in the life of the aspirant) a recapitulation of the triple process which we could call the "processes of unfoldment of the Lemurian, Atlantean, and Aryan consciousness." On the Path of Probation, the ray of the physical body must become subordinated to the potencies emanating from those soul rays which stream forth from the outer tier of petals in the egoic lotus. (See *A Treatise on Cosmic Fire*.) These are the knowledge petals. On the Path of Discipleship, the astral body is brought into subjection by the ray of the soul as it pours through the second tier of petals, the love petals. Upon the Path of Initiation, until the third initiation, the ray of the mental body is subdued by the force of the petals of sacrifice, found in the third tier of petals. Thus the three aspects of the personality are brought into subjection by the energy emanating from the nine petals of the egoic lotus. After the third initiation, the whole personality, composed of the three aspects, becomes sensitive to the energy of pure electric fire or life, as it pours through the "closed bud at the heart of the egoic lotus."

The value of the above information consists in the fact that it gives, symbolically, a synthetic picture of man's unfoldment and higher relations. Its danger consists in the capacity of the human intellect to separate and divide, so that the process is regarded as proceeding in successive stages, whereas in reality there is often a paralleling activity going on, and much overlapping, fusing and inter-relating of aspects, of rays and of processes, within the time cycle.

Such is the program for humanity, as it concerns the unfoldment of the human consciousness. The whole emphasis of the entire evolutionary process is, in the last analysis, placed upon the development of conscious, intelligent awareness in the life animating the various forms. The exact state of awareness is contingent upon the age of the soul. Yet the soul has no age from the standpoint of time, as humanity understand it. It is timeless and eternal. Before the soul there passes the kaleidoscope of the senses, and the recurring drama of outer phenomenal existence; but throughout all these occurrences in time and space, the soul ever preserves the attitude of the Onlooker and of the perceiving Observer. It beholds and interprets. In the early stages, when the "Lemurian consciousness" characterises the phenomenal man, that fragmentary aspect of the soul which indwells and informs the human form, and which gives to the man any real human consciousness which may be present, is inert, inchoate and unorganised; it is devoid of mind as we understand it, and is distinguished only by a complete identification with the physical form and its activities. This is the period of slow tamasic reactions to suffering, joy, pain, to the urge and satisfaction of desire, and to a heavy subconscious urge to betterment. Life after life passes, and slowly the capacity for conscious identification increases, with a growing desire for a larger range of satisfactions; the indwelling and animating soul becomes ever more deeply hidden, the prisoner of the form nature. The entire forces of the life are concentrated in the physical body, and the desires then expressed are physical desires; at the same time there is a growing tendency towards more subtle desires, such as the astral body evokes. Gradually, the identification of the soul with the form shifts from the physical to the astral form. There is nothing present at this time which could be called a personality. There is simply a living, active physical body, with its wants and desires, its needs and its appetites, accompanied by a very slow yet steadily increasing shift of the consciousness out of the physical into the astral vehicle.

When this shift, in course of time, has been successfully achieved, then the consciousness is no longer entirely identified with the physical vehicle, but it becomes centred in the astral-emotional body. Then the focus of the soul's attention, working through the slowly evolving man, is in the world of desire, and the soul becomes identified with another response apparatus, the desire or astral body. His consciousness then becomes the "Atlantean consciousness." His desires are no longer so vague and inchoate; they have hitherto been concerned with the basic urges or appetites,— first, his urge to self-preservation; then to self-perpetuation through the urge to reproduce; and next, to economic satisfaction. At this stage we have the state of awareness of the infant and the raw savage. Gradually, however, we find a steadily growing inner realisation of desire itself, and less emphasis upon the physical satisfactions. The consciousness slowly begins to respond to the impact of the mind and to the power to discriminate and choose between various desires; the capacity to employ time somewhat intelligently begins to make its presence felt. The more subtle pleasures begin to make their appeal; man's desires become less crude and physical; the emerging desire for beauty begins to appear, and a dim sense of aesthetic values. His consciousness is becoming more astral-mental, or kama-manasic, and the whole trend of his daily attitudes, or his modes of living, and of his character begins to broaden, to unfold, and to improve. Though he is still ridden by unreasoning desire most of the time, yet the field of his satisfactions and of his sense-urges are less definitely animal and more definitely emotional. Moods and feelings come to be recognised, and a dim desire for peace and the urge to find that nebulous thing called "happiness" begin to play their part. This corresponds to the period of adolescence and to the state of consciousness called Atlantean. It is the condition of the masses at this present time. The bulk of human beings are still Atlantean, still purely emotional in their reactions and in their approach to life. They are still governed predominantly by selfish desires and by the calls of the instinctual life. Our earth humanity is still in the Atlantean stage, whereas the intelligentsia of the world, and the disciples and aspirants, are passing rapidly out of this stage, for they reached individualisation on the moon chain, and were the Atlanteans of past history.

Workers in the world today should have these facts and sequences most carefully in mind, if they are rightly to appreciate the world problem, and correctly guide and teach the people. They should realise that, speaking generally, there is little true mentality with which to work when dealing with the submerged masses; that they need to be oriented towards the truly desirable, more than towards the truly reasonable, and the right direction of the energy of desire, as it expresses itself in the untutored, easily-swayed masses, should be the effort of all who teach.

In the more advanced people of the world today, we have the functioning of the mind-body; this is to be found in a large scale in our Western civilisation. The energy of the ray of the mental body begins to pour in, and slowly to assert itself. As this happens, the desire nature is brought under control, and consequently the physical nature can become more definitely the instrument of mental impulses. The brain consciousness begins to organise and the focus of energies begins to shift gradually out of the lower centres into the higher. Mankind is developing the "Aryan consciousness" and is reaching maturity. In the more advanced people of the world, we have also the integration of the personality and the emergence into definite control of the personality ray, with its synthetic, coherent grip of the three bodies and their fusing into one working unit. Later, the personality becomes the instrument of the indwelling soul.

The above is a simple and direct statement of a long and difficult evolutionary unfoldment. Its very simplicity will indicate that we have only dealt with the broad outlines, and have ignored the infinite detail of process. The work starts at Individualisation, and continues through the two final stages of Initiation and Identification. These three stages mark the progress of the soul consciousness from that of identification with the form to that of identification with the *Self*. These three words—*individualisation, initiation* and *identification,*—cover the whole process of man's career from the time he emerges into the human kingdom till he passes out of it at the third initiation, and functions freely in the fifth kingdom, the kingdom of God. By that time, he has learnt that consciousness is free and unlimited, and can function in form or out of form according to the behest of the soul, or as the Plan can best be served. The soul is then in no way conditioned by form. Just as man can express himself in what is called three-dimensional living, so, by the time he takes the third initiation, he can function actively and consciously in four dimensions, and in the final stages of the Path of Initiation he becomes active fifth-dimensionally.

As we consider these various degrees of expanding awareness, the significant fact to be borne in mind is that through it all there is one steady, sequential unfoldment taking place. The life of the soul, in this great life cycle which we call human incarnation, passes on the phenomenal plane through all the stages with the same direction, power, steadiness in growth and in the adaptability of form to circumstance and environment, as does the life of God as it flows through the various kingdoms in nature from age to age. The thread of the unfolding consciousness can be traced with clarity in all. Forms are built, used and discarded. Cycles of lives bring the forms into certain phases of unfoldment needed by the progressively inclusive consciousness. Other and later cycles demonstrate the definite and specific effects of this developed consciousness, for some lives are predominantly fruitful in producing causes (which is a paradoxical sentence with deep meaning) and others in working off the effects of the earlier initiated causes. This is a point not often emphasised. Still later cycles of lives bring these two aspects—consciousness and form—into a greater rapport, and thus produce an entirely different type of life. The correspondence to these cycles can be seen working out in the life and consciousness of the planetary Logos, as that great Life seeks expression through the medium of the four kingdoms in nature.

However, (and this is the fact of supreme importance), all this activity, all this directed unfoldment, all this evolving purpose and livingness, all the events in all the kingdoms of nature, and all the phases of life-conditioning in the human family, plus the kaleidoscope of events, the emergence of characteristics and tendencies, the appearance of forms with their unique colouring, qualities and activities, the syntheses and fusions, the urges, instincts and aspirations, the manifested loves and hates (as expressions of the great law of attraction and repulsion), the producing of civilisations, of the sciences and arts in all their wonder and beauty,—all this is but the expression of the will-to-be of certain Beings or Lives. Their consciousness so far transcends the human that only the initiate of high degree can enter into Their true Plan. What we see today is only the expression of Their energies in the processes of form-making and of the evolution of consciousness. The Plan, as it is sensed by the world disciples, in the attempt to work and cooperate with it, is only the sensing of that portion of it which concerns the human consciousness. We have not yet been able to catch even a glimmer of the vastness of the synthetic Plan for evolutions other than human, both superhuman and subhuman; nor can we grasp the fabric of God's ideal as it underlies the sum total of the manifested processes, even upon our little planet. All we really know is the fact of the Plan, and that it is very good; that we are enfolded within it and subject to it.

Herein may be found a clue to the difficult problem of free will. It might be said that within the limits of the intelligent direction of the intelligent man there *is* free will, as far as activity in the human kingdom is concerned. Where no mind activity is present and where there is no power to discriminate, to analyse and to choose, there is no free will. Within the vaster processes of the Plan, however, as it includes the entire planetary evolution, there is, for the tiny unit, man, no free will. He is subject, for instance, to what we call "acts of God", and before these he is helpless. He has no choice and no escape. Herein lies a hint upon the working of karma in the human kingdom; karma and intelligent responsibility are inextricably woven and interwoven.

As we close our discussion of the three steps of *Individualisation*, *Initiation* and *Identification*, which mark the progress of the soul from identification with form until it loses itself and its own identity in a higher identification with the Absolute One, let us carry our thoughts forward to that point in time and space wherein the spiritual consciousness releases itself from all the categories of awareness and all differentiations, and from the final sense of selfhood, and merges itself in that sublime condition in which self-centredness (as we understand it) disappears. We shall later consider the stages wherein the soul—impelled thereto by its peculiar ray qualities—appropriates to itself (for purposes of experience) those forms which can be expressive of, and responsive to, the many types of divine awareness.

It should be noted here, therefore, that there are, literally, two points of identification in the long experience of the soul. One marks the stage wherein form, matter, substance, time and space are controlling factors, and imprison the soul within their types of consciousness. This connotes *identification with form life*. The other connotes *identification with all that lies outside of form expression and is released from it*. What that may be lies beyond the grasp of our present advanced humanity, and is only known in its true significance by such great Existences as the Christ, the Buddha and Those of analogous rank in the Hierarchy of Lives. The qualities generated and developed through the first of these identifications persist and colour the conscious realisation, and it must be remembered that the final identification is the result of the experience gained through the medium of the first. These qualities will vary according to the dominance of one or other of the ray energies, but there will be—in the final stages—no consciousness of quality or ray type, but simply a state of Being or of livingness that realises identification with the *Whole* and which, at the same time, holds in solution (if one may use so unsatisfactory a term) all the results of the lesser identifications, the various differentiations and distinctions, and the many ray instincts, impulses, and intuitions. The garnered and expressed qualities, and the possible actions and reactions and awarenesses are equally eternally present and capable of re-acquisition at will, but they are all held below the threshold of consciousness. Livingness, Being, Wholeness and Unity are the distinctive characteristics of this highly evolved stage, which is, in its turn, the foundation for that higher evolutionary cycle of which we know nothing but which is hinted at in *A Treatise on Cosmic Fire* and in all references to the seven Paths which open up before the adept of the fifth initiation. Absorption into the One Life is the nature of this elevated state of consciousness. Freedom from all that is implied in the use of the words Form and Ego is the major characteristic, and, therefore, many ancient Scriptures, when attempting to deal with and explain this supernormal and superlative condition, are forced back into the use of negatives, and the so-called "doctrine of negation". Only by indicating what this state or condition of awareness is *not*, can any idea be conveyed of what it essentially *is*. The negations thus met with (and frequently misunderstood by the occidental reader) are, therefore, the result of the futility and inadequacy of language to express the Reality then known.

After the major initiations are undergone, the state of consciousness of the illumined and liberated adept is such that language serves only to blind and to hinder true understanding. The consciousness of the initiate is of so lofty a nature that it can only be described in terms of release, of negation, and through the emphasis of that which it is *not*. It is a state of No-thing and Non-ego, for all egoic awareness is superseded by a state of Being and of consciousness which is only capable of comprehension and expression when form life is of no further use to the perfected spiritual life. It is a state of non-individuality, yet with the subconscious knowledge and gains of the individual experience. The centre of consciousness is so far removed from any individual separate identity that that particular factor has faded entirely out, and only the macrocosmic life is sentiently realised. It is a state of non-activity from our present angle of vision, because all individual reactions to the activity of matter or to that state of being which we call egoic, have dropped away, and Life and Mind can no longer be swept into motion by any of the factors which have hitherto produced what we have called soul activity and form existence.

Nevertheless, though the consciousness is other than all that has been hitherto known, and though it can only be expressed in terms of negation, the truth must be borne constantly in mind that the greater awareness must always include the lesser awarenesses. Consequently all possible actions and reactions, identifications and focussings, awarenesses and contacts, ray impulses, approaches and withdrawals, and all possible expressions of the divine activity and qualities, phenomenal and non-phenomenal, are included in the state of Being which is now the natural state of the liberated and enlightened spiritual Existence. All are possible of recovery through the will or in response to a need, but the spiritual Being is no longer held by them or identified with them. Each of the stages on the great Path of Liberation or Enlightenment with which we have been concerned—Individualisation, Initiation and Identification—have led the Life or the spiritual, interior man, from point to point, from quality to quality, from realisation to realisation, from phenomenal appearance to spiritual living, from physical awareness to sentient, emotional awareness, and from that to mental differentiation and separateness. He has been carried from hell to heaven, from heaven to Nirvana, from the life-conditioning of the personal Ego to that of the group soul, and thence to that of the liberated state of pure intuitional life. He has passed from form experience as a whole to that complete freedom from all vibratory impressions which it is the nature of pure Being (divorced from phenomenal existence) to demonstrate. But at the same time, nothing is lost of capacity, or quality or of sentient awareness. This is beautifully expressed for us in the words of the *Old Commentary*, found in the archives of the Masters.

> "The quality of life fades out. It flickers and is gone. Yet the Blessed Ones reveal at will that quality. The colour pure remains.
> The nature of life in form fails to appear. It flashes forth a little while, then disappears. The Blessed Ones, at will, can take a form, yet are not then the form.
> The seven great rays sweep into manifested life. They are,

and then are not. All is and all is not. But the Blessed Ones at any time can sweep forth into manifested light. They carry then the potencies of spirit to meet the need expressed. Light holds Them not; Their purpose is not imprisoned; Their will is not subdued. They appear and disappear at will."

(An expression of the truth of this can be seen demonstrating in the world each full moon of May, when the Buddha flashes forth into manifestation, for the fulfilment of the Plan and at the urgent behest of His own spiritual will.)

"Naught holds the Blessed Ones. Neither the deities nor form; neither desire nor mind; nor any quality of life. Pure life they are; pure being and pure will; pure love and pure intent; this is all that unenlightened man can grasp, and only that in part.

The Blessed Ones are not, and yet They are.
The Blessed Ones know naught, and yet know all.
The Blessed Ones love not, yet offer love divine.
The Blessed Ones remember not, yet all is recollection.
The Blessed Ones remain in isolation pure; and yet at will can take a form.
The Blessed Ones dwell ever in the high and lofty place, yet oft can walk on earth in light phenomenal.
The Blessed Ones manifest not through form; yet are all forms and all intents."

Then the *Old Commentary* runs through what would constitute many pages of writing, shewing that the Blessed Ones are naught and yet are all there is; that They possess nothing and yet are in Themselves the expression of all reality; that They dwell nowhere and yet are found everywhere; that They have faded out and yet are shining in full radiance and can be seen. Negation after negation is piled up, only promptly to be contradicted in an effort to shew how divorced from, and yet inclusive of, form is the life of the Blessed Ones. It ends with the wonderful injunction:—

"Therefore be full of joy, O pilgrim on the Way towards

enlightened Being, for gain and loss are one; darkness and light eternally reveal the True; love and desire eternally invoke the Life.

Naught disappears but pain. Nothing remains but bliss,—the bliss of knowledge true, of contact real, of light divine, the Way to God."

Such is the true goal, as yet unrealisable by us. What is it that we are endeavoring to do? We are treading the *Way of Release*, and on that way, all drops from our hands; everything is taken away, and detachment from the world of phenomenal life and of individuality is inevitably forced upon us. We are treading the *Way of Loneliness*, and must learn eventually that we are essentially neither ego nor non-ego. Complete detachment and discrimination must finally lead us to a condition of such complete aloneness that the horror of the great blackness will settle down upon us. But when that pall of blackness is lifted and the light again pours in, the disciple sees that all that was grasped and treasured, and then lost and removed, has been restored, but with this difference —that it no longer holds the life imprisoned by desire. We are treading the *Way that leads to the Mountain Top of Isolation*, and will find it full of terror. Upon that mountain top we must fight the final battle with the Dweller on the Threshold, only to find that that too is an illusion. That high point of isolation and the battle itself are only illusions and figments of unreality; they are the last stronghold of the ancient glamour, and of the great heresy of separateness. Then we, the Beatific Ones, will eventually find ourselves merged with all that is, in love and understanding. The isolation, a necessary stage, is itself but an illusion. We are treading the *Way of Purification* and step by step all that we cherish is removed,—lust for form life, desire for love, and the great glamour of hatred. These disappear and we stand purified and empty. The distress of emptiness is the immediate result; it grips us and we feel that the price of holiness is too high. But, standing on the Way, suddenly the whole being is flooded with light and love, and the emptiness is seen as constituting that through which light and love may flow to a needy world. The purified One can dwell then in that place where dwell the Blessed Lords, and from that place go forth to "illumine the world of men and of the deities".

There are four ways which stretch before the disciples of the Lord of the World. They must all be trodden before the inner Being is released, and the liberated Son of God can enter, at will, what are symbolically called "the four gates into the City of Shamballa",—that city of the Most High God, which is ever swept by the Life of Those who have achieved liberation through loneliness, detachment, isolated unity, and purification. A realisation of the goal and the way to that goal is of service at this time, and it is to this realisation that the teachers of humanity seek to stimulate the Sons of God.

According to the ray type or quality, so will be the reaction of the life to the great stages of Individualisation, Initiation, and Identification. This is a major occult platitude, but it is one that is much in need of consideration and reflection. Let us bear in mind always that we are considering qualities which govern appearances and express the life. What is called in the Eastern literature "the Blessed One" refers to One who is perfectly expressing some ray quality through some chosen phenomenal appearance, which is assumed at will for purpose of service, but which in no way constitutes a limitation and in no way holds the Blessed One a prisoner, because His consciousness is in no way identified with the phenomenal appearance, nor with the quality it expresses.

a. Individualisation and the Seven Ray Types

We will express the reaction of these seven ray types to the process of Individualisation (which is the process of identification with form) by seven occult statements which can, if properly understood, give the keynote of the new psychology. They state the major impulse, the native quality, and the technique of unfoldment.

Ray One

"The Blessed One flies like an arrow into matter. He destroys (or ruptures) the way by which he might return. He grounds himself deeply in the depths of form.

He asserts: 'I will return. My power is great. I will destroy all obstacles. Nothing can stop my progress to my goal. Around me lies that which I have destroyed. What must I do?'

The answer comes: 'Order from chaos, O Pilgrim on the way of death, this is the way for you. Love you must learn. Dynamic will you have. The right use of destruction for the furtherance of the Plan, must be the way for you. Adherence to the rhythm of the planet will release the hidden Blessed One and order bring.' "

Ray Two

"The Blessed One built him an ark. Stage by stage he built it, and floated upon the bosom of the waters. Deeply he hid himself, and his light was no more seen,—only his floating ark.

His voice was heard: 'I have built and strongly built, but am a prisoner within my building. My light is hidden. Only my word goes forth. Around me lie the waters. Can I return from whence I came? Is the word strong enough to open wide the door? What shall I do?'

The answer came: 'Build now an ark translucent, which can reveal the light, O Builder of the ark. And by that light you shall reveal the lighted way. The power to build anew, the right use of the Word, and the using of the light,—these will release the Blessed One, deep hidden in the ark.' "

Ray Three

"The Blessed One gathered force. He hid himself behind a veil. He rolled himself within that veil, and deeply hid his face. Naught could be seen but that which veiled, and active motion. Within the veil was latent thought.

The thought reached forth: 'Behind this veil of maya I stand, a Blessed One, but unrevealed. My energy is great, and through my mind I can display the glory of divinity. How can I, therefore, demonstrate this truth? What shall I do? I wander in illusion.'

The word went forth: 'All is illusion, O Dweller in the shadows. Come forth into the light of day. Display the hidden glory of the Blessed One, the glory of the One and Only. The glory and the truth will rapidly destroy that which has veiled the truth. The prisoner can go free. The rending of the blinding veil, the clear pronouncing of the truth, and practice right will render to the Blessed One that golden thread which will provide release from all the maze of earth existence.' "

Ray Four

"The Blessed One rushed forth to combat. He saw existence as two warring forces, and fought them both. Loaded with the panoply of war, he stood midway, looking two ways. The clash of battle, the many weapons he had learned to use, the longing not to fight, the thrill of finding those he fought were but brothers and himself, the anguish of defeat, the paean of his victory,—these held him down.

The Blessed One paused and questioned: 'Whence come the victory and whence defeat? Am I not the Blessed One Himself? I will invoke the angels to my aid.'

The trumpet sound went forth: 'Rise up and fight, and reconcile the armies of the Lord. There is no battle. Force the conflict to subside; send for the invocation for the peace of all; form out of two, one army of the Lord; let victory crown the efforts of the Blessed One by harmonising all. Peace lies behind the warring energies.' "

Ray Five

"The Blessed One came forth in ignorance. He wandered in a darkness deep of spirit. He saw no reason for this way of life. He sought among the many threads that weave the outer garment of the Lord, and found the many ways there be, leading to the centre of the web eternal. The forms that weave that web hide the divine reality. He lost himself. Fear entered in.

He asked himself: 'Another pattern must be woven; another garment formed. What shall I do? Shew me another way to weave.'

The Word for him came forth in triple form. His mind responded to the vision clear evoked:—'The truth lies hidden in the unknown Way. The Angel of the Presence guards that Way. The mind reveals the Angel and the door. Stand in that Presence. Lift up thine eyes. Enter through that golden door. Thus will the Angel, who is the shadow of the Blessed One, reveal the open door. That Angel too must disappear. The Blessed One remains and passes through that door into the light sublime.' "

Ray Six

"The Blessed One caught the vision of the Way, and followed the Way without discretion. Fury characterised his efforts. The way led down into the world of dual life. Between the pairs of opposites, he took his stand, and as he swung pendent between them, fleeting glimpses of the goal shone forth. He swung in mid-heaven. He sought to swing into that radiant place of light, where stood the door upon the higher *Way*. But ever he swung between the pairs of opposites.

He spoke at last within himself: 'I cannot seem to find the Way. I try *t*his way, and tread with force that way, and always with the keenest wish. I try all ways. What shall I do to find *The Way*?'

A cry went forth. It seemed to come from deep within his heart: 'Tread thou, O Pilgrim on the Way of sensuous life, the middle, lighted way. It passes straight between the dual worlds. Find thou that narrow, middle way. It leads you to your goal. Seek that perceptive steadiness which leads to proved endurance. Adherence to the chosen Way, and ignoring of the pairs of opposites, will bring this Blessed One upon the lighted way into the joy of proved success.' "

Ray Seven

"The Blessed One sought the pathway into form, but held

with firmness to the hand of the Magician. He sought to reconcile the Pilgrim, who was himself, to life in form. He sought to bring the world of disorder in which he found himself into some kind of order. He wandered far into the deepest depths and became immersed in chaos and disorder. He could not understand, yet still held to the hand of the Magician. He sought to bring about that order that his soul craved. He talked with all he met, but his bewilderment increased.

To the Magician thus he spoke: 'The ways of the Creator must be good. Behind all that which seems to be, must be a Plan. Teach me the purpose of it all. How can I work, immersed in deepest matter? Tell me the thing that I must do?'

The Magician said: 'Listen, O Worker in the furthest world, to the rhythm of the times. Note the pulsation in the heart of that which is divine. Retire into the silence and attune yourself unto the whole. Then venture forth. Establish the right rhythm; bring order to the forms of life which must express the Plan of Deity.'

For this Blessed One release is found in work. He must display his knowledge of the Plan by the sounding of those words which will evoke the Builders of the forms and thus create the new."

It might be of value, if here were summarized in more simple and less occult terms, the significance of the above esoteric stanzas, to express their true meaning in a few succinct and terse phrases. The stanzas are of no use unless they convey to the ray types among the students of this Treatise some useful meaning, whereby they can live more truly.

The individualised Spirit expresses itself through the various ray types in the following manner:—

Ray One
    Dynamic one-pointedness.
    Destructive energy.
    Power realised selfishly.
    Lovelessness.
    Isolation,

A longing for power and authority.
Desire to dominate.
Expressed strength and self-will,

leading to

A dynamic use of energy for the furtherance of the Plan.
The use of destructive forces in order to prepare the
    way for the Builders.
The will to power in order to cooperate.
Power realised as the major weapon of love.
Identification with the rhythm of the Whole.
The cessation of isolation.

Ray Two

The power to build for selfish ends.
Capacity to sense the Whole and to remain apart.
The cultivation of a separative spirit.
The hidden light.
The realisation of selfish desire.
Longing for material well-being.
Selfishness, and subordination of all soul powers to this
    end,

leading to

Building wisely, in relation to the Plan.
Inclusiveness.
A longing for wisdom and truth.
Sensitivity to the *Whole*.
Renunciation of the great heresy of separativeness.
The revelation of the light.
True illumination.
Right speech through generated wisdom.

Ray Three

Force manipulation through selfish desire.
Intelligent use of force with wrong motive.
Intense material and mental activity.
The realisation of energy as an end in itself.
Longing for glory, beauty and for material objectives,
Submergence in illusion, glamour, and maya,

leading to

The manipulation of energy in order to reveal beauty and truth.

The use of forces intelligently for the furtherance of the Plan.

Ordered rhythmic activity in cooperation with the *Whole*.

Desire for right revelation of divinity and light.

Adherence to right action.

The revelation of glory and good will.

Ray Four

Confused combat.

The realisation of that which is high and that which is low.

The darkness which precedes form expression.

The veiling of the intuition.

The sensing of inharmony, and cooperation with the part and not the whole.

Identification with humanity, the fourth Creative Hierarchy.

Undue recognition of that which is produced by speech.

Abnormal sensitivity to that which is the Not-Self.

Constant points of crisis,

leading to

Unity and harmony.

The evocation of the intuition.

Right judgment and pure reason.

The wisdom which works through the Angel of the Presence.

I would here point out a constant misconception on the part of esotericists. This Fourth Ray of Harmony, Beauty and Art is *not* the ray, per se, of the creative artist. The creative artist is found equally on all rays, without exception. This ray is the ray of the intuition and of the harmonising of all that has been achieved through the activity of form life, as later synthesised and absorbed by the solar angel; it manifests eventually as all that can be evoked and evolved through the power of the One Life (the Monad) working through form expression. It is the point of meeting for all the energies flowing through the higher spiritual triad and the lower triplicity.

Ray Five

The energy of ignorance.
Criticism.
The power to rationalise and destroy.
Mental separation.
Desire for knowledge. This leads to material activity.
Detailed analysis.
Intense materialism and temporarily the negation of Deity.
Intensification of the power to isolate.
The implications of wrong emphasis.
Distorted views of truth.
Mental devotion to form and form activity.
Theology,

leading to

A knowledge of reality.
The realisation of the soul and its potentialities.
Power to recognize and contact the Angel of the Presence.
Sensitivity to Deity, to light and to wisdom.
Spiritual and mental devotion.
The power to take initiation. (This is a point of real importance.)

Ray Six

Violence. Fanaticism. Wilful adherence to an ideal.
Short sighted blindness.
Militarism and a tendency to make trouble with others and with groups.
The power to see no point except one's own.
Suspicion of people's motives.
Rapid reaction to glamour and illusion.
Emotional devotion and bewildered idealism.
Vibratory activity between the pairs of opposites.

Intense capacity to be personal and emphasise personalities,

leading to

Directed, inclusive idealism.
Steadiness of perception through the expansion of con-
sciousness.
Reaction to, and sympathy with, the point of view of
others.
Willingness to see the work of other people progress
along their chosen lines.
The choosing of the middle way.
Peace and not war. The good of the *Whole* and not the
part.

Ray Seven

Black magic, or the use of magical powers for selfish
ends.
The power to "sit upon the fence" till the selfish values
emerge.
Disorder and chaos, through misunderstanding of the
Plan.
The wrong use of speech to bring about chosen objec-
tives.
Untruth.
Sex magic. The selfish perversion of soul powers,

leading to

White magic, the use of soul powers for spiritual ends.
The identification of oneself with reality.
Right order through right magic.
Power to cooperate with the *Whole*.
Understanding of the Plan.
The magical work of interpretation.
Manifestation of divinity.

A close study of the above suggested phrases, showing as
they do the wrong and the right major expressions of ray
force, will aid the student correctly to comprehend his own
ray nature, and also whereabouts he stands in his development. One of the major faults of disciples today is the paying

of too close attention to the faults, errors and activities of
other disciples, and too little attention to their own fulfilment
of the law of love, and to their own dharma and work. A
second failing of disciples (and particularly of the working
and accepted disciples in the world at this present time) is
incorrect speech, conveying ambiguous meanings and motivated by criticism, or by an individual desire to shine. In
olden days, the neophyte was forced into a prolonged silence.
Speech was not permitted. This was inculcated as a check
upon physical utterance of wrong words and ideas, based on
inadequate knowledge. Today, the neophyte must learn the
same lesson of attention to personal perfection and to personal work through the means of that inner silence which
broods over the disciple and forces him to attend to his own
work and business, leaving others free to do the same, and so
learn the lesson of experience. A great deal of present right
activity is hindered by the speech interplay between disciples,
and much time is lost through wordy discussion of the work
and activities of other disciples. Humanity, as a whole, needs
silence at this time as never before; it needs time in which to
reflect, and the opportunity to sense the universal rhythm.
Modern disciples, if they are to do their work as desired and
to cooperate with the Plan correctly, need that inner reflective quiet which in no way negates intense outer activity but
which does release them from wordy criticisms, feverish
discussions, and constant preoccupation with the dharma the
motives and the methods of their fellow disciples.

b. THE RAYS AND INITIATION

It will not be possible for me to make clear the ray reactions to the final process which we have considered briefly,
namely the stage in the liberation of the spirit which we call
Identification. All that is possible, even in the case of Initia-

tion, is to give the elementary stanzas which convey to accepted disciples some of the significance of the first initiation. As regards identification, the reactions of the illumined initiate are made available to his intelligence in symbolic form, but if these forms were described, they would be completely misunderstood. When the third initiation takes place and the wider open door looms before the initiate, he will then discover the meaning of that type of realisation which is here called (for lack of a better name) Identification.

Ray One

"The Angel of the Presence stands within the light divine —the centre and the meeting place of many forces.

These forces meet and blend. They focus in the head of him who stands before the Angel.

Eye to eye, and face to face, and hand to hand, they stand. Will reinforces will, and love meets love. The will-to-power merges with the will-to-love and strength with wisdom meets. These two are one. From that high spot of unity, the One who is released stands forth and says:—

'I return from whence I came; from the formless to the world of form I make my way. I will to be. I will to work. I will to serve and save. I will to lift the race. I serve the Plan with will, the *Whole* with power.'"

Ray Two

"The Angel of the Presence draws the wanderer to him. Love divine attracts the seeker on the Way. The point of merging is achieved.

Mouth to mouth, the breath is drawn forth, and the breath is drawn in. Heart to heart, the beating of these twain is merged in one. Foot to foot, the strength is passed from the greater to the less, and thus the Way is trodden.

Force inspires the Word, the Breath. Love inspires the heart, the life. Activity controls the treading of the Way. These three produce the merging. All then is lost and gained.

The Word goes forth: 'I tread the Way of Love. I love the Plan. Unto that Plan, I surrender all I have. Unto the

Whole, I give my heart's deep love. I serve the Plan; I serve the *Whole* with love and understanding.' "

Ray Three

"The Angel of the Presence stands within the centre of the whirling forces. For ages long, thus has he stood, the centre of all energies from above and from below.

With intelligence, the Angel works to make the *One* Who is above and the one who is below to blend and be as one. With twelve clear notes, the hour sounds forth, and then the two are one. The Angel stands entranced.

Ear to ear, breast to breast, right hand to left, the two (who are the three) produce the merging of their lives. Glory shines forth. Truth is revealed. The work is done.

Then man, who is the soul, cries forth with power:—'I understand the Way—the inner Way, the silent Way, the manifested Way, for these three *Ways* are one. The Plan proceeds upon the outer Way; it shews itself. The *Whole* will stand revealed. That Plan I know. I *will*, with love and mind, to serve that Plan.' "

Ray Four

"The Angel of the Presence stands in his beauty rare upon the lighted Way. The glory of the Presence pours throughout the field of combat and ends, in peace, the strife.

The warrior stands revealed. His work is done. Back to back, the Angel and the Warrior stand, their auras meeting in a radiant sphere of light. The two are one.

The Voice goes forth:—'Harmony is restored and the beauty of the Lord of Love shines forth. Such is the Plan. Thus is the Whole revealed. The higher and the lower meet; form and the formless merge and blend, and know themselves as one. In harmony with all united souls, I serve the Plan.' "

Ray Five

"The Angel of the Presence serves the three—the One above, the one below, and the One who ever is. [This refers to the fact that on the fifth plane the Angel is definitely met and known, and the three aspects of the higher triad, buddhi, the abstract mind and spirit, plus the ego in the causal body, and the lower mind are here blended and fused.]

The great Triangle begins its revolutions, and its rays reach out in all directions, and permeate the *Whole*.

The man and Angel face each other, and know themselves to be the same. The light that radiates from the heart, the throat, and from the centre which stands midway meet and merge. The two are one.

The Voice that speaks within the silence can be heard: 'The power that reaches from the highest point has reached the lowest. The Plan can now be known. The Whole can stand revealed. The love that stretches from the heart, the life that issues forth from God, have served the Plan. The mind that gathers all with wisdom into the boundaries of the Plan has reached the outer limits of the sphere of God's activity. That power informs my life. That love inspires my heart. That mind enlightens all my world. I therefore serve the Plan.' "

Ray Six

"The Angel of the Presence reaches down, and, at the midway point, pierces the fog of glamour. The Path stands clear.

The One who treads the path and stops to fight, who wrestles blindly with the two who seek to hinder and to blind, sees the Way free. It stands revealed. He ceases from the clamour and the fight. He finds his way into the Presence.

Knee to knee, and foot to foot, they stand. Hand to hand, and breast to breast, forehead to forehead, see them stand. And thus they merge and blend.

The trumpet call goes forth: 'The warfare is no more. The battle ends. The glamour and the clouds have disappeared. The light and glory of the *Day* is here. That light reveals the Plan. The Whole is with us now. The purpose is revealed. With all I have, I serve that Plan.' "

Ray Seven

"The Angel of the Presence lifts one hand into the blue of heaven. He plunges deep the other into the sea of forms. Thus he connects the world of form and formless life. Heaven to earth he brings; earth into heaven. This the man, who stands before the Angel, knows.

He grasps the meaning of the painted sign which the Angel holds aloft. [Then follows a phrase which is incapable of translation into modern language. It signifies that complete merging which the mystic endeavours to express in terms of the "marriage in the heavens", and which has been wrongly twisted into the false teaching anent sex magic. This phrase, expressed by a painted symbol, symbolises complete unity between the outer and the inner, the objective and the subjective, between spirit and matter, and between the physical and the essential.]

The two are one. Naught more remains to grasp. The Word is manifest. The work is seen complete. The Whole is visioned. The magic work is wrought. Again the two are one. The Plan is served. No word need then be said."

These phrases are an attempt to express some of the realisations of the true initiate when he stands—at the third initiation—before the Angel and sees that Angel also pass away, so that naught is left but conscious knowledge and realisation. Although this statement may signify but little to us at present, it will, nevertheless, serve to demonstrate the futility of dealing with the secrets of the mysteries and with initiation through the medium of words. When this is better realised, the true work of the Masonic dramas will begin to measure up to the need.

This section expresses some of the basic emerging truths which will carry meaning to the senior disciples and the initiates of the world, who are battling, at this time, in the service of the Plan. They are present in the world at this time, and their work is bearing fruit, but they need at times the incentive of the future achievable glory to aid them to carry on.

This treatise is, therefore, somewhat abstruse and quite symbolical. It may appear difficult to comprehend, and it may mean little to some and nothing at all to others. If the disciples of the world are truly struggling and if they are applying practically the teaching given, as far as in them lies, they will find as time elapses, and their reason and intuition awaken, that such symbolic and abstruse statements become clearer and clearer, serving to convey the intended teaching. When this happens, the Angel of the Presence approaches ever closer, and lights the disciple on his way. The sense of separateness diminishes until, at last, light permeates the darkness, and the Angel dominates the life.

2. *The Two Cycles of Egoic Appropriation*

We shall now enter upon a somewhat technical consideration of the relation of the Ego and its ray to the sheaths or vehicles through which it must express itself, and through which it must enter into contact with certain phases of divine experience. The foundation of what is here elaborated in relation to the cycles of appropriation, will be found briefly touched upon in *A Treatise on Cosmic Fire* (pages 787-790), and the following statements, gathered from those pages, will be elucidated in the succeeding pages.

1. As the ego or soul appropriates to itself a sheath for expression and experience, points of crisis will inevitably occur:—

   a. The work of passing onto a particular plane for purposes of incarnation is one such point. This concerns the passing down to a lower plane, or from a lower plane onto a higher. Indications of the importance and the crucial nature of such transition can be seen in certain formulas which are used when passing from one degree in Masonry to another, as in raising a Lodge from a lower to a higher degree.

   b. Another such point of crisis occurs when the mental body is swept into activity and the etheric body is similarly vitalised.

2. Relationship between the ego or soul and the dense physical body is established when

   a. Matter of the three lowest subplanes of the physical
      plane is built into the etheric body, prior to physical
      incarnation, and the potential channels of communi-
      cation and of exit are established. These are the main
      channel or line of communication found between the
      centre at the base of the spine and that in the head,
      via the spleen.

   b. A corresponding activity takes place in the process of
      liberation upon the Path of Return in which the
      bridge (or the antahkarana) is established between
      the lower mental body, the causal body, and the
      higher mental worlds.

When the work under the first category is accomplished
upon the physical plane and its technique is understood, man
can then achieve escape from the physical body in full, waking continuity of consciousness. When a similar work has
taken place on the higher plane and the "bridge" is satisfactorily built, then the "initiate" can escape from the limitations of
form life and enter into that state of consciousness called *Nirvana*, by the Buddhist. This high state of being has to be entered also in full continuity of consciousness. Both these major
crises in the life of the soul,—one leading to physical incarnation and one producing the liberation of the soul from that
condition,—are, and must always be, the result of group
vibration, of group impulse, group incentive and group
impetus. One impetus originates in the group of souls, of
which an incarnating ego is an integral part; the other is the
result of the activity of the groups of atoms which are vibrating in response to (but not in unison with) that egoic impulse. In this phrase is summed up the work and opportunity

of the soul, for it works towards the regeneration of matter and not towards the consummation of its own salvation. It might be stated that the liberation of the soul or ego comes about when its work of salvaging matter (through utilising it and building it into forms) has been carried forward to a desired point. It is not primarily due to the attainment of a certain spiritual stature by the man and the demonstration of certain spiritual qualities. This desired stature and these spiritual qualities are manifested when the vehicles have been "occultly saved", and matter has thus been transformed, transmuted and symbolically "raised up into heaven". When the vehicles vibrate in unison with the soul, then is liberation achieved.

a. THE POINTS OF CRISIS

Just as there are five points of crisis in the life of a man as he achieves the goal of initiation (which we call the five Initiations), so there are five similar points of crisis in the process of taking form in the three worlds, with three of more importance,—the first, the third and the fifth. When (speaking again in symbols) a soul, functioning under divine impulse, comes into incarnation and undergoes racial experience in order to develop certain manifested qualities, there are five points of crisis. I am here speaking in terms of humanity as a whole, as mankind expresses what we call the "human state of consciousness". I am not speaking in terms of an individual soul, if such a misnomer may be permitted. These five points of crisis mark the transfer of soul life from one race to another. Each time such an event happens, there is racial unfoldment, and the appropriation, more or less consciously, by the race of another vehicle of expression. The following tabulation shows the appropriations marking the five racial crises.

1. In the Lemurian civilisation . . . . the appropriation of the physical body, with its five senses.

2. In the Atlantean civilisation . . . . the appropriation of the astral body.

3. In the present Aryan world . . . . the appropriation of the mental body, with consequent intellectual unfoldment.

4. In the coming race . . . . conscious appropriation and integration of the threefold personality.

5. In the final race . . . . the expression, in fullest measure, of the soul and its vehicles, plus some measure of spiritual manifestation.

Here, therefore, we have five points of crisis in the life of the individual, in conjunction with the whole, with the first stage (called individualisation) in Lemuria, the third stage in our race, and a final stage at the end of the age. These stages are carried forward over so long a period of time, and are so closely interrelated, that one stage and period makes possible that of another, and only the analytical mind sees or seeks differentiation. The reflection of this fivefold experience in any individual life takes place in the following order in the life of the average intelligent aspirant, who responds to, and takes advantage of the civilisation and education of the present time.

1. Appropriation of the physical sheath.
    This takes place between the fourth and seventh year, when the soul, hitherto overshadowing, takes possession of the physical vehicle.

2. A crisis during adolescence, wherein the soul appropriates the astral vehicle. This crisis is not recognised by the general public and is only dimly sensed, from its evidenced temporary abnormalities, by the average psychologist. They do not recognise the cause but only the effects.

3. A similar crisis between the twenty-first and twenty-fifth years, wherein the mind vehicle is appropriated. The man should then begin to respond to egoic influences, and in the case of the advanced man, he frequently does.

4. A crisis between the thirty-fifth and forty-second years, wherein conscious contact with the soul is established; the threefold personality then begins to respond, as a unit, to soul impulse.

5. For the remaining years of life, there should be an increasingly strong relationship between the soul and its vehicles, leading to another crisis between the fifty-sixth or the sixty-third years. According to that crisis will depend the future usefulness of the person and whether the ego continues to use the vehicles on into old age, or whether there is a gradual withdrawal of the indwelling entity.

There are many corresponding cycles of crisis in the life history of any soul down through the ages, but these major five crises can be traced with clarity from the standpoint of the higher vision.

One of the ways in which the life story of a soul is charted in the archives of the Masters (under the present planetary experiment) is by means of graphs, which give these crises—racial and individual. Sometimes, with the more advanced aspirants, even the physiological crises of importance are charted. The entire story of the relationship of a soul with its several vehicles of expression in the three worlds, is the story of the various types of energy which are being magnetically related to each other and which are temporarily subordinated to varying aspects of force, in order to produce those fields of magnetic activity wherein certain needed rates of vibration may be established. From the angle of the initiates of the Ageless Wisdom, the story of man, the aspirant, is the story of his response to, or repulse of, applied energies. The fact that the interplay between different types of energy results in the formation of those aggregations or condensations of force which we call bodies, sheaths or vehicles (material or immaterial) is incidental to the main issue, which is the development of a conscious response to the life of God.

Small units of energy, relatively speaking, are swept into contact with great fields of force, which we call planes. According to the extent of the impact (and this is determined, —symbolically speaking,—by the power of the originating will, the so-called age of the soul, the potency of group activity, and planetary or group karma), so will be the response between the unit of energy and the field contacted, and so will be the quality and vibratory activity of the atoms of matter which are attracted and held together. They will thus constitute a temporary form from which can be seen as externalised and as relatively tangible, and which can function as a mode or medium whereby the soul can contact larger forms of divine life and expression. The more intricate the organisation of the form and the more complex and perfect the response apparatus, the more clearly will be indicated the age of the soul and the perfected intent or potency of its will, the freer it will be from the limiting karma of an unevolved conditioning vehicle.

A close study of this subject is not possible here. The appropriation by a soul of those energy units which will constitute its body or sheath, as it passes from one plane to another and from one state of consciousness to another, is a study so abstruse and complicated that only those initiates whose development equips them and whose interest impels them to work with the application of the law of karma (which is identified in time and space with substance and force), can readily comprehend the complexities of the subject.

Two words are emerging today in connection with modern psychology which have a close relation to this difficult law; they indicate two basic ideas with which these trained initiates work. The idea of *patterns* and the idea of *conditioning* hold definite occult implications. The workers in this department of esoteric work deal primarily with the world of patterns which underlie all the activities of the Oversoul and the individual souls. Forget not that this term "individual souls" is but a limiting phrase, used by the separative mind to indicate the aspects of one reality.

Patterns are, in the last analysis, only those types of energy which are struggling to emerge into material expression and which eventually subordinate the more superficial and obvious energies (which have worked their way through to the surface in the process of manifesting) to their newer imposed rhythm. Thus they produce the changed types, new forms and different notes, tones and appearances. These patterns are literally the divine ideas, as they emerge from the subjective group consciousness and take those mental forms that can be appreciated and appropriated by the mind and brain of man during any particular epoch. It might, therefore, be thought that these patterns or fundamental ideas which take shape and appear to control the "way of a man on earth", as it is esoterically called, produce the conditioning here discussed. Literally and curiously, this is *not* so. From the angle of esoteric thought, conditioning (if rightly understood) concerns the response, innate and inherent, of matter or substance, to the pattern. It might be said that the pattern evokes and awakens response, but that the conditioning of the resultant activity is determined by the quality of the response apparatus. This quality is inherent in the substance itself, and the interplay between the pattern and the conditioned material produces the type of sheath which the soul appropriates in time and space, in order to experiment and gain experience. It will appear more clearly, therefore, as one studies this subject and ponders deeply upon its implications, that as a man advances on the path of evolution and nears the status of an initiate, the conditioning of the form, innate and inherent, will continuously approach nearer and nearer to the requirements of the pattern. It might also be stated that the pattern is relatively immutable and unchangeable in its own inherent nature, as it comes forth from the mind of either the macrocosmic Deity or the microcosmic thinker, but that the process of the inner conditioning of matter is mutable and in a state of continual flux. When, at the third initiation, union of the pattern and the conditioned form is achieved, the Transfiguration of the initiate takes place, leading to that final crisis wherein the two are known as one, and the form nature (including in this phase the causal body as well as the lower vehicles) then is dispersed and disappears.

The early stages of human development are—as in all else in nature,—apparently inchoate and formless, from the angle of the true pattern, existing eternal in the Heavens. There is a physical form, but the inner, fluid, subjective nature, emotional and mental, in no way conforms to the pattern, and, therefore, the outer form is also inadequate. But crisis after crisis occurs, and the inner form nature responds more definitely and precisely to the outer impact of the soul impetus (note this paradoxical phrase), until the astral vehicle and the mental body are consciously appropriated, and as consciously used. It must never be forgotten that evolution (as we understand it and as it must be studied by the human intellect) is the story of the evolution of consciousness and not the story of the evolution of form. This latter evolution is implicit in the other and of secondary importance from the occult angle. Consciousness is literally the reaction of active intelligence to the pattern. Today, it is as if we were responding consciously and with an increasingly intelligent purpose to the design as laid down by the Master Builder upon the tracing board. As yet we do not and cannot enter into that Cosmic Mind and vibrate in conscious unison with the divine Idea nor grasp the Plan as it is sensed and seen by the cosmic Thinker. We have to work with the design, with the pattern, and with the Plan, for we are only as yet in process of being initiated into that Plan and we are not aware of the true significance of those great *Identifications* which enabled the Carpenter of Nazareth to say: "I and my Father are one."

But it must also be remembered (and herein lies the clue to world unfoldment and to the mystery of past, present and future) that we are dealing with matter-substance and with forms which are already conditioned, and which were conditioned when the creative process began. The material to be found in the quarries of manifested purpose is, symbolically speaking, *Marble* and is thus conditioned. It is not clay or slate. It is from this marble, with all the inherent attributes of marble, that the Temple of the Lord must be built, in conformity to the design or pattern. This conditioned substance must be accepted as existing and must be dealt with as it is. Such is the parable of the ages. The design, the material, and the future temple are all subjectively related, and it is this that the soul knows. For the soul is the One who appropriates the material (already conditioned and qualified), and for ages the soul wrestles with that material, building it into tentative forms, discarding it at will, gathering together again the material needed, and steadily making more adequate models as the pattern is visioned. Some day, the model will be discarded, the pattern will be seen as it really is, and the worker, the soul, will then begin to build consciously the Temple of the Lord, out of the conditioned and prepared material which, for long ages, it has been preparing in the quarry of the form life, the personal life.

Here, therefore, are indicated two crises in the subjective life of the soul:—

1. The crisis wherein the soul, blinded, limited and handicapped by form, begins to work in the quarry of experience, far from its own country, with inadequate tools, and in complete temporary self-imposed ignorance of the design, or pattern.

2. The crisis which comes very much later in the soul's experience, wherein the soul knows more clearly the design, and in which much material has been prepared. The soul is no longer blind, and can now work in collaboration with other souls in the preparation of the material for the final Temple of the Lord. The soul, incarnate in human form, places in that Temple his particular contribution to the whole, which might be stated symbolically to be

   a. A stone placed in the foundations, typical of the consecrated physical life.

   b. A column in the Temple itself, typical of the desire or aspirational life.

   c. A design upon the tracing board, which coincides with

the Great Pattern or Design, and which is that fragment of that design which the individual had to supply
and in search of which he went forth.

d. A radiance or light, which will augment the Shekinah,
the light which "ever shineth in the East".

Three things emerge in connection with the task of the soul
as it appropriates sheath after sheath for expression:—

1. The condition of the substance of the sheaths which determines the equipment.
2. Responsiveness to the pattern, which is dependent upon
the stage of conscious development.
3. Ability to work in connection with the Plan, which is
dependent upon the number and quality of the crises
undergone.

All this takes place as the soul passes, time after time, through
the experience of physical incarnation; later, progress is
made consciously from plane to plane and this is undertaken
with clear intent. The work is facilitated and progresses with
increased rapidity as the soul, actively, intelligently and
intuitively, begins to work with the pattern, transmitting from
crisis to crisis (each marking an expansion of consciousness)
a newer reach of development and a fresh grasp of the great
Design, coupled with a better and more adequate equipment
through which to carry on the work.

In our consideration of the second part of the statement in
this treatise, which deals with the relationship of the soul to
its instrument,—the mechanism whereby or wherewith it expresses quality, activity and eventually divinity (whatever
that vague word may mean)—we have to approach the subject in two ways:

First, we must consider the utilisation of the mechanism on the Path of Outgoing.

Second, the utilisation of the mechanism upon the Path of Return.

In the first case, we are dealing with what might be regarded as the physiological aspect, for it is in the physical nature that the consciousness is primarily focussed; in the second case, we are concerned with the purely mental apparatus, though the word "apparatus" is basically unsuitable.

It might be well to interrupt here for a moment and deal with the idea of mechanism and divinity, for these are apt to be a materialising of the idea of divinity, particularly in the West. The divinity of Christ, for instance, is frequently illustrated by reference to His miracles, and to those supernormal powers which He so often evidenced. Supernormal powers are, of themselves, no evidence of divinity at all. Great exponents of evil can perform the same miracles and demonstrate the same capacity to create and to transcend the normal faculties of man. These powers are inherent in the creative aspect of Divinity, the third or matter aspect, and are linked to an intelligent understanding of matter and to the power of the mind to dominate substance. This power is, therefore, neither divine nor non-divine. It is a demonstration of the capacity of the mind, and can be used with equal facility by an incarnated Son of God, functioning as a World Saviour or Christ, and by those Beings who are on the path of destruction, and who are called (by those who know no better) Black Magicians, Evil Forces and Devils.

Divinity (using the word in its separative sense) connotes the expression of the qualities of the second or building aspect of God,—magnetism, love, inclusiveness, non-separativeness, sacrifice for the good of the world, unselfishness, intuitive understanding, cooperation with the Plan of God, and many other such qualitative phrases. Mechanism, after all, implies the creation of a form out of matter and the infusing of that form with a life principle which will show itself in the power to grow, to reproduce, to preserve identity of some kind, to flower forth into certain instinctual reactions, and to preserve its own specific qualitative nature. Life resembles the fuel which, in conjunction with the mechanism, provides the motivating principle and makes activity and the needed movement possible. But there is more to manifestation than forms which possess a life principle. There is a diversity running through nature and a qualifying principle which differentiates the mechanisms; there is a general synthesis and purpose which defies the powers of man to emulate it creatively, and which is outstandingly the major characteristic of divinity. It expresses itself through colour and beauty, through reason and love, through idealism and wisdom, and through those many qualities and that purpose which, for instance, animate the aspirant. This is—briefly and inadequately expressed—Divinity. It is, however, a relative expression of Divinity. When each of us stands where stand the Masters and the Christ, we will regard this whole question from another point of view. The developing of virtues, the cultivation of understanding, the demonstration of good character and high aims, and the expression of an ethical and moral point of view are all necessary fundamentals, preceding certain definite experiences which usher the soul into worlds of realisation which are so far removed from our present point of view that any definition of them would be meaningless. What we are engaged in is the development of those qualities and virtues which will "clear our vision", because they produce the purification of the vehicles so that the real significance of divinity can begin to emerge in our consciousness.

b. Certain Basic Premises

With this preamble, we will pass on to the consideration of the mechanism and of that which infuses it and motivates it with life and intelligence.

Certain basic premises are recognised and can, therefore, be very briefly mentioned:—

1. The soul informs the mechanism in two ways and through two points of contact in the body:—
   a. The "thread of life" is anchored in the heart. The life principle is there to be found, and from that station it pervades the entire physical body through the medium of the blood stream, for "the blood is the life".
   b. The "thread of consciousness" or of intelligence is anchored in the head, in the region of the pineal gland, and from that station of perception it orders or directs the physical plane activities, through the medium of the brain and the nervous system.

2. The directive activity of the soul, or its authoritative grasp upon the mechanism of the body, is dependent for its extent upon the point of development, or upon the so-called "age of the soul". The soul is ageless from the human angle, and what is really meant is the length of time that a soul has employed the method of physical incarnation.

3. The result of this twofold hold upon the mechanism during the past ages has been the conditioning of the material, in conjunction with its own inherent conditioned nature. A form is produced which is adequate to the temporary need of the soul and which is a reflection, in time and space, of its "relative age" or point of develop-

ment. This, therefore, produces the type of brain, the conformation of the body, the condition of the endocrine system, and consequently the set of qualities, the type of mental reaction, and the character with which any given subject enters into life upon the physical plane. From that point, the work proceeds. This work might be regarded as an effort to intensify the hold which the divine Thinker has upon the mechanism. This will lead to a wiser, fuller direction, a deeper realisation of the purpose, and an effort to clear the way for the soul by the institution of those practices which tend towards right conduct, right speech, and good character. The thought underlying this paragraph links the conclusions of the materialistic school of psychologists with the introspectionist school and those schools which posit a self, a soul or a spiritual entity, and shows that both groups are dealing with facts, and that both must play their united parts in training the aspirant in the New Age.

4. As the introspective method is pursued, and as we study the human subject, we discover that underlying the human body in all its parts, and constituting a definite part of the human apparatus, there is a vehicle which has been called the "etheric body", composed entirely of threads of force which, in their turn, form the channels along which still more subtle and varying types of energy flow. These are, in their turn, "conditioned" during manifestations by the status of the soul. These threads underlie and interpenetrate the entire body and the nervous system and are in reality the actuating power of the nervous system. Their responsiveness to impacts, outer and inner, is unbelievably great. The nervous reactions of the disciple and highly developed person,

whose etheric body is in close rapport with his nervous system, is beyond the average comprehension.

5. The sum-total of the nerves, with the millions of nadis or "thread counterparts" in the etheric body, form a unit, and this unit, according to the teaching of the Ageless Wisdom, has in it points of focus for different types of energy. These are called "force centres", and upon these depend the life experience of the soul and its expression, and not upon the body. They are the factors which condition the glandular system of the body.

6. This subjective and objective system governs the manifestation of the soul on the physical plane. It indicates to those who can see in truth, the grasp or hold that the soul has upon its instrument; it can be seen whether that grasp is occasional and partial or whether it is entire and whole. This is most wonderfully indicated in a certain Masonic grip, which marks a climax in the experience of the candidate to the mysteries.

I previously referred to the main channel of communication between the soul and its mechanism as being:—

a. The centre at the base of the spine.

b. The centre at the top of the head, where the most important centre in the body is situated, from the standpoint of the soul. There is its point of entry and exit; there is the great radio station of reception, and the distributing centre for direction.

c. The spleen. This is a subsidiary centre and organ in connection with the heart centre.

It is through the spleen that a linking up takes place between the life principle (seated in the heart) and the consciousness system, interlinking all the material organs and the atomic substance of the physical body. This statement indicates that, in the location in the human body where the spleen is found, along with its corresponding subjective force centre, two great currents of energy cross: these are the current of physical vitality or life and the current of the consciousness of the atoms which construct the form. It will be observed that we are here discussing the group subconscious life and not the conscious life and the self-consciousness. The spleen is the organ in which planetary prana or vitality is received and passed. This enters in through "the open gateway" of the splenic force centre, and passes to the heart. There it merges with the individual life principle. Through the splenic centre also passes the conscious life of the sum-total of the bodily cells, which are, in their turn, the recipients of the energy of the consciousness aspect or principles of all atoms and forms within the fourth kingdom of nature. This we cannot be expected to comprehend as yet, but the truth will be appreciated later on in the racial development. A hint can here be found as to the excessive sensitivity of the solar plexus centre to surrounding group impacts and impressions of an astral kind. There is a close rapport between the splenic centre and the solar plexus, as well as with the heart.

7. These two subjective and subconscious streams of energy cross each other in the region of the spleen and there form a cross in the human body, as they traverse each other's lines of force. This is the correspondence in the human body to the cross of matter, spoken of in connection with Deity. Consciousness and life form a cross. The downpouring stream of life from the heart and the stream of life-giving energy from the spleen pass on (after crossing each other and producing a whirl-pool of force) into the solar plexus region; from thence

they are very definitely drawn together as one stream at a certain stage in the life of the advanced aspirant. There they merge with the sum-total of energies, using the three points referred to—the head, the base of the spine and the spleen—as a definite mode of communication, of distribution and of control, and finally of ultimat withdrawal, consciously or unconsciously, at the moment of death or in the technique of inducing that stage of control known as *Samadhi*.

8. When the directing Agent in the head, deliberately and by an act of the will, raises the accumulated energies at the base of the spine, he draws them into the magnetic field of the centres up the spine and blends them with the dual energy emanating from the spleen. The spinal tract with its five centres then awakens into activity, and finally all the forces are gathered together into one fused and blended stream of energy. Three things then happen:

   a. The kundalini fire is raised and immediately burns away all the etheric webs which are the protective barriers, separating the various centres.

   b. The etheric body intensifies its vitality, and the physical body is consequently powerfully vitalised, galvanised, and energised.

   c. The entire aura is coordinated and illumined, and the soul can then, at will, withdraw from its physical vehicle in full waking consciousness, or stay in it as an incarnated Son of God, Whose consciousness is complete on the physical plane, the astral plane, and on the mental levels, as well as in the three aspects of lower mind, causal consciousness and nirvanic realisation. This process finds its consummation at the third initiation.

In the life of the aspirant, the power to cause this tremendous happening is dependent upon the carrying forward of the inner subjective and spiritual work previously described as the "building of the bridge on the mental plane" between the above mentioned three aspects. For the race of men *as a whole*, this work began in the middle of our Aryan race, and is today going forward very rapidly. For the individual aspirant, the work has always been possible right down the ages, and it is the major task undertaken by disciples at this time. It might be added here that the New Group of World Servers is composed of those who are engaged in this work for the race, and every person who builds his bridge joins this group of occult "bridge-builders". There is, therefore, something symbolic about the work of our modern bridge builders who join the chasms and span the waters and thus give concrete evidence of the work being done today by advanced humanity.

It now becomes possible to consider the process whereby a man bridges the gulf or gap (speaking symbolically) which exists between the personal lower self and the higher Self, as the latter functions in its own world. This has to be bridged before at-one-ment can be achieved and complete integration of the entire man can be brought about. To understand clearly what occurs, it will be wise to define more accurately what that higher nature is, and of what it consists.

We have seen in our studies that the soul is a dual blend of energies—the energy of life and the energy of mind—as far as its relation to the mechanism is temporarily concerned. The merging of these two energies in the human mechanism produces what we call consciousness—at first self-consciousness and finally group-consciousness. The mechanism is, in its own nature, also a blend or fusion of energies—the energy of substance itself which takes the form of the atomic structure of the physical body, plus the vitality which animates that body, and, secondly, the energy of that body which we call the astral body, distinguished by sensitivity, emotional activity, and that magnetic force which we call desire. There is, finally, the energy of mind itself. These four types of energy form what we call the lower personal self, but it is the higher mental aspect of the mind which links, subjectively, this personality and the soul. It is the lower consciousness which (when developed) enables a man eventually to make conscious contact with the higher. It is the lower concretising mind which must be awakened, understood and used with definiteness before the higher mind can become the medium through which knowledge can be gained of those realities which constitute the kingdom of God. Intellect must be unfolded before the intuition can be correctly evoked.

We have, therefore, in the case of man, two groups of major energies dominating, as a result of a long experience of incarnation in form, the energy of the astral or desire nature and the energy of mind. When these are fused and blended, thoroughly organised and utilised, then we see a functioning and powerful Personality. Seeking to impose itself upon these energies and to subordinate them to higher and different aims is to be found that blended energy-unit which we call the soul. Its two energies (mind and love, the latter being also a dual form of energy) are anchored, if one may use this word in a symbolic and esoteric sense, in the human brain, whilst the life principle, as we have seen, is anchored in the human heart. The four energies of the lower self—atomic energy, vital energy, feeling energy and mental energy—plus the two energies of the soul, make the six energies used by man in his life experience; but the energy of the atom is usually not counted as a human energy, as it is uniform in its usage in all forms of life in all kingdoms, and therefore man is regarded as a sum total of five energies, and not of six energies.

The human soul (in contradistinction to the soul as it functions in its own kingdom, free from the limitations of human life) is imprisoned by and subject to the control of the lower energies for the major part of its experience. Then, upon the Path of Probation, the dual energy of the soul begins to be increasingly active, and the man seeks consciously to use his mind, and to express love-wisdom on the physical plane. This is a simple statement of the objective of all aspirants. When the five energies are beginning to be used consciously and wisely in service, a rhythm is then set up between the personality and the soul. It is as if a magnetic field were then established, and these two vibrating and magnetic units, or grouped energies, begin to swing into each other's field of influence. In the early stages, this happens only occasionally and rarely. Later it occurs more constantly, and thus a path of contact is established which eventually becomes the line of least resistance, "the way of familiar approach", as it is sometimes esoterically called. Thus the first half of the "bridge", the antahkarana, is constructed. By the time the third initiation is undergone, this way is completed, and the initiate can "pass to higher worlds at will, leaving the lower worlds far behind; or he can come again and pass upon the way that leads from dark to light, from light to dark, and from the under, lower worlds into the realms of light".

Thus the two are one, and the first great unison upon the path of return is complete. A second stage of the way has then to be trodden, leading to a second union of still greater importance in that it leads to complete liberation from the three worlds. It must be remembered that the soul, in its turn, is a union of two energies, plus the energy of spirit, of which the lower three are the reflection. It is a synthesis of the energy of Life itself (which demonstrates as the life-principle within the world of forms), of the energy of the intuition, or spiritual love-wisdom or understanding (which demonstrates as sensitivity and feeling in the astral body), and of spiritual mind, whose reflection in the lower nature is the mind or the principle of intelligence in the form world. In these three energies we have the atma—buddhi—manas of the theosophical literature. They are that higher triplicity which is reflected in the lower three, and which focusses through the soul body on the higher levels of the mental plane before being "precipitated into incarnation", as it is esoterically called.

Modernising the concept, we might say that the energies which animate the physical body and the intelligent life of the atom, the sensitive emotional states, and the intelligent mind have eventually to be blended with, and transmuted into, the energies which animate the soul. These are the spiritual mind, conveying illumination; the intuitive nature, conferring spiritual perception; and divine livingness.

After the third initiation the "Way" is carried forward with great rapidity, and the "bridge" is finished which links perfectly the higher spiritual Triad and the lower material reflection. The three worlds of the soul and the three worlds of the Personality become one world wherein the initiate works and functions, seeing no distinction, viewing one world as the world of inspiration and the other world as constituting the field of service, yet regarding both together as forming one world of activity. Of these two worlds, the subjective etheric body (or the body of vital inspiration) and the dense physical body are symbols on the external plane.

How is this bridging antahkarana to be built? What are the steps which the disciple must follow? We are not here considering the Path of Probation whereon the major faults should be eliminated and whereon the major virtues should be developed. Much of the spiritual instruction given in the past has laid down the rules for the cultivation of the virtues and qualifications for discipleship, and also the necessity for self-control, for tolerance and for unselfishness. But these are elementary stages and should be taken for granted by all students of this Treatise. Such students are presumably occupied not only with the establishment of the character aspect of discipleship, but with the more abstruse and difficult requirements for those whose goal is initiation.

It is with the work of the "bridge-builders" that we are concerned. First, let it be stated that the real building of the antahkarana only takes place when the disciple is beginning to be definitely focussed upon mental levels, and when therefore his mind is intelligently and consciously functioning. He must begin at this stage to have some more exact idea than has hitherto been the case as to the distinctions existing between the Thinker, the apparatus of thought, and thought itself, beginning with its dual esoteric function which is:

1. The recognition of, and receptivity to, *Ideas*.
2. The creative faculty of conscious thought-form building.

This necessarily involves a strong mental attitude and a re-orientation of the mind to reality. As the disciple begins to focus himself on the mental plane (and this is the prime intent of the meditation work) he starts working in mental matter and trains himself in the powers and uses of thought. He achieves a measure of mind control; he can turn the searchlight of the mind in two directions—into the world of human endeavor, and into the world of soul activity. Just as the soul makes a way for itself by projecting itself in a thread or stream of energy into the three worlds, so the disciple be-

gins consciously to project himself into the higher worlds.
His energy goes forth, through the medium of the controlled
and directed mind, into the world of higher spiritual mind
and into the realm of the intuition. A reciprocal activity is
thus set up. This response between the higher and lower mind
is symbolically spoken of in terms of light, and the "lighted
way" (a term frequently employed) comes into being between
the personality and the spiritual Triad, via the soul body, just
as the soul came into definite contact with the brain via the
mind. This "lighted way" is the illumined bridge. It is built
through meditation; it is constructed through the constant
effort to draw forth the intuition, through subservience and
obedience to the Plan (which begins to be recognised as soon
as the intuition and the mind are en rapport) and through a
conscious incorporation into the group in service and for purposes of assimilation into the whole. All these qualities and
activities are based upon the foundation of good character
and the qualities developed upon the Probationary Path.

The effort to draw forth the intuition requires directed
occult (but not aspirational) meditation. It requires a trained
intelligence, so that the line of demarcation between intuitive
realisation and the forms of the higher psychism may be
clearly seen. It requires a constant disciplining of the mind,
so that it can "hold itself steady in the light", and the development of a cultured right interpretation so that the intuitive
knowledge which has been achieved may then clothe itself
in the right thought forms.

Subservience or obedience to the Plan involves something
else than a vague and misty realisation that God has a Plan
and that we are included in it. It is more than a hiding of
oneself in the shadow of the will of God. It necessitates a wise
differentiation between:

1. The general perspective and the large world Plan for the planet, and
2. Those immediate stages of the Plan in which intelligent cooperation is, at this time, and in the immediate present, demanded.

A deep interest in the final root races and speculation as to the life going forward on other planets may be of interest, but it is relatively futile and useless; it fertilises unduly the imagination, causing love of uncheckable detail, loss of time in wild surmises, and the chimeras of an unenlightened intellect. That part of the Plan which relates to its immediate application is of interest and usefulness. Obedience to the immediate purpose and duty is distinctive of the trained disciple. Those who know far more of the Plan than we can, refuse to let Their minds dwell on the unprovable, yet possible, hypotheses for future racial development. They focus Their attention on that which must be attended to at this immediate time. I would urge all disciples to do the same, for in so doing it is possible to bridge the gap and link the two shores of the higher and the lower stages of consciousness, between the old age and the new, between the kingdom of God and the kingdom of men, and thus to take their place in the ranks of the New Group of World Servers, whose arduous task calls for our sacrificing effort. Conscious incorporation in the group necessitates the cessation of personality life, and brings out the subordination of the little self to the work of the whole. These words are easily written and read; they embody, however, the task of all disciples at this time. Where this incentive and realisation are lacking, the disciple is still a long way from his goal.

It might also be stated here that the construction of the bridge whereby the consciousness can function with facility both in the higher worlds and in the lower, is primarily brought about by a definitely directed life-tendency, which steadily drives the man in the direction of the world of spiritual realities, and certain dynamic movements of planned and carefully timed and directed orientation or focussing. In this last process, the *gain* of the past months or years is closely assessed; the *effect* of that gain upon the daily life and in the bodily mechanisms is as carefully studied; and the *will-to-live* as a spiritual being is wrought into the consciousness with a definiteness and a determination that make for immediate progress.

Disciples in the groups of some of the Masters (not of all) are encouraged, every seven years, to do this and to subject themselves to what is esoterically called a "crisis of polarisation". This process is in the nature of a review, such as one imposes on the consciousness at night, only it is carried over a period of years instead of hours. This thought merits consideration.

This building of the antahkarana is most assuredly proceeding in the case of every dedicated aspirant. When the work is carried on intelligently and with full awareness of the desired purpose, and when the aspirant not only recognises the process, but is alert and active in its fulfilment, then the work proceeds apace and the bridge is built.

One thing only need be added in connection with this building of the antahkarana, and that is the statement of the significant fact that the more people can achieve this linking of the higher and lower aspects of the human nature, the more rapidly will the task of salvaging the world proceed. The more painstakingly and persistently this work is carried forward, the sooner will the Hierarchy of the planet resume Its ancient task and status in the world, and the sooner will the Mysteries be restored and the world function, therefore, more consciously in line with the Plan. Every single unit of the human family who achieves success upon the Path of Discipleship may be, in himself, relatively of small importance. But the massed units are of tremendous potency. I tell you at this time for your cheering and encouragement that the numbers of the disciples in the world are greatly increasing. Suffering and trouble, apprehension and the processes whereby detachment and dispassion are enforced, are doing their needed work. Here and there throughout the world, in every nation and practically every week, men and women are stepping off the Path of Probation on to the Path of Discipleship. In this lies the hope of the world today. In this fact is to be found the greatly increased activity of the Masters.

This event, or this transition, never takes place before the first fine strand of energy (like the first steel cable on a physical bridge) has anchored itself on the further shore; thus a delicate and (at first) almost nebulous channel of communication is established between the higher nature and the lower, between the world of the soul and the worlds of human affairs. Each month, at the time of the full moon, the Masters are intensifying Their efforts, and men and women are being prepared for the process of Initiation with as much rapidity as is safely possible. Remember that understanding must always parallel the intellectual grasp of a subject, and it is this that holds back some disciples from this great step forward.

In the performance of the next duty, in the establishing of the dedicated life tendency towards reality, in the dispelling of illusion, and in the performance of service with love and understanding,—thus is the work carried forward. Is this effort beyond the reach of any of us? Or are its implications beyond our comprehension? I do not think so.

c. Seven Ray Methods of Appropriation

As we have seen, this process of appropriation is a dual matter, or rather, it involves a dual activity—that of taking and giving, of grasping and relinquishing, of establishing a hold upon that which is desired, and of detaching oneself from that which has been held. The various types of human beings who come forth along one or other of the seven rays, have each their specific way of doing this. These I shall indicate. At the same time, it must be borne in mind that the true significance of that which is portrayed and the meaning of what happens can only be understood by those who are in the process of this relinquishment. The stage of appropriation is undergone blindly and unconsciously. Man knows not what he does. It is only towards the end of his long pilgrimage and process of appropriation that he discovers how tired he actually is of grasping the non-essential and the material, and how ready he is for the work of detachment. In the life of every human being on the physical plane, who has lived fully and to the full term of years, this dual process can be symbolically seen. In youth the thoughtless (and all are thoughtless, for such is nature's way) hold on to life and give no thought to the time when there must be a relinquishment of the hold on physical existence. The young forget, and rightly forget, the inevitability of that final symbolic detachment which we call Death. But when life has played its part and age has taken its toll of interests and strength, the tired and world-weary man has no fear of the detaching process and seeks not to hold on to that which earlier was desired. He welcomes death, and relinquishes willingly that which earlier engrossed his attention.

In considering the processes of appropriation, the following phrases should be studied, as they throw a light upon the various stages from different angles:—

1. The stage of concretisation and materialisation. The soul takes to itself what it needs and desires for form building.

2. The stage of incarnation, taken at this time blindly.

3. The period wherein satisfaction of the desires is the major goal. These range all the way from physical desire and its satisfaction to a general and undefined desire for release.

4. The processes, in detail, of appropriating
   a. A body or bodies.
   b. A sheath or sheaths.
   c. A vehicle or vehicles.
   d. A form or forms.

5. Immersion in darkness. This was the result of desire. The darkness of ignorance was chosen and man started, through desire, to work his way from darkness to light, from ignorance to knowledge, from the unreal to the Real. Such is the great symbolic work of Masonry. It is an elucidation of the Way of Relinquishment.

6. The Path of outgoing in order to possess.

7. Selfishness, the major characteristic of the self in relation to, and identified with, the not-self.

8. Love of possession, the prostitution of spiritual love.

9. Acquisitiveness, the illusion of material need.

10. The period called in the Bible, that of "riotous living" on the part of the Prodigal Son.

11. The application and use of energy for personal, selfish intent.

12. Personality life, with all that is therein implied,—ambition, selfish purpose, etc.
13. Attachment to the seen, the known, and the familiar, external, objective forms.
14. The stage wherein thought forms are built, at first ignorantly, and then with deliberate selfishness.
15. The period of engrossment in the things of the kingdom of earth.
16. The world, the flesh, and the devil.

On the side of soul expression, which is governed by detachment, the following phrases and sentences will give an idea of the progress and intent:—

1. The stage of spiritualisation and of de-materialisation. The soul functions with the purpose of liberation before it, and not of further physical plane experience.
2. The relinquishment of form life.
3. The period wherein satiety is experienced; the desires have been so dominant and so often satisfied that they no longer attract.
4. The process, in detail, of liberation from
    a. A body or bodies.
    b. A sheath or sheaths.
    c. A vehicle or vehicles.
    d. A form or forms.
5. Emergence into light, a symbolic way of expressing the reverse of immersion in darkness.
6. The Path of Return, motivated by the wish to appropriate nothing for the separated self. The beginning of group consciousness and of group work.
7. Selflessness, the major characteristic of the Soul or Self.
8. Freedom from the desire to possess, freedom from acquisitiveness, and therefore the state of desirelessness.

9. The establishing of the sense of reality as the ruling principle of the life.

10. The return of the Prodigal Son to the Father's home.

11. The application and use of energy for group purpose and in cooperation with the Plan for the whole.

12. The life of the soul with all that is implied in that phrase.

13. Love of God in contradistinction to love of self.

14. Attachment to the unseen, the true, the subjective and the Real, which is only possible when there has been detachment from the seen, the false, the objective and the unreal.

15. Complete liberation from the control of the lower mind.

16. The period wherein the centre of interest is the kingdom of God and of the soul.

17. Reality. Formlessness. God.

It should be remembered, when considering the seven ray methods of appropriation and the reverse stages, that we are dealing with energies. Occult students must increasingly think and work in terms of energy. These energies are spoken of esoterically as "having impulsive effects, magnetic appeals, and focussed activities." The streams or emanations of energy exist, as is well known, in seven major aspects or qualities. They carry the sons of men into incarnation and withdraw them from incarnation. They have their own specific qualities and characteristics, and these determine the nature of the forms constructed, the quality of the life which is expressed at any particular time or in any particular incarnation, the length of the life cycle, and the appearance and disappearance of any of the three form aspects. Certain brief paragraphs will suffice to define each of the stages of appropriation. The paragraphs which detail the methods of detachment have been given earlier in *A Treatise on White Magic*.

Ray One. The Energy of Will or Power. The Destroyer Aspect.

Souls on this ray are spoken of occultly as "crashing their way into incarnation." They appropriate dynamically that which they require. They brook no hindrance in the satisfactions of their desires. They stand alone in a proud isolation, glorying in their strength, and their ruthlessness. These qualities have to be transmuted into that intelligent use of power which makes them powerful factors in the Plan, and magnetic centres of force, gathering workers and forces around them. An illustration of this can be seen in the work of the Master Morya, Who is the centre, the magnetic attractive centre, of all esoteric groups, conferring on them, by His power, the capacity to destroy that which is undesirable in the life of the disciples. Forget not that the work of stimulating that which is needed is one of the major tasks of a Master, and the power of a disciple to destroy that which limits him is greatly needed. Souls of this ray, as they come into incarnation through desire, *grasp*. This expresses the nature of the force demonstration employed. There is a measure of violence in their technique. They eventually "take the kingdom of heaven by force."

Ray Two. The Energy of Love-Wisdom

Souls on this ray use the method of "gathering in", or "drawing into". The soul sets up a vibration (little as we may yet grasp the real significance of that word) and that vibration affects its environment, and atoms of substance on all three planes are attracted to the central point of energy. The method is relatively gentle, when compared to the method of the first ray, and the process is somewhat longer whilst the overshadowing (carried forward prior to entering into the three worlds for purposes of appearance) is very much longer. This refers to that overshadowing of the substance to be built into form, and not to the overshadowing of the completed form, i.e. the child in the mother's womb. In the first case, it might be said that souls on the first ray are sudden and rapid in their desire to incarnate, and in the methods employed. Souls on the second ray are slower in coming to that "impulsive" action (in the sense of impulse to action and not impulse in time) which leads to the occult manufacture of an appearance with which to manifest.

Souls on this ray, as they come into incarnation through desire, *attract*. They are magnetic more than they are dynamic; they are constructive, and they work along the line which is, for all lives and forms, the line of least resistance within our universe.

Ray Three. The Energy of Active Intelligence

Just as the grasping and attracting are terms applicable to the methods of the two first rays, so a process of "selective manipulation" is characteristic of this third ray. This method is totally different in its technique to that of the two mentioned above. It might be said that the note which generates the activity set up by souls on this ray, is such that atoms of the different planes are moved as if consciously responding to a selective process. The vibratory activity of the soul makes itself felt, and atoms collect from widely different points in response to a certain quality in the vibration. It is far more selective than in the case of the second ray.

Just as souls in the first case seem to *grasp* indiscriminately what they need, and force the substance thus grasped into the form or appearance required, enduing it with the quality needed in a dynamic and forceful way, and just as souls on the second ray set up a motion which gathers material out of the immediately surrounding environment, and imposes on it, through *magnetic attraction*, the desired quality, so in the case of souls on the third ray the required material is chosen here and there, but that chosen already has the needed quality (note this difference) and nothing whatever is imposed. It will be apparent, therefore, that substance itself exists in three major categories, and that these three categories are the correspondences in substance to the three Persons of the Trinity or to the three bodies of incarnated man. They are also the analogy in the third aspect of divinity (the life of the third Person of the Trinity) to the quality of the three periodical vehicles through which manifestation takes place.

One division or type of this substance is *dynamically electrified* and from this all first ray egos choose the material needed in the three worlds. Another type of substance is *magnetically electrified*, and from it all second ray egos select what they, in time and space, require in order to manifest. The third type of substance is *diffusively electrified* (I know of no better word to express the intent), and all third ray egos take from it their needed quota of substance from which to build the forms for manifestation.

As regards the methods, techniques and types of substance used by souls on the remaining four minor rays, they are necessarily qualified by the characteristics of the third major ray, which eventually synthesises them.

The following tabulation is an attempt to define that which it is almost impossible to make intelligible in words. From the angle of the illumined occultist it is meaningless, even more than it is to the average student because as yet the mystery of electricity and the true nature of electrical phenomena (than which there is naught else) is at this time an unrevealed secret, even to the most advanced of the modern scientists.

Ray	Energy	Technique	Quality	Source
1	Power or Will	Grasping	Dynamic Purpose	Dynamically electrified forms.
2	Love-Wisdom	Attracting	Love	Magnetically electrified forms.
3	Intelligent activity	Selecting	Intellect	Diffusively electrified forms.
4	Beauty or Art	At-one-ing	Unification	Harmonising electrified forms.
5	Science	Differentiating	Discrimination	Crystallising electrified forms.
6	Idealism	Responding	Sensitivity	Fluidic electrified forms.
7	Organisation	Coordinating	Appearance	Physical electrified forms.

That there is such a thing as electricity, that it probably accounts for all that can be seen, sensed and known, and that the entire universe is a manifestation of electrical power,—all this may be stated and is, today, coming to be recognised. But when that has been said, the mystery remains, and will not be revealed, even in partial measure, until the middle of the next century. Then revelation may be possible, as there will be more initiates in the world, and inner vision and inner hearing will be more generally recognised and present. When man arrives at a better understanding of the etheric body and its seven force centres (which are all related to the seven rays, and in their expression show the seven characteristics and techniques which are here tabulated anent the rays) then some further light can intelligibly be thrown upon the nature of the seven types of electrical phenomena which we call the seven rays.

On the Path of Return and in connection with the process of detachment, which marks the progress of the soul towards release and the ending of the period of appropriation, certain passages in *A Treatise on White Magic* give clearly the intended technique. They are as follows, and are found on pages 288 and 289.

Ray One:—"Let the Forces come together. Let them mount to the High Place, and from that lofty eminence, let the soul look out upon a world destroyed. Then let the word go forth: 'I still persist!' "

Ray Two:—"Let all the life be drawn to the Centre, and enter thus into the heart of Love Divine. Then from that point of sentient Life, let the soul realise the consciousness of God. Let the word go forth, reverberating through the silence: 'Naught is but Me!' "

Ray Three:—"Let the army of the Lord, responsive to the word, cease their activities. Let knowledge end in wisdom. Let the point vibrating become the point quiescent, and all lines gather into One. Let the soul realise the One in Many, and let the word go forth in perfect understanding: 'I am the Worker and the Work, the One that Is.' "

Ray Four:—"Let the outer glory pass away and the beauty of the inner Light reveal the One. Let dissonance give place to harmony, and from the centre of the hidden Light, let the soul speak: Let the word roll forth: 'Beauty and glory veil Me not. I stand revealed. I am.' "

Ray Five:—"Let the three forms of energy electric pass upward to the Place of Power. Let the forces of the head and heart and all the nether aspects blend. Then let the soul look out upon an inner world of light divine. Let the word triumphant go forth: 'I mastered energy for I am energy Itself. The Master and the mastered are but One.' "

Ray Six:—"Let all desire cease. Let aspiration end. The search is over. Let the soul realise that it has reached the goal, and from that gateway to eternal Life and cosmic Peace, let the word sound: 'I am the seeker and the sought. I rest!' "

Ray Seven:—"Let the builders cease their work. The Temple is completed. Let the soul enter into its heritage and from the Holy Place command all work to end. Then in the silence subsequent, let him chant forth the Word: 'The creative work is over I, the Creator, Am. Naught else remains but Me.' "

II. The Seven Laws of Soul or Group Life

We come now to a section of our study of the soul and its life which is of real moment to all who live (or begin to live) and function as *conscious* souls, through definite alignment and at-one-ment. This section will, however, be relatively abstruse to all those whose lives are centred in the personality. Down the ages, the Scriptures of the world and those who have attempted to elucidate them, have been occupied with imparting to humanity an understanding of the nature of those qualities and characteristics which should distinguish all true believers, all true aspirants and all sincere disciples, whether Christian or otherwise. The teaching has always been given in terms of good behavior and of right action, and therefore given in terms of *effects*, produced by inner causes which have not always been specified. Basically, all such virtues, good inclinations and attempted sound qualities represent the emergence into expression upon the physical plane of certain energies and tendencies, inherent in the soul itself. These, in their turn, are governed by *energies and laws which are of a nature different from those governing personalities.* It is important to emphasise this and to bear in mind that the powers of the soul, as they are appearing in the world today, constitute (in their working out) a body of phenomena which would have been regarded as magical, impossible and superhuman several centuries ago. The discoveries of science, the adaptation of the laws governing matter and directing material energy to the service and the growing needs of mankind, the subtle and delicate apparatus of the human body and the steadily increasing sensitivity of the human mechanism, have brought about a world consciousness and a civilisation which—in spite of its glaring defects, all based on the separative and selfish attitudes of the personalities through which the soul has yet to work—are a guarantee of the innate divinity of man, with all that may be inherent in, and inferred from that phrase.

What has not yet been grasped is that these emerging "godlike" qualities, these beneficent characteristics, and the slowly appearing virtues of humanity are only indications of hidden potentialities, which have not been scientifically studied. The qualities of goodness are so called because they are, in essence, the energies controlling group relations; the powers, called superhuman, are fundamentally the powers which express group activity, and the virtues are only effects of group life, rightly handled, which are attempting to express themselves on the physical plane. The growing science of social relations, of social responsibility, or coordinated civic life, of scientific economics and of human inter-relations, the steadily developing sense of internationalism, of religious unity, and of economic interdependence, are all of them indications of the energies of soul life upon the physical plane, and within the human family. Hence the conflict of ideals in the world today; hence the massed dualism which produces such bewilderment; hence the compromises and hence the inconsistencies. Here is to be found the cause of all the divergencies in the world of civilised ideals, and the conflicting and widely differing motives which impel people of good motive and intention and of high principle into antagonistic activities.

Two sets of principles are to be found controlling human life—the selfish and the unselfish, the individual good and the group good, the objective goal and the subjective goal, the material incentive and the spiritual impulse, national patriotism and the world ideal, separative religious belief and the federation of religions, and all the many massed dualities which simply indicate the realism of people who are personalities (integrated and separative) or of souls (aligned and group-conscious). Here is the major divergence in the world today; with the weight of the power on the side of separation, as it is the line of least resistance, and of critical differentiations. A balancing of the two will gradually take place, with the weight of world idealism gradually shifting into the realm of soul unification, until eventually (but not for quite a while) the emphasis of world thought will be definitely and permanently on "the side of the angels." Note the occult truth of that familiar phrase. Therefore we can look for the new laws, governing soul life, which is group life, to begin to function and make their presence felt. This will at first increase the world difficulty; hence the need to make the meaning of these laws clear, their objectives simple and their potencies understandable.

1. *The Law of Sacrifice*

The section upon which we now enter in our studies will be difficult and controversial. The thread which will guide us out of the bewildering maze of thought into which we must perforce enter, is the golden one of *group* love, *group* understanding, *group* relations and *group* conduct.

No.	Exoteric Name	Esoteric Name	Symbol	Ray Energy
1.	The Law of sacrifice.	The Law of those who choose to die.	A rosy Cross with a golden bird.	Outpouring fourth ray, at-one-ing energy.

This law of sacrifice, which is the first of the laws to be grasped by the human intelligence, and is therefore the easiest for man to understand (because he is already governed by it and, therefore, aware of it) came to its first major expression during this slowly disappearing age, the present age, the Piscean age. This law has always been functioning and active in the world, for it is one of the first of the inner subjective laws to express itself consciously, and as an active ideal, in human life. The theme of all the world religions has been divine sacrifice, the immolation of the cosmic Deity, through the process of universal creation, and of the world Saviours, by Their death and sacrifice as a means of salvation and eventual release and liberation. Such is the blindness and such is the contaminating influence of the lower separative man, that this divine law of sacrifice is wielded with the selfish intent of personal and individual salvation. But the travestied truth remains the unsullied truth on its own plane, and this dominant world law governs the appearing and the disappearing of universes, of solar systems, of races and of nations, of world leaders and world rulers, of incarnating human beings and of revealing Sons of God.

Let us see if we can interpret or define the true significance of this law, which is in reality the expression of a divine impulse, leading to a defined activity, with its consequent and subsequent results and effects. It was this aspect of sacrifice which led to the creation of the worlds and to the manifestation of the divine Creator.

It might help to a better understanding of the Law of Sacrifice if it were expressed through synonymous words and terms.

a. THE SIGNIFICANCE OF THE LAW OF SACRIFICE

It means *the impulse of giving*. The whole secret of the doctrines of "the forgiveness of sins" and of the "at-one-ment" lies hid in this simple phrase. It is the basis of the Christian doctrine of love and sacrifice. Hence the emphasis laid, in the Piscean Age and through the influence of Christianity, upon just these two things,—forgiveness and atonement. That man, as usual, distorted and misinterpreted the teaching and the truth, and that it fell, as does all else at present, under the glamour and illusion of the astral plane, plus the Piscean influence, is true. Man's thought dominated and distorted the ideal and produced such a damnable doctrine as the elect of God, the chosen of the Lord, or the sole people to benefit by the sacrifice and death of the great Son of God, and who pass, due to the merits of that vicarious death, into a state of bliss in heaven, simply because of an emotional choice, which ignores millions of those who have made no such choice, nor had the opportunity to do so. The symbolic activity of the great Teacher of Nazareth will be properly understood and its significance will be properly appreciated only when group implications are more carefully studied, the meaning of sacrifice and of death come into their rightful place in the human consciousness, and the law of giving, with all that that entails, is correctly understood and applied. Those who thus sacrifice are:

The solar Deity who gave His life to the universe, to the solar system, to the planet, and the manifested worlds consequently appeared. The cosmic Deity has likewise done the same. But what does this mean to us? Naught, except a symbol. It was His impulse, His will, His desire, His incentive, His idea and purpose to appear. The creative act then took place, and the process of manifestation began its cyclic evolutionary existence. The Cosmic Christ was crucified upon the cross of matter, and by that great sacrifice opportunity was offered to all evolving lives in all kingdoms of nature and in all created worlds. Thus they could progress. The work, in space and time, and the stupendous march of living beings towards an at present unrealised goal, began. We can give no reason for the choice made by Deity thus to act. We do not know His ultimate purpose or plan; and only aspects of His technique and method begin to appear to the illuminated mind. It has been hinted by Those Who know so much more than we, owing to their longer life cycle and experience, that some glimmering of that eternal and cosmic Intent is beginning to dawn in the consciousness of Those who have taken some of the higher initiations. Their nature must necessarily remain incomprehensible to mankind. All that the intelligent human being can grasp as he looks back over the history of the planet (as far as modern history can give it to him) is that there has been:

1. Progress in the human power to be conscious.
2. A growing and paralleling refinement of the forms of life in the various kingdoms of nature.
3. An intensification of conscious activity, on a developing scale of rapid living, that tends constantly to transcend time as we know it.
4. An expanding realisation of progress from one dimension to another, until today we talk in terms of a fourth dimensional state of consciousness and can grasp the fact that five or six dimensions are beautifully possible.
5. An increasingly scientific control of the elements in which we live, and of the forces of nature. Today we talk in terms of air mastery just as five hundred years ago (when such a thing was deemed impossible) they talked in terms of the mastery of oceans. We are offsetting the gravitational pull of the earth so that we can "fly into the face of the sun."
6. From the instinctual life of sense consciousness in material forms, we have progressed to the intellectual life of self-conscious human beings and to the intuitive

realisations of those who are beginning to function as superhuman entities.

All this has been brought about as the result of the determined, conditioned activity of a Great Life, Which chose to make a major sacrifice and to be crucified upon the cardinal Cross of the Heavens, and thereby pass through a cosmic initiation; Which, from our minor and relatively uninformed angle, stands today crucified upon the fixed Cross in the Heavens, and through the medium of the mutable Cross is nevertheless producing changes in the evolutionary cycle, in order to bring about the developed consciousness, the increasing refinement of form, and that intensification of life which distinguishes His creation.

A study of those expressed objectives—

1. A development of consciousness.
2. A refining of forms.
3. An intensification of realised life.

will convey to the earnest student a meagre understanding of the lowest aspects of the divine purpose. The wonder of the idea staggers human imagination. If this is a statement of fact, and if these ideas are but the expression of still deeper and more beautiful cosmic purposes, may not the goal be realised as being far beyond human computation, when its *lowest expression* embraces the highest intuitive and abstract concepts of which the most elevated human consciousness is capable? I commend this thought to your deep consideration.

It will be apparent, therefore, why it is the energy of the fourth ray which is related to this Law of Sacrifice, and why in this fourth planetary scheme and in our fourth globe, (the Earth globe) so much emphasis is laid upon this Law of Sacrifice, "the Law of those who choose to die." The fourth ray of conflict (conflict with a view to eventual harmony) is at present not one of the manifesting rays, yet—in the light of the larger cycle—this ray is a major controlling factor in our earth evolution and in the evolution of our solar system, which is one of the fourth order. The realisation of this may indicate why our little planet, the Earth, is of such apparent importance in the solar system. It is not simply because we choose to think so and thus feed our own arrogance, but it is so primarily because the fourth ray of conflict and this first law are—in time and space—dominating factors in the fourth kingdom in nature, the human kingdom. Our planet, the fourth in the series of divine expression with which we are associated, has a peculiar relation to the position of our solar system in the series of solar systems which constitute the body of expression for The One About Whom Naught May Be Said.

It must never be forgotten that this fourth ray of conflict is the ray whose energies, rightly applied and understood, bring about harmony and at-one-ment. The result of this harmonising activity is beauty, but it is a beauty that is achieved through struggle. This produces a livingness through death, a harmony through strife, a Union through diversity and adversity.

The sacrifice of the solar angels brought the fourth kingdom in nature into being. The "returning nirvanis" (as they are called in esoteric literature), with deliberation and full understanding, took human bodies in order to raise those lower forms of life nearer to the goal. These were and are ourselves. The "Lords of Knowledge and Compassion and of ceaseless persevering Devotion" (who are ourselves) chose to die in order that lesser lives might live, and this sacrifice has made possible the evolution of the indwelling consciousness of Deity. This consciousness, having worked its way through the subhuman kingdoms in nature, needed the activity of the solar angels to make further progress possible. Herein lies

a. Our service to God, through sacrifice and death;
b. Our service to other souls, through deliberate self-sacrificing purpose;
c. Our service to other forms of life in other kingdoms.

All this involves the death and sacrifice of a Son of God, a solar angel, for, from the angle of Deity, descent into matter, manifestation through form, the taking of a body, extension of consciousness through the process of incarnation, are all occultly considered to be death. But the angels "chose to die, and in dying, lived." Through their sacrifice, matter is lifted up into Heaven. It is this theme which fills the pages of *The Secret Doctrine*, and which is discussed in greater elaboration in *A Treatise on Cosmic Fire*. The sacrifice of the angels, the death of the Sons of God, the immolation of the mystic Christ, the crucifixion in time and space of all living entities, called souls—this is the theme of those books. This is the mystery hinted at in the world of Scriptures, and this is the secret of the ages, which is only discovered by the souls of men as each of them enters individually into conscious relation with his own soul and discovers that which he has joyously done in the past, and so arrives at the realisation of that supreme sacrifice which he made with deliberation in the early dawn of time itself and which, at some point in his career as a soul on earth, he consciously and symbolically re-enacts for the benefit of other souls, in order to hasten their progress towards their goal. Then comes a life wherein, in some form or another, he portrays or works out within himself, but also before the watching world, that great symbolic drama which we call

The Sacrifice of a World Saviour. This is the theme of the historical romance of all those great Sons of God who down the ages, have arrived at an understanding of the significance of the divine purpose of God, of the *Word* incarnated through a planet, of those solar angels who are themselves, the Word incarnate through a human form. Whether they enact this drama, as did the Christ, so as to present to man the symbolism of death and sacrifice, or whether they enact this drama, as did the Buddha, so as to demonstrate to man the sacrifice and death of personal desire (to mention only two of the manifested Sons of God, the Christ and the Buddha), the theme remains the same,—the death of that which is lower in order to release that which is higher, or—on a larger scale—the death of that which is higher in the order and scale of being, in order to release that which is lower.

But the lesson needs to be learned (and it is the lesson which man is now engaged in learning) that death as the human consciousness understands it, pain and sorrow, loss and disaster, joy and distress, are only such because man, as yet, identifies himself with the life of the form and not with the life and consciousness of the soul, the solar angel, whose awareness is potentially that of the planetary Deity, Whose greater awareness (in His turn) is potentially that of the solar Deity. The moment a man identifies himself with his soul and not with his form, then he understands the meaning of the Law of Sacrifice; he is spontaneously governed by it; and he is one who will with deliberate intent *choose to die*. But there is no pain, no sorrow, and no real death involved.

This is the mystery of illusion and glamour. From these two imprisoning factors all World Saviours are free. They are not deceived. It is well, in passing, to point out here that in the New Age, we shall enlarge our concept of this term *World Saviour*. At present we apply it predominantly to those souls who emerge upon the teaching ray, the second or

Christ ray. They enact the drama of salvation. But this is an error, due to the overpowering emotional glamour of the Piscean Age. This astral influence has its roots in the past Atlantean civilisation, which preceded ours. In that age, the astral body was the subject of attention. Much that happens today, and which may develop, has its roots in that aspect of energy. Seeds sown at that time are now brought to flower. This is very good and necessary, even if distressing in experience.

But the World Saviours must be recognised as coming forth to serve the race, with sacrifice of some kind along many lines and in many forms. They may be great rulers, or dictators, politicians, statesmen, scientists and artists. Their work is the work of salvage, of restitution, or renovation and revelation, and, through the sacrifice of themselves, they accomplish it. As such, they must be recognised for what they are. Now they are misunderstood, misinterpreted, and judged by their mistakes more than by their aims. But they are dedicated souls. They rescue; they lift; they integrate; they illumine; and the net result of their work, from the angle of ultimate history, is *good*.

This Law of Sacrifice and the impulse to give can also be traced throughout every kingdom in nature. It is typified for us in the basic sacrifices which take place between the various kingdoms. The essential qualities of the minerals and chemicals of the earth are an instance in point. They are needed by other forms of life and are donated to man through the medium of the vegetable kingdom and through the water which he drinks, and thus, even in the first and densest kingdom in nature (whose consciousness is so far removed from ours) does this *process of giving* hold good. But the tracing of this Law of Sacrifice in the subhuman kingdoms is not possible here, and we must confine our attention to the world of human living and consciousness.

b. The Work of Salvage or Salvation

The Law of Sacrifice means also salvage and underlies all the evolutionary processes and particularly does this emerge into clear significance in the human family. The instinct to betterment, the urge to progress (physical, emotional and intellectual), the effort to ameliorate conditions, the tendency to philanthropy which is so rapidly taking hold of the world, and the sense of responsibility which does make men realise that they are their brother's keeper, are all expressions of this sacrificial instinct. This factor, though not unrecognised by modern psychology, is of far wider significance than has yet been realised. This instinctual tendency is the one that itself governs the Law of Rebirth. It is the expression of a still greater factor in the creative process. It is the major determining impulse which impelled the Soul of God Himself to enter into form life; which impels life, upon the involutionary arc, to progress down into matter, producing thus the immanence of God. It is that also which drives humanity forward into its wild struggle for material well-being. It is that too which urges man eventually to turn his back upon the "world, the flesh and the devil," as the New Testament puts it, and orient himself to the things of spiritual import. The prodigal son sacrificed the Father's home when he chose to wander forth into the far country. He wasted and sacrificed his substance through the use he made of the experience of life on earth, until he had exhausted all his resources and there was naught left but the eventual sacrifice of what he held so dear, but had discovered to be so unsatisfying. For these things of lesser values, he had sacrificed the higher values, and had to return again whence he came. Such is the life story of all the sons of God who came into incarnation, as given to us under the symbolism of the Bible. But the theme in all the world Bibles is the same.

This urge to sacrifice, to relinquish this for that, to choose one way or line of conduct and thus sacrifice another way, to lose in order eventually to gain,—such is the underlying story of evolution. This needs psychological understanding. It is a governing principle of life itself, and runs like a golden pattern of beauty through the dark materials of which human history is constructed. When this urge to sacrifice in order to win, gain or salvage that which is deemed desirable is understood, then the whole clue to man's unfoldment will stand revealed. This tendency or urge is something different to desire, as desire is academically understood and studied today. What it really connotes is the emergence of that which is most divine in man. It is an aspect of desire, but it is the dynamic, active side and not the feeling, sensuous side. It is the predominant characteristic of Deity.

It is of interest, however, for students of esotericism to note that this urge to salvage and to sacrifice in order to redeem works out in different ways in the different planetary schemes. Each Ray Lord of a scheme, manifesting through a planet, expresses this urge in varying ways, and each expression is so different from the others that it is hard for a human being to do more than sense that method which exists on our own particular planet. Initiates know that the varying psychological characteristics of the ray Lives condition most peculiarly the method of expressing sacrifice, during the course of manifestation. The great stream of living energy which is manifesting itself in our Earth scheme of evolution is conditioned by a temperament, an attitude and an orientation that is that of a "Divine Rebel." It is only rebellion that produces pain and sorrow, but this rebellion is inherent and innate in the Deity of our planet Himself, the "One in Whom we live and move and have our being." It is, therefore, a tendency greater than the individual unit. It is only possible to express this amazing truth about the planetary Life under a veil of symbology and in terms of human thought. In this there is ever a risk, for men interpret all they read and hear and experience in terms of themselves.

The Old Commentary says:

"He entered into life and knew it to be death.

"He took a form and grieved to find it dark.

"He drove Himself forth from the secret place and sought the place of light, and light revealed all that he sought the least.

"He craved permission to return.

"He sought the Throne on high and Him who sat thereon. He said 'I sought not this. I looked for peace, for light, for scope to serve, to prove my love and to reveal my power. Light there is none. Peace is not found. Let me return.'

But He Who sat upon the Throne turned not his head. He seemed not e'en to listen nor to hear. But from the lower sphere of darkness and of pain a voice came forth and cried: 'We suffer here. We seek the light. We need the glory of an entering God. [I can find no other words except these last two to express the ancient symbol from which I am translating.] Lift us to Heaven. Enter, O Lord, the tomb. Raise us into the light and make the sacrifice. Break down for us the prison wall and enter into pain.'

The Lord of Life returned. He liked it not, and hence the pain."

The same conditions which blend the Law of Sacrifice with pain and sorrow and difficulty are found also on the planet Mars and on the planet Saturn. They are not found on the other planets. Those who have read *The Secret Doctrine* and *A Treatise on Cosmic Fire* with understanding know that our Earth is not a sacred planet. However, Saturn, Mars and our Earth constitute, in a curious esoteric manner, the personality of a stupendous ray Life, Whose energy is that of the third Ray. There are, as has been stated elsewhere, seven sacred planets but ten planetary schemes, and in three cases, (those of the three major rays) three planets constitute the personality of each ray Life. Some esoteric thinkers believe that there are twelve planets to be considered in our solar system, and there is a basis for their conclusion. The personality of this third ray Life functions through the following planets:

1. The mental body expresses itself through the medium of the planet Saturn.
2. The astral body expresses itself through the planet Mars.
3. The physical body expresses itself through the planet Earth.

The potency of this Life is such that He requires three complete schemes—all three closely allied and interdependent—through which to express Himself. Uranus, Jupiter and Venus are similarly allied in order to manifest or express a great Life.

These facts constitute a tremendous mystery, and in no way negate the truth that Venus has a peculiar and intimate relation to the Earth. The point here being stressed is difficult to express, but of great importance. Let me be more explicit, by means of the following statements:

1. Only three planetary schemes are aware of pain and sorrow as we understand those terms; none of them know it so well or feel it so much as does our planetary Logos.
2. Pain and sorrow are the result of rebellion, and of divine discontent. The instinct to betterment, based on discontent, has necessarily involved the planetary temperament or attitude which recognises the dualities.

3. There is a stage to be reached in the human consciousness, where that which lies behind the dualities—the stage of essential oneness—can, and will be recognised.

4. When this takes place, the consciousness of our humanity will then merge with that underlying consciousness of the whole, which recognises no pain or sorrow and has, therefore, slipped out of the realisation which predominantly governs the consciousness of the three great Lives in our solar system.

5. It is this dimly sensed truth which lies behind the highest type of metaphysical thought, such as Christian Science, Unity, Divine Science, and the emphasis laid by Christianity and the esoteric schools upon the at-one-ment.

This instinct towards betterment through sacrifice is itself diverse.

There is, first of all, the instinct towards individual betterment, which leads to selfishness, to a grasping, and to an orientation of the materially-minded towards material possessions.

There is, secondly, the instinct towards an ameliorating of the conditions of other people, first from a selfish motive (the avoiding of personal distress at the sight of suffering), and secondly, through pure, disinterested service, which is a quality of the soul.

There is, finally, the active application and the complete sacrifice of the lower separated self through the power to "stand in spiritual being" which necessarily infers that one has reached that state of consciousness which transcends what may be called, symbolically the "Earth, Saturn and Mars" state of consciousness.

Let it not, however, be forgotten that the contribution to these three great planetary Lives, as They embody pre-eminently the Law of Sacrifice, through pain and rebellion, is a major contribution to the whole, and greatly enriches the sum total. The units of divine life and the atoms of electrical energy who pass through these three planetary schemes are subject to them in order to acquire that psychic sensitivity which would otherwise be impossible. Only those units of life who are coloured predominantly by the third ray of activity pass for any length of time through these three schemes. A hint is here conveyed as to the prevalence of third ray Monads among the sons of men. The ray of active intelligence, expressing itself through the seven ray types, is above everything else the ray upon which the majority of human monads will, particularly, at this time, be found. We shall, therefore, find the following psychological types colouring the bulk of our humanity, and the ray of active intelligence expressing itself through

1. Will, evoking divine purpose.
2. Love, expressing divine quality.
3. Intellect, as the reflector of the Intuition.
4. Conflict, producing harmony.
5. Knowledge or science, leading to radiance.
6. Idealism, establishing the divine pattern.
7. Ritual or organisation, manifesting Deity.

Therefore, psychologically speaking, and when greater knowledge has been gained of the energies determining the type of a man, a person, for instance, whose Monad is presumably upon the third ray, his ego being on the fourth ray, and his personality on the seventh ray, will be described as a Three, IV.7. Within this simple formula there will be lesser differentiations and a seventh ray personality may have a first ray mental body, a fifth ray astral body, and a third ray physical body. The formula which would describe him would be

$$\text{Three, IV. 7.} \quad \left\{ \begin{array}{c} 1 \\ 5 \\ 3 \end{array} \right.$$

This, when interpreted, means

> Monad .... third ray.
> Ego .... fourth ray.
> Personality .... seventh ray.
> Mental body .... first ray.
> Astral body .... fifth ray.
> Physical body .... third ray.

Students may find it of value to study themselves and others in conformity with the above, and to establish their personal formulae. This should be done in conjunction with a consultation of their horoscopes. This will be discussed more at length after we have considered the astrological implications of the rays, in the succeeding volume.

The Law of Sacrifice, therefore, can never be eliminated in our Earth scheme, as far as the human and subhuman reactions to sorrow and pain are concerned, nor can it be eliminated on the planets Saturn and Mars. It is relatively unknown in the other schemes. Bliss and Sacrifice are synonymous terms as far as our solar Logos is concerned, and also for the majority of the planetary Logoi. This must be remembered. A touch of this freedom from the limitations of pain and sorrow can be found among the more advanced sons of men on Earth, who know the ecstasy of the mystic, the exaltation of the initiate, and the exquisite agony of sacrifice or of any feeling which is carried forward to the point of sublimation. When this point has been reached, the mechanism of suffering and the ability to register sensuous perception is transcended, and momentarily the man escapes on to the plane of unity.

Here there is no pain, no sorrow, no rebellion and no suffering. When the living, vibrating antahkarana or bridge is built, this "way of escape" becomes the normal path of life. Escape from pain is then automatic, for the centre of consciousness is elsewhere. In the cases mentioned above, and where the antahkarana is not a consummated, established fact, the tiny thread of the partially constructed "way of escape", under tremendous pressure and excitation, shoots forward like a quivering band of light, and momentarily touches the light that is the Self. Hence ecstasy and exaltation. But it does not last, and cannot be *consciously* recovered until the third initiation has been taken. After that the "way of escape" becomes the "way of daily livingness" (to translate inadequately the occult and ancient phrase). Then pain is steadily transcended, and the pairs of opposites—pleasure and pain—have no longer any hold over the disciple.

All this constitutes the theme of esoteric psychology and, when rightly understood, will explain

1. The Saturnian influence in human life.
2. The cessation of rebellion, or the ending of the Martian influence.
3. The building of the antahkarana, which releases the man from the control of personality life.
4. The evocation of the group consciousness.
5. The consequent negation of pain and sorrow.
6. Entrance into Nirvana, and the beginning of the *real Way*.

The Law of Sacrifice means also

c. THE RELINQUISHING OF GAIN

This is the basic theme of *The Bhagavad Gita*. In that treatise on the soul and its unfoldment, we are taught to "perform action without attachment," and thereby lay the foundation for later relinquishings which can be effected without pain and the sense of loss, because we have acquired the power, latent ever within ourselves, to detach ourselves from achieved possessions.

This law works out in many ways, and it is not possible to do more than indicate a few of those general significances which embody the major lessons of every disciple.

First, the soul must relinquish the personality. For ages, the soul has identified itself with the lower personal self, and through the agency of that lower self has gained experience and acquired much knowledge. The time has to come when that agency is "no longer dear" to the soul, and their respective positions are reversed. No longer is the soul identified with the personality but the personality becomes identified with the soul and loses its separate quality and position. All that has been acquired through age-long struggle and strife, through pain and pleasure, through disaster and satisfied desire, and all that the wheel of life, which has turned ceaselessly, has brought into the possession of the soul—*All* has to be relinquished. Life, for the disciple, becomes then a series of detaching processes, until he has learnt the lesson of renunciation.

The sequence is, first *dispassion*, then *discrimination*, and finally *detachment*. On these three words must all disciples meditate, if they are ever to reap the fruits of sacrifice.

"Having pervaded the worlds with a fraction of Myself, I remain." Such is the theme of the soul's endeavor, and such is the spirit which must underlie all creative work. In this thought lies the clue to the symbol of the Law of Sacrifice —a rosy cross with a bird flying over it. This is the loved cross (rose being the colour of affection), with the bird (symbol of the soul) flying free in time and space.

Secondly, the soul has also to relinquish not only its tie and its gain through contact with the personal self, but it has most definitely to relinquish its tie with other personal selves. It must learn to know and to meet other people only on the plane of the soul. In this lies for many a disciple a hard lesson. They may care little for themselves and may have learnt much personal detachment. Little may they cherish the gain of contact with the lower personal self. They are learning to transcend all that, and may have transcended to a great degree, but their love for their children, their family, their friends and intimates is for them of supreme importance and that love holds them prisoners in the lower worlds. They do not stop to recognise that their love is primarily love for the personalities, and only secondarily for the souls. Upon this rock, many disciples are for lives broken, until the time comes when, through pain and suffering and the constant losing of that which they so much cherish, their love enters into a newer, a higher and a truer phase. They rise above the personal, and find again—after felt loss and suffering—those whom now they love as souls. Then they realise that there has been gain and not loss, and that only that which was illusory, ephemeral and untrue has disappeared. The real Man has been gained and can never be lost again.

This is most frequently the problem of parents who are upon the Path of Discipleship, and it is through their children that the lesson is learnt which can release them for initiation. They hold their children to them, and this, being counter to the law of nature, works out disastrously. It is the height of selfishness. And yet, did they but know and see aright, they would realise that to hold, one must detach, and to keep, one must release. Such is the law.

The soul has also to learn to relinquish the fruits or gains of service and learn to serve without attachment to results, to means, to persons or to praise. This I will deal with later.

In the fourth place, the soul has to relinquish also the sense of responsibility for that which other disciples may do. So many earnest servers hold on to their fellow workers, and do not relinquish their hold upon them or upon their activities upon the outer plane. This is a subtle error, for it masks itself behind a sense of righteous responsibility, an adherence to principles as they appear to the individual, and the accumulated experience of the disciple,—which is necessarily incomplete experience. The relation between disciples is egoic and not personal. The link is of the soul and not of the mind. Each personality pursues its own course, must shoulder its own responsibilities, work out its own dharma, and fulfil its own karma, and so answer for itself to its Lord and Master, the Soul. And answer there will be. Does this itself sound of the nature of separation and aloneness? It does, as far as outer activities are concerned. Only as servers cooperate from the standpoint of an inner subjective linking can a united work be carried forward.

At this time in the history of the world and its periodical salvaging from conditions which are wrecking the current civilisation, it is necessary that aspirants grasp the fact that that salvaging process must be carried on under the Law of Sacrifice, and that only a relative outer unity can be at this time achieved. Not as yet is the vision seen with a sufficient clarity by the many servers, to make them work with perfect unanimity of purpose and objective, of technique and method, or complete understanding and oneness of approach. That fluid, perfect cooperation lies as yet in the future. The establishing of an inner contact and relationship, based on a realised oneness of purpose and soul love, is magnificently possible, and for this all disciples must struggle and strive. On the outer plane, owing to the separative mind during this age and time, a complete accord on detail, on method, and on interpretation of principles is not possible. But—the inner relationships and cooperation *Must* be established and developed, in spite of the outer divergences of opinion. When the inner link is held in love, and when disciples relinquish the sense of authority over each other and of responsibility for each other's activities, and at the same time stand shoulder to shoulder in the One Work, then the differences, the divergences, and the points of disagreement will automatically be overcome. There are three rules which are important to disciples at this time.

First, see to it that you permit no rift to appear in the inner relation in which you stand to each other. The integrity of the inner band of servers must be preserved intact.

Secondly, pursue your own duty and task, shoulder your own responsibility, and then leave your fellow disciples to do the same, free from the impact of your thought and criticism. The ways and means are many; the points of view vary with every personality. The principle of work is love for all men and service to the race, preserving at the same time a deeper inner love for those with whom you are destined to work. Each soul grows into the way of light through service rendered, through experience gained, through mistakes made, and through lessons learnt. That necessarily must be personal and individual. But the work itself is one. The Path is one. The love is one. The goal is one. These are the points that matter.

Thirdly, preserve ever in work the attitude of mind which must grow out of the two rules above, faithfully followed. Your point of view and consciousness are your own, and therefore, are for you, right. Not necessarily is that which seems so clear to you and of such vital importance to you, of the same value or importance to your brothers. Your important principle may be realised by an abler mind than yours and **by** a more advanced disciple as embodying an aspect of a greater principle, an interpretation of a principle, correct and proper at a certain time, but capable of a different application at another time, and by another mind. Under the Law of Sacrifice these three rules might be interpreted thus:

1. Relinquish or sacrifice the age-old tendency to criticise and adjust another's work, and thus preserve the inner group integrity. More plans for service have gone astray and more workers have been hindered by criticism than by any other major factor.

2. Relinquish or sacrifice the sense of responsibility for the actions of others, and particularly of disciples. See that your own activity measures up to theirs, and in the joy of struggle and on the way of service the differences will disappear and the general good will be achieved.

3. Relinquish the pride of mind which sees its way and its interpretations to be correct and true, and others' false and wrong. This is the way of separation. Adhere to the way of integration which is of the soul and not of the mind.

These are hard sayings, but they are the rules by which the Teachers on the inner side, guide Their actions and Their thoughts, when working with each other and with Their disciples. The inner integrity is necessarily a proven fact to Them. To the disciple it is not. But to the inner Teachers, the outer differences are abhorrent. They leave each other free to serve the Plan. They train Their disciples (no matter what their degree) to serve that Plan with freedom, for in freedom and in the sense of joy and in the strength of inner cooperative love is the best work done. It is sincerity for which They look. The willingness to sacrifice the lesser when the greater is sensed is that for which They search. The spontaneous relinquishing of long-held ideals when a greater and more inclusive presents itself is Their guide. The sacrifice of pride and the sacrifice of personality when the vastness of the work and the urgency of the need are realised, sway Them to cooperation. It is essential that the disciples shall learn to sacrifice the non-essential in order that the work may go forward. Little as one may realise it, the many techniques and methods and ways are secondary to the major world need. There are many ways and many points of view, and many experiments and many efforts—abortive or successful, and all of them come and go. But humanity remains. All of them are in evidence of the multiplicity of minds, and of experiences, but the goal remains. Difference is ever of the personality. When this Law of Sacrifice governs the mind, it will inevitably lead all disciples to relinquish the personal in favor of the universal and of the soul, that knows no separation, no difference. Then no pride, nor a short and myopic perspective, nor love of interference (so dear to many people), nor misunderstanding of motive will hinder their cooperation with each other as disciples, nor their service to the world.

2. *The Law of Magnetic Impulse*

No.	Exoteric Name	Esoteric Name	Symbol	Ray Energy
2.	The Law of Magnetic Impulse.	The Law of Polar Union.	Two f i e r y b a l l s and triangle.	Radiatory Energy. Second Ray manifesting Energy.

It would be well to remember that we are not considering here that aspect of the second ray which is peculiarly concerned with form, and which constitutes the cohering, magnetic agent in any form, whether atom, man or solar system. We are not here concerned with the relation between forms, even though due (as is essentially the case) to second ray energy. Nor are we occupied with considering the relation of soul to form, either that of the One Soul to the many forms, or of an individualised soul to its imprisoning form. The laws we are considering are concerned entirely with inter-soul relationship, and with the synthesis underlying the forms. They govern the conscious contact existing between the many aspects of the One Soul. I have expressed this phrase with care.

This Law of Magnetic Impulse governs the relation, the interplay, the intercourse, and the interpenetration between the seven groups of souls on the higher levels of the mental plane which constitute the first of the major *form* differentiations. These we can only study intelligently from the angle of the seven ray groups, as they compose the spiritual aspect of the human family. This law governs also the relationships between souls, who, whilst in manifestation through form, are en rapport with each other. It is a law, therefore, which concerns the inter-relation of all souls within the periphery of what the Christians call "the Kingdom of God." Through a right understanding of this law, the man arrives at a knowledge of his subjective life; he can wield power subjectively, and thus work consciously in form and with form, yet holding his polarisation and his consciousness in another dimension, and functioning actively *behind the scenes*. This law concerns those inner esoteric activities which are not primarily related to form life.

This law is of major importance because of the fact that Deity itself is on the second ray; because this is a second ray solar system, and therefore all rays and the varying states or groupings of consciousness, and all forms, in or out of physical manifestation, are coloured and dominated by this ray, and therefore again finally controlled by this law. The Law of Magnetic Impulse is in the soul realm what the Law of Attraction is in the world of phenomena. It is, in reality, the subjective aspect of that Law. It is the Law of Attraction as it functions in the kingdom of souls, but because it is functioning on those levels where the "great heresy of separateness" is not to be found, it is difficult for us—with our active, discriminating minds—to understand its implications and its significance. This Law governs the soul realm; to it the Solar Angels respond, and under its stimulation, the egoic lotuses unfold. It could perhaps be best understood if it is considered as—

a. The impulsive interplay between souls in form and out of form.
b. The basis of egoic recognition.
c. The factor which produces reorientation in the three worlds.
d. The cause of the magnetic rapport between a Master and His group, or a Master and His disciple.

It has an occult name, and we call it "the Law of Polar Union." Yet when I say to you that this implies the binding of the pairs of opposites, the fusion of the dualities, and the marriage of souls, I have uttered meaningless words, or words which—at the best—embody an ideal which is so closely tied up with material things in the mind of the aspirant, and so connected with the processes of detachment (at which disciples work so strenuously!) that I despair of presenting the truth as it concerns souls and soul relationships.

This law governs also the relation of the soul of a group to the soul of other groups. It governs the interplay, vital but unrealised yet as a potency, between the soul of the fourth kingdom in nature, the human, and the soul of the three subhuman kingdoms, and likewise that of the three superhuman kingdoms. Owing to the major part which humanity has to play in the great scheme or Plan of God, this is the law which will be the determining law of the race. This will not, however, be the case until the majority of human beings understand something of what it means to function as a soul. Then, under obedience to this law, humanity will act as a transmitter of light, energy and spiritual potency to the subhuman kingdoms, and will constitute a channel of communication between "that which is above and that which is below." Such is the high destiny before the race.

Just as certain human beings have, through meditation, discipline and service, most definitely made a contact with their own souls, and can therefore become channels for soul expression, and mediums for the distribution into the world of soul energy, so men and women, who are oriented to soul living in their aggregate, *form a group of souls*, en rapport with the source of spiritual supply. They have, as a group, and from the angle of the Hierarchy, established a contact and are "in touch" with the world of spiritual realities. Just as the individual disciple stabilises this contact and learns to make a rapid alignment and then, and only then, can come into touch with the Master of his group and intelligently respond to the Plan, so does this group of aligned souls come into contact with certain greater Lives and Forces of Light, such as the Christ and the Buddha. The aggregated aspiration, consecration and intelligent devotion of the group carries the individuals of which it is composed to greater heights than would be possible alone. The group stimulation and the united effort sweep the entire group to an intensity of realisation that would otherwise be impossible. Just as the Law of Attraction, working on the physical plane, brought them together as men and women into one group effort, so the Law of Magnetic Impulse can begin to control them when, again as a group and only as a group, they unitedly constitute themselves channels for service in pure self-forgetfulness.

This thought embodies the opportunity immediately before all groups of aspirants and allied men of good will in the world today. If they work together as a group of souls, they can accomplish much. This thought illustrates also the significance of this law which *does produce polar union*. What is needed to be grasped is that in this work, there is no personal ambition implied, even of a spiritual nature and no personal union sought. This is not the mystical union of the scriptures or of the mystical tradition. It is not alignment and union with a Master's group, or fusion with one's inner band of pledged disciples, nor even with one's own Ray life. All these factors constitute preliminary implications and are of an individual application. Upon this sentence I ask you to ponder. This union is a greater and more vital thing *because it is a group union*.

What we are seeking to do is to carry forward a group endeavor which is of such moment that, at the right time, it could produce, in its growing momentum, such a potent, magnetic impulse that it will reach those Lives Who brood over humanity and our civilisation, and Who work through the Masters of the Wisdom and the assembled Hierarchy. This group endeavor will call forth from Them a responsive and magnetic impulse, which will bring together, through the medium of all the aspiring groups, the overshadowing beneficent *Forces*. Through the concentrated effort of these groups in the world today (who constitute subjectively *One* Group) light and inspiration and spiritual revelation can be released in such a flood of power that it will work definite changes in the human consciousness and help to ameliorate conditions in this needy world. It will open men's eyes to the basic realities, which are, as yet, only dimly sensed by the thinking public. Humanity itself must apply the necessary correctives, believing it can do so in the strength of its own sensed wisdom and strength; yet all the time, behind the scenes, stand the grouped world aspirants, working silently, in unison with each other and the Hierarchy, and thus keeping the channel open through which the needed wisdom, strength and love can flow.

There are, therefore, to be found in this great task the following relations and groupings. These must be considered, and are as follows:

1. The Forces of Light and the Spirit of Peace, embodied Lives of tremendous group potency.
2. The Planetary Hierarchy.
3. The Buddha.
4. The Christ.
5. The New Group of World Servers.
6. Humanity.

You will note that the Buddha focusses in Himself the downpouring forces, whilst the Christ focusses in Himself the outgoing demand and the spiritual aspirations of the entire planet. This makes a planetary alignment of great potency. Should the needed work be accomplished, the needed adjustments in the world can be made. The success or failure lies largely in the hands of those scattered but spiritually aligned men and women whom we call the New Group of World Servers.

In the above tabulation, there is portrayed a little of what is implied in the words "The Law of Polar Union." The whole process concerns consciousness, and the results worked out in consciousness, with the subsequent physical plane happenings, dependent upon the conscious realisations of the men of good will in, or out of, the New Group of World Servers.

This work, carried forward successfully and intelligently, should make it possible to inaugurate a new relation between the Hierarchy and mankind. This effort could mark (and let us hope it will) the beginning of a new type of mediatory work—a work carried forward by a salvaging group of servers, who are in training for the establishing of that group which will eventually save the world under the Law of Sacrifice. This mediatory work, however, involves the recognition of the Law of Magnetic Impulse, and a desire to understand it, and to cooperate with Those Who wield it. Through its medium and the right understanding of the Law, it should be possible to establish the needed union between the liberated souls (who are in themselves the symbol of the Soul in all forms) and the souls in prison. Much of the success of this planned endeavor depends upon the intellectual grasp of the members of the New Group of World Servers in connection with the necessary technique. It will depend also upon their willingness to accept the idea of the opportunity, and upon their readiness to work along the indicated lines. They have no guarantee as to the accuracy of claims made regarding the importance of this period, nor have they any personal knowledge of the situation as it is here described. Some do not even know that there is a watching Hierarchy, but they are consecrated and selfless souls, and as such, belong to the New Group of World Servers. If they can aspire, pray, meditate and serve, focussing always in unison with all other servers, the salvaging of humanity will go forward with much greater speed than heretofore, and to this call many will respond.

For the individual disciple, the significance of this Law of Magnetic Impulse and the corresponding relationships in his own life might also be shown in tabulated form:—

1. The world of souls on the higher mental levels.
2. The Master of his group.
3. The solar angel.
4. The aspiring disciple on the lower mental levels.
5. The personality, integrated and often troublesome.
6. The aspirant's environing associates.

It is useful for students to have these analogies in mind, for they can often arrive at release from the limitations of their lives and at a truer comprehension of the larger issues, when they see that their little, unimportant lives are only the reflection of greater and more important factors.

It is wise always to remember that on the plane of soul existence there is no separation, no "my soul and thy soul." It is only in the three worlds of illusion and of maya that we think in terms of souls and bodies. This is an occult platitude and well known, but the re-emphasis of the well known truth will sometimes serve to bring home to you its exactitude.

The second illustration which may perhaps make clearer the meaning and purpose of this law, and which will be of deep interest to esotericists, is to be found in connection with the symbol that specifies this law in the sacred records and in the archives of the Lodge. It is the symbol of the two balls of fire and the triangle. This has not only a planetary and cosmic significance, but has a very definite relation to the individual unfoldment (in the physical body) of the spiritual life of the disciple. Let me put it very simply. Students know that there are in the head two centres, the ajna centre and the head centre,—two balls of fire, symbolic of the fiery consciousness of the soul, and not of the animal consciousness of the body.

These two centres (externalised by the two glands, the pineal gland and the pituitary body) become vibrant and alive and intensely active, through service and meditation and right aspiration. A line of contact between them is eventually set up and established with increasing potency. There is also another line of outgoing fiery power toward the top of the spinal column. As the life of the soul gets stronger, the radiance of the centres increases, and the periphery of their sphere of influence is set up, creating a dual magnetic field. Speaking esoterically they are "magnetically impelled towards each other" and towards the stored up energy to be found in the spine, and localised in the five centres up the spine. Eventually the interplay is so powerful that a triangle of force appears within the radius of the magnetic field, and this triangle of light, of living fire, links the three "laya centres." The symbol is then completed, and the indication is that the disciple is now controlled by the subjective side of his nature. He is now governed by the Law of Magnetic Impulse (as the linking of the head centres demonstrates) and the two aspects of his nature, higher and lower, which constitute the two poles with which he is concerned, are now united. The polar union has been brought about.

The subject of this magnetic interplay offers food for thought and indicates the way of group, and of individual service. As the individual aspirants lose sight of self in service, and as they arrive at the stage of indifference to personality claims and happenings, they learn to cherish a spirit of confidence, of joy and of love, deep and lasting, for each other; they learn to work together whole-heartedly for the helping of the world and the assistance of the Hierarchy.

3. *The Law of Service*

No.	Exoteric Name	Esoteric Name	Symbol	Ray Energy.
3.	Law of Service.	Law of water and the fishes.	A man with a pot of water.	Outpouring Energy Sixth Ray. Vivifying Life.

We come now to the consideration of the third Law of the Soul, which is intended to govern all soul activity. It is the Law of Service. However, before we elaborate this theme, there are three things which I seek to say and which merit our careful attention.

First, is the fact that the result of all contact achieved in meditation and the measure of our success, will be determined by the ensuing service to the race. If there is right understanding, there will necessarily be right action.

It has previously been pointed out that the three great sciences which will come to the fore in the New Age, and which will lead humanity from the unreal to the real, and from aspiration to realisation are

1. The science of Meditation, the coming science of the mind.
2. The science of Antahkarana, or the science of the bridging which must take place between higher and lower mind.
3. The science of Service, which is a definite technique of at-one-ment.

We shall now consider the broad outlines of this science, for it is the major releasing factor in the disciple's life.

Secondly, this Law of Service is something which may not be escaped. Evasion brings its penalties, if that evasion is conscious. Ability to serve marks a definite stage of advance upon the Path, and until that stage is reached, spontaneous service, rendered in love and guided by wisdom, cannot be given. What is found up to that time is good intention, mixed motives, and oft fanaticism. This we will later elucidate.

This law is the imposition upon the planetary rhythm of certain energies and impulses which emanate from that sign of the zodiac into which we are steadily moving. Therefore, there is no escape. It is the effect of this force which, in some countries, is regimenting the masses in such a way that the individual serves the group by a forced negation of his personal self. His own ideas, his own personal well being and his own individuality are subordinated to the whole, and he is rendered relatively futile from the angle of his soul unfoldment. He is forced to conform, willingly or unwillingly, to group conditions. This is one of the lowest manifestations of the impact of this law upon the human consciousness. In its highest expression, we have the service rendered upon the planet in all the kingdoms of nature by the Hierarchy of Masters. Between these two extreme expressions, there is a vast distinction, but both are equally brought about by response (the one consciously rendered and the other unconsciously directed) to the Law of Service.

Thirdly, this Law of Service was expressed for the first time fully by the Christ two thousand years ago. He was the forerunner of the Aquarian Age, and hence His constant emphasis upon the fact that He was the "water of life", the "living water" which men needed. Hence the esoteric name of this law is that of "water and the fishes." The Piscean age slowly, very slowly, prepared the way for the divine expression of service, which will be the glory of the coming centuries. Today, we have a world which is steadily coming to the realisation that "no man liveth unto himself", and that only as the love, about which so much has been written and spoken, finds its outlet in service, can man begin to measure up to his innate capacity.

The sign for the Aquarian Age is that of a man, carrying on his shoulders a jar of water so full that it pours over to all and sundry, and yet it diminishes not. The sign for this Law of Service is very similar, but the difference lies in this; that the man stands, perfectly balanced in the form of a cross, with arms stretched out and with the water pot upon his head. In this difference there lies much of real significance. The jar of water, posed upon the shoulders, is a sign of the burden of service. It is not easy to serve. Man is today only beginning to learn how to serve. The jar of water upon the head of the man, who has been upon the cross of sacrifice for so long a time that the position has become to him perfectly natural, indicates that the cross, which has upheld him for so long, has now disappeared. The man with the water jar upon his head indicates to us poise, equilibrium and balance. For this balance, the understanding of the Law of Magnetic Impulse has prepared him. That is the Law of Polar Union and its symbol is the originator of the zodiacal sign for the constellation Libra—balance and service. These are the two expressions of Divinity which are, today, man's next great objective.

Service is usually interpreted as exceedingly desirable and it is seldom realised how very difficult service essentially is. It involves so much sacrifice of time and of interest and of one's own ideas, it requires exceedingly hard work, because it necessitates deliberate effort, conscious wisdom, and the ability to work without attachment. These qualities are not easy of attainment by the average aspirant, and yet today the tendency to serve is an attitude which is true of a vast majority of the people in the world. Such has been the success of the evolutionary process.

Service is frequently regarded as an endeavor to bring people around to the point of view of the one who serves, because what the would-be server has found to be good and true and useful, must necessarily be good and true and useful for all. Service is viewed as something we render to the poor, the afflicted, the diseased and the unhappy, because we think we want to help them, little realising that primarily this help is offered because we ourselves are made uncomfortable by distressing conditions, and must therefore endeavor to ameliorate those conditions in order ourselves to be comfortable again. The act of thus helping releases us from our misery, even if we fail to release or relieve the sufferers.

Service is frequently an indication of a busy and over-active temperament, or of a self-satisfied disposition, which leads its possessor to a strenuous effort to change situations, and make them what he feels they should be, thus forcing people to conform to that which the server feels should be done.

Or again, service can grow out of a fanatical desire to tread in the footsteps of the Christ, that great Son of God Who "went about doing good", leaving an example that we should follow in His footsteps. People, therefore, serve from a sense of obedience, and not from a spontaneous outgoing towards the needy. The essential quality for service is, therefore, lacking, and from the start they fail to do more than make certain gestures. Service can likewise be rendered from a deep seated desire for spiritual perfection. It is regarded as one of the necessary qualifications for discipleship and, therefore, if one is to be a disciple, one must serve. This theory is correct, but the living substance of service is lacking. The ideal is right and true and meritorious, but the motive behind it all is entirely wrong. Service can also be rendered because it is becoming increasingly the fashion and the custom to be occupied with some form of service. The tide is on. Everybody is actively serving in welfare movements, in philanthropic endeavors, in Red Cross work, in educational uplifts, and in the task of ameliorating distressing world conditions. It is fashionable to serve in some way. Service gives a sense of power; service brings one friends; service is a form of group activity, and frequently brings far more to the server (in a worldly sense) than to the served.

And yet, in spite of all this which indicates wrong motives and false aspiration, service of a kind is constantly and readily being rendered. Humanity is on its way to a right understanding of services; it is becoming responsive to this new law and is learning to react to the steadily imposing will of that great Life who informs the constellation Aquarius, just as our solar Logos informs our solar system and our planetary Logos informs our earth planet.

The idea of service is, at this time, the major idea to be grasped for (in grasping it) we open ourselves wide to the new incoming influences. The Law of Service is the expression of the energy of a great Life, who, in cooperation with Him "in Whom we live and move and have our being", is subjecting the human family to certain influences and streams of energy which will eventually do three things:—

1. Awaken the heart centre in all aspirants and disciples.
2. Enable emotionally polarised humanity to focus intelligently in the mind.
3. Transfer the energy of the solar plexus into the heart.

This unfolding of what we might call "the consciousness of the heart" or the development of true feeling is the first step towards group awareness. This group awareness and this identification with the feeling aspect of all groups is the quality which leads to service—a service to be rendered as the Masters render it, and as the Christ demonstrated it for us in Galilee.

a. SOME QUESTIONS ON SERVICE

Therefore, the service rendered today is what it is because the response of men to these new Aquarian influences is being registered at present in the astral body and is working out through the solar plexus. This accounts for the emotional nature of most of the service rendered in the world at this time; it is responsible for the hatred engendered by those who react sensitively to suffering and who, because of their emotional identification with suffering, lay the blame for the distressing conditions encountered upon a person or a group of persons. It is responsible also for the generally unsatisfactory nature of much of that which is now being done to relieve conditions. It is unsatisfactory from the higher angle of the soul.

When, however, the service rendered is based upon a mental response to humanity's need, then the whole problem is lifted out of the veil of illusion and out of the valley of the world glamour. Then the impulses to serve are registered in the heart centre and not in the solar plexus, and when this is more generally the case, then we shall have a happier and more successful demonstration of service.

In this Treatise I seek to be intensely practical, for this new science of service must be based on right foundations and on sound understanding. Perhaps the simplest way in which I can handle a theme so new and yet so hackneyed is by formulating certain questions and then answering them as fully and as concisely as possible.

1. How do we define the word "service"?
2. What is the field of this science and why do we call it a science?
3. What are the characteristics of the true server?
4. What effect does service have
   a. On the mind?
   b. On the emotions?
   c. On the etheric body?
5. Does this science prove that the seven key or ray types employ distinctive methods in their service?

The consideration of these questions will enable me to do three things:

1. Show in my answers to each question that service is not a sentiment or an ideal, but that it is an effect and a scientific procedure at the same time.
2. Indicate the need today for the right understanding of a technique which, when applied by the New Group of World Servers, will lead humanity into the world of true meaning and of real values. I will seek to show how the New Group of World Servers will work.
3. Give some idea of how certain groups of the Masters of the Wisdom serve upon our planet at this time.

In answering these questions, we will proceed to take them one by one.

How do we define the word "Service"?

The definition of this word is not easy. There has been too much attempt to define it from the angle of personality knowledge. Service can be briefly defined as the spontaneous effect of soul contact. This contact is so definite and fixed that the life of the soul can pour through into the instrument which the soul must perforce use upon the physical plane. It is the manner whereby the nature of that soul can demonstrate in the world of human affairs. Service is not a quality or a performance; it is not an activity towards which people must strenuously strive, nor is it a method of world salvage. This distinction must be clearly grasped, or else our whole attitude to this momentous demonstration of the success of the evolutionary process in humanity will be at fault. Service is a life demonstration. It is a soul urge, and is as much an evolutionary impetus of the soul as the urge to self-preservation or to the reproduction of the species is a demonstration of the animal soul. This is a statement of importance. It is a soul instinct, if we may use such an inadequate expression and is, therefore, innate and peculiar to soul unfoldment. It is the outstanding characteristic of the soul, just as *desire* is the outstanding characteristic of the lower nature. It is group desire, just as in the lower nature it is personality desire. It is the urge to group good. It cannot, therefore, be taught or imposed upon a person as a desirable evidence of aspiration, functioning from without and based upon a theory of service. It is simply the first real effect, evidenced upon the physical plane, of the fact that the soul is beginning to express itself in outer manifestation.

Neither theory nor aspiration will or can make a man a real server. How then is it that there is so much activity in service demonstrating in the world today?

Simply because the life, words and deeds of the world's first Great Server, of the One Who came to make clear to us what service essentially is, has necessarily had an effect, and men today are earnestly attempting to imitate His example, little realising that imitation does not net them the true results, but only indicates to them a growing possibility.

All these laws of the Soul (and the Law of Service is no exception) manifest inevitably in two ways. First, there is their effect upon the individual. This occurs when the soul has been definitely contacted and the mechanism of the soul begins to respond. Evidence of this should work out now among the esoteric students, scattered over the world, for they have reached a point where the true server can emerge from their ranks, and give evidence of an established soul contact. Secondly, these soul laws are beginning to have a group effect in humanity itself, and to influence the race of men as a whole. This effect is somewhat in the nature of a reflection in the lower nature of a higher consciousness, and therefore today we have much running after service, and much philanthropic effort. All of it is, however, deeply coloured by personality, and it often produces much harm, for people seek to impose their ideas of service and their personal techniques upon other aspirants. They may have become sensitive to impression, but they oft-times misinterpret the truth and are biassed by personality ends. They must learn to lay the emphasis upon soul contact and upon an active familiarity with the egoic life, and not upon the form side of service. May I beg those of you who respond to these ideas and are sensitive to soul impression (oft-times misinterpreting the truth, being biassed by personality ends) to lay the emphasis upon soul contact and not upon the form side of service. Activity of the form side lays stress upon personality ambition, veiling them with the glamour of service. If care over the essential of service—soul contact—is taken, then the service rendered will flow with spontaneity along the right lines and bear much fruit. Of this, the selfless service and the deep flow of spiritual life, which have been demonstrated in the world work of late, is a hopeful indication.

What is the field of this science, and why do we call it a science.

The next point to consider is the field of this service, and its nature as a science. The field of service, first of all, demonstrates as the life of the Spirit, working within the region of a man's own nature. The first thing the soul has to do when contact has been made and the man knows it in his brain consciousness and owing to the active impression of the mind, is to make the man aware that he is a living principle of divinity, and then to prepare the lower threefold nature so that it can automatically submit to the Law of Sacrifice. Then it will offer no impediment to the life which must and will pour through it. This is the first and hardest task, and with this task the aspirants of the world are at this time engaged. This indicates, does it not, the point of evolution reached by the majority? When the rhythm of this law has been imposed and the natural impetus of the man in incarnation is to be an expression of the soul, and when this rhythm can be established as a natural daily expression, the man begins to "stand in spiritual being" and the life which pours through him, gently and naturally, will then have an effect upon his environment and his associates. This effect can then be called a "life of service."

Too much emphasis has been laid upon the *process* whereby the lower nature is to be subjugated to the higher Law of Service, and the idea of sacrifice, in its worst implications, has been developed. This idea emphasises the necessary and inevitable clashing between the lower nature, working under its own laws, and the higher aspects as they work under the spiritual laws. Then the sacrifice of the lower to the higher assumes great proportions, and the word becomes quite suitable. There is sacrifice. There is suffering. There is a painful process of detachment. There is a long effort to let the life flow through, whilst steadily the personality throws up one barrier and obstruction after another. This stage and attitude we can view with sympathy and understanding, for there are those who have so much theory about service and its expression that they fail to serve and also fail to comprehend with understanding the period of pain which ever precedes enlarged service. Their theories block the way to true expression and shut the door on real comprehension. The mind element is too active.

When the personal lower self is subordinated to the higher rhythms and obedient to the new Law of Service, then the life of the soul will begin to flow through the man to others, and the effect in a man's immediate family and group will be to demonstrate a real understanding and a true helpfulness. As the flow of life becomes stronger through use, the effect will spread out from the small surrounding family group to the neighborhood. A wider range of contacts becomes possible, until eventually (if several lives have been thus spent under the influence of the Law of Service) the effect of the out-pouring life may become nationwide and worldwide. But it will not be planned, nor will it be fought for, as an end in itself. It will be a natural expression of the soul's life, taking form and direction according to a man's ray and past life expression; it will be coloured and ordered by environing conditions,—by time, by period, by race and age. It will be a living flow, and a spontaneous giving forth, and the life, power and love demonstrated, being sent forth from soul levels, will have a potent, attractive force upon the group units with which the disciple may come in contact in the three worlds of soul expression. There are no other worlds wherein the soul may at this time thus express itself. Nothing can stop or arrest the potency of this life of natural, loving service, except in those cases wherein the personality gets in the way. Then service, as the Teachers on the inner side of life understand it, gets distorted and altered into busy-ness. It becomes changed into ambition, into an effort to make others serve as we think service should be rendered, and into a love of power which hinders true service instead of into love of our fellow men. There is a point of danger in every life when the theory of service is grasped, and the higher law is recognised; then the imitative quality of the personality, its monkey nature, and the eagerness of a high grade aspiration can easily mistake theory for reality, and the outer gestures of a life of service for the natural, spontaneous flow of soul life through its mechanism of expression.

The need for an increasing subtlety of discrimination is constant, and all dedicated students are urged to take stock of themselves at this time. They face a new cycle of service and must avail themselves of a new day of opportunity. There is a great need to stand in spiritual being; where there is this poised standing, there will be no need for others to incite one to service. Let the "Forces of Light" flow through, and the ranks of the world servers will be rapidly filled. Let the "Spirit of Peace" use the lower nature as an instrument, and there will be peace and harmony within the personal field of service. Let the "Spirit of Good Will" dominate our minds and there will be no room for the spirit of criticism and the spreading of destructive discussion. It is for this reason and in order to develop a group of servers who can work along true and spiritual lines, that there must be increasing emphasis upon the need for *Harmlessness*. Harmlessness prepares the way for the inflow of life; harmlessness dissipates the obstructions to the free outpouring of love; harmlessness is the key to the release of the lower nature from the grip of the world illusion and from the power of phenomenal existence.

We have expressed our belief that one of the major sciences of the coming age will be built up around the active rendering of service. We have used the word "Science" because service, as a spiritual quality, will rapidly be recognised as the phenomenal expression of an inner reality, and along the line of a right understanding of service will come much revelation as to the nature of the soul. Service is a method of producing phenomenal outer and tangible results upon the physical plane; I call your attention to this as an evidence of its creative quality. By right of this creative quality, service will eventually be regarded as a world science. It is a creative urge, a creative impulse, a creative momentous energy. This creativity of service has already been vaguely recognized in the world of human affairs under varying names, such as the science of vocational training. Recognition of the impetus coming from a right understanding of social relations and their study is not lacking. Much is also being studied along this same line in connection with criminology and the right handling of the youth of any nation and national group.

Service is, par excellence, the technique of correct group relations, whether it be the right guidance of an anti-social child in a family, the wise assimilation of a trouble-maker in a group, the handling of anti-social groups in our big cities, the correct technique to be employed in child guidance in our educational centres or the relation between the religious and political parties, or between nation and nation. All of this is part of the new and growing Science of Service. The imposition of this soul law will eventually bring light into a distracted world, and release human energies in right directions. It is not here possible to do more than indicate this briefly. The theme is too large, for it includes the awakening of the spiritual consciousness with its responsibilities, and the welding of the individual into an awakened group; it involves the imposition also of a newer and a higher rhythm upon world affairs. This constitutes, therefore, a definitely scientific endeavor and warrants the attention of the best minds. It should also eventually call forth the consecrated effort of the world disciples.

What are the characteristics of the true server?

These characteristics can be easily and briefly noted. They are not exactly what one may have been led to believe. I am not here speaking of the qualifications required for the treading of the Path of Discipleship or the Probationary Path. These are well known. They are the platitudes of the spiritual life, and constitute the battleground, or the Kurukshetra of most aspirants. We are here concerned with those qualities which will emerge when a man is working under the impulse of the Law of Service. They will appear when he is a real channel for the life of the soul. His major characteristics will then be three in number:—

1. He will be distinguished, as might be expected, by the quality of *harmlessness*, and by an active refraining from those acts and that speech which might hurt or cause any misunderstanding. By no word, suggestion, implication, innuendo or voiced dissatisfaction will he hurt his group. You will note that I do not say "will not hurt any individual." Those working under the Law of Service need no reminder not to hurt any individual. They often need, under the exuberance of spiritual stimulation and the intensity of their aspiration, to be reminded to demonstrate group harmlessness.

2. The second characteristic is *a willingness to let others serve as seems best to them,* knowing that the life flowing through the individual server must find its own

channels and outlets, and that direction of these currents can be dangerous and prevent the rendering of the intended service. The server's efforts will be turned in two directions:—

1. To the task of helping others to "stand in spiritual being", as he himself is learning to stand.
2. To aiding the individual to express his service in his chosen field as he desires to express it, and not as the onlooking helper deems that he should do it.

One point might here be made clear. The task of those who are working under the Law of Service is not exerted primarily with that group in the world today which is working under the effect of that general response to which we earlier referred. These effects are easily shepherded into those activities which, en masse, work out as philanthropic endeavor, as educational experiments, or social efforts in the life of the community. The name of those who thus respond is legion, and the will to serve in this particular way needs no impetus. The remarkable response to the many recent campaigns to good will definitely evidenced this. But the work of the new type of server is directed towards those who are establishing soul contact and who can therefore work under the new incoming Aquarian Law. This centres around the capacity to stand, not only in spiritual being, but *together with* others, working with them subjectively, telepathically, and synthetically. This distinction merits attention for one can easily waste effort by entering fields already well handled from the point of view of the attainment of the units in that field.

3. The third characteristic of the new server is *joyfulness*.

This takes the place of criticism (that dire creator of misery) and is *the silence that sounds.*

It would be well to ponder on these last words, for their true meaning cannot be conveyed in words, but only through a life dedicated to the newer rhythms and to the service of the whole. Then that "sounding joy" and that "joyful sounding" can make its true meaning felt.

What effect does service have upon the mind, the emotions and the etheric body?

It must be remembered that it is through its effects that the scientist of the future will begin to deduce the effectual existence of an inner cause, of an inner reality, or of a self or soul. We have seen that service is not simply an activity of some person or group doing something with good intention for another person or group. Service itself is definitely the result of a tremendous inner happening, and when that result is brought about, it will be found to have produced a number of creative secondary causes. These are, primarily, a change in the lower consciousness, a tendency to turn away from the things of the personal self to the larger issues of the group, a reorientation which is real and expressive and a power to change conditions (through creative activity) which is the demonstration of something dynamically new. As this inner event stabilises into an equilibrised inner condition, the demonstration of the above changes becomes more regular and less spasmodic and the effects of the new forces flowing into the personality, to be later used creatively, will be seen in all three bodies. Thus the true server comes into possession of his instruments for service, and thenceforth creative work in accordance with the Plan can go forward on all three planes. Thus has God, in His wisdom, chosen to limit Himself, and the work of evolution proceeds solely through the medium of His chosen builders and under the direction—on this planet—of those men whose lives are being transformed through soul contact and creative service, and who constitute the planetary Hierarchy.

When alignment has been effected, when the at-one-ment has been more constantly made, and when the antahkarana (the bridge connecting the higher and the lower) is in definite process of construction, the true nature of service, as *practiced by any individual*, begins to emerge. The first effect of the inflowing force of the soul, which is the major factor leading to demonstrated service, is to integrate the personality, and to bring all the three lower aspects of the man into one serving whole. This is a difficult and elementary stage from the angle of the student in the Hall of Wisdom. The man becomes aware of his power and capacity, and, having pledged himself to service, he begins furiously to serve; he creates this, that and the other channel for the expression of the force which is driving him; he tears down and destroys just as fast as he creates. He temporarily becomes a serious problem to the other servers with whom he may be associated, for he sees no vision but his own, and the aura of criticism which surrounds him and the strenuous push of the assertive force within him produces the stumbling of the "little ones" and there has to be constant repair work undertaken (on his behalf) by older, more experienced disciples. He becomes the victim, for the time, of his own aspiration to serve, and of the force which is flowing through him. This stage will in some cases fan into flame the latent seeds of ambition. This ambition is, in the last analysis, only the personality urge towards betterment, and in its right place and time is a divine asset, but it has to be rooted out when the personality becomes the instrument of the soul. In other cases, the server will come into a wider and more loving vision, and, taking his eyes off his own accomplishment, will go to work in silent unison with the groups of all true servers. He will submerge his personality tendencies, his ideas and his ambitions in the greater good of the whole, and self will be lost to sight. Perhaps no better suggestion can be made to the man or woman who seeks to function as a true server than to ask them to repeat daily, with their whole hearts and minds behind the words, the dedication at the conclusion of the Esoteric Catechism, which is included at the end of *Initiation, Human and Solar*. I would remind such servers that if they revolt or are dismayed by the ideas embodied in the words, that is perhaps an indication of how much they need the impression of this life objective upon their consciousness. That pledge runs as follows:

> "I play my part with stern resolve; with earnest aspiration; I look above, I help below; I dream not, nor I rest; I toil; I serve; I reap; I pray; I am the Cross; I am the Way; I tread upon the work I do, I mount upon my slain self; I kill desire, and I strive, forgetting all reward. I forego peace; I forfeit rest, and, in the stress of pain, I lose myself and find Myself and enter into peace. To all this I solemnly pledge myself, invoking my Higher Self."

As the work of learning to serve proceeds and the inner contact becomes more sure, the next thing which will occur will be a deepening of the life of meditation, and a more frequent illumining of the mind by the light of the soul. Thereby the Plan is revealed. This will not be the shedding of that light upon the plans of the server either for his own life or upon his chosen field of service. This must be clearly grasped. That might only indicate (if it seems to occur) the mental agility of the server to find means for the justification of his own ambition. It will be the recognition, in the mind, of the Plan of God for the world at the particular time in which the server is existing, and the part that he may play in furthering the ends of those who are responsible for the carrying forward of that Plan. He then becomes willing to be a tiny part of a greater Whole, and this attitude never varies, even when the disciple has become a Master of the Wisdom. He is then in contact with a still vaster concept of the Plan and His humility and His sense of proportion remain unchanged.

An integrated, intelligent personality is adequate to deal with the working out of the server's part in the active work of the world, provided his vision is not blurred by personal ambition nor his activity such that it degenerates into a sense of rush and a display of busy feverishness. It takes the soul itself to reveal to the poised and peaceful mind the next step to be taken in the work of world evolution, through the impartation of ideas. Such is the Plan for humanity.

As the force pours through the personality and gives to the server this necessary vision and the sense of power which will enable him to cooperate, it finds its way into the emotional or astral body. Here again the effect will be dual, owing to the condition of the server's astral body and his inner orientation. It may enhance the glamour and deepen the illusion, swinging the server into the psychic illusory effects there to be found. When this happens, he will emerge upon the physical plane glamoured by the idea, for instance, of his amazing personal contacts, whereas he has only contacted some group thought-form of the Great Ones. He will be under the illusion that he is a chosen vessel or mouthpiece for the Hierarchy, when the truth is that he is deceived by the many voices, because the Voice of the Silence has been dimmed by the clamour of the astral plane; he will be deluded by the idea that there is no other way but his way. Such an illusion and deception is common among teachers and workers everywhere today, because so many are definitely making a contact with their souls, and are being swept then into the desire for service; they are not yet free, however, from ambition, and their orientation is still basically towards personality expression, and not to the merging of themselves in the Group of World Servers. If however they can avoid glamour, and can discriminate between the Real and the unreal, then the in-flowing force will flood their lives with effective unselfish love and with devotion to the Plan, to those whom the Plan serves, and to Those Who serve the Plan. Note the sequence of these attitudes, and govern yourselves accordingly. There will then be no room for self-interest, self-assertiveness, or selfish ambition. All that is considered is the need and the driving necessity to take the next immediate step to meet that need as it demonstrates before the server's eyes.

With the heart and mind then functioning together (either in selfish coalition for the presentation of an active personality, or in dedicated selflessness and the attitude which is oriented towards soul guidance) the force, flowing through the server will galvanise his etheric body into activity. Then, automatically, the physical body will respond. There is, consequently, a great need for the server to pause upon the astral plane, and there, in a holy and controlled silence, wait, before permitting the force to pour through into the centres in the etheric body. *This point of silence is one of the mysteries of spiritual unfoldment.* Once the force or energy of the soul—preserved in its purity, or tainted and sidetracked on its way through into physical manifestation—has reached the etheric body, there is nothing more to be done by the average disciple. The result, when it reaches that point, is inevitable and effective. The inner thought and the desire life determine the activity which will be expressed physically. When the force comes through in purity, it brings the centres above the diaphragm steadily into activity; when it comes through, tainted by personality trends, it uses primarily the solar plexus, and then sweeps into manifestation all the astral illusions, the grandiose delusions and the glamours of egoistic phenomena, using the word "egoistic" in its usual worldly, psychological connotation. This can easily be seen today among the leaders of various groups.

b. DISTINCTIVE METHODS OF RAY SERVICE

Does this science prove that the seven ray types employ distinctive methods in service?

As time goes on this will be proved decidedly, and each ray worker and server will be found to render his service along peculiar and specific lines. These indicate for him the line of least resistance and, consequently, of the greatest efficiency. These methods and techniques will constitute the inner structure of the coming Science of Service, and they will be discovered through the admission of the Ray hypothesis and an observation of the methods employed by these clearly isolated Ray types and groups. These differing ways of service, all of them, work in conformity with the Plan, and together produce a synthetic whole. The ray or rays in manifestation at any one time will determine the general trend of the world service, and those servers whose egoic ray is in incarnation, and who are endeavoring to work with right activity, will find their work facilitated if they understand that the trend of affairs is with them and that they are following the line of least resistance at that period. They will work with greater facility than will the disciples and aspirants whose egoic ray is out of manifestation. This recognition will lead to a careful study of times and seasons, thus there will be no waste effort, and real advantage can be taken of the qualifications and aptitudes of the servers available. All will be in conformity with the Plan. A consideration of the rays in or out of manifestation, and a recognition of the disciples and servers available on the physical plane at any one time, is part of the work of the Masters in the Hierarchy.

The emergence of the New Group of World Servers today is an indication that there are enough egoic ray types in physical manifestation, and that a sufficient number of personalities are responding to soul contact, so that a group can be formed that can be definitely *impressed as a group*. This is the first time that such a situation has been possible. Up till this century, individuals could be impressed, here and there, in different parts of the world, and at widely separated times and periods. But today *a group can respond* and their numbers are relatively so great that there can be formed upon the planet a group composed of a number of persons of such radiatory activity that their auras can meet and contact each other. Thus one group—subjective and objective—can be functioning.

There are today enough centres of light, scattered all over the world, and enough disciples and aspirants, that the little beams or threads of light (speaking symbolically) which radiate from each of them, can meet and interlace, and form a network of light in the world. This constitutes the magnetic aura of the New Group of World Servers. Each individual in the group is sensitive to the Plan, either through his own personal knowledge through contact with his soul, or because his intuition tells him that what the Group, which attracts him, accepts as its immediate work is for him true and right, and with it all that is highest and best in him can cooperate. Each individual in that Group will work in his own particular surroundings according to his ray and type. That again will be coloured by his race and nation. But the work is the better carried forward as the units in the Group meet the need in their own peculiar environment, in the manner that is, for them, the simplest and best way, belonging as they do by habit and training in that particular setting. This should be remembered.

The seven ray types will work in the following ways, which I am stating very briefly for to do more than that might limit the expression of those who do not know enough to be discriminating as to their characteristics, and might unduly qualify and colour the experience of those servers who recognise (as some already do) their ray. They might, with entirely good intention, seek to force the ray qualities of their souls into dominance before the personality ray is adequately known or controlled. Other servers frequently confuse the two rays and deem their soul ray to be of a particular type, whereas it is only their personality ray to which they predominantly conform, and by which they are pre-eminently governed. Is it not possible for us to observe here the care with which the Teachers of these truths and the custodians of the coming revelation, must proceed? They have to guard the aspirants from premature knowledge, which they might theoretically grasp but which they are not yet ready practically to apply.

Ray I. Servers on this ray, if they are trained disciples work through what might be called the imposition of the Will of God upon the minds of men. This they do through the powerful impact of ideas upon the minds of men, and the emphasis of the governing principles which must be assimilated by humanity. These ideas, when grasped by the aspirant bring about two developments. First, they initiate a period of destruction and of a breaking up of that which is old and hindering, and this is later followed by the clear shining forth of the new idea and its subsequent grasping by the minds of intelligent humanity. These ideas embody great principles, and constitute the New Age ideas. These servers, therefore, work as God's destroying angels, destroying the old forms, but nevertheless, behind it all lies the impetus of love.

With the average aspirant, however, who is on the first ray, the activity is not so intelligent. He grasps the idea that is needed by the race, but he will seek to impose it primarily as his idea, something which he has seen and grasped and which impatiently he seeks to impose upon his fellow men for their good, as he sees it. He inevitably destroys as fast as he builds, and finally destroys himself. Many worthy aspirants and disciples in training for service at this time work in this sad way.

Some of the Masters of the Wisdom and Their groups of disciples are actively engaged at this time in an endeavor to impose certain basic and needed ideas upon the races of men, and much of Their work is being prepared for by a group of Destroying Disciples, and also by a group of Enunciating Disciples, for these two types of work carry forward their task as a unit. The idea to be dominant in the future is proclaimed in writing and by the voice, by one Group. The Group of Destroyers takes it up, and proceed to break up the old forms of truth so as to make room and way for the new emerging idea.

Ray II. Servers on this ray ponder, meditate upon and assimilate the new ideas associated with the Plan, and by the power of their attractive love, they gather together those who are at that point in their evolution where they can respond to the measure and rhythm of that Plan. They can select, and train those who can "carry" the idea deeper into the mass of humanity. We should not forget that the work of the Hierarchy at this time, and the task of the New Group of World Servers is primarily associated with ideas. The disciples and servers on the second Ray are "busy building habitations for those dynamic entities whose function it has ever been to charge the thoughts of men and so to usher in that new and better age which will permit the fostering of the souls of men." So runs the *Old Commentary*, if I thus modernise its ancient wording. By magnetic, attractive, sympathetic understanding, and the wise use of slow action, based on love, do the servers on this ray work. Today their power is becoming dominant.

Ray III. The servers on this ray have a special function at this time in stimulating the intellect of humanity, sharpening it and inspiring it. They work, manipulating ideas so as to make them more easy of comprehension by the mass of intelligent men and women who are to be found in the world at this time and whose intuition is not yet awakened. It is to be noted how the work of the true servers is largely with the new ideas and not with the business of organisation and of criticism (for these two go hand in hand). Ideas are taken by the third ray aspirant, as they emerge from the elevated consciousness of Those for whom the first ray works and are rendered attractive by the second ray worker (attractive in the esoteric sense) and adapted to the immediate need and rendered vocal by the force of the intellectual third ray types. In this lies a hint for many of the third ray personalities to be found working in various fields of service at this time.

Ray IV. This ray is not in incarnation at the time and therefore few fourth ray egos are available in world service There are, however, many fourth ray personalities and they can learn much by the study of the work of the New Group of World Servers. The major task of the fourth ray aspirant is to harmonise the new ideas with the old, so that there can be no dangerous gap or break. They are those who bring about a "righteous compromise", and adapt the new and the old so that the true pattern is preserved. They are engaged with the bridging process, for they are the true intuitives and have a capacity for the art of synthesis so that their work most definitely can help in bringing forward a true presentation of the divine picture.

Ray V. The servers on this ray are coming rapidly into prominence. They are those who investigate the form in order to find its hidden idea, its motivating power, and to this end they work with ideas, proving them either true or false. They gather into their ranks those whose personalities are on this ray and train them in the art of scientific investigation. From the sensed spiritual ideas, lying behind the form side of manifestation, from the many discoveries in the ways of God with man and nature, from the inventions (which are but materialised ideas) and from the witness to the Plan which law portrays, they are preparing that new world in which men will work and live a more deeply conscious, spiritual life. Disciples working along these lines in every country today are more active than at any other time in human history. They are, knowingly and unknowingly, leading men into the world of meaning, and their discoveries will eventually end the present era of unemployment, and their inventions and improvements, added to the steadily growing idea of group interdependence (which is the major message of the New Group of World Servers) will eventually ameliorate human conditions so that an era of peace and leisure can supervene. You will note that I do not say "will supervene", for not even the Christ Himself can predict exactly the time limit within which changes can eventuate, nor the reaction of humanity to any given point of revelation.

Ray VI. The effect of the activity of this ray, during the past two thousand years, has been to train humanity in the art of recognising ideals, which are the blue prints of ideas. The main work of the disciples on this ray is to capitalise on the developed tendency of humanity to recognise ideas, and —avoiding the rocks of fanaticism, and the dangerous shoals of superficial desire—train the world thinkers so ardently to desire the good, the true and the beautiful, that the idea which should materialise in some form on earth can shift from the plane of the mind and clothe itself in some form on earth. These disciples and servers work consciously with the desire element in man; they work scientifically with its correct evocation. Their technique is scientific because it is based upon a right understanding of the human material with which they have to work.

Some people have to be galvanised into activity by an idea. With these the first ray disciple can be effective. Others can be reached more easily by an ideal, and will then subordinate their personal lives and wishes to that ideal. With these the sixth ray disciple works with facility, and this he should endeavor to do, teaching men to recognise the truth, holding steadily before them the ideal, restraining them from a too energetic and fanatical display of interest, in the need for the long pull. The sixth ray, it should be remembered, when it constitutes the personality ray of a man or a group, can be far more destructive than the first ray, for there is not so much wisdom to be found, and, as it works through desire of some kind, it is following the line of least resistance for the masses, and can therefore the more easily produce physical plane effects. Sixth ray people need handling with care, for they are too one-pointed and too full of personal desire, and the tide of evolution has been with this type for a very long time. But the sixth ray method of evoking desire for the materialising of an ideal is indispensable, and, fortunately, there are many aspirants and disciples on this ray available today.

Ray VII. This ray provides at this time an active and
necessary grouping of disciples who are eager to aid the Plan.
Their work lies naturally on the physical plane. They can
organise the evoked ideal which will embody as much of the
idea of God as the period and humanity can evidence and
produce in form upon the earth. Their work is potent and
necessary and calls for much skill in action. This is the ray
that is coming into power. None of these ray participants in
the hierarchical crusade today can really work without each
other, and no group can carry on alone. The difference between the methods of the old age and that of the new can be
seen expressed in the idea of leadership by one and leadership by a group. It is the difference between the imposition
of an individual's response to an idea upon his fellow men
and the reaction of a group to an idea, producing group
idealism and focalising it into definite form, carrying forward
the emergence of the idea without the dominance of any one
individual. This is the major task today of the seventh ray
disciple, and to this end he must bend every energy. He must
speak those Words of Power which are a group word, and
embody the group aspiration in an organised *movement*,
which, it will be noted is quite distinct from an organisation.
A striking instance of the use of such a Word of Power being
enunciated by a group has lately been given in the Great
Invocation which has been used with marked effect. It should
continue to be used, for it is the inaugurating mantram of
the incoming seventh ray. This is the first time such a mantram has been brought to the attention of humanity.

   All these rays work today for the carrying out of a specific
group idea of seven Masters Who, through Their picked
and chosen servers, are actively participating in the work
which is the initiatory work of the seventh ray. It is also
linked up with the incoming Aquarian influence. The Masters,

with their large group of disciples, functioning on all the five planes of human unfoldment, have studied minutely Their accepted disciples, the disciples under supervision and not yet accepted, and the aspirants of the world. They have selected a number of them to weld together into a group upon the outer physical plane. The basis of this selection is:—

a. Sensitivity to the Aquarian influence.
b. Willingness to work in a group as an integral part of the group, and having no idea of personal ambition or any wish to be a leader. Where the desire to be a leader exists, that disciple is automatically (though only temporarily) disqualified for this particular endeavor. He can still do good work, but it will be secondary work, and more closely affiliated with the old age than with the work of the New Group of World Servers.
c. A dedication that holds nothing back that can *rightly* be given.
d. A harmlessness which, though not yet perfected, exists as an ideal towards which the aspirant is constantly striving.

In this work many can have a part. The Law of Service has been thus outlined in an endeavor to make one of the most esoteric influences in the solar system somewhat clearer in our minds. I call you to service, but would remind you that the service discussed here will only be possible when we have a clearer vision of the goal of meditation, and learn to preserve, during the day, the attitude of inner spiritual orientation. As we learn to obliterate and efface out of our consciousness ourselves as the central figure in our life drama, then and then only can we measure up to our real potentialities as servers of the Plan.

4. *The Law of Repulse*

We have here a most interesting law to consider. It is one of the major divine laws with which the Pilgrim has much to do on his weary, age-long way, back to the centre. It is the fourth law governing or controlling the life of the soul.

No.	Exoteric Name	Esoteric Name	Symbol	Ray Energy
4.	Law of Repulse.	The Law of all Destroying Angels.	The Angel with the Flaming Sword.	The Rejecting Energy of the First Ray.

First of all, it is well to realise that this law has certain characteristics and basic effects which might be briefly enumerated as follows:—

1. The energy displayed is dissipating in its effect. This law works as a dispersing agent.

2. When in active expression, it causes an active scattering or rejection of the aspects of form life.

3. It produces a discriminating contact which leads eventually to what is esoterically called "the Way of divine refusal."

4. It is, nevertheless, an aspect of the Law of Love, of the Vishnu or Christ aspect, and concerns an attitude of the soul, whose essential nature is love.

5. This law expresses itself through the mind nature, and therefore can only make its presence and influence felt upon the Path of Discipleship.

6. It is the prime pre-requisite to true self-knowledge. It reveals at the same time that it divides or scatters.

7. It works through love and for the interest of the unit,—the form and the existence which finally repulses the form.

8. It is an aspect of one of the greatest cosmic laws, the Law of the Soul, which is the cosmic Law of Attraction, for that which is attracted in time is automatically and eventually repulsed by that which attracted it in the first instance.

This law is one which primarily begins to impress the divine purpose upon the consciousness of the aspirant, and dictates to him those higher impulses and those spiritual decisions which mark his progress upon the Path. It is the demonstration of the first ray quality (a subray influence of the second ray), for it should be remembered that to repulse a form, a situation or a condition may be the evidence of spiritual love in the agent of repulsion. This is well pictured for us in the ancient symbol of the Angel with the flaming sword, who stands before the gate of Paradise to turn away those who seek the fancied security of that shelter and condition. This angel acts in love, and has so acted down the ages, for that state of realisation which we call Paradise is a place of essential danger for all, save those who have earned the right to sojourn there. The angel protects the unready aspirant (not the place which he seeks to enter) and safeguards him from the risks and perils of that initiation which must be undergone before he can pass through the five divisions of Paradise to the place where light dwells and the Masters of the Wisdom live and work. This is the thought which lies behind the Masonic procedure whereby the Tyler stands outside the door of the Lodge with a drawn sword to protect the secrets of the Craft from the unready.

I would remind you also that as this law is an aspect of the fundamental Law of Love, it concerns the psyche or soul, and therefore its function is to further the spiritual interests of the true man, and to demonstrate the power of the second aspect, the Christ consciousness, and the power of divinity. It "rejects the undesirable in order to find that which the heart craves, and thus leads the weary pilgrim from one rejection to another, until with unerring choice he makes the Great Decision." This is quoted from the *Old Commentary*.

We will divide what we have to say about the functioning and effect of the Law of Repulse into three parts:—

a. The Law of Repulse, and the function and quality of desire.
b. The Law of Repulse, as it expresses itself upon the Paths of Discipleship and Initiation.
c. The Law of Repulse, as it "drives in seven directions, and forces all that it contacts back unto the bosom of the seven spiritual Fathers."

This law works through the soul in all forms. It does not literally affect matter, except in so far as form is affected when the soul "withdraws", or occultly "repudiates." It will be apparent, therefore, that our understanding of its activity will depend largely upon the measure of soul force of which we may individually be aware, and the extent of our soul contact. Our point upon the ladder of evolution will govern our manipulation of this law (if such a term may be used), and determine our capacity to be sensitive to its impact. If we are unable to respond to its influence in any measure, that in itself is sufficient to indicate our development. Unless the mind is active, and unless we are beginning intelligently to use the mind, there is no medium or channel through which this influence can flow or work. Never let it be forgotten that this influence or law of our spiritual being is that which reveals the will, plan or purpose of the divine life, as it expresses itself in the individual or in humanity as a whole. Let us never forget that unless there is a thread of light to act as a channel, that which this law can convey will remain unknown, unrealised and useless. These laws are the laws which govern predominantly the Spiritual Triad, that divine Triplicity which expresses itself through the medium of the soul, just as the three aspects of the soul, in their turn, reflect themselves through the personality.

Therefore, all that can be imparted in connection with this law can be comprehended only by the man who is beginning to be spiritually awakened. The three laws which we have already considered deal with the specific spiritual influences which emanate from the three tiers of petals which compose the egoic lotus. (See page 823 of *A Treatise on Cosmic Fire*.)

1. The Law of Sacrifice............The Petals of Sacrifice. The sacrificial will of the Soul.
2. The Law of Magnetic Impulse....The Petals of Love.
3. The Law of Service.............The Petals of Knowledge.

This fourth Law of Repulse works through the first Law of Sacrifice and carries to the aspirant the quality, influence and tendency of the Spiritual Triad, the threefold expression of the Monad. Its full force is felt only after the third initiation, in which the power of the Spirit is, for the first time, consciously felt. Up to that time it has been the growing control of the soul which was primarily registered. Therefore we have:—

1. The Law of Repulse............Atma. Spiritual Will. This
   Fourth Law   influence comes via the egoic petals of sacrifice and the subsidiary Law of Sacrifice.
2. The Law of Group Progress.....Buddhi. Spiritual Love.
   Fifth Law   This comes via the love petals of the egoic lotus,

<table>
<tr><td></td><td></td><td>and the subsidiary Law
of Magnetic Impulse.</td></tr>
</table>

3. The Law of Expansive Response..Manas. Higher spiritual
   Sixth Law mind. It comes via the
   knowledge petals and
   the subsidiary Law of
   Service.

These higher spiritual laws reflect themselves in the three lower spiritual laws, finding their way into the lower consciousness via the egoic lotus and the antahkarana. This statement is the second basic postulate in connection with our study of this Law of Repulse, the first postulate being the earlier statement that unless there is a thread of light to act as a channel, that which this law conveys will remain unknown and unrealised.

These six laws give us the key to the entire psychological problem of every human being, and there is no condition which is not produced by the conscious or unconscious reaction of man, to these basic influences—the natural and spiritual laws. If psychologists would accept the three basic laws of the universe, and the seven laws through which they express their influence, they would arrive at an understanding of the human being far more rapidly than is now the case. The three major laws are, as has been stated elsewhere:—

1. *The Law of Economy*. This governs primarily the instinctual nature of man.
2. *The Law of Attraction*, which governs the soul aspect in man and in all forms of life, from an atom to a solar system.
3. *The Law of Synthesis*, which will govern man when he has arrived at the Path of Initiation, but which as yet means but little in his development.

There are, then, the seven minor Laws which produce the

evolutionary unfoldment of man, the person, and man, the soul. These are:

1. The Law of Vibration, the atomic law of the solar system.
2. The Law of Cohesion, an aspect of the Law of Attraction.
3. The Law of Disintegration.
4. The Law of Magnetic Control, governing the control of the personality by the spiritual nature, via the soul nature.
5. The Law of Fixation. By means of this law the mind controls and stabilises.
6. The Law of Love, whereby the lower desire nature is transmuted.
7. The Law of Sacrifice and Death.

(*A Treatise on Cosmic Fire*, p. 569.)

These seven laws concern the form side of life. To these ten laws must be added the seven laws of the soul which we are here considering. These begin to play upon the man and produce his more rapid spiritual unfoldment after he has been subjected to the discipline of the Probationary Path, or the Path of Purification. He is then ready to tread the final stages of the Path.

These seven laws are the basis of all true psychological understanding and, when their influence is better grasped, man will arrive at real self knowledge. He will then be ready for the fourth initiation which releases him from all further need for rebirth. This is the truth which underlies the Masonic teaching, which is given under the symbolism of the first eighteen degrees. These can be divided into four groups of degrees:—Entered Apprentice, Fellow Craft, (followed by the Mark degree) Master Mason (followed by the H.R.A.) and the grouped degrees, four to seventeen, in the Scottish Rite. These seventeen degrees prepare the man for the fourth or fundamental degree, *taken by the man who is a Master Mason.* It can only be taken when the Master is in possession of the true Lost Word. He has risen from the dead; he has been entered, passed, and raised, and now can be perfected. Herein lies a great mystery. These seventeen degrees, leading to the first great step, (taken by the risen Master) are subjectively related to the seventeen laws which we have been considering. There is a parallelism worth noting between:—

1. The eighteen laws:—
    a. The three major laws of the universe,
    b. The seven minor laws of the solar system,
    c. The seven basic laws of the soul,
        plus what we might call the great law of Deity Itself, the law of God's synthetic purpose.
2. The eighteen subplanes through which man makes his way:—
    a. The seven physical subplanes.
    b. The seven astral or emotional-desire subplanes.
    c. The four lower mental subplanes.
3. The eighteen degrees in Masonry, from that of the Entered Apprentice to that of the perfected initiate of the Rose Croix Chapter.
4. The eighteen centres of force with which the spiritual man has to work:
    a. The seven centres in the etheric body.
    b. The seven centres in the astral body.
    c. The three rows of petals in the egoic lotus.
    d. The "Jewel in the Lotus", at the heart of the "flower of the soul", which makes the eighteenth centre.

An understanding of these symbolic relations will do much to clarify the way of the soul in a body, and will constitute the basis of all true esoteric psychological study.

a. The Law of Repulse and Desire

The section with which we have now to deal will concern itself specifically with the major problem of humanity. We shall, however, touch upon it most briefly, and will deal particularly with the aspect of it which shifts from the problem as it concerns the aspirant to the problem of the disciple. Underlying the entire psychological problem of humanity as a whole lies that major attitude towards existence which we characterise as *Desire*. All lesser complexities are based upon, subservient to, or are emergent from, this basic urge. Freud calls this urge "sex," which is, nevertheless, only another name for the impetus of attraction for the not-self. Other psychologists speak of this dominant activity as the "wish-life" of humanity, and account for all allied characteristic tendencies, all emotional reactions and the trend of the mental life, in terms of the underlying wishes, longings and acquisitive aspirations as "defence mechanisms," or "ways of escape" from the inevitability of environing conditions. To these longings and wishes and the labour incidental to their fulfilment, all men give their lives; and everything done is in an effort to meet the realised need, to face the challenge of existence with the demand for happiness, for heaven, and for the eventual fulfilment of the hoped-for ideal state.

Everything is governed by some form of *urgency towards satisfaction*, and this is distinctive of man's search at every stage of his development—whether it is the instinctual urge to self-preservation, which can be seen in the savage's search for food or in the economic problems of the modern civilised man; whether it is the urge to self-reproduction and the satisfaction of that appetite which works out today in the complexity of the sex life of the race; whether it is the urge to be popular, loved and esteemed; whether it is the urge for intellectual enjoyment and the mental appropriation of truth, or the deep-seated desire for heaven and rest which characterises the Christian, or the aspiration for illumination which is the demand of the mystic, or the longing for identification with reality which is the "wish" of the occultist. All this is desire in some form or another, and by these urges humanity is governed and controlled; I would say most definitely controlled, for this is only a simple statement of the case.

It is this realisation of man's fundamental bias or controlling factor that lies behind the teaching given by the Buddha, and which is embodied in the Four Noble Truths of the Buddhist philosophy, which can be summarised as follows: —

The Four Noble Truths

  a. Existence in the phenomenal universe is inseparable from suffering and sorrow.
  b. The cause of suffering is desire for existence in the phenomenal universe.
  c. The cessation of suffering is attained by eradicating desire for phenomenal existence.
  d. The Path to the cessation of suffering is the noble eightfold path.

It was the realisation of the urgency of man's need to be delivered from his own desire-nature which led Christ to emphasise the necessity to seek the good of one's neighbor in contra-distinction to one's own good, and to advise the life of service and self-sacrifice, of self-forgetfulness and love of all beings. Only in this way can man's mind and "the eye of the heart" be turned away from one's own needs and satisfaction to the deeper demands of the race itself.

Until a man stands upon the Path of Perfection, he cannot really grasp the imperative demand of his own soul for release from the search for outer, material, tangible satisfaction, and from desire. It has been this demand which indicated the soul's need to incarnate and to function, for a needed period, under the Law of Rebirth. As the work of purification proceeds upon the Path of Purification, this demand for release becomes stronger and clearer, and when the man steps out upon the Path of Discipleship, then the Law of Repulse can, for the first time, begin to control his reactions. This takes place unconsciously at first, but it becomes more potent and more consciously appreciated as the disciple takes one initiation after another, with increasingly pointed understanding.

It is not our intention in this Treatise to deal with the development of the unevolved and undeveloped man in connection with these Laws of the Soul. I seek only to clear the way of the highly intelligent man, the aspirants of the world and the world disciples. The progress of the undeveloped and the average man can be covered by the following statements, taken sequentially and describing the stages of his progress under the promptings of desire:

1. The urge to experience, to exist, and to satisfy the instinctual nature.
2. Experience, grasping, existing, followed by renewed demand for more satisfying compliances of fate or destiny.
3. Cycle after cycle of demand for satisfaction, a period of satisfaction of a temporary nature, and then further demands. This is the story of the race.
4. Experience, steadily sought and pursued upon the three planes of human evolution.
5. Then the same experience, but this time as an integrated personality.

6. Demand met until satiety is reached, for in time all men do eventually achieve that which they demand.
7. Then comes the demand for inner spiritual compliances, happiness and bliss. The "heaven wish" becomes powerful.
8. A vague realisation that two things are needed; purification and the power to choose aright, which is right discrimination.
9. A vision of the pairs of opposites.
10. The realisation of the narrow path which leads between these pairs of opposites.
11. Discipleship and the repulsing or repudiation (over a long period of time), of the not-self.

Such, briefly and inadequately stated, is the story of man as he searches for happiness, for joy and for bliss, or (expressing it in terms of realisation) as he progresses from the life of the instincts to that of the intellect, and then from that intellectual apprehension to the stage of illumination and final identification with reality, when he is henceforth freed from the Great Illusion.

Two things determine the rapidity with which he can—upon the Path of Discipleship—bring the Law of Repulse into play. One is the quality of his motive. Only the desire to *serve* is adequate to bring about the necessary reorientation and subjection to the new technique of living. The other is his willingness, at all costs, to be *obedient* to the light which is in him and around him. Service and obedience are the great methods of release, and constitute the underlying causes which will bring the Law of Repulse into play, thus aiding the aspirant to attain the longed-for liberation. Service releases him from his own thought life and self determination. Obedience to his own soul integrates him into the larger whole, wherein his own desires and urges are negated in the interest of the wider life of humanity, and of God Himself. God is the Great Server and expresses His divine life through the Love of His heart for humanity.

Yet, when these simple truths are enunciated and we are urged to serve our brother and to obey our soul, it seems to us so familiar and so uninteresting that it can evoke but little response. If we were told that the following of a prescribed form of meditation, the practicing of a definite formula of breathing, and regular concentration upon a specific centre would release us from the wheel of life and identify us with the spiritual self and its world of being, gladly and willingly and joyously would we follow out instructions. But when, in the terms of the occult science, we are told to serve and obey, we are not interested. Yet service is the mode, *par excellence*, for awakening the heart centre, and obedience is equally potent in evoking the response of the two head centres to the impact of soul force, and unifying them into one field of soul recognition. So little do men understand the potency of their urges! *If the urge to satisfy desire is the basic urge of the form life of man, the urge to serve is an equally basic urge of the soul in man.* This is one of the most important statements in this section. It is as yet seldom satisfied. Indications of its presence are ever to be found, nevertheless, even in the most undesirable types of human beings; it is evoked in moments of high destiny, or immediate urgency, and of supreme difficulty. The heart of man is sound, but oft asleep.

Serve and obey! These are the watchwords of the disciple's life. They have been distorted into terms of fanatical propaganda and have thus produced the formulas of philosophy and of religious theology; but these formulas do, at the same time, veil a truth. They have been presented to the consideration of man in terms of personality devotions and of obedience to Masters and leaders, instead of service of, and obedience to, the soul in all. The truth is, however, steadily emerging, and must inevitably triumph. Once the aspirant upon the Probationary Path has a vision of this (no matter how slight it may be), then the law of desire which has governed him for ages will slowly and surely give place to the Law of Repulse, which will, in time, free him from the thralldom of not-self. It will lead him to those discriminations and that dispassionate attitude which is the hallmark of the man who is on his way to liberation. Let us remember, however, that a discrimination which is based upon a determination to be free, and a dispassion which is the indication of a hard heart, will land the aspirant in the prison of a crystallized shell, which is far harder to break than the normal prison of the life of the average selfish man. This selfish spiritual desire is oft the major sin of so-called esotericists and must be carefully avoided. Therefore, he who is wise will apply himself to serve and obey.

b. The Law of Repulse upon the Paths of Discipleship
and Initiation

When the discriminating sense (the spiritual correspondence of the sense of smell, the last of the five senses to emerge in humanity) has been adequately developed in the aspirant, and he *knows* the pairs of opposites and has gained a vision of that which is neither of them, then he can pass on to the Path of Discipleship and enter upon the arduous task of cooperating with the spiritual laws, particularly with the Law of Repulse. At first, he hardly recognises the influence of this Law. It is as difficult for him to grasp its implications and to measure its possible effects as it would be for the average working man, with a mediocre education and a total ignorance of esotericism, to grasp the significance of such an occult truth as that expressed in the words: "The construction of the antahkarana between higher and lower manas by the divine Agnishvatta, the solar angel, functioning through the egoic lotus, is the task to be carried forward during the contemplative stage of meditation." This statement is relatively simple to grasp intellectually by the average occult student, but is utterly meaningless to the man of the world. The Law of Repulse is equally difficult of understanding by the disciple as he enters upon the Path. He has to learn to recognise its influence; then he must himself learn to do three things:—

1. Through service, steadily to decentralise himself and thus begin occultly to "repulse" the personality. He must see to it that his motive is love for all beings, and not desire for his own release.

2. Through an understanding of the pairs of opposites, he begins, esoterically, to "isolate" the "noble middle path" of which the Buddha spoke.

3. Through comprehension of the words of Christ, enjoining men to "let their light shine," he begins to construct the "path of light" which leads to the centre of life and guides him out of darkness into light, from the unreal to the real, and from death to immortality. This is the true path of the antahkarana, which the disciple weaves from out of himself (speaking symbolically), just as the spider weaves his thread.

Service, an understanding of the Way, and the building of the true line of escape—that is the task to be carried forward upon the Path of Discipleship. Such is the object set before all the students of the esoteric sciences at this time,— provided they desire it enough, and can train themselves to work selflessly for their fellow men. As they succeed in doing this and approximate ever more closely to that which is *not* the pairs of opposites (and thus achieve "the Central Way"), steadily the Law of Repulse begins to swing into operation. When the third initiation is taken, this law will begin to hold the dominant place in the ruling of the life.

The word "repulse" has an unfortunate connotation in many minds, and this revulsion against the word itself indicates man's innately spiritual bias. Repulsion, the desire to repudiate, and repulsive attitudes, words and deeds evoke in our minds all that is unpleasant to contemplate. Yet, spiritually considered and scientifically viewed, the word "repulse" indicates simply "an attitude towards that which is not desirable." This, in its turn (as we seek to determine that which is desirable), calls into activity the virtues of discrimination, dispassion and discipline in the disciple's life, as well as the power to decentralise. These words indicate the urge to devaluate the unreal and the undesirable, to discipline the lower nature till those choices are readily and easily made which lead to the discarding of that which imprisons or impedes the soul. The major concepts are the definitely and carefully chosen way or procedure which will free the soul from the world of forms and identify it, first of all, with itself (thus freeing it from the world illusion), and then with the world of souls, which is the consciousness of the Oversoul.

There is no need to enlarge here upon the technique whereby this choice is to be made. The way of discrimination, the method of dispassion and the discipline of the life have been made plain and clear by the teachings of the past two thousand years, and through the many books written to emphasise the teaching of the Christ and of the Buddha. Through a right understanding of these, right choice can be made, and that which should not be cherished or desired can be "repulsed". Many an earnest student (such as those who will read this Treatise) has found it of advantage to write down for himself his own personal understanding of the four words:—

1. Discrimination,
2. Dispassion,
3. Discipline,
4. Decentralisation.

One page given to each definition should suffice, if it embodies truly one's highest thought. Students will realise that as they practice these four virtues, the prime characteristics of a disciple, they are thereby automatically calling into play the Law of Repulse, which, upon the Path of Initiation, brings revelation and realisation. The expression of this law upon the Path of Initiation is too advanced for those who are not yet versed in the basic discriminations, and who are still far from being dispassionate. Is there need therefore to enlarge upon this law as it works out in the life of the initiate? I think not. The disciple seeks to achieve, without passion, pain or suffering, the distinction which lies between:

1. Right and wrong,
2. Good and evil,
3. Light and dark, spiritually understood,
4. Prison and liberty,
5. Love and hate,
6. Introversion and extraversion. We do well to ponder on this duality
7. Truth and falsehood,
8. Mystical and occult knowledge,
9. The self and the not-self,
10. Soul and body.

Many, many other dualities can thus be listed. Having then discovered the fact of these pairs of opposites, the task of the disciple is to discover *that which is neither of them*. It is this central, intermediate way that is revealed to the initiate, through the working of the Law of Repulse which occultly enables him to "push with either hand, to a distance afar from his way, that which intrudes and veils the central way of light. For neither on the right nor on the left lies safety for the man who seeks that lighted way." Does this sentence really mean aught to most of us? Let us seek to express to ourselves in words the qualifications and name of that third or central way which is, for instance, neither light nor dark, and neither love nor hate. We cannot with clarity see what it could be, nor will we until the increased stimulation which is released in us upon the Way of Initiation does its appointed work. Some idea of what it means may appear, however dimly, to our vision as we deal with our third division.

c. The Law of Repulse and the Pilgrim on the Way of Life

We shall base our thoughts upon the words earlier quoted:

> "The Law of Repulse drives in seven directions, and forces all it thus contacts back to the bosom of the seven spiritual Fathers."

We have come definitely to a consideration of the Way of Repulsion, governed by this law, which is the way or technique for each ray type. Though the same law can be seen working in all seven cases and in all seven directions, yet the results will differ, because the quality and the phenomenal appearance upon which the law of the divine will makes its impact and consequent impression, differ so widely. The complexity of the problem is therefore great. These seven soul laws lie behind all the various presentations of truth as they have been given out by the world Teachers down the ages. It requires much spiritual insight, however, to enable the average disciple to see the correspondence or the trend of ideas which link, for instance:

1. The beatitudes (enunciated by the Christ) and these seven laws.
2. The stages of the Noble Eightfold Path and these soul potencies.
3. The eight Means to Yoga or union of the soul, and this septenate of influences.
4. The Ten Commandments of the Semitic religion, and these seven spiritual laws.

Students would find it of interest to test their understanding of the esoteric relationships existing between these groups of teaching and see if they can, for themselves, trace the basic meanings. Let us, by way of illustration, trace or indicate the relation between the seven laws and the eight means to Yoga, because this will give us an illustration of the difference existing between the means to Yoga as understood by the average yogi or esotericist, and as they can be understood by the trained disciple or initiate.

1.
The five Commandments .... Second ray force...The Law of Magnetic Impulse.
The universal duty.   Inclusion. Attraction.

2.
The Rules .... Fourth ray force...The Law of Sacrifice.
For self training.   "I die daily."

3.
Posture .... Sixth ray force.....The Law of Service.
A poised attitude to   Right relations and
the world.   right ideals.

4.

Pranayama	Seventh ray force...	The Law of Group
The law of rhythmic living.		Progress. The Law of spiritual development.

5.

Abstraction	First ray force.....	The Law of Repulse.
Pratyahara. Withdrawal from desire.		The repudiation of desire.

6.

Attention	Third ray force....	The Law of Expansive
Correct orientation.		Response.

7.

Meditation	Fifth ray force.....	The Law of the Lower
Right use of the mind.		Four. "The soul is in deep meditation."

8.

Result	Contemplation	Complete spiritual detachment.

A close study of these relationships will be found suggestive to the disciple and illuminating to the initiate. Let us not, however, confuse illumination with a new or bright idea! It is something far different to that. The difference is that between the light of a star, and the light of a steadily waxing sun. One reveals the fact of night. The other reveals the world of daylight and of conscious Being.

d. The Seven Directions of the Law of Repulse

It must be remembered that the Law of Repulse, which is the Law of the destroying Angels, works in seven directions; that it produces effects upon seven different types of beings and men, and that by reason of its activity, it draws the prodigal son back to the Father's home. It causes him to "arise and go." But we must remember that, when Christ was relating this story, He made it abundantly clear that there was no impulse to return until the pilgrim in the far country had come to himself or to his senses, as a result of satisfied desire, through riotous living. This was followed by consequent satiety and loss of contentment, and then by a period of intense suffering, which broke his will to wander or to desire. A study of this story will be found revealing. In no Scripture is the sequence of events (as they deal with the pilgrim's existence and life in a far country and his return) so concisely or so beautifully treated. Seek out your Bibles, and study this tale, and read for yourselves the pilgrim's way.

The effect of this Law of Repulse, as it works out in the world of discipleship and destroys that which hinders, sends the pilgrim hurrying back consciously along one of the seven rays that lead to the centre. This cannot be handled in detail here. Our present task is that of treading the Path of Probation or of Discipleship and of learning discipline, dispassion, and the other two necessities on the Way,—discrimination and decentralisation. It is possible, nevertheless, to indicate the goal and point out the potency of the forces to which we shall be increasingly subjected as we pass—as some of us can so pass—on to the Path of Accepted Discipleship. This we will do in the form of seven stanzas which will give a hint (if one is an aspirant) of the technique to which one will be exposed; if one has passed further on the Way, they will give one a command which, as a disciple with spiritual insight one will obey, because one is awakened; if one is an initiate, they will evoke the comment: "This I know."

The Direction of Ray I.

> "The garden stands revealed. In ordered beauty live its flowers and trees. The murmur of the bees and insects on their winged flight is heard on every side. The air is rich with perfume. The colours riot to the blue of heaven. . . .
> The wind of God, His breath divine, sweeps through the garden. . . . Low lie the flowers. Bending, the trees are

devastated by the wind. Destruction of all beauty is followed by the rain. The sky is black. Ruin is seen. Then death. . . .

Later, another garden! but the time seems far away. Call for a gardener. The gardener, the soul, responds. Call for the rain, the wind, the scorching sun. Call for the gardener. Then let the work go on. Ever destruction goes before the rule of beauty. Ruin precedes the real. The garden and the gardener must awake! The work proceeds."

The Direction of Ray II.

"The Scholar knows the truth. All is revealed to him. Surrounded by his books, and sheltered in the world of thought, he burrows like a mole, and finds his way into the darkness; he arrives at knowledge of the world of natural things. His eye is closed. His eyes are opened wide. He dwells within his world in deep content.

Detail on detail enter into the content of his world of thought. He stores the nuggets of the knowledge of the world, as a squirrel stores its nuts. The storehouse now is adequately full. . . . Sudden a spade descends, for the thinker tends the garden of his thought, and thus destroys the passages of mind. Ruin arrives, destroying fast the storehouse of the mind, the safe security, the darkness and the warmth of a satisfied enquiry. All is removed. The light of summer enters in and the darkened crannies of the mind see light. . . . Naught is left but light, and that cannot be used. The eyes are blinded and the one eye seeth not as yet. . . .

Slowly the eye of wisdom must be opened. Slowly the love of that which is the true, the beautiful and good must enter the dark passages of worldly thought. Slowly the torch of light, the fire of right must burn the garnered treasures of the past, yet show their basic usefulness. . . .

The seven ways of light must wean away the attention of the Scholar from all that has been found and stored and used. This he repulses and finds his way into that Hall of Wisdom which is built upon a hill, and not deep under ground. Only the opened eye can find this way."

The Direction of Ray III.

"Surrounded by a multitude of threads, buried in folds and folds of woven goods, the Weaver sits. No Light can enter where he sits. By the light of a tiny candle, carried upon the summit of his head, he dimly sees. He gathers handful after handful of the threads and seeks to weave the carpet of his thoughts and dreams, his desires and his aims. His feet move steadily; his hands work swiftly; his voice, without cessation, chants the words: 'I weave the pattern which I seek and like. The warp and woof is planned by my desire. I gather here a thread and here a colour. I gather there another. I blend the colours and I mix and blend the threads. As yet I cannot see the pattern, but it will surely measure up to my desire.'

Loud voices, and a movement from outside the darkened chamber where the Weaver sits; they grow in volume and in power. A window breaks and, though the Weaver cries aloud, blinded by the sudden light, the sun shines in upon his woven carpet. Its ugliness is thus revealed. . . .

A voice proclaims: 'Look from out thy window, Weaver, and see the pattern in the skies, the model of the plan, the colour and the beauty of the whole. Destroy the carpet which you have for ages wrought. It does not meet your need. . . . Then weave again, Weaver. Weave in the light of day. Weave, as you see the plan.' "

The Direction of Ray IV.

" 'I take and mix and blend. I bring together that which I desire. I harmonise the whole.'

Thus spoke the Mixer, as he stood within his darkened chamber. 'I realise the unseen beauty of the world. Colour I know and sound I know. I hear the music of the spheres, and note on note and chord on chord, they speak their thought to me. The voices which I hear intrigue and draw me, and with the sources of these sounds I seek to work. I seek to paint and blend the pigments needed. I must create the music which will draw to me those who like the pictures which I make, the colours which I blend, the music which I can evoke. Me, they will therefore like, and me, they will adore. . . .'

But crashing came a note of music, a chord of sound which drove the Mixer of sweet sounds to quiet. His sounds died out within the Sound and only the great chord of God was heard.

A flood of light poured in. His colours faded out. Around him naught but darkness could be seen, yet in the distance loomed the light of God. He stood between his nether darkness and the blinding light. His world in ruins lay around. His friends were gone. Instead of harmony, there was dissonance. Instead of beauty, there was found the darkness of the grave. . . .

The voice then chanted forth these words: 'Create again, my child, and build and paint and blend the tones of beauty, but this time for the world and not thyself.' The Mixer started then his work anew and worked again."

The Direction of Ray V.

"Deep in a pyramid, on all sides built around by stone, in the deep dark of that stupendous place, a mind and brain (embodied in a man) were working. Outside the pyramid, the world of God established itself. The sky was blue; the winds blew free; the trees and flowers opened themselves unto the sun. But in the pyramid, down in its dim laboratory, a Worker stood, toiling at work. His test tubes and his frail appliances he used with skill. In rows and rows, the retorts for fusing, and for blending, for crystallising and for that which sought division, stood with their flaming fires. The heat was great. The toil severe. . . .

Dim passages, in steady progress, led upward to the summit. There a wide window stood, open unto the blue of heaven, and carrying one clear ray down to the worker in the depths. . . . He worked and toiled. He struggled onwards toward his dream, the vision of an ultimate discovery. He sometimes found the thing he sought, and sometimes failed; but never found that which could give to him the key to all the rest. . . . In deep despair, he cried aloud unto the God he had forgot: 'Give me the key. I alone can do no more good. Give me the key.' Then silence reigned. . . .

Through the opening on the summit of the pyramid, dropped from the blue of heaven, a key came down. It landed at the feet of the discouraged worker. The key was of pure gold; the shaft of light; upon the key a label, and writ in blue, these words: 'Destroy that which thou has built and build anew. But only build when thou has climbed the upward way, traversed the gallery of tribulation and entered into light within the chamber of the king. Build from the heights, and thus shew forth the value of the depths.'

The Worker then destroyed the objects of his previous toil, sparing three treasures which he knew were good, and upon which the light could shine. He struggled towards the chamber of the king. And still he struggles."

The Direction of Ray VI.

" 'I love and live and love again,' the frenzied Follower cried aloud, blinded by his desire for the teacher and the truth, but seeing naught but that which lay before his eyes. He wore on either side the blinding aids of every fanatic divine adventure. Only the long and narrow tunnel was his home and place of high endeavor. He had no vision except of that which was the space before his eyes. He had no scope for sight,—no height, no depth, no wide extension. He had but room to go one way. He went that way alone, or dragging those who asked the way of him. He saw a vision, shifting as he moved, and taking varying form; each vision was to him the symbol of his highest dreams, the height of his desire.

He rushed along the tunnel, seeking that which lay ahead. He saw not much and only one thing at a time,—a person or a truth, a bible or his picture of his God, an appetite, a dream, but only one! Sometimes he gathered in his arms the vision that he saw, and found it naught. Sometimes, he reached the person whom he loved and found, instead of visioned beauty, a person like himself. And thus he tried. He wearied of his search; he whipped himself to effort new.

The opening dimmed its light. A shutter seemed to close. The vision he had seen no longer shone. The Follower stumbled in the dark. Life ended and the world of thought was lost . . . Pendent he seemed. He hung with naught below, before, behind, above. To him, naught was.

From deep within the temple of his heart, he heard a Word. It spoke with clarity and power: 'Look, deep within, around on every hand. The light is everywhere, within thy heart, in Me, in all that breathes, in all that is. Destroy thy tunnel, which thou has for ages long constructed. Stand free, in custody of all the world.' The Follower answered: 'How shall I break my tunnel down? How can I find a way?' No answer came. . . .

Another pilgrim in the dark came up, and groping, found the Follower. 'Lead me and others to the Light,' he cried. The Follower found no words, no indicated Leader, no formulas of truth, no forms or ceremonies. He found himself a leader, and drew others to the light,—the light that shone on every hand. He worked and struggled forward. His hand held others, and for their sake, he hid his shame, his fear, his hopelessness and his despair. He uttered words of surety and faith in life, and light and God, in love and understanding. . . .

His tunnel disappeared. He noticed not its loss. Upon the playground of the world he stood with many fellow-players, wide to the light of day. In the far distance stood a mountain blue, and from its summit issued forth a voice which said: 'Come forward to the mountain top and on its summit learn the invocation of a Saviour.' To this great task the Follower, now a leader, bent his energies. He still pursues this way. . . ."

The Direction of Ray VII.

"Under an arch between two rooms, the seventh Magician stood. One room was full of light and life and power, of stillness which was purpose and a beauty which was space. The other room was full of movement, a sound of great activity, a chaos without form, of work which had no true objective. The eyes of the Magician were fixed on chaos. He liked it not. His back was towards the room of vital stillness. He knew it not. The arch was tottering overhead. . . .

He murmured in despair: 'For ages I have stood and sought to solve the problem of this room; to rearrange the chaos so that beauty might shine forth, and the goal of my desire. I sought to weave these colours into a dream of beauty, and to harmonise the many sounds. Achievement lacks. Naught but my failure can be seen. And yet I know there is a difference between that which I can see before my eyes and that which I begin to sense behind my back. What shall I do?'

Above the head of the Magician, and just behind his back, and yet within the room of ordered beauty, a magnet vast began to oscillate. . . . It caused the revolution of the man, within the arch, which tottered to a future fall. The magnet turned him round until he faced the scene and room, unseen before. . . .

Then through the centre of his heart the magnet poured
its force attractive. The magnet poured its force repulsive.
It reduced the chaos until its forms no longer could be seen.
Some aspects of a beauty, unrevealed before, emerged. And
from the room a light shone forth and, by its powers and
life, forced the Magician to move forward into light, and
leave the arch of peril."

Such are some thoughts, translated from an ancient metrical
arrangement, which may throw some light upon the duality
of personality and the work to be done by the beings found
upon the septenate of rays. Know we where we stand? Do
we realise what we have to do? As we strive to enter into
light, let us count no price too great to pay for that
revelation.

We have studied an interesting sequence of Laws. *In Law
One*, we find that three major ideas emerge:

First of all, that the Eternal Pilgrim, of his own free will
and accord, chose "occultly" to die and took a body or series
of bodies in order to raise or elevate the lives of the form
nature which he embodied. In the process of so doing, he
himself "died", in the sense that, for a free soul, death and the
taking of a form and the consequent immersion of the life in
the form, are synonymous terms.

Secondly, that in so doing, the soul is recapitulating on a
small scale what the solar Logos and the planetary Logos
have likewise done, and are doing. These great Lives come
under the rule of the laws of the soul during the period of
manifestations, even though they are not governed or controlled by the laws of the natural world, as we call it. Their
consciousness remains unidentified with the world of phenomena, though ours is identified with it until such time
that we come under the rule of the higher laws. By the occult
"death" of these great Lives, all lesser lives can live and are
proffered opportunity.

Thirdly, that through death, a great at-one-ing process is carried forward. In the "fall of a leaf" and its consequent identification with the soil on which it falls, we have a tiny illustration of this great and eternal process of at-one-ing, through becoming and dying as a result of becoming.

In Law Two, the sacrificing unit—again freely and by choice—comes under the influence of the method whereby this death is brought about. By the impact of the pairs of opposites and through his being "pendent" 'twixt the two, he knows the outer darkness as Christ knew it finally at the Crucifixion, where He hung, symbolically pendent 'twixt heaven and earth, and through the potency of His own inner vibration and magnetism, has drawn and will draw all men to Himself. This is the first great idea emerging. The second emerging idea concerns the balancing of the forces which have been mastered. The symbol of the scales is here appropriate, and, of this truth, the three Crosses on Mount Golgotha are also symbols. Libra governs this law, and certain forces from that constellation can be sensed when the soul consciousness comes under the influence of the law. These forces are quiescent where the personality is concerned; their effect does not register, even though necessarily present.

In Law Three, the sacrificing God and the God of the dualities come under certain influences which produce more easily recognised effects. By his death and by his victory over the pairs of opposites, the disciple becomes so magnetic and vibrant, that he serves the race by becoming what he knows he is. Immersed, physically, from the angle of the personality, in the waters of earthly existence, yet at the same time he is aware—in consciousness—of other conditions, of his essential purpose in dying for other lives, and aware also of the method which he must employ in achieving and attaining the releasing equilibrium. When these ideas are dominant in the mind, he can serve his fellow men. These laws have this effect only as they emerge in the consciousness of the man who is building the antahkarana and who is proceeding with the Science of Union.

It is when *the fourth Law* of Repulse is beginning to produce its effects that the disciple becomes aware of the Angel with the Flaming Sword, Who stands before the portal of initiation. By this portent, he knows that he can now enter; but, this time, not as a poor blind candidate, but as an initiate in the mysteries of the world. The truth of this has been summed up for us in an ancient chant which used to be sung in the ante-chamber of the Temples. Some of the words may be roughly expressed as follows:

> "He enters free, he who has known the prison walls. He passes into light with open eyes, he who for aeons long has groped the darkened corridor. He passes on his way, he who has stood for ages before a fast closed door.
>
> He speaks with power the *Word* which opens wide the Gate of Life. He stands before the Angel and takes away his sword, releasing thus the Angel unto a higher task. He himself guards the doorway into the Holy Place.
>
> He died. He entered the strife. He learnt the way of service. He stands before the door."

5. *The Law of Group Progress*

No.	Exoteric Name.	Esoteric Name.	Symbol.	Ray Energy.
5.	The Law of Group Progress.	The Law of Elevation.	The Mountain and the Goat.	Progressive Energy. Seventh Ray. Factor of Evolution.

This law begins to function and to be registered in the personal consciousness when the aspirant has achieved certain definite realisations, and knows certain ideals as facts in his experience. These might be listed in a very simple way and would then connote to the superficial student the simplest achievement of the **Prob**ationary Path. It would, however, be well if we could grasp this fact with clarity, that this simple formulation of requirements and their achievement within the aspirant's consciousness, demonstrate as the outer and veiled reactions of his mind to some deeply esoteric cosmic truths. This statement contains the very essence of the esoteric knowledge. The quite ordinary formulations of loving living and of daily instinctive self-sacrifice suffer from being so vitally familiar and yet—if we could only realise it—they are only on the outer fringe of the deepest world truths. They are the A.B.C. of esotericism and through them, and only through them, shall we arrive at the words and sentences which are, in their turn, the essential key to the highest knowledge.

A brief example will serve to illustrate this, and we can then consider some simple facts which indicate that the aspirant is beginning to function as a soul and is ready for conscious life in the kingdom of God.

The disciple in training for these higher realisations is urged to practice the faculty of *discrimination*. You have been so urged. The initial and normal interpretation and the immediate effect of the practice is to teach the disciple to distinguish between the pairs of opposites. Yet just as the disciple in his early training discovers that the discriminating process has naught to do with the choice between recognised evil (so-called) and recognised good, but concerns the more subtle pairs of opposites such as right and wrong silences, right and wrong speech, right understanding and right indifference and their opposites, so the man who is reacting to these higher laws discovers that the discrimination to be shown is again still more subtle and is—for the bulk of the aspirants in the world today—still a meaningless objective. This type of discrimination is not even being evoked. It is that which must be shown in relation to the following subtle contacts:

1. The vibration of the soul itself.
2. The vibration of the inner group with which he is, even if unconsciously, affiliated.
3. The vibration of the Master as the focal point of the group.
4. His ray vibration, as sensed via his soul and the Master.
5. The vibration resulting from the interplay between his soul and his personality.
6. The three different vibrations of his vital body, his emotional body and the mind.
7. The vibration of the groups or the group with which he must work upon the outer plane.
8. The soul vibration of other people whom he contacts.
9. The vibration of such a group as the New Group of World Servers.

These are only some instances of the type of discriminations which are required. These he will learn to distinguish instinctively when he is further developed. I would like to remind you that it is when we try to discriminate entirely mentally that the problem seems insuperable. When the rule of the soul and the recognition of the soul have been firmly established, these different recognitions become instinctual reactions. *Intuitional response* is the name we give to the instinctual life of the soul—the higher correspondence to the instinctual life of the human body. In the above paragraphs we have a simple summary of some of the deeper significances of the simple injunction: "Learn to discriminate." How much have we truly understood this injunction? Intellectually, the mind may give assent. Practically, the words frequently mean nothing. Do they signify to us the power of the soul to separate vibrations into differing categories? Yet we are told that the soul knows naught of separation! Such are some of the paradoxes of esotericism to the uninitiate.

The Law of Group Progress can only begin to have a conscious effect in the life of the disciple who has been pledged and accepted. When he has established certain rhythms, when he is working effectively along certain well recognised group lines, and when he is definitely and in understanding consciousness preparing himself for the expansions of initiation, then this law begins to sway him and he learns to obey it instinctively, intuitively and intellectually. It is through obedience to this law that preparation for initiation is instituted by the disciple. The previous sentence is so worded because it is important that all should grasp the self-initiated necessity of initiation. Do we understand this importance? Some of the effects earlier mentioned in the initial discussion of this fifth law can here be enumerated. Let us not forget their esoteric and unseen significances.

1. The disciple will then learn effectively to decentralise himself. This means that

    a. He will ask nothing for the separated self. One can therefore easily see why aspirants are taught to pledge allegiance to their Higher Self, and to foreswear all claims of this separated self. One can see also why so many react against it. They are not ready for it, and such a pledge therefore acts as a great discriminating agent. To those for whom the standard of selflessness is set too high, it is neither understood nor desired. Therefore the unready criticise it. Later these will come back and with understanding take this obligation in the light.

    b. His eyes are towards the light and not towards desire for contact with the Master. This, therefore, rules out that spiritual selfishness which has been expressed by the desire, innate and deep, for recognition by one of the Great Ones. When this freedom from the personal is found, then the Master can dare to make a contact and to establish a relation with the disciple. It would be well for us to ponder on this.

2. He will have learnt to serve instinctively. He may, and usually does, need to learn to discriminate in his service; but his attitude to life and toward all men is a divine rushing forth to aid, to lift, to love and to succour.

3. He will have learnt to use the mind in two directions, increasingly and at will, and instantaneously:

    a. He can cast the search-light of the mind into the world of the soul, and know and recognise those truths which must, for him, become his experienced knowledge.

    b. He can also cast it into the world of illusion and dispel the glamours of the personal. When he can do that, then he begins to dispel the world glamours for he is nearing initiation.

a. THE LINK OF THE WORLD GROUPS

It would be possible to go on listing the various developments which indicate to the onlooking Hierarchy that a disciple, or a group of disciples, are now ready for "more light." The major indication is, however, their reaction to the Law of Group Progress. It is this Law which is the coming new law to be sensed by the world disciples and which is already becoming more effective in its potency, even though this will not be realised by humanity for a long while yet. It will bring into activity the work of the world groups. In the past, groups have been formed for mutual benefit, for mutual interest and study, for mutual strengthening. This has been their glory, and also their curse, for great and good though their motives may have been, yet these groups have been basically and primarily selfish, with a form of spiritual selfishness most difficult to overcome, and calling for the expression of the true discrimination to which I have earlier referred. Such groups have ever been battlegrounds wherein the least able and the least integrated have been absorbed and standardised or regimented, and the most powerful have dominated eventually, and the indefinite ones have been eliminated and rendered totally quiescent. The successful group has eventually turned out to be one composed of kindred souls who are all thinking alike, because no one thinks with intuition, but who are governed by some school of thought, or because some central figure in the group dominates all the rest, hypnotising them into an instinctual, quiescent, static condition. This may be to the glory of the teacher and of the group, but it certainly is not to the glory of God.

Today the new groups are slowly and gradually coming into being and being governed by these soul laws. They will, therefore, strike a different note and produce groups which are welded together by a united aspiration and objective. Yet they will be constituted of free souls, individual and developed, who recognise no authority but that of their own souls, and submerge their interests to the soul purpose of the group as a whole. Just as the achievement of an individual has, down the ages, served to raise the race, so a paralleling achievement in group formation will tend to raise humanity still more rapidly. Hence this law is called that of Elevation.

The time has now come when this method of raising the race can begin to be tried. Those who have entered upon the Path of Probation have attempted to raise humanity and have failed. Those who have passed upon the Path of Discipleship have also tried and failed. Those who have themselves mastered circumstance and the illusion of death, and have consequently been raised unto life, can now attempt the task in united formation. They will succeed. The word has gone forth with the request for this united activity, and the urge to bend every effort to raise the dead body of humanity. A great and possible achievement of the Lodge of Masters is now imminent and all aspirants and all disciples can be swung into a synthetic recognition of power and of opportunity.

It is for this end that the teaching anent the New Group of World Servers was given out broadcast. This is the first attempt to form a group which would work as a group and attempt a world task. They can act as an intermediate group between the world of men and the Hierarchy. They stand between what is occultly called the "dead Master" and the "living Masters." Masons will understand what is here described. The true esotericist will also see the same truth from another angle.

I would like here to give you some thoughts anent the new groups which come into functioning activity under the Law of Group Progress. It must be constantly remembered, as one considers these coming new groups, that they are primarily an experiment in *Group Activity*, and are not formed for the purpose of perfecting the individual member in any group. This is a fundamental and essential statement, if the objectives are rightly to be understood. In these groups the members supplement and fortify each other, and, in the aggregate of their qualities and capacities, they should eventually provide groups capable of useful spiritual expression, and through which spiritual energy can flow, unimpeded, for the helping of humanity. The work to be done is very largely upon mental levels. The spheres of daily service of the individual members of the new groups remain as their destiny and inner urge indicates upon the physical plane; but—to the differing fields of individual effort—there will be added (and this is the point of importance) a group activity which will be a joint and united service. Each person in such groups has to learn to work in a close mental and spiritual cooperation with all the others, and this takes time, given the present point of evolutionary development of the world aspirants. Each has to pour forth love on all, and this is not easy. Each has to learn to subordinate his own personality ideas and his personal growth to the group requirements, for at present some will have to hasten their progress in certain directions, and some must slow it down as a service to the others. This process will take place automatically as the group identity and integration becomes the dominant thought in the group consciousness, and the desire for personal growth and spiritual satisfaction is relegated to a secondary place.

This contemplated group unity will have its roots in group meditation, or in the contemplative life (in which the soul knows itself to be one with all souls). This in its turn will work out in some form of group activity which will constitute the distinguishing contribution of any particular group to the raising of the human race esoterically. Within the group life, the individual will not be dealt with as such by those who seek to train, teach and weld the group into an instrument for service. Each person will be regarded as a transmitter of the type of energy which is the predominant energy in any ray type,—either egoic or personality rays. Each can in time learn to transmit the quality of his soul ray to the group, stimulating his brothers to greater courage, clearer vision, finer purity of motive, and deeper love, and yet avoid the danger of vitalising his personality characteristics. This is the major difficulty. To do this effectively and correctly, we must all learn to think of each other as souls, and not as human beings.

Therefore, as a preliminary statement, we have the following objectives in the group work of the New Age, as they make their tentative beginnings at this time. The later and more esoteric objectives will emerge as the earlier ones are reached:

1. *Group Unity*. This must be achieved through the practice of love, which is part of the practice of the Presence of God, through the subordination of the personality life to the group life, and constant, loving, living service.

2. *Group Meditation*. These groups will eventually be grounded in the kingdom of souls, and the work done will be motivated and carried forward from the higher mental levels in the demonstration of the contemplative life. This involves the dual activity of the life of the disciple, wherein he functions consciously both as a personality and as a soul. The life of the personality should be that of intelligent activity; that of the soul is loving contemplation.

3. *Group Activity*. Each group will have some distinguishing characteristic and this will be dedicated to some specific form of service.

When the groups are properly established (and the time is imminent) and after they have worked together subjectively for a certain necessary period of time (to be determined by the quality of the life of the individuals composing it, and their selflessness and service) then they will begin to function outwardly and their life aspect will begin to make its presence felt. The various lines of activity will emerge when the group vibration is strong enough to make a definite impact on the consciousness of the race. Therefore, it will be apparent that the first and foremost requirements are group integrity and group cohesion. Nothing can be accomplished without these. The subjective linking of each group member with each, and the emergence of a group consciousness is a vital objective for the next few decades. Thus there will emerge a group circulation or transmission of energy which will be of real value in world salvage. For the individual it should be remembered that purity of body, control of the emotions, and stability of mind are fundamental requirements and should be the goal of the daily practice. Again and again we must come back to these prime character requirements, and tiresome as the reiteration may be, I urge upon you the cultivation of these qualities. Through these groups it may be possible to restore some of the ancient Mysteries, and some of the groups mentioned previously in *Letters on Occult Meditation*, will be found among the emerging New Age groups.

b. The Characteristics of the New Groups

This brief summary will serve to give some of the elementary requirements and, by means of a broad generalisation, to indicate the major reasons why such groups are being formed. We can now perhaps widen our vision a little and at the same time look at the groups in greater detail.

One of the characteristics distinguishing the groups of world servers and knowers, is that the outer organisation, which will hold them integrated, will be so nebulous and fine that, to the outer observation, it will be practically non-existent. The group will be held together by an inner structure of thought and a close telepathic interrelation. The Great Ones, Whom we all seek to serve, are thus linked, and can at the slightest need and with the least expenditure of force, get into rapport with each other. They are all attuned to a particular vibration, and so must these groups be attuned. There will be thus collected together, people demonstrating the wide difference in nature, who are found on differing rays, who are of varying nationalities, and the product of widely separated environments and heredity. Besides these factors, which immediately attract attention, there will also be found an equal diversity in the life experience of the souls concerned. The complexity of the problem confronting the group members is also tremendously increased when one remembers the long road which each has travelled, and the many factors and characteristics, emerging out of a dim and distant past, which have tended to make each person what he now is. When, therefore, one dwells on the difficulties and the possible barriers to success, the question will arise and rightly so: What makes it possible to establish this group inter-relation? What provides a common meeting ground? The answer to these questions is of paramount importance and necessitates a frank handling.

We find in the Bible the words: "In Him we live and move and have our being". This is the statement of a fundamental law in nature, and the enunciated basis of the relation which exists between the unit soul, functioning in a human body, and God. It determines also, *in so far as it is realised*, the relation between soul and soul. We live in an ocean of energies. We ourselves are congeries of energies, and all these energies are closely interrelated and constitute the one synthetic energy body of our planet.

It must be carefully borne in mind that the etheric body of every form in nature is an integral part of the substantial form of God Himself—not the dense physical form, but what the esotericists regard as the form-making substance. We use the word "God" to signify the one expression of the One Life which animates every form on the outer objective plane. The etheric or energy body, therefore, of every human being, is an integral part of the etheric body of the planet itself and consequently of the solar system. Through this medium, every human being is basically related to every other expression of the Divine Life, minute or great. The function of the etheric body is to receive energy impulses and to be swept into activity by these impulses or streams of force, emanating from some originating source or other. The etheric body is in reality naught but energy. It is composed of myriads of threads of force or tiny streams of energy, held in relation to the emotional and mental bodies and to the soul by their co-ordinating effect. These streams of energy, in their turn, have an effect on the physical body and swing it into activity of some kind or another, according to the nature and power of whatever type of energy may be dominating the etheric body at any particular time.

Through the etheric body, therefore, circulates energy emanating from some mind. With humanity in the mass, response is made unconsciously to the rulings of the Universal Mind; this is complicated in our time and age by a growing responsiveness to the mass ideas—called sometimes public opinion—of the rapidly evolving human mentality. Within the human family are also found those who respond to that *inner group of Thinkers*, Who, working in mental matter, control from the subjective side of life, the emergence of the great Plan and the manifestation of divine purpose.

This group of Thinkers falls into seven main divisions and is presided over by three great Lives or super-conscious entities. These Three are the Manu, the Christ and the Maha-chohan. These three work primarily through the method of influencing the minds of the adepts and initiates. These latter, in Their turn, influence the disciples of the world and these disciples, each in his own place and on his own responsibility, work out their concept of the Plan and seek to give expression to it as far as possible. These disciples have hitherto worked very much alone except when karmic relationships have revealed them to each other and telepathic intercommunication has been fundamentally confined to the Hierarchy of adepts and initiates, both in and out of incarnation, and to Their individual work with Their disciples.

These groups, therefore, which have hitherto worked entirely subjectively, can and will be duplicated externally, and the new groups will come into being largely as an externalisation—experimental as yet—of the groups which have functioned behind the scenes, motivated from the central group, the Hierarchy of Masters.

This experiment is primarily as yet one of group integration and the method whereby it can be developed. The reason why Those on the Inner Side are now experimenting with this group idea is because it is definitely a New Age trend. They are seeking to utilise the increasing bias of the human being towards coherence and integration. It must be remembered, however, and with constancy, that unless there is a subjective coherence, all outer forms must eventually disintegrate or never cohere at all. It is only the subjective links and the subjective work that determines success, and these must (particularly in the new group work) be based on egoic relations and not on personal attachments and predilections. These help where there is at the same time a recognition of the egoic relation. Where that exists, then something can be formed which is immortal and as lasting as the soul itself.

One practical point should be made clear. These groups will for some time be what might be called "pattern-groups" and, therefore, must be formed very slowly and with much care. Each person forming part of the new groups will be tested and tried and subjected to much pressure. This will be necessary if the groups are to stand through this transition period of the present. It will not be easy for disciples to form these groups. The methods and techniques will be so different to those of the past. People may evince real desire to participate in the group life and to form part of the group activity, but their real difficulty will consist in bringing their personal life and vibration into conformity with the group life and rhythm. The narrow path which all disciples have to tread (and in the early stages these groups will consist primarily of those on the Probationary Path or the Path of Discipleship) requires obedience to certain instructions which have been handed down to us from the ancient past. These are followed willingly and with the eyes open, but no rigid adherence to the letter of the law is ever asked or expected. Flexibility within certain self-imposed limits is always needed, yet that flexibility must not be set in motion by any personality inertia or mental questioning.

This great group training experiment, now being initiated on earth through a new activity of the Hierarchy, will demonstrate to the watching Guides of the race just how far the disciples and aspirants of the world are ready to submerge their personal interests in group good; how sensitive they are, as a group, to instruction and guidance; how free the channels of communication are between the groups on the outer plane and the Inner Group, and between them also and the masses whom they are expected eventually to reach. A Master's group of disciples, on the inner side of life, forms an integrated organism, characterised by mutual love, life and interplay. The relationships in that group are entirely mental and astral, and hence the limitations of the etheric force body and of the physical brain and dense physical body are not felt. This leads to a greater inner facility in understanding and to a reciprocal interplay. It is wise here to remember that the astral potency is far more strongly felt than on the physical levels, and hence the emphasis laid upon emotional-desire control in all treatises on discipleship and on preparation for that state.

Now an effort is being made to see if such a group activity and interplay can be set up on the physical plane, which will consequently include the physical body apparatus and the brain. The difficulties are, therefore, great. What has to be the technique employed in handling this more difficult situation, which is only possible because the work of the Masters' groups has been so effective? Much may depend upon just how far we will react to this interplay and how much it will mean to us in our lives. This embodies a most practical occult method of work. The astral-physical brain reactions should be regarded as non-existent and allowed to lapse below the threshold of the group consciousness, there to die for lack of attention. The emphasis is held steadily on mental and egoic relations.

c. The Experimental Nature of the Groups

I have said that these groups constitute an experiment. This experiment is fourfold in nature and a concise statement about it may clarify conjecture:

I. *They are an experiment in founding or starting focal points* in the human family through which certain energies can flow out into the entire race of men. These energies are ten in number.

II. *They are an experiment in inaugurating certain new techniques in work and in modes of communication.* It is to be noted that in these last three words is summed up the whole story. These groups are intended to facilitate interrelation or communication as follows:

1. They will be occupied with an endeavor to facilitate communication between individuals so that the rules

and methods whereby speech can be transcended may become known and the new way of intercourse be brought about. Eventually communication will be from:

a. Soul to soul, on the higher levels of the mental plane. This involves complete alignment, so that soul-mind-brain are completely at-one.

b. Mind to mind, on the lower levels of the mental plane. This involves the complete integration of the personality or lower self, so that mind and brain are at-one.

Students must remember these two distinctive contacts, and bear in mind also that the greater contact need not necessarily include the lesser. Telepathic communication between the different aspects of the human being is entirely possible at varying stages of unfoldment.

2. They will work at the establishment of communication between that plane which is the plane of illumination and pure reason (the buddhic plane) and the plane of illusion which is the astral plane. It should be remembered that our great task is to dispel the world illusion through the pouring in of illumination or of light. When enough groups have been started that have this for their objective, there will then be found upon the physical plane, those channels of communication which will act as the mediators between the world of light and the world of illusion. They will be transmitters of that type of energy which will break up the existing maya or illusion and dissipate the ancient thought-forms. They will release the light and peace which will illumine the astral plane and so dispel the illusory nature of its life.

3. Through other groups another type of energy must flow, producing another type of interrelation and communication. These groups will bring about the right healing of the personalities of individuals, in all aspects of their nature.

The work intended is the intelligent transmission of energy to various parts of the nature—mental, astral and physical—of the human being, through the right circulation and organisation of force. Healing must eventually be carried forward by groups which act as the intermediaries between the plane of spiritual energy (either soul energy, intuitional energy, or will energy) and the patient or group of patients. This last point is to be noted. The *group* idea must always be remembered, for this will distinguish the New Age methods from the past; the work will be group work for the group. The members will work as souls and not as individuals. They will learn to communicate healing energy from the reservoir of living force to the patients.

4. Other groups of communicators will act as transmitters of two aspects of divine energy,—knowledge and wisdom. These must be thought of in terms of energy. Their work will concern itself with the education of the masses, as a direct intermediary between the higher mind and the lower mind, and with the building of the antahkarana; and their task is that of linking the three points of interest upon the mental plane,—the higher mind, the soul, and the lower mind—so that there is established a group antahkarana between the kingdom of souls and the world of men.

5. Political work will occupy other groups more specifically than does any other branch of work. These groups communicate the "quality of imposition" and an authority that is lacking in many other branches of this divine group activity. The work is largely first ray work. It embodies the method whereby the divine *Will* works out in the consciousness of races and nations. Members of this group will have much first ray in their constitution. Their work is to act as channels of communication between the department of the Manu and the

race of men. It is a noble thing to be channels of the *Will* of God.

6. Some groups will be, in a pronounced sense, channels between the activity of the second ray, that of the World Teacher (at the present time, the Christ holds this office) and the world of men. The energy of the second ray must pour through such groups of students and believers and allied groups of thinkers and workers, and there will be many of these. This fact is to be noted. There will be many such groups. The platform of the new world religion will be built by them.

7. A few groups will have an interesting function, but one which will not materialise for a long while, or not until the work of the building forces of the Universe are better understood. This will be coincident with the development of etheric vision. These groups will act as channels of communication or intermediaries between the energies which constitute the forces which construct the forms, the fabricators of the outer garment of God, and human spirits. The possibility is, therefore, to be noted that the main initial work will be concerned with the problem of reincarnation. That problem deals with the taking of an outer garment or form under the Law of Rebirth. Therefore, when these groups are organised, it will be with that subject that the members will at first work. They will make a deeper and different study than has heretofore been undertaken on the Law of Rebirth.

8. Some groups of energy communicators and transmitters will carry illumination between groups of thinkers. They are *Illuminators of group thoughts.* They transmit energy from one thought centre to another. They transmit, above everything else, the energy of ideas. That is their major function. The world of ideas is a world of dynamic force centres. This should not be forgotten. These ideas have to be contacted and

noted. Their energy has to be assimilated and transmitted and this is the function of those force centres which will express themselves along these lines of activity.

9. Groups working in another category will have for their specific work the stimulating of the minds of men so that alignment can take place. They act primarily as channels of communication between the soul of man and the soul in any form. They will be the great psychometrical workers, for a psychometrist is one whose soul is sensitive to the soul in other forms of life,—human and non-human. They evoke the soul of the past, primarily, linking it with the present, and finding it also indicative of the future.

10. Members of other groups will be communicators between the third aspect of Deity as it expresses itself through the creative process and the world of human thought. They will link or blend life and form creatively. Today, unknowingly and without any true understanding, they bring about a concretisation of the energy of desire, which, in its turn, brings about the concretisation of money. This, consequently, necessitates the materialisation of *things*. They have a most difficult task and that is why it is only during the past one hundred and fifty years that the science of world finance has made its appearance. They will deal with the divine aspect of money. They will regard money as the means whereby divine purpose can be carried forward. They will handle money as the agency through which the building forces of the universe can carry forward the work needed; and (herein lies the clue) those building forces will be increasingly occupied with the building of the subjective Temple of the Lord rather than with the materialising of that which meets man's desire. This distinction merits consideration.

III. *They are an externalisation of an inner existing condi-*

tion. It must be realised that these Groups are not a cause but an effect. That they may themselves have an initiatory effect as they work upon the physical plane is no doubt true, but they themselves are the product of inner activity and of subjective aggregations of force which must perforce become objective. The work of the group members is to keep, *as a group*, in close rapport with the inner groups, which form· nevertheless, one large, active group. This central group force will then pour through the groups in so far as the group members, *as a group*—

a. Keep en rapport with the inner sources of power;
b. Never lose sight of the group objective, whatever that objective may be;
c. Cultivate a dual capacity to apply the laws of the soul to the individual life, and the laws of the group to the group life;
d. Use all forces which may flow into the group in service, and learn, therefore, to register that force and use it correctly.

Would the following sequence of statements convey anything to our minds in this connection? It is a statement of fact and is not in the least symbolic in its terminology, except in so far as all words are inadequate symbols of inner truths.

1. Each group has its inner counterpart.
2. This inner counterpart is a complete whole. The outer result is only partial.
3. These inner groups, forming one group, are each of them expressive of, or governed by, certain laws, embodying the controlling factors in group work. A law is only an expression or manifestation of force, applied under the power of thought by a thinker or group of thinkers.

4. These inner groups, embodying differing types of force, and working synthetically to express certain laws, are an effort to bring in new and different conditions, and hence produce a new civilisation. This is the New Age that the Aquarian Age will see consummated.

5. The outer groups are a tentative and experimental effort to see how far humanity is ready for such an endeavor.

IV. *They are also an experiment which has for its objective the manifestation of certain types of energy* which will produce cohesion, or an at-one-ment, upon earth. The present distraught condition in the world, the international impasse, the religious dissatisfaction, the economic and social upheaval of the past few decades, are all the result of energies that are so potent—owing to their immense momentum—that they can only be brought into rhythmic activity by the imposition of stronger and more definitely directed energies. When the groups are functioning adequately and have achieved, not only an internal group unity, but also harmony between the groups themselves, then some peculiar and esoteric work can be done.

Such are some of the plans which the Hierarchy are attempting to carry forward and in which all true disciples and aspirants can have a part. They are brought to our attention in order to evoke our lasting cooperation.

d. Astrology and the New Groups

This Law of Group Progress embodies one of the energies which have gradually been released over the past two centuries. A fuller tide was swept into activity at the time of the May, 1936, full moon and now the growth of the group idea, both in its good and bad aspects, can be imminently expected. As has several times been pointed out to students, this law is connected with a certain realised impulse in the minds of men, and this is, in its turn, the effect of various types of energy, which are playing upon the earth. The name "Law of Group Progress" is the phrase given by human beings to a particular type of energy which is producing the *coherence of units in a group*, thus forming them into one living organism. The recognitions eventuating are those of group affinity, group objective, and group goal. It is, in the last analysis, the emergence into the subjective consciousness of the same type of energy which produces that aspect of cohesive action which demonstrates as tribal, national or racial unity. In this case, however, the determining factor is not of a physical connotation nor have these groups a physical plane basis. They are based on a group idealism which can only be consciously registered when the units in the group are beginning to function upon the mental plane and are developing the capacity to "think things through"—that is, to register in the brain that which the soul has imparted to the mind. We have here a definition of the meditation process as it should be followed by those who, through alignment, have made some measure of soul contact. These groups are functioning entirely through a subjective relation, which produces a subjective integration and activity.

When we come to study the astrological implications in connection with these laws, we shall discover that the energies of the zodiacal signs have a specific effect upon the energy of a Being, Whose purpose works out into manifestation through these laws, which are regarded by us as great and inevitable natural laws and also spiritual laws. This effect produces a blending of energies which is both balancing and, at the same time, impelling.

In December, 1935, the energies of Capricorn were augmented by the pouring in of forces from a still greater constellation which is—to our zodiac—what the zodiac is to the earth. This augmentation will take place again in 1942. It must be remembered that, from certain angles, the circle of twelve signs or constellations constitutes a special unity which revolves within our universe of heavens as our planet revolves in the centre of our circle of influences. By means of this augmentation—during the coming Aquarian zodiacal cycle—groups on earth can avail themselves of the tide of Capricornian influences which will flow into our radius of registration every seven years. The one just past, gave a tremendous impetus to the work of the New Group of World Servers, and was the cause of the very good reaction in the world to their particular impulse. This worked out in every nation and in every group as a marked tendency to good will. In 1942, there will come another planetary inflow of which we all are begged to avail ourselves, and for which we are urged to make due preparation. This "week of group impact" occurring every seven years, will run from December 21st till December 28th, and if this should at any time fall at the period of the full moon, the opportunity will be most significant. This possibility must be watched. This week should be regarded as pre-eminently the "festival week" of the New Group of World Servers, and after 1942 advantage must be taken of this period, and special preparation made. This fact invites the attention of all of us.

These new groups are appearing everywhere all over the world. The groups upon the outer plane, with their diversity of names and stated aims, are not connected with this inner group which is sponsoring or "projecting" the new groups except in so far as they have a definite, even if nebulous connection. This becomes always possible where there are three members of the New Group of World Servers found in any one exoteric group; it then becomes "linked by a triple thread of golden light" to the New Group of World Servers, and can in some measure be used. This great and spiritual grouping of servers is, on the physical plane, only very loosely linked. On the astral plane the linking is stronger and is based upon love of humanity; on the mental plane the major linking takes place, from the angle of the three worlds as a whole. It will be apparent, therefore, that certain developments must have taken place in the individual before he can consciously become a functioning member of the New Group of World Servers, which is the principal group at this time definitely working under the Law of Group Progress.

1. He must have the heart centre awakened, and be so outgoing in his "behaviour" that the heart is rapidly linked up with the heart centres of at least eight other people. Groups of nine awakened aspirants can then be occultly absorbed in the heart centre of the planetary Logos. Through it, His life can flow and the group members can contribute their quota of energy to the life influences circulating throughout His body. The above piece of information is only of interest to those who are spiritually awakened, and will mean little or nothing to those who are asleep.
2. The head centre must also be in process of awakening, and the ability to "hold the mind steady in the light" must be somewhat developed.
3. Some forms of creative activity must likewise be found and the server must be active along some humanitarian, artistic, literary, philosophic or scientific lines.

All this involves personality integration and alignment and that magnetic, attractive appeal which is distinctive of all disciples in some form or another. In this way, from the standpoint of esotericism, certain great triangles of energy will be found in the individual and consequently increasingly in humanity. Then too the "forces of creative life" will circulate from the "point within the head" (the head centre) along the "line to the heart" and then, with the throat centre, form a "triangle of fiery light". Such is the Way of Group Progress, and when this is being consummated, then the Law of Group Progress begins definitely to function and to control. It might be of interest, if we here listed the recognised effects of the five laws with which we have been dealing:

LAW	EFFECT	GENERAL PHYSICAL EFFECT	REACTION	QUALITY
1. Sacrifice	World Saviours The Christ	Deliberate death. "I die daily."	Love for the Saviour. Desire to *follow*.	Selflessness.
	Physical Plane Unity.		*The Masses.*	
2. Magnetic Impulse	World Religion Schools of Thought.	Churches Organisations	Love of Ideas. Philosophy.	Devotion. Idealism.
	Etheric or Vital Unity.		*The Aspirants.*	
3. Service.	Humanitarian Activity.	The Red Cross and allied activities.	Love of Humanity.	Sympathy. Compassion.
	Astral Unity.		*The Probationers*	
4. Repulse.	The fight against evil.	Crusades of all kinds.	Love of Good.	Discrimination.
	Mental Unity.		*The Disciples.*	
5. Group Progress.	New Groups	New Group of World Servers.	Love of Synthesis.	Inclusiveness.
	Soul Unity.		*The Initiates.*	

6. The Law of Expansive Response

We can now, with great brevity, however, touch upon the sixth law and the seventh, for we will speak of them together. The other five laws have worked out into a definite activity upon the physical plane. The effect or consequences of the impulses behind them produce the working out of the purpose of the Most High, and can be recognised upon the plane of phenomena. They can all be so recognised, but at this time, the conscious awareness of humanity is such that only in five instances can the effect of these laws be noted, and then only by the most advanced of the world aspirants. The disciple and the initiate can dimly begin to recognise the effect of the sixth and the seventh laws, but no one else at this time.

These two laws are not capable of interpretation as above, because only those who are initiated or in preparation for initiation can begin to understand them. The enlightenment which is the result of initiation is necessary before one can touch the idea behind these expressions of purpose. We shall not, therefore, take any time dealing with *The Law of Expansive Response*, or with *The Law of the Lower Four*, beyond giving two ancient stanzas which will convey much to the initiate but may only be sounding words and meaningless symbolic phrases to the average reader and student.

> "The Sun, in all its glory, has arisen and cast its beams athwart the Eastern sky. The union of the pairs of opposites produce, in the cycles of the time and space, both clouds and mists. These veil a mighty conflagration. . . .
> The flood pours forth. The ark floats free . . . the flames devour. The three stand free; and then again the mists envelop.
> Above the clouds of earth, a sign shines forth. . . . Only the eye of vision sees this sign. Only the heart at peace can hear the thunder of the Voice which issues from the dark depths of the cloud. Only an understanding of the law which elevates and lifts can teach the 'man of fire and son of water' to enter into mist. From thence he climbs on to the mountain top and there again stands free.
> The triple freedom thus achieved has naught to do with earth, or water, or with fire. It is a freedom, triple in its kind, which greets the man who passes freely from the sphere of earth into the ocean of the watery sphere, and

thence on to the burning ground of sacrifice. The sun aug-
ments the fire; it dissipates the mist and dries the earth. And
thus the work is done."

7. The Law of the Lower Four

"Four sons of God went forth. But only one returned. Four
Saviours merged themselves in two, and then the two became the *One*."

These two ancient writings—one mystical and the other
occult—convey but little to most minds, and this we can
easily see. Therefore it does not profit us to consider them
too carefully. The time is not yet. These are given us, however, because they contain a magnetic potency which will
aid in stimulating comprehension.

We stand today on the verge of great things. Humanity is
on its way with renewed impetus. It stands no longer at the
crossroads, but irrevocable decisions have been made, and the
race is moving forward along a path which will lead it eventually into light and peace. It will find its way into "the peace
which passeth understanding" because it will be a peace which
is independent of outer conditions and which is not based
upon what present humanity defines as peace. The peace
which lies ahead of the race is the peace of serenity and of
joy—a serenity, based upon spiritual understanding; and a
joy which is untouched by circumstance. This joy and
serenity is not an astral condition but a soul reaction. These
qualities are not achieved as the result of disciplining the
emotional nature, but demonstrate as a natural, automatic reaction of the soul. This is the reward of a definitely achieved
alignment. These two qualities of the soul—serenity and joy
—are the indications that the soul, the ego, the One Who
stands alone, is controlling or dominating the personality, circumstance, and all environing conditions of life in the three
worlds.

III. The Five Groups of Souls

We now begin our study of the five groups of souls. For purposes of classification and comparison, we shall divide our earth humanity into the following groups:

1. Lemurian Egos . . . . our true Earth Humanity.
2. Egos which came in . . . . on Atlantis.
3. Moon chain Egos . . . . from the moon.
4. Egos . . . . from other planets.
5. Rare and advanced Egos . . . . awaiting incarnation.

We enter, therefore, upon a brief consideration of a subject that, to the ordinary psychologist and student who is not familiar with the occult teaching and terms, will sound fanciful and unintelligent. The reason for this is that we are considering the *origin* of the souls which are expressing themselves through human beings, of the selves who are functioning through form and are therefore intangible and—scientifically speaking—non-provable. They are only to be inferred by those who can accept inference, deduction and conclusions which cannot be demonstrated, with the type of human equipment now in use. Modern psychology, speaking generally, regards the soul in one or another of the following ways:—

1. Either non-existent, the only obvious and provable thing being the intelligent mechanism.

2. As being the sum total of the conscious reactions of the cells of the body—the sentiency of the organism, in other words.

3. As a gradually evolving self, conveying life and, as time elapses, awareness; it is regarded as being conditioned by the body and as a product of the evolution of that

body during the ages. It does not, however, exist in the lower types of human beings, and it possibly possesses immortality, but that is not provable and may not be posited as a fact.

4. As a definite Self, an entity, informing a body, functioning at various levels of human consciousness, and having continuity, immortality and potentiality.

The occult teaching accepts all these hypotheses as correct, but as relative in time and space, and as having reference to different forms of divine life and to differing aspects of those forms. It is with the occult teaching, right or wrong, that we are at present engaged, and our premises and conclusions can be stated in the following propositions:

1. Every human being, in or out of incarnation, is a "fragment of divinity," and an outpost of the divine consciousness, functioning in time and space for purposes of expression.

2. All these souls, selves, or human beings are found, as we have seen, on one or other of the seven emanations of spiritual energy, issuing forth from God at the beginning of an era of creative activity. They return to their emanating Source when that particular cycle is brought to a close.

3. In the interim between emanation and reabsorption, these souls pass through various experiences until such time as they can "shine forth in all their exactitude of truth."

4. They are called, as has been stated, in *A Treatise on Cosmic Fire*, (See page 855.)

      1. Lotuses of revelation.
      2. Lotuses with perfume.
      3. Radiant lotuses.

4. Lotuses wherein the flower is on the point of
   opening.
5. Lotuses of closed and sealed condition.
6. The colourless lotuses.
7. Lotuses in bud.

5. These souls, cycling through various forms of life in the
long evolutionary process arrive eventually at full, self-
conscious existence. By this we mean that they are
self-determined, self-conditioned, and self-aware. They
are also conscious of and responsive to their environment.

6. Once this conscious awareness is achieved, then progress
becomes more rapid. It should be borne in mind that
many human beings are not thus aware. The groupings
which arise out of this awareness (limiting our ideas
entirely to those within the radius of the human family)
can be expressed as follows:—

1. The souls who live but whose consciousness
   sleeps. These are the dormant human beings
   whose intelligence is of such a low order,
   and their awareness of themselves and of life
   is so dim and nebulous, that only the lowest
   forms of human existence come into this
   category. Racially, nationally, and tribally
   they do not exist as pure types, but occasionally such a person emerges in the slums of
   our great cities. They are like a "throw
   back" and never appear among what are
   called the natural savages, or the peasantry.
2. The souls who are simply aware of physical
   plane life and of sensation. These people are
   slow, inert, inarticulate, bewildered *by their*

environment, but they are not bewildered, as are the more advanced and emotional types, *by events*. They have no sense of time or of purpose; they can seldom be trained along any mental line, and they very rarely exhibit skill in any direction. They can dig and carry, under direction; they eat, sleep and procreate, following the natural instincts of the animal body. Emotionally, however, they are asleep, and mentally they are totally un-awakened. These too are relatively rare, though several thousands of them can be found upon our planet. They can be recog-nised through their complete incapacity to respond to emotional and mental training and culture.

3. The souls who are beginning to integrate and who are emotionally and psychically alive. In them, of course, the animal nature is awake and the desire nature is becoming rampant. These people are to be found in all races to a small extent, and a number of them can be found among the negroes, which race con-tains a large number of those who are today relatively children. These are child souls, and though the mental equipment is there and some of them can be trained to use it, the preponderance of the life emphasis is entirely upon physical activity as it is motivated by the desire for satisfaction of some kind, and by a shallow "wish-life" or desire nature, almost entirely oriented towards the phys-

ical life. These souls are the modern correspondences to the old Lemurian cultures.

4. The souls who are primarily emotional. The
mind nature is not functioning strongly, and
only rarely does it swing into activity, and
the physical body is slipping steadily into the
realm of the unconscious. In every race and
nation there are millions of such souls in
existence. They may be regarded as the
modern Atlanteans.

5. Those souls who can now be classed as intelligent human beings, capable of mental application, if trained, and showing that they can
think when need arises. They are still, nevertheless, predominantly emotional. They constitute the bulk of modern humanity at this
time. They are the average citizens of our
modern world,—good, well-intentioned,
capable of intense emotional activity, with
the feeling nature almost over-developed,
and oscillating between the life of the senses
and that of the mind. They swing between
the poles of experience. Their lives are spent
in an astral turmoil, but they have steadily
increasing interludes wherein the mind can
momentarily make itself felt, and thus at
need effect important decisions. These are
the nice good people, who are, nevertheless,
largely controlled by the mass consciousness,
because they are relatively unthinking. They
can be regimented and standardised with
facility by orthodox religion and govern-

ment, and are the "sheep" of the human family.

6. The souls who think, and who are minds. These are steadily increasing in number and gaining in power as our educational processes and our scientific discoveries bring results, and expand human awareness. They constitute the cream of the human family, and are the people who are achieving success in some department of human life. They are writers, artists, thinkers in various fields of human knowledge and aspiration, politicians, religious leaders, scientists, skilled workers and artisans, and all those who, though in the front rank, yet take ideas and propositions and work with them for the ultimate benefit of the human family. They are the world aspirants, and those who are beginning to get the ideal of service into their consciousness.

7. Those souls whose sense of awareness on the physical plane is now of such an order that they can pass on to the Probationary Path. They are the mystics, conscious of duality, torn between the pairs of opposites, but who are yet unable to rest until they are polarised in the soul. These are the sensitive, struggling people, who long for release from failure and from existence in the world to-day. Their mind natures are alive and active but they cannot yet control them as they should and the higher illumination remains as yet a joyous hope and final possibility.

8. Souls whose intelligence and love nature is becoming so awakened and integrated that they can begin to tread the Path of Discipleship. They are the practical mystics, or the occultists, of modern times.

9. The souls who are initiate into the mysteries of the kingdom of God. These are souls who are not only conscious of their vehicles of expression, the integrated personality, and conscious also of themselves as souls, but they know, past all controversy, that there is no such thing as "my soul and your soul," but simply "the Soul". They know this not only as a mental proposition, and as a sensed reality, but also as a fact in their own consciousness.

10. The souls who have achieved release from all the limitations of the form nature and who dwell eternally in the consciousness of the One Soul, withdrawn from identification with any aspiration of the form life, no matter how highly developed. They can and do use the form at will for the purposes of the general good. These are the Masters of Life, the perfected adepts.

Higher than this we need not go, except by inference. A detailed analysis is not, however, in order, owing to the limitations of men's minds. The above is only a wide generalisation, and the various groupings shade into each other in a bewildering way. The varieties of intermediate types are myriad, but this analysis will serve as a skeleton structure upon which to build.

7. In the development of the race at this time, we can now study the types, the qualities of these souls, the apparatus of response which they must use, and the nature of the mechanism of contact which they have constructed in order to enable them to function in the world as we know it today. Science and religion together are producing that latest of the sciences which we call psychology. For this, the time is now ripe.

8. All these manifesting souls have come forth from some Source at some time in their cyclic expressions. This, to the modern thinker, is purely speculative, and can be regarded probably unprofitable; it may also be interesting, but is presumably imaginative. May I say here that the occultist regards all the above affirmative statements as constituting an exact and proven science, but as being presented in symbolic form for the consideration of the minds of men. Esotericists and theosophists would do well to remember this, and to realise that their divisions and groupings, their affirmations and statements about occult teaching, and their pronouncements as to time and place are largely symbolical and must be thus considered.

9. The process whereby the soul nature and the form nature meet and blend is termed *individualisation*.

> 1. *Individualisation* is the emergence of the soul upon the path of outgoing, through the medium of a form. Thus through the use of a form, expression in the three worlds becomes possible.
>
> 2. *Initiation* is the process whereby a soul, having exhausted the resources of form life, and

having thus achieved mastery and expression, returns again to its source. This the soul does through the medium of five stages, steps or initiations which are the correspondence in the interior life of the soul to the five stages whereby expression is developed in the strictly human races, beginning with the Lemurian stage, passing through the Atlantean and the Aryan, and so on through the two final races upon our planet in this world cycle.

In connection with individualisation the following points should be remembered:—

1. Individualisation upon the moon chain took place in the fifth race of the third round.

2. In Lemurian days, individualisation took place because it was the third root race and the fourth round.

3. In Atlantis, the door of initiation opened, and forced initiation became the objective of the best of the human family. Those who could or can thus become initiate are the "lights which ever radiate." In Lemurian days it was the "lights which ever burn" that came into being.

4. In our race we find the "lights which ever shine." This is the individualisation of the sixth race types who came in in the second round.

It is well to remember that the soul who came into incarnation in old Atlantis individualised upon that chain which is called the moon chain. This was a period of unfoldment so much earlier than that of our earth that we know nothing about it. These egos, therefore, did not individualise on our earth at all but came into our cycle of evolution as human beings,—of a low order as far as the lowest of our present humanity is concerned, but somewhat higher than the egos which individualised upon ancient Lemuria.

It might be of interest here to note that Christ was the first of our earth humanity to achieve the goal, whereas the Buddha was the last of the moon chain humanity to do so. As far as the development of these two sons of God was concerned, so rapid was the development of the Christ that in Atlantean days He found Himself upon the Path of Probation as did also the Buddha. He, coming into incarnation from the moon chain (having been held in what the occult teaching calls "pralaya" till that time), entered upon the probationary Path a very short time ahead of His Brother, the Christ. From the angle of evolution the rapid unfoldment of the evolution of Christ was, and has been, *totally unparalleled*. It has never been duplicated, though there are people living today upon the planet who are beginning to develop *now* with equal rapidity (but not earlier, so that they have a background of slow individual development, which is only now being accelerated). This rapidity is, however, a different matter altogether, for many of the disciples today came into this earth evolution from the moon chain where already much had been unfolded. They have not worked up to their present point from Lemurian times as the Christ has done. He, therefore, stands uniquely alone.

Just how and why egos come into our planetary evolution from earlier cycles and from other planetary systems is a subject of the greatest interest, but it is of no real importance to the students of this Treatise. We shall not therefore consider it or deal with it. It is of a speculative nature and utterly past their possible corroboration or capacity to check. There is no standard of comparison nor can they judge by inference what is important. All that can be said is that the three major monadic types came into being, either from the moon chain or during the Lemurian stage of individualisation, and that these three determine much that is transpiring today. All that it is here possible to do is to give some information which may throw a light on the subject, and colour our general thought, but which it is impossible either to check or accept except as being inferential or possible. All this can later be determined by the student when his knowledge and powers are greater than they are at present and adequate for that purpose.

The three major types are, as is well known, those of will or power, of love-wisdom and of active intelligence. The following facts must, therefore, be remembered:—

1. That egos of all types individualised upon the moon chain, but that the egos of active intelligence constituted 75% of the total, the remaining 25% being divided between the other two.
2. That in Lemurian times, the egos of love-wisdom preponderated, and in their turn constituted 75%, with the remaining 25% being the egos of active intelligence. Very few indeed, practically a negligible number, individualised along the line of power or will at that time.
3. There was a very large influx of individualising egos in early Atlantean days and they were practically all of the power-will type. It might be stated that 80% of those who entered human evolution at that time were egos who were expressing the will aspect of deity, and that the remaining 20% were along the line of love-wisdom.

These all, with the egos which individualised upon the moon chain and which came in steadily, as the planetary conditions fitted them, until the final stages of the Atlantean period, constitute the bulk of our modern humanity, plus some rare egos which drift into our planetary evolution for some reason or other, and never become properly adapted to or fitted into our planetary life. They persistently remain abnormalities.

Two happenings of great import will occur before so very long. The door will be opened, for the admittance of rare and peculiar souls who will bring into our world civilisation new aspects and rare and new qualities of Deity, though it will not be opened for ordinary individualisation. These rare and unexpected types will cause much bewilderment to our psychologists. It should here be pointed out that *individualisation is a crisis and not an unfoldment*. This is of real importance and should be borne in mind in all consideration of this difficult subject. It is the result of development, but such development need not lead to this particular crisis. What causes this crisis in the lives of souls remains as yet hidden in the consciousness of the planetary Logos and is only revealed at initiation. There are as yet characteristics and qualities of the planetary Logos which remain incomprehensible to us.

When the animal kingdom, viewing it from the angle of the whole and not from the angle of species, had reached a particular stage of development, then there was an inrush into the planetary life of the energy of all the seven rays simultaneously. This occurs very rarely and the tremendous stimulation then undergone by the sensitive forms of life (and of these the animal was at that time the most sensitive), produced the emergence of a new form, that of infant humanity. It was the reaction of that kingdom, as expressed through its indwelling life, the animal Being (who is the informing Life of that kingdom in nature), which produced individualisation in the more advanced animal-man of the time.

The statements found in occult books that dogs and other

animals responded to the divine impulse through an activity of the will or of love, may be symbolic in nature, but are not correct literally, as so many devout occult students may think. Such specific forms of life did not exist in those far off times, particularly upon the moon chain. The consideration of species and of types may not be permitted; it is futile and a waste of time. What really occurred was a reaction throughout the entire animal kingdom to the inpouring of the three major types of energy, which expressed themselves through the usual seven types and thus called forth response from those forms of life which were energised through the medium of the three major centres—heart, head and throat— of the Being who is the informing life. A tremendous surging upward and a going-forth in response ensued, which enabled a new kingdom to emerge.

A creative act is ever the result of inspiration being seized upon, recognised for what it is, and developed by the form side, and understood and fostered by the brain and the heart of man. Some new thing is thus produced. The instinctive creative act of the physical body is not here discussed. In this way, through a response to inspiration, the animal kingdom came into being. First, there was the pouring in of energy, stimulating and inspiring; then there came the recognition of the responding form, resulting in an initiated activity, and then there was the production of that which had not been theretofore. Thus a new kingdom in nature appeared.

This same thing it is that is again happening today in the world. There is a pouring in of spiritual energy, vitalising, transforming, and rendering humanity creative. Initiatory work becomes possible and a new and higher kingdom can appear upon the earth. But all this is due, as before, to the pouring in of a triple energy in seven ways. The potency of these forces lies behind the disruption of the present time, but a new kingdom in nature will be born.

The interest of this, psychologically speaking, does not lie in the historicity of the facts stated, but in the appearance upon earth today of the higher types at present found amongst men everywhere. Egos of will are relatively and naturally few; egos of love are becoming more frequent in appearance; intelligent egos are widely distributed. There is a balance now being established between the egos of love and of intelligence, and these together must and will inaugurate the new civilisation which will be the field for the culture of the kingdom of God on earth. The coming of this kingdom will be as much a precipitation of an inner reality as an unseen factor, such as a germ, working within a human body. This precipitation and culturing of the germ kingdom is slowly happening.

IV. Rules for Inducing Soul Control

In considering the rules which can induce soul control, it is not my intention to recapitulate the many rules which the aspirant must follow as he perseveres in his endeavor to tread the path to the source—that path to what the Buddhists call Nirvana. This Path is, in fact, but the beginning of that higher Way which leads to a life incomprehensible, even to the most developed of the Beings in our planetary Hierarchy. Nor is it essential that we emphasize the details of living which must control the man who is seeking to function as a soul in command of the personality. These have oft been adequately outlined by disciples down the ages, and reduced to many words. They have also been dealt with in my earlier book *A Treatise on White Magic* and other books. Our immediate problem is the application of these rules for discipleship and a steady progress in their practical technique. My present purpose is a far more difficult one, for this Treatise is written for the future more than for present students. I seek to indicate the basic rules determining the hierarchical government, and conditioning, therefore, world affairs. We are here concerned therefore with the subtle activities of energies which, on the inner side, actuate the outer activities and bring about those events in the world of men which later form history.

The problem before the Hierarchy is twofold and can be expressed in two questions:—

1. How can the consciousness of humanity be expanded so that it can be developed from the germ of self-consciousness (such as it was at individualisation) and be brought up to that of complete group consciousness and identification as occurs when the final initiation is undergone?

2. How can the ascending energy of the fourth kingdom in nature be brought into such close rapport with the descending energy of spirit that another great expression—a group expression—of Deity may emerge through man into manifestation?

Two points should therefore here be noted:—First, that the attention of the members of the Hierarchy who work at this time with mankind is not centred upon the individual aspirant in any manner which could be interpreted as personal interest. Interest in him is evoked just in so far as he is occupied with matters which concern group good. The second point is one well known and often stressed of late. At this time we are passing through a period of unprecedented opportunity and crisis, and the attention of the Hierarchy is consequently focussed upon men in an exceedingly one-pointed manner as They attempt to capitalise, for the benefit of man, upon this opportunity. Herein lie both responsibility and the ground for hope.

The rules, therefore, which we are to consider are not the laws of the soul or the laws controlling the stages of human development upon the Path. They have a much wider scope, and pertain to the broad sweep of the evolutionary cycle as it concerns the human family as a whole, particularly in relation to its contribution to the entire evolutionary scheme. However—owing to the lack of trained understanding—we shall have to confine ourselves to the consideration of these rules solely as they govern human unfoldment.

What we are seeking to reveal (if possible) is some of the factors which govern the effort which the Hierarchy of Control and the Custodians of the Plan utilise, as They proceed to work with the factors already present in man, and the energies already in objective use on this planet. What we shall say will not be of great simplicity, for it is hard, even for the advanced disciple, to see the purpose of certain of these factors. That which is here set forth on these matters must await later developments during the coming century, and certain lines of scientific and spiritual unfoldment must eventuate before the hidden implications can be adequately comprehended. If it seems simple and clear it might be wise to distrust the obvious interpretation. The matter is abstruse. It is well to ponder on the thought here presented, but not to be quick to assume understanding. There are many ways in which the work of the Hierarchy can be expressed, and according to the type of mind will be the interpretation.

1. The Aim of These Rules

The objectives can (for our purposes) be stated as four in number, but each of these is capable of re-expression in a number of ways. They simply indicate the four major goals which the Workers with the Plan have set Themselves. Let us state them succinctly, and later we can somewhat elaborate them:—

1. The first aim and the primary aim is to establish, through the medium of humanity, an outpost of the Consciousness of God in the solar system. This is a correspondence, macrocosmically understood, of the relationship existing between a Master and His group of disciples. This, if pondered on, may serve as a clue to the significance of our planetary work.

2. To found upon earth (as has already been indicated) a powerhouse of such potency and a focal point of such energy that humanity—as a whole—can be a factor in the solar system, bringing about changes and events of a unique nature in the planetary life and lives (and therefore in the system itself) and inducing an interstellar activity.

3. To develop a station of light, through the medium of the fourth kingdom in nature, which will serve not only the planet, and not only our particular solar system, but the seven systems of which ours is one. This question of light, bound up as it is with the colours of the seven rays, is as yet an embryo science, and it would be useless for us to enlarge upon it here.

4. To set up a magnetic centre in the universe, in which the human kingdom and the kingdom of souls will, united or at-oned, be the point of most intense power, and which will serve the developed Lives within the radius of the radiance of the *One About Whom Naught May Be Said*.

In these four statements we have sought to express the wider possibility or occasion as the Hierarchy sees it today. Their plans and purposes are destined and oriented to a larger accomplishment than it is as yet possible for normal man to vision. If it were not so, the unfoldment of the soul in man would be a prime objective in the planet. But this is not the case. It may be so from the point of view of man himself, considering him as an essentially separable and identifiable unity in the great cosmic scheme. But it is *not* so for that greater whole of which humanity is only a part. Those great Sons of God, Who have passed beyond the point of development of those Masters Who work entirely with the human kingdom, have plans of a still vaster and broader sweep, and Their objectives involve humanity only as an item in the Plan of the Great Life *"in Whom we live and move and have our being."*

One may ask (and rightly ask) wherein all this information can be of use to us in the midst of a troubled and bewildered world. For obvious reasons, a vision of the Plan, nebulous as it must necessarily be, confers a sense of proportion and also of stability. It leads to a much-needed re-adjustment of values, indicating as it does, that there is *purpose* and *objective* behind all the difficult happenings of daily life. It broadens and widens and expands the consciousness, as we study the great volume of the planetary life, embracing as it does the detail and the finished structure, the item man, and the entire life of the planet, with their relation to the greater Whole. This is of far more importance than the minute detail of the human being's individual capacity to grasp his own immediate place within the larger picture. It is easy and natural for man to emphasise those aspects of the hierarchical work which concern himself. The Masters of the Wisdom Who are advanced enough to work upon the larger areas of the spiritual plan are oft amused at the importance which the disciples and aspirants of the world attach to Them, and at the manner in which They are overestimated. Can we not realise that there are members of the Hierarchy Whose grasp of truth and Whose knowledge of the divine Plan is as much in advance of the Masters known to us as They are in advance of the savage and of the undeveloped man? We do well to ponder on this fact.

It is not, however, a profitless task for the disciples and aspirants to catch the dim outline of that structure, that purpose and that destiny which will result from the consummation and fruition of the Plan on earth. It need evoke no sense of futility or of endless striving or of an almost permanent struggle. Given the fact of the finiteness of man and of his life, given the tremendous periphery of the cosmos and the minute nature of our planet, given the vastness of the universe and the realisation that it is but one of countless (literally countless) greater and smaller universes, yet there is present in men and upon our planet a factor and a quality which can enable all these facts to be seen and realised as parts in a whole, and which permits man (escaping, as he can, from his human self-consciousness) to expand his sense of awareness and identity so that the form aspects of life offer no barrier to his all-embracing spirit. It is of use also to write these words and to deal with these ideas, for there are those now coming into incarnation who can and will understand, when present readers are dead and gone. I and you will pass on to other work, but there will be those on earth who can vision the Plan with clarity, and whose vision will be far more inclusive and comprehending than ours. Vision is of the nature of divinity. Expansion is a vital power and prerogative of Deity. Therefore let us struggle to grasp what is possible at our particular stage of development, and leave eternity to reveal its hidden secrets.

The factors which determine this peculiar process of hierarchical work, and which therefore constitute the major rules of the evolving life of God in the human family, are seven in number. These—if we may so express it—determine hierarchical activity, leaving wide scope for individual effort, but providing the vital active trends beyond which no worker with the Plan will dare to go. We should be aware that there are forces and energies which are kept in abeyance as the result of the interposition, consciously effected, by the Hierarchy. It is possible for us to grasp the fact that there are lives and types of activity which have been unable to manifest (fortunately for the planet) since the Hierarchy was founded upon the earth. There has not always been a Hierarchy of perfected souls, and this concept opens up vistas in the realms of immature expression (from the angle of human vision) as difficult to comprehend as those opened up when we pass, in dim and nebulous imaginative consciousness, beyond the department of the Hierarchy which deals with human affairs, and catch faint glimpses of the other departments which work on broader and more inclusive lines.

2. *The Seven Rules*

The seven factors or "Rules for Inducing Soul Control" are:—

1. *The tendency, innate and ineradicable, to blend and synthesise.* This is a law or rule of life itself.

   a. This tendency results, on the form side, in destruction and wreckage, with its accompaniments of pain and sorrow. On the life side, it results in release, liberation and subsequent expansion.

b. This tendency is the basic cause of all initiation—individual, racial, planetary and systemic.

c. It is the result of an act of the will, and is caused by the impulsion of the sensed and innate purpose of God. However (and this is a point oft forgotten) this tendency is motivated by the recognition of the planetary Logos, that His plan is conditioned in its turn, and is an integral part of a still larger plan—that of the solar Deity. God, the solar Logos, is likewise conditioned by a still higher life purpose.

2. *The quality of the hidden vision.*

a. This quality, on the form side, produces physical sight, astral illusion and concrete knowledge. On the life side it produces illumination. This includes the widespread illumination reflected by our planet in the heavens, as well as that which makes an individual man a light-bearer, and which will eventually enable humanity, (as a whole) to constitute a station of light upon earth.

b. This quality is the basic cause of all sensory perception and is the instinctive urge to consciousness itself, in all its many phases. With this quality the Hierarchy has to work, intensifying it and giving it magnetic power.

c. It is the high result of desire, which is itself intrinsically founded on the will to form a plan and a purpose.

3. *The instinct to formulate a plan.* This instinct governs all activity which, in process of evolution, divides itself into instinctual activity, intelligent activity, intuitional or purposive activity, and illumined activity, as far as mankind is concerned. This includes that department of the

Hierarchy which works with humanity. The higher phases of planned activity are many and diverse, and are all synthesised under the third ray activity, at present focussed in the seventh ray.

a. Viewed from the form side, this faculty of planning leads to separative and selfish activity. Viewed from the life side, it leads to a blended cooperation which swings each unit of energy in every form, in all its subjective and unified aspects, into the task of unification. This is potently taking place in the world today. It is the tendency to at-one-ment which leads the human being, first of all, to the development of an integrated personality, and then to the submergence of that personality in the good of the greater whole.

b. This constitutes the basic cause of evolution itself—individual, planetary and systemic.

c. This instinct is the result of the development of manas, or mind, and the emergence of the intelligence. It is the peculiar quality or instinctual nature through the means of which humanity expresses the first Ray of Willed Intent, fostered by desire, and transmuted into intelligent activity.

4. *The urge to creative life, through the divine faculty of imagination.* This urge is, as can easily be seen, closely connected with the fourth Ray of Harmony, producing unity and beauty, won through conflict.

a. This, on the form side, leads to warfare, struggle and the building of forms which must later be destroyed. On the life side, it leads to quality, vibratory radiance and the revelation upon earth of the *world of meaning.*

b. It is therefore the basic cause of that subtle essence or revelation which is seeking expression through every form in each kingdom in nature. There seems to be no better term by which to express this hidden wonder which must be revealed than the *revelation of meaning*. This is beginning to happen today.

c. It is the result of the ability—sometimes adequate and sometimes inadequate—of the inner consciousness to reveal its measure of control by the Plan, and its response to the larger intent. It is upon this response that the Members of the Hierarchy are today counting, as They endeavor to bring the hidden meaning to the fore in the consciousness of man.

5. *The factor of analysis.* This factor may surprise those who suffer from the misuse of the power to discriminate, to analyse and to criticise. It is, however, a basic, divine quality, producing wise participation in the Plan and skill in action.

a. On the form side, it manifests as the tendency to separate, divide and to place in contradictory positions. On the life side, it leads to that understanding which tends to identification, through the wider choice and comprehension.

b. It is the basic cause and impulse which will lead to the eventual appearance of the kingdom in nature, higher than the human, which is strictly that of the soul, and will produce the manifestation upon earth of the fifth kingdom in nature, that of the kingdom of gods. This phrase should be noted.

c. It is the result of the active work of the sons of God, the sons of mind, and is the part which they are contributing to the total planetary contribution, as part of the great systemic Plan. The Hierarchy itself is the outer and inner manifestation of the sacrifice of the divine Manasaputras (as They are called in *The Secret Doctrine*), and its members respond to Their sensed vision of the Plan for the whole. The Hierarchy is essentially the germ or nucleus of the fifth kingdom in nature.

6. *The quality, innate in man, to idealise.* This is founded upon the success of the Plan itself. This Plan sought originally to awaken in man the following responses:— right desire, right vision and right creative activity, based upon right interpretation of ideals. This triplicity of purpose merits thoughtful consideration.

   a. On the form side, this has worked out as material desire, leading eventually to cruelty and frequently to an extreme sadistic expression. On the life side, it has led to sacrifice, one pointed purpose, progress on the path, and devotion.

   b. It is the basic cause of all organisation and of cooperation. The ideal before the Hierarchy is the realised Plan. This is brought to humanity in the form of ideas, which become, in time, ideals—to be desired and fought for. In order to materialise these ideals, the trend to organise comes into being.

   c. It is the result—curiously enough—of the work of a peculiar group of world workers, who are recognised by humanity under the name of World Saviours. These are the Founders of those forms through which the divine ideas become the ideals of the masses, in all realms of human thought. Every great world leader is necessarily a "suffering Saviour."

7. The seventh rule or controlling force with which the

Hierarchy works is *the interplay of the great dualities.* Through the activity engendered by this interplay, and through the results achieved (producing always a third factor), the whole manifested world is swept into line with the divine Purpose. This does not become apparent to the man who is immersed in the detail of life, but could we see the planetary life as it can be seen by the Masters Themselves, we would note the pattern emerging in all its beauty, and the structure of God's thought for the universe appearing today in clearer outline and greater synthesis and beauty of detail than ever before.

a. On the form side, this produces the sense of being imprisoned by the time factor, the victim of speed, and the implacable forces of all life activity, as they play upon the imprisoned human being. On the life side, it results in rhythmic living and conscious adaptation of energy to the immediate purpose and goal.

b. It is necessarily the basic cause of the appearance and the disappearance of forms, human and humanly constructed.

c. It is the result of at-one-ments wrought out on the physical plane, thus producing the lower unifications, just as the at-one-ments wrought out hitherto in the human consciousness, have produced unification with the soul. The higher at-one-ments, hitherto effected on the plane of mind, have to be expressed eventually on the plane of physical life.

In the preceding introductory outline, we have considered very briefly the rules which can induce on earth that soul control which is the immediate goal of the evolutionary process. We have seen that we are considering no simple exercises or discipline, nor are we dealing with the development of those required characteristics which precede the stage of technical Initiation. We are, in reality, concerned with those basic trends and those innate tendencies in the divine expression which will ultimately bring about the manifestation of the Oversoul upon our planet. We have seen also that these governing tendencies are already beginning to be expressed and realised, and that the fourth kingdom in nature, the human, occupies a unique position in this development. In the downward and the upward flow of the divine life, as it expresses itself through the involutionary and evolutionary urges, humanity constitutes one of the fundamental "original centres of force" which can and will form an outpost of the divine Consciousness, an expression of the divine Psyche, manifesting eventually those three outstanding psychological characteristics of divinity: Light, Energy, and Magnetism. In the human being, the microcosmic reflection of the Macrocosm, these qualities are expressed by the words: Illumination or Wisdom, Intelligent Activity, and Attractiveness or Love. It is well to ponder on this attempt to simplify the divine potencies into words, and thus to indicate how they may express themselves in and through a human vehicle.

We can now enlarge somewhat upon the previous statements, so as to give a clearer idea upon two matters:—

1. The relationship of these divine qualities as they can be apprehended and developed in man.
2. The future responsibility of an enlightened humanity, as it passes on into the New Age. We shall thus lay the foundation for the teaching to be given later in this treatise.

One of the points which I have sought to bring out in all the previous writings already published, is that the Laws of the Universe, the Laws of Nature and those basic controlling factors which determine all life and circumstance, remaining for us fixed and unalterable, are the expression—as far as man can understand them—of the *Will* of God. The rules or living factors which we are now considering and which (when understood and obeyed) will induce soul control in the individual and in the universe, are the expression of the *Quality* or Nature of God. They will ultimately lead to the full expression of the divine Psyche. They will bring into evidence the instinctual, emotional nature of Deity, if such human words can in any way express the divine qualitative potencies.

The Laws of the Universe express the divine Will, and lead to the manifestation of divine Purpose. This is wisdom. They ordain and nurture the Plan.

The Rules for Inducing Soul Control express the divine quality and lead to the revelation of God's Nature, which is love.

The Laws of Nature, or the so-called physical laws, express the stage of manifestation or the point reached in the divine expression. They concern multiplicity, or the quality aspect. They govern or express that which the divine Spirit (which is will, functioning in love) has been able to effect in conjunction with matter for the production of form. This emerging revelation will produce the recognition of beauty.

The first category, the Laws of the Universe, are touched upon in *A Treatise on Cosmic Fire* and occasionally mentioned in the other writings. Modern science has done much to bring about an understanding of the Laws of Nature, and can be trusted to do so, for the soul drives all things on to knowledge. In what is here presented I seek to lay the basis for the new science of psychology which must be founded upon a broad and general understanding of the divine Psyche as it seeks expression through the manifested Whole, the solar system, and, for our purposes, the planet and all that is upon it.

When the potency of the divine psychology and its major trends and characteristics are recognised, and when modern psychology shifts its attention away from the minute study of the psyche of the individual man (and usually an abnormal individual) to a concentrated consideration of the psychological attributes of the greater Whole of which we are but a part, we shall arrive at a new comprehension of Deity and of the relation of the microcosm to the Macrocosm. This has been left too much to the department of philosophy in the past, but must now engross the attention of the psychologist. This desirable event will be brought about when the true meaning of history is grasped, when the wide sweep of human unfoldment down the ages is understood, and when the soul is seen to be functioning through all parts of all forms. At present, man alone is really credited with a soul, and the soul of all things is overlooked. Yet man is but the macrocosm of the other kingdoms in nature.

The seven rules which we are now studying are, therefore, of supreme importance, for they embody the key ideas which will reveal Deity in operation as the Soul of all things; They will reveal the nature and method of activity of the Cosmic Christ, and will indicate the governing qualitative tendencies which determine the psychical life of all forms—from a universe to an atom—in the body of any so-called material revelation of life. Let us bear these thoughts in mind as we read and study.

These rules express themselves with equal potency on all the seven rays, and they produce the manifestation of consciousness on earth in any and every form. We shall first deal mainly with the greater Whole, without emphasising the differentiation into rays. The seven rays, as has often been stated, colour or qualify the divine instincts and potencies, but that is not all. They are themselves determined and controlled by these potencies. It must never be forgotten that the rays are the seven major expressions of the divine quality as it limits (and it does so limit) the purposes of Deity. God Himself hews to a pattern, set for Him in a still more distant vision. This purpose or defined will is conditioned by His instinctual quality or psyche, in just the same way as the life purpose of a human being is both limited and conditioned by the psychological equipment with which he enters into manifestation. I have earlier stated that we were dealing with abstruse and difficult matters, and that much presented might lie beyond our immediate concrete understanding. The above statement is, however, relatively simple, if interpreted in terms of one's own life purpose, and quality.

One point might here be touched upon before we proceed with our study of the seven psychological tendencies of Deity.

We have spoken here of God in terms of *Person*, and we have used therefore the pronouns, He and His. Must it therefore be inferred that we are dealing with a stupendous Personality which we call God, and do we therefore belong to that school of thought which we call the anthropomorphic? The Buddhist teaching recognises no God or Person. Is it, therefore, wrong from our point of view and approach, or is it right? Only an understanding of man as a divine expression in time and space can reveal this mystery.

Both schools of thought are right and in no way contradict each other. In their synthesis and in their blending the truth as it really is can begin—aye, dimly—to appear. There is a God Transcendent Who "having pervaded the whole universe with a fragment of Himself" can still say: "I remain." There is a God Immanent Whose life is the source of the activity, intelligence, growth and attractiveness of every form in all the kingdoms in nature. There is likewise in every human being a transcendent soul which, when the life cycle on earth has come and gone and when the period of manifestation is over, becomes again the unmanifest and the formless, and which can also say: "I remain." In form and when in manifestation, the only way in which the human mind and brain can express its recognition of the conditioning divine life is to speak in terms of Person, of Individuality. Hence we speak of God as a Person, of His will, His nature and His form.

Behind the manifested universe, however, stands the formless One, *That* which is not an individual, being free from the limitations of individualised existence. Therefore the Buddhist is right when he emphasises the non-individualised nature of Deity and refuses to personalise Divinity. The Father, Son and Holy Spirit of the Christian theology, embodying as they do the triplicities of all theologies, disappear also into the One when the period of manifestation is over. They remain as One, with quality and life untouched and undifferentiated, as they are when in manifestation.

An analogy to this appears when a man dies. Then his three aspects—mind or will, emotion or love, and physical appearance—vanish. There is then no person. Yet, if one accepts the fact of immortality, the conscious being remains; his quality and purpose and life are united with his undying soul. The outer form with its differentiations into a manifested trinity, has gone—never again to return in exactly the same form or expression in time and space.

The interplay of soul and mind produces the manifested universe, with all that is therein. When that interplay is persisting, either in God or in man, we use (for how else can we speak with clarity?) terms of human origin and therefore limiting, such is our present stage of enlightenment—or should we say, unenlightenment? Thus the idea of individuality, of personality, and of form is built up. When the interplay ceases and manifestation ends, such terms are no longer suitable; they have no meaning. Yet the undying one, whether God or man, persists.

Thus in human thought, preserved for us by the great Teacher of the East, the *Buddha*, we have the concept of the transcendent Deity, divorced from the triplicities, the dualities and the multiplicity of manifestation. There is but life, formless, freed from the individuality, unknown. In the teaching of the West, preserved for us and formulated for us by the *Christ*, the concept of God immanent is preserved,— God in us and in all forms. In the synthesis of the Eastern and the Western teachings, and in the merging of these two great schools of thought, something of the superlative Whole can be sensed—sensed merely—not known.

a. THE TENDENCY TO SYNTHESIS

The first of the factors revealing the divine nature and the first of the great psychological aspects of God is *the tendency to synthesis*. This tendency runs through all nature, all consciousness, and is life itself. The motivating urge of God, His outstanding desire, is towards union and at-one-ment. It was this tendency or quality which Christ sought both to reveal and to dramatise for humanity. As far as the fourth kingdom in nature is concerned, His tremendous utterances, expressed for us in St. John XVII, are the call to synthesis, and urge us towards our goal.

> "And now I am no more in the world, but these are in the world, and I come to thee. Holy Father, keep through thine own name those whom thou has given me, that they may be one, as we *are*. . . .
> I have given them thy word; and the world hath hated

them because they are not of the world, even as I am not of
the world.

I pray not that thou shouldest take them out of the world
but that thou shouldest keep them from the evil.

They are not of the world, even as I am not of the world

Neither pray I for these alone, but for them also which
shall believe on me through their word;

That they all may be one; as thou, Father, *art* in me, and
I in thee, that they also may be one in us; that the world
may believe that thou hast sent me.

And the glory which thou gavest me I have given them
that they may be one, even as we are one;

Father, I will that they also, whom thou has given me, be
with me where I am; that they may behold my glory, which
thou hast given me; for thou lovedst me before the founda
tion of the world."

Here we have the synthesis of soul with spirit pointed out
to us, and the synthesis of soul with matter also emphasised
thus completing the unification and the desired at-one-ment

But the synthesis of Deity, His tendency to blend and fuse
is far more inclusive and universal than any possible expres
sion in the human kingdom, which is, after all, but a small
part of the greater whole. Man is not all that is possible, nor
the consummation of God's thought. The sweep of this in
stinct to synthesis underlies all universes, constellations, solar
systems, planets, and kingdoms in nature, as well as the activ
ity aspect and achievement of man, the individual. This in
stinct is the governing principle of consciousness itself, and
consciousness is the psyche or soul, producing psychical life
it is awareness—sub-human, human and divine.

In connection with man, we have the following psycholog
ical expressions postulated:

1. *Instinct*, lying below the level of consciousness, but pro
   tecting and governing most of the habits and life of the
   organism. Much of the emotional life is thus governed

Instinct controls, via the solar plexus and the lower centres.

. *Intellect*, which is intelligent self-consciousness, guiding and directing the activity of the integrated personality, via the mind and brain, and working through the throat and ajna centres.

. *Intuition.* This is predominantly concerned with group consciousness and will eventually control all our relations with each other, as we function in group units. It works through the heart and the heart centre, and is that higher instinct which enables a man to recognise and submit to his soul and to its control and life impression.

. *Illumination.* This is a word which should really be applied to the designation of the super-human consciousness. This divine instinct enables a man to recognize the whole of which he is a part. It functions via a man's soul, utilising the head centre, and eventually flooding with light or energy all the centres, thus linking a man in consciousness with all the corresponding parts of the divine Whole.

Thus the trend to synthesis is an instinct inherent in the entire universe, and man is today only awakening to its immediacy and potency.

It is this divine attribute in man which makes his physical body an integral part of the physical world; which makes him psychically gregarious and willing to herd (of choice or perforce) with his fellow man. It is this principle, working or functioning through the human consciousness, which has led to the formation of our huge modern cities—symbols of coming higher civilisation which we call the kingdom of God, wherein the relationship between men will be exceedingly close psychically. It is this instinct to unify which underlies all mysticism and all religions, for man seeks ever a closer union with God and naught can arrest his at-one-ment (in consciousness) with Deity. It is this instinct which is the basis of his sense of immortality, and which is his guarantee of union with the opposite pole to the personality—the Soul.

Being an attribute of Deity, and being a divine instinct and, therefore, part of the subconscious life of God Himself, it will be obvious that, given the original premise that there is a God, transcendent and immanent, we have, therefore, no cause for real fear or foreboding. God's instincts are stronger and more vital and pure than are those of humanity, and must eventually triumph, coming forth into full flower and expression. All the lower instincts with which man battles are but the distortions (in time and space) of reality, and hence the value of the occult teaching that by pondering upon the good, the beautiful and the true, we transmute our lower instincts into higher divine qualities. The attractive power of God's instinctual nature, with its capacity to synthesise, to attract and to blend, cooperates with the unrealised potencies of man's own nature, and makes his eventual at-one-ment with God, in life and purpose, an inevitable, irresistible occurrence.

This instinct or trend towards synthesis and unification can be linked up by students with the laws of the universe and of nature. It is closely related to the Law of Attraction and to the Principle of Coherence. Later, we shall see much study done along these relations. This series of text books of occultism and of the occult forces which I have written are intended to act as sign posts, and as beacon lights upon the way to knowledge. They contain hints and suggestions, but must be interpreted by each student according to the measure of light which is in him. Let him study what is going on around him in the light of the Plan and of the knowledge here imparted, and let him seek to trace for himself the emergence of the instinctual psychical nature of Deity in world affairs and in his own life, for it is happening all the time. He must ever remember that he himself possesses a psychical nature which is a part of a greater whole, and, therefore, subject to impression from divine sources. Let him cultivate in himself the trend to synthesis; let him make the words, "I will not be separative in my consciousness," one of the key thoughts of his daily life.

One point here should be noted. This instinct to synthesis (concerning as it does the psychical nature of Deity) has nothing to do with the physical expression of sex. This is governed by other laws and is under the control of the physical nature. Let us not forget that H.P.B. has said (and truly) that the physical body is not a principle. These seven basic trends which we are considering are purely psychical or psychological in nature.

The comprehension of the nature of these compelling psychical attributes of God should enable a man to throw the weight of his psychical aspiration on the side of these emerging qualities. He will, for instance, in his daily life, work toward at-one-ment with all beings, seeking to penetrate to the heart of his brother; endeavoring to be at one with the life in all forms; rejecting every tendency to separative reactions, because he knows that they concern the innate, inherited psyche of the atoms of matter and substance which constitute his form nature. These have been brought over and reassembled and rebuilt into the forms found in the present manifestation of God. They carry with them the seeds of psychical material life from an earlier universe. There is no other evil.

We have been taught much anent the great heresy of separativeness; it is this that is offset when a man permits the "trend towards synthesis" to pour through him as a divine potency, and thus to condition his conduct. These divine trends have constituted the basic, subconscious urges since the dawn of evolution. Today humanity can consciously adjust itself to them, and thus hasten the time wherein truth, beauty and goodness will reign.

The disciples of the world and the New Group of World Servers, as well as all intelligent and active aspirants, have today the responsibility of recognising these trends, and particularly this trend to unification. The work of the Hierarchy at this time is peculiarly connected with this, and They, and all of us, must foster and nurture this tendency, wherever found. The standardisation and regimentation of nations is but an aspect of this move towards synthesis, but one that is being misapplied and prematurely enforced. All moves towards national and world synthesis are good and right, but they must be consciously and willingly undertaken by intelligent men and women, and the methods employed to bring about this fusion must not infringe the law of love. The swing at this time towards religious unity is also a part of the emerging beauty, and though forms must disappear (because they are a source of separation) the inner, spiritual synthesis must be developed. These two outstanding instances of this divine trend, as they emerge in the human consciousness, are here mentioned because they must be recognised, and all awakening souls must work for these ends. The moment there is knowledge and a flash of understanding, that moment a man's responsibility begins.

Let us study, therefore, the tendencies in the world today, which indicate the active presence of this trend, and foster it where we can. It will be discovered to be a practical and hard task. The imposition cf a sensed, divine, psychical attribute upon the form life (with its own psychical habits) will test the powers of any disciple. To this we are called, for the sake of the greater Whole.

b. The Quality of the Hidden Vision

The next emerging trend is one most difficult to express. It is not easy to discover the right words to define its meaning. It is the *quality of the inner vision*. This cannot readily be expressed in words that man can comprehend, for we refer not to man's vision of God but to God's own vision of His purpose. Down the ages, men have sensed a vision; they have seen it, and have merged themselves with it after much struggle and effort; they have then passed out of human life into the silence of the unknown. The mystic and the occultist have both testified to this vision, and to it all that is beautiful and colourful in the world of nature and of thought also bears silent witness. But what is it? How define it? Men are no longer satisfied to call it God, and they are right, for *it is*, in the last analysis, *that to which God bends every effort*.

Yet the quality and the nature of the vision which is God's own vision, dream and thought, have held His purpose steady throughout the aeons and have motivated His creative processes. Great Sons of God have come and gone and challenged us to follow the light, to seek the vision of reality, to open our eyes and see truth as it is. Down the ages, men have sought to do this and have called the method of their search by many names—life-experience, scientific research, philosophic questionings, history, adventure, religion, mysticism, occultism and many other terms applied to the adventurous excursions of the human mind in search of knowledge, of reality, of God. Some have ended up in a maze of astral phenomena, and must continue their search later when they emerge, chastened, from the depths of the Great Illusion. Others have wandered back into the dark cave of a pronounced materialism, of phenomenalism, and must likewise return and reorient themselves, or rather perhaps, complete the circle, for who shall say that God is here or there, or from what point His vision can be seen? Some lose themselves in thought processes and self-induced imaginings, and the vision gets hidden behind a multitude of words, both spoken and written. Still others find themselves lost in the clouds of their own devotion and self-awareness, and in the misty speculations of their own minds and desires. They are at a standstill, lost in the fog of their own dreams of what the vision should be and thus it eludes them.

Others—the theologians of any school of thought—have sought to define the vision, and have endeavored to reduce God's hidden goal and intent to forms and rituals and to say, with emphasis: "We know." Yet they have never touched the reality, and the truth is as yet unknown to them. The possibility of the *Vision* which lies beyond, or behind the vision of the mystic is forgotten in the forms built up in time; and the symbols of the teachings of those Sons of God Who *have* seen the reality is lost to sight in rituals and ceremonies, which (though they have their place and teaching value) must be used to reveal and not to obscure.

The vision is ever on ahead; it eludes our grasp; it haunts our dreams and our high moments of aspiration. Only when a man can function as a soul, and can turn the developed inner eye outward into the world of phenomena and inward into the world of reality, can he begin to sense God's true objective and purpose, to catch a brief glimpse of God's Own pattern and the Plan to which he so willingly conditions His own Life, and for which the Eternal Sacrifice of the Cosmic Christ is essential.

With these two divine trends (towards synthesis and towards the vision) the Hierarchy is at this time primarily occupied. Their watchwords are *unification* and *sight*. For humanity, these developments will produce the integration of the soul and the personality, and the awakening of that inner vision which will permit a flash of the Reality to enter into man's consciousness. This is not a flash of his own divinity, or a sensing of God as Creator. It is a flash of the divinity inherent in the Whole, as it works out a vaster scheme of evolutionary process than any hitherto grasped or sensed by the keenest minds on earth. It concerns the vision granted when a man achieves Nirvana, and enters upon the first stage of that endless Path which leads towards a beauty, comprehension and unfoldment, untouched as yet by the highest type of human insight.

It would be well to point out here that beyond the stage of illumination, as it can be achieved by man, lies that which we might call the unfoldment of divine *Insight*. We have, therefore, the following unfoldments and possible developments, each of which constitutes an expansion in consciousness, and each of which admits man more closely and more definitely into the heart and mind of God.

$$\left.\begin{array}{l} \text{Instinct} \\ \text{Intellect} \\ \text{Intuition} \\ \text{Illumination} \end{array}\right\} \text{All of them leading up to } \textit{Insight.}$$

In these words, sequentially presented, there is perhaps made clearer to us the fact of God's own vision. More is not possible until each of those words signifies something practical in our own inner experience.

This quality of the inner vision with which the Hierarchy are seeking to work and to develop in the souls of men (it would be of use to ponder on this last phrase, as it presents an aspect of hierarchical endeavor not hitherto considered in occult books) is an expression of the Principle of Continuance, which finds its distorted reflection in the word so often used by disciples:—*Endurance*. This principle of continuance constitutes the capacity of God to persist and "to remain." It is an attribute of the cosmic Ray of Love as are all the principles which we are now considering in connection with these soul rules or factors—these trends of divinity and these tendencies of the divine life. Let us not forget that all the seven rays are subrays of the cosmic Ray of Love. We shall therefore, see why these principles are determining *soul* activities, and can only come into play when the kingdom of God, or of souls, begins to materialise on earth.

This principle of continuance is based upon the clearer vision of Deity and upon the consequent continuity of God's plan and purpose which results when the objective is clearly seen by Him and developed in plain and formulated outline. It is the macrocosmic correspondence to the continuance and the continuity found in man when—after a night of sleep and of unconsciousness—he proceeds with his daily avocation and consciously resumes his planned activities.

From the hints given above it will be seen how the work of the Hierarchy in connection with mankind falls into two parts:—the work with individual human beings, in order to awaken them to soul consciousness, and then the work with them, as souls, so that (functioning then on soul levels and as conscious units in the kingdom of God) they can begin to vision the objective of God Himself. This second division of Their effort is only now becoming possible on a wide scale as men begin to respond to the trend towards synthesis, and to react to the divine principle of coherence, so that (stimulated by their group relation) they can unitedly sense the vision and react to the principle of continuance. A hint is here given as to the true and future purpose of group meditation. More on this subject is not possible.

c. The Urge to Formulate a Plan

The third divine instinct or hidden inner trend is *the urge to formulate a plan*. It will be apparent that this urge grows out of, or is dependent upon, the previous two trends considered. It finds its microcosmic reflection in the many plans and projects of finite man as he lives his little life or runs busily about the planet in connection with his tiny personal affairs. It is this universal capacity to work and plan which is the guarantee that there exists in man the capacity to respond eventually and in group formation to God's plan, based on God's vision. All these basic, developing, divine instincts and expressions of God's consciousness and awareness find their embryonic reflections in our modern humanity. It is no part of my purpose to indicate my understanding of God's Plan. This is limited naturally by my capacity. Only dimly do I sense it, and only occasionally and faintly does the outline of God's stupendous objective dawn on my mind. This Plan can only be sensed, visioned and known in truth by the Hierarchy, and then only in group formation and by those Masters Who can function in full monadic consciousness. They alone are beginning to comprehend what it is. Suffice it for the rest of those in the Hierarchy—the initiates and disciples in their ordered ranks and various gradings—to cooperate with that immediate aspect of the Plan which they can grasp and which comes down to them through the inspired minds of their Directors at certain stated times, and in certain specific years. Such a year was 1933. Such another will be the year 1942. At those times, when the Hierarchy meets in silent conclave, a part of God's vision, and His formulation of that vision for the immediate present, is revealed for the next nine year cycle. They then, in perfect freedom and with full mutual cooperation lay Their plans to bring about the desired objectives of the Heads of the Hierarchy, as They in Their turn cooperate with still higher Forces and Knowers.

The above information will probably evoke much interest from those students who are not as yet attuned to the higher values. For all who read this, could they but grasp it, this is the least important part of the chapter and carries for them the minimum of usefulness. It has for us, you will note, no practical application. Some might enquire then and rightly: Why then give out this information? Because this Treatise is written for the future disciples and initiates, and all that is here set forth is part of a revelation of truth which it is desired should be given out. It comes today through many channels and from many sources—such is the wonder of the power behind the present world adjustments!

This instinct of Deity is closely connected with the Law of Economy and is an expression of the Principle of Materialisation. For man, it has to be studied, grasped, and wrought out through the right use of the mental body, working under the influence of Atma or Spirit. The principle of Continuance has to be wrought out into conscious knowledge by the right use of the astral or desire nature, working under the influence of Buddhi. The Trend to Synthesis has finally to be wrought out in the brain consciousness upon the physical plane, under the influence of the Monad, but its real expression and man's true response to this urge only become possible after the third initiation. So it is easily to be seen that this Treatise is indeed written for the future.

We have here received much upon which to ponder, to

think and to meditate. Let us search for the thread of gold which will lead us, in waking consciousness, into the treasure house of our own souls, and there let us learn to be at-one with all that breathes, to sense the vision for the whole, as far as we can, and to work in unison with God's plan as far as it has been revealed to us by Those Who know.

These ancient rules, or determining factors—the essential conditioning laws in the life of the Soul—are in their nature basically psychological. For that reason, they warrant our study. On its own plane, the soul knows no separation, and the factor of synthesis governs all soul relations. The soul is occupied not only with the form that the vision of its objective may take, but with the quality or the meaning which that vision veils or hides. The soul knows the Plan; its form, outline, methods and objective are known. Through the use of the creative imagination, the soul creates; it builds thought-forms on the mental plane and objectifies desire on the astral plane. It proceeds then to externalise its thought and its desire upon the physical plane through applied force, creatively actuated by the imagination of the etheric or vital vehicle. Yet because the soul is intelligence, motivated by love, it can (within the realised synthesis which governs its activities) analyse, discriminate and divide. The soul likewise aspires to that which is greater than itself, and reaches out to the world of divine ideas, and thus itself occupies a midway position between the world of ideation and the world of forms. This is its difficulty and its opportunity.

In this way the life of the soul is affirmed in terms of its conditioning factors. The value of this lies in the fact that, upon the Path of Discipleship, these factors must begin to play their part in the life of the personality. They must begin to condition the lower man so that his life, his habits, his desires and his thoughts are brought into line with the higher impulses initiated by the soul. This is only another way of dealing with those expressions of the spiritual life which every initiate must demonstrate.

Every aspirant must, as time elapses, develop the power to see the whole and not only the part, and to view his life and sphere of influence in terms of its corporate relationships and not in terms of the separated self. He must not only see the vision (for that the mystic has always done) but he must penetrate behind it to those essential qualities which give meaning to the vision. The instinct to formulate plans, inherent in all and so dominant in the highly evolved, must give way to the tendency to make plans in tune with the Plan of God, as expressed through the planetary Hierarchy. This in time will produce the urge to create those forms, conveying meaning, which will transmute evil into good and produce the transfiguration of life.

But to do this within the Plan and at the same time to recognise the basic synthesis in which we live and move, the disciple must learn to analyse, discriminate and discern those aspects, qualities and forces which must be creatively used in the materialisation of the intuited Plan, based on the sensed vision. We might well ponder on this rapport between the man, and the Hierarchy, via a man's own soul. The Hierarchy exists in order to render possible in form that sensed Plan and divine Vision. To produce this emergence of truth, the man stands also at the midway point, and in handling the great dualities of life, must produce the new world.

As we study these rules of soul control, it should not be necessary constantly to affirm the three basic relationships of the soul:

1. The relationship to other souls within the enveloping life

of the Oversoul. Only through an understanding of this relation do we arrive at a practical knowledge that all souls are one Soul.

2. The relationship to the Hierarchy of governing souls. Though this Hierarchy has in it all the seven elements which constitute the primary differentiation to which the One Life, as consciousness, submits itself, yet it must be borne in mind that this Hierarchy is essentially an embodiment of the will aspect of the Logos—the will to good, the will to love, the will to know, the will to create. This will is served by the Universal Mind of Deity, but it is the expression of a still higher consciousness in which that Deity shares. This concept is necessarily beyond our comprehension, but we must bear in mind that this section of the book is for use in days to come and not merely for today's understanding.

3. The relationship to the Plan of God as it is working out at the present time.

These thoughts will serve to set the stage for what should now be made clear. It is of use at times to swing the consciousness back to the centre, when the orbit the mind travels is of vast extent. The synthesis of the divine concept, the vision of its structural outline and the plan for its materialisation—these are the factors which govern souls on their plane, condition their activity, and, within the limits wherein they work, are the factors which (in time and space) condition and limit Deity, for such is His divine Will. Looking at the whole subject from another angle, it is these rules of soul contact which set the rhythm and determine the pulsation of the life of God as it steadily beats upon the lower rhythms and will finally obliterate them. This happens in the case of individual human beings; it will happen in the case of humanity, as a whole, some day; it will determine finally the life, purpose and activity of all forms in and upon our planet.

d. The Urge to Creative Life

This realisation brings us to the consideration in a little more detail of our fourth point, which is the *urge to creative life through the divine use of the imagination*. As we have seen, it is necessary for humanity to recognise that there is a world of meaning behind the world of appearances, of form —behind what has been called the "world of seeming." It is the revelation of this world of inner meaning that lies immediately ahead of the race. Hitherto we have—as a race—been occupied with the symbol and not with that for which it stands, and of which it is the outer appearance. But we have today largely exhausted our interest in the tangible symbol, and are searching—again as a race—for that which the outer world of appearance is intended to express.

Much is heard today of the New Age, of the coming revelation, of the imminent leap forward into an intuitive recognition of that which has hitherto been only dimly sensed by the mystics, the seer, the inspired poet, the intuitive scientist and the occult investigator who is not too preoccupied with the technicalities and the academic activities of the lower mind. But one thing is oft forgotten in the great expectancy. There is no need for too great an upward straining or too intense an outward looking, to use terms which the usual limited point of view can grasp. That which is to be revealed lies all around us, and within us. It is the significance of all that is embodied in form, the meaning behind the appearance, the reality veiled by the symbol, the truth expressed in substance.

Only two things will enable man to penetrate into this inner realm of causes and of revelation. These are:

First, the constant effort, based on a subjective impulse, to create those forms which will express some sensed truth; for thereby and through this effort, the emphasis is constantly shifted from the outer world of seeming to the inner side of phenomena. By this means, a focussing of consciousness is produced which eventually becomes stable and withdrawn from its present intense exteriorisation. An initiate is essentially one whose sense of awareness is occupied with subjective contacts and impacts and is not predominantly preoccupied with the world of outer sense perceptions. This cultivated interest in the inner world of meaning will produce not only a pronounced effect upon the spiritual seeker himself but will eventually bring about the emphasis, recognised in the brain consciousness of the race, that the world of meaning is the sole world of reality for humanity. This realisation will, in its turn, bring about two subsequent effects:

1. A close adaptation of the form to the significant factors which have brought it into being on the outer plane.
2. The production of a truer beauty in the world and, therefore, a closer approximation in the world of created forms to the inner emerging truth. It might be said that divinity is veiled and hidden in the multiplicity of forms with their infinite detail, and that in the simplicity of forms which eventually will be seen, we shall arrive at a newer beauty, a greater sense of truth and at the revelation of God's meaning and purpose in all that He has accomplished from age to age.

Secondly, the constant effort to render oneself sensitive to the world of significant realities and to produce, therefore, those forms on the outer plane which will run true to the hidden impulse. This is brought about by the cultivation of the creative imagination. As yet, humanity knows little about this faculty, latent in all men. A flash of light breaks through to the aspiring mind; a sense of unveiled splendour for a moment sweeps through the aspirant, tensed for revelation; a sudden realisation of a colour, a beauty, a wisdom and a glory beyond words breaks out before the attuned consciousness of the artist, in a high moment of applied attention, and life is then seen for a second as it essentially is. But the vision is gone and the fervour departs and the beauty fades out. The man is left with a sense of bereavement, of loss, and yet with a certainty of knowledge and a desire to express that which he has contacted, such as he has never experienced before. He must recover that which he has seen; he must discover it to those who have not had his secret moment of revelation; he must express it in some form, and reveal to others the realised significance behind the phenomenal appearance. How can he do this? How can he recover that which he has once had and which seems to have disappeared, and to have retired out of his field of consciousness? He must realise that that which he has seen and touched is still there and embodies reality; that it is he who has withdrawn and not the vision. The pain in all moments of intensity must be undergone and lived again and again until the mechanism of contact is accustomed to the heightened vibration and can not only sense and touch, but can hold and contact at will this hidden world of beauty. The cultivation of this power to enter, hold and transmit is dependent upon three things:

1. A willingness to bear the pain of revelation.
2. The power to hold on to the high point of consciousness at which the revelation comes.
3. The focussing of the faculty of the imagination upon the revelation, or upon as much of it as the brain consciousness can bring through into the lighted area of external

knowledge. It is the imagination or the picture-making faculty which links the mind and brain together and thus produces the exteriorisation of the veiled splendour.

If the creative artist will ponder upon these three requirements—endurance, meditation, and imagination—he will develop in himself the power to respond to this fourth rule of soul control, and will know the soul eventually as the secret of persistence, the revealer of the rewards of contemplation and the creator of all forms upon the physical plane.

This use of the creative imagination and the fruits of its endeavor will work out into the many fields of human art according to the ray of the creative artist. We must not forget that the artist is found on all rays; there is no particular ray which produces more artists than another. The form will apparently take spontaneous expression when the inner life of the artist is regulated, producing the outer organisation of his life forms. True creative art is a soul function; the primary task, therefore, of the artist is alignment, meditation and the focussing of his attention upon the world of meaning. This is followed by the attempt to express divine ideas in adequate forms, according to the innate capacity and the ray tendencies of the artist in any field which he may choose and which is for him the best medium for his endeavor. It is paralleled by the effort, constantly made upon the physical plane, to equip, instruct, and train the mechanism of brain and hand and voice through which the inspiration must flow, so that there may be right expression and a correct externalisation of the inner reality.

The discipline involved is great and it is here that many artists fail. Their failure is based on various things—on a fear that the use of the mind will cripple endeavor, and that spontaneous creative art is, and must be primarily emotional and intuitive, and must not be crippled and handicapped by too great an attention to mental training. It is based on inertia which finds creative work the line of least resistance and which seeks not to understand the way in which the inspiration comes, or how the externalisation of the vision becomes possible, or the technique of the inner activities, but simply follows an impulse. Again it indicates an uneven, unbalanced development which results from the fact that, through specialisation or focussed intense interest over a period of lives, there comes a capacity to make a soul contact *along one line of endeavor*, but not the capacity to be in contact with the soul. This is facilitated by the fact that the artist for many lives comes under the influence of one particular personality ray. Hence the occult paradox stated above, which warrants the attention of artists. Another factor upon which failure is often based is the supreme conceit and ambition of many artists. There is the ability to excel in some field and, in that one particular, to evidence greater capacity than the average man. But there is not the ability to live as a soul and the vaunted excellence is only in one direction. There is frequently no life discipline or self-control but instead there are flights of genius, stupendous achievement in the chosen line of art, and a life lived in contradiction to the divinity expressed through the artistic achievement. The understanding of the significance and technique of genius is one of the tasks of the new psychology. Genius is ever the expression of the soul in some creative activity, thus revealing the world of meaning, of divinity, and hidden beauty which the phenomenal world usually veils but will some day indicate in truth.

e. The Factor of Analysis

The fifth conditioning quality or activity of the soul is *the factor of analysis*. It constitutes a law, governing humanity.

This must ever be remembered. Analysis, discrimination, differentiation, and the power to distinguish are divine attributes. When they produce a sense of separateness and of difference, they are then stimulating personality reactions and are consequently personally misused and misapplied. When, however, they are preserved within the sense of synthesis and used in the application of the Plan for the whole, they are soul qualities and laws and are essential to the right unfolding of divine purpose. The Plan of God comes into being through *the right use of emphasis*, and when we emphasise one aspect or quality, temporarily we exclude or relegate into brief abeyance another aspect or aspects. This is a major part of the activity of the law of cycles with which the Masters work. It involves, on Their part, the constant use of the faculty to analyse, and the power to discriminate.

The fact that in time and space the pairs of opposites hold sway and that they are used by the Masters to weave the web of life is indicative of this primary differentiation of the One into the two, and the two into three, the three into the basic seven and these seven into the many. From unity to diversity the work proceeds and all of it emerges under the soul law which is the law of analysis within the field of synthesis.

The "seeds of difference", as they are called, are major factors used in producing the phenomenal world. The Hierarchy works with the seeds, as a gardener works with the seeds of flowers, and from these seeds the needed differentiated forms appear, producing still further distinctions. The sowing of these seeds, their care and nurturing is part of the phenomenal task of the Hierarchy, particularly at the inauguration of a New Age, as is the case today. The Masters have to understand, first of all, what is the meaning which the will of God is seeking to express in any particular world cycle. They must comprehend the significance of the impulses emanating from sources higher than Their own field of expression and of dharma, and They must see to it that the seeds of the new forms are adequate to the desired intent. They must appreciate the nature of the reality which any age must reveal in the progressive unfoldment of divine purpose; and then They have the responsibility of so working that the outer reality approximates (in appearance and in quality) the inner truth. All this is made possible through an understanding of the factor or rule of analysis, regarding it as a law governing or producing soul control, both on soul levels and on the level of appearances. This is one of the major tasks of the Hierarchy, and involves the keenest type of mind control, of intuitive apprehension and of analytical desire. We would do well to ponder upon these terms.

It should be remembered that analysis governs the emergence of the fifth kingdom in nature, the Kingdom of God, upon the phenomenal plane. This appearing presupposes a distinction between the fifth kingdom and the other four kingdoms. It is, however, a distinction in one direction only and that is in the direction of consciousness. Herein lies its major interest, for in this respect the fifth kingdom differs from the other kingdoms. The other four kingdoms have separate phenomenal types and differentiated groups of forms. The phenomena of the vegetable kingdom, for instance, and that of the animal kingdom are vastly unlike each other. In the fifth kingdom, however, a new condition or state of affairs will be found. The outer phenomenal appearance will be retained as far as the form is concerned, though refinement and quality will be intensified. The kingdom of God materialises in and through humanity. But in the realm of consciousness a very different state of affairs will be found.

A Master of the Wisdom appears phenomenally to be a human being. He has the physical attributes, functions, habits and mechanism of the fourth kingdom in nature, but within the form, the consciousness is entirely changed. The analysis, therefore, referred to in these pages relates to a distinction in consciousness and not to a distinction in form. The symbol persists unchanged though perfected upon the outer plane, but its quality and state of awareness is as much changed as is that existing between a human being and a vegetable. This is somewhat a new thought and its implications are stupendous. It is the secret of the entire shift at this time into the world of meaning and involves a new awareness and a fresh appreciation by humanity of a greater world of values. But—and here is a point of interest—it is an awareness carried forward into a new kingdom in nature whilst remaining a part of the old. It is here that the new synthesis and fusion takes place.

It is not a part of the plan of God for a constant cyclic appearance of new and unpredictable forms to continue indefinitely. Humanity will go on perfecting the human mechanism so as to keep pace with the growth of the divine consciousness in man, but because in man the three lines of divinity meet and blend, there is no need for further drastic distinctions to continue to appear in the outer world of phenomena as further states of consciousness are attained. In the past each great unfoldment of consciousness has precipitated new forms. This will no longer occur. The consciousness of God working in and upon substance in the mineral kingdom produced totally different forms to those which the same consciousness, working upon higher substance, employed in the animal and human kingdoms. Under the divine plan for this solar system, this form-differentiation has its limitations and cannot proceed beyond a certain point. This point was reached in the human kingdom for this world cycle. Now, in the future, *the consciousness aspect of Deity will continue to perfect the forms in the fourth kingdom in nature through the instru-*

mentality of those whose consciousness is that of the fifth kingdom. This is the task of the Hierarchy of Masters. This is the delegated task of the New Group of World Servers who, upon the physical plane, can become the instrument of Their will. Through this group, the inner divine qualities of good will, peace and love can increase and express themselves through human beings, functioning in the forms of the fourth kingdom.

These points of interest have been discussed as it is essential that some understanding of the factor of analysis within the field of synthesis should be grasped. Analysis is too often confused with separativeness. The problem is complex and difficult, but an understanding of the underlying implications will emerge as the race grows in wisdom and in knowledge. We are here concerned with the concept of the Plan as initiates have grasped it.

f. The Quality, Innate in Man, to Idealise

It is interesting to note how automatically and naturally the factors inducing soul control, as outlined up to this point, have brought us to the sixth law or rule, the power—innate, inherent, and spiritually instinctual—to idealise. Instinct, intellect, intuition, ideation, and illumination—these are but differentiations and distinctive aspects of one great inherent capacity in man, and are found in all forms in all kingdoms in varying degree. Whether it is the power of the tiny seed, deeply hidden in the dark earth, to penetrate through its surrounding barriers and to emerge into the light, or whether it is the power of a human being to rise from death in matter to life in God, and to penetrate into the world of the Real from the realm of the unreal, it is all the one basic factor of idealism. Anthropology and history give us an account of the evolution of individual man and of nations and their activities upon the plane of appearances. But there is a history which today is slowly being formulated which is the history of the seed of consciousness in nature and the growth of the power to recognise ideas and to push forward towards their fulfilment. This is the new history which—as might be expected—is carrying us steadily into the world of meaning and revealing to us gradually the nature of those impulses and tendencies which have led the race steadily forward from the densest point of concrete, primitive life into the world of sensitive perception.

It is in this field that the Masters work and in which They call Their disciples to be active. The power of ideas is only today beginning to be understood. The potency of ideation, the forms which ideas must take, and the promotion of the cult of right ideas is one of the major problems to be tackled in the New Age.

g. The Interplay of the Great Dualities

The seventh of these Rules—that of *the interplay of the great dualities*—is one of the basic rules of soul control and it is by no means an easy one for the student to grasp. It is a fundamental law of soul life. The reason why it is so hard to understand the paradox of soul unity through duality is that in speaking of the pairs of opposites, emphasis has for ages been laid upon the astral dualities and the need for humanity to choose the narrow path which runs between them. Upon the battlefield of the dualities he stands and must find the razor-edged path which opens up before him and lands him before the portal of initiation. But, essentially, these pairs of opposites are only reflections of a higher and divine corre-the .. The law here considered is that which governs ter. ... tween life and form, between spirit and mat-not here enlarge for only those initiates who have, in their own lives, transcended the lower reflection of the dualities can even begin to grasp the true spiritual significance of this rule for soul control in its wider and more essential meaning. There is, therefore, no need for us to enter upon that abstruse question in this Treatise.

Ours is rather the task to gain a wise understanding of the vision, as far as the capacity of each of us will permit. Only in this way will there come to us not only eventual release, but also the strength to live in this world and to be of service to our fellow men.

CHAPTER II

The Ray of Personality

As we start this new part of our study, we can proceed to consider man as he is upon the physical plane, in the majority of cases. Speaking with a broad generalisation, we could say that human beings can be grouped into four classes:

1. A few who are under the influence of their souls, or who are rapidly becoming susceptible to this influence.
2. Personalities, of whom there are many today.
3. A vast number of people who are awakening to mental consciousness.
4. The great mass of humanity, who are the unawakened human beings and the bulk of the population of the world.

In every phase of human history, the *quality* of the civilisation is the only thing that can in any way be conditioned by the Great White Lodge. The Members of the Lodge are only permitted to work with the emerging qualitative aspects of the divine nature. This is, in its turn, slowly conditioning the form life, and in this way the form aspect is steadily altered and adapted, as it progresses towards an increasing perfection. This conditioning process is carried forward through the souls who are returning to incarnation, for just in so far as they are awakened or are in process of awakening, is it possible for the Hierarchy to prevail upon them or influence them to regard the time factor as a definitely important matter in considering the subject of incarnation.

The majority of the souls in the human family come into incarnation in obedience to the urge or the desire to experience, and the magnetic pull of the physical plane is the final determining factor. They are, as souls, oriented towards earth life. Increasingly, awakening souls, or those who are (occultly speaking) "coming to themselves", enter into physical life experience only dimly aware of another and higher "pull." They are, therefore, without as true an orientation to the physical plane as are the bulk of their fellow men. These awakening souls are the ones who can at times be influenced to retard or delay their entry into physical life in order to effect a conditioning of the processes of civilisation. Or again, they can be prevailed upon to hasten their entrance into life so as to be available as agents for such a conditioning process. This process is not carried forward by them through any emphasised or intelligently appreciated activity, but it is naturally brought about by the simple effect of their living in the world and there pursuing their life objectives. They thus condition their surroundings by the beauty, the power, or the influence of their lives, and are themselves frequently quite unconscious of the effect that they are having. It will be apparent therefore, that the needed changes in our civilisation can be brought about rapidly or slowly, according to the number of those who are living as *souls in training*.

About the beginning of the eighteenth century, after a

meeting of the Hierarchy at its great centennial gathering in 1725, an effort was determined upon which would bring a more definite influence to bear upon a group of souls awaiting incarnation, and thus induce them to hasten their entry into the life of the physical plane. This was done, and the civilisation of modern times came into being, with both good and bad results. The era of culture which was the outstanding characteristic of the Victorian age, the great movements which awakened the human consciousness to a recognition of its essential freedom, the reaction against the dogmatism of the Church, the great and wonderful scientific developments of the immediate past, and the present sexual and proletarian revolutions now going on, are the result of the "impulsive" hastenings into incarnation of souls whose time had not truly come but whose conditioning influence was needed if certain difficulties (present since 1525) were to be averted. The bad effects above mentioned are indicative of the difficulties incident to premature development and to the undesirable unfoldments of what might be termed (injudiciously nevertheless) evil.

These incoming souls have, through their highly developed understanding and by means of their "self-willed power," frequently wrought havoc in various directions. However, if we could look on, as can Those on the inner side and if we were in a position to contrast the "light" of humanity as it is today with what it was two or three hundred years ago, we would recognise that enormous strides had been made. This is evidenced by the fact that the emergence of a band of "conditioning souls", under the name of the New Group of World Servers, has been possible since 1925. They can now come in because of the work already done by the group of souls who hastened their entrance into incarnation, under the impulse of the Hierarchy. The words "condition" or "conditioning" are here used quite frequently because of the aptness of the phrase to indicate function. These souls, because of their point in evolution, because of their stage in unfoldment and because of their impressibility to the group idea and to the Plan, can come into incarnation and begin, more or less, to work out that Plan and evoke a response to it in the human consciousness. They are thus in a position to "prepare the way for the coming of the Lord." This latter is a symbolic phrase indicating a certain level of spiritual culture in humanity. They are sometimes dimly conscious of this stupendous task, but they are, in the majority of cases, quite unconscious of their "qualifying" destiny. As souls, under the guidance of the Hierarchy and prior to incarnation, they are conscious of the impulse to "go in and help the sorrowing planet and thus release the prisoners held in durance hard by low desire" (quoting from the *Old Commentary*), but once the garment of flesh has been assumed, that consciousness too dies out and in the physical brain they are not aware of that which their souls have purposed. Only the urge for specific activities remains. The work nevertheless proceeds.

A few souls come into incarnation of their own free will and accord; they work with clear knowledge and proceed to the task of the day. They are the key people in any age, and the determining factors, psychologically, in any historical period. It is they who set the pace and do the pioneering work. They focus in themselves both the hatred and the love of the world; they work as the Builders or as the Destroyers, and they return eventually to their own place, carrying with them the spoils of victory in the shape of the freedom which they have won for themselves or for others. They bear the scars, psychologically speaking, which have been given to them by opposing workers, and they bear also the assurance that they have carried forward the task to which they have been assigned and which they have successfully undertaken.

This first category of people in incarnation has been greatly augmented during the past century and it is for this reason that we can look for the rapid development of the characteristics of the incoming Aquarian Age.

The second category of human beings, who are here designated as *personalities*, is also becoming powerful. It merges with both the first group and the third.

We have in the world today the following types of personalities:

1. Personalities who are rapidly shifting into the category of "conditioning souls."
2. Personalities who are integrated, coordinated men and women, but who are not yet under the influence of the soul. Their "self-will and self-love" is such a powerful factor in their lives that they exert a determining influence upon their environment. It would be well to note the esoteric difference between *conditioning* and *determining*. The first leaves the subject (be it a man or a race, or a civilisation) free. It simply provides the influence and the conditions wherein the best in the race can flower forth to a state of perfection. The second does not leave the subject free, but "determines" through the exercise of power, selfishly applied and utilised for personality ends, the way that a person, a race, or a civilisation shall go.
3. Awakening personalities are also found. These merge with our third classification and are the cream or the best expression of the third group.

It is with these personalities in their three groups that we are primarily to deal in this division of our treatise. The word, however, is very loosely used, and it might be of value to give here a list of definitions of the word "personality", both those in common usage and those used in the true spiritual significance. It is of value (is it not?) if students know the many ways in which this word is used, both correctly and erroneously. Let us here list them:

A personality is a separated human being. We could perhaps equally well say a *separative* human being. This is the poorest and most loosely used definition; it applies to common usage, and regards each human being as a person. This definition is consequently *not true.* Many people are simply animals with vague higher impulses, which remain simply impulses. There are those also who are primarily nothing more or less than *mediums.* This term is here used to apply to all those types of persons who go blindly and impotently upon their way, swayed by their lower and dense desire nature, of which the physical body is only the expression or medium. They are influenced by the mass consciousness, mass ideas, and mass reactions, and therefore find themselves quite incapable of being anything definitely self-initiated, but are standardised by mass complexes. They are, therefore, mediums with mass ideas; they are swept by urges which are imposed upon them by teachers and demagogues, and are receptive—without any thought or reasoning—to every school of thought (spiritual, occult, political, religious and philosophical). May I repeat that they are simply mediums; they are receptive to ideas which are not their own or self-achieved.

A personality is one who functions with coordination, owing to his endowment and the relative stability of his emotional nature, and his sound and rounded out glandular equipment. This is aided by his urge to power and the proper environing conditions. The above situation can work out in any field of human endeavor, making a man either a good fore-man in a factory or a dictator, according to his circumstances, his karma, and his opportunity. I am not here referring in any sense whatever to the desirable coordination of soul and body, which is a later development. I am simply postulating a good physical equipment, and a sound emotional control and mental development. It is possible to have a superlative inner development and yet have such a poor instrument on the physical plane that coordination is not possible. In such cases the subject seldom affects his environment in any per-manent or powerful sense. He cannot bring through or radiate out his inner power because he is blocked at every point by his physical equipment. A man of much less inner development but with a responsive physical body and glands which are functioning well will frequently prove a more effective agent of influence in his environing circumstances.

A personality is a man with a sense of destiny. Such a man has sufficient will power to subject his lower nature to such a discipline that he can fulfil the destiny of which he is sub-consciously aware. These people fall into two groups:

a. Those with no soul contact of any kind. Those peo-ple are urged forward to their destiny by a sense of power, by self-love, by exalted ambition, by a superiority complex, and by a determination to reach the top of their particular tree.

b. Those with a small measure of soul contact. These are people whose methods and motives are therefore a mixture of selfishness and of spiritual vision. Their problem is a difficult one, as their measure of soul contact does bring in an inflow of force which stimulates the lower nature, even whilst increasing soul control. It is not, however, powerful enough to subordinate the lower nature entirely.

A personality is a completely integrated human being. In this case, we have a man whose physical, emotional and mental natures can be fused and can subsequently function as one, and thus produce a mechanism which is subordinated to the will of the personality. This can take place with or without a definite soul contact, and it is at this stage that there comes a predisposition to the right, or to the left hand path. The coordination proceeds as follows:

a. Coordination of the emotional or astral nature with the physical body. This took place in the racial sense in Atlantean times; it is going on today among the lower groupings in the human family. It should be the objective of the development of children from the ages of seven to fourteen.

b. Coordination of the physical, astral and mental natures into one blended whole. This is taking place racially in the Aryan race today and the process will be completed (for the bulk of humanity) when the sun enters the zodiacal sign, Sagittarius, just as now it is entering Aquarius. This coordination is going on rapidly among the advanced members of the human family and should be the objective of the training of all adolescents between the ages of fourteen and twenty-one.

c. Next, coordination is commenced between the soul and the personality, with the focus of the soul's attention upon the astral or desire nature. This is the immediate task of the world aspirants at this time, and will be the goal of the next race succeeding to that of the Aryan.

d. Coordination between soul, mind and brain to the exclusion of the body of illusion, the astral body. This is the peculiar goal of the world disciples.

e. Coordination then has to be established between the soul, the purified personality and the Hierarchy. This is the goal of the initiates in the world at this time, and of all who are in preparation for the first, the second and the third initiations. This consummation is finally achieved at the Transfiguration initiation.

f. Coordination between the soul, the personality and the spirit. This takes place via the Hierarchy of Souls—a phrase which only initiates can properly interpret and understand. This process is carried on after the third initiation.

A man can be regarded as a personality in truth when the form aspect and the soul nature are at-one. When the soul influences the personality and pervades all the lower manifestation, then and only then, does the personality measure up to its true significance, which is to constitute the mask of the soul, that which is the outer appearance of inner spiritual forces. These forces are expressions of the soul, and the soul is the central identity or fundamental focus upon the mental plane of the life of God Himself. Essence, consciousness and appearance are the three aspects of divinity and of man; the personality, when fully developed, is the "appearance of God on earth." Life, quality, and form is another way of expressing this same triplicity.

These definitions have been made of a real simplicity and also exceedingly brief. Intricacy of definition does not necessarily ensure correctness, and the clear outlines of a truth are oft lost in a maze of words.

1. *The Appropriation of the Bodies*

The final definition which is given here, leads up to our consideration of the subject of the rays. *The personality is the fusion of three major forces and their subjection (finally and after the fusion) to the impact of soul energy.* This impact is made in three different stages or in what are occultly termed "three impulsive movements"—using the word "impulsive" in its true connotation and not in the usual emotional and enthusiastic significance. These impulsive movements are:

a. The impact of the soul at the stage of human evolution which we call individualisation. At that time, the form becomes aware for the first time of the touch of the soul. This is called in the language of esotericism the *"Touch of Appropriation."* The soul then appropriates its vehicle.

This stage is succeeded by a long period of adjustment and of gradual development and unfoldment. This takes place upon the way of experience, and during that period the soul tightens its hold upon its instrument, the lower form nature.

b. The impact of the soul is called forth by the dilemmas and through the emergencies of the later stages of the path of experience. During this stage, the urgency of the need, and the dilemmas brought about by the forces of opposition, lead the man to submit to a higher influence. He calls then in desperation upon the soul and upon the spiritual resources laid up in his divine nature and hitherto remaining unused. This impact is called the *"Touch of Acquiescence,"* and marks the acceptance by the soul of the demand of the personality for help and

light. The soul acquiesces in the plea of the personality for guidance.

It is to be noted that we are here considering the
attitude of the soul to the personality and not that
of the personality to the soul, which is the attitude
usually under consideration. We are dealing primarily in this treatise with the reactions and activities of the soul through its ray energy, and its response to the demand of the forces—focussed,
combined and integrated—of the personality.

c. The impact of the soul at the time of the various and
sequential initiations to which the disciple is eventually subjected, as he transits out of the fourth into
the fifth kingdom in nature. This stage is called the
"Touch of Enlightenment," and through the bringing together of the forces of the purified personality and those of the "approaching" soul, a "light is
engendered which fadeth not away."

In these three impacts,—

1. The touch of appropriation on the physical plane,
2. The touch of acquiescence on the astral plane,
3. The touch of enlightenment upon the mental plane,
there is summarised clearly and concisely the attitude of the
soul towards its rapidly preparing instrument.

The great Touch of Appropriation lies racially in the past.
The Touch of Acquiescence takes place upon the battlefield
of the emotional nature, and the Touch of Enlightenment is
effected through the mind.

The first three initiations are expressions of these three
stages or impacts, and it might also be stated that the Lemurian, the Atlantean and the Aryan races are also expressions of man's reactions to these three soul approaches.

The third initiation sees the soul and the personality perfectly blended so that the light blazes forth and the great Approaches between soul and form are consummated.

Today, in this particular cycle and in this Aryan race, the Hierarchy (as an expression of the kingdom of souls) is recapitulating these three inevitable steps and making certain advances or approaches to the race. We can therefore divide humanity into three groups and relate humanity to the three major approaches.

a. *The Approach of Appropriation will express the effect* of the present stimulation *upon the unevolved masses.* Thousands and thousands of men and women are in process of awakening and during the next few years will come to soul consciousness, for the soul of each individual is intensifying its initial appropriation at the Lemurian crisis of individualisation, and the ancient enterprise is again being re-enacted as a needed recapitulatory endeavor. All this today lies almost entirely in the realm of consciousness. The great appropriation was made millions of years ago. Today, in consciousness, there will come a great awakening to the significance of what was, at that time, largely a physical event, and masses of men will become aware—in their brain consciousness—of that early appropriation. This is being brought about by a fresh approach by the soul and an advance towards its reflection, the personality, and it produces in time a consequent recognition upon the part of man.

b. *The Approach of Acquiescence* will be equally well recognised by *the intelligent and more highly evolved sons of men.* They will awaken to the relationship which exists between their personalities and the soul, and between the forces of the lower nature and the energy of the soul. It is with this particular task that the New Group of World Servers is primarily occupied,—looking at their activities from the standpoint of the Hierarchy. Their work is to facilitate the entrance of soul energy, which energy expresses itself in love and in good will. This in its turn results in peace—individual, racial and planetary—and the great group aspect of the approach will be brought about, and is today in process of being carried forward.

c. *The Approach of Enlightenment* carries the disciple through the gate of initiation, and is the effect of the same energy playing upon the personalities of the disciples of the world, and transforming their spirit of aspiration into the light of initiation.

The Mysteries of the world, the flesh and the devil (to use the symbolic formal terminology of Christianity) are to be transmuted with rapidity into those of the Mysteries of the Kingdom of God, the energy of the soul, and the revelation of divinity. The secret hid by the inverted lotus (the world) is to be revealed by the opened lotus of the kingdom of souls. The secret of the flesh, which is the prison of the soul, is revealed by the perfume of the unfolding lotus of the soul. The mystery of the devil will eventually be seen to be that of the light of God's countenance, which reveals that which is undesirable and must be changed and renounced, and which thus transforms life by the light that God's nature pours forth.

It would be of use to us all to study these three soul approaches—individual or hierarchical—and to ponder upon them and put ourselves in training, so that we may make the needed recognitions. Let us also ponder upon the following triplicities:—

1. Mass Consciousness. Self-consciousness. Group-consciousness.
   These lead, in due time, to
2. Appropriation .... Acquiescence .... Enlightenment.
   through the racial stages of

3. Lemurian experience. Atlantean experience. Aryan experience.
   and the individual stages of
4. Experience . . . . Discipleship . . . . Initiation.
   producing, in their turn,
5. Racial probation. . . . . Racial discipleship. . . . . Racial initiation.
   and individually
6. The probationer. . . . . The Disciple. . . . . The Initiate.
   which lead eventually to
7. The New Group of World
   Servers. . . . . . The Hierarchy. . . . . . The Kingdom of God.

A comparative study of these stages and phases will reveal how the relationship of the ego and the personality emerges, and that the distinctive feature between the two, as far as the aspirant is concerned, is the focus or the concentration of the life aspect. In the personality the focus of consciousness is *Form*. In the individuality, that focus is transferred to the *Soul*. It is all a question of where lies the centre of attention. The "approaches" which take place between the soul and the personality are the processes of relationship in the periods of transition. In connection with the race, these are called the Great Approaches of the Hierarchy, and they represent the soul of humanity within the racial form. The New Group of World Servers is that body of men and women who have responded to one of these major approaches. As soon as they have done this, they become a bridging or a linking group between the Hierarchy and the race, thus facilitating the task of the planetary Hierarchy.

The revelation of these Approaches, during the time in which they are going on, is only now possible. At the first Great Approach in Lemurian days, when the race of men individualised, only the members of the approaching Hierarchy were in any way aware of the purpose. Those who were approached registered dimly a deepened urge to rise to better things. Aspiration was born—conscious aspiration, if such a word can be employed in connection with the vague yearning of animal man. Today, such is the progress made through the effect of evolution that many people can and do consciously register the influence of the soul and the nearing approach of the Hierarchy. This ability to register the Approach, or the Touch of Enlightenment, is largely due to the successful work of the Christ when He came down to the earth some two thousand years ago. He accustomed us to the idea of divinity—an entirely new concept as far as man was concerned. He thus paved the way for the nearer approach, upon a large scale, of the Kingdom of Souls, through its agent, the Hierarchy and the hierarchical agency, The New Group of World Servers. This may convey something of an understanding of an aspect of Christ's work which is frequently overlooked.

Today, as the seventh ray comes into manifestation, we shall see the approaches between the two higher kingdoms of men and of souls greatly facilitated, as the magical work in the producing and bringing about of relationship begins to go forward as desired. It is the work of the Ray of Magical Order which will bring about sensitivity to one of the Major Approaches which is being now attempted. Only as history is made and we learn later the amazing nature of the epoch through which the race is passing, will humanity appreciate the significance of the work of the present Hierarchy, and the magnitude and the success of its achievement since 1925, as a result of the initial impulse instituted in 1875.

No more need be said on this point except to observe that the first indications of the work done during the Wesak Festival of 1936 and the response engendered among humanity would warrant the assumptions of success. Let us all stand poised and ready, unafraid and sure, thus preserving the gain of past effort and (in company with all true servers throughout the world) ensuring to us a positive focal point for the transmission of spiritual energy.

It would be well, before we proceed with our consideration of the Ray of the Personality, to add a word more to the information given above anent the three great Approaches of the soul or the three Touches which are transforming or initiating agencies in the life of the personality. Students would do well to remember that there must ever be an analogy or a correspondence carried out in the life of the little self—a reflection of the activities of the greater Self. Just as the soul makes three approaches towards its instrument or reflection, a human being, so the integrated personality approaches also towards union with the soul by three similar or related *touches*. It might be of interest if we were to enlarge somewhat upon this matter.

The corresponding activity in the personality to the *Approach of Appropriation* comes as a result of the reorientation and the readjustment which takes place in the personality life when upon the probationary path. Then the individual aspirant—after much struggle and effort—suddenly "touches", for one brief moment, the level of the soul, and knows the meaning of the words "soul contact." That contact is no longer a desire, a vision or a theoretical belief or hope. It is experience and fact. The terms "soul contact" and "sensing the vibratory quality of the soul" are phrases oft used. It should prove useful to students if they could learn to appreciate the fact that when "in meditation deep" a certain sudden and recognised relationship is established, the personality has responded for the first time in such a manner that the "appropriation" by the soul of its instrument (called individualisation) is duplicated by the appropriation by the personality of the inspiring and overshadowing soul. This experience marks a significant moment in the life of the soul and the personality, and the man is never again the same. He has participated in a soul activity. This great event, when looked at from this angle, should throw new light and a fresh spirit of enterprise into the meditation work of the aspirant. Just as the soul through a planned activity, individualised itself in a human form, so the probationary aspirant, also as a result of a planned activity, takes the first step in individualising himself in a spiritual form, and the shift of consciousness from a body nature into a body "not made with hands, eternal in the heavens" takes place. The little self repeats the activity of the great Self. An event upon the path of ascent explains the significance of what occurred on the way of descent.

We are told that a long time transpires between the first initiation (wherein the crisis of appropriation on the Path of Ascent, finds its culmination) and the second initiation. Here again there is a correspondence to earlier happenings, for much time has transpired since individualisation, technically understood, has taken place. That individualisation, the first great soul approach took place either in Lemurian days or in a still earlier crisis upon that dead planet, the moon. Today, just as the form of animal man had to reach a certain level of development, so the human form has to reach the level of personality integration before the reenactment of the Approach of Appropriation can be consciously carried forward.

Next there comes a period in the life of the aspirant when he shifts off the probationary path and moves on to the path of discipleship. This is the result of an activity which is a reflection in his individual personality life of the Approach of Acquiescence. This takes place upon the battlefield of the astral plane. There the disciple acquiesces consciously in the inevitable process of transmutation which takes place before the personality can be a fit instrument for the soul. He stands between the pairs of opposites, learning the secret of duality, and like Arjuna (fixed at the midway point) he seeks the way out, eventually acquiescing in the task ahead. This is the stage of submission to which every disciple subjects himself.

It is through *acquiescence* that the astral aspect of the personality is brought into line with the divine purpose of the indwelling soul. This is not, a negative, weak submission, or a sad, sweet acceptance, so-called, of the will of God, but it is a positive, dynamic assumption of a certain position or attitude upon the battlefield of life. This attitude recognises rightly, as did Arjuna, the demands of both armies (the army of the Lord and the army of the Personality) and whilst acquiescing in the *facts* of the case, the disciple stands up and fights as best he may for the privilege of right understanding and right activity. Just as the soul in far off days acquiesced, and gave the touch of acquiescence in the obligation assumed when the approach of appropriation took place and the demands of the personality upon the soul became steadily more definite, so now the personality reverses the process, and recognises the demands of the soul. This marks, as may well be seen, a very definite stage in the life of the aspirant, and is the cause of that unhappy sense of duality which produces distress and sorrow in the life of all disciples. It is at this point upon the *Way* that many very well-meaning disciples fall. Instead of standing in spiritual being and taking a firm position upon the middle way between the pairs of opposites, and thus intensifying the touch of appropriation and endeavoring to make the approach of acquiescence, they fall into the illusions of self-pity. These prevent the process of appropriation. A furious conflict then ensues in the endeavor to change the theme of their lives, and the disciples forget that that theme is the embodiment of the Word of their souls in any particular incarnation, and that no theme—calling as it does, particular conditions into being—could provide the right and needed circumstances for full and complete development. They become so occupied with the theme that they forget the composer of that theme.

The dramatic rehearsal by the personality of the Approach or Touch of Enlightenment (as enacted by the soul) takes place upon the Path of Initiation. It has been portrayed for us by the Buddha when He took illumination and became the Enlightened One.

There is one peculiarly interesting point which can perhaps be made clear. God, or whatever word anyone may employ to express the Originator of all that exists, constantly re-enacts these dramatic approaches for His people. In so doing and as history proceeds, two great classes of Avatars must inevitably emerge, or have emerged. There are, first of all, Those Who embody in Themselves the great major soul approaches. There will be (and I would ask you to note the change of tense) Those Who will embody the human approaches, or the corresponding activities of the personality to the soul approaches. These are called in the language of esotericism "the Avatars of logoic descent upon the radiant path of . . ." and "the Avatars of divine descent upon the Claiming Way." I cannot translate these terms more clearly, nor can I find an adequate word for the phrase which qualifies the radiant path.

On the Way of Descending Approaches, the *Buddha* from the mental plane and also upon it, embodied in Himself the blazing enlightenment which is the result of a rare occurrence—a *Cosmic Touch*. He challenged the people to the Path of Light, of which knowledge and wisdom are two aspects. These, when brought into relationship with each other, produce the light. In a curious and esoteric manner, therefore, the Buddha embodied in Himself the force and activity of the third ray, of the third aspect of divinity—the divine cosmic principle of Intelligence. By its fusion with the ray of our solar system (the ray of Love) He expressed perfectly the significance of light in matter, of the intelligence principle as found in form, and was the Avatar Who carried in Himself the fully ripened seeds of the past solar system. We should not forget that our present solar system is, as was stated in *A Treatise on Cosmic Fire*, the second in a series of three systems.

Then came the next great Avatar, the Christ, Who, enfolding in Himself all that the Buddha had of light and wisdom (being fully enlightened in the occult and spiritual sense) on the Way of Descending Approach, embodied also the peace of inclusiveness, which comes from the *Touch of Divine Acquiescence*. He was the embodied force of submission, and He carried the divine approach to the astral plane, the plane of feeling.

Thus two great stations of energy and two major powerhouses of light have been established by these two Sons of God, and *the descent* of the divine life into manifestation has been greatly facilitated. The *Way* is now opened so that the *ascent* of the sons of men can become entirely possible. It is around these two ideas of divine descent and of human corresponding ascent that the coming new religion must be built.

Stations of power exist and have been founded through the work of the various World Saviours. These stations of power must be contacted by humanity as time transpires, through their individual re-enactment (on a tiny scale) of the cosmic approaches, or the touches of divinity, dramatically engineered by the cosmic Avatars, the *Buddha* and the *Christ*. It is because the Christ has approached closer to humanity by focussing divine energy upon the astral plane through His divine acquiescence that He is the First Initiator.

From one point of view, these two centres of force constitute the Temples of Initiation through which all disciples have to pass. This passing is the theme of the coming new religion.

Mankind has entered into the Temples at the great cosmic *Approach of Appropriation* in Lemurian times. Certain of the more advanced sons of men were passed in Atlantean times and still more will be passed in the immediate future, whilst a fair number will also be raised to immortality, but from the angle of the race it is the initiation of passing which is ahead for a very large number, and not the initiation of being raised. I am not here speaking of the so-called five major initiations, but of certain group events which are predominantly cosmic in nature. The major initiations which are the goal of human endeavor are individual in nature, and constitute, as it were, a preparatory period of expansions of consciousness. There were, if I might so express it, seven steps or approaches on the part of the life of God in the subhuman kingdoms prior to the *Approach of Appropriation* when humanity individualised. There are, as we know, five initiations ahead of the world disciples and these are steps towards the *Approach of Acquiescence* which will become possible on our planet before long. There are—after these seven and five steps—three more to be taken before the cosmic *Approach of Enlightenment* can take place in a far distant future. So humanity enters into the outer Court of God's love, passes into the Holy Place and is raised in the Secret Place of the Most High.

Later, the Avatar will emerge Who will embody in Himself all that the Buddha had of enlightenment and all that Christ had of acquiescing love. He will, however, also embody the energy which produced the *Approach of Appropriation*, and when He comes forth, there will transpire a great appropriation by humanity of its recognised divinity, and the establishing upon earth of a station of light and of power which will make possible the externalising of the Mysteries of Initiation upon earth. This approach is the cause of much of the present turmoil, for the Avatar is on His way.

Much of the above can mean but little to those who are not yet upon the path of accepted discipleship. We are here dealing with some of the major mysteries. But a mystery only remains a mystery when ignorance and unbelief exist. There is no mystery where there is knowledge and faith. The coming of the Avatar Who will fuse in Himself three principles of divinity is an inevitable future happening, and when He shall appear "the light that always has been will be seen; the love that never ceases will be realised, and the radiance deep concealed will break forth into being." We shall then have a new world—one which will express the light, the love and the knowledge of God.

These three Temples of the Mysteries (of which two are already existing, and the third will later appear) are each of them related to one of the three divine aspects, and the energy of the three major rays pours through them. In the corresponding approaches upon the path of ascent by humanity, it is the energy of the four minor Rays of Attribute which produce the power to make the needed approach. Through the active work and the guidance of the "presiding guardians" of these temples, the fifth kingdom in nature will be brought into manifested being. Over the Temple upon the mental plane, the *Buddha* presides and there will consummate His unfinished work. Over the Temple upon the plane of sentient feeling and of loving aspiration, the Christ presides, for this is the Temple of the most difficult initiatory processes. The reason for this difficulty and for the importance of this Temple is due to the fact that our solar system is a system of *Love*, of sentient response to the love of God, and of the development of that response through the innate faculty of feeling or sentiency. This calls for the cooperation of a Son of God who will embody two divine principles. Later will come an Avatar Who will achieve neither the full enlightenment of the Buddha nor the full expression of the divine love of the Christ, but Who will have a large measure of wisdom and of love, plus that "materialising power" which will enable Him to found a divine powerhouse upon the physical plane. His task, in many ways, is far more difficult than that of the two preceding Avatars, for He carries in Himself not only the energies of the two divine principles, already "duly anchored" upon the planet by His two great Brothers, but He has also within Himself much of a third divine principle, hitherto not used upon our planet. He carries the will of God into manifestation, and of that will we, as yet, know really nothing. So difficult is His task that the New Group of World Servers is being trained to assist Him. Thus an aspect of the first ray principle will be anchored by Him upon earth.

All that the student can grasp is that the *Plan* will be the dynamic impulse of this third and vital energy which will pervade the outer court of the Temple, constituting a Temple of Initiation upon the physical plane, thus externalising the activities of the Hierarchy in certain possible respects. The first initiation will then take place upon earth. It will be then no longer a veiled secret. This is the initiation of the outer court, wherein the approach of the soul upon the Way of Descent into manifestation, and the subsequent appropriation of the proffered divine energy by the personality upon the Way of Ascent will take place.

The Holy Place is the place where the second initiation is enacted, and this will some day be given upon the astral plane when the illusion there persisting has been somewhat dissipated. Over this second initiation, the Christ presides and, as was said above, it is for us the most difficult and most transforming of the initiations. The acquiescence of the soul to the demands of the personality for spiritual life, and the submission of the personality to the soul, find therein their consummation.

Finally will come the initiation of the Transfiguration, wherein the light breaks forth, the *Touch of Enlightenment* is given, and the soul and the personality stand forth as one. This process requires also the aid of the Buddha and the inspiration of the Christ, and it is "occultly guarded" by the Avatar of the physical plane.

In all the above information there is given a hint as to what will take place when human personalities are actively functioning and steadily awakening. The rapid coming of the Avatar Who will found the station of light and power upon the physical plane is dependent upon the rapid unfoldment and appearance of integrated personalities who love and think and seek to serve. There has here been given a new hint upon one of the more esoteric aspects of the work of the New Group of World Servers, and a hint at the same time as to the reason that this *Treatise upon the Seven Rays* has been written. An understanding of the rays and of the impelling forces in, through, and with which the personality has to work was essential if the work of this third Avatar from cosmic sources, was to be made possible.

We have thus endeavored to outline something of the problems of the personality from the angle of the larger issues. We have, as the occult law dictates, begun with the relation of the form to the soul, with the descent of life and the ascent of the sons of God, and we have carried the thought forward to the fact of the Hierarchy, working under the same law, and its relation to the New Group of World Servers. Information on initiation has hitherto been primarily occupied with the relations of the individual man to the soul and to the Hierarchy. There are here presented some of the *group implications*. The New Group of World Servers is related to the Hierarchy as body to soul, and they in their turn as a group of souls are similarly related to the human family. Therefore we have:

1. Soul ....Body.
2. The Fifth Kingdom ....The Fourth Kingdom.
3. The Hierarchy ....The New Group of
                                        World Servers.
4. The New Group of World Servers......Humanity.
5. A Soul ....A Personality.

The one unit descends towards the ascending related unit, (speaking in terms of an approach from two directions). This takes place under divine impulse and human aspiration, and both act equally under:

1. The Law of Karma.
2. The Law of Necessity.
3. The Law of Cycles.
4. The Law of Attraction.

Let us now return to the level of practical understanding. Although we turn aside to deal with these momentous matters at times, such discussions are not primarily intended for the present generation of readers but for those who are coming into incarnation and who will read with a more accurate understanding than is possible at this time to the average interested aspirant who studies these pages.

Three types of energy, as has been said, meet and blend in the personality, finding their expression through the medium of an outer tangible form which is itself coloured, motivated and conditioned by a fourth type of energy—the energy of basic matter. This basic matter is the product of the first solar system, and the energy of which it is composed does not, therefore, belong to our solar system at all, except through an act of appropriation, performed by our planetary Logos at the dawn of the creative activity of God. Seeking to impress, impel and motivate this group of four energies is the energy of the informing, indwelling soul. This fifth type of energy is itself dual in nature, being the transcendent archetype of both mind and emotion, or will and love. These six energies in their turn are animated or impelled by the life of God Himself, thus making the seven energies now in manifestation. This is, of course, well known, as the theory constitutes the very bones of the occult body of truth, and in this statement is formulated the essential structure upon which esotericism is built. I have stated it purely in terms of energy, and not of principles or bodies, so as to bring the Ageless Wisdom into line with modern truth and scientific conclusions. We therefore have:

The Personality.

1. *The energy of mind.* The force of manas. The reflection of divine will and purpose. Motivation. The impulse to plan, under the Law of Synthesis.
2. *The energy of sentiency.* The capacity to respond. Emotional feeling, astral energy. The reflection of love. The force of desire. The impulse to aspire. The divine evolutionary urge. The tendency to attract, to be magnetic, under the Law of Attraction.
3. *The energy of life.* The capacity to integrate, to coordinate. The force of the vital or etheric body. The reflection of intelligent activity or divine movement.

The impulse to act, to be energetic, under the Law of Economy.

4. *The energy of dense matter.* Externalised activity. The automatic reactions of the outer sheath. The densest point of unity. The lowest aspect of synthesis.

The Soul.

5. *The energy of buddhi.* The force of divine, reasoning love. The intuition. This is part of the flower of attractive energy and focusses itself in the "love petals of the egoic lotus." Its reflection is found in the astral, emotional, sentient consciousness of the personality.

6. *The energy of atma.* The force of the divine will. The embodiment of divine purpose. This focusses itself in the "sacrifice petals of the egoic lotus." Its reflection is found in the mind nature of the personality.

The Spirit.

7. *The energy of life itself.*

These energies constitute the human being, a unit of energy. They make him *essentially* an active, intelligent, loving, living, human being. They are unfolded sequentially in time and space and, as a result of the great experiment of evolution, bring him eventually to the full flowering of his nature, and to a full expression of the seven types of energy which condition him.

The question arises as to when man can become aware in his own personal and separated consciousness (as registered in the waking brain) of the truth of the existence of this septenate of energies. I would reply as follows:

1. Unevolved man, and low grade human beings are aware

of the urges of the automatic physical nature and the impulses of the vital or etheric body.

2. Awakening human beings are coordinating and becoming aware of both these primitive urges and impulses, plus the sentient and emotional reactions of the emotional or astral body.

3. Intelligent humanity is, in due time, conditioned by the urges, impulses and sentiency of the three lower types of energy, plus the energy of the mind. When this has really been achieved, the man is then definitely an aspirant upon the probationary path.

4. Aspirants are now becoming aware of the fifth type of basic energy—that of the soul. This response to soul energy, and the blended activity of the soul energies (buddhi-atma) produce the unfolding of the outer layer of petals, the knowledge petals, which are formed of three types of force.

a. Manasic energy. The energy of the abstract levels of the mental plane, inherent in the soul.

b. Mental energy. This is the energy of the concrete levels of the mental plane, and is definitely a contribution of the human being himself.

c. The energy of the mind found in matter itself. This is inherent mind, and is inherited from an earlier solar system.

These three aspects of mind energy are thus blended and are a synthesis of the intelligent force of deity. They embody as much of the mind of God as a human being can embrace in time and space, for they are

a. The energy of intelligent life, coming from God the Father.

 b. The energy of intelligent soul or consciousness, coming from God the Son.

 c. The energy of intelligent matter coming from God the Holy Spirit.

5. The disciples of the world are occupied with the integration of the personality with the soul, or with the synthesis of the first five aspects of energy as the lotus petals of love come into conscious recognition, and the intuition begins faintly to function. These petals of love, which are only symbolic forms of expressing energy, have a dual activity—they attract upward the planetary energies and bring downward the energies of the Spiritual Triad, the expression of the Monad.

6. Initiates are becoming conscious of the sixth type of energy, that of atma, the will aspect of Spirit. This causes them to work with the Plan and through the lotus petals of sacrifice to bring the service of the Plan into being. This is ever the aim of the initiate members of the Hierarchy. They understand, express and work with the Plan.

7. After the third initiation, the disciple begins to work with, and to understand the significance of Spirit and his consciousness shifts gradually out of the Soul into that of the Monad in the same way as the consciousness of the personality shifted out of the lower awareness into that of the soul.

This is the second panel, if one might so express it, of the picture here being drawn, of the divine life as it manifests through the consciousness of humanity. I am seeking to give it in such terms that comprehension may ensue. The first panel gave some of the universal implications. This was elaborated in *A Treatise on Cosmic Fire*. The second panel, contained in this *Treatise on the Seven Rays*, gives a general view of the synthetic unfoldment of man. The third panel entered the realm of synthetic work and was embodied in a *Treatise on White Magic*.

It would be useful to bear in mind here what was earlier pointed out:

1. The mental body is governed by Rays 1, 4, 5.
2. The astral body is governed by Rays 2, 6.
3. The physical body is governed by Rays 3, 7.

This is often forgotten and people will have to readjust their ideas in this matter. It is by an understanding of these dominant types of force as they condition the various vehicles that the true nature of the problem of psychology will emerge and the right clue to the solution will appear. The above tabulation and statement is one of the most important ever made in this Treatise in connection with psychology.

Gradually it will be noted that certain ray meditations can be used to bring in the influence of the soul and these will be later discussed. Some simple yet powerful meditation formulas will be given, which can be used by the man who is an integrated personality, in order to bring one or another of his vehicles into alignment and consequent control.

It will be observed that the rays governing the mind include one which links the mind nature with the ray of the solar system, which is the cosmic ray of love. This one is the Ray of Harmony, the fourth ray, but it is also Harmony through Conflict. It is a most important ray, for it gives us the clue to the whole problem of pain and of suffering. Our attention should be directed to this ray and to the mind nature which is related to it. In an understanding of this relationship, we have indicated to us the way out, or the use of that type of force which will lead humanity out. Every man who has reached the point of personality integration has eventually to call in this fourth type of energy when upon the Path, in order rightly to condition his mind and through the mind, his personality.

In considering the personality, therefore, and its conditioning rays we will study:

1. *The appropriation of the bodies:*

    a. Their building psychologically, or their coherent construction.
    b. Their development and eventual alignment.
    c. Their inter-relation in the life of the personality.

2. *The coordination of the personality:*

    a. The techniques of integration, seven in number.
    b. The technique of fusion, leading to the emergence of the ray of the personality.
    c. The technique of duality, divinely understood, or the relation of the ray of the personality and the ray of the soul.

3. *Some problems of psychology,* arising from the point in evolution of the personality.

    a. The technique of appropriation. Physical and etheric integration.
    b. The technique of acquiescence. Astral or psychic healing.
    c. The technique of enlightenment. Mental education.

We have before us in this study much food for thought. The subjects touched upon are deep, difficult to understand, and hard to grasp. Careful reading, however, quiet reflection, and a practical application of the sensed truth and of the intuited idea will gradually bring enlightenment and lead to acquiescence in the techniques of the soul, and the appropriation of the teaching.

a. Building and Construction of the Bodies

In theosophical literature, there is much talk anent the various elementals or lunar lords which compose, constitute and control the lower nature. These, in their triple totality, form the personality. They are of man's own creation, and form the basis of the problem which he, as a soul, has always to face until the final liberation is achieved. The mental elemental, the astral elemental and the physical elemental have a definite life of their own which is coloured by the rays upon which these various bodies or elementals have their being, until the man has reached a relatively high point in evolution.

The elementals composing the mental body are spoken of in the *Old Commentary* in the following terms:

> "The Lord of Will took being. His dim reflection followed in His steps. The little lord of force manasic appeared on earth.
> The Lord Who sought for harmony took form. The little lord, who loved to fight for what he sought, followed with swiftness in His wake.
> The Lord Who in this world of ours knew mind and thought, swept into incarnation. He was not, then He was. The little lord of mental stuff also took form. Man's troublous journey then began."

These old phrases bear out the statement earlier made that the mental body of every human being is composed of substance which is governed by the rays, one, four and five. Exceptions to this rule appear, sometimes, upon the Path of Discipleship, and are the result of the direct and intelligent action of the Soul, prior to incarnation. The soul builds a body of mental substance or attracts to it that particular type of mental energy which will enable it to possess (whilst in incarnation) the type of vehicle which will make a *chosen* experience possible. This freedom of choice never occurs except in the case of the awakening disciple. The reason for this will be seen if it is realised that the energy of these three rays, when focussed in a personality, provides exactly the right impulse to govern the lower life, both in the case of an undeveloped human being and of a man in the early stages of discipleship and aspiration. It might be well for us to elaborate this a little by means of certain tabulations:

THE MENTAL BODY

This provides (in the case of the unevolved or the highly developed) the following possibilities:

Ray One

IN UNEVOLVED MAN

1. The will to live or to manifest upon the physical plane.
2. The impulse which works out, therefore, as the instinct to self-preservation.
3. The capacity to endure, no matter what the difficulties.
4. Individual isolation. The man is always the "One who stands alone."

IN THE ADVANCED MAN

1. The will to liberation or to manifest consciously upon the plane of the soul.
2. The capacity to react to the plan, or to respond to the recognised will of God.
3. The principle of immortality.
4. Perseverance or endurance upon the *Way*.

Ray Four

IN UNEVOLVED MAN

1. Aggressiveness and that needed push towards the sensed goal which distinguishes the evolving human being. This goal, in the early stages, will be of a material nature.
2. The fighting spirit or that spirit of conflict which finally

brings strength and poise, and which produces eventual integration with the first ray aspect of deity.

3. That coherent force which makes a man a magnetic centre, whether as the major force in any group unity, such as a parent or a ruler, or a Master in relation to his group.

4. The power to create. In the lower types, this is connected with the impulse, or the instinct, to reproduce, leading consequently to the sex relation; or it may lead to construction of thought-forms or creative forms of some kind, even if it is only the hut of a savage.

IN THE ADVANCED MAN

1. The Arjuna spirit. This is the urge towards victory, the holding of a position between the pairs of opposites, and the eventual sensing of the middle way.

2. The urge to synthesis (again a first ray impulse) blended with a second ray tendency to love and to include.

3. The attractive quality of the soul as it expresses itself in the relation between the lower and higher selves. This eventuates in the "marriage in the Heavens."

4. The power to create forms, or the artistic impulse.

It will be noted in this connection how accurate was the earlier statement that the artist is found upon all the rays, and that the so-called Ray of Harmony or Beauty is not the only ray upon which the creative worker is found. The mental body of every human being, at some time or another, is found upon the fourth ray and usually when the man is nearing the probationary path. This means that the mental vehicle is governed by an elemental of fourth ray nature or quality and that, therefore, creative, artistic activity is the line of least resistance. We then have a man with an artistic tendency or we have a genius along some line of creative work. When, at the same time, the soul or the personality is also upon the fourth ray, then we will find a Leonardo da Vinci or a Shakespeare.

Ray Five

1. The power to develop thought.
2. The spirit of materialistic enterprise, the divine urge, as it evidences itself in the early stages.
3. The tendency to enquire, to ask questions and to find out. This is the instinct to search and to progress, which is, in the last analysis, the urge to evolve.
4. The tendency to crystallise, to harden, or to have an "idée fixe." In this connection, it will usually be discovered that the man who succumbs to an "idée fixe" has not only a fifth ray mental body but either a sixth ray personality or a sixth ray emotional body.

1. The true thinker, or mental type—awake and alert.
2. The one who knows the Plan, the purpose and the will of God.
3. The one whose intelligence is being transmuted into wisdom.
4. The scientist, the educator, the writer.

I have given the above in connection with the rays of the mental body in order to enable us to grasp not only the complexity of the problem but also the inevitability of success through the play of the many energies upon and through any one single human mind. It is not necessary here to elaborate upon the energies which create and form the emotional body, or the physical body. The second and the sixth rays colour the astral body of every human being, whilst the physical body is controlled by the third and the seventh rays.

It is interesting to remember that the etheric body is uniquely constituted; it is the *instrument of life*, predominantly, more so than the *instrument of quality*. It is the factor which produces and sustains the *instrument of appearance*, the physical body. It will be recalled that in Volume One of this Treatise, the human being was differentiated into the three divine aspects: Life, Quality, and Appearance. Through the seven centres in the etheric body, the seven ray energies make their appearance and produce their effects, but at the very heart of each chakra or lotus, there is a vortex of force to be found which is composed of pure manasic energy, and, therefore, is purely energy of the first three rays. This energy is quiescent until an advanced stage of discipleship is reached. It only sweeps into its divine rhythm and activity when the three tiers of petals, found in the egoic lotus (the higher correspondence), are beginning to unfold, and the centre of the egoic lotus is becoming vibrant. Though the etheric body of man is an expression of the seven ray qualities in varying degrees of force, the etheric body of a Master is an expression of monadic energy, and comes into full activity after the third initiation.

It will be obvious, therefore, that when the psychologist takes into consideration the various types of energy which go to the constitution of a human being and can distinguish (from study and investigation, plus an understanding of the rays) what the energies are which are conditioning a patient, then great strides will be made in handling people. The nature of the human equipment and its internal relationship, as well as the external effects, will be better comprehended. Speaking technically, the extreme psychological position (as it is expressed in the Behaviouristic School, which is essentially sound where the dense material mechanism of man is concerned) will fall into its rightful place. Materialistic psychologists have been dealing with the substance energies and with the instinctual life of the organism. These constitute the sum total of the available energies, organised into the form of the automatic physical body, coloured as its atoms are by the tendencies and qualities developed in a previous solar system. In our solar system, we are arriving at an understanding and a development of the consciousness aspect of divinity, its qual‑ity and characteristic, just as instinctual intelligence or auto‑matic activity was the contribution of the earlier manifesta‑tion of God, in which the third aspect was dominant.

The problem can be posited and its extent made clear by the following tabulation which gives the rays that may be supposed or imagined to govern or control a problematical or hypothetical man in a particular incarnation.

1. The Ray of the Monad.........Second Ray of Love-
   (the *life* aspect) Wisdom.
2. The Ray of the Soul...........First Ray of Will or
   (the *consciousness* aspect) Power.
3. The Ray of the Personality....Second Ray of Love-
   (the *matter* aspect) Wisdom.
   a. Ray of the mental body...Fifth Ray of Concrete
      Science.
   b. Ray of the astral body....Sixth Ray of Devotion.
   c. Ray of the physical body..Second Ray of Love-
      Wisdom.

Certain ideas should here be considered. They are here given in the form of statements, but we will not elaborate them, simply leaving them to the student for his pondering and careful thinking.

1. Only initiates are in a position to sense, determine, or discover the nature of their monadic ray or that of their disciples. The monadic ray is that life element in man with which They have definitely to deal as They seek to prepare him for initiation. It is the "unknown quan‑tity" in a man's nature. It does not, however, greatly complicate his problem in the three worlds of ordinary human endeavor, as it remains relatively quiescent until after the third initiation, though it basically conditions the etheric body itself.

2. The three rays (termed, in *The Secret Doctrine*, "the

three periodical vehicles") are therefore the rays of the monad, the ego and the personality, and are essentially three streams of energy, forming one great life stream. These relate a human being to the three aspects or expressions of divinity in manifestation:

a. The monadic ray is the energy which, when consciously employed, relates the initiate to the Father or Spirit aspect and gives Him "the freedom of the solar system".

b. The egoic ray, when consciously utilised, relates the disciple to the second aspect of divinity and gives him the "freedom of the planetary sphere".

c. The personality ray, again when consciously governed and employed, relates a man to the matter or substance aspect of divinity and gives him the "freedom of the three worlds" and of the subhuman kingdoms in nature.

3. Taking the hypothetical chart given above, students should notice how the rays of the personality relate them, within the sphere or periphery of their own manifestation, to the major rays of the monad, ego or personality. This is a correspondence (within the microcosmic manifestion) to the macrocosmic situation, touched upon in the previous paragraph. In the case cited (which is one of quite usual occurrence) we find that

a. The fifth ray of the mental body relates the man to his egoic ray, thereby facilitating soul contact. Had it related him to his monadic ray a very different situation would have eventuated.

The line of 1.3.5.7. must ever be remembered.

b. The sixth ray of the astral body relates the man to his

monadic ray, and it will finally constitute his astral-buddhic approach to life, and will be employed when he takes the fourth initiation. This ray relates him also to his personality and intensifies his natural problem.

The line of 2.4.6. must also be carefully borne in mind.

c. The second ray quality of his physical body relates him both to the personality and finally to the monad. It is, therefore, for him a great problem, a great opportunity, and a great "linking" energy. It makes the life of the personality exceedingly dominant and attractive, and at the same time facilitates the future contact (whilst in a physical body) with the monad. His problem of *soul* consciousness will not, however, be so easily solved.

You will note also that the monad (2nd ray), the astral body (6th ray) and the physical body (2nd ray) are all along the same line of activity, or of divine energy, creating a most interesting psychological problem. The soul (1st ray) and the mental body (5th ray) are along another line entirely, and this combination presents great opportunity and much difficulty.

4. In the lower expression of the man whose psychological chart we are considering, the psychologist will find a person who is intensely sensitive, inclusive and self-willed. Because of the fact that the second ray personality and the physical body are related by similarity of ray, there will also be a clearly pronounced tendency to lay the emphasis upon *material* inclusiveness and tangible acquisition, and there will, therefore, be found (in this person) an exceedingly selfish and self-centred man.

He will not be particularly intelligent, as only his fifth
ray mental body relates him definitely and directly to the
mind aspect of Deity, whilst his first ray egoic force
enables him to use all means to plan for himself, and to
use the will aspect to acquire and to attract the material
good he desires or thinks he needs. His predominant
second ray equipment, however, will eventually bring
the higher values into play.

In the higher expression of the same man and when the
evolutionary cycle has done its work, we will have a sensitive,
intuitive, inclusive disciple whose wisdom has flowered forth,
and whose vehicles are outstandingly the channel for divine
love.

Many such charts could be drawn up and studied, and
many such hypothetical cases could present the basis for
occult investigation, for diagram, and for the study of the
Law of Correspondences. Students would find it of interest
to study themselves in this way, and, in the light of the information given in this *Treatise on the Seven Rays*, they could
formulate their own charts, study what they think may be
their own rays and the consequent ray effect in their lives,
and thus draw up most interesting charts of their own nature,
qualities and characteristics.

It might be of interest to mention the fact that the moment
a man becomes an accepted disciple, some such chart *is*
prepared and placed in the hands of his Master. In fact, four
such charts are available, for the rays of the personality vary
from one cycle of expression to another and necessitate the
keeping of the personality chart up to date. The four basic
charts are:

1. The chart of a man's expression at the time of his in-

dividualisation. This is of course a very ancient chart. In it, the rays of the mental body and of the emotional body are most difficult to ascertain as there is so little mental expression or emotional experience. Only the ray of the soul and of the physical body are clearly defined. The other rays are regarded as only suggestive.

This is the chart of the *man who is asleep*.

2. The chart of a man's expression when the personality reaches its highest independent point of development;— that is, before the soul has taken over *conscious* control and is functioning at all dominantly.

This is the chart of *the man who dreams*.

3. The chart of a man's expression at that peculiar moment of determining crisis when the soul and personality are at war, when the battle for reorientation is at its highest and the aspirant knows it. He knows that upon the issue of that battle much depends. He is Arjuna upon the field of Kurukshetra.

This is the chart of *the man awakening*.

4. The chart of a man's expression during the life wherein the orientation has been altered, the emphasis of the life forces changed, and the man becomes an accepted disciple.

These four charts, depicted or drawn in colour according to ray, form the *dossier* of a disciple, for the Master only deals with general tendencies and never with detail. General trends and predispositions and emphasised characteristics concern Him, and the obvious life patterns.

I would call to your attention the increasing use by the psychologists and thinkers of the race of the word "pattern". It is a word which has a deep occult significance. One of the exercises given to the disciple upon the inner planes is connected with these psychological charts or these life patterns. He is asked to study them with care, all four of them, and then to draw up the pattern which embodies for him the goal as far as he, at his present point of development, can sense it. When he takes the first initiation, then the Master adds another pattern or chart to the dossier of the disciple, and the latter can then study:

a. The chart of his condition at the time he became an accepted disciple.

b. The hypothetical chart which he himself drew up earlier in his training as an accepted disciple.

c. The chart of his general psychological condition at the time he took the first initiation.

By a careful analysis and comparison of the three charts, he can discover the accuracy or the inaccuracy of his own diagnosis, and thus develop a better sense of proportion as to his own mental perception of himself.

It would be interesting later, if students could be set some such task as drawing up an analysis of themselves which could be embodied in a chart, giving the rays that they believe govern their equipment, and stating the reasons for assigning these ray qualities.

When the psychologist of the future employs all the available sciences at his disposal and, at the same time, lays the emphasis upon those sciences which deal with the subjective man and not so predominantly with the objective man (though that should *not* be omitted) we shall then have a fundamental change in the handling of the human problem or equation. This is today a problem which is seriously confronting and distressing the psychologist, the psychiatrist, the neurologist, the social worker and the humanitarian.

The psychologist will then employ:

1. The modern exoteric science of psychology, with its emphasis upon equipment, upon the glands and their effects, upon dreams and their occasional effect, upon instinctual behaviour (which is largely a reaction of the physical body) and upon all the latest conclusions of the investigating material scientists the world over.
2. Esoteric psychology, such as is embodied in this *Treatise on the Seven Rays*. This indicates the types of energy and the forces which govern, control and determine the varying aspects of the average man's equipment, and condition his consciousness.
3. Astrology, with its indications (little realised as yet) of a man's place "in the sun", and in the general scheme of things. These relate him to the planetary whole and give much information anent the time factors which govern every individual, little as he may think it.

It will be recognised that the astrology with which we are here concerned and which I will later somewhat elaborate, does not deal with the expression of the personality. It is the planetary and racial astrology which Those who work on the inner side, know to be of deep significance. It is the astrology of discipleship and the relation of the stars to the activities of the soul which They regard of importance. It is the astrology of initiation with which They are most profoundly concerned. Though the time is not yet, we shall some day be able to cast the horoscope of the soul, and make more clear to the awakening human being the way that he should go. Of this more anon.

It will also be apparent that, as the relationships of the different aspects of a man's manifested life appear, his seven centres are related to the seven aspects or qualities which embody a man's essential divinity. The following is therefore of interest:

1. The head centre........Monad. Life. First aspect.
2. The heart centre.........Soul. Consciousness. Second aspect.
3. The ajna centre.........Personality. Substance. Third aspect.

These are the three major centres for the advanced man.

4. The throat centre........Mind. The mental aspect and energy.
5. The solar plexus centre..Emotion. The astral aspect and energy centre.
6. The sacral centre........Physical.
7. The centre at base of the spine.............Life itself. Monadic centre.

The latter centre is only awakened in its true and final sense at the third initiation. At that time the circle is completed. As was earlier stated, the etheric body is related to the monad and is the exteriorisation of the life aspect. It is the etheric body, with all its seven centres, which is swept into activity when the basic centre is awakened, and the kundalini fire is aroused. It might be of value to students to point out that frequently when a student is under the impression or belief that the kundalini fire has been aroused in him, all that has really happened is that the energy of the sacral centre (i.e. the sex centre) is being transmuted and raised to the throat, or that the energy of the solar plexus centre is being raised to the heart. Aspirants do, however, love to play with the idea that they have succeeded in arousing the kundalini fire. Many advanced occultists have mistaken the raising of the sacral fire or of the solar plexus force to a position above the diaphragm for the "lifting of the kundalini" and have therefore regarded themselves or others as initiates. Their sincerity has been very real and their mistake an easy one to make.

C. W. Leadbeater frequently made this mistake, yet of his sincerity and of his point of attainment there is no question.

The abstruseness and the difficulty of all of the above is very real and, living as the disciple does in the world of glamour and illusion, it is not easy for the average aspirant to sort out his ideas on these matters, or to see the extent of the subject with the perspective that is necessary. He has to start, first of all, by accepting the premise of the rays, and this he cannot prove, though he may do two things:—

1. Correlate the idea of these ray energies with the modern teaching of exoteric science that there is nothing but energy as the underlying substance of all phenomenal appearance.

2. Regard the theory as one which, though as yet for him only an hypothesis, fits the facts as he knows them better than any other. He will then, one can safely predict, eventually change his hypothesis into a living fact, if he studies himself with care. One of the first things a disciple has to learn is that he is, indeed, the microcosm of the macrocosm, and that within himself has to be found the open door to the universe.

What is here presented is of sufficient difficulty and of adequate interest to merit careful consideration.

I wonder if the students have any idea how the ideals I seek to bring to their attention could illumine their lives if they took them into their "brooding consciousness" for the space even of a month. This aspect of consciousness is the correspondence *in the soul body* to the mother aspect, as it broods over, guards and eventually brings to the birth the Christ aspect. Lives are changed primarily by reflection; qualities are developed by directed conscious thought; characteristics are unfolded by brooding consideration. To all this I call your attention.

I diverged briefly for a moment and took up the subject of the rays of the three bodies of the personality before completing the detail of the outline previously given on the ray of personality. This I did with deliberation, as I was anxious to have clearly established the difference which will be found existing between the rays governing the elementals of the three lower bodies and that of the personality. The life of these three elementals is founded primarily in the three lowest centres in the etheric body:

1. The sacral centre.............the mental elemental life
                    Transferred later to the throat centre.
2. The solar plexus centre.........the astral elemental life.
                    Transferred later to the heart centre.
3. The centre at the base of the spine. .the physical elemental life.
                    Transferred later to the head centre.

The life of the indwelling soul is focussed in the three higher centres.

1. The head centre.........the mental consciousness.
2. The throat centre.......the creative consciousness.
3. The heart centre........the feeling consciousness.

Two important stages in the life of the man take place during the evolutionary process:—

First: The stage wherein there comes the first great fusion or "assertion of control" by the soul. At this time the ajna centre comes alive. This stage precedes a man's passing on to the Probationary Path and is the stage which distinguishes the average man and woman at this time in the world.

Second: The stage wherein there comes a more definite

spiritual awakening. At this time the centre at the base of the spine comes into rapport—through its circulating life—with all the centres in the etheric body. This step precedes what is called initiation and signalises the arousing into activity of the central focus of power at the heart of each of the chakras or etheric lotuses. In all the previous stages, it has been the petals of the various lotuses, chakras or vortices of force which have come into increased motion. At this later stage, the "hub" of the wheel, the "point in the centre" or the "heart of the lotus" comes into dynamic action and the whole inner force-body becomes related in all its parts and begins to function harmoniously.

This is of value to remember and upon this the teaching of esoteric psychology is based. We have therefore, three stages of activity spread over a long evolutionary cycle, and differing according to ray and to the karmic conditions engendered.

1. The stage of being alive. This is the earliest and simplest stage wherein the man functions as an elementary human being. During this period all the centres are necessarily active in a slow and rhythmic way. All have a light in them, but it is dim and feeble; all have the three petals (not more) functioning and this the clairvoyant can see. As time goes on *all* the petals in the centres below the diaphragm become active, but they are not dynamic in the essential sense, nor are they brilliant focal points of light.

2. The stage of the first fusion as related above. Then all the centres have their petals vibrant. They are, at the same time, conditioned by

   a. The fact as to whether the *drive* of the life is above or below the diaphragm.

b. The nature of the particular ray energy.

c. The stage already reached upon the evolutionary way.

d. The type of physical mechanism, which is itself conditioned by the karma of the person and the field of service chosen in any one life.

e. The quality of the aspiration and many other factors.

3. The stage of the second fusion, in which the initiate expresses himself through all the centres and in which both the group of petals and the central point of energy are fully and dynamically alive.

Christ symbolically expressed these three stages for us at the Birth experience, the Transfiguration enlightenment, and the Ascension liberation.

In summarising, it might be said:

1. At the *stage of individualisation*

a. The centres throughout the body awaken and begin to function faintly.

b. The centres below the diaphragm receive the major impact and effect of the incoming life.

c. Three of the petals in all centres are "awake" and demonstrate activity, quality and light.

2. At the *stage of intellection* wherein a man is a self-conscious, self-directed being, and a definite personality,

a. All the petals in all the centres are awake, but the central focal point of each centre is quiescent. It glows with a faint light, but there is no true activity.

b. The centres above the diaphragm, with the exception of the ajna and head centres, are receptive to impact and inflow of life.

3. At the *stage of discipleship*, when the individuality and the personality are beginning to merge,

   a. The two head centres are becoming increasingly active.
   b. The petals are all vibrant, and the dynamic life of the soul is beginning to sweep the centre of the lotus into activity.
   c. The light of the petals in the centres below the diaphragm is beginning to dim, but the centre of the lotus is becoming more and more brilliant and living.

All the above process takes much time, and it includes the Path of Probation or Purification and the Path of Discipleship.

4. At the *stage of initiation* when complete at-one-ment is established.

   a. The four centres above the diaphragm become dominantly active.
   b. The centre at the base of the spine comes into awakened activity and the three fires of the matter aspect, of the soul, and of the spirit (fire by friction, solar fire, and electric fire) merge and blend.
   c. All the centres in the body of the initiate can be intensified electrically at will and used simultaneously, or one at a time, according to the demand and the need which must be met by the initiate.

All the above takes place progressively upon the Path of Initiation. This same truth can also be expressed in terms of the rays:

At the stage of *Individualisation*, the rays governing the physical and emotional bodies are dominant. The soul ray is scarcely felt and only flickers with a dim light at the heart of each lotus.

At the stage of *Intellection*, the ray of the mental body

comes into activity. This second process is itself divided into two stages:

1. That in which the lower concrete mind is developing.
2. That in which the man becomes an integrated, coordinated person.

At each of these latter two stages, the rays of the lower nature become increasingly powerful. Self-consciousness is developed, and then the personality becomes clearer and clearer, and the three elementals of the lower nature, the force of the so-called "three lunar Lords" (the triple energies of the integrated personality) come steadily under the control of the ray of the personality. At this stage, therefore, four rays are active in the man, four streams of energy make him what he is and the ray of the soul is beginning, though very faintly, to make its presence felt, producing the conflict which all *thinkers* recognise.

At the stage of *Discipleship*, the soul ray comes into increased conflict with the personality ray and the great battle of the pairs of opposites begins. The soul ray or energy slowly dominates the personality ray, as it in its turn has dominated the rays of the three lower bodies.

At the stage of *Initiation*, the domination continues and at the third initiation the highest kind of energy which a man can express in this solar system—that of the monad, begins to control.

At the stage of individualisation, a man comes into being; he begins to exist. At the stage of intellection, the personality emerges with clarity and becomes naturally expressive. At the stage of discipleship, he becomes magnetic. At the stage of initiation, he becomes dynamic.

In reference to the pairs of opposites and their conflict, it might be of interest to note the following facts:

Students would do well to bear in mind that there are several pairs of opposites with which they have sequentially to deal. This is a point oft forgotten. Emphasis is usually laid upon the pairs of opposites to be found upon the astral plane, whilst those to be found upon the physical plane and the mental levels are omitted from the recognition of the aspirant. Yet it is essential that these other pairs of opposites receive due recognition.

Etheric energy, focussed in an individual etheric body, passes through two stages prior to the period of discipleship:

1. The stage wherein it assimilates the force latent in the dense physical form—the energy of atomic substance, thus producing a definite fusing and blending. This causes the animal nature to conform entirely to the inner impulses—emanating from the world of pranic influence, where the entirely undeveloped man is concerned, and from the lower astral world where the more developed or the average man is concerned. It is this truth which lies behind the statement frequently made that the dense physical body is an automaton.

2. The moment, however, that an inner orientation towards the world of higher values takes place, then the etheric or vital force is brought into conflict with the lowest aspect of man, the dense physical body, and the battle of the lower pair of opposites takes place.

It is interesting to note that it is during this stage that the emphasis is laid upon physical disciplines, upon such controlling factors as total abstinence, celibacy and vegetarianism, and upon physical hygienes and exercises. Through these, the control of the life by the form, the lowest expression of the third aspect of divinity, can be offset and the man set free for the true battle of the pairs of opposites.

This second battle is the true *kurukshetra* and is fought out in the astral nature, between the pairs of opposites which are distinctive of our solar system, just as the physical pairs of opposites are distinctive of the past solar system. From one interesting angle, the battle of the opposites upon the lower spiral (in which the physical body in its dual aspect is concerned) can be seen taking place in the animal kingdom. In this process, human beings act as the agents of discipline (as the Hierarchy in its turn acts towards the human family) and the domestic animals, forced to conform to human control, are wrestling (even if unconsciously from our point of view) with the problem of the lower pairs of opposites. Their battle is fought out through the medium of the dense physical body and the etheric forces, and in this way a higher aspiration is brought into being. This produces in time the experience which we call *individualisation*, wherein the seed of personality is sown. On the human battlefield, the *kurukshetra*, the higher aspect of the soul begins to operate and eventually to dominate, producing the process of divine-human integration which we call *initiation*. Students might find it of use to ponder upon this thought.

When an aspirant reaches that point in his evolution wherein the control of the physical nature is an urgent necessity, he recapitulates in his own life this earlier battle with the lower pairs of opposites, and begins to discipline his dense physical nature.

Making a sweeping generalisation, it might be stated that, for the human family *en masse*, this dense-etheric conflict was fought out in the world war, which was the imposition of a tremendous test and discipline. We should ever remember that our tests and disciplines are self-imposed and grow out of our limitations and opportunities. The result of this test was the passing on to the Path of Probation of a very large number of human beings, owing to the purging and the purification to which they had been subjected. This purificatory process in some measure prepared them for the prolonged conflict upon the astral plane which lies ahead of all aspirants, prior to achieving the goal of initiation. It is the "Arjuna" experience which lies definitely ahead of many today. This is an interesting point upon which to think and reflect; it holds much of mystery and of difficulty in the *sequence* of human unfoldment. The individual aspirant is prone to think only in terms of himself, and of his individual tests and trials. He must learn to think in terms of the mass activity, and the preparatory effect where humanity, as a whole is concerned. The world war was a climaxing point in the process of "devitalising" the world maya, as far as humanity is concerned. Much force was released and exhausted, and much energy also was expended. Much was consequently clarified.

Many people are occupied today, in their individual lives, with exactly the same process and conflict. On a tiny scale, that which was worked out in the world war is being worked out in their lives. They are busy with the problems of maya. Hence today we find an increasing emphasis upon the physical cultures, disciplines, and upon the vogue for physical training, which finds its expression in the world of sport, in athletic exercises, military training and preparation for the Olympic Games. These latter are in themselves an initiation. In spite of all the wrong motives and the terrible and evil effects (speaking again with a wide generalisation), the training of the body and organised physical direction (which is taking place today in connection with the youth of all nations) is preparing the way for millions to pass upon the Path of Purification. Is this a hard saying? Humanity is under right direction, e'en if, during a brief interlude, they misunderstand the process and apply wrong motives to right activities.

There is a higher duality to which it is necessary that we refer. There is, for the disciples, the duality which becomes obvious when the Dweller on the Threshold and the Angel of the Presence face each other. This constitutes the final pair of opposites.

The Dweller on the Threshold is oft regarded as a disaster, as a horror to be avoided, and as a final and culminating evil. I would here remind you, nevertheless, that the Dweller is "one who stands before the gate of God", who dwells in the shadow of the portal of initiation, and who faces the Angel of the Presence open-eyed, as the ancient Scriptures call it. The Dweller can be defined as the sum total of the forces of the lower nature as expressed in the personality, prior to illumination, to inspiration and to initiation. The personality *per se*, is, at this stage, exceedingly potent, and the Dweller embodies all the psychic and mental forces which, down the ages, have been unfolded in a man and nurtured with care. It can be looked upon as the potency of the threefold material form, prior to its conscious cooperation and dedication to the life of the soul and to the service of the Hierarchy, of God, and of humanity.

The Dweller on the Threshold is all that a man is, apart from the higher spiritual self; it is the third aspect of divinity as expressed in and through the human mechanism. This third aspect must be eventually subordinated to the second aspect, the soul.

The two great contrasting forces, the *Angel* and the *Dweller*, are brought together—face to face—and the final conflict takes place. Again, you will note, that it is a meeting and battle between another and a higher pair of opposites. The aspirant, therefore, has three pairs of opposites with which to deal as he progresses towards light and liberation:

THE PAIRS OF OPPOSITES

1. Upon the physical plane....The dense and etheric forces.
   These are faced upon the Path of Purification.

2. Upon the astral plane........The well-known dualities.
   These are faced upon the Path of Discipleship.

3. Upon the mental plane......The Angel of the Presence and the Dweller on the Threshold.
   These are faced upon the Path of Initiation.

b. DEVELOPMENT AND ALIGNMENT OF THE BODIES

After these preliminary remarks, we can come now to a study of the previous tabulation in connection with the method whereby the soul appropriates the various bodies, how they are developed and inter-related, and finally how coordination and alignment is brought about. The last part of the tabulation was outlined in such a manner that many of the problems facing the psychologist at this time can be dealt with from an esoteric angle, and perhaps some light on these problems may then be forthcoming.

In the current occult literature, the careful student will come to the conclusion that the emphasis has been laid upon the process whereby the ego or soul draws to itself the form, utilising for that purpose a mental unit and two permanent atoms, thus anchoring itself in three worlds of human experience. The matter, or rather the substance, aspect has been the subject of immediate importance. Hence this subject was covered in my earlier books which are intended to aid in the bridging process between the older "techniques of understanding" and the esotericism which the new age will sponsor. We should, however, bear in mind two things:

1. That such terms as "mental unit", "permanent atom", etc.,

are simply symbolic ways of expressing a difficult truth. The truth is that the soul is active on all the three lower planes, and that it is a type of energy, functioning in a field of force, thus producing an activity of some kind.

2. That the permanent atoms are not really atoms at all, but simply focal points of energy, which are of sufficient power to attract and hold coherently together the substance required by the soul with which to create a form of expression.

The soul itself is a major centre of experience in the life of the monad; the lower bodies are centres of expression in the life of the soul. As the consciousness of the man shifts continuously into the higher bodies through which expression can become possible, the soul gradually becomes the paramount centre of experience *in consciousness* and the lesser centres of experience (the lower bodies) assume less and less importance. The soul experiences less through them, but uses them increasingly in service.

This same thought must be carried into our concept of the soul as a centre of consciousness. The soul uses the bodies in the earlier stages of evolution as centres of *conscious* experience, and upon them and upon the experience is the emphasis laid. But as time progresses, the man becomes more soul-conscious and the consciousness which he experiences (as a soul in the three bodies) is of decreasing importance, until finally the bodies become simply instruments of contact through which the soul comes into understanding relationship with the world of the physical plane, of the feeling, sentient levels, and with the world of thought.

In considering, therefore, the section with which we are now concerned, it is essential for right understanding and eventual psychological usefulness, that we remember constantly that we shall be talking always in terms of conscious-ness and of soul energy, and are only dealing with sentient substance from the point of view of its usefulness in terms of time and space, or of manifestation. In thinking of the focal points of soul energy upon the mental, astral and phys-ical planes, we will not think of the permanent atoms as ma-terial centres, or as germs of form, which is the prevailing idea. We will think of them simply as an expression—attrac-tive or magnetic in quality as the case may be—of soul energy, playing upon energies which have in them the quality of responsiveness to the positive aspects of energy with which they are brought in contact. In elucidating this most difficult problem it might be said that the problems of psychology fall into two major groups:

1. A group of difficulties wherein the psychologist has to deal with those people whose vehicles of expression, as centres for the gaining of experience, are not adequately responsive to their environment for the creative, in-dwelling soul. When this is the case, the centres in the etheric body are diversely but only partially awakened, and the glandular system, therefore, is correspondingly mediocre and irregular.

2. Another group of difficulties concerns those human beings whose vehicles of expression, as centres of experience, are over-developed and over-stimulated without adequate *conscious* control by the soul. This development is, at this time, primarily focussed in the astral body, leading to over-sensitivity of the solar plexus centre or of the throat centre, and occasioning consequent difficulty. Much of the thyroid instability of the present time is based upon this.

There is a third class of difficulties which concern those who are on the Path of Discipleship, but these we will not consider here. In these latter cases there is an abnormal over-sensitivity in the vehicles, the rush of force through from the soul, via the centres, presents real difficulty, and responsiveness to the environment is over-developed in many cases.

These conditions are governed, as will be recognised, by the point in evolution, the ray type, the quality of past karma, and the present family, national and racial inherited characteristics. As we study, let us bear clearly in mind that *it is the soul as a centre of consciousness* and *the vehicles as centres of experience* with which we are concerning ourselves. We should seek to eliminate from our minds the more material connotations which past teachings have emphasised. Annie Besant in her *Study in Consciousness* sought to avoid the error of materialism and to voice a real vision of the truth, but words themselves are limiting things and oft veil and hide the truth. Her book, therefore, is of definite value. Remember also that a man's consciousness is first of all, and usually, centred sequentially in the three bodies, and the centres of experience for him are primarily the field of his consciousness. He is identified for long with the field of experience and not with the real self. He has not yet identified himself with the conscious subject, or with the One Who is aware, but as time goes on, his centre of identification shifts, and he becomes less interested in the field of experience and more aware of the soul as the conscious, thinking Individual.

The comprehension of each of us will depend upon *where* we each, as individuals, lay the emphasis, and *where* we are awake and alive, and of *what* we are conscious. When we have achieved the experience of the third initiation and are no longer identified with the vehicles of expression, then—on a higher turn of the spiral—another shift in the life expression and experience will take place. Then neither the centre of experience, the soul, nor the vehicles of expression, the lower threefold man, will be considered from the angle of consciousness at all. The *Life* aspect will supersede all others. Of what use is it for us to discuss this stage when for many of us, as yet, the lower expressions of divine manifestations are dominant (or should one say "rampant"?) and even the soul fails to assume vital control?

It was for this reason (when giving the earlier tabulation) that the words "building psychologically" were used, with the intent to direct the attention of the student to the soul or psyche as the building agency, but at the same time to negate or offset the material concept of *body*-building. Occultism is the science of energy manipulation, of the attractive or the repulsive aspect of force, and it is with this that we shall concern ourselves.

In this soul activity is to be found the source or the germ of all the experiences which—on the physical plane today—are recognised and considered by the psychologist. In this thought is to be found the fact that there is no difficulty in the vehicles of expression but finds its correspondence and higher truth in the centre of experience which we call the soul.

Take, for instance, the emphasis which is laid by certain psychologists upon the idea that all that we have inherited of truth (the idea of God, the concept of a future heaven, the ancient and exploded (?) belief around which the thoughts of men have superstitiously centred) are only the outer expression or formulations of a hidden "wish life." This wish life is, we are told, based upon an inner and often hidden and unrealised sense of frustration, of disillusionment, of trouble; all the ideas which the race has prized down the ages and whereby most of its nobler souls have lived, are founded on illusion. With the formulation of these various "wish-fulfil-ments" in the life of the individual, with the fact that they lead to many difficulties and strains and stresses which require careful adjustment, and with the belief that in these concepts is mixed much of a childish superstition, the Teachers upon the inner side would find Themselves in hearty agreement in many cases. But They make the following reservation. They state that the centres of expression through which the soul gains needed experience and becomes conscious in worlds of being, otherwise unknown, have come into manifestation as the result of the "wish" or the desire of the soul. It is the "wish-life" of the soul and not the frustrations of the personality which have brought about the situation with which man is today contending. Therefore, the emerging into the public consciousness (through the teaching of certain schools of psychologists) of knowledge anent this wish life and its increasing prevalence is definitely founded upon the fact that humanity is becoming soul-conscious and, therefore, slowly becoming aware of the *wishes* of the soul. But as man's basic identifications remain as yet in the centres of expression and not in the centre of experience—the soul, there is an unavoidable, though temporary, distortion of the truth.

We can approach another psychological problem in the same manner. Much is being written today which is the result of the development of the science of psycho-analysis. This is the problem of what is commonly called a "split personality". This division in the continuity of consciousness (for that is what it basically is) takes many forms and sometimes produces more than simply a duality. The great expression of the continuity of desire is voiced for us by Paul, the initiate, in The Epistle to the Romans where he refers to the constant battle between the will-to-good and the will-to-evil, as it takes place within the periphery of consciousness of a human being. From certain angles this passage is prophetic, for the writer (perhaps unknowingly) was looking *forward* to that period in the evolution of mankind when the "battle of the opposites" would be waged in its full strength, both individually and within all nations and races. Such a time is now upon us. As far as the individual is concerned, the psychologist is attempting to deal with the problem. As far as the race is concerned, the great social, philanthropic, political and religious movements are equally concerned with the same problem. This should be of interest to all for it indicates that the planetary *kurukshetra* is now being fought out and, therefore, that present affairs must be viewed from the angle of a basic psychology, which is expressive—in time and space—of that great centre of soul expression which we call the human family. It indicates also the advanced point of attainment *in consciousness* upon the path of evolution. When the battle is successfully fought, and there is a realisation in consciousness of the nature of the issue involved (and such an awareness is most rapidly developing), then we shall have a bridging of the gap and the fusing of the fundamental pairs of opposites (the soul and the form). This will bring in the new era of spiritual attainment or of soul contact.

The thought which should be dominant in our minds today, in order that we may rightly understand the correct use of this whole section is simply this:—that the right appropriation of form by the soul is the result of an initial *wish* or desire. It is the result of a fundamental *outgoing* impulse on the part of the centre of energy. This tendency outwards is expressed in many differing words or expressions in the literature of the world, such as:

    a. The desire to manifest.
    b. The creative impulse.
    c. The evolutionary urge.

    d. The wish to incarnate.

    e. The attraction of the pairs of opposites. This is posi ·
tive energy having an attractive effect upon negative energy.

    f. The outgoing tendency.

    g. The fall of man.

    h. The "sons of God came in unto the daughters of men".

                                 (The Bible)

    i. The "corn of wheat falling into the ground".

Many such expressions can be found, having in them symbolic
quality and which are not to be interpreted literally, or with
a physical connotation. Each idea, however, involves a duality,
and the concept that there is "that which is manifesting
through the form of the manifest". This is "the soul and the
form", and many other similar phrases are familiar to all of us.

    I would urge you to preserve, as far as possible, the thought
of the psychological implications, considering this whole section from the angle in sentiency, for in sentiency (as you well
know) lies the entire psychological problem. It is always and
in every case the problem of response to environment and
opportunity, and in this idea lies much for the esoteric psychologist. In sensitive awareness lies the secret of progress for
the psyche, and also the secret of the many states of consciousness which the sentient or feeling factor, the soul, experiences on the path of evolution as it expands—

    a. The sphere of its contacts,

    b. The range of its influence,

    c. The field of its conscious activity.

I have expressed these three in the order of their appearance.

    We are apt to consider these appearances from the point
of view of man upon the physical plane. It is necessary to

consider them from the point of view of the soul and the process of experiencing. This is an angle of vision which is only truly possible to the man who is beginning to function *as a soul*.

It is here that the ray nature of any specific soul is first of all brought into activity, for its colouring, tone, quality and its basic vibration determine psychologically the colour, tone, quality and basic vibration of the mind-energy demonstrated. It conditions the sentient form attracted and the vital body which constitutes the attractive agency upon the physical plane, drawing to itself the type of negative energy or substance through which the quality, tone or vibration of the specific centre of experience can be expressed, and the environment contacted. In the early stages of manifestation, it is the nature of the form or of the vehicle which dominates and is the outstanding characteristic. The nature of quality, of the underlying soul, is *not* apparent. Then the form or vehicle is sentient in two directions: outwards towards the environment, which leads (as evolution proceeds) to the perfecting of the vehicle, and inwards towards the higher progressive impulse, which leads to the definite expansion of consciousness. These higher impulses are progressive in their appearance. It might, in this connection be stated that:

1. The physical nature becomes responsive to

    a. Desire,
    b. Ambition,
    c. Aspiration.

The fusion of the sentient, astral body and the physical body then becomes complete.

2. This basic duality then becomes responsive to

    a. The lower concrete mind,

    b. The separative impulses of the selfish mental body,

    c. The intellect, the synthesis of mind and instinct,

    d. The promptings of the soul.

This produces an integration of the three energies which constitute the threefold lower man.

3. This triplicity then becomes responsive to

    a. Itself, as an integrated personality. Then the rhythm set up by the fusion of the lower energies (the astral and the mental) becomes dominant.

    b. The Soul, as the fundamental centre of experience. The personality gets a vision of its destiny, which is to be an instrument of a higher force.

    c. The intuition.

    d. The source of inspiration, the monad.

A few students may get the symbolic significance of the process, if they grasp the fact that, in the earlier stages upon the evolutionary path, the Monad is the source of the exhalation or of the expiration which brought the soul into being upon the physical plane: upon the Path of Return, with which we are concerned in the latter stage, the Monad is the source of inhalation or of the inspiration.

    In the process of exhalation or of the breathing-out, a certain type of divine energy focussed itself as a centre of experience in that type of sentient substance which we call higher mental matter. This eventually formed that aspect of man which we call the soul. In its turn, the soul continued in this process of exhalation or breathing-out, initiated by the monad, or the One Life. The energy thus sent forth forms centres of experience in the three worlds through the process of "attractive appropriation" of qualified material or substance. Through these centres, the needed experience is gained, the life process is intensified, the range of experience through contact with an ever-widening environment becomes possible, leading to successive expansions of consciousness which are called initiations in the later stages, when consciously undergone and definitely self-initiated. Thus the field of soul influence is steadily enlarged. Whilst this soul activity is proceeding, a paralleling activity in the material substance is going on, which steadily brings the negative aspect of matter or substance up to the positive requirements of the soul. The vehicles of expression, the mechanism of manifestation and the centres for experience improve as the consciousness widens and deepens.

From the standpoint of psychology, this means that the glandular equipment, the physical apparatus, and the response instrument become increasingly efficient, whilst an inner co-ordination and integration proceeds apace. The dilemma of the psychologist today is largely due to the fact that the law of rebirth is not yet recognised scientifically or among the intelligentsia. He is therefore faced with the problems of the inequalities in the physical equipment, everywhere prevalent. There is a widespread failure to recognise the underlying cause which is responsible for the "appearance", for the mechanism. There is, therefore, no scientific proof (as the word is understood at this time) of the field of experience. There is—in time and space—no *synthesis* (esoterically understood) permitted, but simply the isolated appearance of a human being, making up hosts of human beings, variously equipped, greatly limited by that equipment, and faced also with an environment which seems antagonistic, lacking inner synthesis, coordination and integration, except in the case of the highly intelligent and deeply spiritual people, those who are definitely functioning souls. For these latter, the average psychologist has no adequate explanation.

The integration of an individual into his environment is proceeding apace, and the psychological adjustment of man to his field of experience will steadily improve. Upon this, humanity can count, and to this, the history of man's development as a *knowing* being testifies. But the integration of the human being into time has not been accomplished and even this statement will be little understood. Man's origin and his goal remain largely unconsidered, and he is studied from the angle of this one short life, and from the point of view of his present equipment. Until he is integrated into time as well as into his environment and until the Law of Rebirth is admitted as the most likely hypothesis, there will be no real understanding of the process of evolution, of the relationships of individuals, and the nature of the unfoldment of the equipment. There will be no true wisdom. *Knowledge* comes, as the individual integrates into his environment. *Wisdom* comes as he becomes coordinated into the processes of time. The mechanism is related to the environment, and is the apparatus of contact and the means through which the experiencing soul arrives at a full awareness of the field of knowledge. This soul is the identity which is time-conscious in the true sense of the word, and which views the period of manifestation *as a whole*, gaining thus a sense of proportion, an understanding of values and an inner sense of synthesis.

Little by little the triple mechanism is developed and the centre of experience expands in knowledge. Today this knowledge is of a very high order, and the world is full of personalities. Supplementing our earlier definitions, a personality might be simply defined as:

> a. An equipment which is becoming adequate in three directions of contact. The experiencing soul can now begin to use the instrument effectively.

b. An expression of the creative power of the soul which is ready to transmute knowledge into wisdom.

c. An incarnate soul, which is now ready to work consciously with the time factor, for, having learned how to work with the factor of environment, the soul can now begin to control circumstances and environment from the standpoint of time. This means, in the first instance, the right use of time and opportunity and then the establishing of continuity of consciousness.

It is not my intention to deal with the building of the various bodies. I seek here to generalise and to take up the theme from the point of attainment of modern humanity. Hints are given in *A Treatise on Cosmic Fire* which, if duly studied, will serve to elucidate the early problem of the soul's impulse to creation. We will, therefore, accept the fact of the initial creation of the forms, based upon the wish or desire to manifest, and proceed with our theme along the idea of *experience*, *expression*, and *expansion*, dealing with modern man and his problems from the standpoint of the psychological development of his problems.

c. Inter-relations of the Personality Life

In dealing now with the esoteric aspect of the appropriation of the vehicles through which a manifesting Son of God can express himself, it is impossible to avoid the use of some form of symbolic rendering of words. So long, however, as the student remembers that they are symbolic, there is no real danger of a basic misunderstanding. The analytical, intelligent mind uses forms of speech in order to limit the concept intuited within terms which can be comprehended, and abstract ideas are thereby brought down to the level of the understanding.

We have seen that our major consideration must be that of *the soul as a centre of consciousness* and of *the bodies as a centre of experience*, and with this postulate we lay the foundation for our future psychological investigations. We are not here dealing with the question of why this is so, or of how it may have come about. We accept the statement as basic and fundamental, and take our stand upon the premise that the nature of life in the world is experience-gaining, because we see this happening around us on every side and can note it occurring in our own lives.

We can divide people into three groups:

1. Those who are unconsciously gaining experience, but are at the same time so engrossed with the processes of the results of experiencing, that they remain unaware of the deeper objectives.

2. Those who are dimly awakening to the fact that adaptation to the ways of living to which they are subjected, and from which there seems no escape, means for them the learning of some lesson which

   a. Enriches their lives, usually in the practical and material sense.
   b. Intensifies their sensitive perception.
   c. Permits of the development of quality and the steady acquiring of characteristics, facilities and capacities.

3. Those who are awakened to the purpose of experience, and who are consequently bringing to every event an intelligent power to extract from the happenings to which they are subjected some gain to the life of the soul. They have learnt to regard the environment in which they find themselves as the place of purification and the field of their planned service.

This is a rough and broad generalisation, but it accounts for human experience and consequent attitudes in the three major groupings.

It is of interest to bear in mind that the process of the appropriation of the bodies, presents similar stages with respect to the evolution of the form and to the evolution of the indwelling life. In the history of the material aspect of manifestation, there have been (as the occult books teach) the following stages:

1. The stage of involution, or of appropriation, and of construction of the vehicles of expression upon the downward arc, where the emphasis is upon the building, growth and appropriation of the bodies, and not so much upon the indwelling, conscious Entity.
2. The stage of evolution, or of refinement and the development of quality, leading to liberation upon the upward arc.

It is the same in the psychological history of the human being. There too we find a somewhat similar process, divided into two stages, marking the involution and the evolution of consciousness.

Hitherto in the occult books (as I earlier pointed out) the emphasis has been upon the development of the form side of life, and upon the nature and quality of that form as it responds, upon different levels of the planetary life, to the impact of the environment in the early stages and to the impress of the soul at the later stages. In this Treatise with which we are now engaged, our primary aim is to point out the effect upon the soul of the experiences undergone in the bodies, and the process whereby the consciousness aspect of divinity is expanded, culminating as it does in what is technically called an initiation. Each of the two major divisions of this process—involution and evolution—could be divided into six definite expansions of consciousness. Those upon the upward arc differ from those upon the downward arc in objective and motive and in scope, and are essentially sublimations of the lower aspects of the unfoldment of consciousness. These six stages might be called:

1. The stage of Appropriation.
2. The stage of Aspiration.
3. The stage of Approach.
4. The stage of Appearance.
5. The stage of Activity.
6. The stage of Ambition.

Each stage, when at its height of expression, involves a period of crisis. This crisis precedes the unfoldment of the next stage in the conscious awakening of man. We here are viewing *Man* as a conscious thinker, and not man as a member of the fourth kingdom in nature. Ponder upon this distinction, for it marks the points of emphasis and the focus of the identification.

In the first stage of *appropriation*, we have the soul or the conscious thinker (the divine son of God, or manasaputra) doing three things:

1. Consciously registering the desire to incarnate. This is the will to exist or the will-to-be upon the physical plane.
2. Consciously focussing attention on the processes involved in the decision to "make an appearance".
3. Consciously taking the necessary steps to appropriate the needed substance through which to appear and thereby satisfy the demand for existence.

With these processes, formulated as theories, we are familiar. The speculations and pronouncements of teachers everywhere, and down the ages, have familiarised us with the many symbolic ways of dealing with these matters. Upon them there is no need to enlarge. The whole series of events involved in the decision are to be considered here only from the angle of consciousness and of a defined involutionary procedure.

The second stage of *aspiration* concerns the aspiration or the desire of the soul to appear, and brings the consciousness down on to what we call the astral plane. The inclination of the soul is towards that which is material. We must not forget this fact. We have been apt to regard aspiration as the consummation or the transmutation of desire. However, in the last analysis, it might be said that aspiration is the basis or root of all desire and that we have only used the word "desire" to signify aspiration which has a natural object in the consciousness of man, confining the word "aspiration" to that transmuted desire which makes the soul the fixed objective in the life of the man in incarnation. But all phases of desire are essentially forms of aspiration and, on the involutionary arc, aspiration shows itself as the desire of the soul to experience in consciousness those processes which will make it conscious and dynamic in the world of human affairs.

When this conscious realisation is established and the soul has appropriated a form upon the mental plane through the will to exist, and one also upon the astral plane through aspiration, then the third stage of *approach* takes place upon etheric levels. The consciousness becomes focussed there, preparatory to the intense crisis of "appearing", and there takes place what might be regarded as a ranging or a gathering of all the forces of the consciousness in order to force the issue and thus emerge into manifestation. This is a vital moment in consciousness; it is a period of vital preparation for a great spiritual event—the coming into incarnation of a son of God.

This involves the taking of a dense physical body which will act either as a complete prison for the soul or as a "form for revelation", as it has been called, in the cases of those advanced men whom we regard as the revealed sons of God.

The crisis of approach is one of the most important and one of the least understood of the various stages. Students should find it of interest to make a comparative study of the approaches which have previously been mentioned in connection with such episodes in human history as those occurring at the time of the Wesak Full Moon. There is a close underlying relationship between the approaches upon the path of involution and those upon the path of evolution, and also between those taken by an individual and those by a group.

Then, when the gathering of forces during the stage of approach is consummated, the fourth stage takes place, that of *appearance*, and the man emerges into the light of day and runs his little cycle upon the physical plane, developing increased sensitivity in consciousness, through the medium of experience gained through the processes of life in a physical body. After appearing in form, he becomes (with each new appearance) increasingly active and alive and awake, and the stage of *activity* grows in intensity until the consciousness of the man is swept by *ambition*.

The two final stages of activity and of ambition are those covered by the ordinary man and dealt with by the ordinary psychologist. This is itself of interest, because it shows how very little of the life of the real man, of the conscious thinking Being is touched by the orthodox, exoteric psychologist. The four stages of man's development which lie behind his active appearance upon the physical plane are not considered at all. The intensity of the process of approach which preceded that appearance is not dealt with, yet it is basically a determining factor. But this activity upon the physical plane and the nature of his desire life (which is only translated into terms of ambition later on in his life experience) are the dominant factors to be considered. It is, of course, exceedingly difficult for there to be a true understanding of man until the theory of rebirth is admitted and man is accounted for in terms of a long preceding history. In this age of intensest separative thinking and attitudes, it is the individual life of the individual man, separate in time and space from all that has gone before, and from all that surrounds him in the present, which is considered as of importance and as constituting a man. Man, as an expression of a soul process, is not dealt with in any way.

Thus we have the stages succeeding each other from the initial appropriation upon the mental plane until the man, in consciousness, has worked his way down through the planes and back again to the mental plane, which brings him to the stage of the coordination of the personality, and the emergence into full expression of what we call the personality ray. Life after life takes place. Again and again, the soul incarnates and, in consciousness, passes through the stages outlined above. But gradually a higher sense of values supervenes; there comes a period when desire for material experience and for ambitious personality satisfactions begins to fade out; newer and better values and higher standards of thought and desire begin slowly to appear.

The consciousness aspect then passes through all the stages upon which we have touched but in reverse order, and this time upon the upward arc, corresponding to the evolutionary stage in the great cycle of natural processes, concerned with the form life. It expands slowly from the consciousness of ambition through activity and the succeeding unfoldments, to the stage of approach to the divine reality upon the mental plane and that of the final appropriation, wherein the consciousness of man, becomes merged in that of the soul upon its own level, and finally appropriates in full awareness (if one can use so paradoxical a phrase) the *One*.

When the consciousness of the soul, incarnate in a human form, arrives at a realisation of the futility of material *ambition*, it marks a high stage of personality integration and precedes a period of change or of a shift in *activity*. During this second stage upon the Path of Return, the shift of the consciousness is away from the physical body altogether, into the etheric or vital body, and from thence into the astral body. There duality is sensed and the battle of the pairs of opposites takes place. The disciple makes his *appearance* as Arjuna. Only after the battle and only when Arjuna has made his fateful decisions, is it possible for him to make his *approach* upon the mental plane to the soul. This he does by

1. Realising himself as a soul and not as the form. This involves a process of what is called "divine reflection", which works out in two ways. The soul now begins definitely to reject the form, and the man, through whom the soul is experiencing and expressing itself, is himself rejected by the world in which he lives.

2. Discovering the group to which he belongs, blocking his way of approach until he discovers the way of approach by service.

3. Identifying himself with his group upon his own ray and so earning the right to make his approach, because he has learnt the lesson that "he travels not alone".

Then comes that peculiar stage of transcendent *aspiration*, wherein desire for individual experience is lost and only the longing to function as a conscious part of the greater Whole remains. Then and only then can the conscious soul *appropriate* the "body of light and of splendour, the expression of the glory of the One" which, when once assumed, makes all future incarnations in the three worlds impossible, except as an act of the spiritual will. The significance of the above may be found difficult of comprehension for it is one of the mysteries of a higher initiation.

Therefore, it will be seen that we begin and we end with an expansion of consciousness. The first one led to the inclusion of the material world, and the second one includes or appropriates, consciously and intelligently, the spiritual world. We see the desire consciousness transmuted into aspiration for the spiritual realities and the focussed, vital approach to the kingdom of God. We see the appearance on the physical plane of the imprisoned consciousness, limited and confined for purposes of defined, intelligent development, within an evolving form, and the final emergence upon the mental plane of the enriched, released consciousness into the full freedom of the Mind of God. We see the activity of the conscious mind of man slowly expanding and intensifying, until it becomes the activity of the illumined mind, reflecting the divine consciousness of the soul. We see the ambition of the conscious man transformed at first into the spiritual ambition of the pledged disciple and finally into the expression of the Will of God or of the Monad, in the initiate.

Thus the three aspects of divinity are released upon earth through the medium of an incarnated and fully developed consciousness, that of a Son of God. From the conscious appropriation of form back again to the conscious appropriation of divinity is the work carried forward and the plan of Deity worked out. Laying the ground, as we are now proposing to do, for the study of integration in connection with the human being, it will not be necessary for us to deal in detail with the many phases of the various stages we have been considering. Thousands of human beings, indeed perhaps millions, will be found on our planet, at any one time, who will illustrate in their lives and activities some one point or other upon the downward or the upward arc. For the majority, the expert assistance of the modern trained educator and psychologist, the churchman or the physician, will suffice to give the needed aid, particularly when three happenings eventuate, which will inevitably be the case before so many decades have gone by:

1. These four types of experts—educators, psychologists, churchmen and physicians—will work in conjunction with each other, and each will place his skill and his peculiar point of view and interpretation of conditions at the disposal of his fellow workers.
2. The fact of the soul will be admitted as a reasonable hypothesis, and the fact that there may be an indwelling entity, seeking to control in some measure the mechanism, will also be accepted.
3. The Law of Rebirth will be regarded as a law in nature, and place will be given in the thoughts of these four groups of human helpers, for a man's past and his rapidly developing future.

In this Treatise, we are considering those more advanced people who constitute the intelligentsia of the world, who are beginning to use the mind, who are upon the probationary path, or who are nearing the Path of Discipleship. When this is the case (and it seldom occurs before, unless to the eye of the initiate) the personalities are so refined that the personality ray and the egoic ray permit of analysis and definition. Until there is sufficient *pronounced* development to allow of a true diagnosis, it is not possible to say definitely what is the ray of the personality. The defining of the egoic ray comes later still and can only be surmised at first from the nature of the conflict of which the personality is aware, based as it will be on a growing sense of duality. It will also be capable of expert diagnosis from certain physical and psychical characteristics which indicate the quality of the higher nature of the person concerned, and also through a study of the type of a man's group affiliations as they begin to appear upon the physical plane. A man who—being, through personality predilection, a creative artist—suddenly takes a deep and profound interest in mathematics, might be inferred to be coming under the influence of a second ray soul; or a man, whose whole personality was definitely upon the sixth ray of fanatical idealism or devotion to an object of his idealism, and who had functioned during life as a religious devotee, and who then switched the centre of his life interest into scientific investigation, might be, therefore, responding to a fifth ray soul impression.

We shall, therefore, study the process of coordination and the methods whereby two great integrations take place:

1. The integration of the personality, or the means whereby the consciousness of the person
   a. Shifts out of one body into another, so that a definite expansion of consciousness takes place.
   b. Begins to be active in all the three personality vehicles simultaneously.
2. The integration of the personality and the soul so that the soul can
   a. Function through any one body at will, or
   b. Function through all the three bodies which constitute the personality simultaneously.

This will lead us to confine ourselves to the study of the more advanced or pronounced types, which are primarily the mystic, the aspirant, the notable people, and those who constitute the people with psychological problems of our present time and period.

Step by step, the various bodies have been developed, utilised, refined and organised; step by step the sensory apparatus of man has been sensitised and used, until the world today is full of men and women whose response apparatus, and whose instruments of contact are as far removed in effectiveness from those of primitive man as are the vehicles of the average modern man from those of the Christ and the Buddha, with Their immensely wide range of subjective and divine awareness. Step by step, the unfoldment of the nervous system has paralleled that of the inner psychical apparatus, and the glandular equipment has faithfully reflected that of the great centres of force, with their inter-connecting lines of energy. Step by step, the consciousness of man has shifted from:

1. That of the purely animal, with its emphasis upon the natural physical appetites, into that of the vital, personal being, responding to the impacts of an environment which he does not intelligently understand but in which he finds himself. This is the primitive and so-called savage state of consciousness and lies far behind us today, in a distant racial history. This primitive stage saw the birth of that religious direction to which we give the name of animism.

2. That of a vital, primitive being into that state of consciousness which is coloured almost entirely by desire for material satisfaction. This in time transmutes itself into that of an emotional response to the environing conditions, leading thus to an intensified "wish-life", a development of the imaginative faculty. It ends finally in the production of the *Mystic*, with his aspiration, his sense of

duality, and his reaching out after God, plus an intense devotion to an ideal of some kind or another.

3. That of the vital, emotional, desire emphasis and state of longing into that of a mental consciousness,—intelligent, enquiring, intellectually sensitive, responsive to thought currents and reacting with increasing steadiness, vigour and sensitivity to the impact of ideas.

4. That of one or another of these states of consciousness, alternating in their emphasis, or predominantly active in some one or other of these lower aspects, to that of integrated personality, selfishly occupied with self-emphasis, self-interest, self-expression, and so demonstrating as a great or intrepid individual, demonstrating power and purpose in a world which he exploits for his own selfish ends.

When this stage is reached, the focus of the life is predominantly material, and the man is ambitious, effective, and powerful. Yet there slowly arises in him a divine discontent; the savor of his life experience and enterprises begins to prove unsatisfactory. Another shift in consciousness takes place, and he reaches out—at first unconsciously and later consciously—to the life and significance of a dimly sensed reality. The soul is beginning to make its presence felt, and to grip in a different sense than hitherto, and in a more active manner, its vehicles of expression and of service.

In this summary, we have sketched the broad general outlines of the process. It will be obvious that there will be gradations in the process and men will be found on earth at every stage of consciousness. One will be equipped with vehicles in which the emphasis is upon the sensory life. In some cases there will be found a consciousness which is shifting its emphasis out of one vehicle into another, and so becoming awake and more inclusive in its range of contacts and in its awareness. Others again will be possessed of a consciousness which is organising itself for full expression as a man, as an integrated personality and as a worker for material ends, bringing to bear upon those objectives all the force and power of an integrated functioning person. There will be those whose consciousness is gradually awakening to a new and higher sense of values, and is slowly at first and more rapidly as facility is acquired, shifting its focus of attention out of the world of material, selfish living into that of true spiritual realities.

Little by little, the consciousness of the third aspect of divinity is coordinated with that of the second, and the Christ consciousness is aroused into activity through the medium of experience in form. Man begins to add to the gained personality experience of the three worlds of human endeavour, the intuitive spiritual perception which is the heritage of those who are awake within the kingdom of God. Paralleling this development of the consciousness in man is the evolution of the instruments whereby that consciousness is brought en rapport with a rapidly expanding world of sensory perception, of intellectual concepts and of intuitive recognitions. With the development of this form aspect we will not concern ourselves, beyond pointing out that, as the consciousness shifts from one body to another and its range of contacts, therefore, steadily expands, the centres in man's etheric body (three below and four above the diaphragm) are awakened in three major stages, though through the medium of many smaller awakenings.

1. They begin to develop from that of the "closed bud to that of the opened lotus". This takes place during the period of ordinary evolution.

2. The petals of the lotus become vibrant and alive. This is the stage of personality integration.
3. The heart of the lotus, "the jewel in the lotus" also becomes actively alive. This is the period of the final stages upon the Path.

This process of unfoldment is itself brought about by five crises of awakening, so that we have a threefold process and a fivefold movement.

1. The centres below the diaphragm are the controlling and dominant factor. The stage of dense materiality, of lower desire and of physical urge is in full expression. This was carried to its higher point of development in Lemurian times. The sacral centre was the controlling factor.
2. The centres below the diaphragm become fully active, with the major emphasis in the solar plexus centre. This centre eventually becomes the great clearing house for all the lower forces and marks the period of the shift into a higher body, the astral body. This was characteristic of Atlantean racial development.
3. The awakening of the throat centre and the shift of much of the lower energy into the throat activity. The ajna centre also begins to become active, producing integrated and creative personalities. This stage is characteristic of the present Aryan race.
4. The awakening of the heart centre and the shift of the solar plexus energy into that centre, thus producing groups and the entrance of a new and fuller sense of spiritual energy. The shift of emphasis is then into those states of awareness which reveal the kingdom of God. The fifth kingdom in nature becomes creatively active

on earth. This will be characteristic of the consciousness of the next great race.

5. The awakening of the head centre, with the consequent arousing of the kundalini fire at the base of the spine. This leads to the final integration of soul and body, and the appearance of a perfected humanity upon earth. This will express the nature of the final race.

Forget not that there are at all times those who are characteristically expressing one or another of all of these various stages and states of consciousness. There are but a few on earth today who are capable of expressing as low a state of relative development as the Lemurian consciousness. There are a few at the extreme end of the *Way* who are expressing divine perfection, and in between these two extremes are all possible grades of development and unfoldment.

Man is therefore (from the angle of force expression) a mass of conflicting energies and an active centre of moving forces with a shift of emphasis constantly going on, and with the aggregation of the numerous streams of energy presenting a confusing kaleidoscope of active inter-relations, interpenetration, internecine warfare, and interdependence until such time as the personality forces (symbolic of divine multiplicity) are subdued or "brought into line" by the dominant soul. That is what we really mean by the use of the word "alignment". This alignment results from:

1. The control of the personality by the soul.
2. The downpouring of soul energy, via the mental and the emotional bodies, into the brain, thus producing the subjugation of the lower nature, the awakening of the brain consciousness to soul awareness, and a new alignment of the bodies.

3. The right arrangement, according to ray type, of the energies which are motivating and dynamically arousing the centres into activity. This leads eventually to a direct alignment of the centres upon the spine, so that soul energy can pass up and down through the centres from the directing centre in the head. Whilst this process of soul control is being perfected (and the time consumed is, from the angle of the limiting personality consciousness, of vast duration), the ray types of the vehicles steadily emerge, the ray of the personality begins to control the life, and finally the soul ray begins to dominate the personality ray and subdue its activity.

Eventually, the monadic ray takes control, absorbing into itself the rays of the personality and of the soul (at the third and fifth initiations) and thus duality is finally and definitely overcome and "only the *One Who Is* remains."

We can now deal with the coordination of the personality, with its three types of techniques previously mentioned, which are the techniques of integration, the techniques of fusion and the techniques of duality. We will then pass on to a consideration of some of the problems with which psychology has to deal, arising as they do, out of the shifting consciousness, the intensification of the energy reception by the centres, and the inflow of soul potency. This will bring us to a point in our Treatise in which the rays and the human being will have been somewhat considered, and where we can eventually and with profit deal with that point, the third pertaining to the Ray of Personality, which we are in process of completing. It concerns education, the psychological training of aspirants and disciples, and the trends to be found emerging in the new esoteric psychology.

2. *The Coordination of the Personality*

We have considered, cursorily I realise, the fact that the ego appropriates to itself forms, through which expression can be made possible upon the various levels of divine manifestation. We observed that these forms, in due process of time, become embodiments of the will and purpose of their divine Indweller. This Indweller is the soul. As the evolutionary cycle runs its course, three developments take place:

1. The forms for expression are developed, little by little as a result of:

   a. Successive incarnations.
   b. The impulse and consequent activity of desire.
   c. The interpretation of experience, intensifying and becoming more correct and adequate as time passes.

2. The self within, or identified with, the form nature,

   a. Becomes slowly conscious and consequently intelligently active in the three worlds of human evolution.
   b. Shifts its focus of attention successively from one body to another, passing, in consciousness, into higher and higher states of awareness until the Path of Pursuit becomes the Path of Return, and desire for identification with form changes into aspiration for self-awareness. Later, comes identification with Self on its own level of consciousness.
   c. Reorients itself and thus occultly "leaves behind the hitherto desirable and aspires to that which has not hitherto been seen."

3. The aspirant passes through an intermediate stage in the

process of evolution wherein "divine attraction" supersedes the attraction of the three worlds. This stage falls into five parts:

a. A period wherein duality and lack of control are realised.

b. A period wherein an assertion of self-control takes place, through the following process:

 1. Decentralisation.
 2. Comprehension of the task ahead.
 3. An investigation, by the divine Observer of the nature of form life.
 4. Divine expression, through the medium of the form, understandingly practised.

c. A period wherein alignment takes place, and (through understanding and practice) the form is gradually subordinated to the requirements of the Self, and begins to work in unison with that Self.

d. A period wherein the forms, aligned at increasingly frequent intervals, are
 1. Integrated into a functioning, active personality;
 2. Swept by the power of their own dominant, integrated, personality life;
 3. Gradually controlled by the Self, and fused into an instrument for effective world service;
 4. Unified, in intent and purpose, with the soul.

e. A period wherein the personality ray and the soul ray are blended into one united energy, and the personality ray becomes a quality of, and complementary to, that of the soul, making soul purpose in the three worlds possible.

It is thus that we progress, and in this manner form and consciousness, appearance and quality, are brought together and divine unity is achieved, thus ending the duality hitherto sensed, which up till this time has handicapped the aspirant.

Two angles of this matter warrant our attention. One is that covering the processes of the past evolutionary cycle which, as it has transpired, has brought the aspirant to the point of a sensed duality, of consequent struggle, and of a hardly achieved reorientation towards reality. That period has been adequately covered, for all present purposes, by science, exoteric and esoteric. The other is the period of ultimate perfection which is finally achieved as a result of the struggle. One period lies far behind us, and intelligent humanity has travelled far towards the period of realisation; the other period lies far ahead. We will confine our studies to the task of the aspirant as he reorients himself upon the probationary path, and becomes increasingly aware of the world of higher values, and of the existence of the kingdom of God. On this path he senses his duality in an almost distressing manner, and begins to aspire towards unity. This is the task today of the vast numbers of world aspirants. So widespread is the desire for this reorientation that it has produced the present world upheaval, and is the spiritual source of the specific cause of the ideological conflicts now going on in every country.

We will deal with the work of the disciples of the world as, having endeavoured to bring about the desired reorientation, they learn the basic necessity of integrating the personality, and from that pass on to achieve contact or fusion with the Self, the ego or soul. It will be wise to keep these three stages carefully in mind, because all the many modern psychological problems are founded upon—

1. The process of reorientation with its consequences of personality upheaval and disorders.

2. The process of integration which is going on within the lower nature of intelligent humanity, leading inevitably to duality and conflict.

3. The fusion of the personality and the soul *in consciousness*, with its physiological and personality effects, producing the problems and psychological dilemmas of the highly developed aspirant and disciple. In this stage, the so-called "diseases of mystics" become pronounced.

We will also touch very briefly upon the efforts of the initiate as he works through and with the subdued mechanism of the personality in the service of the Plan. He in his turn—as a functioning soul and body, united, aligned and used—becomes gradually aware of a still higher synthesis. After the third initiation, he enters upon a renewed effort to produce a more inclusive fusion and integration,—this time with the monad or life aspect. About this later stage, little can be profitably said. Teaching which would be intelligible to an initiate of the third degree would be profitless and unintelligible even to the highly integrated and intelligent disciple, especially as such teaching is given necessarily through the use of most abstract and complicated symbols, requiring careful analysis and interpretation. None of this higher teaching is given through the medium of words, either spoken or written.

a. Seven Techniques of Integration

Let us now proceed to a consideration of the seven techniques of integration, bearing in mind that we shall here be dealing with the *integration* of the threefold lower nature into an active, conscious personality, prior to its *fusion* into a unity with the soul. We must remember that we are here dealing with the consciousness aspect of manifestation and its apprehension and appreciation of purpose and of truth. We are so apt always to think in terms of form and form activity, that it seems necessary again and again to reiterate the necessity for thinking in terms of consciousness and awareness, leading to an eventual realisation. This purpose and truth, when grasped, brings into direct conflict the will of the personality (the separative individual, governed by the concrete, analytical mind) and the will of the soul, which is the will of the Hierarchy of Souls, or of the Kingdom of God. In the fourth kingdom, the human, the controlling factor is that of desire, ending in aspiration. In the fifth kingdom, the spiritual, the controlling factor is that of divine purpose or the will of God. Then we find this purpose, though free from what we call desire, is actuated by love, expressed through devotion and service, wrought out into full expression upon the physical plane.

As may be naturally surmised, there is a technique for each of the seven rays. It is the ray of the ego or soul, slumbering in the early stages within the form, which occultly applies these modes of integration. The soul is essentially the integrative factor, and this shows in the early and unconscious stages as the coherent power of the life principle to hold the forms together in incarnation. In the later and conscious stages, it shows its power by applying these methods of control and unification to the personality. They are not applied, nor can the man avail himself of them, until such time as he is an integrated personality. This has often been forgotten, and men have claimed the rights of discipleship and the powers of initiation before they have even become integrated persons. This has led to disaster, and the falling into disrepute of the whole problem of discipleship and initiation.

It is difficult to make easily comprehensible the nature and purpose of these techniques. All that it is possible to do is to indicate the seven ray techniques as they are applied to the rapidly aligning bodies of the lower man. We will divide our theme, for the sake of clarity and for an understanding of the significance, into two parts. The first one is that in which the first ray aspect of the technique is applied to the form nature, producing destruction through crystallisation. This brings about the "death of the form" in order that it may "again arise and live". The other is the second ray aspect of the technique, wherein the rebuilding, reabsorption, and recognition of the form takes place in the light which is thrown around, over and upon the personality. In that light, the man sees Light, and thus becomes eventually a light-bearer.

What I have to say concerning each ray and its work with the individuals upon it in integrating the personalities, will be conveyed by means of a formula of integration. This will itself be divided into two parts, dealing with those processes in time and space which bring about the integration of the personality.

The words, covering the process in every case, are *Alignment, Crisis, Light, Revelation, Integration*. Under the heading of each ray we shall have therefore:

1. The formula of integration.
2. Its dual application of destruction and rebuilding, with a brief indication of the process and the result.
3. The final stage of the process wherein the man

   a. Brings the three bodies into *alignment*.

   b. Passes through a *crisis* of evocation, thus, as the Bhagavad Gita says, becoming "manifest through the magical power of the soul".

c. Enters into a phase of *light*, wherein the man sees clearly the next step to be taken.

d. Receives the *revelation* of the Plan and of what he has to do in connection with it.

e. *Integrates* the three bodies into one synthetic whole, and is therefore ready for the Technique of Fusion, which is suited to his ray type.

This will bring us to our second point which concerns the *Technique of Fusion* and the emergence into activity of the personality ray.

Just what do we mean by *Integration?* We are apt to bandy words about with unthinking lightness and inexactitude, but, dealing as we are with a development which is becoming increasingly prevalent in the human field, it might profit us for a moment to define it and seek to understand one or two of its major implications. It has to be regarded as an essential step, prior to passing (in full and waking consciousness) into the fifth, or spiritual kingdom. We regard the physical body as a functioning aggregate of physical organs, each with its own duties and purposes. These, when combined and acting in unison, we regard as constituting a living organism. The many parts form one whole, working under the direction of the intelligent, conscious Thinker, the soul, as far as man is concerned. At the same time, this conscious form is slowly arriving at a point where integration into the larger whole becomes desirable and is finally achieved—again in the waking consciousness. This process of conscious assimilation is carried forward progressively by the gradual integration of the part into the family unit, the nation, the social order, the current civilisation, the world of nations, and finally into humanity itself. This integration is, therefore, both physical in nature, and an attitude of mind. The consciousness of the man is gradually aroused so that it recognises this relation of the part to the whole, with the implied inter-relation of all parts within the whole.

The man who has awakened to full consciousness in the various aspects of his nature—emotional, mental and egoic—realises himself first of all as a personality. He integrates his various bodies with their different states of consciousness into one active reality. He is then definitely a personality and has passed a major milestone on the Path of Return. This is the first great step. Inevitably, the evolutionary process must bring to pass this phenomenal occurrence in the case of every human being, but it can be produced (and is increasingly so produced today) by a planned mental application to the task, and an intelligent consideration of the relation of the part to the whole. It will be found that the purely selfish, material personality will eventually arrive at the condition wherein the man will be conscious of integrated activity and power, because he

1. Has developed and integrated his own separative "parts" into one whole.
2. Has studied and used his environment, or the whole of which his personality is but a part, in such a way that it contributes to his desire, his success, and his emergence into prominence. In doing this, he necessarily has had to make some living contribution to the whole, in order to evoke its integrating power. His motive, however, being purely selfish and material in objective, can only carry him a certain distance along the path of the higher integration.

The unselfish, spiritually oriented man also integrates the various aspects of himself into one functioning whole, but the focus of his activity is *contribution*, not acquisition, and, by the working of the higher law, the Law of Service, he becomes integrated, not only as a human being within the radius of the prevalent civilisation, but also into that wider and more inclusive world of conscious activity which we call the Kingdom of God.

The progress of humanity is from one *realised* integration to another; man's basic integrity is, however, in the realm of consciousness. This is a statement of importance. It might be remarked—speaking loosely and generally—that

1. In Lemurian times, humanity achieved the integration of the vital or etheric body with the physical body.
2. In Atlantean times, humanity added to the already achieved synthesis still another part, that of the astral nature, and psychic man came definitely into being. He was alive and at the same time sensitive and responsive to his environment in a wider and more specialised sense.
3. Today, in our Aryan race, humanity is occupied with the task of adding still another aspect, that of the mind. To the achieved facts of livingness and sensitivity, he is rapidly adding reason, mental perception and other qualities of mind and thought life.
4. Advanced humanity upon the Probationary Path is fusing these three divine aspects into one whole, which we call the personality. Many hundreds of thousands stand at this time upon that Path, and are acting, feeling and thinking simultaneously, making of these functions one activity. This personality synthesis comes upon the Path of Discipleship, under the direction of the indwelling entity, the spiritual man.

This integration constitutes alignment and—when a man has achieved this—he passes eventually through a process of reorientation. This reveals to him, as he slowly changes his direction, the still greater Whole of humanity. Later, upon the Path of Initiation, there will dawn upon his vision, the *Whole* of which humanity itself is only an expression. This is the subjective world of reality, into which we begin definitely to enter as we become members of the Kingdom of God.

5. Upon the Probationary Path, though only during its later stages, he begins to serve humanity consciously through the medium of his integrated personality, and thus the consciousness of the larger and wider whole gradually supersedes his individual and separative consciousness. He knows himself to be but a part.

6. Upon the Path of Discipleship, the process of integration into the Kingdom of God, the Kingdom of Souls, proceeds until the third initiation is undergone.

All these various integrations work out into some definite form of activity. First, there is the service of the personality, selfish and separative, wherein man sacrifices much in the interests of his own desire. Then comes the stage of service of humanity, and, finally, the service of the Plan. However, the integration with which we shall primarily deal as we study the seven *Techniques of Integration* is that of the personality as it integrates into the whole of which it is a part, through service to the race and to the Plan. Bear in mind that these ray techniques are *imposed by the soul upon the personality after it has been somewhat integrated into a functioning unity* and is, therefore, becoming slightly responsive to the soul, the directing Intelligence.

Ray One

"*The love of power* must dominate. There must also be repudiation of those forms which wield no power.
The word goes forth from soul to form; 'Stand up. Press

outward into life. Achieve a goal. For you, there must be not a circle, but a line.

Prepare *the form*. Let the eyes look forward, not on either side. Let the ears be closed to all the outer voices, and the hands clenched, the body braced, and mind alert. Emotion is not used in furthering of the Plan. Love takes its place.'

The symbol of a moving point of light appears above the brow. The keynote of the life though uttered not, yet still is clearly heard: 'I move to power. I am the One. We are a Unity in power. And all is for the power and glory of the *One*.' "

Such is the pattern of the thought and the process of the life of the man upon the first ray who is seeking first of all to control his personality, and then to dominate his environment. His progress is that of "achieved control; that of being controlled, and then again controlling." At first, his motive is that of selfish, separative achievement, and then comes failure to be satisfied. A higher achievement then takes place as a result of the service of the Plan, until the time eventually comes when the first ray man can be trusted to be God's Destroying Angel—the Angel who brings life through the destruction of the form. Such integrated personalities are frequently ruthless at first, selfish, ambitious, self-centered, cruel, one-pointed, implacable, undeviating, aware of implications, of significances, and of the results of action but, at the same time, unalterable and undeviating, moving forward to their purposes. They destroy and tear down in order to rise to greater heights upon the ruin they have wrought. They do thus rise. They trample on other men and upon the destinies of the little person. They integrate their surroundings into an instrument for their will and move relentlessly forward upon their own occasions. This type of man will be found expressing these qualities in all walks of life and spheres of action, and is a destroying force in his home, business or in the nation. All this is made possible because the first ray has at this stage integrated the personality vehicles and has achieved their simultaneous control. The man functions as a *whole*.

This process and method of work brings him eventually to a *point of crisis*,—a crisis based upon the unalterable fact of his essentially divine nature or being, which cannot remain satisfied with the gaining of power in a personality sense and in a material world. Power selfishly used exhausts its user and evokes a display of power antagonistic to him; he is thereby destroyed, because he has destroyed. He is separated off from his fellow men because he has been isolated and separative in his nature. He walks alone because he has cried forth to the world: "I will brook no companion; I am the one alone."

This crisis of evocation brings him to an inner point of change which involves an alteration in his direction, a change of method, and a different attitude. These three changes are described in the *Old Commentary* (in which these techniques are to be found) in the following terms:

> "The one who travels on a line returns upon his way. Back to the centre of his life he goes, and there he waits. He reaches out his arms and cries: I cannot stand and walk alone. And standing thus, a cross is formed and on that cross he takes his place—with others."

The change of direction takes him back to the centre of his being, the heart; a change of method takes place, for, instead of moving straight forward, he waits in patience and seeks to feel. A change of attitude can be noted, for he reaches out his arms to his fellow men—to the greater whole—and thus becomes inclusive.

Standing thus in quietness at the centre, and searching within himself for responsiveness to his environment, he thus loses sight of self and the light breaks in. It is as if a curtain were raised. In that light, the first thing which is revealed to him is the devastating sight of that which he has destroyed.

He is subjected to what has esoterically been called "the light which shocks." Slowly and laboriously, using every power of his aligned personality and, in his realised desperation, calling in the power of his soul, he proceeds one-pointedly to rebuild that which he has destroyed. In rebuilding, he lifts the entire structure on to a higher level than any he has hitherto touched. This is the task of the destroyers and of those who work with civilisations and who can be trusted to act as agents of destruction under the Plan.

It is interesting to note that when this stage is reached (the stage of rebuilding as the first ray man understands it), he will usually pass through four incarnations in which he is first of all "the man at the centre," a focal point of immobile power. He is conscious of his power, gained whilst functioning as a selfish destroyer, but he is also conscious of frustration and futility. Next he passes through a life in which he begins to reorganise himself for a different type of activity, and it will be found that in these cases he will have a third or a seventh ray personality. In the third incarnation he definitely begins rebuilding and works through a second ray personality until, in the fourth life, he can function safely through a first ray personality without losing his spiritual balance, if we might use such a phrase. Through this type of personality, his first ray soul can demonstrate, because the disciple has "recovered feeling, gained divine emotion, and filled his waiting heart with love." In such cases as this, the astral body is usually on the second ray, the mental body upon the fourth ray, and the physical body upon the sixth ray. This naturally tends to balance or offset the intensity of the first ray vibrations of the personality and soul. It is in the third life of reorientation that he gains the reward for the arresting of his selfish efforts, and aspects of the Plan are then revealed to him.

Ray Two

" 'Again I stand; a point within a circle and yet myself.'
The love of love must dominate, not love of being loved.
The power to draw unto oneself must dominate, but into the
worlds of form that power must some day fail to penetrate.
This is the first step towards a deeper search.

The word goes forth from soul to form: 'Release thyself
from all that stands around, for it has naught for thee, so look
to me. I am the One who builds, sustains and draws thee
on and up. Look unto me with eyes of love, and seek the
path which leads from the outer circle to the point.

I, at the point, sustain. I, at the point, attract. I, at the
point, direct and choose and dominate. I, at the point, love
all, drawing them to the centre and moving forward with
the travelling points towards that great Centre where the
One Point stands.' What mean you by that *Word?*"

In reference to this second ray, it is advisable to recollect
that all the rays are but the subrays of the second Ray of
Love-Wisdom. The One in the centre, Who is the "point
within the circle" of manifestation, has three major qualities:
life or activity in form, love and the power of abstraction. It
is these last two qualities of Deity with which we are concerned in these formulas and (in connection with the second
ray) the dualities of attraction and abstraction emerge, both
latent and both capable of perfected activity in their own
field.

There comes ever the moment in the life of the aspirant
when he begins to consider with wonder the significance of
that familiar reaction of finding no satisfaction in the familiar
things; the old life of desire for well known forms of existence and expression ceases to attract his interest. The pull or
attractive power of the *One* at the centre (Who is his true
self) also fails. It is not yet a familiar "call." The aspirant is
left, unsatisfied and with a deepening sense of futility and
emptiness, "pendent upon the periphery" of the divine "ring-

pass-not" which he has himself established. It is at this point and in this situation that he must reflect upon and use this formula.

The question might here be interjected: What should now be the procedure and right use? Upon this it is not possible here to enlarge, beyond pointing out that all the meditation processes connected with the Raja-Yoga system are intended to bring the aspirant to a point of such intense inner focussing and alert mental detachment that he will be in a position to use these formulas with understanding, according to his ray type, and to use them with efficacy and power. His meditation has produced the needed *alignment*. There is therefore a direct way or line (speaking symbolically) between the thinking, meditative, reflective man upon the periphery of the soul's influence and the soul itself, the One Who is at the centre. The crisis of evocation succeeds, once this line of contact, this antahkarana, has been established and recognised, and a crisis of intense activity ensues, wherein the man occultly "detaches himself from the furthest point upon the outer rim of life, and sweeps with purpose towards the central Point." Thus speaks the *Old Commentary*, which is so oft quoted in these pages.

It is not possible to do more than put these ideas into symbolic form, leaving these mysteries of the soul to be grasped by those whose soul's influence reaches to that periphery, and is there *recognised for what it is*. This crisis usually persists for a long time, a far longer one than is the case with the aspirant upon the first ray line of activity. However, when the second ray aspirant has understood and has availed himself of the opportunity and can see ahead the line between himself and the centre, then the "light breaks in."

It is this period of crisis which presents the major problem to the advanced aspirants of today and evokes consequently the concern of the psychiatrist and psychologist. Instead of treating the difficulty as a sign of progress and as indicating a relatively high point in the evolutionary scale and therefore a reason for a sense of encouragement, it is treated as a disease of the mind and of the personality. Instead of regarding the condition as one warranting explanation and understanding but no real concern, the attempt is made to arrest the difficulty by elimination and not by solution, and though the personality may be temporarily relieved, the work of the soul is for that particular life cycle arrested, and delay ensues. With this problem we will later deal.

Light reveals, and the *stage of revelation* now follows. This light upon the way produces vision and the vision shows itself as:

1. A vision, first of all, of defects. The light reveals the man to himself, as he is, or as the soul sees the personality.
2. A vision of the next step ahead, which, when taken, indicates the procedure next to be followed.
3. A vision of those who are travelling the same way.
4. A glimpse of the "Guardian Angel," who is the dim reflection of the Angel of the Presence, the Solar Angel, which walks with each human being from the moment of birth until death, embodying as much of the available light as the man—at any given moment upon the path of evolution—can use and express.
5. A fleeting glimpse (at high and rare moments) of the Angel of the Presence itself.
6. At certain times and when deemed necessary, a glimpse of the Master of a man's ray group. This falls usually into two categories of experience and causes:

   a. In the early stages and whilst under illusion and glamour, that which is contacted is a vision of the astral, illusory form upon the planes of glamour and illusion. This is not, therefore, a glimpse of the Master Himself, but of His astral symbol, or of the form built by His devoted disciples and followers.

b. The Master Himself is contacted. This can take place when the disciple has effected the needed integrations of the threefold lower nature.

It is at this moment of "integration as the result of revelation" that there comes the fusion of the personality ray with the egoic ray. This we will consider later, but at this point a fact should be mentioned which has not hitherto been emphasised or elucidated. This point is that *the personality ray is always a subray of the egoic ray*, in the same sense that the seven major rays of our solar system are the seven subrays of the Cosmic Ray of Love-Wisdom, or the seven planes of our system are the seven subplanes of the cosmic physical plane. We will suppose, for instance, that a man's egoic ray is the third ray of active intelligence or adaptability, and his personality ray is the second ray of love-wisdom. This personality ray is the second subray of the third ray of active intelligence. Then, in addition, there might be the following rays governing the three personality vehicles:

Egoic Ray—3rd Ray of Active Intelligence

I	2	3	4	5	6	7
	Personality					
				Mental body		
					Astral body	
						Physical body

This is a valuable point for all who are real students to remember and to grasp. Ponder upon it, for it is self-explanatory and an understanding of it will make it possible to solve the problems of:

1. Alignment
2. The lines of least resistance.
3. The processes of substitution.
4. The alchemy of transmutation.
5. The fields of
   a. Service
   b. Avocation
   c. Vocation.

The lack of balance will also emerge if the chart is studied and man can then arrive at an understanding of what he has to do. A study of the two formulas of the first and second rays will make it clear why in humanity (and in the solar system also) these two major rays are always so closely associated, and why all esoteric schools throughout the world are predominantly expressions of these two rays. At a certain stage upon the Path all the rays governing the mental body shift their focus onto rays one and two, doing this via the third ray. This ray holds the same position to the other rays that the solar plexus centre does to the other six centres, for it constitutes a great clearing house. The first ray penetrates, pierces and produces the line along which Light comes; the second ray is the "light-carrier," and supplements the work of the first ray. A study of the activities and the cooperative endeavours of the Master M. and the Master K.H. may serve to make this clearer. Their work is indispensable to each other, just as life and consciousness are mutually indispensable, and without them form is rendered valueless.

Ray Three

" 'Pulling the threads of Life, I stand, enmeshed within my self-created glamour. Surrounded am I by the fabric I have woven. I see naught else.

'*The love of truth* must dominate, not love of my own thoughts, or love of my ideas or forms; love of the ordered process must control, not love of my own wild activity.'

The word goes forth from soul to form: 'Be still. Learn to stand silent, quiet and unafraid. I, at the centre, *Am*. Look up along the line and not along the many lines which, in the space of aeons, you have woven. These hold thee prisoner. Be still. Rush not from point to point, nor be deluded by the outer forms and that which disappears. Behind the forms, the Weaver stands and silently he weaves.' "

It is this *enforced* quiet which brings about the true alignment. This is the quiet not of meditation but of living. The aspirant upon the third ray is apt to waste much energy in perpetuating the glamourous forms with which he persistently surrounds himself. How can he achieve his goal when he is ceaselessly running hither and thither—weaving, manipulating, planning and arranging? He manages to get nowhere. Ever he is occupied with the distant objective, with that which may materialise in some dim and distant future, and he fails ever to achieve the immediate objective. He is often the expression and example of waste energy. He weaves for the future, forgetting that his tiny bit of weaving is an intrinsic part of a great Whole and that time may enter in and frustrate—by change of circumstance—his carefully laid plans, and the dreams of earlier years. Therefore futility is the result.

To offset this, he must stand quiet at the centre and (for a time at any rate) cease from weaving; he must no longer make opportunities for himself but—meeting the opportunities which come his way (a very different thing)—apply himself to the need to be met. This is a very different matter and swings into activity a very different psychology. When he can do this and be willing to achieve divine idleness (from the angle of a glamoured third ray attitude), he will discover that he has suddenly achieved *alignment*. This alignment naturally produces *a crisis* which is characterised by two qualities:

a. The quality of deep distress. This is a period of difficulty and of real concern because it dawns upon his consciousness how useless, relatively, are his weaving and his manipulations, and how much of a problem he presents to the other Weavers.

b. The quality which might be expressed as the determination to stand in spiritual being and to comprehend the significance of the ancient aphorism, given frequently to third ray aspirants:

> "Cease from thy doing. Walk not on the Path until thou hast learnt the art of standing still.
> Study the spider, brother, entangled not in its own web, as thou art today entangled in thine own."

This crisis evokes understanding, which is, as many will recognise, an aspect of *light*. The aspirant slowly begins to work with the Plan as it is, and not as he thinks it is. As he works, *revelation* comes, and he sees clearly what he has to do. Usually this entails first of all a disentangling and a release from his own ideas. This process takes much time, being commensurate with the time wasted in building up the agelong glamour. The third ray aspirant is always slower to learn than the second ray, just as the first ray aspirant learns more rapidly than the second ray. When, however, he has learnt to be quiet and still, he can achieve his goal with greater rapidity. The second ray aspirant has to achieve the quiet which is ever present at the heart of a storm or the centre of a whirlpool. The third ray aspirant has to achieve the quiet which is like to that of a quiet mill pond, which he much dislikes to do.

Having, however, learned to do it, integration then takes place. The man stands ready to play his part.

It is interesting to note that the first result of the use of these three formulas can each be summed up in one word, for the sake of clarity. These words embody the first and simplest steps upon the way of at-one-ment. They embody the simplest aspects of the necessary technique.

> Ray One ....Inclusion.
> Ray Two ....Centralisation.
> Ray Three ....Stillness.

The above will suffice for the techniques of integration of these three major rays. We will now take the formulas which will embody the techniques of integration for the four minor rays, and glimpse the possibilities which they may unfold. We will emphasize in connection with each of them the same five stages of the technique we are studying:

> 1. Alignment.
> 2. A crisis of evocation.
> 3. Light.
> 4. Revelation.
> 5. Integration.

At the same time, we will bear in mind that the alignment with which we have hitherto been occupying ourselves is that of a form of expression and that this is achieved through discipline, meditation, and service. These techniques of integration, however, refer to the establishing of a continuity of consciousness, within the aligned forms. Therefore we begin with alignment in these cases and do not end with it.

Ray Four

" 'Midway I stand between the forces which oppose each other. Longing am I for harmony and peace, and for the beauty which results from unity. I see the two. I see naught else but forces ranged opposing, and I, the one, who stands within the circle at the centre. Peace I demand. My mind is bent upon it. Oneness with all I seek, yet form divides. War upon every side I find, and separation. Alone I stand and am. I know too much.'

The love of unity must dominate, and love of peace and harmony. Yet not that love, based on a longing for relief, for peace to self, for unity because it carries with it that which is pleasantness.

The word goes forth from soul to form. 'Both sides are one. There is no war, no difference and no isolation. The warring forces seem to war from the point at which you stand. Move on a pace. See truly with the opened eye of inner vision and you will find, not two but one; not war but peace; not isolation but a heart which rests upon the centre. Thus shall the beauty of the Lord shine forth. The hour is now.' "

It is well to remember that this fourth ray is preeminently the ray of the fourth Creative Hierarchy, the human kingdom, and therefore has a peculiar relation to the functions, relationships and the service of man, as an intermediate group, a bridging group, upon our planet. The *function* of this intermediate group is to embody a type of energy, which is that of at-one-ment. This is essentially a healing force which brings all forms to an ultimate perfection through the power of the indwelling life, with which it becomes perfectly at-oned. This is brought about by the soul or consciousness aspect, qualified by the ray in question. The *relation* of the human family to the divine scheme, as it exists, is that of bringing into close rapport the three higher kingdoms upon our planet and the three lower kingdoms of nature, thus acting as a clearing house for divine energy. The *service* humanity is to render is that of producing unity, harmony, and beauty in nature, through blending into one functioning, related unity the soul in all forms. This is achieved individually at first, then it takes place in group formation, and finally it demonstrates through an entire kingdom in nature. When this takes place, the fourth Creative Hierarchy will be controlled predominantly by the fourth ray (by which I mean that the majority of its egos will have fourth ray personalities, thus facilitating the task of fusion), and the consciousness of its advanced units will function normally upon the fourth plane of buddhic energy or intuitional awareness.

It is this realisation which will provide adequate incentive for alignment. This alignment or sense of oneness is not in any way a mystical realisation, or that of the mystic who puts himself *en rapport* with divinity. The mystic still has a sense of duality. Nor is it the sense of identification which can characterise the occultist; with that there is still an awareness of individuality, though it is that of an individual who can merge at will with the whole. It is an almost undefinable consciousness of *group* fusion with a greater whole, and not so much individual fusion with the whole. Until this is experienced, it is well nigh impossible to comprehend, through the medium of words, its significance and meaning. It is the *reflection*, if I might so express it, of the Nirvanic consciousness; the reflection I would point out, but not that consciousness itself.

When this fourth ray alignment is produced and the disciple becomes aware of it, *a crisis* is evoked. The phrase "the disciple becomes aware of it," is significant, for it indicates that states of consciousness can exist and the disciple remain unaware of them. However, until they are brought down into the area of the brain and are recognised by the disciple in waking, physical consciousness, they remain subjective and are not usable. They are of no practical benefit to the man upon the physical plane. The crisis thus precipitated leads to fresh illumination when it is properly handled. These crises are produced by the bringing together (oft the clashing together) of the higher forces of the personality and soul energy. They cannot therefore be produced at a low stage of evolutionary development, in which low grade energies are active and the personality is neither integrated nor of a high grade and character. (Is such a phrase as "low grade energies" permissible? When all are divine? It conveys the idea, and that is what is desired.) The forces which are involved in such a crisis are the forces of integration at work in a personality of a very high order, and they are themselves necessarily of a relatively high potency. It is the integrated personality force, brought into relation with soul energy, which ever produces the type of crisis which is here discussed. These constitute, consequently, a very difficult moment or moments in the life of the disciple.

This fourth ray crisis, evoked by a right understanding and a right use of the fourth ray formula, produces the following sequential results:

1. *A sense of isolation.* Putting this into more modern language, a complex is produced of the same nature as that which temporarily overcame Elijah. He was overwhelmed with a sense of his clarity of vision in relation to the problem with which he was faced, of his unique response to it, and also with a sense of aloneness which devastated him.

2. *A sense of despairing futility.* The forces arraigned against the disciple seem so great and his equipment so inadequate and feeble!

3. *A determination to stand* in the midst and, if not victorious, at least to refuse to admit defeat, taking with determination the position which St. Paul expressed in the words: "Having done all, to stand."

4. *A sudden recognition* of the Warrior within, Who is invisible and omnipotent but Who can only now begin His real work when the personality is aligned, the crisis recognised, and the will-to-victory is present. We would do well to ponder on this.

When, therefore, this state of mind is achieved, and the disciple and inner Master, the soldier and the Warrior are known to be at-one, then there takes place what has been called in some of the ancient books "the breaking forth of the light of victory"—a victory which does not inflict defeat upon those who are at war, but which results in that triple victory of the two sides and of the One Who is at the centre. All three move forward to perfection. This is typical of a fourth ray consummation, and if this thought is applied with due reflection to the problem of the fourth kingdom in nature, the fourth Creative Hierarchy, humanity itself, the beauty of the phrasing and the truth of the statement must inevitably appear.

With this blazing forth of light comes the revelation expressed for us so adequately in the closing words of the fourth ray formula. Man sees and grasps the final purpose for the race and the objective ahead of this fourth kingdom in the great sweep of the divine manifestation. It is valuable also to remember that this revelation comes to the race in three stages:

1. *Individually*, when the disciple "relinquishes the fight in order to stand, thereby discovering victory ahead,

achieving oneness with the enemy, the Warrior and the *One*."

2. *In group formation.* This approach to the revelation is today going on in the world, and is producing a moment of extreme crisis in connection with the work of the New Group of World Servers. Their moment of crisis lies immediately ahead.

3. *In the human family as a whole.* This revelation will come to the race at the end of the age and with it we need not for the moment, therefore, concern ourselves. It is essentially the revelation of the *Plan* as a whole, embodying the various aspects of the Plan as—from cycle to cycle—the race has grasped the smaller aspects and revelations and succeeded eventually in bringing them into concrete manifestation. It is a revelation of the purposes of Deity—past, present and future purposes—as grasped by those who have developed the divine aspects and are, consequently, in a position to understand.

This series of spiritual happenings or unfoldments of consciousness in the life of the individual and the group produces a definite integration upon the three levels of personality work (mental, emotional and physical). It also lays the ground for those processes of fusion which will blend the rays of the personality and of the soul. If you will carry this concept of integration (achieved upon the three levels of the three worlds of human endeavour) into the activities and relationships of groups, you will find much of interest and of informative value anent the work of the New Group of World Servers. This group is, if I might so express it, an effort at an externalisation of the group personality of the disciples, connected with the Hierarchy. If we ponder on this, the function and relation will be apparent.

Let us now add to the three words expressing the three ray formulas already given, the word for this ray: *Steadfastness.* Therefore we have:

Ray One ....Inclusion.
Ray Two ....Centralisation.
Ray Three ....Stillness.
Ray Four ....Steadfastness.

As we brood on these words and on the remaining three which are indicated hereafter, we shall bring clearly into our consciousness the keynote for the disciples of the world at this time, who are in a position to discover that their personalities or their souls are on some one or other of these rays. The use of these words by those who are not pledged disciples in connection with their personality rays and personality expression might be definitely undesirable. The third ray personality, emphasising *stillness*, for instance, might find himself descending into the sloughs of lethargy; the first ray personality, seeking to develop *inclusiveness* might go to extremes, deeming himself a centre of inclusiveness. These are Words of Power, when used by a disciple, and must be employed in the light of the soul or may have a striking harmful effect.

Ray Five.

> " 'Towards me I draw the garment of my God. I see and know His form. I take that garment, piece by piece. I know its shape and colour, its form and type, its parts component and its purposes and use. I stand amazed, I see naught else. I penetrate the mysteries of form, but not the *Mystery*. I see the garment of my God. I see naught else.'
> *Love of the form* is good but only as the form is known for what it is—the veiling vase of life. Love of the form must never hide the Life which has its place behind, the *One* who brought the form into the light of day, and preserves

it for His use,—The *One* Who lives, and loves and serves the form, the One Who *Is*.

The Word goes forth from soul to form: 'Behind that form, I am. Know Me. Cherish and know and understand the nature of the veils of life, but know as well the One Who lives. Know Me. Let not the forms of nature, their processes and powers prevent thy searching for the Mystery which brought the mysteries to thee. Know well the form, but leave it joyously and search for Me.

'Detach thy thought from form and find Me waiting underneath the veils, the many-sided shapes, the glamours and the thought-forms which hide my real Self. Be not deceived. Find Me. Know Me. Then use the forms which then will neither veil nor hide the Self, but will permit the nature of that Self to penetrate the veils of life, revealing all the radiance of God, His power and magnetism; revealing all there is of form, of life, of beauty and usefulness. The mind reveals the *One*. The mind can blend and fuse the form and life. Thou art the One. Thou art the form. Thou art the mind. Know this.' "

This fifth ray formula is of exceeding potency at this time and should be used often, but with care, by those upon this line of divine energy. It has most powerful integrating properties, but the person who employs it must be mindful to visualise and hold in his mind's eye the even, balanced, equilibrised distribution of the divine energy set in motion by the use of this fifth ray formula so that the three aspects of the spiritual entity concerned—the mind, the One Who uses it (the Self) and the form nature—may be equally stimulated. This statement means, for instance, that if all the emphasis of the soul energy available is poured into the lower nature, the natural man, it might result in the shattering of the form and the consequent uselessness of the man in service. If all of it, on the other hand, is poured into the receiving chalice of the astral nature, it might only serve to intensify the glamour and to produce fanaticism.

1. The lower psychic man—physical and astral—must receive a balanced quota of force.
2. The mind must receive its share of illuminating energy.
3. A third part of that energy must be retained within the periphery of the soul nature to balance thus the other two.

This is a replica of the experience of the Monad when coming into manifestation, for the monad retains a measure of energy within itself, it sends energy forth which is anchored in that centre of energy which we call a soul. Still more energy pours forth also, via the soul, for the production of a human being—an expression of the soul upon the physical plane, just as the soul is an expression of the monad upon the mental plane, and both are expressions also of that one monad.

The use of this formula, which produces eventually a definite relation between the soul and the various aspects of the form, brings about a needed alignment, and again (as in the other cases considered previously) produces also, and evokes, *a crisis*. This crisis must be regarded as producing two lesser crises in the consciousness of the personality:

1. That in which there comes the achieving of equilibrium and what might be called a "balanced point of view." This balanced vision causes much difficulty and leads to what might be called the "ending of the joy-life and of desire." This is not a pleasant experience to the disciple; it leads to much aridness in the life-experience and to a sense of loss; it often takes much wise handling, and frequently time elapses before the disciple emerges on the other side of the experience.
2. This balanced condition in which the not-Self and the Self, the life-aspect and the form-aspect, are seen as they

essentially are (through the aid and the use of the discriminating faculty of the mind), leads eventually to a crisis of choice, and to the major task of the disciple's life. This is the detaching of himself from the grip of form experience, and consciously, rapidly, definitely and with intention preparing himself for the great expansions of initiation.

When this dual crisis is over and that which it has evoked has been rightly handled, then the light streams forth, leading to the revelation of the relationships of form to soul. These two are then seen as one in a sense never before realised and are then regarded as possessing a relation quite different to the theoretical relationships posited in ordinary occult and religious work. It will be apparent, therefore, how a new relationship and a new type of integration then becomes possible and how the mind quality of the fifth ray (critical, analytical, separative and over-discriminating) can become, what in the middle ages it used to be called, the "common sense."

When this takes place, form and life are indeed one unity and the disciple uses the form at will as the instrument of the soul for the working out of the plans of God. These plans are at-one with the intention of the Hierarchy. We now have five words for disciples upon the five rays to study:

Ray One	Inclusion.
Ray Two	Centralisation.
Ray Three	Stillness.
Ray Four	Steadfastness.
Ray Five	Detachment.

Ray Six.

" 'I see a vision. It satisfies desire; it feeds and stimulates its growth. I lay my life upon the altar of desire—the seen, the sensed, that which appeals to me, the satisfaction of my need—a need for that which is material, for that which feeds emotion, that satisfies the mind, that answers my demand for truth, for service, and my vision of the goal. It is the vision which I see, the dream I dream, the truth I hold, the active form which meets my need, that which I grasp and understand. *My* truth, *my* peace, *my* satisfied desire, *my* dream, *my* vision of reality, *my* limited ideal, *my* finite thought of God;—for these I struggle, fight and die.'

Love of the truth must always be. Desire and aspiration, reaching out for that which is material or soaring upward towards the vision of reality must ever find their satisfaction. For this men work, driving themselves and irking others. They love the truth as they interpret it; they love the vision and the dream, forgetting that the truth is limited by mind—narrow and set, one-pointed, not inclusive; forgetting that the vision touches but the outer fringe of mystery, and veils and hides reality.

The word goes out from soul to form: 'Run not so straight. The path that you are on leads to the outer circle of the life of God; the line goes forward to the outer rim. Stand at the centre. Look on every side. Die not for outer forms. Forget not God, Who dwells behind the vision. Love more your fellow men.' "

It will be apparent, therefore, that the sixth ray disciple has first of all to achieve the arduous task of dissociating himself from his vision, from his adored truth, from his loved ideals, from his painted picture of himself as the devoted follower and disciple, following his Master unto death, if need be; forcing himself (from very love of form) and forcing all his fellowmen to dedicate themselves to that which he sees.

It must be recognised that he lacks the wide love of the second ray disciple which is a reflection of the love of God. He is all the time occupied with *himself*, with *his* work, *his* sacrifice, *his* task, *his* ideas, and *his* activities. He, the devotee, is lost in his devotion. He, the idealist, is driven by his idea. He, the follower, runs blindly after his Master, his chosen ideal and loses himself in the chaos of his uncontrolled aspirations and the glamour of his own thoughts. Curiously enough, there is a close relation between the third and the sixth rays, just as there is between the first and the second rays, and the second and the fourth. The fourth, fifth, sixth and seventh rays have no such paralleling relations. 1 added to 1 equals 2, 2 added to 2 equals 4, 3 added to 3 equals 6. Between these pairs of rays there is a line of special energy flowing which warrants the attention of disciples who are becoming conscious of their relationships. This relation and interplay only becomes active at a relatively high stage of evolution.

The problem, therefore, of the sixth ray aspirant is to divorce himself from the thralldom of form (though not from form) and to stand quietly at the centre, just as the third ray disciple has to learn to do. There he learns breadth of vision and a right sense of proportion. These two qualities he always lacks until the time comes when he can take his stand and there align himself with all visions, all forms of truth, all dreams of reality, and find behind them all—God and his fellow men. Then and only then can he be trusted to work with the Plan.

The alignment evoked by this "peaceful standing still" naturally produces *a crisis* and it is, as usual, a most difficult one for the aspirant to handle. It is a crisis which seems to leave him destitute of incentive, of motive, of sensation, of appreciation by others and of life purpose. The idea of "my truth, my master, my idea, my way" leaves him and as yet he has nothing to take its place. Being sixth ray, and therefore linked with the world of astral psychic life, the sixth plane, he is peculiarly sensitive to his own reactions and to the ideas of others where he and his truths are concerned. He feels a fool and considers that others are thinking him so. The crisis therefore is severe, for it has to produce a complete readjustment of the Self to the self. His fanaticism, his devotion, his furious driving of himself and others, his wasted efforts, and his lack of understanding of the point of view of others have all gone, but as yet nothing has taken their place. He is swept by futility and his world rocks under him. Let him stand still at the centre, fixing his eyes on the soul and ceasing activity for a brief period of time until the light breaks in.

It is interesting here to note that the Master Jesus, as He hung upon the Cross, experienced (on a much higher turn of the spiral than is possible to the disciple) the acme and the height of this crisis, though in His case—being attuned to God and to all God's children—there swept over Him the sum total of the dilemma of the world disciples and all the agony of the astral awareness of this dilemma, voicing itself in the agonising words: "My God, My God, why hast Thou forsaken Me."

But by facing futility and himself and by surrendering himself to the life at the centre and there holding himself poised and still, yet alert, the light will break in and reveal to the disciple that which he needs to know. He learns to express that inclusive love which is his major requirement and to let go the narrow, one-pointed attitude which he has hitherto regarded as love. He welcomes then all visions, if they serve to lift and comfort his brothers; he welcomes all truths, if they are the agents of revelation to other minds; he welcomes all dreams if they can act as incentives to his fellow men. He shares in them all, yet retains his poised position at the centre.

Thus we can see that the essential integration of this unit into his group can now take place.

The problem of the disciple upon this ray is greatly increased by the fact that the sixth ray has been the dominant ray for so many centuries and is only now passing out. Therefore the idealistic, fanatical thought-forms, built up by the devotees upon this ray, are powerful and persistent. The world today is fanatically idealistic, and this is one of the causes of the present world situation. It is hard for the man who is the one-pointed devotee to free himself from the prevailing influence, for the energy thus generated feeds that which he seeks to leave behind. If he can, however, grasp the fact that devotion, expressing itself through a personality, engenders fanaticism and that fanaticism is separative, frequently cruel, often motivated by good ideals, but that it usually overlooks the immediate reality by rushing off after a self-engendered vision of truth, he will go far along the way to solving his problem. If he can then realise that devotion, expressing itself through the soul, is love and inclusiveness plus understanding, then he will learn eventually to free himself from the idealism of others and of himself and will identify himself with that of the Hierarchy, which is the loving working out of God's Plan. It is free from hatred, from intense emphasis upon an aspect or a part, and is not limited by the sense of time.

Ray Seven.

" 'I seek to bring the two together. The plan is in my hands. How shall I work? Where lay the emphasis? In the far distance stands the One Who *Is*. Here at my hand is form, activity, substance, and desire. Can I relate these and fashion thus a form for God? Where shall I send my thought, my power the word that I can speak?

'I, at the centre, stand, the worker in the field of magic. I know some rules, some magical controls, some Words of Power, some forces which I can direct. What shall I do? Danger there is. The task that I have undertaken is not easy of accomplishment, yet I love power. I love to see the forms emerge, created by my mind, and do their work, fulfill the plan and disappear. I can create. The rituals of the Temple of the Lord are known to me. How shall I work?

'*Love not the work*. Let love of God's eternal Plan control your life, your mind, your hand, your eye. Work towards the unity of plan and purpose which must find its lasting place on earth. Work with the Plan; focus upon your share in that great work.'

The word goes forth from soul to form: 'Stand in the centre of the pentagram, drawn upon that high place in the East within the light which ever shines. From that illumined centre work. Leave not the pentagram. Stand steady in the midst. Then draw a line from that which is without to that which is within and see the Plan take form.' "

It is not possible to be more explicit than this. This great and powerful ray is now coming into manifestation and it brings new energies to man of so potent a nature that the disciples of today must move and work with care. They are literally handling fire. It is the children who are now coming into incarnation who will eventually work more safely and more correctly with these new potencies. There is much, however, to be done in the meantime, and the disciples upon this seventh ray can ponder on this formula and seek their own interpretation of it, endeavouring first of all to stand in the East, within the protection of the pentagram. As he realises the task to be carried out and the nature of the work to be done by the seventh ray worker, and appreciates the fact that it is the magical work of producing those forms on earth which will embody the spirit of God (and in our particular time, this necessitates the building of new forms), each seventh ray disciple will see himself as a relating agent, as the one who stands in the midst of the building processes, attending to his portion of the task. This, if really grasped and deeply considered will have the effect of producing alignment. The moment that this alignment is achieved, then let the disciple remember that it will mean a tremendous inflow of power, of energy from both the aligned points, from both directions, converging upon him, as he stands in the midway place. Ponder deeply upon this truth, for it is this fact which always evokes a seventh ray crisis. It will be obvious what this crisis is. If the man concerned is materially minded, selfishly ambitious and unloving, the inpouring energy will stimulate the personality nature and he will immediately be warring furiously with all that we mean by the instinctual, psychic, intellectual nature. When all these three are stimulated, the disciple is often for a time swung off the centre into a maelstrom of magical work of the lower kind— sex magic and many forms of black magic. He is glamoured by the beauty of his motive, and deceived by the acquired potency of his personality.

If, however, he is warned of the danger and aware of the possibility, he will stand steady at the centre within the mystical pentagram, and there *suffer* until the light in the East rises upon his darkness, discovering him still at the midway point. Then comes the revelation of the Plan, for this has ever to be the motivating power of the seventh ray disciple. He works on earth, upon the outer plane of manifestation, with the construction of those forms through which the divine will can express itself. In the field of religion, he works in collaboration with the second and sixth ray disciples. In the field of government he labours, building those forms which will enable the first ray activity to be expressed. In the field of business, he cooperates with third ray energies and the executives of the Plan. In the field of science, he aids and assists the fifth ray workers. He is the expression of the builder, and the creator, bringing into outer manifestation God's Plan. He begins, however, with himself, and seeks to bring into expression the plan of his soul in his own setting and worldly situation. Until he can do this, he is unable to stand in the East within the pentagram.

It is occultly said that "the pentagram is open and a place

of danger when the disciple knows not order within his own life, and when the ritual of the soul is not imposed and its rhythm not obeyed. The pentagram is closed when order is restored and the ritual of the Master is imposed." The writing goes on to say that "if the disciple enters through the open pentagram, he dies. If he passes over into the closed pentagram, he lives. If he transmutes the pentagram into a ring of fire, he serves the Plan."

b. The Techniques of Fusion and Duality

We come now to the consideration of a very practical matter where the world disciples are concerned, and one with which I intend to deal very simply. The point which we are to study is the Technique of Fusion, leading, as it inevitably does, to the emergence (into controlling prominence) of the Ray of the Personality. After a brief study of this we will refer briefly to the Technique of Duality. The brevity is necessary because only disciples of some experience and initiates will really comprehend the things whereof I speak. A study of the Technique of Duality would serve to elucidate the relationship which should exist between the two rays of manifesting energy, which constitute that phenomenal being we call man. Therefore, it will be apparent to you from the start, how necessary it will be to deal with these abstruse subjects in the simplest way. Our study of the Techniques of Integration was definitely abstruse and couched in language quite symbolic. We were there dealing with the relationship of five rays: Those of the personality, of the ego or soul, and of the rays of the three personality vehicles, prior to their integration into a functioning whole.

It might be of value here if I pointed out to you that the three words: Integration, Fusion and Duality when dealt with, as they are, in connection with the final stages of the Path of Evolution, are significantly different. For one thing it might be said that

1. The Technique of Integration, a sevenfold technique, is applied upon the Path of Probation.
2. The Technique of Fusion is applied upon the Path of Discipleship.
3. The Technique of Duality is applied upon the Path of Initiation.

I am here using these three terms only in relation to what we call the Aryan Race, or to what might be more adequately called the Aryan consciousness, for that consciousness demonstrates in a two-fold manner as mental power and personality force. It is found at a certain stage in every human being and in every race; it must therefore be remembered that I am not using the word Aryan as synonymous with Nordic but as descriptive of the intellectual goal of humanity, of which our Occidental civilisation is in the early stages, but which men of all time and all races have individually demonstrated. The Aryan state of consciousness is one into which all men eventually pass.

Integration here refers to the bringing into one field of resultant magnetic activity of five differing types of energy:

1. Physical and emotional sentient energy (2 energies therefore) are brought together and eventually form one expressive force.
2. Physical, emotional-sentient and mental energy (3) are also brought into relationship; one potent vortex of force is then set up which eventually becomes so systematised and integrated that we call its aggregated expression *Personality*, (4) and in time this aggregate

becomes a realised potency and thus completes the four-fold lower man.

3. These four types of energy are then brought into relationship with the ego or soul. This brings then into play another and higher type of energy expression, and thus the five energies integrate, blend and fuse.

These five energies, when rightly related to each other, produce one active force centre, through which the Monad can work, using the word Monad to express the first differentiation of the One Life, if such a paradoxical phrase can be employed. Its use is only permissible from the standpoint of the personal self, still limited and imprisoned in the "I" consciousness.

The Technique of Fusion deals with the production of a close interplay of the five above enumerated aspects of energy which have been, in due time, integrated into a unity. It is really a fusion of the four forces and the one energy. This fusion produces:

1. A demonstration of personality activity when, in response to the Technique of Integration, there is

   a. Response and interplay between the threefold lower man.

   b. A gradual emergence of the dominant note of the lower man which will, in time, indicate the nature of the personality ray.

   c. The quality of the personality ray, in its higher aspects, emerges into living expression. Great beauty of character or great forcefulness will then appear.

2. Gradually, the qualities of the personality energy are transmuted into those of the ego or soul and the fusion of the two energies—soul and body—is then complete.

This Technique of Fusion might be better understood by all of you if it were called the Technique of Transmutation, but it must be remembered that the transmutation referred to is not that of bad qualities into good or of bad characteristics into good ones (for this should take place quite definitely upon the Path of Probation) but the transmutation of the higher aspects of the personality ray into those of the soul. When this has been to a great extent carried forward satisfactorily, then the Technique of Duality comes into play—a duality differing greatly from that to which we refer when we speak of the higher and lower selves. It is a duality which is utilised upon the Path of initiation by Those Who Know no sense of separativeness, and signifies one wherein the transmuted and purified personality qualities and characteristics are used by the initiate in the three worlds for service and the furthering of the Plan. The egoic energies are only brought into play when needed for group benefit and within the confines (again a paradoxical term and only of significance in consciousness from the standpoint of the lesser minds) of the Kingdom of God.

It will be seen, therefore, that we are dealing here with relatively advanced stages of human development. What I have now to say will veil, under extremely simplified phrases, truths which will be apparent to two groups of aspirants:

1. Accepted disciples, who will comprehend the significances of the Technique of Fusion.
2. Initiates, who will work with the Technique of Duality

It should be remembered also that we are here dealing with the primordial duality of spirit and matter and not with the secondary duality of soul and body. This point is of deep importance and will bear most careful consideration.

The man who will seek to use the Technique of Fusion is

the disciple who is conscious of personality power, owing to the fact that his mind is beginning to dominate his sentient emotional nature, much in the same way as his emotional-sentient nature has, for ages, controlled his physical body. The use of the mind is becoming "second nature" to certain advanced types of men, and it is called into play, when they reach this stage, almost automatically. The result is that the integration of the three energies is proceeding fast. At the same time, the man is definitely oriented to soul contact and knowledge, and frequently the mind (when it is the controlling personality factor) is itself brought suddenly and dynamically under the control of the soul.

This accounts for the intense difficulty of the life of every disciple at this stage. Several processes are simultaneously going on:

1. The mind factor is steadily becoming more dominant, increasingly clarified and usable.
2. The three aspects of the lower nature are working in closer unity all the time, each growing at the same time in individual potency.
3. The personality ray is making its presence felt, and the expressed power of the man (within his environment) is equally increasing.
4. The soul ray is, at times, projecting itself and this produces in the early stages those difficult upsets and turmoils which are usually of a distressing kind.

It is at this stage therefore that the Technique of Fusion can profitably be used, preserving at the same time the realised integrity of the motive which, if correctly apprehended, should be

1. The motive of a realised objective of soul control in response to a living reaction to its sensed pull or call.

2. The motive of service, in response to a sentient realisation of humanity's need.

3. The motive of cooperation with the Plan, in response to an intelligent appreciation of its nature and existence.

Again you will note that we have swung back to our three major themes: Soul control, Service, and the Plan.

It might, therefore, seem that this particular technique will be a sevenfold one like the Technique of Integration, but in this you would be mistaken. It is a threefold technique based upon the fact that all souls are eventually divided (again a paradoxical phrase when dealing with souls, but what can be done when modern language proves inadequate to the demands of soul knowledge) into three major groups, or rather distinguished by three major qualities, those of the first, second and third rays. Life, the One Life, manifests through these three major qualities, which condition its sevenfold appearance, and which are essentially Will, Love and Intelligence.

This Technique of Fusion evokes these three qualities in relation to the soul, to service and to the Plan. At the same time, it brings illumination to the mind (thus revealing the soul and the kingdom of God); it brings increased imagination (creative and dynamic) to the emotional sentient nature, the astral body (thus revealing relationship and responsibility); it brings likewise inspiration to the physical life, to the physical body, via the brain (revealing actual capacity to cooperate intelligently with the Plan). Therefore, we shall have to consider a technique which will do three things:

1. Bring *Illumination*, through the evocation of the Will or first aspect of divinity.

2. Bring *Imagination*, through the evocation of Love, the

second aspect or of sentient response to the world soul in all forms.

3. Bring *Inspiration*, through the evocation of the Intelligence, the third aspect.

If we study this triplicity with care, we shall see that the process outlined brings the higher aspect of the personal self, the mind, to the lowest point of contact and into control of the physical body; we shall see that it brings the soul into conscious control of the astral, desire-sentient body, and that it also brings the will aspect (the highest aspect of divinity) into control of mind.

There are, therefore, two thoughts which we will have in our minds as we study this Technique of Fusion. First, that it is a threefold technique and is coloured by and conditioned by the qualities of the first, second and third major rays. Secondly, that this technique of whichever of these three natures it may be, will be of such a kind that it will produce illumination through the evocation of the will. It is right here that esotericists will recognise the importance of the teaching in connection with the centre at the base of the spine. It is awakened by an act of the will, which really means by the mind, functioning forcefully, under the influence of the spiritual man, through the medium of the brain.

It infers also that this technique will so stimulate the faculty of the imagination that an ever expanding or an all inclusive love will increasingly be expressed, and therefore that the heart centre will be forcefully affected and awakened into full activity. It infers also that the spiritual plane life of the disciple, as it expresses itself in his environment will become inspired and creative through the full and conscious use of the intelligence. This, in its turn, brings about the rounded out activity of the throat centre, and thus the three major centres, which are aroused into activity upon the Path of Discipleship, are brought to full and measured and controlled activity. Upon the Path of Initiation, the awakening and full-conditioned functioning of the two head centres is completed. This is the result of the use of the Technique of Duality by the initiate. One head centre, the thousand-petalled lotus, represents the spirit or life aspect; the other, the ajna centre, represents matter or the form aspect. Thus the work carried forward upon the paths of evolution, of probation, and of discipleship is completed upon the path of initiation, and thus, when the rays are understood, you have the possibility of a new system of awakening the centres, or chakras. But this system concerns only the awakening of the central part of the centre or lotus of force. The teaching given in the oriental and theosophical books refers primarily to the awakening and right relation of the centres when the aspirant is upon the probationary path. The teaching which I have here given has not before been so explicitly made public and has hitherto only been communicated orally. One half of the centre, the outer half (therefore one half of the lotus petals) is brought into increased activity upon the probationary path; the other half begins its intensified vibratory activity upon the path of discipleship, but the intensification of the centre of the lotus (though the One Life controls both soul and body) only takes place when the two later techniques of fusion and of duality are carried successfully forward.

Certain questions therefore arise:

1. What are the techniques, producing fusion upon the three major rays.
2. How do these techniques bring about
   a. Illumination of the mind.

b. Imaginative capacity of the sentient body.

c. An inspired life.

Another point should here be made; Disciples upon the minor rays likewise employ one or other of these three major techniques. Fourth ray disciples employ the second ray technique, as do sixth ray disciples; disciples upon the fifth ray employ the first ray technique. It is interesting to note that (prior to the first initiation) the personalities of all aspirants to this great expansion of consciousness will be found upon the third ray, which is—like the solar plexus centre—a great clearing house for energies, and a great transmuting station, if I may use this term.

The first ray technique must, therefore, do the following things and produce the following results:

1. The divine will must be evoked, of which the mind aspect is the reflection, and the brain (or the phenomenal appearance) the shadow. This brings into functional activity upon the physical plane what is called in theosophical books, Atma, or the first qualified differentiation of the monadic Life. The quality is often called the spiritual will.

2. The evocation of this will produces an illumination of the mind, differing from the illumination achieved through ordinary meditation and about which much has been written in the mystical books. This latter illumination is essentially the evocation of the intuition, which brings the illumination of direct knowledge to the mind. The one to which I here refer is, symbolically speaking, related to the state of consciousness of the Creator when He sent forth the phenomena-producing fiat: "Let there be *Light*."

3. This illumination, coming from the highest aspect which

man can conceive follows a direct line of approach, or pours down through a direct channel from

a. The level of Atma, or that centre of spiritual will which is dynamic and effective but seldom called into play, to the will petals of the egoic lotus, upon which I touched in *A Treatise on Cosmic Fire*. These petals are the reflection in the soul of this particular aspect of energy.

b. From this layer of petals to the mind body.

c. From the mind body to the brain.

d. From the brain, in due and set time, to the centre at the base of the spine, thus arousing the kundalini fire.

It will interest students to note how the first ray disciple, when employing this first ray technique of fusion, ends by producing second ray characteristics of which illumination, producing understanding love and sympathetic cooperation, is the predominant note. The second ray disciple, through rightly applied technique, produces curiously enough, third ray results, of which the use of the creative imagination is the outstanding characteristic. The third ray disciple through the development of the "power to inspire" adds to his innate qualities certain definitely first ray potencies. All are, however, subordinated to the second ray nature of the divine expression in this solar system.

The technique of Fusion, employed by the second ray disciple, will produce the following results:

1. Increased sentient response to the world soul and to the environment in which the disciple finds himself will increasingly be achieved.

2. This is largely done through the cultivation of the creative imagination. This is one of the great building attributes

of deity. It is brought about by the evocation of the love nature and, as earlier noted, brings in soul power in full tide. In the world of phenomenal appearance, the soul is the creating agent, the major building factor, the constructor of forms, and, through the Technique of Fusion, the power to imagine or to use imaginative thought power (in conjunction with the faculty to visualise, to wish, to dream into being) is definitely and scientifically developed.

3. This creative tension or one-pointed focus of imaginative dreaming swings the astral body into complete subordination to the soul. This fact is hinted at in *The Bhagavad Gita* where, upon the battle field of Kurukshetra, Arjuna suddenly sees the form of God wherein all forms constitute the One Form. The battle is then over. The soul is in complete control; no sense of separativeness is again possible.

4. The channel through which this synthesising and creative energy pours down is as follows:

   a. From the Monad to the love petals of the egoic lotus.
   b. From these love petals to the astral vehicle, energising all astral matter found in the equipment of the phenomenal man. "The spirit of God moves upon the face of the waters."
   c. From thence to the solar plexus centre.
   d. From that centre to the heart centre. The needed duality connected with the astral body thus appears. We have here also a correspondence to the descent of the fire of the will to the base of the spine with its subsequent raising, along the spinal column, to the head.

The third ray disciple, employing the Technique of Fusion, finds that:

1. It evokes a full functioning of the divine creative faculty. It will be apparent at this point how important is *motive*, for it determines the line of activity and differentiates man's activity into what is called (by esotericists) black and white magic. It is interesting also to note that it is the very rare man indeed who swings into the field of so-called black magic. This indicates, does it not, my brother, the extraordinarily triumphant work of the Great White Lodge.

2. The fiat which initiated this creative activity, as far as it relates to man, has been inadequately couched in the words: "Let the earth bring forth abundantly", thus inaugurating the age of creativity. This creative fecundity has steadily shifted during the past few thousand years into the creation of those effects of which ideas are the cause, producing within the creative range of man's mind:

   a. That which is useful and so contributing to man's present civilisation.

   b. That which is beautiful, thus gradually developing the aesthetic consciousness, the sense of colour, and the recognition of the use of symbolic forms in order to express quality and meaning.

3. As a result of the disciple's use of this technique, there is brought about an increased vital livingness, and a dynamic inflow of spiritual life into the physical plane experience. The disciple becomes "inspired" by the fire of love, and this evokes the "service of creation" as an expression of that love.

4. The power which inspires him and which makes him dynamic and creative in his environment comes likewise from the will aspect of the Monad, sweeping the higher

mind into activity upon the higher mental level which is that on which the creative ideas of God emerge in form to be recognised by the human consciousness.

5. The channel of approach or of downflow is as follows:

a. From the will aspect of the monadic life to that level of consciousness and of energy which we call that of the higher mind.

b. From the higher mind to the knowledge petals of the egoic lotus.

c. From these vortexes of force to the lower or concrete mind—that in which the average intelligent man familiarly works—to the throat centre and from thence immediately to the sacral centre (the centre of physical plane creation or reproduction). From there it is raised again to the throat centre where the creative physical urge is transmuted into artistic or literary creation in some form or another, and later still into the power to create groups or organisations which will express some idea or some thought which emanates from the Mind of God, and which demands immediate precipitation upon earth.

The result of this inflow of supremely high energies is that the processes set in motion by the Technique of Integration are completed and the rays of the lower man are welded or fused into the Personality Ray. This itself is later blended with the egoic ray, enabling that spiritual Identity which we recognise as standing behind phenomenal man to work through both these rays, thus bringing about a correspondence to that grouping within the divine expression which we call the major and minor rays. The rays of the triple lower nature then form one single avenue through which the soul, and later the energy of spirit can contact the larger *Whole* in manifestation upon the physical, astral and mental planes. When the Techniques of Integration and Fusion have done their intended work, this spiritual Identity can work in service to humanity and in cooperation with the Plan in the three worlds of human endeavour and in the five states of consciousness, human and superhuman. This brings the disciple to the period wherein the third initiation can be taken; then still higher forces can be brought into play and the Technique of Duality can be considered, mastered and used. It will be obvious to you that I cannot give you the rules of this technique, as they constitute part of the veiled secrets of initiation. Though duality is emphasised, it is a duality which produces simplification, merging and synthesis. Man is then viewed as a duality of spirit and matter and not as the well known triplicity of spirit, soul and body.

Now let us for a moment consider the Technique of Fusion. The keynotes of the three techniques are as follows:

First Ray .... Isolated Unity.
Second Ray .... Inclusive Reason.
Third Ray .... Presented Attributes.

The first thing the disciple who seeks to use these techniques undertakes is to arrive at an understanding (practical, experimental and subjective) of the appropriate phrase for his ray. Let me paraphrase or elucidate each of them, inadequately perforce owing to the lack of comprehension and the limited evolution of the average disciple, but in any case in order to bring suggestion to your minds.

Isolated Unity is that stage of consciousness which sees the whole as one and regards itself, not theoretically but as a realised fact, as identified with that whole. It is a whole which is "isolated" in the consciousness of the man, and not the man himself who regards himself as isolated. The word "isolated" refers to that complete organised organism of which the man can feel and know himself to be a part. The word "unity" expresses his relationship to the whole. It will be apparent therefore that this whole is something progressively realised. For the bringing about of this progressed realisation the great expansions of consciousness, called initiations, have been temporarily arranged as a hastening or forcing process. This progression of realised "isolations in unity" may begin with the disciple's group, environment or nation and, through right use of the understanding, will end by enabling him to isolate the whole divine scheme or living structure, and to identify himself with it in an active capable manner.

The result of meditation upon this theme will be:

1. A definite illumination of the mind, for it will then be at-one with the Universal Mind and all the ways of God and the plans of God will stand revealed to him.
2. The creative imagination will be powerfully evoked in response to this revelation, and modes and methods of cooperation will be *sentiently* developed and the disciple will become a creative cooperator and not just an obedient servant of the Plan.
3. His life will be then inspired by the desire to serve humanity and to cooperate with the Custodians of the Plan. This will bring in the full tide of soul life, producing temporarily a violent conflict between the personality ray and the soul ray, but also producing a steady subordination of the lower to the higher, of the minor to the major.

I cannot too strongly call to your attention that I am not here dealing with the normal service and the self-enforced cooperation of the aspirant—a cooperation based upon theory and a determination to prove theory and plan and service to be evolutionary facts—but with that spontaneous illumination, creativity and inspiration which is the result of the use of the Technique of Fusion *by the soul*—by the soul, and not by the aspiring struggling disciple. Here lies the clue to meaning. We are dealing consequently with that stage of development wherein, in deep contemplation, the man is consciously merged with the soul and that soul, in meditation, decides, plans and works. He functions as the soul and has achieved a definite measure of success in living as a soul, consciously upon the physical plane.

This particular technique of meditation involves the use of the head centre, demands the ability to focus the consciousness in the soul form, the spiritual body, and, at the same time, to preserve soul consciousness, mind consciousness and brain consciousness—no easy task for the neophyte and something which lies far ahead for the majority of students who read these words. This condition has been described as "the intensest reflection of the man, isolated in God Who is the negation of isolation and is nevertheless the Whole which is set apart from other Wholes." When this state of awareness has been achieved (and Patanjali hints at it in the last book of the Sutras) the disciple becomes invincible upon the physical plane, for he is completely unified and linked up with all aspects of himself in the greater Whole of which he is a part, is fusing all attributes and is at-one with the Whole, not simply subjectively and unconsciously (as are all human beings) but in full, waking, understanding awareness.

Inclusive Reason, which is the theme for the initiatory meditation of the second ray disciple, produces that inherent divine capacity which enables the detail of the sensed Whole to be grasped in meticulous entirety. This wide, yet detailed, scope or universal recognition is extremely difficult for me to explain or for you to understand. The second ray has been called the Ray of Detailed Knowledge and where this term has been employed, the beginner has necessarily laid the emphasis upon the word "detail". It might rather be called the Ray of Detailed Unity or the Ray of the Divine Pattern, or of beauty in relationship. It involves on the part of the disciple a very high point of synthetic comprehension.

You will note how, in all these three keynotes for advanced meditation, there is the calling of the disciple's attention to those related arrangements which constitute the whole when brought into relation with each other. The word "isolated", the words "detail" and "presented" would seem to indicate separative recognition, but this is emphatically not so. They simply indicate and refer to the intricate internal life of the organised creation of God wherein the consciousness (released from all material pettiness and self-centredness) sees not only the periphery of the Whole but the beauty and purpose of every aspect of the inner structure. Just as the average, yet unthinking human being knows that he is a person of intricate design, of multiple interior organisms which produce an aggregate of living forms, co-related and functioning as a unity, but of which he in fact knows nothing except their general nature, so the aspirant upon the probationary path may see the whole of which he is similarly a part. Just as the intelligent student of humanity and the highly educated thinker knows in greater detail and fuller comprehension the general equipment and more detailed purpose of the organised whole which we call a man, so the disciple, in the early stages of his career upon the path of discipleship, comes to see and grasp wider aspects of the inner relationships of the organised organism through which Deity is working out His Plans and Purposes. Just as the trained physician, who is also a trained psychologist (a rare thing to find) views the human body and its energies, so the disciple upon the later stages of the Path also grasps the plans, purposes and materialised ideas of God. This is but a feeble effort in my attempt to show the vastness of the knowledge required when a man begins to use these three seed thoughts in meditation. The living structure as it expresses ideas, the intricate beauty of the inner relationships within the expressing Whole, the circulation of the energy which is working out the divine *Idea*, the points of force and focal points of energy which act as power and light stations within that Whole—all these stand revealed to the man who is permitted, as a soul, to meditate upon such a phrase as *inclusive reason*.

The reason here referred to is that pure intuitional infallible comprehension which grasps cause and effect simultaneously, and sees why and whence and to what end all things are moving. It is not possible for the aspirant to take these words into his meditation and profit greatly thereby, for he will be meditating as an aspiring mind, and not as a soul. No matter, therefore, how great his effort, it will be the material more than the consciousness aspect and pattern which will engross his attention. When he has reached the point where he can meditate both as a soul and as a mind, involving also the brain reaction, then he will understand the purpose of these words and will view both the symbol, the inner living structure and the emerging conscious ideas with a synthetic comprehension and a simultaneity of reception which it is impossible for me to put into words.

You might well ask me here of what profit is it then for me to write these things at all, and to say much that I have said in this Treatise. I would reply: There are a few today, and there will be an increasing number in the next two decades, who—grasping the beauty of the presented idea—will be urged by their souls to work towards these ends. By so doing, they will succeed in raising the consciousness of the entire human family.

The results of using this meditation on the synthetic detail of the manifested Life will be

1. The realisation of the true significance of Light and the revelation of the meaning of what has been called in esoteric books, "the heart of the Sun", which is the inner point of life in all manifested forms. Illumination of the mind will be seen to be direct and infallible and will usurp the place of the present theoretical knowledge and belief.

2. The creative imagination will be occupied with those measures which will "throw the light" into the dark and unrelieved places in the (as yet) incomplete creative process. The man then works consciously in the light, as a Light bearer. Perhaps my meaning will emerge more clearly to some of you when I point out to you that the disciple usually sees himself as a point of intensified light within the light of the world and then seeks to use that light (which is in him atomic, etheric and that acquired as a soul) for the furtherance of the Plan.

3. This necessarily produces an intensified service to "those in dark places". The disciple will seek to bring the light of knowledge to them first of all, and then the light of Life. Ponder deeply on this distinction.

Presented Attributes may appear to you a more simple phrase upon which to meditate and easier for the average aspirant to contemplate and understand. Perhaps this apparent simplicity may be due to your failure to comprehend the significance and meaning of the word "attribute".

This third ray meditation concerns itself essentially with inherent forces, and students would do well to recognise the fact that there are inherent or innate qualities and attributes in the divine Whole which remain as yet unrevealed, and are as much unexpressed as are the divine tendencies in the majority of human beings. It is with these mysterious and slowly emerging energies that the man, ready for initiation, will have to deal, and of them he will become increasingly aware. He has to learn to occupy himself with the task of cooperating with those great Lives Who, working on formless levels, are busy with the development of an inner and as yet unrealised development within the Whole, and which can only be contacted and sensed by those on, or nearing, the Path of Initiation. There is a mystery within the mystery. The four minor rays, or rays of attribute, are concerned with the attributes which *are* definitely and slowly coming into expression and to fruition—knowledge, synthesis, beauty, science, idealism and order. But there are others, further back behind the scenes, held in latency for the proper period and time (if I may speak of these things in terms of modern usage), and these are the theme of this higher meditation. Only those who have freed themselves from the thralldom of the senses can truly thus meditate. The attributes of Deity might be divided into three main groups:

1. *Expressing Attributes*—those which are steadily emerging, —of which we are becoming conscious, and which will constitute the major qualities and attributes of the fourth kingdom in nature, when the evolutionary cycle has done its work.

2. *Presented Attributes*—those which (again using human phraseology) have presented themselves to the consciousness of the advanced disciple, which are as yet not capable of interpretation nor can they be comprehended by average human beings, but which are attributes of

the Kingdom of Souls, and which will distinguish that kingdom in its final stages. These latent attributes can be gradually comprehended and brought into activity by those who can function as souls.

3. *Undefined Attributes* are those of which the Christ, the planetary Logos and Those great Lives of Whose consciousness we can have no conception are becoming aware (note that phrase). For these attributes we have no words, and it is needless for us even to guess at their nature or to ponder upon their significance. They are as remote from our understanding as the aesthetic sense, group philanthropy and world states are from the consciousness of the aboriginal savage.

In connection with the problem of "presented attributes", it might be stated that those which characterise the soul and which cannot express themselves until the soul is consciously known and steadily achieving control, could be illustrated through attention to the word *Love*. Love is such a presented attribute, and it took a great Avatar, such as the Christ, to grasp for humanity and present to humanity its significance. It has taken two thousand years for this presented attribute to take even the form it has in the consciousness of the human family, and those of us who are students of world affairs well know how unknown real love is. Even today, in relation to the entire planetary population, there is only a very small group (a few million would be an optimistic speculation) who have even a beginner's grasp of what the love of God really is.

Love is the presented attribute which is at this time working into manifestation. *Wisdom* began to emerge in the time of the Buddha, and was the specified forerunner of love. *Synthesis* is another of the presented attributes and is only now making its appeal for recognition—an appeal which can only evoke response from the higher types of men, even though centuries have elapsed since Plato endeavoured to picture forth the completeness of the Whole and the intricacy of the ideas which have come forth as an expression of that Whole. Such great Revealers of emerging divine attributes as are Plato, the Buddha or Christ differ radically from other Avatars in that They are so constituted that They are focal points through which a new presented attribute can emerge as a thought form, and, therefore, impinge definitely upon the minds of the racial thinkers. These Avatars are *possessed* by the attribute; They intelligently comprehend it and are used to "anchor" the attribute in human consciousness. There then ensues a long period of adjustment, development and emergence before the presented attribute becomes the expressed attribute. The above few comments may serve to simplify your thought on these abstruse matters, and give you a better idea of the true scope of these advanced meditations.

The result of using this meditation on the presented attributes will be:

1. The attributes already expressing themselves somewhat will achieve an intensified livingness in the daily life-expression of the disciple, and consequently in the lives of all whom he may touch. They will form the stepping-stones across the river of life down which the new attributes may come, presenting themselves in the Persons of Those Who are destined to reveal them eventually to man. Just as, symbolically speaking, the meditation on Inclusive Reason opens the way to the "heart of the Sun", so this meditation brings in certain agencies and forces from the "central spiritual Sun", and these energies find their focal point through the medium of some re-

vealing Agent. Thus the problem of Avatars or of the Messengers from the Most High, the Embodied Principles, and the Revealers of Divine Attribute will gradually come to be understood in a new light, and grasped and understood as a possible goal for certain types of men.

2. This theme opens up a wide range wherein the creative imagination can roam, and provides a fertile source of specialised divine expression. The purer the agent, the better should be the functioning of the imagination, which is essentially the planned activity of the image-making faculty. By its means, subtle divine attributes and purposes can be presented in some form to the minds of men, and can thus in time achieve material expression. This involves the higher sensitivity, power to respond intuitionally, intellectual ability to interpret that which is sensed, focussed attention in order to "bring down" into manifestation the new potentiality and possibility of the divine nature, and an organised stability and purity of life. Ponder on this.

3. This use of the creative imagination will appear to you immediately as constituting, in itself, a definite field of service. Of this service, the highest of which you can know anything is that of the Group of Contemplatives, connected with the inner planetary Hierarchy, Who are called Nirmanakayas in the ancient books. They are entirely occupied with the task of *sensing* and with the endeavour to express the presented attributes which must some day be as familiar to men (theoretically, at least) as are the gradually expressing attributes of Love, Beauty or Synthesis today. On a much lower plane, those of you who are occupied with the effort to make soul quality expressed factors in your lives are beginning

to perform, on your level of consciousness, a task somewhat similar to that of the Divine Contemplatives. It is good training for the work you may have to do as you prepare for initiation. The small lesson mastered (and many of you are finding it a hard lesson) leads inevitably to wider opportunity in Service.

I have given enough information on which deeply to think and reflect. I have pointed out a goal which is impossible of achievement as yet, but one which leads eventually to that assured faith which is based upon direct knowledge and vision. I have briefly indicated the triple techniques of Integration, Fusion and Duality, and have shown you how, by means of them, the three rays of the Personality, the Ego and the Monad can be fused and blended until Deity, the essential divine Life, is revealed and from a materialised Triplicity only an eventual Unity can be seen. We will next take up some of the problems of Psychology, studying them from the angle of the soul.

3. *Some Problems of Psychology*

INTRODUCTION

What I have here to say should be of general interest. I intend to write with great simplicity, avoiding the technical terms of academic psychology, and putting the human psychological problem so plainly that real help may eventuate to many. These days are fraught with difficulty and it would sometimes appear that the necessary environmental adjustments are so hard and the equipment so inadequate to the demanded task that humanity is being asked to perform the impossible. It is as if the human frame had accumulated so much physical disability, so much emotional stress and had inherited so much disease and over-sensitivity that men fall back defeated. It is as if the attitude of man to the past, to the present and to the future was of such a nature that there seems no reason for existence, that there is nothing toward which to look, and no help to be found in retrospection.

I am, therefore, widely generalising. There are those to whom this generalisation does not apply, but even they, if they are students of human affairs, of sociological conditions, and of human equipment, are prone to question and at times to despair. Life is so difficult these days; the tension to which men are subjected is so extreme; the future appears so threatening; and the masses of men are so ignorant, diseased and distressed. I am putting this gloomy picture before you at the start of our discussion in order to evade no issue, to paint no silly optimistic and glamourous situation, or to portray no easy way of escape which would only lead us deeper into the gloomy forest of human error and illusion.

Yet, could we but know it, present conditions indicate their own cause and cure. I trust that by the time we have studied the problem (cursorily, I realise, for that is all that is possible) I shall have been able to indicate a possible way out and to have offered such practical suggestions that light may appear in the dense darkness, the future hold much promise, and the present much of experiment, leading to improvement and understanding.

The major science today is Psychology. It is one that is yet in its infancy but it holds the fate of humanity in its grasp and it has the power (rightly developed and employed) to save the race. The reason for its greatness and usefulness lies in the fact that it lays the emphasis upon the relation of the unit to the whole, to the environment and contacts; it studies man's equipment and apparatus of such contact, and seeks to produce right adaptation, correct integration and coordination and the release of the individual to a life of usefulness, fulfilment and service.

Some of the difficulties which have to be faced as one considers the conclusions of the many, many schools of Psychology are based upon the fact of their failure to relate the many points of view to each other. The same cleavage and even warfare is to be found within the confines of this science as are found in the individual man or in the religious field. There is to be found a lack of synthesis, a failure to correlate results, and a tendency to over-emphasise one aspect of the ascertained truth to the exclusion of others equally important. The outstanding weakness or weaknesses in an individual's equipment or presentation of life (and also those of the group or social order) are considered to the exclusion and even negation of other weaknesses not so obvious but equally crippling. Prejudice, dependent upon a biassed scholastic training, often frustrates the outlook so that the weakness in the psychologist's own equipment negates his efforts to aid the patient. The failure of education today to take into consideration the whole man, or to allow scope for the activity of an integrating centre, a central point of consciousness, and a determining factor within the mechanism of the one who must be helped to adapt himself to his life condition— this above everything else is responsible for much of the trouble. The assertion of the purely materialistic and scientific attitude which recognises only the definitely proven, or that which can be proved by the acceptance of an immediate hypothesis, has led to much loss of time. When again the creative imagination can be released in every department of human thought we shall see many new things brought to light that are at present only accepted by the religiously inclined and by the pioneering minds. One of the first fields of investigation to be benefited by this release will be that of psychology.

Organised religion has, alas, much to answer for, because of its fanatical emphasis upon doctrinal pronouncements, and its penalisation of those who fail to accept such dicta has served to stultify the human approach to God and to reality. Its over-emphasis upon the unattainable and its culture of the sense of sin down the centuries have led to many disastrous conditions, to interior conflicts which have distorted life, to morbidity, sadistic attitudes, self-righteousness and an ultimate despair which is the negation of truth.

When right education (which is the true science of adaptation) and right religion (which is the culture of the sense of divinity) and right scientific unfoldment (which is the correct appreciation of the form or forms through which the subjective life of divinity is revealing itself) can be brought into right relation to each other and thus supplement each other's conclusions and efforts, we shall then have men and women trained and developed in all parts of their natures. They will then be simultaneously citizens of the kingdom of souls, creative members of the great human family, and sound animals with the animal body so developed that it will provide the necessary instrument upon the outer plane of life for divine, human and animal revelation. This, the coming New Age, will see take place and for it men are today consciously or unconsciously preparing.

We will divide the problems of psychology into the following groupings:

1. The Problems of Cleavage, leading frequently to the many ways of escape, which constitute the bulk of the modern complexes.

2. The Problems of Integration, which produce many of the difficulties of the more advanced people.
3. The Problems due to Inheritance, racial, family, etc., involving the problems of inherited diseases, with consequent crippling of the individual.

With this third group I shall deal very little. There is not much to be done save to leave to time and greater wisdom much of the solution, coupled with an effort to bring amelioration to the individual thus afflicted, to supply glandular deficiency, training in self-control if possible, and the bringing of the physical vehicle to as high a point of development as may be possible within limits. The time is coming when every infant will early be subjected to certain tests and become the recipient of skilled care so that the apparatus of contact may be as usable as possible, as adaptive as may be, and as sound as it can be rendered. But I would here remind you that no physical equipment can be brought beyond a certain point of development in any one life—a point determined by the stage reached under the evolutionary process, by racial factors, by the quality of the subtle or subjective nature, by past experience and by soul contact (distant, approaching or already made), and by the mental equipment.

For the right understanding of our subject, and of my method of handling it, I would like to lay down four fundamental propositions:

1. That in time and space, man is essentially dual, consisting of soul and body, of intelligent life and form, of a spiritual entity and the apparatus of contact—the body nature whereby that entity can become aware of worlds of phenomena and states of consciousness of a nature different to those on its own level of awareness.
2. That this body nature consists of the physical outer form,

the sum total of vitality or the etheric body (which science today is rapidly coming to recognise), the sensitive, emotional, desire body, and the mind. Through the physical body contact is made with the environing tangible world; through the vital body the impulses come which produce direction and activity upon the physical plane; through the sensory vehicle the astral or emotional nature originates the bulk of those desires and impulses which direct the undeveloped or average man, and which can be called desire-impulses or the wish-life of the individual; through the mind comes eventually intelligent understanding and a life directed by purpose and planning instead of desire.

3. That human unfoldment proceeds by a series of integrations, of processes of coordination or synthesis, involving as they do (particularly when the intelligence is beginning to control) a sense of cleavage and of duality. These integrations, as far as humanity is concerned, either lie far behind in the past, are proceeding at this time, or lie ahead in the future.

> *Past Integrations.*
>> Between the animal body and the vital body.
>> Between these two and the sensitive desire nature.
>> Between these three and the lower concrete mind.
>
> *Present Integrations.*
>> Between these four aspects thus producing a coordinated personality.
>
> *Future Integration.*
>> Between the personality and the Soul.

There are other and higher integrations but with these we

need not here concern ourselves. They are reached through the processes of initiation and of service. The point to be remembered is that in racial history, many of these integrations have already taken place unconsciously as the result of life-stimulation, the evolutionary urge, the normal processes of living, experience through contact with the environment, and also of satisfaction leading to satiety of the desire nature. But there comes a time in racial unfoldment, as in the lives of individuals, when the blind process of evolutionary acquiescence becomes the living conscious effort, and it is right at this point that humanity stands today. Hence the realisation of the human problem in terms of modern psychology; hence the widespread suffering of human units everywhere; hence the effort of modern education; and hence also the emergence in every country on a wide scale and in increasingly large numbers of three kinds of people:

Those conscious of cleavage.

Those achieving integration with much pain and difficulty.

Personalities, or integrated and therefore dominant people.

4. That at the same time in every country, men and women are proceeding towards a still higher synthesis and achieving it:—the synthesis of soul and body. This produces a sense of destiny, individual and racial; a sense of purpose, and of plan. It produces also the unfoldment of the intuition (the sublimation of the intellect, as that was the sublimation of the instinctual nature) and the consequent recognition of the higher ideas and idealism, and of those basic truths which when disseminated among the thinking people of the world, will produce great mental and material changes, with their transitory accompaniments and upheaval, of chaos, experiment, destruction and re-building.

Humanity provides a cultural field for all types, i. e. for those who are today expressions of past integrations, and those who are in process of becoming thinking human beings. The two earliest integrations, between the vital body and the physical form, and between these two and the desire nature, are no longer represented. They are universal and lie below the threshold of conscious activity and far behind in racial history. The only field in which they can be studied is in those processes of recapitulatory history of infancy wherein one can see the power to move and respond to the sensory apparatus, and the power to express desire, most clearly demonstrated. The same thing can also be noticed in infant and savage races. But the third stage of integration, that of gradual mental development, is proceeding apace and can be, and is being, most carefully studied. Today, modern education is occupied almost exclusively with this stage and when educators cease to train the brain cells or to deal with the evocation of memory, and when they cease to regard the brain and the mind as one, but learn to differentiate between the two, then great strides forward will be made. When the child receives training in mind control and when that mind is taught to direct the desire nature and the brain, producing direction of the physical vehicle from the mental level, then we shall see these three integrations carried forward with precision and with rapidity. Attention will then be given to the integration of the personality, so that all three aspects shall function as one unit. We have, therefore:

1. The *child* state, in which the three first integrations are brought about, and the objective of the educational procedure will be to effect this with the minimum of difficulty.
2. The *human* state, dealing with the integration of all the

aspects into one functioning self-conscious, self-directed personality.

3. The *spiritual* state, dealing with the integration of the personality and the soul, thus evoking the consciousness of the *Whole*. When this is accomplished, group consciousness is added to self-consciousness, and this is the second great step on the way to God consciousness.

The difficulty today is that we have on every hand people at all different stages in the integrative process; all of them in a "state of crisis" and all of them therefore providing the problems of modern psychology.

These problems may be divided more precisely into three major groupings:

a. *The Problems of Cleavage.* These in their turn are of two kinds:

1. The problems of integration.
2. Those arising out of a sense of duality.

This sense of duality, as the result of realised cleavage, ranges all the way from the "split personality" difficulties of so many people to those of the mystic with his emphasis upon the lover and the loved, the seeker and the sought, upon God and His child.

b. *The Problems of Integration*, which produce many of the difficulties of the more advanced people.

c. *The Problems of Stimulation.* These arise as the result of an achieved synthesis and integration, producing consequently an inflow of unaccustomed energy. This inflow may express itself as a high voltage ambition, as a sense of power, as desire for personality influence or as true spiritual power and force. In every case, however, comprehension of the resultant phenomena is required, and most careful handling.

Arising from these problems we find also—

1. *Mental Problems.* Certain definite complexes occur when the integration of the mind with the three lower aspects has been brought about, and some clear thought about them will be useful.

2. *The Diseases of Mystics.* These are concerned with those attitudes of mind, those complexities of idea and those "spiritual enterprises" which affect the mystically inclined or those who are aware of the spiritual dualism of which St. Paul wrote in the Epistle to the Romans. He wrote as follows:

> "For we know that the law is spiritual: but I am carnal, sold under sin.
>
> For that which I do I allow not: for what I would, that do I not; but what I hate, that do I.
>
> If then I do what I would not, I consent under the law that *it is* good.
>
> Now then it is no more I that do it, but sin that dwelleth in me.
>
> For I know that in me (that is, in my flesh), dwelleth no good thing: for to will is present with me; but *how* to perform that which is good I find not.
>
> For the good that I would, I do not: but the evil which I would not, that I do.
>
> Now if I do that I would not, it is no more I that do it, but sin that dwelleth in me.
>
> I find then a law, that, when I would do good, evil is present with me.
>
> For I delight in the law of God after the inward man:
>
> But I see another law in my members, warring against the law of my mind, and bringing me into captivity to the law of sin which is in my members.

O wretched man that I am! Who shall deliver me from the body of this death?" (Romans VII, 14-24)

These difficulties will call for increasing attention as the race proceeds towards personality integration and from thence to soul contact.

It will be apparent to you, therefore, how wide is our subject and of what real importance. It will be obvious to you also that much of our nervous disease, our inhibitions, suppressions, submissions, or their reverse aspects, are tied up with this whole process of successive syntheses or fusions.

Two points should be touched upon here: First, that in any consideration of the human being—whether we regard him simply as a man or as a spiritual entity—we are in reality dealing with a most complex aggregate of *differentiated energies*, through which or among which the consciousness plays. This consciousness is, in the early stages, nothing more than a vague diffused awareness, undefined, unidentified and free from any definite focus of attention. Later, it becomes more awake and aware and the focus becomes centred in the realm of selfish desire, and its satisfaction and assuagement. To this condition we can give the general name of the "wish life" with its objective, personal happiness, leading eventually to consummated desire, but a consummated desire postponed till after death and to which we have given the name "heaven". Later (again as the mind nature integrates with the other more developed aspects), we have the emergence of a definitely self-conscious entity, and a strictly human being, characterised by intelligence, comes into active expression. The focus of attention is still· the satisfaction of desire, but it is the desire to know, the will to understand through investigation, discrimination and analysis.

Finally comes the period of personality integration wherein

there is the will-to-power, with self-consciousness directed to the domination of the lower nature, and with the objective of the domination of the environment, of other human beings in small or large numbers, and of circumstance. When this has been grasped and understood, the focus of attention shifts into the realm of the higher energies, and the soul factor becomes increasingly active and prominent, dominating and disciplining the personality, interpreting its environment in new terms, and producing a synthesis, hitherto unrecognised, between the two kingdoms of nature—the human and the spiritual.

Throughout all these processes we see the bringing together of many types of energy, all of them distinguished by quality of some kind or another, which—when brought into relation with each other—produce first of all a period of chaos, of anarchy and of difficulty. Later ensues a period of synthesis, of organised activity and of a fuller expression of divinity. But there remains for a long time the need for recognition of energy and its right use.

The second point I seek to make is that these inner energies make their contact through the medium of the vital or etheric body, which is composed of energy streams; these work through seven focal points or centres of force in the etheric body. These centres of energy are found in close proximity to, or in relation to, the seven sets of major glands:

1. The pineal gland.
2. The pituitary body.
3. The thyroid and para-thyroid glands.
4. The thymus gland.
5. The pancreas.
6. The adrenals.
7. The gonads.

These centres are:

1. The head centre.
2. The centre between the eyebrows.
3. The throat centre.
4. The heart centre.
5. The solar plexus centre.
6. The centre at the base of the spine.
7. The sacral centre.

These centres are closely concerned with the endocrine system, which they determine and condition according to the quality and source of the energy which flows through them. With this I have dealt at length in my other books, and so shall not here enlarge upon it beyond calling your attention to the relation between the centres of force in the etheric body, the processes of integration, which bring one centre after another into activity, and the eventual control of the soul, after the final at-one-ment of the entire personality.

Only when modern psychologists add to the amazingly interesting knowledge they have of the lower man, an occidental interpretation of the oriental teaching about the centres of force through which the subjective aspects of man—lower, personal and divine—are to be expressed, will they solve the human problem and arrive at an understanding of the technique of unfoldment and of integration which will lead to intelligent comprehension, a wise solution of the difficulties, and a correct interpretation of the peculiarities with which they are so frequently confronted. When to this acceptance can be added a study of the seven major types, the science of psychology will be brought another step nearer its eventual usefulness as a major instrument in the technique of human perfecting. They will be greatly helped also by a study of astrology from the angle of energy contacts, of the lines of least resistance, and as one of the determining influences and characteristics of the type under consideration. I refer not here to the casting of a horoscope with the objective of discovering the future or of determining action. This aspect of astrological interpretation will become less and less useful as men achieve the power to control and to govern their stars and so direct their own lives. I refer to the recognition of the astrological types, of their characteristics and qualities and tendencies.

Bearing in mind the analysis earlier made of the various aspects of the human being, which—during the evolutionary process—are gradually fused into one integrated person, let us remember that the fusion effected and the changes brought about are the result of the steady shift of the consciousness. It becomes increasingly inclusive. We are not dealing here with the form aspect as much as with the conscious realisation of the dweller in the body. It is in this region that our problems lie, and it is with this developing consciousness that the psychologist has primarily to deal. From the angle of the omniscient soul, the consciousness is limited, disturbed, exclusive, self-centred, distorted, erratic and, in the early stages, deceived. It is only when the processes of development have been carried forward to a relatively high point and the awareness of duality is beginning to emerge, that the real problems and the major difficulties and dangers are encountered and the man becomes aware of his situation. Before that time, the difficulties are of a different nature and revolve largely around the physical equipment, are concerned with the slowness of the vital reactions and the low grade desires of the animal nature. The human being is, at that stage, largely an animal, and the conscious man is deeply hidden and imprisoned. It is the life principle and urge which dominate and the instinctual nature which controls. The solar plexus is the seat of the consciousness and the head and brain are inactive.

It should also be remembered here (as I have oft pointed out) that the reality which we call the soul is basically an expression of three types of energy—life, love and intelligence. For the reception of these three energies, the triple lower nature has been prepared and the intelligence aspect reflects itself in the mind, the love nature in the emotional desire body, and the life principle in and through the etheric or vital body. As regards the physical body in its more dense expression (for the etheric body is the more subtle aspect or expression of the physical body), the soul anchors itself in two streams of energy at two points of contact: the life stream in the heart and the consciousness stream in the head. This consciousness aspect is itself dual, and that which we call self-consciousness is gradually unfolded and perfected until the ajna centre, or the centre between the eyebrows, is awakened. The latent group-consciousness, which brings realisation of the greater Whole, is quiescent for the greater part of the evolutionary cycle, until the integrative process has proceeded to such a point that the personality is functioning. Then the head centre begins to awaken and the man becomes conscious in the larger sense. Head and heart then link up, and the spiritual man appears in fuller expression.

This, I know, is familiar teaching to you but it is of value briefly to recapitulate and get the picture clear. Bearing these premises in mind, we will not deal with the earliest difficulties but will begin with those of modern man, and with those conditions with which we are all too sadly familiar.

a. PROBLEMS OF CLEAVAGE

Thinkers are today awakening to this particular type of difficulty and finding the cleavages in human nature so widespread and so deep seated in the very constitution of the race itself that they are viewing the situation with much concern. These cleavages seem basic, and produce the divisions we find everywhere between race and race and between religion and religion, and can be traced back to the fundamental condition of manifestation which we call the relationship of positive and negative, of male and female and, esoterically speaking, of the sun and the moon. The mystery of sex itself is bound up with the re-establishment of the sense of unity and of balance, of oneness or of wholeness. In its higher human aspect, this sexual differentiation is only the symbol or lowest expression of the cleavage or separativeness of which the mystic is aware and which makes him seek at-one-ment or union with what he calls divinity. In between this physical cleavage and this spiritual recognition of divinity lie a large number of lesser cleavages of which man becomes aware.

Behind all of this is to be found a still more fundamental cleavage—that between the human kingdom and the kingdom of souls—a cleavage in consciousness more than in fact. The cleavage between the animal and the human kingdom has been largely resolved through the recognition of the physical identity of the animal nature and the uniformity in expression of the instinctual nature. Within the human family, the various cleavages of which man is so distressingly aware will be bridged and ended when the mind is trained to control and to dominate within the realm of the personality and is correctly used as an analytical, integrating factor instead of as a critical, discriminating, separative factor. The right use of the intellect is essential to the healing of the personality cleavages. The cleavage between personality and the soul is resolved by the right use of:

1. The *instinctual* sense of divinity which leads to reorientation in the right direction. This leads to—
2. The *intelligent* use of the mind so that it becomes consciously aware of the soul and of the laws which govern soul unfoldment.
3. The *intuitive* recognition of reality, which resolves the differentiated parts into a unit, producing illumination.
4. This *illumination* reveals the essential oneness which exists on the the inner side of life and negates the outer appearance of separativeness.

Thus it will be apparent to you that the cleavages are "healed" by a right and intelligent use of the quality aspect of the form nature:

1. *Instinct* distinguishes the automatic physical nature, the vital or life vehicle and the desire nature. It works through the solar plexus and the organs of reproduction.
2. *Intelligence* distinguishes the mind aspect or mental vehicle, and works through the clearing house of the brain, and through the ajna and throat centres.
3. *Intuition* distinguishes the soul nature and it works through the mind, the heart centre and the head centre. From these three major points the soul governs eventually the personality.

I commend these ideas to your careful consideration and assure you that rightly understood they will aid in the solution of the problems connected with the various cleavages in human nature.

There is no cleavage to be found today between the vital body and the physical body. There is only at times a partial cleavage and what one might call a "loose connection". The two streams of living energy—life and consciousness—are usually anchored in the head and heart. In the case of certain forms of idiocy however, the consciousness stream is not anchored at all in the body, but only the life stream has made its contact in the heart. There is, therefore, no self-consciousness, no power of centralised control and no capacity to direct action or to provide in any way a life programme or plan. There is only responsiveness to aspects of the instinctual nature.

Certain forms of epilepsy are due to what we might call "a loose connection", the consciousness stream or thread of energy is subject at times to withdrawal or abstraction, and this produces the familiar epileptoid symptoms and the distressing conditions seen in the usual fit. In a lesser degree, and producing no permanent, dangerous results, the same basic cause produces the so-called "petit mal" and certain types of fainting fits; these are caused by the brief and temporary withdrawal of the thread of consciousness energy. It should be remembered that when this withdrawal takes place and there is a separation of the consciousness from the vehicle of conscious contact, all that we understand by the term consciousness, such as self-consciousness, desire and intelligence, is abstracted and only life and the consciousness inherent in the physical body cells remain.

As a rule, however, the average man today is a closely knit and functioning unit. (This is true whether one is considering the unevolved masses or the materialistically minded citizens of the world.) He is firmly integrated physically, etherically and emotionally. His physical body, his vital body and his desire nature (for emotion is but expressed desire of some kind or another) are closely knit. At the same time there can be a weakness in the etheric integration, of such a nature that there is a low vitality, a lack of desire impulses, a failure to register adequate dynamic incentives, immaturity and sometimes obsession or possession. Frequently what is called a lack of will and the labelling of a person as "weak-willed" or "weak-minded" has in reality nothing to do with the will, but is apt to be the result of this feeble integration and loose connection between the consciousness and the brain which renders the man negative to the desire impulses which should normally stream through into his brain, galvanising his physical vehicle into some form of activity.

The will, which usually demonstrates itself through a programme or ordered plan, originates in the mind and not on the desire levels of awareness, and this programme is based on a sense of direction and a definite orientation of the will to a recognised objective, and it is not, in these cases, the cause of the difficulty. The trouble is simpler and lies nearer home. The handling of these difficulties and their right solution is of a definitely material nature, and the trouble is frequently overcome by increasing the vitality of the body, building up the etheric body, through sunshine, vitaminous foods and exercise, plus correct treatment and balancing of the endocrine system. Along these lines much work is being done today and the less serious forms of etheric cleavage are rapidly yielding to treatment. Lack of vitality, immaturity, depression based upon a weak vital connection and lack of interest in life (so prevalent at this time) will become less frequent.

I cannot here deal at length with the problems of obsession, due to the withdrawal of the self-conscious aspect of the dweller in the body. This process of abstraction leaves only a living shell, an empty house. Too much would have to be considered for a treatise such as this. It is not easy for the scientific psychological investigator to accept the premise of the substitution of the consciousness of another entity in the place of the consciousness of the one who has been unable to hold the link within the brain with adequate positiveness. But, speaking as one who knows, such cases frequently occur, leading to many of the problems of so-called "split personality" which is in reality the ownership of a particular physical body by the two persons—one providing the life stream (anchored in the heart) and the other providing the stream of consciousness (anchored in the brain) and thus controlling the body, directing its activities and expressing itself through the organs of speech. Sometimes this possession alternates between the two individuals concerned. Sometimes more than two are concerned, and several persons upon the inner side of life use the same physical body. Then you have multiple personalities. This is however due to a definite weakness in the etheric connection of the original dweller; or again it may be due to that dweller's great dislike for physical incarnation; again it may be caused by some shock or disaster which suddenly severs the link of consciousness, and in this latter case there is no hope of restoration. Each case has to be diagnosed and dealt with on its individual merits and preferably by dealing directly with the real dweller when he is "at home in his own dwelling". Furthermore, the consciousness of this dweller is sometimes so strongly orientated in directions other than those of physical existence that a process of abstraction has taken place, with the focus of the conscious interest elsewhere. This is the undesirable side or expression of the same power of abstraction which enables the mystic to see his visions and to participate in heavenly happenings, and which enables the advanced adept to enter into the state of Samadhi. In the one case, the vehicle is left unguarded and the prey of any passing visitor; and in the other it is left duly guarded and positively attentive to the call and the note of its owner.

It is not possible for me to do more than hint at these various explanations and so start investigators with open minds and the willingness to accept unusual hypotheses, along a trail which may lead them into the valley of understanding. The clue to success in eliminating these types of difficulty lies in pre-natal care and study of hereditary taints; syphilis and the other venereal diseases are potent predisposing causes. The right culture of the body nature after birth and the development in the child of a positive sense of himself, thus making him positive in thought and training his sense of self-identity —all these are sound helps towards the elimination of this type of trouble. The tendency today to emphasise the vitamins in food and to give a balanced diet is all to the good.

The true sense of cleavage and really serious difficulty comes, however, when two things have occurred. These might be stated to be as follows:

1. The self-consciousness of the man has reached a point where his desires are so dominant and compelling that he becomes aware of their strength, and also simultaneously of his inability truly to satisfy them, coupled with the recognition that there is an aspect of himself which does not truly want to do so. The sense of frustration then descends upon him and he becomes painfully aware of what he wants and of what he would be if his desires were met and satisfied. He is then torn in two directions: his desire-mind keeps him dwelling in the realm of longing, of hope and of wish, whilst his brain and his physical nature bring to him the conviction that nothing he wants is possible and if possible, does he really want it? This is true of the man whose objective is the satisfaction of his material longings or of the man who is responding to the desire for intellectual or spiritual satis-

faction. In the one case the cleavage begins to appear in the lower aspects of his desire nature. In the other it appears in the higher aspects, but in both cases the lines of the cleavage are clear. The conflict has begun and two possibilities lie ahead:

a. Eventual acquiescence of a nature which ends the life in futility, deep depression and a sense of frustration which runs all the way from a submissive life of acceptance to those many ways of escape which push a man into the dream world, into the land of illusion, into a state of negativity and even over the border to death through self-destruction.

b. A furious conflict, based on a refusal to be moulded by circumstance or environment. This drives a man on to success and to achievement of his desire or it breaks him on the wheel of life, either physically or mentally.

2. Cleavage comes also when the man fails to use his God-given intellect and so is unable to choose between the essentials and the non-essentials, between right direction and wrong goals, between the various satisfactions which appeal to the various aspects of his lower nature and eventually between the higher and the lower duality. He must learn to grasp the distinction between:

a. Submission to the inevitable and submission to the urge of his own desire.

b. Recognition of capacity and recognition of potentiality. Many conflicts would be solved through the summation, understanding and right use of recognised assets, thus eliminating impossible goals and the consequent inevitable frustration. When this part of the conflict has been overcome, then potentiality can emerge in recognition and become power in expression.

c. Recognition of individual goals and group goals, between the ability to be social or anti-social. Much is being done along these lines but the emphasis is still upon the individual and not upon the group. When this is the case, we become responsible for anti-social groups.

I have mentioned only three of many possible recognitions but the resolution of the cleavage for which these are responsible will result in the liberation of a large majority of sufferers. It might perhaps be said that the release of many whose cleavage lies primarily in the realm of the desire nature, leading to the sense of frustration and a break in the life continuity of interest, can be cured by—

1. Attention first of all to the physical equipment and to the glands, particularly to the thyroid gland, plus the regulation of the diet.

2. Attention to the physical coordination of the patient, for physical coordination is the outer expression of an inner process of integration and much can be done by training.

3. Interpretation of the life and the environment, given in terms of appreciation. Ponder on this.

4. Decentralisation through—

a. The providing of right interests and the right kind of education and vocational training.

b. Cultivation of the power to recognise and meet surrounding need, thus evoking the desire to serve and providing the sense of satisfaction which comes from accomplishment and appreciation.

   c. The careful and slow transmutation of desire into aspira‑‑
     tion.

5. Reorientation to higher goals and the development of the
   sense of right direction. This involves

   a. The cultivation of a wider vision.
   b. The formulation of an inner programme, intelligently
     compiled, and suitable for the point in evolution but
     not so advanced as to be impossible.
   c. The avoidance of those steps and activities which are
     doomed to failure.

6. Later, when the above is somewhat grasped, there must be
   the search for, and the development of, any creative
   faculty, thus meeting the desire to be noticed and to
   contribute. Much artistic effort or literary and musical
   effort is based on the desire to be the centre of attention
   and is not based on any true creative ability. It is the
   sense of "I, the dramatic actor". This rightly used and
   developed, is of real value and importance.
7. The elimination of the sense of sin, of disapprobation, with
   its concomitants, revolt, suspicion and an inferiority
   complex.

One point I feel the need definitely to re-emphasise and
that is the necessity, when considering the human being and
his expression and existence, to remember that we are really
considering *energy*, and the relation or non-relation of forces.
As long as this is carefully borne in mind, we shall not go
astray as we deal with our subject. We are considering related units of energy, functioning in a field of energy; remembering this always, we shall (at least symbolically) be
enabled to get a fairly clear idea of our theme. As long as we
regard our problem as consisting of the inter-relation of

many energies, their fusion and their balancing, plus the final synthesis of two major energies, their fusion and their balancing, we shall arrive at some measure of understanding and subsequent solution. The field of energy which we call the soul (the major energy with which man is concerned) absorbs, dominates or utilises the lesser energy which we call the personality. This it is necessary for us to realise; and to remember, at the same time, that this personality is itself composed of four types of energy. According to our ray type, so will be our use of the words "absorbs, dominates and utilises". I would here remind you, as I have oft done before, that words fail to express and language handicaps rather than aids the objective that I have in view. Human thought is now entering a field for which there exists, as yet, no true language-form, for we have no adequate terms, and in which word-symbols mean but little. Just as the discovery of the automobile, and the radio have necessitated the formulation of an entirely new set of terms, phrases, nouns and verbs, so in the years that are coming the discovery of the fact of the soul will necessitate a new language approach. It is true, is it not, that a man of the Victorian age, listening to the technical jargon of the present radio laboratory or the ordinary garage, would be completely in the dark? So the psychologist of today is in the dark very often and understands not what we are trying to convey, for the new language is not yet evolved and the old terms are inadequate. I am, therefore, unable to do more than employ the terms which seem to me to be the most suitable, knowing that I am failing to express the true significance of my ideas, and you are consequently gaining only an approximate understanding and conception of the concepts I am endeavoring to expound.

We have already somewhat considered the problem of the

cleavages to which man is subject, and we saw that the human evolutionary process was, in the last analysis, a series of at-one-ments; each step forward meant the bringing together of certain types of energy in order that their fusion might produce a more complete person. May I state here an interesting point? The problem itself is brought about by the fact that there *Is* an Observer. This Observer, at certain points in the normal development of the man, comes to the realisation that there are cleavages. This Observer suffers because of their existence in his self-awareness. He realises that he is the victim of the divisions in his nature. Yet—and this is of importance—the man upon the physical plane is unable either to understand them or, apparently, to heal them without aid from the soul, the Observer, the higher aspect of himself. For instance, a man suffering from dissociation between the emotional, sentient part of himself and the mental aspect is aware of need, of frustration and of intense suffering and difficulty, yet needs the understanding help of a trained psychologist or of his own soul before fusion can be made and he, as an individual, can "be made *whole*".

This same truth exists in connection with all the cleavages found in man, but three of these cleavages are of major importance:

1. The cleavage between the mind and the rest of the lower nature—physical, vital, astral or emotional.
2. The cleavage between the man and his environment which—when once healed and bridged—makes him a responsible human being and a good citizen who accepts his environment and gives to it of his best. Thus he grows in character and capacity, as a result of a definite interplay between the two—himself and his environment.

3. The cleavage between the man (the personality) and the soul. This produces sequentially:
   a. A dominant selfish personality.
   b. A practical mystic, conscious of the need for fusion and for unity.

Parallels to these states of consciousness are found in the adolescent. They are found also in the man who is integrating into his life work, and also in the thinking aspirant. This is true, whether his thoughts, purposes and ambitions are self-ishly polarised or spiritually inclined. The sense of cleavage, the need for orientation, the bridging process and the ultimate sense of achievement are identical in both cases.

In dealing with these situations certain general rules should govern the psychologist, and certain general premises should eventually be accepted by the man who constitutes the problem case. These same rules and premises can be considered and accepted by the man who, without the aid of a trained psychologist, manages to train himself and to bridge his realised cleavages. These basic premises are:

1. That any psychological difficulty is universal and not unique. It is the sense of uniqueness—with its separative tendency and its realised loneliness—which is often the all-engrossing factor. It makes the personality too important, and this should be definitely negated.

2. That the crisis faced indicates progress and opportunity, and that it does not indicate disaster and failure. It must be realised by the patient (can I use that term?) that the race has progressed to its present point in evolution by just such crises. So does the individual human unit progress. In the last analysis, psychological crises are indicative of progressive steps upon the *Way*, bringing with them the need for effort and at the same time a

sense of gain and of freedom, when surmounted, overcome and solved.

3. That the power to produce the needed integration and to end a cycle of sensed duality lies within the man himself because:

  a. His discomfort, lack of coordination, pain and distress are symptoms of aspiration, unrealised perhaps but none the less there. They are the reaction of the integrated aspects to that aspect which is seeking integration.

  b. The aspect to be integrated is essentially more powerful than the lower *waiting* aspects, for they are negative or receptive whilst that which should be realised and accepted is positive and dynamic. Hence the sensed discomfort.

4. That the capacity, innate in that imaginative creature, man, to act "as if", holds the solution to the problem. By the use of the creative imagination, the bridge between the lower aspect and higher can be built and constructed. "As a man thinketh, hopeth and willeth" so is he. This is a statement of an immutable fact.

When modern psychologists comprehend more fully the creative purpose of humanity, and seek to develop the creative imagination more constructively, and also to train the directional will, much will be accomplished. When these two factors (which are the signal evidence of divinity in man) are studied and scientifically developed and utilised, they will produce the self-releasing of all the problem cases which are found in our clinics at this time. Thus we shall, through experiment, arrive at a more rapid understanding of man. Psychology can count definitely upon the innate ability of the human unit to understand the use of the creative imagination and the use of directed purpose, for it is found frequently even in children. The development of the sense of fantasy and the training of children to make choices (to the end that ordered purpose may emerge in their lives) will be two of the governing ideals of the new education. The sense of fantasy calls into play the imagination, perception of beauty, and the concept of the subjective worlds; the power of choice, with its implications of why and wherefore and to what end (if wisely taught from early days), will do much for the race, particularly if, at the time of adolescence, the general world picture and the world plan are brought to the attention of the developing intelligence. Therefore:

1. The sense of fantasy
2. The sense of choice
3. The sense of the whole
          plus
4. The sense of ordered purpose

should govern our training of the children which are coming into incarnation. The sense of fantasy brings the creative imagination into play, thus providing the emotional nature with constructive outlets; this should be balanced and motivated by the recognition of the power of right choice and the significance of the higher values. These, in turn, can be developed selflessly by a due recognition of the environing whole in which the individual has to play his part, whilst the entire range of reactions are increasingly subordinated by the understanding of the ordered purpose which is working out in the world.

These are the basic premises which should emerge in the new techniques which psychology will use when it has reached the point of accepting (or at least experimenting with) the above ideas. By their use, it will be found that the problem case itself can be brought into functioning right activity, for all the innate, and unused faculties of man will be swept into integrating activity. The process is always and inevitably the same:

1. Cleavage.
2. A recognition of duality, either subjectively or in the waking consciousness.
3. A period of wild unrest, of frustration and futility, leading sometimes to disaster, to forms of nervous or mental breakdown, and to generally chaotic and undesirable conditions.
4. An intelligently applied bridging process, gradually carried forward, *once the point of cleavage is determined.*
5. The achievement of periods of recognised fusion, integration or *true* normality. A process of analysis would here be useful. It will later be found that psycho-analysis will come into its real usefulness when it comes to the aid of a man in *explaining his achievement* rather than in unearthing the detail of his apparent disaster. There is no real disaster. There is only an unrecognised point of crisis, a moment of unrealised fulfilment. The disaster comes when this point of crisis is not utilised and understood, for it then serves to increase the cleavage instead of being recognised as a moment of opportunity.
6. The establishment of a definite rhythm composed of the creative imagination, of discriminating choice, of the value of the relation of the part to the whole, and of the acceptance of group purpose. This rhythm, when duly established in a life or in a series of lives, leads eventually to
7. Integration.

I would like to stop here and point out that the foundation of the new psychology must inevitably be built upon the premise that this one life is not man's sole opportunity in which to achieve integration and eventual perfection. The great Law of Rebirth must be accepted and it will then be found to be, in itself, a major releasing agent in any moment of crisis or any psychological problem case. The recognition of further opportunity and a lengthened sense of time are both quieting and helpful to many types of mind; its interpretative value will be found illuminating as the patient grasps the fact that behind him lie points of crisis wherein it can be demonstrated by his present equipment that he achieved integration, thus guaranteeing to him victory in his present point of crisis and of difficult conflict. The light which this throws on relationships and environment will serve to stabilise his purpose and make him comprehend the inevitability of responsibility. When this great law is understood in its true implications and not interpreted in terms of its present childish presentation, then man will shoulder the responsibility of living with a daily recognition of the past, an understanding of the purpose of the present, and with an eye to the future. This will also greatly lessen the growing tendency towards suicide which humanity is showing.

It will be apparent to you, therefore, that the time element can enter into the problem most helpfully and it is here that a real understanding of the Law of Rebirth, or of the Law of Opportunity (as I would prefer to call it) will be of definite usefulness. Above everything else, it will bring into the attitude of both psychologist and problem case, the idea of hope, the thought of fulfilment and of ultimate achievement.

It will also be essential that the psychologist of the future should arrive at a recognition and an admittance of the inner structure of the human being—of his emotional vehicle, his mind body and their close inter-relation through the medium of the vital or etheric body which serves ever as the *linking web* between the dense physical body and the other bodies. The soul and its triplicity of energies (life itself, expressing will or purpose, love and intelligence) work through the seven major centres, whilst the mind body and the astral body work through many other centres, though possessing also within themselves seven centres which are the transmitting counterparts of those found in the etheric body. The integrations which evolution eventually effects are carried out through the medium of all these centres. Through the heightening of vibration, through the swinging into activity of the centres, and through the subsequent and consequent development of the human response apparatus, new avenues of approach to reality, new qualities of awareness, new sensitivity to that which has hitherto been unrecognised, and new powers begin to open up.

Each man is, therefore, *within himself*, a hierarchy, a reflection of a great chain of being—the Being which the universe expresses. Psychology has to recognise eventually:

1. The fact of the soul, the integrating agent, the self.
2. The Law of Opportunity or Rebirth.
3. The nature of the inner structure of man and its relation to the outer tangible form.

It is interesting to note that practically all the teaching given anent rebirth or reincarnation has emphasised the material phenomenal side though there has always been a more or less casual reference to the spiritual and mental gains acquired in the school of life upon this planet, from incarnation to incarnation. The true nature of the unfolding awarenesses and the growth in the inner consciousness of the true man have been little noted; the gain of each life in added grasp of the mechanism of contact, and the result of increased sensitivity to the environment (which are the only values with which the self concerns itself), are seldom, if ever, stressed. Details of living conditions, statements about possible material situations, descriptions of places, clothes, and of personality human relations are imaginatively displayed, and the "recovery of past incarnations" has usually been the so-called recovery of dramatic episodes which feed the innate sense of individuality of the reincarnating man, and usually feed his vanity as well. This curious presentation has been due to several things. First of all, to the fact that the world of illusion is the dominating factor as yet in the lives of the best of men; secondly, that the point in evolution has been such that the writer or speaker has not been able to view the life cycle from the angle of the soul, detached and undeluded, for had he done so, the material phenomenal descriptions would have been omitted and probably not even perceived, and only the *values*—spiritual and mental—and those matters which concern the group interior life would have been emphasised. The methods used to present this age-old doctrine of rebirth, and the false emphasis laid upon the form aspect to the exclusion of the soul values, have brought about a bad reaction to the whole subject in the minds of intelligent people and of the scientific investigator. Yet, in spite of this, real good has been accomplished, for the whole theory has been seeping steadily into the racial consciousness, becoming an integral part of it and, therefore, moving on to popular and finally scientific recognition.

In considering the inner structure of man and those factors which produce the outer appearance and quality and condition it, thus producing the resultant behaviour and conduct, psychologists will have to study the following subjects, beginning with the lowest aspect and expanding their ideas to include the highest possible. These might be grouped and listed as follows:

1. *The outer response apparatus,* acting under impulses received from the outer environment and the inner subjective realms. These come, according to the esoteric theories, via

   a. The brain, from whence certain aspects of the nervous system are directed and controlled, first by mental influence and then by conscious soul direction.

   b. The endocrine or glandular system, acting under impulses entering the physical body via the seven centres in the etheric body; of these centres, the glandular system is simply the externalisation, or physical counterpart. The glands condition the man through the blood stream, being in their turn conditioned by the centres.

   c. The solar plexus, directing and controlling certain aspects of the nervous system, and which is in large part the instinctual or animal brain.

   d. The heart, the centre of life.

2. *The vital or etheric body.* This is the major energising factor and is an exact replica or counterpart of the outer form, being the true intermediary between the inner worlds and the outer man. The *nadis* (lines or threads of force) underlie every nerve in the human body and the centres which they form at certain points of intersection or juncture are the background or motivating agency of every ganglion or plexus found in the human body. Certain of these centres, major and minor, are of unique evolutionary importance. These are as follows:

a. The head centre is the seat of soul energy, or the centre through which the conscious, *spiritual* man functions.

b. The heart centre is the seat of life, of the highest principle which expresses itself through man.

c. The solar plexus centre is the seat of the instinctual life, of the animal soul, and of the highly developed emotional nature.

d. The centre at the base of the spine is the major integrating centre and comes into functioning activity when two major fusions have been effected: that of the fusions of the three bodies into one coordinated personality, and when soul and body are at-oned.

3. *The emotional or sentient body*, which is often called the astral body. From this vehicle emanate the desires, impulses, aspirations and those conflicts of duality which so oft afflict and hinder the disciple. It is the seat also of the creative, imaginative life of man. It also possesses centres of force which are counterparts of those to be found in the etheric body, but for the majority of people it is energised mainly from the world of illusion and from the astral plane. It is from this plane of illusory awareness, that the advanced man has to learn to withdraw himself.

4. *The mind nature*, which works through four centres and only four.

5. *The soul itself*, or the true spiritual man, the self in manifestation; working through or seeking to work through, its phenomenal appearance, the fourfold lower man.

If the above is carefully studied, it will become apparent that the cleavages which exist in man are cleavages in certain inherent or basic relations:

1. *Found within the man himself,* in one or other of these various focal points of realisation or awareness:

   a. Unrecognised by the man himself or by those around him. When this is the case, the man is unevolved and the cleavages or gaps in his consciousness do no real harm relatively, either to himself or to those in his environment. They simply indicate lack of development.

   b. When recognised, they produce distress and difficulty and the man becomes in need of sound psychological help. Correct information along the lines here laid down can be given in those cases where the intellectual type is involved; the psychologist is then dealing with people who should be able and willing to help themselves.

   c. When the man has effected the necessary bridging and unification, he then becomes a unified personality. Then the mystic can emerge. This means that he has achieved the point wherein the higher bridging between the integrated personality and the soul becomes possible. Finally, a Master of the Wisdom, Who is an exponent of the Christ consciousness, in its unifying, salvaging and constructive aspects, appears.

   The at-oning of the higher and the lower nature will produce results which will be determined in their field of expression by a man's ray. These ray conditions will result in a man's finding his right field of usefulness and right expression in the political, religious, or scientific fields, and in other modes of divine manifestation.

2. *Found between a man and his environment.* The effect of this may mean that he is an anti-social human being, or unpopular, full of fear of life, or expressing, in many

other forms, his inability to tune in on his surroundings. Lack of understanding, of right relationship, and inability correctly to blend the inner and the outer forms of the life structure, will be evidenced. The cause of the cleavage in this case is usually found somewhere within the astral body itself.

3. *Found between a man and his life task*, or the life activity to which fate ordains him and pre-disposition inclines him. The difficulty here lies in a definite break or failure of continuity between the mind nature, determining purpose, and the astral nature, governing impulse.

4. *Found between a man and his overshadowing* (*and slowly dominating*) *soul*. This leads to much realised unhappiness, dire conflict, and the eventual and symbolic "death of the personality."

Here again I would like to pause and to point out that the concepts of death, of substitution, of the vicarious at-one-ment and of sacrifice, will—in the New Age—be superseded by the concepts of resurrection or of livingness, of spiritual unity, of transference and of service, so that a new note will enter into human life, bringing hope and joy and power and freedom.

b. Problems of Integration

One of the first things which happens when a man has succeeded (alone or with academic psychological aid) in healing or bridging certain cleavages is the recognition of an immediate sense of well-being and of demand for expression. This in its turn, brings its own problems among which are these:

A sense of power, which makes the man, temporarily at least, selfish, dominant, sure of himself and full of arrogance. He is aware of himself as facing a larger world, a wider horizon, and greater opportunities. This larger sense can bring, therefore, serious troubles and difficulties. This type of person, under the influence of this extension of consciousness, is often beautifully motivated and actuated by the highest intentions, but only succeeds in producing inharmony in his surroundings. These tendencies, when allowed to rule unchecked, can lead eventually to a serious state of ego-mania, for ego-mania is outstandingly a problem of integration. All these difficulties can be obviated and offset if the man can be brought to realise himself as an integral part of a much greater whole. His sense of values will then be adjusted and his sense of power rightly oriented.

A tendency to over-emphasis may also show itself, turning the man (as a result of integration and a sense of well-being or power and capacity) into a fanatic, at any rate for a time. Again with the best motives in the world, he seeks to drive everyone the way that he has come, failing to recognise the differences in background, ray type, point in evolution, and tradition and heredity. He becomes a source of distress to himself and to his friends. A little learning can be a dangerous thing, and the cure for many ills, particularly of a psychological nature, is the recognition of this. Progress can then be made on the Path of Wisdom.

The over-development of the sense of direction or of vocation, if you like to call it so, though the two are not identical, for the sense of direction is less definite than the recognition of vocation. In the schools of esoteric psychology, a phrase is sometimes used in connection with this sense of direction or inner guidance which runs as follows: "the bridging of the gaps induces a man continuously to run across the bridge." Certain aspects of the man are now *consciously* recognised, and the higher of these constantly attracts him. When, for instance, the gap between the astral or emotional body and the mind has been bridged, and the man discovers the vast field of mental activity which has opened up before him, he may for a long time become materialistically intellectual and will tune out as far as he can all emotional reactions and psychic sensitivity, glamouring himself with the belief that they are, for him, non-existent. He will then work intensively on mental levels. This will prove only a passing matter from the point of vision of the soul (e'en if it last an entire incarnation or several incarnations); but it can cause definite psychological problems, and create in the man's perception of life, "blind spots." However, much trouble is cured by leaving people alone, provided the abnormality is not too excessive.

Once the fact of the soul is admitted, we shall see an increasing tendency to leave people to the directing purpose and guidance of their own souls, provided that they understand what is happening to them and can discriminate between:

a. The upward surging of the subconscious self into the lighted area of consciousness,
b. The play and force and recognitions of the immediately conscious self.
c. The downflow of the superconscious self, the soul, carrying inspiration, higher knowledges and intuitions.

These words—subconscious, conscious and super-conscious—need definition, for the purpose of this treatise; they are bandied about so freely and mean different things according to the school of psychological thought to which the student belongs.

I use the term *subconscious* to signify the entire instinctual life of the form nature, all the inherited tendencies and innate predispositions, all the acquired and accumulated characteristics (acquired in past incarnations and frequently lying dormant unless suddenly evoked by stress of circumstance) and all the unformulated wishes and urges which drive a man into activity, plus the suppressed and unrecognised desires, and the unexpressed ideas which are present, though unrealised. The subconscious nature is like a deep pool from which a man can draw almost anything from his past experience, if he so desire, and which can be stirred up until it becomes a boiling cauldron, causing much distress.

The *conscious* is limited to that which the man knows himself to be and have in the present—the category of qualities, characteristics, powers, tendencies and knowledges of all kinds which constitute a man's stock in trade and of which he is definitely aware or of which the psychologist is aware. These are displayed in his window for all to see, and they make him what he apparently is to the outer onlooking world.

By the *super-conscious*, I mean those potencies and knowledges which are available but which are as yet uncontacted and unrecognised and, therefore, of no immediate use. These are the wisdom, love and abstract idealism which are inherent in the nature of the soul but which are not yet, and never have been a part of the equipment available for use. Eventually, all these powers will be recognised and used by the man. These potencies and realisations are called in *The Yoga Sutras of Patanjali* by the interesting name of "the raincloud of knowable things." These "knowable things" will eventually drop into the conscious aspect of a man's nature and become an integral part of his intellectual equipment. Finally, as evolution proceeds and the ages pass away, they will drop into the subconscious aspect of his nature, as his power to grasp the super-conscious grows in capacity. I might make this point clearer to you if I pointed out that just as the instinctual nature is today found largely in the realm of the subconscious, so in due time, the intellectual part of man (of which he is at this time becoming increasingly aware) will be relegated to a similar position and will drop below the threshold of consciousness. The intuition will then take its place. For most people, the free use of the intuition is not possible, because it lies in the realm of the super-conscious.

All these movements within the realm of consciousness,—from the subconscious to the immediately conscious and from thence to the super-conscious—are essentially crises of integration, producing temporary situations which must be handled. I would like here to point out that when an individual becomes aware of the higher aspect of himself which is demanding integration and is conscious of its nature and of the part which it could play in his life expression, he frequently becomes afflicted with an inferiority complex. This is the reaction of the lower, integrated aspects to the higher one. He experiences a sense of futility; the comparison which he makes within himself of the possible achievement and the point already attained leaves him with a sense of failure and of impotence. The reason for this is that the vision is at first too big, and he feels that he cannot make the grade. Humanity today has made so much progress upon the path of evolution that two groups of men are thus powerfully affected:

1. The group which has recognised the need for bridging the cleavage between the emotional nature and the mind

and has thus, through their integration, reached the level of intelligence.

2. The group that has already bridged this cleavage and is now aware of a major task which is the bridging of the gap between the personality and the soul.

These groups include a very large number of people at this time; the sense of inferiority is very great and causes many types of difficulty. If, however, the cause is more intelligently approached and handled, it will be found that the growth of a truer perspective will be rapid.

Another real difficulty in the field of achieved integration is to be found in the case of those who have integrated the entire lower nature and have fused the energies of the personality. All the energies involved in this fusion have *quality*, and the combination and interplay of these qualities (each determined by some particular ray energy) constitute the character of the person. For a long while after integration has been reached there will frequently be much conflict, strictly within the realm of character and within the Man's immediate consciousness. First one energy and then another will assert itself and battle for the supremacy. It might be of value here if I posited a hypothetical case, giving you the governing ray energies and reminding you that their fusion is the objective. In the case in point the subject has fused the personality vehicles into one functioning whole and is definitely a personality, but the major fusion of soul and personality has not been made.

Major Energies

Egoic energy ....Ray 1. The energy of will or power.

Personality energy ....Ray 4. The energy of harmony through conflict.

Minor Energies

Mental energy .... Ray 3. The energy of intelligence.

Astral energy .... Ray 6. The energy of devotion. Idealism.

Physical energy .... Ray 1. The energy of will or power.

Here we have a fivefold field of energy in which all factors are active except the energy of the ego or soul. They have been definitely fused. There is at the same time a growing awareness of the need for a still higher or more inclusive fusion and the establishing of a definite relation with the soul. The process has been as follows: First, the man was simply an animal, aware only of physical energy. Then he began to include within his field of awareness the emotional nature, with its desires, demands and sensitive reactions. Next, he discovered himself as a mind, and mental energy proceeded to complicate his problem. Finally, he arrived at the life expression we are hypothetically considering in which he has (and this is the point of real interest).

a. A first ray physical body, with a brain dominated and controlled by a third ray mind. This means capacity for intellectual achievement of a very varied kind.

b. An emotional nature which, being governed by sixth ray energy, can be rapidly swung into fanatical orientations and is easily idealistic.

c. The whole problem is further complicated by the rapidly emerging fourth ray energies of the personality. This means that the personality goal is the achievement of harmony, unity and skill in living, through an intensity of conflict, waged within the fourfold field of energy which constitutes the lower self.

You will, therefore, have a man who is ambitious for power, but with right motive, because he is truly idealistic; who will fight intelligently to achieve it, but will fight fanatically to bring about these ends because his fourth ray personality and sixth ray astral body will force him to do so, and his first ray body and brain will enable him to put up a strong fight. At the same time, his first ray soul energy is seeking to dominate, and will eventually do so through the medium of third ray mental energy, influencing the first ray brain. The first result of soul influence will be an intensification of every thing in the personality. The trouble will be localised in the mental body or in the brain and can range all the way down from idée fixe and mental crystallisation to insanity (if the stimulation becomes unduly powerful or the heredity is not good.) He can express arrogant success in his chosen field of work, which will make him a dominant and unpleasant person, or he can express the fluidity of the third ray mind which will make him a scheming manipulator or a fighter for immense schemes which can never really materialise. In this analysis I have not considered the tendencies evoked in past lives and lying hidden in the subconscious, or his heredity and environment. I have simply sought to show one thing: that the conflict of energies within a man can produce serious situations. But most of them can be corrected through right understanding.

It will be apparent to you, therefore, that one of the first studies to be made in this new approach to the psychological field will be to discover:

1. Which rays, major and minor, are conditioning and deter-

mining the nature of the man, and evoking the quality
of his daily life.

2. Which of these five energies is (at the time of the difficulty) the most dominant, and through which body or
vehicle it is focussed.

3. Which of these ray energies is struggling against the imposed dominance, mentioned above. These can be either:

a. Varying aspects of the same energy within their own
particular field.

b. Higher energies which are endeavouring to control the
lower energies and therefore indicating a cleavage in
the man's nature.

c. The energy of the fusion process itself, which unifies
the lower energies into one functioning personality.

d. The adjustment of the bridging process between the
two major energies. This will result in the at-one-
ment of soul and of the personality.

These constitute the larger areas of difficulty, and in each
of these fields of conflicting energies there are lesser centres
of conflict. These are frequently brought about by environing circumstances and events.

Given all these factors, and considering our hypothetical
case as being that of a man with a highly intelligent nature
and a good equipment for daily expression, how would the
esoteric psychologist proceed? How would he deal with the
man and what would he do? On what broad and general
principles would he proceed? I can but briefly indicate some
of them, reminding you that, in the case which we are considering, the subject is definitely cooperating with the psychologist and is interested in bringing about the right results.
The answers to the following questions will be the goal of
the psychologist's effort:

1. What are your reasons for wanting to be "straightened out"? This phrase, though an ordinary colloquialism, has deep significance, for it indicates the recognition of the need of *alignment*.

2. What brought this need to your attention and evoked in you the desire for a specific process of interior adjustment?

3. Realising the nature of the inner constitution of man, in which vehicle is there the need for the bridging process? Where is the point of cleavage, and, therefore, the point of present crisis? Is this difficulty a major or a minor crisis?

4. What are the five ray energies conditioning the subject?

5. How far does the man's life pattern, his life vocation and his innate coherent desires, co-incide with the trend set by

   a. The soul ray type of energy,
   b. The personality ray type?

   With disciples much of the difficulty will be found to lie in this area of expression.

6. In what period of the present life expression did the cleavage make its appearance? Or has an achieved integration brought about the difficult situation? Is this problem

   a. One of cleavage, requiring a bridging process, and leading thus to a fusion of energies?
   b. One of integration, requiring right understanding of what has happened, and leading to right adjustment of the fused powers to environing conditions?

7. Is the man at the point where he should be

   a. Integrated as a personality and, as a result, becoming more strictly human.

b. Developed as a mystic and taught to recognise the higher aspect and its relation to the lower, with a view to their unification.

c. Trained as an occultist and brought mentally to such a state of consciousness that the higher and the lower natures or aspects begin to function as one? This involves the blending of the forces of the personality and the energy of the soul, and fusing them into one divine expression of "the part within the whole."

8. What, in the last analysis, must be done to make "the lighted area" of the immediate consciousness of such a nature that the subconscious part of the man can be "lighted at will by the ray of the mind", and the mind itself can become a search light, penetrating into the super-consciousness and thus revealing the nature of the soul? It is in fact the problem of the expansions of consciousness. A wide field of psychological investigation lies ahead in connection with the use of the mind as constituting the "path of light between the subconscious nature and the superconscious nature, and yet focussing both as a brilliant point of light within the conscious nature."

To esotericists, this whole problem of the at-one-ment is closely connected with the building of the antahkarana. This name is given to the line of living energy which links the various human aspects and the soul, and it holds the clue to the occult truism that "before a man can tread the Path, he must become the path itself." When the cleavages are all bridged, the various points of crisis have been surmounted and passed, and the required fusions (which are simply stages in process) have taken place, then unification or at-one-ment occurs. New fields of energy then are entered, recognised and mastered, and then again new areas of consciousness open up before the advancing pilgrim.

The great planetary achievement of Christ was expressed by St. Paul in the words that He made "in himself of twain one new man, so making peace." (Ephesians II. 15)

In the two words "peace" and "good will" you have two keywords which express the bridging of two cleavages: One in the psychic nature of man, particularly that between the mind and the emotional vehicle which means the attainment of *peace*, and the other between the personality and the soul. This latter is the resolution of a basic "split", and it is definitely brought about by the *will-to-good*. This bridges not only the major cleavage in individual man, but it is that which will bring about the great and imminent fusion between intelligent humanity and the great spiritual centre which we call the spiritual Hierarchy of the planet.

It has been the almost unconscious recognition of these cleavages and of the need for their fusion which has made marriage, and the consummating act of marriage, the great mystical symbol of the greater inner fusions.

May I remind you also that these cleavages are cleavages in consciousness or awareness and not in fact? Is that too difficult a matter for us to grasp? Let us ponder upon it.

c. Problems of Stimulation

We now come to what is the most interesting part of our psychological study, for we will take up and consider the results of stimulation.

This theme is of outstanding interest at this time because of the mystical tendency and the spiritual urge which distinguishes humanity as a whole, and because of the definite results—some of them bad, many of them good—which the growing practice of meditation is bringing about in the world of men. These results of mystical and spiritual aspiration and of applied occult or intellectual meditation (in contradistinction to the mystical approach) must be faced and understood or a great opportunity will be lost and certain undesirable developments will appear and need later to be offset.

It surprises you, does it not, when I speak of the mystical tendency of humanity? Yet never before has the aspiration of mankind been of so high and general an order. Never before have so many people forced themselves on to the Path of Discipleship. Never before have men set themselves to discover truth in such large numbers. Never before has the Approach to the Hierarchy been so definite and so real. This situation warrants certain reactions. Of what nature should these reactions be? How shall we meet and deal with the opportunity with which we are confronted? By the development of the following attitudes: By a determination to avail oneself of the tide which is forcing humanity to approach the world of spiritual realities in such a way that the results will be factual and proven; by a realisation that what men seek in their millions is worth seeking and is of a reality, hitherto unknown; by a recognition that now is the day of opportunity for all disciples, initiates and workers, for the tide is on and men can be influenced for good at this time but perhaps not later. There are not always times of crisis, for they are the exception, not the rule.

This is, however, a time of unusual crisis. One point, nevertheless, seems impressed upon my mind, and I would like to emphasise it. In these times of crisis and consequent opportunity, it is essential that men should realise two things: first, that it is a time of stimulation, and also that it is a time of crisis for the Hierarchy as well as for men. This latter point is oft forgotten; the hierarchical crisis is of great importance, owing to its relative rarity. Human crises are frequent and—

from the time angle—of almost regular occurrence. But this is not the case where the Hierarchy is concerned. Also when a human crisis and a hierarchical crisis coincide and are simultaneous, there emerges an hour of dominant opportunity, and for the following reasons:

1. The attention of the Great Ones is entirely focussed owing to planetary affairs, in one particular direction. A synthesis of planned effort appears.
2. These occasions are so rare that when they do occur, they indicate a solar, as well as a planetary, significance.
3. Certain forces and powers, exterior to the government of the solar system, have been called into play, owing to the planetary emergency. This emergency is of such importance (from the angle of consciousness) that the solar Logos has seen fit to invoke external agencies to aid. And, They are aiding.

If you couple to these facts the reoriented and focussed attention of humanity upon what is called "modern idealism", you have a most interesting moment or event—for these two words are synonymous.

Men everywhere are aspiring towards freedom, towards mutual understanding, towards right group and personal conditions of living and of thinking, and towards right external and internal relationships. This is a fact generally recognised. Humanity is weary and tired of unwholesome ways of living, of the exploitation of the defenceless, of the growth of discontent, and of the centralisation of power in wrong and selfish hands. They are anxious for peace, right relations, the proper distribution of time and the understanding and right use of money. Such indications are unusual and of a deeply spiritual nature.

What is the result of these developments in the world of

subjective spiritual government and in the world of human affairs?

First of all and pre-dominantly, the evocation of a joint Approach: one being the longing and the desire of the Hierarchy for the solution of the human problem and the adjustment of human misery, and also for a right emergence of spiritual government (the government of correct values) and the other being the determination of man to bring about right conditions and proper environing situations wherein human beings can develop, and wherein the true values also may register and be recognised. It is at this point that the Hierarchy and humanity are at-one. That many human beings are too undeveloped to record these aspirations correctly is non-essential. They are unconsciously working towards the same ends as is the Hierarchy.

Where these two allied situations simultaneously exist, the result is necessarily a synchronous response, and this (equally necessarily) produces stimulation. The situation in relation to humanity as a whole is exactly the same as the situation in the life of an individual mystic. This must be carefully borne in mind, because the trend of human aspiration is mystical and *not* occult. Hence the world wide appositeness of what I am saying and its opportuneness.

I intend, however, to confine myself to the problems of the individual mystic and leave my readers to draw the necessary parallels.

It might be of value if, first of all, we defined the word *stimulation*, dealing with it from the occult standpoint and not just from the technical dictionary standpoint. Stimulation is the crux of our problem and we might as well face it and understand whereof we speak and what are the implications.

I have consistently emphasised the necessity for our recognition of the existence of energy. In occultism (or esoter-

icism) we use the word "energy" to connote the living activity of the spiritual realms, and of that spiritual entity, the
soul. We use the word "force" to connote the activity of the
form nature in the realms of the various kingdoms in nature.
This is a point of dominant interest and of implied distinction.

Stimulation might, therefore, be defined as *the effect* which
energy has upon force. It is the effect which soul has upon
form, and which the higher expression of divinity has upon
what we call the lower expression. Yet all is equally divine
in time and space and in relation to the point in evolution
and the whole. This energy has the following effects and
I state these effects in various ways in order to produce clarification in the many differing types of minds:

1. An increased rate of rhythm and vibration.
2. A capacity to offset time and, therefore, to do more in
   one hour of so-called time than the average person can
   do in two or three hours of time.
3. An upheaval in the personality life which leads—if correctly met—to a clear sighted meeting of karmic obligations.
4. An intensification of all reactions. This includes all reactions emanating from the world of daily living (and,
   therefore, from the environment), from the world of
   aspirational life, from the mind and from the soul, the
   great Reality in the life of the incarnated individual
   (even if he does not know it).
5. A clarification of life objectives, and hence a dominant
   emphasis upon the importance of the personality and
   the personality life.
6. A developing process of destruction which involves issues
   with which it seems beyond the capacity of the personality to deal.

7. Certain physiological and psychological problems which are based upon the capacity, the inherent weaknesses and strengths and the qualifications of the instruments of reception.

It should be remembered here that all stimulation is based upon the reaction (or the power to receive and register) of the lower nature when brought into relation to the higher. It is not based upon the reaction of the higher to the lower. Upon this reception, there eventuates a speeding up of the atoms which compose the personality vehicles; there follows a galvanising into activity of cells in the brain which have been hitherto dormant and also of the body areas around the seven centres, particularly in the organic and physiological correspondences to the centres, plus a grasp of possibilities and of opportunities. These results may work out either in the form of disastrous failure or in the form of significant development.

To all this, the stimulation of the nervous system of the subject responds and hence the effects are pronouncedly physical. These effects may mean release through the proper expenditure of the inflowing energy and consequently no serious effects, even when there may exist undesirable conditions, or they may mean that the instrument is in such a condition that the energy pouring through will be disruptive and dangerous and all kinds of bad results may be incurred. These include:

Mental problems.

It is with this theme that we shall now deal primarily. Mental stimulation is comparatively rare, if the total population of the planet is considered; nevertheless among the peoples of our Western civilisation and among the cream of the

Eastern civilisation it is frequently to be found. These particular problems can, for the sake of clarity, be divided into three groups or categories:

1. Those problems which arise out of intense mental activity, which produce undue mental focus and emphasis, one-pointed intellectual approach and crystallisation.
2. Those problems which arise out of meditation processes, which have successfully brought about illumination. This, in its due turn, produces certain difficulties, such as—

    a. Over activity of the mind, which grasps and sees too much.
    b. The revelation of glamour and illusion. This leads to bewilderment and the unfoldment of the lower psychism.
    c. Over sensitivity to the phenomena of the inner light, registered in the etheric body.

3. Those arising out of the higher psychic unfoldments, with consequent sensitivity to—

    a. Guidance.
    b. Cooperation with the Plan.
    c. Soul contact.

The last three groups of problems under sensitivity are most definite and real in the experience of disciples.

The first group of problems (those arising out of intense mental activity) are those of the pronounced intellectual and they range all the way from a narrow crystallised sectarianism to that psychological phenomenon called idée fixe. They are largely the problems of thought-form making, and by their means the man becomes the victim of that which he has himself constructed; he is the creature of a Frankenstein of his own creation. This tendency can be seen working out in all schools of thought and of cultures and is primarily applicable to the *leader* type of man and to the man who is independent in his thought life and, therefore, capable of clear thinking and the free movement of the chitta or mind stuff. It is necessary, therefore, in the coming days to deal with this particular problem, for *minds* will be met with increasing frequency. As the race proceeds towards a mental polarisation which will be as powerful as the present astral polarisation from which it is emerging, it will be found increasingly necessary to educate the race in—

1. The nature of mental substance.
2. The triple purpose of the mind:

    a. As a medium for expressing ideas, through the construction of the needed embodying thought forms.
    b. As a controlling factor in the life of the personality through the right use of the creative power of thought.
    c. As a reflector of the higher worlds of perceptive and intuitive awareness.

Creative thought is not the same as creative feeling and this distinction is often not grasped. All that can be created in the future will be based upon the expression of ideas. This will be brought about, first of all, through thought perception, then through thought concretion and finally through thought vitalisation. It is only later that the created thought form will descend into the world of feeling and there assume the needed sensuous quality which will add colour and beauty to the already constructed thought form.

It is at this point that danger eventuates for the student. The thought form of an idea has been potently constructed. It has taken to itself also colour and beauty. It is, therefore, capable of holding a man both mentally and emotionally. If he has no sense of balance, no sense of proportion and no sense of humour, the thought form can become so potent that he finds he is an avowed devotee, unable to retreat from his position. He can see nothing and believe nothing and work for nothing except that embodied idea which is so powerfully holding him a captive. Such people are the violent partisans in any group, in any church, order or government. They are frequently sadistic in temperament and are the adherents of cults and sciences; they are willing to sacrifice or to damage anyone who seems to them inimical to their fixed idea of what is right and true. The men who engineered the Spanish Inquisition and those who were responsible for the outrages in the times of the Covenanters are samples of the worst forms of this line of thought and development.

People tainted with this psychological trouble of blind adherence to ideas and of personality devotions are found in every organisation, every church, religion, in political and scientific bodies and also in every esoteric and occult organisation. They are psychologically unsound and the trouble from which they suffer is practically contagious. They are a menace, just as smallpox is a menace. This type of difficulty is not often regarded as constituting a psychological problem until the time comes when the man is so far afflicted that he becomes a group problem, or is regarded as peculiar or unbalanced. It is, nevertheless, definitely a psychological disorder of a most definite kind, requiring careful handling. It is also peculiarly difficult to handle, as the early stages are apparently wholesome and sound. To work with some group or with some teacher is often regarded as a definite means of psychological salvation, for it tends to extrovert the mystic and thus give proper release for the recognised inflowing energy. As long as it does this and nothing else, there is no real danger, but the moment a man's vision of other and greater possibilities becomes dim or begins to fade out, the moment a body of doctrines or a school of thought or an exponent of any theory engrosses his complete attention to the exclusion of all other points of view or possibilities, that moment the seeds of psychological trouble can be duly noted and the man is in danger.

The moment also that the entire mental powers of which a man is capable are employed in only one direction, such as, for instance, the achievement of business success or of financial dominance, that moment the man becomes a psychological problem.

This is peculiarly one of the problems of integration, for it is due to the stimulation of the mind, as it endeavours to assume control of the personality. A sense of power supervenes. Success feeds the stimulation even if it is only the doubtful success of attracting the attention of some teacher who is idealised or adored, or the pursuit of some transaction in the money market which is successfully carried through.

The time is coming when the whole problem of personality will be much better understood and, when this happens, any *undue emphasis* upon profession, calling, ideology or thought will be regarded as an undesirable symptom, and an effort will then be made to produce two things: a rounded out unfoldment and a conscious fusion with the soul and with the group.

I have no intention of dealing with problems of insanity. These exist and are of constant occurrence, and we esoterically divide them into three divisions:

1. Those which are due entirely to—

    a. Disease of the brain matter.
    b. The deterioration of the brain cells.

    c. Abnormal condition within the brain area, such as tumours, abscesses or growths.

    d. Structural defects in the head.

2. Those which are due to the fact that the ego or soul is not present.

    In these cases, there is to be found a situation wherein:

    a. The true owner of the body is absent. In this case the life thread will be anchored in the heart but the consciousness thread will not be anchored in the head. It will be withdrawn, and, therefore, the soul remains unaware of the form. In these cases you have idiocy, or simply a very lowgrade human animal.

    b. Certain cases of possession or obsession will be found, wherein the life thread is attached to the original owner of the body but the consciousness thread is that of another person, or identity—discarnate and most anxious for physical plane expression. In the average case, where the true owner of the body is not present, the situation is of no real moment, and sometimes serves a useful purpose, for it enables the obsessing entity to continue in possession. I refer to those cases wherein there is a true withdrawal of the incarnating ego and, therefore, a perfectly empty house. These are the rare cases, and present an unresented occupancy, whereas in the average case of possession or obsession there is a dual personality problem and even of several personalities. Conflict then ensues and many distressing conditions result— distressing from the point of view of the true owner of the body. The cases to which I am here referring permit of no cure as there is no ego to call into ac-

tivity by strengthening the will or the physical condition of the human being when ejecting intruders.
In many cases of possession cure is possible but in
those to which I here refer, cure is not possible.

3. Those cases which are due to the fact that the astral
body is of such a nature that it is uncontrollable and
the man is the defeated victim of his own rampant
desire of some kind or another and yet is such an intellectual potency that he can create a dominating
thought form, embodying that desire. These "astral
maniacs" are the most difficult and quite the saddest
types to handle because mentally there is little that
is wrong with them. The mind, however, cannot
control and is definitely relegated to the background;
it remains useless and inert whilst the man expresses
(with violence or subtlety as the case may be) some
basic desire. It may be the desire to kill, or desire to
have abnormal sexual experience, or even the desire to
be ever on the move and thus constantly active. These
sound fairly simple and usual types but I am not here
considering their normal expression but *something
which cannot be controlled* and for which there is
no remedy but the protection of the man from himself and his own actions.

These three forms of insanity, being incurable, will not permit of psychological help. All that can be done is the amelioration of the condition, the providing of adequate care of the
patient and the protection of society until death shall bring
to an end this interlude in the life of the soul. It is interesting
to remember that these conditions are related far more to the
karma of the parents or of those who have charge of the case
than to the patient himself. In many of these cases, there is

no person present within the form at all, but only an animated living body, informed by the animal soul but not by a human soul.

We are primarily engaged with those problems which arise in the mental nature of man and from his power to create in mental substance. There is one aspect of this difficulty to which I have not yet referred, and that is the potency of thought of such a case, and the dynamic stimulation of the mind which we are considering, to evoke response from the desire body and thus swing the entire lower nature into unison with the recognised mental urge and the dominant mental demand. This, when strong enough, may work out on the physical plane as powerful action and even violent action, and may lead a man into much trouble, into conflict with organised society, thus making him anti-social and at variance with the forces of law and order.

These people fall into three groups and it would be wise for students of psychology to study these types with care, for there is going to be an increasing number of them, because humanity is shifting its focus of attention more and more on to the mental plane:

1. Those who remain mentally introverted, and profoundly and deeply pre-occupied with their self-created thought forms and with their created world of thought, centered around the one dynamic thought form they have built. These people work always towards a crisis and it is interesting to note that this crisis may be interpreted by the world—

   a. As the revelation of a genius, such as emerges when some great scientist unfolds to us the conclusions of his focussed attention and period of thought.

b. As the effort of a man to express himself along some creative line.

c. As the violent and often dangerous expressions of frustration in which the man attempts to release the results of his inner brooding along the chosen line.

These all vary in expression, because of the original equipment with which the man began his life of thought upon the mental plane. In the first case, you have genius; in the other (if paralleled by a rich emotional nature) you will have some creative imaginative production, and in the third case, you will have what will be regarded by the world as insanity, curable in time and not permanent in its effects, provided some *form of creative* imaginative emotional release is provided. This is often the struggle point of the 2nd, the 4th and the 6th ray personality.

2. Those who become amazingly self-conscious and aware of themselves as centres of thought. They are obsessed with their own wisdom, their power and their creative capacity. They pass rapidly into a state of complete isolation or separateness. This can lead to acute megalomania, to an intense pre-occupation with and an admiring satisfaction with the self, the lower self, the personality. The emotional, feeling, desire nature is utterly under the control of the dynamic self-centred point of thought which is all of which the man is aware at this time. Consequently, the brain and all the physical plane activities are equally controlled and directed towards the planned aggrandisement of the man. This condition is found in varying degrees, according to the point in evolution and the ray type, and—in the early stages—it is curable. If it is persisted in, however, it makes the man eventually untouchable, for he becomes entrenched in a

rampart of his own thought forms concerning himself and his activities. When curable, the effort should be made to decentralise the subject by the evocation of another and higher interest, by the development of the social consciousness and—if possible—by contact with the soul. This condition is often the struggle point of the first and fifth ray personalities.

3. Those who become strongly extroverted by the desire to impose the conclusions they have reached (through their one-pointed mental focus) upon their fellow men. This constitutes quite often the crux of the difficulty for the third and sixth ray people. These people will be found ranging in consciousness all the way from the well-meaning theologian and dogmatic doctrinaire, found in practically all schools of thought, to the fanatic who makes life a burden to all around him as he seeks to impose his views upon them, and the maniac who becomes so obsessed with his vision that, for the protection of society, he must be locked away.

It will be obvious to you, therefore, how promising the outlook can be if educators and psychologists (particularly those who specialise in the training of young people) would teach them the needed care in the balancing of values, in the vision of the whole, and in the nature of the contribution which the many aspects and attitudes make to the whole. This is of profound usefulness at the time of adolescence when so many difficult adjustments require to be made. It is too late to do this usually when a person is of adult years and has for a long period of time constructed his thought forms and brooded over them until he is so identified with them that he has really no independent existence. The shattering of such a thought form or of a group of thought forms which are holding any man in bondage can result in such serious conditions that suicide, prolonged illness or a life rendered futile through frustration can eventuate.

Only two things can really help: First, the steady, loving presentation of a wider vision, which must be held before the man's eyes by some one who is so inclusive that understanding is the keynote of his life, or, secondly, by the action of a man's own soul. The first method takes much time and patience. The second method may be instantaneous in its effects, as in conversion, or it may be a gradual breaking down of the walls of thought by means of which a man has separated himself off from the rest of the world and from his fellowmen. The trumpets of the Lord, the soul, *can* sound forth and cause the walls of Jericho to fall. This task of evoking soul action of a dynamic character on behalf of an imprisoned personality, impregnably surrounded by a wall of mental matter, will constitute a part of the science of psychology which the future will see developed.

Problems arising from meditation, and its result: Illumination.

I would like first of all to point out that when I use the word meditation in this place I am using it in only one of its connotations. The intense mental focussing, producing undue mental emphasis, wrong attitudes and anti-social living, is also a form of meditation, but it is meditation carried forward entirely within the periphery of the small area of a particular man's mind. This is a statement of fact and of importance. This restricts him and leaves out all contact with other areas of mental perception and induces an intense one-pointed mental stimulation of a particularly powerful kind, and which has no outlet except towards the brain, via the desire nature. The meditation to which we shall refer in this part of our study relates to a mental focussing and attitude which attempts to relate itself to that which lies beyond the individual's mental world. It is part of an effort to put him in touch with a world of being and phenomena which *lie beyond*. I am phrasing this in this manner so as to convey the ideas of expansion, of inclusion, and of enlightenment. Such expansions and attitude should not render a man anti-social or incarcerate him in a prison of his own making. They should make him a citizen of the world; they should induce in him a desire to blend and fuse with his fellowmen; they should awaken him to the higher issues and realities; they should pour light into the dark places of his life and into that of humanity as a whole. The problems which arise as a result of illumination are practically the reverse of those just considered. Nevertheless, they in their turn constitute real problems and, because the intelligent people of the world are learning to meditate today on a large scale they must be faced. Many things are inducing this turning towards meditation. Sometimes it is the force of economic circumstances which forces a man to concentrate, and concentration is one of the first steps in the meditation process; sometimes it is brought about through the urge to creative work which leads a man in pursuit of some theme or subject for creative presentation. Whether men are interested only academically in the power of thought, or whether, through a touch of vision, they become students of true meditation (either mystical or occult) the fact remains that serious problems arise, dangerous conditions appear, and the lower nature evidences in every case the need for adaptation to the higher impulses or demands, or suffers consequences of a difficult nature if it fails to do so. The necessary adjustments must be made or psychological, psychopathic, and nervous difficulties will inevitably supervene.

Again, let me remind you that the reason for this is that the man sees and knows and realises more than he is able to do simply as a personality, functioning in the three worlds, and so oblivious in any true sense to the world of soul activity. He has "let in" energies which are stronger than the forces of which he is usually aware. They are intrinsically strong, though not yet apparently the stronger, owing to the well-established habits and the ancient rhythms of the personality forces with which the soul energy is brought into conflict. This necessarily leads to strain and difficulty, and unless there is a proper understanding of this battle, dire results may be produced, and with these the trained psychologist must be prepared to deal.

With the type and nature of the concentration, with the theme of the meditation, I will not deal, for I am considering here only results and not the methods for producing them. Suffice it to say, that the man's efforts in meditation have opened a door through which he can pass at will (and eventually with facility) into a new world of phenomena, of directed activity, and of different ideals. He has unlatched a window through which light can pour in, revealing that which is, and always has been, existent within the consciousness of man, and throwing illumination into the dark places of his life; into other lives; and into the environment in which he moves. He has released within himself a world of sound and of impressions which are at first so new and so different that he does not know what to make of them. His situation becomes one requiring much care and balanced adjustment.

It will be obvious to you that if there is a good mental equipment and a sound educational training, that there will be a balancing sense of proportion, an interpretative capacity, patience to wait till right understanding can be developed, and a happy sense of humour. Where, however, these are not present, there will be (according to the type and the sense of vision) bewilderment, a failure to comprehend what is happening, undue emphasis upon personality reactions and phenomena, pride in achievement, a tremendous sense of inferiority, too much speech, a running hither and thither for explanation, comfort, assurance, and a sense of comradeship, or perhaps a complete breakdown of the mental forces, or the disruption of the brain cells through the strain to which they have been subjected.

Exhilaration is also sometimes found as a result of the contact with a new world, and strong mental stimulation. Depression is as frequently a result, based upon a sensed incapacity to measure up to the realised opportunity. The man sees and knows too much. He can no longer be satisfied with the old measure of living, with the old satisfactions, and with the old idealisms. He has touched and now longs for the larger measures, for the new and vibrant ideas, and for the broader vision. The way of life of the soul has gripped and attracts him. But his nature, his environment, his equipment and his opportunities appear somehow to frustrate him consistently, and he feels he cannot march forward into this new and wonderful world. He feels the need to temporise and to live in the same state of mind as heretofore, or so he thinks, and so he decides.

These expansions which he has undergone as the result of successful meditation need not be along the line of recognised religious effort, or produced by so-called occult revelation. They may come to him along the line of a man's chosen life activity, for there is no life activity, no vocational calling, no mental occupation and no condition which cannot provide the key to the unlocking of the door into the desired wider world, or serve to lead a man to the mountain top from which the wider horizon can be seen, and the larger vision grasped. A man must learn to recognise that his chosen school of thought, his peculiar vocation, his particular calling in life and his personal trend are only part of a greater whole, and his problem is to integrate *consciously* his small life activity into the world activity.

It is this we call illumination for lack of a better word. All knowledge is a form of light, for it throws light into areas of awareness of which we have hitherto been unconscious. All wisdom is a form of light, for it reveals to us the world of meaning which lies behind the outer form. All understanding is an evocation of light, for it causes us to become aware of, or conscious of, the causes which are producing the outer forms which surround us (including our own) and which condition the world of meaning of which they are the expression. But when this fact is first seen, grasped, and when the initial revelation has come, when the place of the part in relation to the whole is sensed, and when the world which includes our little world is first contacted, there is always a moment of crisis and a period of danger. Then, as familiarity grows and our feet have wandered in and out of the door we have opened, and we have accustomed ourselves to the light which the unshuttered window has released into our little world of daily living, other psychological dangers eventuate. We are in danger of thinking that what we have seen is all there is to see, and thus—on a higher turn of the spiral and in a larger sense—we repeat the dangers (earlier considered) of undue emphasis, of wrong focus, of narrow minded belief, and idée fixe. We become obsessed with the idea of the soul; we forget its need of a vehicle of expression; we begin to live in an abstracted detached world of being and of feeling, and we fail to keep in contact with the factual life of physical plane expression. We thus repeat—again on a higher turn of the spiral—the condition we considered in which the soul or ego was not present, reversing the condition so that there is no form life really present in the focussed consciousness of the man. There is only the world of souls and a desire for creative activity. The handling of daily living on the physical plane drops below the threshold of consciousness, and the man becomes a vague, impractical, visionary mystic. These states of mind are dangerous, if they are permitted to exist.

There are, however, certain phases of this mental trouble which are induced by the illumination of the mind through meditation with which it might be profitable to deal. I can do so only cursorily, as the time is brief and I seek to indicate and not to elucidate in detail. I can only point out to you the general lines of difficulty and the methods whereby a specific difficulty or problem can be met or solved. In the handling of many of these cases, ordinary common sense is of value, and the effort to impress upon the patient that his troubles, though small in the beginning, can open the door to serious situations. There are three of these upon which I will touch.

The first of these is the over-activity of the mind in quite a number of cases, which—sometimes with suddenness and sometimes slowly—grasps and sees too much. It becomes aware of too much knowledge. This produces irregularities in the organisation of the man's life, and interjects so much variation, so much fluidity and so much restlessness that he is forever in a seething turmoil. Throughout it all, he is conscious of himself as the one at the centre, and interprets all the mental activity and contacts, all the fluidity, the constant analysis to which he is prone, and the ceaseless making of plans as indicative not only of mental ability but of real spiritual insight and wisdom. This produces difficult situations for all associated with him, and continues frequently over a long period of time. For as long as this condition lasts, there is little that anyone can do. The constant "permutations of the chitta or mind stuff" and the perpetual "thought form making activity of the mental body" engrosses the man so constantly that nothing else registers in his consciousness. Vast plans, widespread schemes, correlations and correspondences, plus the attempt to impose them on others and to invoke their aid (with consequent criticism if this aid is withheld) for the carrying out of the mass of unrelated ideas occupy him. There is no real effort made to carry these plans and ideas through to completion, for they all remain tentative on the mental plane, in their original vague state. The effort to see more and grasp more and apprehend more of the detail and the inter-relation engrosses all the attention, and there is no energy left to carry even one of them down on to the plane of desire, and thus take the first steps towards the physical materialisation of the visioned plan. If this state of mind continues for too long a period, it produces mental strain, nervous breakdown and sometimes permanent difficulty. The cure, however, is simple.

Let the man thus afflicted realise the futility of his mental life as he is living it. Then, choosing one of the many possible methods of work and one of the many channels of service whereby the sensed plan can be developed, let him force himself to bring it through into physical manifestation, letting all other possibilities drop. In this way, he can begin again to regulate and control his mind and to take his place among those who are accomplishing something—no matter how small the contribution may be. He becomes then constructive.

I have illustrated this type of difficulty in terms of the aspirant who, in meditation, comes into touch with the influences of the Hierarchy, and thus is in a position to tap the stream of thought forms created by Them and by Their disciples. But the same type of difficulty will be found among all those who (through discovery of the mental plane and the use of focussed attention) penetrate into that larger world of ideas which are just ready to precipitate on to the concrete levels of mental substance. This accounts for the futility and the apparent arid fruitlessness of many quite intelligent people. They are occupied with so many possibilities that they end by achieving nothing. One plan carried through, one line of thought developed to its concrete conclusion, one mental process unfolded and presented in consciousness will save the situation, and bring creative usefulness into otherwise negative and futile lives. I use the word "negative" in this place to indicate a negativity in the achievement of results. Such a man is, it is needless to say, exceedingly positive in the implications which he attaches to his so-called mental conceptions and ideas as to how it all should be worked out, and is a constant source of dismay to those around him. His friends or co-workers are the butt of his ceaseless criticism, because they do not work out the plan as he believes it should be worked out, or fail to appreciate the flood of ideas with which he is overwhelmed. It should be realised that the man is suffering from a sort of mental fever, with its accompaniments of hallucination, over-activity, and mental irritability. The cure, as I said above, lies in the patient's own hands. It involves earnest application to one chosen plan to prove its effectiveness, using common sense and ordinary good judgment. The light that can be contacted in meditation has revealed a level of mental phenomena and of thought forms with which the man is unaccustomed to deal. Its manifestation and implications and possibilities impress him as so vast that he argues they must be divine and, therefore, essential. Because he is still in the dramatic centre of his own consciousness and still—even if unconsciously—full of mental pride and spiritual ambition, he feels he has great things to do, and that everybody he knows must aid him in doing it, or else reckon themselves as failures.

The second is *the revelation of the maya of the senses.* This maya is a generic term covering three aspects of the phenomenal life, of the three worlds or the three major results of force activity. These serve to bewilder the man and make difficult the lot of the earnest aspirant. It might be of value if I here defined for you the three terms which are applied to these three phenomenal effects: Illusion, Glamour and Maya.

These three phrases have for long been bandied about among so-called occultists and esotericists. They stand for the same general concept or the differentiation of that concept. Speaking generally, the interpretations have been as follows and they are only partial interpretations, being almost in the nature of distortions of the real truth, owing to the limitations of the human consciousness.

Glamour has oft been regarded as a curious attempt of what are called the "black forces" to deceive and hoodwink well-meaning aspirants. Many fine people are almost flattered when they are "up against" some aspect of glamour, feeling that their demonstration of discipline has been so good that the black forces are interested sufficiently to attempt to hinder their fine work by submerging them in clouds of glamour. Nothing could be further from the truth. That idea is itself a part of the glamour of the present time, and has its root in human pride and satisfaction.

Maya is oft regarded as being of the same nature as the concept promulgated by the Christian Scientist that there is no such thing as matter. We are asked to regard the entire world phenomena as maya and to believe that its existence is simply an error of mortal mind, and a form of auto-suggestion or self-hypnotism. Through this induced belief, we force ourselves into a state of mind which recognises that the tangible and the objective are only figments of man's imaginative mind. This, in its turn, is likewise a travesty of reality.

Illusion is regarded in rather the same way, only (as we define it) we lay the emphasis upon the finiteness of man's mind. The world of phenomena is not denied, but we regard the mind as misinterpreting it and as refusing to see it as it is in reality. We consider this misinterpretation as constituting the Great Illusion.

I would point out here that (generally speaking) these three expressions are three aspects of a universal condition that is the result of the activity—in time and space—of the human mind.

The Problem of Illusion lies in the fact that it is a soul activity, and is the result of the mind aspect of all the souls in manifestation. It is the soul which is submerged in the illusion, and the soul that fails to see with clarity until such time as it has learnt to pour the light of the soul through into the mind and the brain.

The Problem of Glamour is found when the mental illusion is intensified by desire. What the theosophist calls "Kama-manas" produces glamour. It is illusion on the astral plane.

The Problem of Maya is really the same as above, plus the intense activity produced when both glamour and illusion are realised on etheric levels. It is that vital, unthinking, emotional *mess* (yes, that is the word I seek to use) in which the majority of human beings seem always to live. Therefore:

1. *Illusion* is primarily of a mental quality and is characteristic of the attitude of mind of those people who are more intellectual than emotional. They have outgrown glamour as usually understood. It is the misunderstanding

of ideas and thought forms of which they are guilty, and of misinterpretations.

2. *Glamour* is astral in character, and is far more potent at this time than illusion, owing to the enormous majority of people who function astrally always.

3. *Maya* is vital in character and is a quality of force. It is essentially the energy of the human being as it swings into activity through the subjective influence of mental illusion or astral glamour or of both in combination.

The vastness of the subject is overwhelming, and it takes time for the aspirant to learn the rules whereby he can find his way out of the worlds of glamour. I seek here only to deal with the theme as it produces effects in the life of the man who has evoked a measure of light within himself. This has served to reveal the three worlds of lower force to him. This revelation, in the early stages, oft deceives him and he becomes the victim of that which has been revealed. It might justly be remarked that all human beings are the victims of the Great Illusion and of its various correlations and aspects. In the cases which we are here considering, the difference lies in the fact that—

1. The man is definitely and consciously aware of himself.

2. He knows also that he has released a measure of the higher light.

3. That which is revealed to him is interpreted by him in terms of spiritual phenomena instead of in terms of psychical phenomena. He regards it all as wonderful, revealing, true and desirable.

Because he has achieved integration and is able to function in the mind nature; because his orientation is good and right; because he is on the Path of Probation; and because he knows himself to be an aspirant and even a disciple, that which the

lights reveals upon the astral plane, for instance, is naturally
of a very high order. It is, consequently, most deceptive in
its effects. Vast cosmic schemes which have emerged from
the minds of thinkers in the past and which have succeeded
in reaching the astral plane; the ancient forms embodying the
"wish life" and the imaginary conceptions of the race and
which are of such potency that they have persisted in the
desire life of many; the symbolic forms employed down the
ages in the attempt to materialise certain realities; the tentative
and experimental forms of great and good endeavours which
have been or are at this time being worked out, plus the life
activity of the astral plane itself, the dream world of the planet
—all this tends to preoccupy him and to lead him into danger
and error. It retards his progress on the way and sidetracks
his energies and attention.

It should be remembered that this constitutes the line of
least resistance for the man because of the potency of the
astral body in this world period. The result of all this is that
the powers and faculties of the mind become over developed
and what are called the "lower siddhis" (the lower psychic
powers) begin to assert control. The man is, in reality, revert-
ing to states of awareness and to conditions of functioning
which were normal and right in Atlantean times, but undesirable and unnecessary in our day. He is recovering—
through stimulation—ancient habits of psychic awareness
which should lie normally below the threshold of consciousness.

The light has revealed this world of phenomena to him; he
deems it desirable and interprets its activities as a wonderful
spiritual development within himself. This stimulation by the
mind (itself stimulated in meditation) as it turns *downward*
on to the astral plane, evokes the renewed and the re-
awakened active reaction from the lower powers. It is as

definitely a recovery and as definitely undesirable as are some of the Hatha-yoga practices in India which enable the yogin to recover the *conscious* control of his bodily functions. This conscious control was a distinguishing mark of the early Lemurian races but for ages the activity of the body-organs has lain, most desirably and safely, below the threshold of consciousness, and the body performs its functions automatically and unconsciously, except in the case of disease or maladjustment of some kind. It is not intended that the race (when the work of this present cycle is accomplished) should function consciously in forgotten areas of awareness, as did the Lemurian or the Atlantean races. It is intended that men should function as Caucasians, though no really satisfactory term has yet been coined to distinguish the race which is developing under the impact of our occidental civilization. I am referring to states of consciousness and realms of awareness which are the prerogative of all races and peoples at certain stages of development, and I only use the three, scientific, racial nomenclatures as symbols of these stages:

The Lemurian consciousness....................physical.
The Atlantean consciousness.....astral, emotional, sensuous.
The Caucasian or Aryan...........mental or intellectual.

This must never be forgotten.

The man who is suffering from the revelations of light in the three worlds (particularly in the astral world) is, therefore, really doing two things:

1. He is remaining in a relatively static condition as far as his higher progress is concerned; he is looking on at the bewildering kaleidoscope of the astral plane with interest and attention. He may not be active on the plane himself or consciously identify himself with it, but, mentally and emotionally, it is satisfying temporarily his

interest, holding his attention and arousing his curiosity, even if he remains, at the same time, critical. He is, therefore, wasting time and surrounding himself continuously with new layers of thought forms—the result of his thought about what he is seeing or hearing. This is dangerous and should be brought to an end. Intelligent interest in the world of glamour and illusion is required of all wise aspirants and disciples so that they may release themselves from its thralldom, for otherwise it will never be understood and controlled. But a prolonged application to its life and complete engrossment in its phenomena is dangerous and imprisoning.

2. The interest evoked in these undesirable cases is such that the man—

   a. Becomes completely glamoured by it.
   b. Descends (speaking symbolically) to its level.
   c. Reacts sensitively to its phenomena, and often with pleasure and delight.
   d. Evokes the ancient faculties of clairvoyance and clairaudience.
   e. Becomes a lower psychic and accepts all that the lower psychic powers reveal.

I would like to pause here and point out two things which should be borne in mind:

First, that many people are today living in the Atlantean state of awareness, in the Atlantean consciousness and for them the expression of these lower psychic powers is normal, though undesirable. For the man who is a mental type or who is overcoming gradually the psychic nature, these powers are abnormal (or should I say subnormal?) and most undesirable. In this discussion with which we are now engaged, I am not dealing with the man with the Atlantean consciousness but with the modern aspirant. For him to develop the previous racial consciousness and to revert to the lower type of development (which should have been left far behind) is dangerous and retarding. It is a form of atavistic expression.

Secondly: that when a man is firmly polarised upon the mental plane, when he has achieved some measure of contact with the soul, and when his entire orientation is towards the world of spiritual realities and his life is one of discipline and service, then, at times, and when necessary, he can at will call into use these lower psychic powers in the service of the Plan and in order to do some special work upon the astral plane. But this is a case where the greater consciousness includes normally the lesser consciousness. This is however seldom done even by the adepts, for the powers of the soul—spiritual perception, telepathic sensitivity and psychometrical facility —are usually adequate to the demand and the need to be met. I interject these remarks, as there are some enlightened men who use these powers, but it is always along the line of some specific service to the Hierarchy and humanity, and *not* along any line connected with the individual.

When a man has wandered into the bypaths of the astral plane, and has left the secure place of mental poise and intellectual altitude (again I am speaking symbolically) when he has succumbed to glamour and illusion (usually being quite sincerely deceived and well-intentioned) and when he has unfolded in himself—through misapplied stimulation and experiment—old habits of contact, such as clairvoyance and clairaudience, what can he do, or what shall be done to him to bring about right conditions?

Many of these people find their way into the hands of psychologists and psychiatrists; many are to be found today in our sanitariums and asylums, placed there because they "saw things" or heard voices, or dreamed dreams, and because they had unfitted themselves for normal living. They appear to be a danger, both to themselves and to others. They constitute a problem and a difficulty. The ancient habits must be dropped, but because of their antiquity they are very powerful, and to drop them is easier said than done. The practices whereby the lower psychic powers have been developed must be given up. If these faculties of response to an environing astral world appear to have been developed with no difficulty and to be natural to the man, they should nevertheless be discontinued and the avenues of approach to this lower world of phenomena should be closed. If human beings make so poor a success of living consciously on the physical plane and in handling the phenomena there contacted, and if the life of mental attention and mental living is still so difficult to the vast majority, why complicate the problem by trying to live in a world of phenomena which is admittedly the most powerful at this time?

The task of release from the thralldom of astral sensitivity is unique and stupendous. The details of the method whereby it can be done are too numerous for us to consider them here. But certain words hold the keynotes of release and three basic suggestions will aid the psychologist in dealing with these types of difficulty. The words which hold the secret are:

1. Instruction.
2. Focus of attention.
3. Occupation.

The nature of the human response apparatus in the three worlds should be carefully explained to the man who is in difficulty and the distinction between the Lemurian, the Atlantean and the Caucasian consciousness should be made clear to him, if possible. His pride of place upon the ladder of evolution should be evoked at this point again, if possible, and it will prove a constructive evocation. The effort to focus his attention should be progressively and sympathetically attempted. According to his type so will the effort be directed to focussing his attention and directing his interest upon the physical plane or the mental plane, thus directing it away from the intermediate plane. Definite physical or mental occupation (again arranged according to type) should be arranged and the man forced to occupy himself in some chosen manner.

The three suggestions I would make to the psychologist or the mental healer are:

1. Study with care the nature of the rays which presumably constitute the man's nature and provide the forces and energies which make him what he is. I have worded this with care.
2. Determine which of the vehicles of contact is the most powerful, best organised and well developed. It will indicate through which forms the life expression in this particular incarnation is flowing.
3. Investigate the physical condition with care, and where it needs attention see that due care is given. At the same time, take note of the glandular equipment, studying it from the standpoint of its relation to the seven major centres in the body. In many cases, the glands indicate the condition of the centres. Thus an understanding of the force system of the patient will take place.

The Science of the Centres is yet in its infancy, as is the Science of the Rays and the Science of Astrology. But much is being learned and developed along these three lines and when the present barriers are down and true scientific investigation is instituted along these lines, a new era will begin for the human being. These three sciences will constitute the three major departments of the Science of Psychology in the New Age, plus the contributions of modern psychology and the insight into the nature of man (particularly the physical nature) which it has so wonderfully developed.

Problems of guidance, dreams, and depression.

I am dealing with these problems because of their exceeding prevalence at this time, due to the activities of various religiously or psychologically motivated groups, to the trend of certain schools, dedicated to the spread of religion or of psychology, and to the present world situation which has plunged so many sensitive people into a state of lowered spiritual vitality, accompanied usually by lowered physical vitality. This condition is widespread and based on wrong economic conditions. I am dealing with these before we take up our fourth point, The Diseases and Problems of Mystics, as they form an intermediate group, including many intelligent and well-intentioned citizens.

The Problem of Guidance is a peculiarly difficult one to handle, for it is based on an innate instinctive recognition of the fact of God and of God's Plan. This inherent, instinctual, spiritual reaction is being exploited today by many well meaning reformers, who have, however, given no real attention to the subject, or to the phenomena of the outer response to a subjective urge. They are, in the majority of cases, blind leaders of the blind. We might define the problem of guidance as the problem of the method whereby a man, through processes of auto-suggestion, throws himself into a state of negativity and (whilst in that state) becomes aware of inclinations, urges, voices, clearly impressed commands, revelations of courses of conduct which should be pursued or of careers which should be followed, plus a general indication of lines of activity which "God" is proposing to the attentive, negative, receptive subject. In this state of almost sublimated awareness to the insistent demands of the subjective realms of being or of thought, the man is swept into a current of activity which may succeed in permanently orienting his life (often quite harmlessly and sometimes most desirably) or which may have only a temporary effect, once the urge of response has exhausted itself. But in any case, the source of the direction and the origin of the guidance is vaguely called "God", is regarded as divine, is spoken of as the voice of the "Christ within", or as spiritual direction. Many analogous terms are used, according to the school of thought to which the man may belong, or which has succeeded in attracting his attention.

We shall see this tendency towards subjective guidance of some kind or another developing increasingly as humanity becomes more subjectively oriented, more definitely aware of the realms of inner being, and more inclined towards the world of meaning. It is for this reason that I desire to make a relatively careful analysis of the possible sources of guidance so that at least men may know that the whole subject is vaster and more complicated than they had thought, and that it would be the part of wisdom to ascertain the origin of the guidance vouchsafed, and so know, with greater definiteness, the direction in which they were headed. Forget not that the blind, unreasoning subjecting of oneself to guidance (as at present practiced) renders a man eventually a negative impressionable automaton. Should this become universally prevalent and the present methods become established habits, the race would forfeit its most divine possession, i. e., free will. There is no immediate fear of this, however, if the intelligent men and women of the world think this problem out. Also there are too many egos of advanced nature coming into incarnation at this time to permit the danger to grow out of all bounds, and there are too many disciples in the world today whose voices are ringing loudly and clearly along the lines of free choice, and the intelligent comprehension of God's plan.

It might be of profit if I indicated anew the various schools of thought who feature "guidance" or whose methods and doctrines tend to the development of an inner attentive ear, and yet who fail to teach the distinctiveness of the sources of guidance, or to differentiate between the various sounds, voices and so-called inspired indications which that attentive ear may be trained to register.

The emotionally inclined people *in the Churches* of all denominations and persuasions are ever prone to find a way of escape from the troubles and difficulties of life by living always with a sense of the guiding Presence of God, coupled to a blind acquiescence in what is generalised as the "will of God". The practice of the Presence of God is most definitely a desirable and needed step but people should understand what it means and steadily change the sense of duality into the sense of identification. The will of God can take the form of the imposition of life circumstance and conditions from which there is no possible escape; the subject of this imposition accepts it and does literally nothing to improve or truly better (and perhaps avoid) the circumstances. Their destiny and situation is interpreted by them as such that within the imposed ring-pass-not and lines of limitation they determine placidly, submissively to live. A spirit of submission and acquiescence is inevitably developed, and by calling the situation in which they find themselves an expression of God's will they are enabled to bear it all. In some of the more sublimated states of this acquiescence, the sensitively inclined person *voices* his submission, but fails to recognise that the voice is his own. He regards it as God's voice. For them, the way of understanding, the recognition of the great Law of Cause and Effect (working out from life to life) and the interpretation of the problem in terms of a lesson to be mastered would spell release from negativity and blind, unintelligent acceptance. Life does not demand acquiescence and acceptance. It demands activity, the separation of the good and high values from the undesirable, the cultivation of that spirit of fight which will produce organisation, understanding, and eventual emergence into a realm of useful spiritual activity.

People who participate in the activity of those schools of thought which are called by many names such as Mental Science schools, New Thought groups, Christian Science and other similar bodies are also prone to drift into a state of negativity, based on auto-suggestion. The constant re-iteration of the voiced, but unrealised, fact of divinity will eventually evoke a response from the form side of life which (even if it is not worded guidance) is, nevertheless, the recognition of a form of guidance and leaves no scope for free will. This is a reaction on a large scale, from the one dealt with above. Whereas in the one case there is found a blind acceptance of an undesirable lot because it is the will of God and that Will therefore must be good and right, in the second group there is an attempt to stir the subjective man into the acceptance of a definitely opposite condition. He is taught that there are no wrong conditions except as he himself creates them; that there is no pain and nothing undesirable; he is urged to recognise that he is divine and the heir of the ages and that the wrong conditions, limited circumstances and unhappy occurrences are the result of his own creative imagination. He is told they are really non-existent.

In the two schools of thought, the truth about destiny as it works out under the Law of Cause and Effect and the truth about man's innate divinity are taught and emphasised, but, in both cases, the man himself is a negative subject, and the *victim* either of a cruel fate or of his divinity. I am wording this with deliberation because I am anxious for my readers to realise that destiny never intended man to be a helpless victim of circumstance or the self-hypnotised tool of an *affirmed*, but *undeveloped*, divinity. Man is intended to be the intelligent arbiter of his own destiny, and a conscious exponent of his own innate divinity, of the God within.

Again, schools of esotericists, theosophists and rosicrucians (particularly in their inner schools) have also their own forms of this illusion of guidance. It is of a different nature to the two dealt with above, but the results are nevertheless of much the same quality and reduce the student to a condition of being guided, often of being directed, by illusionary voices. Frequently the heads of the organisation claim to be in direct communication with a Master or the entire Hierarchy of Masters, from Whom orders come. These orders are passed on to the rank and file of the membership of the organisation and prompt unquestioning obedience is expected from them. Under the system of training, imparted under the name of esoteric development, the goal of a similar relationship to the Master or the Hierarchy is held out as an inducement to work or to meditation practice, and some day the aspirant is led to believe that he will hear his Master's voice, giving him guidance, telling him what to do and outlining to him his participation in various roles. Much of the psychological difficulties found in esoteric groups can be traced to this attitude and to the holding out to the neophyte of this glamorous hope. In view of this, I cannot too strongly re-iterate the following facts:

1. That the goal of all teaching given in the real esoteric

schools is to put man consciously in touch with his own soul and not with the Master.

2. That the Master and the Hierarchy of Masters work only on the plane of the soul, as souls with souls.

3. That conscious response to hierarchical impression and to the hierarchical plan is dependent upon the sensitive reaction which can be developed and made permanent between a man's own soul and his brain, *via his mind*.

4. That the following points should be borne in mind:

   a. When a man is consciously aware of himself as a soul, he can then be in touch with other souls.

   b. When he is consciously a disciple, he is then in touch with, and can collaborate intelligently with, other disciples.

   c. When he is an initiate, other initiates become facts in his life and consciousness.

   d. When he is a Master, the freedom of the Kingdom of Heaven is his, and he works consciously as one of the senior members of the Hierarchy.

   But—and this is of prime importance—all these differentiations relate to grades of work and not to grades of persons; they indicate soul expansions but not graded contacts with personalities. According to the realised soul development upon the physical plane will be the response to the world of souls of which the occult Hierarchy is the heart and mind.

The guidance to which the adherents of many esoteric schools so often respond is *not* that of the Hierarchy but that of the astral reflection of the Hierarchy; they respond therefore to an illusory, distorted, man-made presentation of a great spiritual fact. They could, if they so chose, respond to the reality.

Apart from the ordinary occult and esoteric schools found in the world today, there are groups of people as well as solitary individuals who are practicing various forms of meditation and of yoga. This is true both of Eastern and Western aspirants. Some of these people are working with real knowledge, and, therefore, quite safely; others are profoundly ignorant not only of techniques and methods but also as to the results to be expected from their efforts. Results there must inevitably be, and the major result is to turn the consciousness inward, to develop the spirit of introspection, and to orient the man or woman to the inner subjective worlds and to the subtler planes of being—usually to the astral realm and seldom to the truly spiritual world of souls. The mind nature is seldom invoked and the processes pursued usually render the brain cells negative and quiescent whilst the mind remains inactive and often unawakened. The only area of consciousness which remains therefore visible is that of the astral. The world of physical and tangible values is shut out; the mental world is equally shut out. I would ask you to ponder on this statement.

The Oxford Group Movement has also laid much stress on the need for guidance, yet seems to have developed no real understanding of the subject or to have given any real attention to the inclusive investigation of the alternative possibilities to the voice of God. Mystics of all kinds, with a natural pre-disposition to the introspective, negative life are today hearing voices, receiving guidance and obeying impulses which they claim come from God. Groups everywhere are occupied with the task of orienting people to the spiritual life or with the task of ascertaining the Plan of God or of cooperating with it in some way or another. Some of these groups are working intelligently and are sometimes correct in their surmises and endeavours, but the bulk of them are incorrect as they are largely astral in nature.

The result of all this is twofold. One is the development of a spirit of great hopefulness among the spiritual workers of the world as they note how rapidly humanity is turning towards the world of right meaning, of true spiritual values and of esoteric phenomena. They realise that in spite of errors and mistakes, the whole trend of the racial consciousness today is "inwards towards the Centre of spiritual life and peace." The other result or recognition is that during this process of re-adjustment to the finer values, periods of real danger transpire and that unless there is some immediate understanding of the psychological conditions and possibilities and that unless the mentality of the race is evoked on the side of understanding and common sense, we shall have to pass through a cycle of profound, psychological, and racial disturbance before the end of this century. Two factors today are, for instance, having a deep psychological effect upon humanity:

1. The suspense, fear and apprehension in every country are most adversely affecting the mass of the people, stimulating them astrally and—at the same time—lowering their physical vitality.

2. The impact of the higher spiritual forces upon the more intelligently inclined and mystically motivated people is producing serious and widespread trouble, breaking down protective etheric barriers, and throwing the doors wide open on to the astral plane. Such are some of the dangers of spiritual stimulation.

Therefore, it is of real value to us to study the sources from which much of this so-called "guidance" can come. For the sake of clarity and impressiveness, I propose to list these sources very briefly and without any prolonged comment.

This will give the earnest and intelligent investigator the opportunity to realise that the whole theme is vaster and far more important than has been surmised and may lead to a more careful analysis of the "types of guidance" and an understanding of the possible directing agencies to which the poor and ignorant neophyte may fall a victim.

1. Guidance or instruction coming from the man or woman upon the physical plane to whom the guided person is, usually unconsciously, looking for help. This is largely a brain relationship, electrical in nature, established by conscious physical plane contacts, and is greatly helped by the fact that the neophyte knows pretty well, exactly what his instructor would say in any given circumstance.

2. The introverted attitude of the neophyte or mystic brings to the surface all his subconscious "wish life." This, as he is mystically inclined and probably aspires normally towards goodness and the life of the spirit, takes the form of certain adolescent tendencies towards religious activity and practices. These, however, he interprets in terms of definite extraneous guidance, and formulates them to himself in such a way that they become to him the Voice of God.

3. The recovery of old spiritual aspirations and tendencies, coming from a previous life or lives. These are deeply hidden in his nature but can be brought to the surface through group stimulation. He thus recovers spiritual attitudes and desires which, in this life, have not hitherto made their appearance. They appear to him as utterly new and phenomenal, and he regards them as divine injunctions coming from God. They have, however, always been present (though latent) in his own nature

and are the result of the age-old trend or tendency towards divinity which is inherent in every member of the human family. It is the prodigal son speaking to himself and saying: "I will arise and go"—a point which Christ makes beautifully and abundantly clear in the parable.

4. The "guidance" registered can also be simply a sensitivity to the voices and injunctions and well-meaning intentions of good people on the path of return to incarnation. The spiritual dilemma of the race today is causing the rapid return of many advanced souls to life on the physical plane. As they hover on the borderland of outer living, awaiting their time to be re-born, they are oft contacted subjectively and unconsciously by human beings in incarnation, particularly at night when the consciousness is out of the physical body. What they say and teach (frequently good, usually indifferent in quality and sometimes quite ignorant) is remembered in the waking hours of consciousness and interpreted by the neophyte as the voice of God, giving guidance.

5. The guidance can also be of an astral, emotional nature, and is the result of the contacts made by the aspirant (firm in his aspiration but weak in his mental polarisation) upon the astral plane. These cover such a wide range of possibilities that it is not possible for me to enlarge upon them here. They are all coloured by glamour, and many well-meaning leaders of groups and organisations get their inspiration from these sources. There is, in them, no true lasting divine guidance. They may be quite harmless, sweet, kindly and well-intentioned; they may feed the emotional nature, develop hysteria or aspiration; they may develop the ambitious tendencies of their victim and lead him down the by-

ways of illusion. But they are *not* the voice of God, or of any Member in the Hierarchy, nor are they divine in nature, any more than the voice of any ordinary teacher upon the physical plane is necessarily divine.

6. The guidance recorded may also be the result of the man tuning in telepathically upon the mind or the minds of others. This frequently happens with the more intelligent types and with those who are mentally focussed. It is a form of direct, but unconscious, telepathy. The guidance, therefore, comes from other minds or from the focussed group mind of some band of workers with which the man may have a realised or an unrealised affinity. The guidance thus given can be consciously or unconsciously imparted, and can be, in quality, good, bad, or indifferent.

7. The mental world as well as the astral world is full of thought forms and these can be contacted by man and be interpreted by him as conveying guidance. These thought forms can be used by the Guides of the race at times in order to help and guide humanity. They can also be used by undesirable entities and forces. They can, therefore, be most useful, but when interpreted by any man as embodying divine guidance and as constituting an infallible leading (thus demanding and evoking blind and unquestioning acceptance) they become a menace to the free activity of the soul and are of no true value.

8. Guidance can come, therefore, from all kinds and types of incarnate or discarnate men, ranging in character from very good to very bad. They can include the help proffered by real initiates and adepts through their working disciples and aspirants to the mental and astral activities of ordinary intelligent men and women, in-

cluding the emotionally and selfishly oriented person. It should be remembered that no true initiate or disciple ever seeks to control any person nor will he indicate to him in the form of a positive command, any action which he should take. But many people tune in on teaching being given by trained minds to disciples, or record telepathically the powerful thought forms, created by world thinkers or Members of the Hierarchy. Hence the many misinterpretations and the so-called recorded guidances. Men appropriate to themselves sometimes that which is intended for a group or a hint given by a Master to a disciple.

9. Guidance also comes from a man's own powerful, integrated personality and he will frequently fail to recognise it for what it is. The ambition, desire, or prideful purposings of a personality may work down from the mental body and be impressed upon the brain, and yet the man, in that brain consciousness, may regard them as coming from some extraneous outer source. Yet all the time, the physical man is responding to the injunctions and impulses of his own personality. This often happens to three types of people:

a. Those whose egos or personalities are upon the sixth ray.

b. Those who have laid themselves open to the glamours of the astral plane through over stimulation of the solar plexus.

c. Those who are susceptible, for some reason or another, to the receding Piscean energy.

10. Guidance can come, as you well know, from a man's own soul when through meditation, discipline and service, he has established contact, and there is consequently a

direct channel of communication from soul to brain, via the mind. This, when clear and direct, is true divine guidance, coming from the inner divinity. It can, however, be distorted and misinterpreted if the mind is not developed, the character is not purified and the man is not free from undue personality control. The mind must make right application of the imparted truth or guidance. Where there is true and right apprehension of the inner divine voice, then—and only then—do you have infallible guidance, and the voice of the inner God can then speak with clarity to its instrument, man upon the physical plane.

11. Once this latter form of guidance has been established, stabilised, fostered, developed and understood, other forms of spiritual guidance then become possible. The reason for this is that they will pass through or be submitted to the standard of values which the factor of the soul itself constitutes. The awareness of the soul is a part of all awarenesses. The recognition of this soul awareness is a gradual and progressive happening where the man upon the physical plane is concerned. The brain cells must be gradually awakened and the correct interpretative response developed. As, for instance, a man becomes aware of the Plan of God, he may regard that Plan as being imparted to him by a Master or by some Member of the Hierarchy; he may regard the knowledge as coming to him through his own immediate contact with a thought form of the Plan. If he achieves and interprets this knowledge in a truly right way, he is perforce simply achieving recognition of that which his own soul inevitably knows, because his soul is an aspect of the Universal soul and an integral part of the planetary Hierarchy.

There are other sources of guidance, of inspiration and of revelation but, for the psychological purposes of our present study, the above will suffice.

We will now touch upon the subject of *dreams*, which is assuming such importance in the minds of certain prominent psychologists and in certain schools of psychology. It is not my intention to criticise or attack their theories in any way. They have arrived at a most important and indicative fact— the fact of the interior, inner subjective life of humanity, which is based on ancient memories, on present teachings, and on contacts of various kinds. A true understanding of the dream-life of humanity would establish three facts:

1. The fact of reincarnation.
2. The fact of there being some activity during sleep or un- consciousness.
3. The fact of the soul, of that which persists and has con- tinuity.

These three facts provide a definite line of approach to the problems which we are considering and they would, if an- alysed, substantiate the position of the esotericists.

The origin of the word "dream" is in itself debateable and nothing really sure and proved is known. Yet what is in- ferred and suggested is of itself of real significance. In a great standard authority, *Webster's Dictionary*, two origins of the word are given. One traces the word back to a Sanskrit root, meaning "to harm or to hurt"; the other traces it back to an old Anglo-Saxon root, signifying "joy or bliss." Is there not a chance, that *both* derivations have in them a measure of truth, and that in their mutual tracing back to some most ancient origin and root we should discover a real meaning? In any case two thoughts emerge from an under- standing study of these derivations.

The first is that dreams were originally regarded as undesirable, probably because they revealed or indicated, in the majority of cases, the astral life of the dreamer. In Atlantean times, when man was basically astral in his consciousness, his outer physical consciousness was largely controlled by his dreams. In those days, the guidance of the daily life, of the religious life, and of the psychological life (such as it was) was founded on a lost science of dreams, and it is this lost science (little as he may like the idea) which the modern psychologist is rapidly recovering and seeking to interpret. Most of the people (though necessarily not all of them) who find themselves needing the care and instruction of the psychologist are Atlantean in consciousness, and it is this fact which has predisposed the psychologist unconsciously to lay the present emphasis upon dreams and their interpretation.

May I point out again that the true psychology will only appear and right techniques be used when psychologists ascertain (as a first and needed measure) the rays, the astrological implications and the type of consciousness (Aryan or Atlantean) of the patient.

However, as time elapsed, the dreams of the more intelligent minds became of an increasingly forward-looking, idealistic nature; these, as they came to the surface and were remembered and recorded, began to control the brain of man so that the Anglo-Saxon emphasis on joy and bliss eventually became descriptive of many so-called dreams. We have then the emergence of the utopias, the fantasies, the idealistic presentations of future beauty and joy which distinguishes the thought life of the advanced human being, and which find their expression in such presented (and as yet unfulfilled) hopes as Plato's *Republic*, Milton's *Paradise Regained* and the best Utopian, idealistic creative productions of our Western poets and writers. Thus Occident and Orient together present a theory of dreams—of a lower astral or higher intuitional nature—which are a complete picture of the wish life of the race. These range all the way from the dirty ideas and the bestial filth, drawn forth at times from their patients by psychologists (thus revealing a wish life and an astral consciousness of a very low order), up to the idealistic schemes and the carefully thought-out paradises and cosmic orders of the higher types of aspirants. All, however, come into the realm of *Dreams.* This is true, whether such dreams are tied up with frustrated sex or unfulfilled idealism; they are all indicative of an urge, a powerful urge, either to selfish satisfaction or group betterment and group welfare.

These dreams can embody in themselves ancient astral illusions and glamours, potent and strong because of ancient origin and racial desire, or they can embody the sensitive response of advanced humanity to systems and regimes of existence which are hovering on the borderland of mani-festation, awaiting future precipitation and expression.

This will indicate to you how vast is this subject, for it includes not only the past astral habits of the race, ready—when given certain pathological conditions or fostered by fretting frustrations—to assert themselves, but they also in-clude the ability of the spiritually-minded aspirant in the world today to touch the intended plans for the race and thus see them as desirable possibilities.

Having thus indicated the scope of our theme, I would like to point out that I seek only, in the limited space at my dis-posal, to do two things:

1. Touch briefly upon the conditions which foster dreams.
2. Indicate the sources from which dreams can come and what produces them.

I do not expect to have these theories accepted by the average psychologist, but there may be somewhere those minds which will be open enough to accept some of the suggestions and thus benefit themselves and certainly benefit their patients.

The major cause of a distressing dream life is, in every case, a frustration or an inability of the soul to impose its wishes and designs upon its instrument, the man. These frustrations fall into three categories:

1. *Sex frustration.* This type of frustration leads in many cases, especially in the average person, to an over-emphasis of the fact of sex, to an uncontrolled sex thought-life, to sexual jealousies (oft unrecognised) and to physical underdevelopment.
2. *Frustrated ambition.* This dams back the resources of the life, produces constant inner fret, leads to envy, hatred, bitterness, intense dislike of the successful, and causes abnormalities of many kinds.
3. *Frustrated love.* This would perhaps be included under sex frustration by the average psychologist, but it is not so viewed by the esotericist. There can be full sexual satisfaction or else complete freedom from its grip and yet the out-going magnetic love nature of the subject may meet only with frustration and lack of response.

Where these three types of frustration exist, you will frequently have a vivid, unwholesome dream life, physical liabilities of many kinds and a steadily deepening unhappiness.

You will note that all these frustrations are, as might be expected, simply expressions of frustrated *desire*, and it is in this particular field (tied up as it is with the Atlantean consciousness) that the work of the modern psychologist primarily and necessarily lies. In an effort to bring the patient to an understanding of his difficulty and in line with that which constitutes the way of least resistance, the psychologist endeavours to relieve the situation by teaching him to evoke and bring to the surface of his consciousness forgotten episodes and his dream life. Two important facts are sometimes forgotten and hence constitute a fruitful source of the frequent failure to bring relief. First, the patient as he descends into the depths of his dream life, will bring to the surface not only those things which are undesirable in his unrecognised "wish-life" but also those which were present in previous lives. He is penetrating into a very ancient astral past. Not only is this the case, but also—through the open door of his own astral life—he can tap or tune in on the astral life of the race. He then succeeds in producing the emergence of racial evil which may have absolutely no *personal* relation to him at all. This is definitely a dangerous thing to do, for it may prove stronger than the man's present capacity to handle.

Secondly, in his desire to be freed from the things in himself which are producing trouble, in his desire to please the psychologist (which is encouraged by certain of them under the method of "transference") and in his desire to produce what he believes the psychologist wants him to produce, he will frequently draw upon his personal imagination, upon the collective imagination or, telepathically, tune in on the imagination of the one who is seeking to treat and help him. He, therefore, produces something which is basically untrue and misleading. These two points warrant careful attention and the patient must be safeguarded from himself, from the environing racial thought life, and also from the psychologist whose aid he is seeking. A difficult thing to do, is it not?

I would like, at this point, to make what I feel to be a needed and suggestive interpolation. There are three main ways in which the person who seeks psychological aid can be helped and this is true of all types and cases. There is, first of all, the method with which we have been dealing. This method delves into the patient's past; it seeks to unearth the basic determining conditions which lie hidden in the happenings of childhood or infancy. These discovered events, it is held, gave a wrong direction or twist to the desire nature or to the thought life; they initiated predisposing germ-complexes, and therefore constitute the source of all the trouble. This method (even if the psychologist does not realise it) can carry over into past lives, and thus open doors which it might be well to leave shut until they can be more safely opened.

The second method which is sometimes combined with the previous one is to fill the present moment with constructive creative occupation and so drive out the undesirable elements in the life through the dynamic expulsive power of new and paramount, engrossing interests. I would like to point out that this method could be more safely applied if the subjective dream life and the hidden difficulties were left untreated—temporarily at least. This method is (for the average ordinary person who is pure Atlantean in consciousness but is just beginning to develop mental activity) usually a sound and safe way to work, provided the psychologist can gain the understanding cooperation of the person concerned.

The third method, which has the sanction of the Hierarchy and which is the one its members employ in Their work, is to bring in *consciously* the power of the soul. This power then pours through the personality life, vehicles and consciousness, and thus cleanses and purifies all aspects of the lower nature. It will be apparent to you, however, that this method is of use only to those who have reached the point in their unfoldment (and there are many such today) where the mind can be reached and trained, and where the soul can consequently impress the brain, via the mind.

If these three methods are studied, you can arrive at an understanding as to the three systems which psychologists could elaborate and develop in order to handle the three types of modern consciousness—the Lemurian, which is the lowest found upon our planet at this time; the Atlantean, which is the commonest found today, and the Aryan, which is developing and unfolding with great rapidity. At present, psychologists are using the lowest type of aid for all groups and states of consciousness. This does not seem wise, does it?

The question now arises as to *the source of dreams*. Again, as in those cases we considered in connection with the sources of guidance, I shall simply enumerate such origins and leave the student of psychology to make adequate application of the information, when faced with a dream problem. These sources are about ten in number and could be enumerated as follows:

1. *Dreams based upon brain activity*. In these cases, the subject is sleeping too lightly. He never really leaves his body and the thread of consciousness is not completely withdrawn as it is in deep sleep or in unconsciousness. He remains, therefore, closely identified with his body, and because of the partial withdrawal of the thread of consciousness, his condition is more like a dazed, benumbed self-recognition than real sleep. This condition may persist throughout the entire night or period of sleep, but it is usually found present only in the first two hours of sleep and for about one hour prior to returning to full waking consciousness. The problems, worries, pleasures, concerns, etc., etc. of the waking

hours are still agitating the brain cells, but the recognition and interpretation of these vague or agitated impressions is uncertain and of a confused nature. No importance whatever need be attached to this type of dream. They indicate physical nervousness and poor sleeping capacity but have no deep psychological significance or spiritual meaning. These dreams are the most common at this time, owing to the prevalence of the Atlantean consciousness and the stress under which people live today. It is easy to attach undue importance to the wild and stupid or jumbled vagaries of a restless brain, yet the sole trouble is that the man is not sleeping soundly enough.

The effort to make people dream and to train them to recover their dream life when they are naturally sound sleepers, and drop easily into deep and dreamless sleep is not good. The evocation of the dream life, as brought about through the methods of certain schools of psychology, should only be brought about forcibly (if one may use this word in that connection) through the determination of the will during the later stages upon the Path. To do so earlier produces frequently a kind of continuity of consciousness which adds the complexities of the astral plane to those of daily living upon the physical plane; few people are competent to handle the two and, when there is persistence in the endeavor to evoke the dream life, the brain cells get no rest and forms of sleeplessness are apt to supervene. Nature wills that all forms of life should "sleep" at times.

We now come to two forms of dreams which are related to the astral or emotional nature and which are of great frequency.

2. *Dreams of remembrance.* These are dreams which are a recovery of the sights and sounds encountered in the hours of sleep upon the astral plane. It is on this plane that the

man is usually found when the thread of consciousness is separated from the body. In this case, the man is either participating in certain activities, or he is in the position of the onlooker who sees actual sights, performances, people, etc., etc., just as any person can see them as he walks down a street in any large city or as he looks out of a window in any environment. These sights and sounds will often be dependent upon the wish-life and the predilections of the subject, upon his likes and dislikes and his desires and recognised attractions. He will seek for and often find those he loves; he will sometimes search for and find those he seeks to damage, and find occasion to hurt those he hates; he will favour himself by participating in the fulfillment of what he desires, which is always imaginatively possible upon the astral plane. Such desires may range all the way from desire for sexual gratification to the longing of the spiritually-minded aspirant to see the Master, the Christ or the Buddha. Thought forms, created by the similar wishes of the multitude, will be found to meet his desire and—on returning to his body in the morning—he brings with him the recollection of that satisfaction in the form of a dream. These dreams, related to astral satisfactions, are all of them in the nature of glamour or illusion; they are self-evoked and self-related; they indicate however real experience, even if only astral in accomplishment and can be of value to the interested psychologist in so far as they indicate the character trends of the patient. One difficulty can, however, be found. These thought forms (to which the man has responded and in which he has found an imaginative satisfaction) embody the expression of the wish-life of the race and exist, therefore, upon the astral plane for all to see. Many people do see and contact them and can identify themselves with them upon returning to waking consciousness. In fact, however, they have really done no more than register these thought forms in the same manner as one can register the contents of a shop window when passing by. A shocked horror can, for instance, induce a person to relate, quite innocently, a dream which is, in reality, no more than the registering of a sight or experience which was witnessed in the hours of sleep but with which the man has no real connection whatever. This experience he relates with dismay and disgust; most feelingly he tells the experience to the psychologist, and frequently receives an interpretation which reveals to him the depths of evil to which his unrealised desires apparently bear witness. His unexpressed longings are "brought to the surface" by the psychologist. He is told that these longings, when faced, will then leave him, and that the ghost of his mental and psychological disorder will then be laid. Unless the psychologist is of real enlightenment, the subject of his care is then saddled with an experience which was never his but which he simply *witnessed*. I give this as an example of great frequency and of much damaging value. Until psychologists recognise the actuality of the life of humanity when separated at night from the physical body, such errors will be of increasing occurrence. The implications are obvious.

3. *Dreams which are recollections of true activity.* These dreams are registrations of true activities. They are not simply witnessed, registered and related by the subject. As soon as a person has reached

    a. A state of real integration of the astral body and the vital or etheric body, plus the physical body, then these three aspects function harmoniously.

    b. A capacity to pursue ordered activity at night or in the hours of sleep. Then the man can impress the physical brain with a knowledge of those activities and on returning to waking consciousness put it to actual use by the physical body.

The man's dreams will then be, in reality, nothing more nor less than the relation of the continuance of the day's activities, as they have been carried forward on the astral plane. They will be simply the record, registered on the physical brain, of his doings and emotions, his purposes and intentions, and his recognised experiences. They are as real and as true as any of those which have been recorded by the brain, during waking hours. They are, nevertheless, only partial records in the majority of cases, and mixed in nature, for the glamours, illusions and the perceptions of the doings of others (as recorded in the second category of dreams above) will still have some effect. This condition of mixed recording, of erroneous identifications, etc., leads to much difficulty. The psychologist has to make allowance for:

a. The age or soul experience of the patient. He has to determine whether the related dream is an illusory participation, a perceived or registered activity, or a real and true happening in the experience of the man during the hours of sleep.

b. The ability of the subject to bring through correctly the related experience. This ability is dependent upon the pre-establishing of continuity of consciousness, so that at the moment of return, the brain of the man concerned is easily impressed by the experience of the true man when out of the body.

c. The freedom of the patient from the desire to make an impression upon the psychologist, his innate truthfulness, his control of the imagination, and his power of verbal expression.

Where advanced aspirants and disciples are concerned, we have a somewhat different situation. The demonstrated integration has involved the mind nature and is involving the soul likewise. The activity, registered, recorded and related, is that of a server upon the astral plane. The activities which interest a world server are, therefore, quite different in nature to those earlier experienced and related. They will be concerned with deeds which are related to other people, to the fulfillment of duties involving other people, to the teaching of groups rather than individuals, etc. These differences, when carefully studied, will be recognised by the psychologist of the future (who will necessarily be also an esotericist) as most revealing because they will indicate in an interesting manner, the spiritual status and hierarchical relationship of the patient.

4. *Dreams which are of a mental nature.* These have their origin upon the mental plane and presuppose a consciousness which is, at least, becoming more sensitive mentally. At any rate, they are not recorded in the waking brain consciousness until there is some measure of mind control. I might add at this point that one of the major difficulties with which a psychologist is confronted, as he attempts to interpret the dream life of his patient, is based not only on his inability esoterically to "place" his patient as to ray type, evolutionary status, astrological indications and inherent characteristics, but also he is confronted with the inability of the patient to relate his dream correctly. What is presented to the psychologist is a confused and imaginative description of brain reactions, astral phenomena, and (where there is a measure of intellectual poise) some mental phenomena also. But there is no capacity to differentiate. This confusion is due to lack of alignment, and of true mental relation between the mind and the brain.

It becomes, therefore, oft a case of the "blind leading the blind".

Dreams which are of mental origin are fundamentally of three kinds:

a. Those dreams which are based on contact with the world of thought forms. This comprises a vast realm of ancient thought forms, of modern thought forms, and those thought forms also which are nebulous and emerging. They are of purely human origin and are definitely a part of the Great Illusion. They constitute, in the bulk of cases, man's effort at the interpretation of life and its meaning down the ages. They merge with the soul of glamour which is astral in nature. It will be obvious to you that these thought forms comprise all possible themes. They do not embody the wish-life of the race, but are concerned with men's thoughts about the ideas and ideals which—down the ages—have controlled human life and which, therefore, form the basis of all history.

b. Those dreams which are geometrical in nature, and in which the subject becomes aware of those basic patterns, forms and symbols which are the blue prints of the archetypes determining the evolutionary process, and which produce eventually the materialising of God's Plan. They are also the great symbols of man's unfolding consciousness. For instance, the recognition of the point, the line, the triangle, the square, the Cross, the pentagon and similar symbols are simply the recognition of a connection with, and a founding upon, certain lines of force which have, to date, determined the evolu·

tionary process. There are seven such forms, evolved and recognised in every race and, for our present purposes, there are, therefore, twenty-one basic symbols which, in geometrical form, embody the concepts which determine the Lemurian, Atlantean and Aryan civilisations. It is interesting to realise that there are fourteen more to come. The symbols which are already evolved are deeply ingrained in the human consciousness, and lead, for instance, to the constant use of the cross in its many diverse forms. Two symbols are at this time taking form as the basis of the coming civilisation. These are the lotus and the flaming torch. Hence the frequent appearance of these two in the life of meditation and the dream life of the world aspirants.

c. Those dreams which are symbolic presentations of teaching received in the hours of sleep by aspirants and disciples in the Hall of Learning on the highest level of the astral plane, and in the Hall of Wisdom on the mental plane. In the first Hall is the best that the race has already learnt through its Atlantean experience and in the world of glamour. Through these, wise choice can be developed. The Hall of Wisdom embodies the teaching which the two coming races will develop and unfold, and thus trains the disciple and the initiate.

I cannot do more than thus indicate the nature of these three basic mental experiences which find their way into the dream life of the man on the physical plane. These are given expression by him in the form of related dreams, creative work, and the expression of the ideals which are building the human consciousness

5. Dreams which are records of work done. This activity
the aspirant carries on at night and when absent from the
body, and it is carried on

a. In the borderland between the astral plane and the
physical plane.
b. In the so-called "summerland" wherein the entire
wish-life of the race is centred and all racial desire
takes form.
c. In the world of glamour which is part of the astral
plane which embodies the ancient past, which fertilises the desire life of the present, and which indicates the nature of the desire life of the immediate
future.

These phases and spheres of activity are very real in nature.
Aspirants who succeed in functioning with any measure of
consciousness on the astral plane are all occupied, at some level
or another, with some form of constructive activity or
work. This activity, selfishly performed (for many aspirants
are selfish) or unselfishly carried forward, constitutes much
of the material of many of the so-called dreams, as related by
the average intelligent citizen. They warrant no more attention or mysteriously applied interpretation or symbolic elucidation than do the current activities and events of daily life
as carried on in waking consciousness upon the physical
plane. They are of three kinds:

a. The activity of the patient himself when freed, in
sleep, from the physical body.
b. His observation of the activities of others. These he
is apt to appropriate unwillingly and quite erroneously to himself because of the ego-centric tendency of the average human mind.

c. Instruction which is given to him by those responsible for his unfoldment and training.

This category of dreams is becoming increasingly prevalent as the alignment of the astral body and the physical body is perfected and continuity of consciousness is slowly developed. The activity involves religious activity, sexual living in its many phases (for not all of them are physical, though all of them are related to the problem of the polar opposites and the essential duality of manifestation) political activity, creative and artistic activity and the many other forms of human expression. They are as varied and as diverse as those in which humanity indulges on the physical plane; they are the source of much confusion in the mind of the psychologist and need most careful consideration and analysis.

6. *Telepathic dreams.* These dreams are simply the record upon the physical brain consciousness of real events which are telepathically communicated from one person to another. Some friend or relation undergoes some experience. He seeks to communicate it to his friend or—at the moment of crisis— he thinks powerfully of his friend. This registers on the friend's mind but is often only recovered in the hours of sleep and is brought through in the morning as a man's own personal experience. Many of the dreams related by people are records of the experiences of other people of which a man becomes aware and which he is appropriating to himself in all sincerity.

We come now to a group of dreams which are a part of the experience of those people who have made a definite soul contact and are in process of establishing a close link with the world of souls. The "things of the kingdom of God" are opening up before them and the phenomena, the happenings, the ideas, and the life and knowledge of the soul realm are being registered with increasing accuracy in the mind. From the mind, they are being transferred to or imprinted upon the brain cells. We have therefore:

7. *Dreams which are dramatisations by the soul.* This type of dream is a symbolic performance by the soul for the purpose of giving instruction, warning or command to its instrument, man, on the physical plane. These dramatic or symbolic dreams are becoming increasingly numerous in the case of aspirants and disciples, particularly in the early stages of soul contact. They can express themselves in the hours of sleep and also during the meditation period or process. Only the man himself, from his knowledge of himself, can rightly interpret this class of dreams. It will be apparent to you also that the ray type of the soul and of the personality will largely determine the type of symbolism or the nature of the dramatisation employed. This must be determined, therefore, by the psychologist before interpretation can be intelligently given and prove useful.

8. *Dreams concerned with group work.* In this type of dream, the soul trains or fits its vehicle, the lower man, for group activity. This type of dream is also the higher correspondence of the dreams dealt with under our fifth heading. The group work involved is not this time carried on in the three worlds of human expression but in the world of soul life and soul experience. Soul knowledges and purposes are involved; work in a Master's group may be registered and regarded as a dream in spite of its reality and basically phenomenal occurrence. The realities of the kingdom of God may for a time seep through into the brain consciousness in the form of dreams. Much of the experiences recorded in the mystical writings during the past few centuries in the Occident, are in this category. This is a point worth careful consideration.

9. *Dreams which are records of instruction.* This type of dream embodies the teaching given by a Master to His accepted disciple. With these I shall not deal. When a man can receive these instructions consciously, either at night when absent from the body or in meditation, he has to learn to direct them correctly from mind to brain and to interpret them accurately. They are communicated by the Master to the man's soul. The soul then impresses them on the mind, which has been held steady in the light, and then the mind, in its turn, formulates them into thought forms which are then thrown down into the quiescent waiting brain. According to the mental development and educational advantages of the disciple so will be his response and his correct use of the communicated teaching.

10. *Dreams connected with the world plan*, the solar plan, and the cosmic scheme. These can range all the way from the insane brain and recorded experiences of the mentally unbalanced to the wise and measured teaching of the World Knowers. This teaching is communicated to the world disciples and can be regarded by them as either an inspired utterance or a dream with a deep significance. It should be remembered in both cases (the mentally unbalanced and the trained disciple) that a similar condition exists; there is a direct line from the soul to the brain. This is true of both types. These dreams or recorded instructions indicate a high stage of evolutionary advancement.

A consideration of all the above will indicate to you the complexity of the subject. The superficial student or the mystically inclined person is apt to feel that all these technicalities are of minor importance. The charge is often made that the "jargon" of occultism and its academic information is of no true importance where knowledge of the divine is concerned. It is claimed that it is not necessary to know about the planes and their various levels of consciousness, or about the Law of Rebirth and the Law of Attraction; it is an unnecessary tax upon the human mind to study the technical foundation for a belief in brotherhood, or to consider our distant origin and our possible future. It is nevertheless just possible that if the mystics down the ages had recognised these truths we might have had a better managed world. It is only today that those forces are being set in motion which will lead to a truer understanding of the human family, a wiser comprehension of the human equipment, and, therefore, to an effort to bring human living into line with the basic spiritual truths. The sorry condition of the world today is not a result of the intellectual unfoldment of man as is often claimed, but it is the working out of the unalterable effects of causes, originated in the past of the Aryan race.

That good can come from evil, that the bad effects of man's mental laziness can be transmuted into teaching points in the future and that humanity is now intelligent enough to learn wisdom will be the result of the widespread dissemination of the academic truths of the esoteric teaching and its correct interpretation by the trained minds in the Occident. The East has had this teaching for ages and has produced numerous commentaries upon it—the work of the finest analytical minds that the world has ever seen—but it has made no mass use of the knowledge, and the people in the Orient do not profit by it, as a whole. It will be different in the West and is already modifying and influencing human thought on a large scale; it is permeating the structure of our civilisation and will eventually salvage it. Be not, therefore, afraid of the technicalities of wisdom but seek for the reason of the undesirable reaction against them in the latent inertia of the mystical mind, plus the lowered vital condition of the entire race.

This brings me to a point I would seek to touch upon: that

of the widespread depression which is so seriously affecting the whole of humanity. The physical vitality of the races is low, or it is being whipped up into a better condition by the imposition of applied thought. Instead of drawing upon the resources of vitality, stored up in the soil, in food, fresh air and outer environing conditions, men are beginning to draw it from the etheric body itself through the galvanising effect of two things: *ideas*, as they are presented to them, thereby aligning mind and brain and incidentally stimulating the etheric body; *mass impetus* or contact which swings the unit into line with mass intention and opens up to him therefore the vast resources of mass intention. This enables him to feed his etheric body at the general etheric centre of power. This can be seen happening in its initial stage in practically every country. In the interim, however, between the establishing of the facility to tap at will the inner sources of vital stimulation and the changing of the old conditions, the masses of the people are left with neither source of sustenance available for their helping. They are consequently depleted, full of fear, and unable to do more than stand ready and hope for a better future for the next generation.

It is during this interim state that the full difficulty of depression can be felt, and it is at this time one of the major problems confronting the Hierarchy. How can the vitality of the human family be restored? How can the ancient joyousness of life, the keenness of spirit and the easy activity which distinguished the ancient races in the earlier phases of civilisation be recovered and humanity lose its depression and its unhappiness?

The whole position is the reverse of the problems of stimulation which constitute the major difficulty of the mystical life. With these we shall later deal.

No general covering solution has yet appeared. But inevitably it will, and when it does it will be the direct result of the activity of the New Group of World Servers. It will be a slow process, for humanity is entering into what may be regarded as a long convalescence. It will be brought about in three ways:

1. The discovery of the unused resources and vital reservoirs of strength, latent in the human being himself.

2. The promulgation of such truths as the potency **of** good will by members of the New Group of World Servers. The healing power of such realisations is immense.

3. Certain potencies and outer forces which the senior Members of the Hierarchy are now in process of invoking to the aid of humanity.

We come now to one of the most valuable and practical parts of our study upon the effects of the seven rays of energy as they make their presence felt in the human unit, and particularly as they affect the aspirant, disciple and mystic. During the past three decades, much has been written upon the pathology of the mystic and the physiological disturbances accompanying the mystical experience; much has also been investigated in connection with the neurotic characteristics which are frequently to be found in the spiritually polarised person and the inexplicable conditions which seem to exist—mentally, emotionally and physically—along with deep spiritual knowledge, definite mystical phenomena and high aspiration for divine contact. These conditions are increasing with great rapidity. More and more people are, for instance, becoming clair-voyant and clair-audient, and these reactions to stimulation and these expressions of innate powers are regarded as evidence of mental derangement, of delusions and hallucinations, and sometimes of insanity. Certain nervous complaints, affecting at times the muscular equipment and other parts of the human body, will be found eventually to have their origin in over-stimulation; instead then of being handled (as they now are) by imposed processes of rest, by the use of soporifics, and other forms of treatment, the patient will be taught methods of divorcing himself temporarily from the source of this mystical or spiritual potency; or he may be taught how to deflect these forces which are pouring into and through the various centres to those centres which can more safely handle them, thus producing a more even distribution of energy. He will also be taught how to use them effectively in outer service. Forms of nervous inflammation and neuritis will be regarded as symptoms of the wrong use made of the energy available in the human equipment or of undue emphasis upon it. We shall discover the sources of certain disorders and find that the difficulty lies in the centres which are found near to the particular organ in the body which seems *outwardly* to be responsible for the trouble. This is noticeably true in connection with certain forms of heart trouble and brain tensions and, of course, all cases of hypertension. It is true likewise in relation to the metabolism of the body which can be seriously thrown out of balance by the over-stimulation of the throat centre, with consequent evil effects upon the thyroid gland— that master gland which is related to the transference of the various forces (found in the body) to the head. There are two major centres definitely connected with the fact of transference:

1. The solar plexus centre which is the transferring centre for all the forces found below the diaphragm to the centres above the diaphragm.

2. The throat centre, which is the transferring centre for all the forces found above the diaphragm into the two head centres.

There are three aspects connected with this whole subject of the diseases and difficulties of the mystical life which it would be well to bear in mind. Those people who are concerned with the education and training of children or with the esoteric training of the world disciples and aspirants should study the matter with care; they should attempt to understand the causes of many of the nervous complaints and pathological conditions found in the advanced people of the world, plus the problems arising out of the premature development of the lower psychic powers as well as the unfoldment of the higher faculties. The problem, therefore, involves people at all stages of unfoldment and they should carefully consider them from the standpoint of energy activity—a thing which has been little done as yet.

The first of these three aspects could be stated as follows: We are passing at this time through a transition period wherein old energies are passing out and new ray influences are coming in. We are transiting into a new sign of the zodiac. Therefore, the impact of the new forces, plus the withdrawal of the old, is apt to produce clearly felt effects upon humanity, as a whole, and upon mystics and aspirants in particular, and cause definite reactions. With these we shall shortly deal when we consider the influence of the rays today and in the Aquarian Age. (*A Treatise on the Seven Rays*, Vol. III and *The Destiny of the Nations*).

Secondly, the present world problem, the fear and deep anxiety, and the suffering and pain which are so widespread, are producing a mixed and dual result. These two results (with all their intermediate stages) are—

1. The extraversion of the mass consciousness.
2. A pronounced introversion of the individual.

There is, therefore, a mass effect and an individual effect and these two must be more carefully borne in mind. This process of externalisation can be seen working out in all the clamour and in the ardent and oft noisy psychology of the great national movements and experiments, going on today all over the world. Simultaneously, individuals in all these countries and in practically every land are learning a needed (and sometimes enforced) suppression, control of speech and other restraining reactions; they are being turned definitely inward through force of circumstances and in such a powerful manner that—if you could see the play of forces as we on the inner side can see them—you would become aware of these two great movements being carried forward in the three worlds of human endeavour, as if they were opposing currents of force:

1. The movement, tending towards the extraversion or the externalisation of the great energies to which the mass consciousness responds. This is being directed or enforced through the activity of the first ray energy. Much of it, therefore, is to be found in the political field and in the realm of the mass will. In these early stages we are witnessing the evocation of that mass will; it is, as yet, unintelligent, inchoate, fluidic and easily imposed upon by the directed will of a group in any land, which can evidence enough power to engross the mass attention. This can also be sometimes done by a dominant and powerful personality. The net result—from the long range point of view—is the bringing to the surface of the deeply hidden and submerged mass consciousness, a silent, hitherto unexpressed and unoriented force, and yet a potency in the planetary life.

2. The movement towards the introversion or the "turning inwards" of the intelligent consciousness (not the mass consciousness this time) of all those men and women in the world today whose minds are awakening and who can function actively and creatively on the three levels of human awareness.

It is this dual movement—outward and inward—which is the source of much of the present world crisis. The effect of this "pull" in two directions is having a serious effect upon sensitive individuals. They are pulled in two directions: outward by the pull of the mass consciousness, and by the force of the political, economic and social life of the race; inwards by the pull of the world of higher values, by the kingdom of souls, by the organised work of the spiritual Hierarchy, aided by the age-old religious consciousness.

Psychologists would do well to study their patients from the angle of these two diverging energies. They would thus offset the tendency to cleavage which is one of the major anxieties of the spiritual Workers at this time. In the stress and strain of modern living, men are apt to think that the major task and the most important duty today is to make life more bearable and thus easier for humanity to live. To the spiritual Hierarchy of our planet, the major task is so to safeguard mankind that, when this period of transition is over and the forces that are withdrawing their influences have ceased entirely to have an effect upon humanity, there will be fusion and not cleavage to be found in the world. Thus the kingdom of God and the kingdom of men will be fusing rapidly into a dual manifesting expression. The incoming force will then be stabilised and its note clearly heard.

The third factor to be considered by the man who is working towards the wellbeing of his fellows is the study of the *effects* of the new incoming forces upon the *present* mechanism of man. This is not yet being done but is a determining factor in the successful development of the human unit. Therefore, it is of vital importance to educators, psychologists, parents and esotericists. There is, however, as yet no real recognition of the fact and the urgency of these incoming forces, nor is there any appreciation of the potency of the energies emanating from—

1. The sign of the zodiac into which we are now passing.
2. The effect of the relation existing between the forces emanating from the sign Aquarius and the sign Leo which is its polar opposite and, therefore, closely related to it. The interplay of the two signs is, at this time, responsible for the appearance of the great and modern human movements, involving vast numbers of men and engineered usually by some dominant personality. It is responsible also for the intense individualism which is manifesting in every department of human life today.
3. The effect of the new zodiacal influences upon the eleven other signs. This is a most interesting theme and one that has been little considered. What effect will the potency of the sign Aquarius (which is becoming increasingly dominant with each decade) have upon a person or a nation which is governed by the sign Taurus, for instance, or by Sagittarius, or Pisces? In coming centuries, this aspect of astrological science will be of definite importance and will be considered by those responsible for the rearing and education of children during the coming centuries. It will be one of the most important themes to be dealt with in all systems of psychological and esoteric service to humanity, and will

eventually cause a reorganisation of the methods employed up to date to aid and liberate man.

This we shall endeavour to elucidate as one of the points in Volume III of *A Treatise on the Seven Rays*, and it will contribute an entirely new approach.

4. The effect of the relation of the seven rays to the zodiacal forces. It should be remembered that there is a close interplay between the seven rays and the twelve signs of the zodiac.

Another task of the psychologist is to investigate the effect or the relation of the seven centres of force, which are to be found in the human body, in the etheric counterpart of the physical body. Many of the modern physical ills and a large number of undesirable psychological conditions will then be traced to their true source. This is the over-stimulation, plus the under-development, of the centres of energy found in the human mechanism and closely connected with the endocrine system. This is part of the new Science of Humanity.

You will see from the above how vast and intricate is our theme. It will not be possible for me to do more than generalise, and point out the way to certain broad trails or lines of investigation along which the modern student and scientist would do well to go. I would like to remind you also that the problem of the human being is essentially and basically the problem of consciousness or awareness. The five aspects of man—

1. The physical body.
2. The vital or etheric body.
3. The astral body.
4. The mental body.
5. The soul body or the egoic lotus,

are basically only open doors into the larger whole of which the individual unit is a part. They put the man into relation with the divine expression and manifestation in the same way that his five senses put him in touch with the tangible world and enable him thus to share the general life.

Many of our present problems (arising out of the mystical or the spiritual life) and a large number of our psychological difficulties are connected with this fact. Many a man also is over-developed in some one of these directions and, therefore, (through this developed sensitivity of some aspect of the fivefold instrument of contact) he becomes aware of a realm of consciousness and of states of awareness with which he is not competent to deal, owing to the under-development of his mind and the lack of soul contact.

4. *Diseases and Problems of Disciples and Mystics*

We will divide what we have to say about our theme, *The Diseases and the Problems of Mystics*, under four headings:

1. Those arising out of the awakening of the centres. These constitute a major difficulty and will, therefore, be dealt with first of all.
2. Those arising out of the unfoldment of psychic powers.
3. Those connected with group conditions and problems.
4. Those related to the outgoing sixth ray forces and the incoming seventh ray influences.

a. Problems Arising Out of the Awakening and Stimulation of the Centres

Those of you who have read my other books and treatises will know how immense is the subject with which we are concerned and how little is yet known and taught anent the centres and their force emanations and the activity of the vital or etheric body which is the receiver and the distributor of energies. These energies determine and condition the circumstances and the physique of the human being and produce (in the last analysis) the phenomenal manifestation of man upon the physical plane, plus his inherent characteristics. All of this information I have earlier given and it can be read and studied by those who are interested to do so. They can thus clarify their knowledge anent the various centres. One thing I would like here to point out and will later elucidate and that is the relation of the various centres to the rays. This is as follows:

Ray one	Power or Will	Head centre.
Ray two	Love-Wisdom	Heart centre.
Ray three	Active Intelligence	Throat centre.
Ray four	Harmony through Conflict	Ajna centre.
Ray five	Concrete Knowledge	Sacral centre.
Ray six	Devotion	Solar plexus.
Ray seven	Ceremonial Order	Base of spine.

Much could be learned if one would gather all the data given on this subject into one book, thus relating what is known about the specific energy points to be found in the human frame. All that I can do here is to give a general idea of the subject, indicate certain lines of development and relationship anent the seven major centres, the seven major glands and the localities and areas in the human body where these glands and centres are to be found. I would also beg you to realise five facts:

1. That undeveloped men are energised and galvanised into outer activity through the medium of the three centres below the diaphragm.

2. That average man is beginning to function primarily through the solar plexus centre and to use it as a transferring centre of force for energies which must be carried from below the diaphragm to above the diaphragm.

3. That the world aspirants are slowly being energised and controlled by the forces which are being transferred from the centres below the diaphragm to the throat centre and from the soul to the throat centre. This leads to creative activity of some kind.

4. That the world disciples are beginning to be governed and controlled by the throat and heart centres and are also beginning to transfer the forces which have been raised to the heart and throat, to the ajna centre between the eyebrows, in the middle of the forehead. When this has been done, the man is then an integrated personality. The soul also stimulates the ajna centre.

5. That the more advanced disciples and world initiates are also energised from two sources: by means of the energies raised up and lifted into the head from all the centres in the body, and by those which pour into the human frame from the soul, via the highest centre at the top of the head.

The whole process is, as you can see, one of development, use and transference, as is the case in all evolutionary development. There are two major transferring centres in the etheric body—the solar plexus and the throat—and one master centre through which the energy of the soul must pour when the right time comes, pouring consciously and with the full awareness of the disciple. That centre is the head centre, called in the Eastern philosophy "the thousand-petalled lotus". The problem of the average man is, therefore, connected with the solar plexus. The problem of the disciple, the advanced aspirant and the initiate of the lower degrees is connected with the creative centre, the throat.

I would here remind students that the following three

points, related to the transference of energy, must be borne in mind:

1. That there is a transference to be made from all the lower centres to higher ones and that this is usually done in two stages. This transference, carried on within the personality, is paralleled by the transference of spiritual energy from that reservoir of force we call the soul to the man on the physical plane. This becomes possible as the man makes the needed transference within himself. These transferences can take place in the course of the evolutionary process, or they can be hastened through the forced training given to disciples of all degrees.

2. That, within this major field of activity, the following transferences will have to be made:

   a. The energy of the centre at the base of the spine (the organ of the personal will) must be raised and carried up the spinal column to the head centre, via the ajna centre.

   b. The energy of the sacral centre (governing the sexual life and the organs of physical creation) must be raised to the throat centre, which becomes the organ of creative activity of a non-physical nature.

   c. The energy of the solar plexus (the organ of self-conscious personal desire) must be raised to the heart and there transmuted into group service.

3. That all these centres are developed and brought into activity in three stages, and thus progressively condition the outer aspects of a man's life:

   a. There is a period wherein the centres are active only in a sluggish and semi-dormant manner: the forces of which they are formed, and which they express, move slowly and with a heavy inert rhythm; the light which can be seen wherever there is a centre is dim; the point of electric potency at the centre (the "heart of the lotus or chakra," the hub of the wheel, as it is esoterically termed in the Oriental teaching) is relatively quiescent. There is just enough energy pouring into the centre to produce the preservation of life, the smooth functioning of the instinctual nature, plus a tendency to react, in a fluctuating and unintelligent manner to stimuli coming from the astral plane, via the individual astral body.

b. A period wherein there takes place a definite heightening and intensifying of force. The light of the centres is brighter and the solar plexus centre, in particular, becomes very active. As yet, all the real life of the man is focussed below the diaphragm. The centres above the diaphragm are dim and dull and relatively inactive; the point at the centre is, however, more electrical and dynamic. At this stage, the man is the average intelligent citizen, predominantly controlled by his lower nature and his emotional reactions, with what mind he has actively employed in bringing satisfaction to his needs. His centres are the receivers primarily of physical and astral forces, but occasionally respond to mental impacts.

c. A period wherein the first transference is being made. This can last a long time and cover several lives. The centres below the diaphragm are fully awakened; their activity is great; their light is vivid; their interrelation is real, so much so that a complete magnetic field has been set up involving the whole area below the diaphragm and becoming potent enough to extend its influence above the diaphragm. The solar plexus becomes the dominant organ in the place of the sacral centre which has so long determined the life of the animal nature. It becomes the recipient of energy streams from below which it absorbs and starts on its task of deflecting them and transferring them to the higher centres. The man is now the highly intelligent citizen and aspirant. He is conscious of the dualism of his nature, of that which is below and of that which is above, as it has been called, and is ready to tread the Probationary Path.

d. A period wherein the transference is continued. The sacral forces are carried to the throat and the solar plexus forces are carried to the heart. The latter transference is as yet of so small a measure that the effect of the transference is almost negligible. This period is a long and very difficult one. Today, most people are going through periods c and d, which are preparatory to the expression of the mystical life.

e. A period wherein the heart and throat centres are brought into activity. The man is creatively intelligent along some line or other and is slowly becoming group conscious. As yet, however, his reactions are still selfishly motivated though—at the same time—he is subject to cycles of vision and periods of spiritual effort. The mystical life is definitely attracting him. He is becoming the mystic.

f. A second period of transference ensues and the ajna centre, which governs the integrated personality, becomes active and dominant. The life of feeling and of mystical effort is, at this time, liable to die down temporarily in its expressed fervour and ardent disciplines, and personality integration, personality ambitions, personality aims and personality expression take its place. This is a right and good change and tends correctly to a rounded out development. It is only temporary, for still the mystic sleeps beneath the outer activity and the intelligent worldly effort, and will emerge again to living endeavour when the mind nature has been fully aroused and is controlling, when desire for mental satisfaction has been satiated and the "son of God is ready to arise and enter the Father's house". During this period, we find the intelligently creative or the powerful man will come to the zenith of his personality life. The centres below the head will all be active and functioning, but the centres below the diaphragm will be subordinated to and controlled by those found above. They are subject then to the conditioning will of the man who is governed at this time by ambition, intellectual expediency and that form of group work which tends to the expression of his personality potency. The ajna centre is vivid and potent; the throat centre is intensely active and the heart centre is rapidly awakening.

g. A period wherein the highest head centre is brought into radiant activity. This occurs as the result of the uprising (in a fresh and more potent manner) of the mystical instinct, plus, this time, an intelligent approach to reality. The result is twofold:

1. The soul begins to pour its energy into all the etheric or vital centres, via the head centre.
2. The point at the heart of each centre comes into its first real activity; it becomes radiant, brilliant, magnetic and forceful, so that it "dims the light of all that lies around."

All the centres in the body are then swept into ordered activity by the forces of love and will. Then takes place the final transference of all the bodily and psychic energies into the head centre through the awakening of the centre at the base of the spine. Then the great Polar opposites, as symbolised and expressed by the head centre (the organ of spiritual energy) and the centre at the base of the spine (the organ of the material forces) are fused and blended and from this time on the man is controlled only from above, by the soul.

There are, consequently, two points to be borne in mind as we study the mystic and his difficulties; first of all, the period of awakening and subsequent utilisation of the centres and, secondly, the period of the transference of energy from the solar plexus to the heart, and then from all the four centres up the spine to the throat centre, prior to the focussing of the energy of all the centres in the ajna centre (between the eyebrows). This centre is the controlling one in the personality life and from it goes all personality direction and guidance to the five lower centres which it synthesises. Each of these stages brings with it its own difficulties and problems. We shall, however, concern ourselves with these problems only as they affect present opportunity or hinder the man who finds himself upon the Path and is, therefore, taking his own evolution in hand. Then he stands "midway between the pairs of opposites" and this means (as far as our particular interest at this time is concerned) that we shall find three stages in the mystical work, each of which will mark a definite point of crisis, with its attendant tests and trials:

1. The stage wherein transference is made of all the lower

energies into the solar plexus, preparatory to carrying them to the throat and heart centres above the diaphragm. This stage covers not only the process of transference but also that of focussing the forces in the higher centres.

Period ....The later stages of the Path of Probation and the early stages of the Path of Discipleship.

Keynote ....Discipline.

Objective ....Idealism, plus personality effort. Purification and control.

2. The stage wherein transference is made into the ajna centre and the personality life becomes integrated and powerful.

Period ....The later stages of the Path of Discipleship and up till the time of the third initiation.

Keynote ....Expression of the soul, through the medium of the personality.

Objective ....The understanding of the Plan and consequent cooperation with it.

Then comes the third and final stage with which we need not concern ourselves wherein there is a complete blending of the bodily forces (focussed through the ajna centre) with the Soul forces, (focussed through the head centre). It is at this time that there comes the final evocation of the personality will (purified and consecrated) which has been "sleeping, coiled like the serpent of wisdom" at the base of the spine; this surges upward on the impulse of devotion, aspiration and enlightened will and thus fuses itself in the head with the spiritual will. This is the final raising, by an act of discriminating determination, of the kundalini fire. This raising takes place in three stages, or impulses:

1. The stage wherein the lower energies are carried to the solar plexus centre.
2. The stage wherein these energies, pouring through to the heart, are blended with it and carried to the throat.
3. The stage wherein all the five lower forms of energy are focussed in the ajna centre in the head.

Students might here ask: Are there any other energies below the diaphragm, except those of the sacral centre and those focussed in the centre at the base of the spine which are carried up to the ajna centre via the solar plexus centre? There are quite a large number of lesser centres and their energies, but I am not specifying them in detail for the sake of clarity; we shall deal here only with the major centres and their effects and inter-relations. The subject is abstruse and difficult in any case without our complicating it unduly. There are energies, for instance, pouring into the spleen from planetary sources as well as into two small centres situated close to the kidneys, one on either side, besides several others and these forces must all be understood, transmuted, transformed and transferred. It is interesting to note that the two little centres close to the kidneys are related to the lower levels of the astral plane and let loose into the system much of the fear, etc., which is the distinguishing factor in those subplanes. They are, therefore, found close to the centre which can control them because even the modern endocrinologist knows that the adrenal glands, when stimulated, produce (as a psychological result of a physical happening) an access of courage and a form of directed will which enables achievements to be carried out that are, at other time, wellnigh impossible.

I would like here to point out that the statement so frequently made in occult books that "kundalini sleeps" is only partially true. The centre at the base of the spine is subject to the same rhythmic life as are the other centres. The specific period wherein "kundalini awakes" refers to that period wherein the "point at the centre" becomes vibrant, potent and active: its forces can then penetrate throughout the entire spinal area until the highest head centre is reached. This, however, would not be possible had there not been three earlier "uprisings of the latent force of will". These uprisings serve to clear the passage up the spine, penetrating and destroying the etheric web which separates each centre and the area it controls from the next above.

All these transferences and interior organisation produce normally and naturally turmoil and conflict in the life of the mystic, causing difficulties of a definitely psychological nature and frequently pathological trouble as well. You have to note consequently, the series of *transference, psychological difficulty* and *pathological results.*

For instance, these ideas may clarify themselves in your mind if I point out certain facts, relating to the *sacral centre* which for so long a period of time governs the animal and physical creative life of the human being. During the processes of evolution, the sacral centre passes through the stages of automatic unconscious use, such as you find in purely animal man; then use under the urge of desire for pleasure and physical satisfaction, wherein the imagination is beginning to exert its influence; next comes the period wherein there is the conscious subordination of the life to the sex impulse. This is of a different nature to the first mentioned. Sex becomes a dominating thought in the consciousness, and many people today are passing through this stage and everybody at some time or in some life passes through it. This is followed by a period of transference wherein the physical pull of sex and the urge to physical creation is not so dominant and the forces begin to be gathered up into the solar plexus. There they will be controlled largely by the astral imaginative life far more than by the unconscious animal or the conscious desire life. They blend there with the forces of the solar plexus itself and gradually are carried up to the throat centre, but always *via the heart centre*. Here we find a major point of difficulty for the mystic who is rapidly coming into being and functioning activity. He becomes painfully conscious of duality, of the pull of the world and of the mystical vision, of divine possibilities and personality potencies, of love in place of desire and attraction, of divine relationship instead of human relations. But this whole subject is still interpreted in terms of duality. Sex is still imaginatively in his consciousness and is not relegated to a balanced place among the other instincts of the human nature; the result is an almost pathological interest in the symbolism of sex and what might be called a spiritualised sex life. This tendency is amply exemplified in the writings and experiences of many of the mystics of the middle ages. We find such expressions as the "bride of Christ", the "marriage in the Heavens", the picture of Christ as the "heavenly bridegroom" and many such symbols and phrases. In the Song of Solomon, you find a masculine rendition of the same basically sexual approach to the soul and its all embracing life.

These and many more unpleasant examples of a sex psychology are to be found, blended with a true and pronounced mystical aspiration and yearning, and a genuine longing for union with the divine. The cause of all this lies in *the stage of transference*. The lower energies are subject, as you can see, to two stages of transference: first, into the solar plexus and from thence to the throat centre. The throat centre is not, at this period, active enough or sufficiently awakened to absorb and utilise the sacral energies. They are arrested in some cases in their upward passage and retained temporarily in the heart centre, producing the phenomena of sex urges (accompanied at times with definitely physical sexual reactions), of religious eroticism and a generally unwholesome attitude, ranging all the way from real sexuality to fanatical celibacy. This latter is as much an undesirable extreme as the other and produces most undesirable results. Frequently in the case of a male mystic there will be over developed sexual expression on the physical plane, perversions of different kinds or a pronounced homosexuality. In the case of women, there may be much disturbance of the solar plexus (instead of sacral disturbances) and consequent gastric trouble and an unwholesome imaginative life, ranging all the way from a feeble pruriency to definite forms of sexual insanity with (frequently) a strong religious bias at the same time. I would remind you here also of the fact that I am definitely dealing with abnormalities, and hence must touch upon that which is unpleasant. In the early stages of mystical development, if there were right guidance of the mental life and of thought, plus courageous explanation of process, a great deal of difficulty would later be avoided. These early stages resemble closely the interest shown by the adolescent both in sex and religion. The two are closely allied in this particular period of development. If right help can be given at this time by educators, parents and those concerned with the training of the young, certain undesirable tendencies —now so prevalent—would never grow into habits and thought states as they now do.

The next question which might most correctly emerge in the student's consciousness could be stated as follows: How can this process of awakening the centres, of using them as channels for force (at first unconsciously and later with increasing consciousness), and finally of transferring the energy to ever higher centres,—produce problems, disease, and the many and varied difficulties of a phenomenal nature to which humanity seems heir, once the mystical experience becomes a goal and appears desirable. I would again remind you that the whole problem must be interpreted in terms of the growth of consciousness and also in terms of the bringing together, in progressive stages, of various types of energy. The human body is, in the last analysis, an aggregate of energy units. In the vital body (thus conditioning the endocrine and lymphatic systems) are certain focal points through which energy pours into the physical body, producing an impression and a stimulation upon the atoms of the body and thus having a powerful effect upon the entire nervous system which it underlies in all parts. The vital or etheric body is the subtle counterpart of the physical body in its nervous structure and the energy centres condition and control the glandular system. Thus energies, influences, potencies and forces pour into and pass through the physical body—consciously in some cases, unconsciously in the majority of cases—from the three worlds of human enterprise and activity. When the heart centre and the head centres are awakened and used by the interior and the exterior forces, you have the beginning of the mystical and occult life.

There are two reasons for this period of excessive difficulty:

1. The thread of consciousness in the head is anchored in the neighborhood of the pineal gland. The thread of life is to be found anchored in the heart. The turning of the forces (found below the diaphragm) into the solar plexus and from thence into the heart and the head brings those two major streams of energy (one coming from the Monad via the soul body to the heart centre, and the other coming from the soul direct to the highest head centre) to the attention of the mystic. He then becomes aware of life possibilities and of the wide field which

consciousness can cover and of the area or the extension of its capacity. This is the period of interior awareness.

2. The inflow of planetary and solar potencies, via the head centre to the heart and from thence to the other centres.

This inflow produces:

a. Stimulation of all the centres, major and **minor,** carried forward according to ray tendencies and influences.

b. The revelation of good and evil, that is, of the worlds of personality expression and of the world of soul expression. This dual process proceeds simultaneously.

c. The existence, therefore, of duality, which when realised and when the great opposites (soul and personality) are blended, can and will produce the at-one-ment.

The result of these realisations in consciousness leads inevitably to struggle, conflict, and aspiration plus constant frustration; this process produces those adjustments which must be made as the man becomes increasingly aware of the goal and increasingly "alive". The life expression (the threefold lower man) has to become accustomed to the new fields of consciousness and the opening areas of awareness, and to become used to the new powers which emerge, making the man able to enter more easily the wider fields of service which he is discovering. It might be stated here in a broad and general sense that—

1. *Stimulation* produces the awakening of the lower psychic powers if the incoming energy is directed to the solar plexus or to the throat centre. It produces the intense activities of the centres and this can, in the early stages,

cause definite psychic trouble. In illustration of this I would like to indicate the general nature of the difficulties to which the mystic can be physically prone:

a. The awakening of *the head centre* can produce serious trouble if brought about prematurely and even lead at times to insanity. Inflammation of certain areas of the brain and certain forms of brain tumours can be induced by a too rapid inflow of the highest form of energy which a man can receive prior to initiation. This takes place, however, only in those cases where the man is a highly developed person and of a mental type. In other cases of premature soul inflow, the energy pours through the opening at the top of the head and finds its way to some one or other of the centres, according to the ray type or stage of unfoldment. Where the greatest attention of the man's consciousness and life force is focussed (even if unconsciously) to that point the incoming energy will almost automatically flow.

b. The awakening of *the ajna centre* which is, as we have seen, primarily the result of the development of a man's personality to the point of integration, can (if the energies involved are not correctly controlled) lead to serious eye trouble, to many aural difficulties, to various forms of neuritis, headache, migraine, and nerve difficulties in various parts of the body. It can produce also many difficulties connected with the pituitary body and psychological trouble emanating from this important controlling gland as well as definite physical trouble.

c. The awakening of *the heart centre* (which is going on very rapidly at this time) is responsible for many forms of heart trouble and for the various difficulties connected with the autonomic nervous system, particularly in relation to the vagus nerve. The prevalence of various forms of heart disease at this time, particularly among the intelligentsia, professional and financial classes, is due to the awakening of this centre and to the discovery of an unrecognised capacity in humanity to become group conscious, and to undertake group service. The thymus gland, which controls in a peculiar manner the life aspect in man, is closely connected with the heart centre, as might be expected. This gland must eventually become more active in the adult than is now the case, just as the pineal gland in the coming human races will no longer be an atrophied organism with its true functions not understood and comprehended, but it will be an active and important part of man's equipment. This will take place normally and naturally as man learns to function as a soul and not just as a personality.

d. Again, much trouble among people is due at this time to the awakening of *the throat centre*. This centre governs and conditions the thyroid gland and the parathyroids. It can produce, when unduly developed or prematurely awakened, hyper-thyroidism with its attendant difficulties and its often dangerous effects upon the heart and upon the metabolism of the body. The psychological effects are well-known and recognised. These difficulties are increased and this higher creative centre unduly stimulated and rendered a danger instead of an aid to expression by the enforced celibacy of many people, owing to the present unfortunate economic conditions. These conditions are such that people refrain from marriage and there is consequently the lack of opportunity to use (or to misuse) the energy flowing through the sacral centre. Mystics are likewise prone to this difficulty. The throat centre is not used creatively nor is the sacral centre turned to its proper uses. The sacral energy is carried prematurely to the throat where it produces an intense stimulation. The equipment of the man concerned has not yet reached the point where it can be turned to creative work in any field. There is no creative expression of any kind as the development of the man does not permit him to be creative *in the higher sense.* The Swiss people, though highly intelligent, are not creative in this sense. The energy flowing through the thyroid gland is not used in creative art, music or writing in any outstanding manner, and hence the prevalence of goitre and thyroid difficulty. There is much energy flowing through and to the thyroid gland and, as yet, but little use made of it.

e. The increased activity and stimulation of *the solar plexus* centre today is a most fruitful source of trouble. It produces a great deal of the nervous difficulties to which women are particularly prone, and many of the stomach ills and liver troubles of the time, as well as intestinal difficulties. One of the most powerful sources of cancer in various parts of the body (except in the head and face) can esoterically be traced to the congestion of the energy of the solar plexus centre. This congestion has a general and widespread effect. Difficulties arising from the awakening of the heart centre and the solar plexus centre (for the two are closely allied and have a reciprocal action for a long time in the mystical experience) produce also a powerful effect upon the blood stream. They are connected with the life principle which is ever "carried upon the waves of desire" (as the ancient writings put it) and this, when prevented from full expression, through lack of development or other causes, leads to cancerous areas in the body wherever there is a weakness in the bodily tissue.

f. The awakening of *the sacral centre* is of such ancient origin that it is not possible at this time to trace the true history of the development of the difficulties connected with sexual expression, nor is it desirable. I have dealt with the subject of sex in my other treatises, particularly in *A Treatise on White Magic.* I call attention to it only because in the course of the mystical life there is often a period of sexual difficulty if the mystic has not previously learnt sexual control and unless it has assumed balanced proportions to his other life activities and natural instincts in his consciousness. Else, as he touches the heights of spiritual contact and brings in the energy of his soul to the personality, that energy will pass straight down to the sacral centre and not be arrested at the throat centre, as it rightly should be. When this occurs, then perversions of the sex life may take place, or an undue importance may be attached to the sex activity, or the sexual imagination can be dangerously stimulated, leading to lack of control and to many of the difficulties known to physicians and psychologists. The result is ever an overactivity of the sex life in some form or another.

g. The awakening of *the centre at the base of the spine* during the final stages of the higher mystical experience carries with it its own dangers. These definitely affect the spine and consequently all the nerves which branch out in all directions from the spinal column.

The raising of the kundalini force—if brought about ignorantly and prematurely—may produce the rapid burning through of the protective web of etheric matter which separates the various areas of the body (controlled by the seven centres) from each other. This causes serious nervous trouble, inflammation of the tissues, spinal disease, and brain trouble.

I have here hinted at some of the difficulties in an effort to give you a general picture of the problem of the mystic.

2. *Utilisation of a centre.* Let me explain this phrase. Certain difficulties also arise when a centre is used to such an extent that the attention is withdrawn from the activity of the other centres and they are thus neglected. In this way, whole areas of consciousness can temporarily cease to be recognised. It should be remembered that the goal of all the mystic's efforts should be to achieve a rounded-out development which brings into use sequentially, correctly and in conformity to right ray methods, all the different centres. Many people, however (once a centre is awakening and is subjectively stimulated) immediately find the utilisation of the centre to be the line of least resistance; they, therefore, begin to function almost exclusively through that centre. This can be well illustrated by two examples.

The solar plexus centre is, at this time, highly active among men and women everywhere. In every country millions of people are over-sensitised, emotional frequently to the point of hysteria, full of dreams, visions and fears, and highly nervous. This produces widespread gastric difficulties, indigestion, stomachic and liver ills and diseases, and intestinal disorders. To all of these the race today is exceedingly prone. To these are often coupled all kinds of skin eruptions. The cause is two-fold:

a. The over-stimulation of the solar plexus centre by its practically exclusive use, and by the consequent inflow of forces from the astral plane, to which the solar plexus is the wide open door.

b. The increased and constant use of this centre as its rhythm and vibration get too powerful to control. The man then succumbs to the temptation to focus his life interest and attention in the astral world and to do this with increasing awareness, interest and phenomenal results.

The man is, therefore, a victim of forces which would otherwise produce a gathering together of that "which is lower" and their necessary transference into that which is higher. A needed purpose would then be served, but—in the case we are considering—these forces are all concentrated in that central area of the body which is intended to be simply the clearing house for that "which is below into that which is above". Instead of this, there is set up a tremendous whirlpool of forces which not only produces physical difficulties of many kinds (as stated above) but which is also a fruitful source of the cleavages with which modern psychology is dealing at the time. So potent are the forces generated by the over use of the solar plexus (which is one of the most powerful of all the centres) and through the consequent flowing in of astral forces of every kind—thus augmenting the difficulties—that they assume eventually complete control of the life. The forces below the diaphragm and those above become *separated* by this vibrant and potent central force centre. Cleavage, astralism, delusions, hallucinations, nervous disorders of every kind and difficulties of a physical nature which definitely involve the intestinal tract, the liver and the pancreas are only some of the problems which arise from the uncontrolled use of the solar plexus centre. The man becomes controlled by it and is not the controlling factor, as he is intended to be.

The second illustration is connected with the unfoldment of the heart centre with its recognition of the group life and consequent group responsibility. This today is rapidly growing and can be seen on every hand. Students are apt to think that the awakening of the heart centre and its consequent group recognitions must be expressed in terms of religion, of love and of divinity. They, therefore, make of it something spiritual, as that much misused word is understood by the orthodox religious man. But it is far more than that. The heart is connected with the life aspect, for there is the seat of the life principle and there is the life energy anchored. It is connected with synthesis, with the monad, and with all that is more than the separated self. Any group which is engineered and controlled by one man or by a group of men, whether it is a nation, or a big business institution or an organisation of some kind or another (such as a great hospital) is connected with the life which is found in the heart. This remains true even when the motive or motives are mixed and undesirable, or purely selfish. A business magnate controlling vast interests who has the lives of many people dependent upon the contingencies of a business which he may have founded and over which he presides, is beginning to work through the heart centre. Hence the prevalence of certain forms of heart trouble to which so many people of influence and power so frequently succumb. The heart becomes over-stimulated by the impact of the energies pouring in on the man who is subjected— among other things—to the directed thoughts of those connected with his organisation. Can you see why, therefore, the senior members of the Hierarchy, Who work through the head and the heart centres, keep Themselves withdrawn from public life and much human contact? These two illustrations may help to clarify in your minds the sense in which I here use the term, "utilisation of a centre".

3. In the period of *transference* wherein the forces of the body are in a state of abnormal flux and mutation, it will be obvious what danger there is for the mystic and the disciple, and how serious can be the results of any transference which is *forced* into effect instead of following the natural course of evolution. This accounts, partially, for the present world upheaval and chaos. The forces flowing through the masses of average intelligent men today (and by that I mean those men who are educated and able to recognise the world news and to discuss world events and trends) are constituting the experimental ground for the transference of the energy of the sacral centre to the solar plexus. This leads inevitably to turmoil, over-stimulation, revolt and many other difficulties.

The problems, therefore, are many but are subject to solution. Let that not be forgotten. The whole theme is vast, but many minds are today seeking to deal with it and are working selflessly and altruistically to bring about the needed changes, a better understanding of man's physical and psychological natures, and a new approach—both to religion and education. When the mystical approach and its consequences—good and bad, material and spiritual—are better understood, through study and experiment, we shall arrive at a more complete comprehension of our problem and a better programme for human unfoldment.

I would like to point out that I am using the words "mystic and mystical" in this section of our treatise because I want what I have to say to meet with the interest of those who recognise the fact of the mystical approach to God and the mystical life of the soul, but who refuse as yet to widen the concept so that it includes also the intellectual approach to divine identification.

The keynotes which the mystic at present recognises and which the religious writer and thinker is also willing to admit are those of feeling, sensitivity to the divine existence, the recognition of a vision of God which will suffice to meet individual need and thus bring relief, peace, understanding and the realisation of divinity without and within, plus the relationship of the man to some extraneous Factor called *God*, or the Self, or the Christ. This attitude is coloured always by a sense of duality; it leads to the attainment of union—a union of which the marriage relation remains still the best symbol and illustration as the writings of the mystics of all periods and nationalities will testify, and which still preserves the consciousness of the two identities.

The keynotes of the occult life have been (and rightly) the notes of knowledge, of the mental approach to the problem of divinity, the recognition of divine immanence and of the fact that "as He is so are we." There is, however, no sense of duality. The goal is the achievement of such an approved and appreciated identification that the man becomes what he is—a God and, eventually, God in manifestation. This is not the same thing as the mystical union.

And yet, the whole theme is mystical and innately subjective. The time must come when the mystic will appreciate and follow the way of the head and not only the way of the heart. He will learn to realise that he must lose his sense of the Beloved in the knowledge that he and the beloved are one and that the vision must and will disappear as he transcends it (note that phrase) in the greatest processes of *identification through initiation*.

The occultist, in his turn, must learn to include the mystical experience in full understanding consciousness as a recapitulatory exercise before he transcends it and passes on to a synthesis and an inclusiveness to which the mystical approach is but the beginning, and of which the mystic remains unaware.

The mystic is too apt to feel that the occultist over-estimates the way of knowledge and repeats glibly that the mind is the slayer of the real and that the intellect can give him nothing. The occultist is equally apt to despise the mystical way and to regard the mystical method as "lying far behind him". But both must learn to tread the way of wisdom. The mystic must and will inevitably become the occultist and this whether he likes the process or not. He cannot escape it in the long run, but the occultist is not a true one until he *recovers* the mystical experience and translates it into terms of synthesis. Note the structure of words I have used in this last paragraph for it will serve to elucidate my theme. I use therefore the words "mystic and mystical" in this section of the treatise to describe the intelligent, highly mental man and his processes upon the Path of Discipleship.

In dealing with the problems and diseases of mystics who are at the point in their evolution where they are making one of the major transferences of force, it should be pointed out that in the earlier stages quite a long period of time may elapse between the first effort to transmute and transfer the energies and that particular life wherein the energies are finally gathered up and "elevated" as the esoteric term usually employed technically expresses it. It is at this point of focussed activity (in the place of the previous fluidic and spasmodic efforts) that one finds a definite point of crisis in the life of the mystic.

The question is often asked: Why is there frequently so

much illness, nervous trouble and various pathological conditions found among the saints of the earth, and among those who are clearly oriented towards the light? The answer is that the strain put upon the physical vehicle by the shift of the forces is usually unduly great and so produces these undesirable conditions. These again are often augmented by the foolish things done by the aspirant as he seeks to bring his physical body under control. It is, however, far better for the undesirable results to work themselves out in the physical vehicle than in the astral or mental bodies. This point is seldom realised and hence the emphasis laid upon the idea that sickness, ill-health, and disease are indicative of individual error, of failure and of so-called sin. They can of course be all of these things, but, in the case of the true aspirant who is endeavouring to discipline and control his life, they are often not due to these causes at all. They are the inevitable result of the clash of forces—those of the awakened energies which are in process of elevation and those of the centre into which the energies are being raised. This clash produces strain, physical discomfort and (as we have seen) many distressing kinds of disorders.

The widespread disease and ill-health found everywhere at this time is caused by a mass transference which is steadily going forward in the race. Through this transference, the solar plexus centre is thrown into an abnormal activity, thereby releasing all kinds of astral forces into the consciousness of man—fear, desire of a wrong kind and many of the emotional characteristics which are causing people so much distress. The process is as follows: the consciousness first of all registers these astral impressions, then formulates them into thought forms and—as energy follows thought—a vicious circle is thus set up, involving the physical body. In the turmoil consequently evoked by these clashing forces which are

  a. Mounting from below into the solar plexus,
  b. Pouring into the solar plexus from the astral plane,
  c. Reacting to the magnetic attractive power of the higher centres,

the interior life of the man becomes a whirlpool of conflicting energies with disastrous effects upon the intestinal tract, upon the liver and upon the other organs found below the diaphragm. The mystic, as is well known, is often dyspeptic and this is not always caused by wrong eating and wrong physical habits. It is brought about in many cases by the processes of transference which are going on.

One of the difficulties which tend also to increase the strain is the inability of the average mystic to divorce his mind from his physical condition. Energy inevitably follows thought and where a distressed area is found, *there* the mind seems to throw all its attention, with the result that the situation is not bettered but surely and steadily made worse. The best mental rule of all mystics should be to keep the mind definitely above and away from the region where the transference is going on, except in those cases where esoteric methods are being employed to force the process, to hasten and facilitate the processes of elevation. Then (under right direction and guidance plus a knowledge of the rules) the mystic can work with the centre in the spine which is concerned. This academic technique, I will endeavor to indicate in a later Instruction, but I want first of all to deal with the psychic difficulties of the mystic, for both the psychic and physical difficulties arise from the same basic cause and can be offset and controlled by the same correct occult and psychological knowledge.

The ills with which we are dealing are, therefore, the result of a large number of causes and it might be of service if I listed them here, reminding you that the centres up the spinal column and in the head govern definite areas in the body. These are affected and controlled by the centres and it is in these regions that one must look for indications of trouble.

Speaking generally, diseases fall into five major categories and it is only with the last of them that we are here occupied. These five groupings of disease are:

1. Hereditary diseases:

   a. Inherent in the planet itself and having a definite effect upon humanity, through contact with the soil and water.

   b. Developed during past ages in mankind itself and handed on from generation to generation.

   c. Characteristic of some particular family and inherited by the member of this family as part of his chosen karma. Souls come into certain families because of this opportunity.

2. Diseases invoked by tendencies in the man himself. These are governed by his astrological sign—either his sun sign or his rising sign and will be considered later.

3. Contagious diseases (epidemic or endemic) which are of group origin and involve the man as a part of his group karma, but are quite frequently unrelated to his personal karma.

4. Acquired diseases and accidents which are the result of injudicious action or unwise habits in this life and definitely condition his future karma. One interesting point in connection with accidents might here be made. Accidents are frequently caused by what might be regarded as "explosions of force". These are generated by a man or by a group of human beings through hatred or

jealousy or vindictiveness, which qualities react or are "turned back" upon the individual life like a boomerang.

5. The diseases of mystics with which we are at this time concerned. Speaking generally, these are caused by the energy of an awakened and active lower centre being transferred into a higher one. This is done in three stages and each stage brings its own physiological difficulties:

a. The stage wherein the energy of the lower centre becomes intensely active *prior* to rising upward. This will produce over-activity of the organs in the physical area governed by the centre, with consequent congestion, inflammation, and usually disease.

b. The stage wherein the "processes of elevation" are taking place, producing intense activity in the higher centre and a lessening of activity in the lower. A fluid period intervenes in which the forces swing back and forth between the two centres, accounting for the uneven life of the mystic in the earlier stages of his unfoldment. This is particularly the case in connection with the solar plexus. The energy is rejected at first by the higher centre and is then re-absorbed into the lower only to be elevated again and again until the higher centre can absorb and transmute it.

c. The stage wherein the energy is raised definitely into the higher centre. This leads to a difficult period of adjustment and of tension, again producing physical ills but, this time, in the area controlled by the higher centre.

When, for instance, the sacral energy is raised to the solar plexus, there will be found many ailments involving, as noted before, the intestinal tract. When the energy of the lesser centres which are found below the diaphragm (but not up the spine) are raised to the solar plexus centre, trouble involving the gall bladder and the kidneys will often be found. Occultly speaking, any process of elevation or of "raising up" automatically involves *death*. This death affects the atoms in the organs involved and causes the preliminary stages of ill-health, disease and disruption, because *death is nothing but a disruption and a removal of energy*. When the science of the transference of energy from a lower centre to a higher is understood, then light will be thrown upon the entire problem of dying and the true Science of Death will come into being, liberating the race from fear.

Students would do well at this stage to pause and consider the following points with care:

1. Which are the areas controlled by the five centres up the spine and the two centres in the head.
2. The three major points of transference:—the solar plexus, the throat centre and the ajna centre in the head. The heart centre and the highest head centre, as points of transference, only concern the initiate.
3. The fluidic and changeable condition produced by the processes of awakening, transference and the focussing of the energy in the higher centre. These three major activities are conditioned by the intermediate stages of:
   a. The active radiation of the lower centre.
   b. The responsiveness of the lower centre to the magnetic pull of the higher.
   c. The succeeding interplay between the higher and the lower centres, conditioned at first by a rhythmic repulsion and attraction. This is a reflection of the play of the dualities in the career of the human being.
   d. This is followed by a concentration of the lower energy in the higher centre.

e. Then comes the control of the lower centre or centres by the higher focal points of energy and their rhythmic interplay.

Between all these different stages come "points of crisis" of greater or lesser moment. This intense interior activity which is going on all the time in the subjective life of humanity produces both good and bad effects, and psychological as well as physiological reactions. Today, the mass transference of the forces of the sacral centre into that of the solar plexus is responsible for many of the modern and physical disabilities of the race. Because also of the slow removal on a racial scale of the sacral force to the solar plexus there is eventuating a condition which is called sometimes "race suicide", necessitating the efforts of many of the different governments to offset the rapidly falling birth rate in their countries.

The above summation of the threefold activity which is going on in the human body all the time will give some idea of the strain under which the individual man labours, and will account, therefore, for much of the discomfort and disease found in those areas in the human body which are governed and controlled by a particular centre. I would like to add the following points to the information given above:

1. The intense activity of *the sacral centre* will often produce diseases and physiological abnormalities, connected with the organs of reproduction (both male and female). These difficulties are of two kinds:

a. Those to which normal humanity is prone and which are well known to the physician, surgeon and psychologist.

b. Those which are the result of over-stimulation, through the successful effort of the mystic to bring in energy from the higher centres and from sources outside the human frame altogether.

2. In all cases of transference, the intense activity produced will cause all kinds of tensions and reactions, resulting in congestions, inflammations and diseases of the organs vitalised. This is particularly the case today in relation to the sacral and solar plexus centres. The glands—major and minor, endocrine and lymphatic—in the abdominal area are powerfully affected and through their hypersensitivity or their "deficiency through abstraction" (as it is esoterically called) they constitute a fruitful source of difficulty.

3. The activity of *the solar plexus centre* at this time, which is a result of this transference, produces the abnormal tension which characterises the race. This tension, with the average man, controls the intestinal tract and its connections, both above and below the diaphragm. With the advanced man, it produces tension in the higher centres, definitely affecting the heart and the vagus nerve. It should be pointed out that many of the diseases inherent in the racial form to which planetary disease predisposes the human being are brought into activity as the result of the stimulation of the solar plexus. As humanity becomes less astral in its consciousness and the solar plexus, therefore, becomes less active and less dominating, these forms of difficulty will die out. As the heart centres and the higher centres assume control, such diseases as cancer, tuberculosis and the various syphilitic complaints (due to the age old activity of the sacral centre) will gradually die out.

4. The activity of *the heart centre* as it

   a. Magnetically attracts the energies out of the solar plexus,

b. Becomes involved in a reciprocal interplay with the solar plexus,

is a fruitful source of nervous trouble to the mystic and advanced aspirant. The heart centre powerfully affects the vagus nerve and the autonomic nervous system with all that that involves and we are only today beginning to understand and deal with these difficulties. Clarification will come once the premise of the existence of the centres and their three "activities of interplay" are admitted —even if only as a possible hypothesis. The little understood thymus gland holds the key to much that concerns the activity and control of the vagus nerve—a fact not yet generally recognised. Later, a carefully controlled process with the object of stimulating the thymus gland and its secretion will be worked out by the medical profession, leading to a much better functioning of the nervous system and of the vagus nerve which controls it. I can but hint at possibilities at present because the basic premise of the existence of the centres of force is not yet recognised. It is interesting to note, however, that the solar plexus (as a great nerve centre) is recognised and this is due to the fact that the bulk of humanity is, at this time, transferring force to that centre. It is, for the masses, the major recipient of forces, both from below the diaphragm, from above, and from the environment.

5. The activity of *the throat centre* is steadily increasing today, owing to the creative activity and the inventive genius (which brings in the higher stimulation) and the idealistic conceptions of the intelligentsia of the world. This activity is responsible physiologically for many of the diseases of the respiratory tract. Energy is carried to the throat but is not adequately used and there is a con-

sequent congestion and similar consequences. But, curiously enough, a great many of the difficulties connected with the entire breathing apparatus are related *to group conditions*. These I will touch upon later. Today, the concentration of energy is producing serious effects upon that master gland, the thyroid gland. These effects disturb the balance of the physical body and involve also the parathyroid glands. The metabolism of the body is upset bringing attendant difficulties. The race is advancing so rapidly in its development that this centre will soon compete with the solar plexus centre for the position of being the most important centre and the major clearing house in the human body. I would commend this statement to your careful consideration for it carries with it much of encouragement. It indicates, nevertheless, much physiological change and many problems and above everything else much psychological difficulty.

6. The activity of *the ajna centre* will increase a great deal during the coming century, bringing with it its own attendant problems. Its close relation to the pituitary body and the growing interplay between

a. The ajna centre and the pituitary body
b. The centre at the top of the head (involving the pineal gland) and the ajna centre

will produce serious problems connected with the brain and the eyes. The ajna centre focusses the abstracted energy of the five centres up the spine and is the seat of personality power. According to the use made of that power and according to the direction of the force sent forth throughout the body by the directed, integrated personality, so will the organs of the body be affected. The solar plexus can be stimulated from that centre with disastrous effects; the heart centre can be swept into undue activity by the imposition of personality force, and its energy deflected downwards in a focussed selfish manner; the solar plexus can be so over-vitalised that all the forces of the personality can be turned downwards and subverted to purely selfish and separative ends, thus producing a powerful personality, but—at the same time —the temporary suspension of the spiritual life of the man. When this suspension takes place, all the forces of the body which have been "elevated" are driven downwards again, putting the man en rapport with the rank and file of humanity who are working through the lower centres; this tends to produce an immense personality success. It is interesting to note that when this takes place, the energies—concentrated in the ajna centre —sweep down into the solar plexus or into the sacral centre, and seldom to the heart centre. The heart centre has a power all its own to produce what is called "occult isolation", because it is the seat of the life principle. The throat centre receives stimulation in this case but seldom to the point of difficulty. The man is a powerful creative thinker, selfishly polarised and with an emotional solar plexus contact with the masses. He frequently also has a strong sexual complex in some form or another.

7. The activity of *the head centre* is as yet little known and there is little that I can profitably say about it, for I would not be credited with speaking the truth. This centre is the central factor in human life, but the focalisation of the lower and the higher bodily forces is not yet located there. Beyond producing hyper-tension (becoming so prevalent today among the more advanced people of the world) and certain forms of brain trouble and nervous disorders, its power is mostly seen in its pro-

nounced psychological effects. With these I shall proceed to deal as we consider the unfoldment of the psychic powers, the evolution of the mystical vision and the revelation of the light and of power. This centre controls the pineal gland and consequently certain areas of the brain. Indirectly also, the vagus nerve is affected. Consciousness and life, sensitivity and directed purpose are the great energies which express themselves through this centre, for consciousness is a form of energy, as well you know, and life is energy itself.

b. Unfoldment of the Psychic Powers

The forces which are responsible for the awakening of the centres are many. The primary one is the force of evolution itself, plus the inherent or innate forward-pressing urge towards greater inclusiveness which is always found in every individual being. This secondary aspect of the evolutionary principle needs careful elaborating. We have for too long been occupied with the effort to develop the form side of nature so that it shall become increasingly sensitive to its environment and thus build an ever improving mechanism. But the twofold idea (should I say *Fact*, for such it is?) of the development of an increasing capacity to include and the fact of the existence of the one interior factor, the Self, which brings about this steady development, needs emphasising. From the standpoint of the occult student, there are three ideas which lie behind this belief:

1. The fact of the Indweller, the Entity within the form who looks on at life as it unfolds, who develops awareness of the environment and who becomes inclusive—eventually to the point of synthesis.
2. The fact of the inherent ability (found in all forms of life

in all kingdoms) to progress towards this greater inclusiveness, passing from kingdom to kingdom in this unfolding process.

3. The fact that humanity constitutes a central point from which this inclusiveness can be *consciously* developed. Hitherto, the development has been natural, normal and part of the evolutionary urge. This it still remains, but the process can be hastened (and frequently is) as man gains control of his mental processes and begins to work (as the conscious Indweller) towards appointed ends.

I wanted to make these points adequately clear because they have a definite bearing on our theme which concerns the psychic difficulties of modern man. These difficulties are rapidly growing and are causing much distress among those who believe that the development of the lower psychic powers is a hindrance to true spiritual development. Certain mystics regard these powers as indications of divine grace, however, and as guarantees of the reality of their endeavour. Others regard them as signifying a definite "fall from grace". It seems to me, therefore, that an analysis of these powers, their correct placing upon the path of development, and a comprehension of the distinction between the higher and the lower powers will be of real value and will enable students in the future to proceed with a greater surety and knowledge. They will thus be more accurately sure of the nature of the contacts of which they become aware and of the means whereby these contacts are approached and gained.

The major idea which I would have you bear in mind is the development of *Inclusiveness*. This inclusiveness is the outstanding characteristic of the soul, or self, whether it is the soul of man, the sensitive nature of the cosmic Christ, or the anima mundi, the soul of the world. This inclusiveness tends to synthesis. It can already be seen functioning at a definite point of fulfilment in man, because man includes in his nature all the gains of past evolutionary cycles (in other kingdoms in nature and in previous human cycles), plus the potentiality of a greater future inclusiveness. Man is the macrocosm of the microcosm; the gains and peculiar properties of the other kingdoms in nature are his, having been resolved into capacities of consciousness. He is, however, enveloped in and part of a still greater macrocosm, and of this greater Whole he must become increasingly aware. Let this word, *Inclusiveness*, govern your thinking as you read this instruction which I am giving you upon the psychic powers and their effect.

The next idea to which I would call your attention is that the human being has the power to be inclusive in many directions, just as a line can be drawn from the point at the centre of the circle to any point upon the periphery. You must remember that for a large part of his career and for the most important part of his human experience, he remains the dramatic actor, holding the centre of the stage and in his own eyes playing the star part; he is always conscious of his acting and of the reactions to that acting. When man was little more than an animal, when he was in the state which we have earlier called the Lemurian consciousness and the early Atlantean consciousness, he lived unthinkingly; life unrolled like a panorama before his eyes; he identified himself with the episodes depicted and knew no difference between himself and that which he seemed to be in the unfolding picture. He simply looked on, played his little part, ate, reproduced, reacted to pleasure and to pain, and seldom, if ever, thought or reflected.

Then comes the period, familiar to all of us, wherein the man becomes the dramatic center of his universe—living, loving, planning, acting, conscious of his audience and his surroundings, and demonstrating to his fullest capacity the later Atlantean and present Aryan characteristics. He is intelligently aware of his power and of a few of his powers; he is a functioning personality and (because the mind is controlling or beginning to control) the lower animal powers and the Atlantean psychism which have distinguished him begin to fade out. He loses these lower powers and has not yet developed the higher ones. Hence the reaction to be seen on every hand today to such powers as clairvoyance, clairaudience, etc.; hence their wholesale condemnation as fraudulent by the intelligentsia of the world.

Next comes the mystical stage wherein the advanced human being, the aspirant and the disciple becomes steadily aware of another realm of nature to conquer, the realm of the Kingdom of God, with its own life and phenomena; he registers the existence of other powers which he can develop and use if he so desires and is willing to pay the price; he recognises another and wider sphere of being which he can include in his own consciousness if he permits himself to be conquered by it.

The inference then is that there are two sets of powers latent in his human equipment—the lower one being recoverable if he deem it desirable, the other and higher one to be developed. These two sets of powers are:

1. The ancient powers and faculties which humanity developed and possessed in past ages which he drove into the background of his consciousness and below the threshold of his current awareness in order to develop the mind and thus become himself a conqueror and a personality.

2. The higher powers and faculties which are the prerogative of the conscious soul. These are greater powers to which the Christ referred when He promised His

disciples that some day they would do greater things than He had done.

It should be remembered, however, that all the psychic powers are the powers, faculties and capacities of the One Soul but that, in time and space, some of them are expressions of the animal consciousness or the animal soul, some of the human soul, and some of the divine soul.

The following tabulation of the developing psychic powers as they blend in consciousness three kingdoms in nature may be of service at this point if careful study is made of the inferred relationships:

Animal.	*Human.*	*Divine.*
1. *The four major instincts.*	*The five major instincts*	*The five transmuted instincts.*
a. Self-preservation.	Creative self-preservation.	Immortality.
b. Sex	Sex. Human love.	Attraction.
c. Herd instinct.	Gregariousness	Group consciousness.
d. Curiosity	Enquiry. Analysis. plus	Evolutionary urge.
	Self-assertion	*Self*-control.
2. *The five senses.*	*The five senses.*	*The five senses.*
a. Touch	Touch. Contact	Understanding.
b. Hearing	Hearing. Sound	Response to the *Word*.
c. Sight	Seeing, Perspective.	The mystical vision.
d. Taste (embryonic)	Taste. Discrimination	Intuition.
e. Smell (acute)	Smell, Emotional idealism.	Spiritual discernment.
3. *Lower psychic powers.*	*The human correspondences.*	*Higher psychic powers.*
a. Clair-voyance	Extension through vision.	The mystical vision.
b. Clair-audience	Extension through hearing.	Telepathy. Inspiration.

	Animal.	Human.	Divine.
c.	Mediumship	Intercourse. Speech.	Mediatorship.
d.	Materialisation	Invention	Creativity.
e.	Divination	Foresight. Planning.	Prevision.
f.	Healing through animal magnetism.	Healing through science.	Healing through spiritual magic.

Extracts from "A Treatise on Cosmic Fire" pp. 188-196

No. 1

MICROCOSMIC SENSORY EVOLUTION

Plane		Subplane	
Physical	1. Hearing	5th	gaseous
	2. Touch, feeling	4th	first etheric
	3. Sight	3rd	super-etheric
	4. Taste	2nd	sub-atomic
	5. Smell	1st	atomic
Astral	1. Clairaudience	5th	
	2. Psychometry	4th	
	3. Clairvoyance	3rd	
	4. Imagination	2nd	
	5. Emotional idealism	1st	
Mental	1. Higher clairaudience	7th	} Form
	2. Planetary psychometry	6th	
	3. Higher clairvoyance	5th	
	4. Discrimination	4th	
	5. Spiritual discernment	3rd	} Formless
	Response to group vibration	2nd	
	Spiritual telepathy	1st	
Buddhic	1. Comprehension	7th	
	2. Healing	6th	
	3. Divine vision	5th	
	4. Intuition	4th	
	5. Idealism	3rd	
Atmic	1. Beatitude	7th	
	2. Active service	6th	

3. Realisation 5th
4. Perfection 4th
5. All knowledge 3rd

It can be noted that we have **not** summed up the two planes of abstraction on the atmic and the buddhic planes, the reason being that they mark a degree of realisation which is the property of initiates of higher degree than that of the adept, and which is beyond the concept of the evolving human unit, for whom this treatise is written.

We might, here, for the sake of clarity, tabulate the five different aspects of the five senses on the five planes, so that their correspondences may be readily visualised, using the above table as the basis:

a. The First Sense............Hearing.
 1. Physical hearing.
 2. Clairaudience.
 3. Higher clairaudience.
 4. Comprehension (of four sounds).
 5. Beatitude.

b. The Second Sense...........Touch or feeling.
 1. Physical touch.
 2. Psychometry.
 3. Planetary psychometry.
 4. Healing.
 5. Active service.

c. The Third Sense............Sight.
 1. Physical sight.
 2. Clairvoyance.
 3. Higher clairvoyance.
 4. Divine vision.
 5. Realisation.

d. The Fourth Sense...........Taste.
 1. Physical taste.
 2. Imagination.
 3. Discrimination.

4. Intuition.
5. Perfection.

e. The Fifth Sense.............Smell.
1. Physical smell.
2. Emotional idealism.
3. Spiritual discernment.
4. Idealism.
5. All knowledge.

Extract 2

Hearing gives him an idea of relative direction, and enables a man to fix his place in the scheme, and to locate himself.

Touch gives him an idea of relative quantity and enables him to fix his relative value as regards other bodies, extraneous to himself.

Sight gives him an idea of proportion, and enables him to adjust his movements to the movements of others.

Taste gives him an idea of value, and enables him to fix upon that which to him appears best.

Smell gives him an idea of innate quality, and enables him to find that which appeals to him as of the same quality or essence as himself.

In all these definitions it is necessary to bear in mind *that the whole object of the senses is to reveal the not-self, and to enable the Self therefore to differentiate between the real and the unreal.*

Extract 3

These three major senses (if I might so describe them) are very definitely allied, each with one of the three Logoi:

Hearing—The recognition of the fourfold word, the activity of matter, the third Logos.

Touch—The recognition of the sevenfold Form Builder, the gathering together of forms, their approximation and interrelation, the second Logos. The Law of Attraction between the Self and the not-self begins to work.

Sight—The recognition of totality, the synthesis of all, the realisation of the One in Many, the first Logos. The Law of Synthesis, operating between all forms which the self occupies, and the recognition of the essential unity of all manifestation by the means of sight.

Extract 4

Hearing	. . . . Beatitude.	This is realised through the **not-self.**
Touch	. . . . . Service.	The summation of the work of the Self for the not-self.
Sight	. . . . . . Realisation.	Recognition of the triplicity needed in manifestation, or the reflex action of the Self and the not-self.
Taste	. . . . . . Perfection	Evolution completed through the utilisation of the not-self and its realised adequacy.
Smell	. . . . . . Perfected Knowledge.	The principle of manas in its discriminating activity, perfecting the interrelation between the Self and the not-self.

A close study of the above will bring to the open-minded student two major points which he would do well to consider:

1. That the instinctual nature, as it develops in the three kingdoms (animal, human and divine) is, in fact, that which develops stage by stage into what we call consciousness; it is in reality, the development of a gradual expansion of capacity to be aware of the environment, whatever that environment may be. The herd instinct of the animal is, for instance, the embryonic unfoldment of what is later recognised by the intellect as group consciousness. These higher developments are brought about by the application of the intellect and a change in the motivating power. The same idea can be traced in connection with all the instincts.

2. That the lower psychic powers, inherent in the animal nature, are in every case embryonic indications of soul capacities.

Once this idea is grasped, the attitude of the sceptic and unbeliever will change and he will see (as he studies these lower powers) that, rightly understood and utilised, they can be direct avenues of approach to certain states of existence, but are incidental to and not substitutes for the higher powers.

I would like to offer two other points to your consideration:

First, that the man or woman who is expressing and interested in these lower powers (which are called the lower siddhis by the oriental philosophy) is demonstrating true powers. They are not however the highest possible powers nor are they the powers which humanity is intended to express unless at the lowest point in evolution and, therefore, allied closely to the animal kingdom; or at the highest point, in which case the greater powers automatically include the lesser. The lower psychic powers are shared with the animal kingdom and with all those human races which are low down in the scale of the human evolution.

This is a fact and a statement which arouses much antagonism among the present day exponents of these powers, both in and out of the spiritualistic and occult movements. Such people are apt to consider these powers as indicative either of an advanced spiritual condition or as a rare and unique possession, setting their owner apart as more gifted, more wise and more able to advise and direct other human beings than is the ordinary man. This attitude is demonstrated by the immense audiences such people can address and gather around themselves, and the willingness of the public to listen to them and to pay money for the privilege and the benefit of the demonstration and the advice.

Secondly, the difficulty of this situation is increased because, as evolution proceeds, certain more or less advanced people *recover* these ancient animal propensities and capacities as their power to become inclusive goes forward; they begin to expand their consciousness so that the past as well as the future is brought within their range of awareness. Knowing that they are aspiring to the higher things and towards the world of mystical realisation (in contradistinction to that of psychical realisation), they interpret some episode, which they may have clairvoyantly apprehended, as appertaining to them as individuals; they regard some clairaudient injunction or happening as appropriately theirs, and some vision of a thought form of the Christ or of one of the Masters as indicative of a direct and personal interview with these advanced leaders. They thus enter into the world of glamour and of delusion from which they must, finally with great difficulty, extricate themselves.

May I also call your attention to the fact that the lines of demarcation between these animal, human and divine states of consciousness are not clear cut as in our tabulation? A recognition of this will call attention to the complexity of the subject and the difficulty of our theme. This complexity can, I think, be well illustrated by a study of the uses of the word *telepathy*. As generally used today it indicates two powers:

1. An instinctual registering of some situation, some call and some impression which impinges upon the solar plexus centre. This power of impression is *Not* controlled; there is no supervised intentional mental perception of a directed message; there is only a tuning in on a state of mind or on a condition and situation connected with the one who is regarded as sending the message. In nine cases out of ten, this message is one of distress and goes forward and produces its effect without any capacity on the part of the recipient to induce the reception of the

message. An illustration of this would be the recognition by a mother that a loved child is in danger.

2. A form of clairvoyance which enables the man to see that which is hidden, such as the number of symbols on a playing card which is laying face downwards upon the table.

True telepathy, however, is a *direct* mental communication from mind to mind and in its more advanced expression is a communication of soul to soul, using the mind later as a formulator of the communication, as in the case of inspiration. It is interesting to note (and instructive also in view of our subject) that in true telepathic registration, the lesser powers may be raised and used at a high level of awareness. It is well known esoterically that

a. Some people simply record telepathically in their minds the information coming from another mind. The registration as well as the communication is wordless and formless. The recipient simply *knows* and the imparted knowledge takes form in the consciousness without any intermediate stages or steps. This is formless telepathy.

b. Other people instantaneously step down into form the knowledge which has been imparted; they will *see* the message, word or information appear before their eyes in written or printed form as if it were imposed upon a moving screen, seen within the head.

c. Others will step the information down into form whereby they *hear* it.

In these two latter cases, the true man is making use of his latent lower powers, raising them to as high a level as possible and subordinating them to mental or soul uses. The difference between this usage of the power of clairvoyant and clairaudient demonstration is that in this case there is full mental control and understanding, and in the other cases the lower powers are automatically employed, are uncontrolled, are occupied with matters of no true importance and are not understood in any way by the one who is employing them.

The one basic sense, as you well know, is that of *touch*. This is the reason why I have not placed psychometry in any particular category in my tabulation of the instincts, senses and powers. Psychometry is essentially the capacity to work with and to get in touch with the soul of the higher grouping to which the unit in the lower grouping aspires, and with the soul that can thus aspire in any form. It concerns, in reality, the "measure" of inclusiveness. This measure will govern, for instance, the relation of the dog or other domesticated animal to a human being, of a man to other men, and of an aspirant to his soul, his master and his group. When this psychometrical inclusiveness is turned towards the world of tangible things—minerals, possessions and other material objects, for instance—we tend to make a magical performance out of it, and to charge money for the demonstration of psychometrical power. We then call this the science of psychometry. Yet it is the same power, turned towards the lower kingdoms as is employed in making contact with the higher. There are three groups of people who use the lower psychic powers, either consciously or unconsciously:

1. Those whose evolutionary stage is low enough to permit of their automatic use.

2. Those who have brought over the capacity to see and hear on astral levels or to "work magic" from another life—from Atlantean times. These powers are natural to them, but are usually neither understood nor controlled by

knowledge and they usually make their owner a victim or an exploiter of these powers.

3. The mystic upon the path of vision who (through the bringing in of energy from the soul through meditation and aspiration) stimulates the solar plexus or throat centres and thus opens a door on to the astral plane.

In all cases, it is the astral plane which stands revealed. The statement can here be made that where there is colour, form and phenomena analogous to or a replica of that to be found upon the physical plane then there is to be seen the "duplicating phenomena" of the astral plane. Where there is materialisation of forms upon the physical plane you see the joint activity of the astral and etheric planes. You do not have the phenomena of the mental or soul levels. Bear this definitely in mind. The astral plane is—in time and space and to all intents and purposes—a state of real being plus a world of illusory forms, created by man himself and by his imaginative creativity. One of the major lessons to be learnt upon the Path of Discipleship is to learn to distinguish that which is real from that which is illusion.

What then, is to be seen and heard by the medium when in trance or when giving an exhibition of clairvoyance and clairaudience? Several possibilities, which I might list as follows:

1. A revelation of the "wish life" of the person or the group to whom the medium is addressing himself. This wish life takes form in proportion to the power of the unexpressed wish or the mental ability of the person or persons concerned.

2. A recognition by the medium of the thought forms or thought form to be found in the aura of the person in the audience or circle. These thought forms have been

built over a space of time and are usually of some one deeply loved or as deeply disliked. They are often so real in appearance that the person can recognise them when described by the medium and the medium can at the same time by a process of telepathy (via the solar plexus centre) become aware of the things which the sitter wishes to hear, which will be in line with the usual mannerisms and methods of speech and thought of the departed or living friend. This accounts for the mediocre calibre of the usual utterance and statement made at a seance. The average person who frequents a seance is not usually of the highest grade of intelligence, unless he is simply there as an investigator.

3. A few rare cases when a soul on the path of return to incarnation or immediately after death is impelled (for good and sufficient purpose) to make a contact with a friend or relative via a medium. Such cases are known and usually presuppose more than average intelligence on the part of the sitter, the communicator and the medium. They constitute however, the exceptional occurrence.

4. The revelation to the clairvoyant and clairaudient worker of much of the phenomena of the astral plane, which parallels that of the physical plane and which is conditioned by the quality and calibre of the circle of people who constitute the audience. This, the medium interprets to them and it usually evokes recognition.

I am here casting no doubt on the sincerity of the performance nor on those mediums who are born with these clairvoyant and clairaudient faculties. I am only pointing out that the phenomena which they are contacting is astral in nature and that anyone looking at a circle from the standpoint of the higher psychic powers would note around each sitter a group of astral forms (self-created) of those who have departed physical life through death, of those who are constantly in his thoughts though still alive, and also a kaleidescopic and changing process of appearing and disappearing forms (some quite nebulous and some quite substantial according to the power of thought) which concern the wish life of the sitter, which are concerned with his home affairs, his business or are built up around his health. The sensitive tunes in on these, connects them with the attendant thought forms and hence the production of the usual performance found in the seance room or with the average audience. The medium is truly and accurately relating just what he sees and hears and therefore is sincere and truthful, but because he receives no real training in the art of interpretation and in the technique of distinguishing the illusory from the real, he is, perforce, unable to do more than describe the phenomena seen and the words heard.

When, however, the mystic opens up these same powers as is sometimes the case, the phenomena seen and the words which are heard can be of a very high order. Nevertheless they are still astral, for they concern happenings and phenomena found upon the higher levels of the astral plane. He comes into contact with the spiritual or religious wish life of the race and according to the basic trend of his individual aspiration at the moment so will be his contacts. If he is an earnest and devoted Christian, he will see one of the beautiful and vital thought forms of the Christ there to be found and in the wonder of that revelation, his love and his imagination and all that is best in him will be evoked in adoration and mystery. Hence some of the inspired writings and illumined visions of the mystic. If he is a Hindu, there may come to him a vision of the Lord of Love, Shri Krishna, or, if a Buddhist, he may see the Lord of Light, the Buddha, in all His radiance. If he is an occult student, or a Theosophist or Rosicrucian, he may see a vision of one of the Masters or of the entire Hierarchy of adepts; he may hear words spoken and thus feel assured, past all controversy, that the Great Ones have chosen him for special privilege and for unique service. And yet, his consciousness has never moved from off the astral plane and his contacts have only been a wonderful and inspiring expression of the phenomena of that plane, released to his inner sight and hearing through his aspiration.

All this is brought about through the over-activity of the solar plexus centre, stimulated by the energy pouring in from the heights he has attained in aspirational meditation. The results are very emotional in their nature, and the reactions developed and the subsequent service rendered are on emotional levels. A great deal of this is to be seen among the teachers in the world at this time in many lands. Such teachers have been and are true aspirants. They have awakened in consciousness upon the higher levels of the astral plane. They have there seen the thought forms which humanity has created of the spiritual Hierarchy or the reflections on those levels of that Hierarchy (a still more potent group of thought forms) and have heard repetitions of that which has been said and thought by the world aspirants of all time—all of it most beautiful, good and true. They then proceed to teach and proclaim what they have thus heard, seen and learnt and frequently do much good—on astral levels. They are, all the same, confusing the reflection with the reality, the reproduction with the original, and the humanly constructed with the divinely created.

Forget not, that the astral plane is that whereon man has

to learn to distinguish truth from error, and the real from the unreal. Thus those who are deceived are only learning a needed lesson. The fact of the astral plane is being steadily recognised and that is good. The fact of the existence of the spiritual Hierarchy and of Masters is being brought to the attention of the masses even if it is being done by those who are confusing the reflection and the thought form with the reality.

The question could here properly be asked: How can the mystic avoid this error and confusion? How can he distinguish the real from the illusory? This constitutes an individual problem for every mystic and there is no one profound and scientific rule whereby he can guide his reactions. The only rules which I can give you are so simple that those who are occupied at this time with teaching and proclaiming that which they have astrally contacted may not like to follow them. The attitude of mind which will guard the mystic from astral delusion and error is:

1. The cultivation of a spirit of true humility. There is a spiritual arrogance which masks itself behind a cloak of humbleness and which is very prevalent at this time. It leads people to regard themselves as the chosen of the Hierarchy to save the world; it leads them to look upon themselves as the mouthpieces of the Masters or of the Christ; it tends to make them separative in their attitudes to other leaders and teachers, refusing to recognise the many aspects of the one work and the many methods which the Mind of God has devised for reaching the masses.

2. The refusal to accept any contact or message which has personality implications or which sets its recipient apart, thus tending to the development of a Messiah complex.

I like that phrase. It is simple and concise and illustrates dramatically the state of mind and describes the assured nature of the consciousness of many of the present teachers of humanity. A true contact with the Hierarchy and the true accolade of service carries with it the conviction of the existence of the many servers in the one Service, of the many messengers carrying the one message, of the many teachers of the many aspects of the one Truth, and of the many and various ways back to the Heart of God. When this all-embracing revelation accompanies the call to service, then the spirit of inclusiveness is developed and the man can be sure that he is truly called to cooperate and convinced of the reality of his vision.

3. The freedom from emotional appeal. The true disciple and mystic is ever mentally polarised. His vision is free from the deluding reactions of the solar plexus centre. His vision awakens the heart centre and evokes the response of his personality energy (focussed in the ajna centre) and produces eventually a "centering in the place of light". This indicates the growing activity of the head centre. He may, later, use controlled emotional appeal in dealing with the masses but he himself seeks to remain free from all emotional control.

We are considering the unfoldment of the psychic powers, producing conditions in the subject which are regarded by the orthodox investigator as pathological in nature or as indicating psychological trouble of a serious kind. However, we are today close to the time when the fact of there being modes of perception other than those of the physical senses will be recognised, and the attitude of medicine and of the psychiatric and neurological sciences will undergo definite changes—much to the assistance and aid of humanity. The development of the psychic powers is basically due at this time (for the whole problem shifts into changing fields as evolution proceeds) to the psychic becoming aware of a field or fields of phenomena which are always present but which remain usually unrecognised because the inner mechanism of perception remains latent or quiescent. In the undeveloped human being or in groups of men who are low down in the racial scale, as also in animals, there is much psychic perception because the sacral centre motivates the physical plane life and the solar plexus centre governs the psychic nature. In these cases, all the higher centres are quiescent and undeveloped. The solar plexus is to the worlds of lower psychic perception what the brain is intended to be in the worlds of higher psychic understanding. In the one case, you have a centre of energy which is so potent that it swings the man into a state of consciousness which is fundamentally astral, thus governing the sex life from the angle of the sentient consciousness; in the other case, you have so close an identification between the head centre in etheric matter and the brain in physical substance that an organ which is definitely physical functions sympathetically, accurately and synchronously with its subjective counterpart, registering impressions from the head centre and the worlds with which that centre puts a man in touch. The two are then as one.

In between these stages of low grade psychic life and the spiritual perception of the initiate there is to be found every possible type of sentient consciousness. These can be divided into three major categories:

1. The unfoldment and use of the psychic powers, both higher and lower.

   This is the stage of *Psychism.*

2. The evolution of the mystical vision.

This is the stage of *Mysticism.*

3. The revelation of light and power.

This is the stage of *Occultism.*

All these expressions of divine knowledge are connected with, and dependent upon, the development of the centres. In the low grade human being, the centres are nothing more than slowly revolving, palpitating disks of dim light. In Lemurian days, the sacral centre was the most active and the brightest. In Atlantean days, the solar plexus centre was by far the most significant. Today, as you know, the higher correspondences are coming into functioning activity and humanity is beginning to reap the benefits derived from experience in three races—the Lemurian, the Atlantean and the Aryan.

The throat centre is now the most active in the majority of cases and the most significant. The time is, however, coming when humanity will function on a large scale and as a mass through the ajna centre; this will take place in the next race for, in the next great cycle of racial development, there will be no people with a Lemurian consciousness to be found anywhere and the "pull" or the activity of the sacral centre will be greatly lessened and controlled. This can be seen happening today among the intelligentsia of the race. The Atlantean state of awareness (which functions primarily through the solar plexus) will be also greatly lessened as the heart centre awakens. Humanity will then be wrestling with difficulties and pathological and psychological troubles which will be based on group conditions and influences and not so much on a man's individual unfoldment. The beginnings of this can already be seen in its lowest phase in the emergence today of what is called "mass psychology"—a thing practically unknown (except in urban centres) a few hundred years ago.

Now it is well nigh planetary in its radius of influence. Public opinion, with its determining and conditioning influence, is another phase of the same emerging factor.

The Aryan state of consciousness, with its coordinating capacity and its mental emphasis, will control the mass of the people, for in the coming race the Atlantean emotional state of consciousness will be to humanity what the Lemurian or low grade type is to the Aryan at this time. The masses will then all come under the category of the intelligentsia, whilst the intelligentsia of today will be the intuitives of tomorrow. In the language of mysticism, the masses will be on the probationary path and the cream of the race will be on the path of discipleship. The number also of the initiates and adepts, present in incarnation in order to carry forward the externalised work of the Hierarchy, will be great. The world will then be full of people who will be completely integrated personalities with all the virtues (and consequently all the vices), the ambitions and problems, incident to that stage of awareness.

It is for this reason that the Hierarchy is working at this time to bring about the fecundation of the race by the cosmic principle of love, so that love and intellect can proceed hand in hand and thus balance each other. It is for this reason that the fact of the existence of the spiritual Hierarchy must be brought to the attention of the masses. This must be done in order to enhance the magnetic power of the love aspect of the hierarchical effort and not in order to awaken fear or awe, for that is of the old order and must disappear.

I might here touch upon the paralleling activity of the forces which are working to prevent the externalisation of the Hierarchy of Light since such a happening as that would mean increased—because proven—power. As you know, on the astral and mental planes centres exist which are called "dark centres" because the emphasis of their activity is upon the material aspect of manifestation and upon the activity of material substance; all energy is subordinated to purely selfish purpose. As I have before stated, the Forces of Light work with the soul, hidden in every form. They are concerned with group purposes and with the founding of the kingdom of God on earth. The dark forces work with the form side of expression and with the founding of a centre of control which will be theirs entirely and which will subdue all the living forms in all kingdoms to their peculiar behests. It is the old story, familiar in Biblical phraseology, of the kingdoms of the world and the kingdom of the Christ, of the power of anti-Christ and the power of Christ. This produced a great climax in Atlantean days and, though the Hierarchy of Light triumphed, it was only by the merest margin. The battle was fought out on the astral plane, though it had its correspondence upon the physical plane, in a great world conflict of which the ancient legend tells us. It ended in the catastrophe of the Flood. The seeds of hate and of separation have been fostered ever since that time and the three modes whereby the forces of darkness seek to control humanity are hatred, aggression and separativeness. The three great spiritual counterparts are love, selfless sharing and synthesis.

However, the hold of the forces which are working against the living principle of love (as embodied in the Hierarchy) is not gaining ground at this time, for the response of humanity to that which is good and synthetic is much more rapid and general than it was a few hundred years ago. There is much reason to hope that there will be a steady waning of the undesired control. The dark forces are ruled on the physical plane by a group of six oriental leaders and six occidental leaders; of these the oriental are the most powerful because they are the oldest racially and therefore the most experienced. They work by the intensification of glamour and by the stimulation of the lower psychic powers. Their particular point of attack at this time is the group of world disciples and initiates, for these latter are responsible for the fostering of love in the world and for the binding of men together in the spirit of unity. If they cannot succeed with this task now, it should be possible to externalise the Hierarchy and thereby greatly lessen the control of the so-called evil forces.

If these evil forces cannot induce the disciples everywhere, in group formation or individually, to succumb in some form to glamour, then they will endeavour to utilise group glamour to negative their efforts and force those with whom the disciples work to believe evil, to impugn motives, and to produce such a convincing story that the struggling disciple will be left to fight almost singlehanded. If this cannot be done, they may then attack the physical bodies of the workers and agents for the Hierarchy, and seek, through the distress of the physical body, to control the disciple's output. This does not always prove successful, as the Master can, and often does, protect His disciple. The dark forces work also through the intensification or stimulation of the psychic mechanism, so that the lower psychic powers become abnormally developed and prematurely assume proportions which are almost uncontrollable. This happened on a large scale in Atlantean days and led to the entire astral plane standing revealed, but not understood. Its undesirable potencies were then let loose upon the physical plane and this led to the war between the two great schools of the mysteries—the Light and the Dark—which culminated in the destruction of the then known world.

Today these potencies, light and dark, are again struggling for physical plane expression and supremacy but this time the result is vastly different. The effort to produce soul contact or to hinder it is working out in the form of nervous diseases and pathological conditions and this is affecting potently the group activity of man. The effort by the dark forces to stimulate the lower psychic powers seems able to reach no deeper into matter and form than the etheric vehicles and from there to condition the physical body physiologically in the form of diseases, lesions, nervous troubles and brain afflictions and the many other ways in which the human being is rendered helpless and unfitted to cope with daily living and modern world conditions. But the mind nature has reached a stage of protective usefulness and some of the great guarding barriers which are flung up around humanity at this time are the spirit of scepticism, and the refusal to recognise the existence or the usefulness of the psychic powers. This is a point to be remembered.

I have several times used the expression "the premature awakening" of the psychic powers. By that I mean the abnormal unfoldment of the powers of clairvoyance and of clairaudience so that the entire lower levels of the astral plane stand revealed, though the possessor of these powers can neither control the phenomena of subtle sight and hearing, nor interpret correctly what he sees and hears. In the earlier animal or savage stage, these faculties are frequently normal and there is no *mental* reaction of any kind and, therefore, no undue strain is put upon the nervous system and the brain. There is what I might call a flat or unemotional acquiescence in the condition which is due to the complete lack of the interpretative sense and of the dramatic self-conscious attitude of the man who is beginning to use his mind. The moment the "I-consciousness" becomes uppermost, then the possession of these lower psychic powers becomes a hindrance and a complication. Temporarily, they must be thrust into the background in order that the mind principle may assert its control and the life of the soul can then flow out into matured and considered expression upon the physical plane. This relegation of the psychic powers to a position below the threshold of consciousness is the intent of the development planned for the Aryan race.

I would like here to point out that I use the word "Aryan" in contradistinction to the majority of the races found in Asia. Speaking generally, we can today classify the races into three groups:

1. The many remnants of the Atlantean or fourth root-race people, plus a very small sprinkling of the Lemurian peoples—so small as to be negligible.
2. The Aryan race itself, which includes the civilisation of India and all Latins, Teutons, Nordics, and Anglo-Saxons, and their various off-shoots.
3. A group which bridges between the Oriental races and the Aryan race which we call the Semitic. This race is neither purely Oriental nor is it Aryan.

The Jews are a group of people in whom the principle of separation is pronouncedly present. For ages they have, with determination and in obedience to the injunctions in the Old Testament, insisted on regarding themselves as a people set apart. For ages they have held themselves separated off from all other peoples in the world. The result is that they are now evoking from the races among whom they are scattered a corresponding desire to force that very separation upon them. Under the law, we draw forth from others what is actually present within ourselves, and to this law, races and nations are no exception. Through the inter-relation of Jew and Gentile, of Semitic and Aryan, and through the solving of the Jewish problem will the great heresy of separateness eventually be fought out.

It is not intended that the Aryan race should be a psychic race. Their goal is bringing the mind nature into prominence. This could not take place if the "drift" of the forces, flowing into the human mechanism was in the direction of the solar plexus—the major centre, governing all lower psychic unfoldment. Just as certain transferences are going on today between the centres below the diaphragm into those above the diaphragm, so the solar plexus (which is like the controlling brain in the animal and the physical-emotional man) must cease finally to control the activities of the human being and the brain must become the seat of the directing agency in its place. Speaking again generally, there are three major controlling factors in the career of a human being:—

1. The solar plexus, corresponding to that stage wherein the play of the forces is physical-etheric-astral.

   This is the stage of *psychic* development.

2. The ajna centre between the eyebrows, corresponding to the period of integration and of personality control, wherein certain areas of the brain become sensitised and used.

   This is the stage of *mental* development.

3. The head centre, involving the entire brain area around the pineal gland, wherein the spiritual man assumes control.

   This is the stage of *soul* control.

It is in this latter stage that the higher psychic faculties come into play and the lower powers can then again be used, if deemed desirable. The initiate has full control of all faculties and powers, and knows both when and how to use them the most profitably and with the least expenditure of energy. It should be noted, however, that the average modern psychic or medium does not come under this category, for the initiates and Masters use all Their powers quietly and behind the scenes and not for demonstration before the public. The majority of psychics today are solar plexus workers, though a few—a very few—are beginning to shift their forces into the ajna centre and to develop mental faculties. This has an integrating effect and temporarily is marked by a complete and necessary cessation of the lower powers. In this sense "the mind is the slayer of the real", but only of the relatively real. That which has seemed real and of importance or which proved interesting and exciting to the average psychic is eventually forced below the threshold of consciousness by the unfoldment of the mind. It is this needed transition period in the case of many of the modern psychics which lies at the root of a number of their undoubted difficulties. They are faced with issues they cannot resolve and which they do not understand as they have no background of occult practice or understanding. They have been brought to the point of discarding the old ways and yet the new techniques of living and of practice mean nothing to them. A future which must be faced without the phenomena which has made the past so exciting, interesting and frequently remunerative does not attract them. Yet, in reality, they are faced with the transition out of the Atlantean state of consciousness into the higher and Aryan state of awareness. They are offered a step forward and need to remember that every step forward in evolution and, therefore, towards the spiritual goal, is always at a cost and through the relinquishing of that which has hitherto been held dear.

The psychical difficulties, which eventually are many, fall into three general categories:

1. Those arising from the premature awakening of the centres. In these cases, the psychic has no control whatsoever over his powers. He simply knows that he sees and hears that which cannot be seen and heard by the average man. His problem is to live consciously and simultaneously upon the physical and astral planes. He cannot stop himself seeing and hearing and his life becomes most complex and complicated. Where there is this premature awakening in the case of the intellectual man, it frequently produces great difficulty, nervous tension, brain disturbance and always misunderstanding from those around. There is many times a definite drift into insanity. In the case of the average unintelligent person, there is usually a shift of the life-emphasis on to the astral plane and away from the physical plane where it is intended that men should express all that is in them. The psychic then lives altogether in the world of glamour and of lower psychic phenomena. What he sees and relates is truly and sincerely what he has noted but there is no interpretative ability. It is seldom of a high order because the psychic is not of a high order of mentality or influence himself,

2. Those arising out of a loose connection existing between the physical body and the etheric body. This produces the various stages of mediumship, of control by entities of some kind or another, of trance conditions and of many kinds of obsession, temporary or permanent.

I do not include in this list the work of the materialising mediums, for their work is of a totally different kind and though not so dangerous to the personality of the medium is perhaps still more undesirable. So completely is the medium divorced (as an astral-mental-soul individual) from his physical body that it becomes dom-

inant in its own field (the material) and can absorb—
through the many etheric orifices—the stuff of which
certain of the lower forms are constituted; it can attract
the primitive substance of a low grade which can be
built into shape (and often is) by the thought, either
of a sitter or of a group of sitters in a so-called "materialising seance". With these the medium is en rapport sub-
consciously. This is not a telepathic rapport but a solar
plexus, a psychic rapport. The subject is too abstruse
for elaboration here and this form of mediumship must
inevitably be discarded as the evolution of the race
proceeds.

3. Those which are indicative of an exceeding sensitivity to
impressions, to conditions and to atmospheres, surrounding the psychic. This sensitivity is of a somewhat inchoate nature and is difficult to define, but it is analogous to the general sense of *Touch*. There is no part
of the human frame which, if it is touched in a certain
manner, will not react. So the sensitive will register
psychic awareness of a more general nature than that of
the defined powers. We have consequently:

Physical	*Psychic*	*Higher Correspondence*
a. Hearing	Clairaudience	This leads eventually to mental telepathy and finally to spiritual knowledge.
b. Sight	Clairvoyance	This leads eventually to spiritual vision and finally to spiritual identification.
c. Touch	Sensitivity	This leads eventually to spiritual aspiration and finally to spiritual impressibility.

It might here be pointed out that *mystical development and
aspiration* are the way of escape from the highest aspect of
the Atlantean consciousness. This is itself astral in nature,

Occultism and science are the way of escape from the highest expression of the concrete mind, and from the Aryan consciousness, which is mental in nature. Sensitivity or the psychic sense of touch is etheric in nature, is general in expression and must eventually give place to that spiritual impressibility which enables a man, like the Christ, simply to "know" what is in his fellow man and to be aware of his condition and of the condition of life in all forms. It is the first step towards that universal spiritual key of which *psychometry* is the lowest expression.

In the above paragraph and differentiations I have given you much food for thought and indicated a sequence of unfoldment which is individual, racial and universal.

If we extend these ideas into their planetary connotations (which is interesting but probably quite useless to you) I would add that:

1. Touch .....is the keynote of the evolution proceeding at this time *on Venus*. It is sensitivity to spiritual impression.
2. Hearing ....is the keynote of the evolution proceeding at this time *on Mars*. It is spiritual telepathy and knowledge.
3. Sight ......is the keynote of the evolution proceeding at this time *on the Earth*. It is spiritual vision leading to identification.

Let us now consider how the abuse of the lower psychic powers may be arrested temporarily until such time as the initiate may seek to use them, in full consciousness and with full control.

The prime difficulty of the natural psychic and of the man who is born as a medium is his inability intelligently to control the phenomena evidenced. Lack of control of the physical powers is deemed highly undesirable. Lack of psychic control should also be relegated to the same category. The medium is either in trance or his psychic powers are brought into expression through the stimulation which comes from his contact with the group of sitters in the seance room or from a large audience. In other cases, he is all the time living on the borderland of consciousness between the physical and the psychic or astral planes. How can this be changed, provided the medium wishes for such a change, which is rare indeed. In three ways only:

1. By ceasing to be interested in the display of these powers, by refusing to use them any more and by this means causing them gradually to die out. This leads to the closing of the solar plexus centre (and consequently of the open door to the lower levels of the astral plane) and the atrophying of that part of the inner mechanism which has made these powers available.

2. By the transference of the attention to the mystical life and to the expression of an intense aspiration towards the spiritual realities. This provides the new interest which eventually becomes dynamically expulsive of the old interests and thus tends to shift the life-emphasis away from the lower levels of the astral plane to the higher levels. This also presupposes a tendency to spiritual orientation on the part of the psychic.

3. By a course of intellectual training and of mental development which would, if persisted in for a sufficient length of time, automatically make the use of the lower powers impossible because the shift of the flow of energy will be into the centres above the diaphragm. It is well known in psychic circles that mental training does bring to a close the psychic cycle.

There are three ancient rules which—in the last period of the Atlantean cycle—were given by the Adepts of the time to Their disciples. You must bear in mind that the problem before the Hierarchy at that time was to bring to an end temporarily the then *normal* psychic emphasis and start the flow of the forces to the upper part of the body. These three rules can be connected in your minds with the three methods touched upon above.

I. Shun the pits of hell, Oh, Chela. Let your feet go hurrying from the lower way and seek the upper reaches of the plane of glamour. Ascend. Choose for your good companions those who live a life of arduous labour upon the plains of earth. Depart. Descend and live the normal life of Earth. Depart.

II. Lift up thine eyes, Oh, Chela, and cleanse thine heart and see the vision of thy soul. Look up, not down; within, not out. Live free and hasten towards the higher goal. Depart and seek the distant secret place where dwells thy soul.

III. Energy follows thought, the ancient rule proclaims. Think, Chela, think and leave behind the realms where thought rules not and where no light revealing can be seen but only self-engendered light and thus deluding. So, therefore, think.

These rules sound simple and familiar but are of profound difficulty to follow, particularly in the case of the average psychic, and this for two reasons; first, he does not truly desire the loss of the power which the use of the powers confers, and secondly, his mental perception is as a rule so undeveloped that the effort to transfer his consciousness into the higher levels of expression proves too arduous a task. But, where the will is active and the peril entailed by continuing to work on the lowest astral levels is adequately perceived, then in due time the needed effort will be made.

The above rules apply to the psychic who is willing enough and intelligent enough to change his orientation and type of work. But what of the man who has drifted into the dangerous ways of the lower psychism when he is an Aryan in consciousness and not an Atlantean? What can he do if the solar plexus centre is over-active and the door to the astral plane stands wide open? He seeks to shut it and to function normally; he distrusts and fears his psychic powers of sight and hearing. There is no one specific or one rule of conduct for much is dependent upon the originating cause, but I will here suggest various rules and remedial lines of behaviour.

1. If the door to the astral plane has been opened by following certain breathing exercises, plus certain postures, and other methods taught by ignorant teachers at this time, I would suggest certain preliminary and necessary steps, as follows:

   a. Let the man drop all such exercises and postures and avoid all contact with the teacher. This is a first and necessary step.

   b. Let him live a full life of physical activity, permitting himself no time for the introspective life. If he is materially minded, let him fulfill his commercial, business or social obligations, by physical plane interests and his due responsibilities with every power he has, permitting himself no backward thought.

   c. Let him focus his attention upon the things of physical living until such time as evolution carries him to the stage of mental focussing and spiritual orientation. Before this can be done, the lower door must be closed. Let him, therefore, control emotion, for emotion serves to keep the door ajar and facilitates astral experience.

d. Let him "learn to work and think with the spine and head and not with the forefront of the body", as the ancient rule can be translated. The idea is that the average psychic regards the solar plexus and throat centres (the only two about which they seem to know anything) as existing in the front and centre of the torso or the front of the throat. This carries the energy downwards by the involutionary route and not upwards by the evolutionary route of the spinal column. This is of moment.

2. If the door to the astral plane is open because of natural birthright, the activity of previous lives and because the flow of the forces normally focusses in the solar plexus, the problem is much more difficult. It will be necessary to gain:

a. Some understanding of the etheric constitution of man and teaching must be given as to the nature of the centres of force so that the Aryan psychic has some intelligent background upon which to work. The effort must be made to build a healthy body.

b. Higher goals must be emphasised and the necessity for the life of service must be stressed. I would remind you that service is a scientific method whereby the forces which awaken, stimulate and control the solar plexus are directed to the heart centre, thus causing the closing of the astral door and a decentralisation of the interests of the psychic. This decentralisation is technically fulfilled when the central plexus is no longer the dominant factor and the thought interests of the man are of a different nature.

c. One other practical hint may be useful here. When the psychic is at the Aryan stage of unfoldment and is not simply at the Atlantean, then much good can come from the frequent use of the colour *yellow*. He should surround himself with that colour, for it serves to keep the inflowing energies in the head or to prevent their descent no lower than the diaphragm. This deprives the solar plexus of a constant inflow of energy and greatly aids in freeing of the psychic from the astral plane. I would point out here that the psychic with the Atlantean consciousness (and they constitute the great majority) is functioning normally when displaying the psychic faculties, though along an arc of retrogression, but the man with the Aryan consciousness who displays these powers is an abnormality.

3. Where the danger is of a serious nature, producing great nervous tension or excessive debility, extreme care must be used. Where there is a violent fight against the psychic activity going on, or where there is a nervous breakdown and loss of mental grip and control, then it is essential that at times the psychic should be forced to take a long rest in bed, with light diet and complete freedom from all contacts. It may be necessary at times to put him under restraint. Today, many such cases—fighting hard for mental equilibrium and seeking to close the astral door—are deemed insane or on the border line of insanity. Their plight is greatly enhanced by the lack of understanding of their friends, and of the consulting physicians and psychologists. Their trouble is not mental but is entirely related to the solar plexus. Only when this is recognised will we begin to have a right handling of these problem cases. It is rare indeed to find a psychologist who would be willing to admit the possibility of these premises.

When psychic difficulties arise in the case of the advanced mystic, the disciple or the occult student, the mode of approach has to be more definitely scientific, for the trouble is more deep-seated owing to the fact that the mind is more involved. Definite work with the centres up the spine and in the head is in order but must be carried forward under careful supervision. I cannot here give the exercises which lead to—

1. The closing of the different centres,
2. The opening of the higher centres,
3. The transference of force from one centre to another.

This treatise is intended primarily for the general public and will be widely read during the next generation. Should I give them here, my readers might experiment with them and only succeed in doing real harm to themselves.

The Science of the Breath, which is the science of laya-yoga or the science of the centres, is one of profound importance and one of real danger as well. It is, in the last analysis, the Science of Energy and teaches the method whereby energy can be controlled, directed and utilised for the expanding of the consciousness, for the establishing of right relations between the man and his environment and, above all (in the case of those affiliated with the Great White Lodge), for the production of white magic. This pranic energy works through the vital body and courses through the many "nadis" found therein. These "nadis" exist in their millions and are minute channels of force which underlie the entire nervous system of man. Of this they are the counterpart and the animating factor, making sensitivity possible and producing that action and reaction which converts the mechanism of man into an intricate "receiver" of energy and "director" of force. Each

of these tiny lines of energy are fivefold in nature and resemble five strands or fibers of force, closely knit together
within a covering sheath of a different force. These forces
are bound together in a cross-sectional relation.

It is to be noted, also, that these five types of energy
form one closely knit unit, and these units form, in their
entirety, the etheric sheath itself. Through these five channels flow the five major pranas—energising, galvanising and
controlling the entire human organism. There is no part of
the physical body which this network of energies does not
underlie or "sub-stand". This is the true form or substance.

Where the lines of force cross and recross, as they repeat
in the microcosm the involutionary and evolutionary arcs
of the macrocosm, there are formed five areas up the spinal
column and two in the head where the energies are more
potent than elsewhere, because more concentrated. Thus you
have the appearance of the major centres. Throughout the
entire body, these crossings and recrossings occur and so the
equipment of energy centres is brought into being:

1. Where the lines of force cross 21 times, a major centre is
   found. Of these there are seven.
2. Where they cross 14 times, you have the appearance of
   the minor centres, to which I earlier referred.
3. Where they cross 7 times, you have tiny centres and of
   these minute centres there are many hundreds.

Some day the entire etheric body will be charted and the
general direction of the lines of force will then be seen. The
great sweep of the energies will be apparent, the point in
evolution more easily established and the psychic situation
infallibly indicated. The intricacy of the subject is, however,
very great, owing to just this difference in the evolutionary
development of the vehicles, the stage of the expanding con-

sciousness and the receptivity to stimulation of the human being. The Science of Meditation will eventually absorb the science of laya-yoga but only in the highest form of the latter. The goal of meditation is to bring about the free play of all the incoming forces so that there is no impediment offered at any point to the incoming energy of the soul; so that no obstruction and congestion is permitted and no lack of power—physical, psychic, mental and spiritual—is to be found in any part of the body. This will mean not only good health and the full and free use of all the faculties (higher and lower) but direct contact with the soul. It will produce that constant renewing of the body which is characteristic of the life expression of the initiate and the Master, as well as of the disciple, only in a lesser degree. It will produce rhythmic expression of the divine life in form. To the clairvoyant view of the adept as He looks at the aspirant or disciple, it causes:

1. *The rhythm of manifestation.* This is the cause of the appearance and the disappearance of the form. The adept, by looking at the body, can tell just how long it has been in incarnation and how long it will still continue to "appear". The state of the pranic channels reveals this accurately, particularly those found below the diaphragm. The centre at the base of the spine, where is found the seat of the will-to-live (governing the seed of the life principle in the heart) reveals this.

2. *The rhythm of the psychic life.* This is, in reality, the revelation of where the man stands in relation to consciousness and its contacts. The adept, when seeking information upon this point, looks first of all at the solar plexus centre and then at the heart and head, for in these three centres and in their relative "light and radiant brightness", the whole story of the individual stands re-

vealed. The head centre, looked at for the average or below average man, is the centre between the eyebrows. In the case of the aspirant, mystic and disciple, it is the highest head centre.

As evolution proceeds and the life forces flow ever more freely along the "nadis" and through the centres—major, minor, and minute—the rapidity of the distribution and of the flow, and the consequent radiance of the body steadily increases. The separating walls within the enclosing sheath of the tiny channels of force eventually dissolve (under the impact of soul force) and so disappear and thus the "nadis" of the advanced disciple take a new form indicating that he is now essentially and consequently dual and is therefore an integrated personality. He is soul *and* personality. Soul force can now flow unimpeded through the central channel of the "nadi" and all the other forces can flow unimpeded around it. It is whilst this process is going on and the forces within the "nadis" are being blended and thus forming one energy that most of the diseases of the mystics make their appearance, particularly those connected with the heart.

Simultaneously with this appearance of duality in the "nadis", the disciple finds himself able to use the two channels—ida and pingala—which are found up the spinal column, one on each side of the central channel. There can now be the free flow of force up and down these two "pathways of the forces" and thus out into the "nadis", utilising the area around any of the major centres as distributing areas and thus galvanising, at will, any part of the mechanism into activity, or the whole mechanism into coordinated action. The disciple has now reached the point in his development where the etheric web, which separates all the centres up the spine from each other, has been burned away by the fires of life. The "sushumna" or central channel can be slowly utilised. This parallels the period wherein there is the free flow of soul force through the central channel in the "nadis". Eventually this central channel comes into full activity. All this can be seen by the clairvoyant eye of the Master.

I have dealt with this in detail as the practice of breathing exercises definitely *moves* the forces flowing through the "nadis" and re-organises them—usually prematurely. It hastens the process of breaking down the walls separating four forces from the fifth energy, and hastens the burning of the protecting etheric webs up the spinal column. If this is done whilst the emphasis of the life is below the diaphragm and the man is not even an aspirant or intelligent, then it will cause the over-stimulation of the sex life, and also the opening up of the astral plane and hence much physical difficulty and disease. It occultly "releases the lower fires and the man will be destroyed by fire"; he will not be then (as is intended) the "burning bush which burns forever and cannot be destroyed". If this burning takes place by a forced process and is not under right direction, there *must* inevitably be difficulty. When the man is on the Path of Purification or Probation or is in the early stages of discipleship, with the emphasis of his intention *above* the diaphragm, then there is much danger of over-development of the sense of egotism, over-stimulation of the heart centre (with the consequent appearance of various forms of heart disease and of emotionalism, evoked over group conditions) and of troubles related to the thyroid gland and the brain, as well as difficulties connected principally with the pituitary body.

I could give you here certain forms of breathing exercises which might prove helpful to some people in the work of re-organising the vital body and consequently the etheric body, but the dangers involved in the case of the majority of my readers negate any such action. The old rule that aspirants must find their way into an esoteric or mystery school still holds good. All I can do—as I have done—is to give certain directions and teach certain safe and generally well-known rules which will lay the foundation for the more advanced work which must be carried forward under careful personal supervision. For this reason, once this present world crisis is duly ended, there must be laid a foundation of true esoteric schools. Such do *Not* as yet exist. Today, aspirants and disciples are working in the modern esoteric schools (such as the Arcane School and the Esoteric Section of the Theosophical Society—to mention two of the most important) and there they learn some of the foundational truths of esotericism; they begin to gain control of the emotional nature and the mind; they learn to purify the body and to apprehend the basic postulates of the Ageless Wisdom. They are then under the direction subjectively of some senior disciple who knows the needed next truth and has unfolded in himself the "sense of contact" and the power of intuitive perception. A few persons, here and there, are definitely working under the direction of one of the Masters. Only where there is direction, a knowledge of a man's governing rays and a grasp of the astrological indications as to a man's "path of life" can the true, but dangerous, rules be given, which will lead to:

1. A right distribution of energy.
2. The focussing of the forces in the centres.
3. The burning of the separating walls and of the dividing etheric webs.
4. The lifting of the energies ever higher in the body by the power of the directed will.

Many of the difficulties of mystics and occultists today are due to the fact that they are literally "playing with fire" and are not aware of it; that they are not preserving the right or ordered sequence of development, as outlined above; that they are following practices for which they are not ready, which have not been modified to suit the occidental type of body, and which they blindly follow without any understanding of the process or results. Unless the basic rule is grasped that "energy follows thought", it is inevitable that dire results must eventuate. The mystic, for instance whose thought is focussed on the Christ, regarding Him as somewhere in Heaven, but as outside himself, and whose aspiration makes Him the objective of all his desire, is frequently debilitated and physically ill. Why is this the case? Because the energy which is seeking to enter him and permeate his whole organism only reaches as far as the heart centre and is from there constantly turned back and driven out of the physical body by the directing power of the mystic's thought. Christ, for him, is elsewhere. Outside himself lies his thought and the energy consequently streams out of his body. It is a much discussed problem among initiates today as to whether the generally debilitated condition of the human race is not due in part to the fact that the aspiration and thought of mankind, having been constantly directed to some outside goal and not (as should have been the case) to the centre of life and love *within* each human being, has drained man of much needed energy. In spite of the fact that he has been taught for centuries that the kingdom of God is within, the peoples in the occident have not accepted the statement or worked on the premise presented, but have sought for reality *without* and have turned their attention to the Personality of the *One* who taught them a major truth. At no time did He desire or seek their devotion. The price of this distortion of the truth has been paid again and again by a devitalised body and by the inability of the average mystic to live a concrete, and yet divine, life upon earth.

There is little more that I can say here in connection with the problems and the difficulties of the psychic powers as they unfold in humanity and on a higher turn of the spiral than in the past. As evolution proceeds, the human and animal psychic faculties become available to the disciple. Humanity has chosen to proceed by means of the "trial and error" method and it is in many ways a sound choice, but it is slow and leads to points of crisis and moments of almost intolerable difficulty in the history of the race. In the case of the mystic and the disciple who is endeavouring to gain control of these inherent instincts, the problem is today enhanced by the fact that the physical vitality of the race is so lowered and also so little understood and the proper care of the body is consequently so poorly rendered that the unhealthy condition of that body releases the lower powers more easily than would otherwise be the case. They therefore unfold prematurely and before their nature and function is understood or the laws of their control grasped. The acceptance of this statement would be found enlightening and much progress would be made if the various premises I have made were accepted as valid hypotheses and acted upon. The result would open the door to a new understanding of the psychic faculties. Psychology and medicine would be thereby enriched.

We come now to two more problems which are related to the higher psychic powers but are of a more advanced kind and dependent upon the development of the mind nature more than upon the solar plexus consciousness.

Problem of the Development of the Mystical Vision

This process of sensing the goal, of contacting the ideal and of visioning the many symbols that veil the soul, which portray pictorially the ultimate destination and the final purpose, are the recognised prerogative of the mystical aspirant. The mystical literature of all the world religions is, as you know, full of these visions, ranging all the way from the more sexual approach of the Song of Solomon or the writings of many of the feminine mystics of the Church to the amazing revelations given in the ancient Puranas or in the Apocalypse. These cover all the ground from the formulation of the high-grade "wish-life" of the mystics to the true prevision as to the future of the race as found in the writings of the prophetical Scriptures. With the detail I do not intend to deal. It has been considered by the modern psychologist and the religious instructor and Church writers and dealt with by them at great length. I want only to touch upon the effects that these experiences have upon the mystic himself. I would ask you also to remember that I am generalising and not being specific.

The difficulties to which such mystics are prone are four:

1. *Devitalisation.* The mystic is drawn so constantly "upwards" (as he regards and terms it) to the land of his dreams, to the person of his idealism or to the spiritual ideal (personified or non-personified) of his aspiration that he reverses the normal and wholesome process of "the Way of the constant materialising of the Real". He lives entirely in the world of his aspiration and thus neglects life on the physical plane, becoming not only impractical but negative to the physical plane. He draws all his life forces upward so that the physical body and life on the physical plane suffers. Technically, the forces of the solar plexus are not drawn upward into the heart centre, as they should be, nor is the energy of the heart poured out in selfless love of humanity; they are all focussed and distributed in the highest level of the astral consciousness and sent to feed the forces of the astral body. They reverse,

therefore, the normal process and the physical body suffers grievously through this.

A study of the lives of the saints and mystics will reveal much of this difficulty, and even in the relatively rare cases where there has been some definite service to humanity, the motives were frequently (I might say, usually) the meeting of a sensed requirement or obligation which would serve the mystic, bringing him emotional satisfaction and reward. This devitalisation was often so excessive that it led not only to nervous debility, trance conditions and other pathological developments, but sometimes to death itself.

2. *Delusion*. The drama life of the mystic and the constant cultivation of the vision (whatever that might be) led also in many cases to serious if unrecognised psychological trouble. The vision absorbed the mystic's whole attention and instead of indicating to him a goal to which he might some day attain, or existing in his consciousness as the symbol of an inner reality which he would some day know, as it in truth was, he lived always within his own thoughtform of this goal. This powerful dream, this defined thoughtform (built year by year through aspiration, worship and longing) ended by obsessing him to such an extent that he finally ended by mistaking the symbol for the reality. Sometimes he died of the ecstasy induced by his identification with his vision. Nevertheless, I would point out here that the true attainment of the mystical goal, so that it is no longer seen but is realised as fact, has never yet killed anyone. It is delusion which kills. It is only when the focus of the life is in the astral body, when the downflow of soul force is there also and when the heart centre is overenergised that the mystic dies as a result of his aspiration. Where death does not take place (and this is somewhat unusual) serious psychological difficulties are apt to be found. These have brought much concern to Churchmen at

all times and to the modern psychologist and have brought the whole subject of the mystical unfoldment into disrepute, particularly in this modern scientific age.

It is the materialising of the vision in astral matter, its development through the power of emotion (masquerading as devotion) and the failure of the mystic either to enter into the realm of mental perception or to bring his idealistic dream down into physical expression which lies at the root of the trouble. The man becomes deluded by the best that is in him; he is the victim of an hallucination which embodies the highest he knows; he is overcome by the glamour of the spiritual life; he fails to distinguish between the vision and the Plan, between the manufactured unreal of the ages of mystical activity and the *Real* which stands ever in the background of the life of the integrated human being.

Forget not that the vision (of Heaven, of God, of Christ, of any spiritual leader or of any millennium) is based in the majority of cases upon the dreams and aspirations of the mystics down the ages who have blazed the mystical trail, who have used the same terminology and employed the same symbols to express that which they sense, and to which they aspire and for which they long so yearningly. They all sense the same Reality, lying behind the glamour of the world aspiration; they all couch their desire and longing in the same symbolic forms—marriage with the Beloved, life in the Holy City, participation in some ecstatic vision of God, adoration of some deified and loved Individuality, such as the Christ, the Buddha, or Shri Krishna, walking with God in the garden of life, the garden of the Lord, the attainment of the mountain top where God is to be found, and all stands revealed. Such are a few of the forms in which their aspiration clothes itself and their sense of duality finds satisfaction. These ideas exist as powerful thought forms on the astral plane and they attract—like magnets—the aspiration of the devotee which follows century after century the same path of yearning search, imaginative expression of a deep-seated spiritual "wish-life" and an emotional surging outward towards divinity, described sometimes as "the lifting of the heart to God."

Devitalisation and delusion are the frequent case history of the purely emotional mystic. When this astral cycle is over and he later (and probably in another life) swings into a frankly agnostic state of mind, there comes a restoration of balance and a more wholesome unfoldment becomes possible. The true and valuable fruits of the mystical experience of the past are never lost. The inner spiritual realisation remains latent in the content of the life, later to be resurrected to its true expression but the vagueness and the sense of duality must eventually be transformed into a realised mental clarity; dualism must give place to the experience of the at-one-ment and the mists must roll away. The mystic sees through a glass darkly but some day must *Know*, even as he is known.

When, in these modern times, the mystically oriented person comes under the care of a wise psychologist, the latter would be well advised gently and gradually to develop in him a cycle of doubt, leading even to a temporary agnosticism. The result would be a rapid establishing of the desired equilibrium. I would call your attention to the words "gently and gradually". The encouraging of a normal physical life, with its ordinary interests, the fulfilling of its obligations and responsibilities and the usual physical functioning of the nature should bring about much wholesome and needed orientation.

3. *Delirium.* I use this powerful word with deliberation when dealing with the dangerous and difficult stages of the mystical life. When the delusions of the mystic and his devitalisation have gone beyond a certain point, he arrives at a stage where he has no real inner control, he develops the

mystical sense to the point where he has no sense of proportion, where the conventions (right or wrong), social training, economic responsibility, human obligations and all the aspects of daily life which integrate the human part into the whole of humanity fail to police the lower nature. His outer expression becomes abnormal and he (from the highest and best sense of values) anti-social. Such an anti-social attitude will range all the way from a relatively usual fanaticism which forces its possessor to see only one point of view out of the many possible, to certain pronounced and recognisable forms of insanity. The mystic is then obsessed by his own peculiar thoughtform of truth and of reality. He has only one idea in his head. His mind is not active, for his brain has become the instrument of his astral nature and registers only his fanatical devotion and his emotional obsession. The ajna centre swings into activity before there is any true integration of the whole man, and any true useful purpose to its activity.

A period ensues wherein the man expresses himself in many undesirable ways which include a too strenuous one-pointedness, real fanaticism, sadistic effort with a supposed spiritual motive, (such as was seen in the Inquisition) and certain forms of mental breakdown. Occultly speaking, "the fiery vision proceeds to burn its victim and thus destroys the thread which holds his mind and brain in friendship close." This burning astral fever necessarily produces an effect upon the physical body as well as on the personality expression, and the trouble can then be recognised by others as real and serious in consequences and effects. Frequently, there is little that can be done; sometimes no attempts to help prove availing. The mystic has, for this one life, done himself irreparable damage. The healing influence of death, and the interlude of the life beyond the physical plane must do their beneficent work before the man can again achieve normality and begin to transmute his Vision of the Good, the Beautiful and the True into working expression upon the plane of daily living; he will then bring his mind to bear upon the problem; he will then discover that the vision is but the reflection of the *Plan* of God. He will know that the power to personalise aspiration must be transformed into the power to depersonalise oneself, prior to world service and cooperation with the Hierarchy.

4. *Detachment.* This is one of the major psychological difficulties which leads to the common phenomenon of cleavage. It is one of the hardest to handle. The mystic who can see naught but his vision, who registers that vision in terms only of symbolic forms, of sexual longing, of agonising aspirations and an intense "wish-life" of dream and desire may eventually succeed in severing all right relations both within himself (with his physical body in one place, his emotional life directed to another and his mind pre-occupied elsewhere) and with his surroundings and environing responsibilities, so that he lives entirely in a world of his own manufacturing—detached, unmoved, and untouched by normal affairs or human calls. This is sometimes also brought about by an unrecognised desire to escape from responsibility, from the pain and irksomeness of daily living or from the clinging hands of those who love him; it can be brought over from another life of mystical experience which should, in this life, be permanently transcended and outgrown, having served its useful purpose and done a needed work. This is a detachment of the wrong kind.

I realise as I give you this teaching upon the difficulties of the mystical life—devitalisation, delusion, delirium and detachment—that those who have gained much from the mystics or those who are at this time mystically inclined will violently disagree. I would seek to make myself clear on these points. The mystical way is the right way for people at a certain stage of evolution, the Atlantean stage, provided it is not carried to the point of insanity, hallucination, furious fanaticism and psychopathic complications. It is, rightly expressed, a useful and needed process whereby the astral body is re-oriented and spiritual aspiration begins to take the place of desire. It is necessary to have vision for "where there is no vision, the people perish". True vision is, in reality, the astral reflection of the divine Plan, reflected into the higher levels of the astral consciousness of the planet and there contacted and sensed by those human beings whose focus in life is of a very high grade nature, whose "intention is towards God and righteousness" but who are introverted at this time, who lack much technical knowledge either of divine law or of the constitution of man or of the planetary life, and whose minds are quiescent and non-questioning except in an emotional sense and for the relief of the mystic's own spiritual distress and desire for peace and satisfaction. There is, for instance, little in the writings of the mystics of the middle ages, (either in the East or in the West) which gives any indication of a sense of world need or of humanity's demand for enlightenment.

The astral reflection of the Plan—such is the vision. There the life forces of the mystical physical nature, of his astral body and of his soul (two forces and one energy) unite and there they produce a powerful expression of focussed desire, deep inchoate longing, vivid imagination and the construction of a thought form, expressing all that the mystic desires to contact or to see expressed.

There will be, as time goes on, less and less of this mystical approach. The work of realising beauty and the instinct to reach out towards divinity are now so deeply rooted in the racial consciousness that the balancing work of the mind and the presentation of the Plan in the place of the Vision can safely proceed. The children of the race who are still Atlantean in consciousness will continue with the mystical approach and the beauty of that contribution will still be the heritage of the race. But the cycle of the mystical effort and experience will be considerably shortened and scientifically controlled because its purpose, its place in racial unfoldment and its contribution to the "doctrine of Reality" will be better understood.

This mystical cycle is the correspondence to the "adolescent" cycle in the life of the young, valuable, visionary and life-giving, spurring on to right orientation and stabilising certain standards and values. Such a cycle will, however, be recognised as undesirable when the time has come that a new and higher set of values and a more spiritual and controlled technique should take its place. A life purpose, a recognised plan and a correctly directed activity must eventually supersede all adolescent yearnings, dreams, imaginative longings and aspiration in the life of the individual and of the race.

Mistake Me Not. The vision is a vision of reality. The Eternal Dreamer dreams and the greatest of all Mystics is the divine Logos Himself. But His dream must be registered in our consciousness as God's Plan and the mystical vision is the necessary though passing development in the human being of the "dreaming" aspect of God's Nature. Ponder on this, for it holds revelation to those who ponder rightly.

Revelation of Light and Power and Attendant Difficulties

The problems with which we must now deal belong in a totally different category. They have no relation at all to emotion or to the astral plane but constitute the specific difficulty of the aspirant or the advanced man or disciple who has learnt to focus himself in the mental nature. They are problems connected with achieved contact with the soul, which results in the illumination of the mind and a definite influx of power.

These difficulties only come to the man in whom the throat centre and the ajna centre are awakening. The moment that any difficulty is sensed in relation to the phenomena of light, the psychologist or the physician can know that the pituitary body is involved and that consequently the centre between the eyebrows is beginning to be active and awake.

The problem of power, sensed by the aspirant and seeking expression in his life, falls into two categories:—

1. The sense of power which comes through the effort to do definite creative work. This necessarily involves the activity of the throat centre. Where there is this inflow of creative force and where there is no real use made of the inflowing energy in the production of creative work, then there is very apt to be difficulty with the thyroid gland.

2. The sense of power which takes the form of ambition, and of an integration which is brought about by the force of that ambition. This frequently succeeds in subordinating the various aspects of the lower nature to that ambition. When this takes place the ajna centre is active and is synchronising its vibration with that of the throat centre. This leads to real difficulty and is one of the commonest forms of ambition to which the aspirant and the disciple succumb.

One can also divide the problem of light into two groups of difficulties if one so desires—one related to the physical registering of the light in the head and the other to the acquiring of knowledge.

This registering of light within the periphery of the skull is connected with the relation to be found between the head

centre and the centre between the eyebrows; that is, between
the area (localised around the pituitary body) and that localised around the pineal gland. The vibratory effect, you know,
of those two centres can become so strong that the two vibrations or their "pulsating rhythmic activity" can swing into
each other's field of action and a unified magnetic field can be
set up which can become so powerful, so brilliant and so pronounced that the disciple—when closing his eyes—can see it
plainly. It can be visually sensed and known. Eventually, and
in some cases, it can definitely affect the optic nerve, not to its
detriment but to the extent of evoking the subtler side of the
sense of sight. A man can then see etherically and can see the
etheric counterpart of all tangible forms. This is physiological
and not a psychic power and is quite different to clairvoyance.
There can be no etheric vision apart from the usual organ of
vision, the eye. The sensing and the registering of this light
in the head can lead to its own peculiar problems when the
process is not correctly understood or controlled, just as the
registering of the energy of power (coming from the mind in
its will aspect or from the soul through the will petals) can
prove definitely detrimental to the personality, when not
consecrated or refined.

Again, this registering of the light falls into certain definite
stages and takes place at certain definite points in the unfoldment of the human being, but is more likely to occur in the
earlier stages than the later. These are:—

1. The sensing of a diffused light outside the head, either
   before the eyes or over the right shoulder.
2. The sensing of this diffused misty light within the head,
   permeating, apparently, the entire head.
3. The concentrating of this diffused light until it has the
   appearance of a radiant sun.

4. The intensifying of the light of this inner sun. This is in reality the recognition of the radiance of the magnetic field, established between the pituitary body and the pineal gland (as expressions of the head and the ajna centres). This radiance can at times seem almost too bright to be borne.

5. The extension of the rays of this inner sun first to the eyes, and then finally beyond the radius of the head so that (to the vision of the clairvoyant seer) the halo makes its appearance around the head of the disciple or aspirant.

6. The discovery that there is, at the very heart of this, a point of dark blue electric light, which gradually grows into a circle of some size. This occurs when the light in the head irradiates the central opening at the top of the head. Through this opening the various energies of the soul and the forces of the personality can be synthesised and thus flow into the physical body, via the major centres. It is also the esoteric "door of departure" through which the soul withdraws the consciousness aspect in the hours of sleep and the consciousness aspect plus the life thread at the moment of death.

The registering of this inner light often causes serious concern and difficulty to the inexperienced person and the intensity of their concern and fear leads them to think so much of the problem that they become what we occultly call "obsessed with the light and so fail to see the Lord of Light and that which the Light reveals". I would point out here that all aspirants and occult students do not see this light. Seeing it is dependent upon several factors—temperament, the quality of the physical cells of the brain, the nature of the work which has been done or of the particular task, and the extent of the magnetic field. There never need be any difficulty if the aspirant will use the light which is in him for the helping of his fellowmen. It is the self-centred mystic who gets into difficulty, as does the occultist who uses the light which he discovers within himself for selfish purposes, and personal ends.

An incidental difficulty is sometimes found when the "doorway out into the other worlds" is discovered and becomes, not a door for rightful and proper use, but a way of escape from the difficulties of life and a short cut out of conscious physical experience. The connection then between the mystic and his physical vehicle becomes less and less firmly established and the link gets looser and looser until the man spends most of his time out of his body in a condition of semi-trance or a deep sleep condition.

Students should make no effort to see the light in the head, but when it is sensed and seen—then there should be a careful regulation and registration of it. Second ray types will respond to this phenomenon more easily and more frequently than first or third ray types. First ray people will register the inflow of force and power with facility and will discover that their problem lies in the control and the right direction of such energies.

Much of the present impasse to be found in the personalities of the aspirants of the world is due to the fact that the light that is in them remains undirected and the power that is flowing through them remains unused or misapplied. Much of the physical blindness and the poor sight to be found in the world today (unless the result of accident) is due to the presence of the light of the head—unrecognised and unused—and thus producing or exciting a definite effect upon the eyes and upon the optic nerve. Technically speaking, the light of the soul—localised in the region of the pineal gland—works through and would be directed through the right eye which is (as you have been told) the organ of the buddhi, whilst the light of the personality—localised in the region of the pituitary body—functions through the left eye. The time has not yet come when this statement means much except to very advanced students, but it should be on record for the future use of disciples and aspirants.

I would also like to point out that one of the difficulties today is that the light of the personality is more active within the head than is the light of the soul and that it has far more of the *quality of burning* than has soul light. The effect of the soul light is stimulating and occultly cool. It brings the brain cells into functioning activity, evoking response from cells at present quiescent and unawakened. It is as these cells are brought into activity by the inflow of the light of the soul that genius appears, accompanied often by some lack of balance or control in certain directions.

This whole subject of light and power is of so vast a nature and is relatively so little undertsood in its true significance as an expression (in dual form) of energy which flows upward from the personality and downward from the soul that it is only as more and more people tread the Path that the problem will emerge in its true light and thus eventually be handled rightly. I will refer here briefly to some of the problems so as to provide the germ or seed of thought from which future study can grow and the future investigation arise. They might be summarised as follows:—

1. The theme of light and energy is closely connected with the problem (for such it is at this time) of the entire glandular system; it is, therefore, of basic importance that there should be understanding of this relation for it is one of the fundamental things upon which the health of the entire body and its right functioning rests.
2. When there is a correct grasp of this subject, it will be

found that the brain and the two head centres (actuating the pituitary body and the pineal gland) are the directing agents for all the activities of the man upon the physical plane. Today, he is largely directed by his animal instincts, by his sexual life and by his emotional reactions or else by his creative activities as they express themselves through the throat centre. A few—very few —of his activities are directed from the heart, but eventually men must control their life expression from the head via the dual organs of the soul and the personality —the ajna centre, working through the pituitary body and expressing the personality life at its highest, and the head centre, working through the pineal gland, responsive to soul impulse. There will then be balance and right direction of all the life forces and a right development (following ray indications) of all the centres in the body.

3. Through this right re-arrangement of the life forces in the body and their consequent "enlightenment and energising", men will be enabled to do two things, speaking symbolically:—

   a. They will "see God" and be in touch with the soul.
   b. They will "know what is in man" and can then act wisely and work constructively.

4. They will be able to "pierce the glamour of the astral plane" and proceed to function without error and can thus bring about the unimpeded illumination of the brain and the dissemination of knowledge in the brain.

You will note from the above how many of the hallucinations, the glamours, the ambitions and the errors of the modern mystic can all be traced to the early stages and the embryonic beginnings of these developments. They are indicative, therefore, of unfoldment. But unfortunately they are not understood for what they are and the available light and energy are misapplied or turned to selfish and personal ends. This cannot as yet be avoided by any but the more advanced and experienced disciples and occultists; and many aspirants must continue for some time destroying themselves (from the personality angle and in this life) in what has been called the "fiery light of their misunderstanding and the burning fire of their personality ambition" until they learn that humility and scientific technique which will make them wise directors of the light and the power which is pouring into and through them all the time.

A study, therefore, of the three types of difficulties, emerging out of the development and the unfoldment of the psychic powers brings me to a wide generalisation, to which you must remember there will be many exceptions:—

1. The appearance of the lower psychic powers usually indicates that the man who is their victim (for we are here only dealing with the abnormalities of the psychic science) is on the third ray or that the third ray is dominant in his personality or a controlling factor in his personality equipment. Frequently an astral body, controlled by the third ray, will be found.

2. The registering of the mystical vision with its attendant difficulties is facilitated when the second ray is controlling and powerful, because the second ray is connected peculiarly with vision and with light.

3. It will be apparent to you that the revelation of power is obviously part of the expression of the first ray type.

In this way, though all experiences come eventually to the disciple, the three major difficulties with which we have been dealing,—the psychic powers, the problems incident to the mystical vision and the revelation of light and power—have a relation to and a connection with the ray expression. This should be borne in mind by the psychologist, the investigator and the physician. Psychic sensitivity, mystical duality, and dominating power—these are the three major problems of the aspirant and should be studied and understood. They affect the three major centres—the head, the heart and the centre between the eyebrows—in the disciple, for psychic sensitivity is related to the heart, mystical duality to the ajna centre and the problem of power to the highest head centre.

In the aspirant or advanced human being, they affect the throat, the solar plexus and the sacral centre, but as they are definitely due to an expansion of consciousness, they have little registered or noticeable effect upon the unevolved man or upon the average man who is pre-occupied with physical plane life and emotional reactions. He is not passing through the stimulating but disrupting processes of re-orientation, of recognising duality and of fusion of the personality. As we have earlier seen, the processes of integration bring their own problems.

As time goes on, the stages of difficulty will be more carefully investigated from the angle of the occult hypotheses and then much progress will take place. This will be peculiarly so, if the problems of adolescence are studied, for they are the problems of the Atlantean consciousness and of the mystical unfoldment.

I would like here to point out that just as the embryo in the womb recapitulates the various stages of animal unfoldment, so the human being, during the years of infancy, adolescence and youth up to the age of 35, recapitulates the various racial stages of consciousness. At 35 years old he should then affirm in himself the stage of the intelligent disciple. Much will be gained by a recognition of this recapitulatory process which

—in the New Age which is upon us—will do much to control and to determine the processes of unfoldment to which the child and youth will be subjected by the wise educator.

c. DISEASES CONNECTED WITH GROUP CONDITIONS

We can only briefly touch upon this theme, owing to the fact that group work (esoterically understood) is relatively new, and because the individual, working at this time in a group, is scarcely affected at all by these factors, owing to his relatively partial integration. I refer here to his integration in the group. People are still so insulated in their personalities that they are shut off, in many cases, from group stimulation, group effects and group impulses. It is only as they become decentralised and, therefore, more easily responsive to the group ideas, the group idealism, and to the group aura (with its out-breathing and its in-breathing and its group livingness) that they can and do succumb to those difficulties which group life imposes. Today it is the central figure in the group life, the dominant personality or soul, who is the one to whom the group life and the group thought turns, with all the consequences of such turning. It is this person, upon whom the group life pivots (if I may use such a term), who is the group victim and it is he who pays the price of any group weakness. The expression of the group attitude finds its outlet in him and he is, at times, practically "killed" by the group. No group today is a perfect group. They are in the experimental stage and are largely composed of a few Aquarians, many Pisceans and a number of people who are in a transition stage between these two. The leader or leaders of the new groups are usually of as pure a type of the new age or Aquarian character as is possible or available at this time. This accounts for the failure of the group, as a rule, either to understand the leader or to cooperate with the new ideals as is desired. The leader is a pioneer in a new field of thought and of intention and, therefore, suffers the penalties of his daring and of his spirit of enterprise.

It is not my intention to deal here with group difficulties, for that is not my theme. I am considering the difficulties (amounting often to physical disease) and the problems of the individual who is sensitive to group pressures and group life —a very different thing to the usual problems of the mystics of the past. These can only be studied and investigated today by a consideration of the lives, physical condition, problems, difficulties and deaths of group leaders. I would call this definitely to your attention. The group members—little as they may like to recognise this fact—are not as yet prone to suffer much from the group life, the group emanation and the group energy for they are not yet sufficiently integrated into the group.

The problem we are considering falls into two major categories and as I seek to deal with them I realise that there is relatively little that I can say. The next century will see the problems more defined and the difficulties more clearly delineated. They are:

   a. Those arising as a result of the directed thought of the group. On this I can say something.
   b. Diseases, connected with the respiratory tract. On these I can say but little.

Let us, therefore, look at these problems. We shall have to study the first from the angle of the one most affected by them—the leader or focal point of the group. These same problems may also affect the three or four people who, with the group leader and in collaboration with him, direct the group policies.

Diseases and Problems Evoked by Directed Group Thought

It will be obvious to you that the first and most important of these difficulties will be those arising from group criticism, either voiced or strongly felt. This criticism can be based on many things, but is usually rooted in jealousy, thwarted ambition, or pride of individual intellect. Each member of any group, particularly those in the immediate circle of the leader or leaders, is prone to sit in judgment. The responsibility is not theirs; they know not the problems as they truly exist and criticism is, therefore, easy. It should here be remembered that criticism is a virulent poison. It damages in every case eventually the one who criticises—owing to the fact of *voiced direction*—it hurts still more the one who is criticised. Where there is purity of motive, true love and a large measure of detachment, the subtler bodies of the one who is under attack may remain immune but the physical effects will be definite and where there is any physical weakness or limitation *there* will be found the localisation of the projected poison.

Unvoiced criticism is very dangerous for it is powerfully focussed and strongly, though not individually directed; it issues continuously and as a steady stream, sent forth on the wings of jealousy, ambition, pride in a personal grasp of a supposed situation and a belief that the one who criticises is in a position to understand correctly and could—given right opportunity—take right action. Where the criticism is voiced and expressed in words, it is consequently strengthened by the cooperation of those influenced by the criticism and the consequences of this group-directed thought may result in the physical undoing, and disruption of the physical body of the leader or leaders. This may be a new thought to some and should cause many in the New Age groups to arrest their thoughts and so release their leaders from the disastrous impact of their criticism.

I refer not here to hate, though that is **often** present, either consciously or unconsciously, but simply to the "sitting in judgment" and to the idle critical gossip which seems necessary to the average group member. It is like the very breath of death and it can not only kill the leader through accumulated poison and distress but it can also kill the group life and render abortive the efforts which could, if given cooperation and time to develop, prove constructive agencies through which the Hierarchy might work.

From every side and in every group there streams in on the group leader directed criticism, poisonous thoughts, untrue formulated ideas, idle gossip of a destructive kind, the imputation of motives, the unspoken jealousies and hates, the frustrated ambitions of group members, their resentments and their unsatisfied desires for prominence or for recognition by the leader or leaders, their desires to see the leader superseded by themselves or by someone else and many other forms of selfishness and mental pride. These produce results in the physical bodies of the leader or leaders and often in the emotional bodies. The responsibility of the group member is, therefore, great and it is one which they seldom recognise or shoulder. It is hard for them to appreciate the dire effects when one person is the target for group criticism and when the directed thought of a number of persons is focussed on one or two individuals.

The more highly evolved the group leader, the greater the pain and suffering. First ray people who have naturally a "technique of isolation" suffer less than many for they know how to shut off these directed streams of force and how to deflect them and—when they are not deeply spiritual people —they can return them to their originators and thus wreak havoc in their lives. Second ray persons do not and cannot work this way. They are naturally absorbers and magnetically attract all that is in their environment which is directed towards them. That is why Christ paid the penalty of death. He was killed, not only by His enemies, but also by His so-called friends.

You might here ask: What can a leader or a group of leaders do in these unfortunately normal and usual circumstances? Nothing, but continue in the work; retreat within themselves; speak the truth with love when occasion occurs; refuse to become bitter over the pain which the group occasions and wait until the group members learn the lessons of cooperation, of silence, of loving appreciation and a wise realisation and understanding of the problems with which all group leaders are faced in these difficult and individualistic days. That time will come.

Then there is the reverse of this problem and one that must be faced by many group leaders. In this reverse situation, the leader is overcome and (if I might use such a phrase) is "smothered" by the devotion of certain of the group members. Group leaders can be almost annihilated by the personality love of people. But this is not of such a poisonous nature as the difficulties above referred to, for—though it is handicapping and leads to many forms of difficulty, misunderstanding and group reaction—it is along the line of love and not of separation and hate. It produces what is esoterically called "the crippling of the one who seeks to serve and the binding of his hands and feet."

One other difficulty I will touch upon for it is important in so far that it is a group activity, carried forward *as a whole* and is not the act of one individual or a small handful of individuals within the group. I refer to the way in which at this time a group drains the life of its leader or leaders. The umbilical cord (speaking symbolically) is seldom cut between the leader and the group. That was the major mistake of the groups in the Piscean age. Always they remained attached to the leader or—when aroused to hate or dislike—they violently disrupted the tie and severed the relationship, causing much distress and unnecessary suffering to the group as well as to the leader. In the New Age the cord will be cut early in the life of the group but the leader or group of leaders will remain for a long time (as does the mother of a child) the guiding inspiration, the loving protecting force and the source of instruction and of teaching. When this is the case, the group can proceed upon its way and live its life as a self-directing agent even when the leader passes over to the other side or there is a change in leadership for some good reason or other.

According to the general flow of group life and activity so will be the effect—emotional and physical—upon any sensitive group member; the more frequent the physical contact between the group members the more definite will be the group problems and difficulties, however. Groups in the New Age will be held together by a subjective link and not so much by the emotional reaction induced by outer contact. I would ask you to ponder carefully upon this last paragraph for it holds the clue to the successful working of the new groups. It is from group life and group atmosphere that much infection arises, leading to difficulties of a physical nature. Disease is largely of group origin and the mystics and sensitives of the world most easily succumb. In these early stages of true group work, the difficulties which arise from group contacts are frequently of a purely physiological nature and are not so deep seated as those with which we have earlier been dealing. This is a point to be remembered. Physical trouble and disease is not of so serious a nature as psychological.

Respirational Diseases of Mystics

There is little to say about this. It will constitute a major difficulty as the groups grow in strength and power. Just in so far as they are objective and not subjective so will this trouble increase. I refer to those diseases affecting the breathing apparatus which arise from group contact; I do not refer to the same difficulties which are brought by the individual to the group. Esoterically, the reason for this should be obvious. Mistakes in speech, idle talk and gossip, the effects of the leaders' words—all these will have a subjective result little grasped or realised by the average student and all these work out as physical effects—either good or bad. Owing to the newness of this theme and the lack of evidence to substantiate my statements, I can only call your attention to the latent possibilities and leave time to demonstrate the accuracy of my position. Curiously enough this whole subject of breathing—individual and group breathing—is evoking its own paralleling solution in the emphasis that is being laid in many esoteric groups upon breathing exercises, upon the sounding of the *Aum* (which is the breath of the soul when correctly sounded) and on the practice (under different formulas) of rhythm. These are all the unrecognised effort on the part of the group—instinctual in nature more than intelligently planned—to offset certain definitely sensed group dangers.

These practices can be beneficial if carefully carried out, but often induce their own peculiar problems. The sounding of the *Aum*, for instance, by the unprepared or by groups who are intrigued by the activity but who have no faintest idea of what they are doing, carries with it definite difficulties. However, the special difficulties of group work in the New Age can be offset by certain esoteric exercises and practices connected with the respiratory tract. More than this I can not say for the new groups are in their infancy and group difficulties have not yet developed on a large scale nor are the future problems (incident to the occult and pronounced mystical nature of these groups) of so defined a nature that they can evoke understanding formulation.

d. PROBLEMS OF MYSTICS CONNECTED WITH PRESENT RAY INFLUENCES

Today we are watching the passing out of the sixth ray energy and the growing power and activity of the seventh ray. The energy which is withdrawing itself from our planet in one of the cyclic crises has for centuries expressed itself through the planetary solar plexus and also, as might be inferred, through the solar plexus centre of the average aspirant. This has led to much of the digestive difficulties, plus the emotional problems (and are they not closely related) from which the majority of people have suffered in this age and generation. The intense one-pointed attitude, the fanatical state of mind, the sacrifice of the personal life to the sensed ideal have all brought about a dangerous condition in those organs of the body which lie below the diaphragm. This should be remembered.

The seventh ray, working as it does through the centre at the base of the spine, will in time have a peculiar effect upon the entire circulatory system, for this basic centre is connected with the life-force and, as you know, the "blood is the life". It works with the highest centre in the body and is therefore related to the entire problem of the polarities. It is consequently one of the factors which will increase the difficulties connected with the various psychological "cleavages" with which we have earlier dealt. It concerns the human triplicity of spirit-soul-body, the duality of soul and personality and the major aspects of Deity, spirit and matter, as well as the many groupings of the pairs of opposites with which the mystic is so constantly concerned and which he has eventually to resolve into a unity. The recognition of this will make clear how complex are the problems and the possibilities arising out of the stimulation which will be felt as the "will to circulate, the will to relate and the will to express" makes its presence felt with the manifestation of the seventh ray. This force, as far as the individual is concerned, will play upon the centre at the base of the spine, arousing it into a hitherto unknown activity. These aspects of the will life are fortunately for humanity far from full development, but much of the present world confusion and the swing between the expressed extremes, are to be attributed to the play of these new forces. Much of the untimely and over-emphasised expression of the *Will* aspect of certain nations and individuals is connected with the coming into manifestation of this seventh ray and the passing out of the old. The problem is greatly increased by the fact that there is apparently a pronounced affinity between the fanatical idealistic will of the sixth ray—which is crystallised, directed, unwavering, emotional emphasis—and the will force of the untrained magical worker who is influenced by seventh ray energy, working through the centre at the base of the spine.

The distinction between these two forces and their expression at this time is subtle in the extreme and most difficult for the neophyte to distinguish. Each one leads to its own difficulties. I only mention them here as they constitute a problem of a mystical nature with which the Hierarchy has to deal but with which the average aspirant need not attempt to cope as yet.

As I conclude this discussion of the problems and diseases of the mystics, I realise far more than you can that I have been able to say little about the last few points, particularly about those connected with group or ray problems. This was unavoidable and inevitable. The new age groups are, as yet, seldom found, though many new age people are coming into manifestation. Only in the middle of the next century will the really new type of group emerge. Tentative beginnings of such groups are to be found today but their success or their failure is an unstable matter and both so ephemeral that it is not easy yet to bring them under law. One ambitious, disloyal person, for instance, can wreck a group; one selfless, non-critical, consecrated person can swing the group into successful work. This will indicate to you the potency of the individual and the fact that he can temporarily and at any given moment prove stronger than the group because the group has yet no true understanding of group activity, group coherency and group vitality. The mystic therefore suffers as a result of this condition, producing diseases and psychological difficulties which are not only personal but are often the result of the fluidity of the conditions in which he has to live.

One of the reasons guaranteeing the power of the Hierarchy and its freedom from any psychological problems inherent in group work and from any mystical or occult disturbances is its stability, its coherency and the surety of its touch on life. The mystic and the occultist are frequently passing through a cycle of insecurity and of transition from doubt as to the future's possible revelations, into a faith that the testimony of the ages is based on incontrovertible fact. The average mystic and occult student therefore lacks stability in his environing conditions and faith in his group affiliations. The greatest contribution to world thought at this time is the emerging recognition everywhere to be found of the finiteness of man's knowledge, of the insufficiency of his accumulated wisdom to cope with the world situation, and of his inability as yet to produce that workable plan which will lead the race out of its present difficulties and impasse. Human beings are neither sure of themselves nor of each other, and the greater their sensitivity the more complex their re-action and the more complicated and disastrous the physiological and psychological effects. Humanity as a whole is becoming mystical in its orientation and consciousness. The intelligentsia of the race are adding to that mystical aware-ness (which is always there, even if unrecognised or repudiated) a rapidly developing sense of occult understanding.

The Atlantean consciousness of adolescent humanity is giving way to the more developed consciousness of the mature human being. The problems, difficulties, diseases and disturbances of the man who is mystically oriented, introspective and enquiring, will, during the next few centuries, give place to the problems and complexities of the man who is becoming group conscious and who is working with an extraverted awareness in a group of some kind or another. I would remind you here that—as a result of the Piscean influence during the past two thousand years—such groups are predominantly idealistic.

This brings us to one of the most interesting parts of our treatise, which is the influence of the rays today and in the Aquarian age which is now upon us. This should prove of practical value. Let us bring to the work of the new cycle which is opening before us a renewed aspiration, a deepened love and a livelier faith, remembering, as we study the future, that *Faith* is one of our major needs, being "the *Substance* of things hoped for, the *Evidence* of things not seen".

III. *Humanity Today*

CHAPTER III

Humanity Today*

---

1. The World Situation

THE bringing into manifestation of the New Age upon earth and the accompanying emergence of the fifth kingdom of souls, is a task which calls for the united and concerted efforts of all those who are applying themselves to achieve this objective. It also needs the cooperative endeavours of that more advanced portion of humanity that is sensitive to these new influences, who can grasp the nature and far reaching potentialities of this momentous happening, and who are, therefore, prepared to share, to the best of their ability, in the response to the need of this crucial moment and to the service which the Great Ones are seeking to render. This cooperative effort by the more receptive portion of humanity is, in reality, what the Hierarchy is seeking to bring about among the sons of men.

The pressure upon the Hierarchy and upon all connected with it upon the Path of Discipleship and the Path of Initiation is today great. There has been necessitated a constant collaboration and an extreme activity, for Those guiding human evolution have been deeply concerned to preserve the balance needed in the world today. If possible, there must be no rapid climaxing of the situation, either into a general con-

* The material for this chapter was written prior to the declaration of war in 1939.

flagration nor (alternatively and quite possibly) into a general seething unrest of such widespread dimensions and of so persistent a character that the peoples of the world would be, in the one case, devastated by war, with its consequences of famine and pestilence, and in the other, worn out by the suffering engendered by economic unrest, destitution and the exploitation of the masses by fanatics, publicity seekers and well meaning but impractical idealists.

The dangers to the race and to its development of a disastrous war or wars, and the equally disastrous condition of no real or definite development, but simply decades of the present impasse and economic bankruptcy, are equally great and equally undesirable. To offset these possibilities and yet produce, during the next ten years, the maximum desired change, has been the objective of the planetary Hierarchy (that hidden band of Workers which the Christian calls the Christ and His Disciples), and constitutes the focal point of their struggle. I use this word "struggle" advisedly. The Hierarchy is struggling hard with the so-called "forces of evil," and the New Group of World Servers is the instrument, at this time, upon the physical plane, with which the Hierarchy has to work. They have no other instrument.

What do we mean by the phrase "forces of evil?" Not the armies of unrighteousness and sinfulness, organised under that figment of the imagination, the devil or some supreme antichrist, for such an army does not exist, and there is no great enemy of God, arraigned in battle against the Most High. There is only suffering, erring humanity, still half-awakened, dimly sensing the vision, and struggling to free itself from the thralldom of the past, with its tarnished allegiances and its unchecked loyalties. The forces of evil are, in the last analysis, only the entrenched ancient ideals and habits of thought which have served their purpose in bringing the race to its present point of development, but which must now disappear if the New Age is to be ushered in as desired. The old established rhythms, inherent in the old forms of religion, of politics and of the social order, must give place to newer ideals, to the synthetic understanding, and to the new order. The laws and modes of procedure which are characteristic of the New Age must supersede the old, and these will, in time, institute the new social order and the more inclusive regime.

The world today is full of experiments, particularly in the realm of government, which are the attempts of men everywhere to apply the new, dimly-sensed approaching ideals. These have to be applied to our modern conditions of living and eventually supersede them. There is no form of national experiment which is not based on some such ideal, and which is not essentially an effort on the part of some school of idealists to better world conditions, or to bring relief to some group of human beings. This is an axiom which must be accepted from the start, and it is one upon which the New Group of World Servers takes its stand. It therefore negates in them all political antagonisms. In the process of materialising the ideal, in the effort to procure its recognition and thus bring about conformity to the life purpose of the idea, the methods employed and the hatreds induced, the cruelties done in its name, the enforced acceptance demanded, and the evils perpetrated in the name of the new goals, have produced a condition of such an inflammatory nature that Those who stand behind world affairs and the development of humanity have been hard put to it to keep matters as quiet as they are.

What have we got in the world at this time?—for the lines of cleavage are daily clarifying, and the situation can be more distinctly grasped. Those with no vision and a myopic outlook upon environing events regard what is happening in the world as steadily becoming worse and more aggravated. They see no light in the darkness, and talk wildly of our civilisation being doomed. Others regard the situation as one in which they have their opportunity to assume prominence, to come to the forefront or surface in some department of world activity. They thus exploit the masses, and twist the situation to their own ends, sometimes with the best intentions, sometimes because they see their chance to arrive at power and prominence, and sometimes because life, destiny, fate or karma (we can use whichever word we like) casts them for that position, and they become men of destiny. They find themselves with their hand upon some ship of state, and are the controlling agent in some party, some group and in some political, religious or economic situation. Yet all the time they are but pawns in the hands of Those who are working to some wider end.

This whole matter might be looked at from two angles, and it may profit us to do so, remembering always that the objective of the new social order, of the new politics and the new religion is to bring about the unfoldment of the human consciousness, to institute and bring to men's attention the higher values, and to end the reign of materialism. It is, after all, the goal which all true knowers and spiritually minded men down the ages have set themselves—to bring in the rule of the Kingdom of God, the control of the soul, whose nature is love, and to carry forward the work which Christ inaugurated,—the era of peace on earth, good will towards men. This is plainly indicated by the widespread emphasis upon world peace, as voiced by the great political leaders and as worked for by the churches everywhere.

The peoples of the world today are divided into four groups, from the angle of Those Who are seeking to guide humanity into the New Age. This is of course a wide generalisation and there are many bridging groups between the four major divisions.

First, *the ignorant masses:* These, through poverty, lack of employment, illiteracy, hunger, distress and no leisure or means for cultural advantages, are in an inflamed condition. They are developed just enough to respond to the mental control and suggestion of slightly more advanced people. They can be easily regimented, influenced, standardised and swept into a collective activity by leaders of any school of thought which is clever enough and emotional enough to appeal to material desires, to love of country, and to hatred of those who possess more than they do. They can be controlled by fear, and thus aroused to action by emotional appeal.

Knowing no better and suffering so much, they are easily swept by the fires of hatred and fanaticism, and so they constitute one of the greatest and most innocent menaces of the present time. They are the playthings of the better informed, and are helpless in the hands of those who seek to use them for any purpose whatsoever. They can be reached most easily by emotional appeals and by promises, whereas ideas can make but little impact upon their consciousness, for they are not yet developed enough to do their own thinking. The bulk of them are young souls, though there are exceptions, naturally. It is not the idealism of the leaders and demagogues which impresses them and impels them into action (usually of a violent nature), but the desire to retaliate, the longing to possess in the material sense, and the determination to be what is colloquially called the "top dog." They embody mob psychology, mob rule, and mob violence. They are helpless, exploited and—because they are an unthinking, unreasonable mass of human beings,—they present a very real problem, as we all well know and as all governments realise. Blind, unthinking violence has hitherto been met by armed force. Such is the case today. The masses fight and die on the urge of inflammatory speeches and seldom know what it is all about. Their conditions *must* be bettered, but not through bloodshed and exploitation.

Secondly, *the middle classes*, so called, both higher and lower. These are the bulk of the nations, the bourgeoisie—intelligent, diligent, enquiring, narrow-minded, essentially religious, though frequently repudiating the forms of religion. They are torn and devastated by the economic conflict, and are, without exception, the most powerful element in any nation, because of their capacity to read, to discuss, to think, to spend money, and to take sides. They form the bulk of the partisans in the world, the fighters for a cause, and are formed into great groups, either for or against this, that, or the other party. They love to recognise and choose a leader, and are ready to die for a cause, and to make endless sacrifices for their ideals, based upon the ideas presented to them by their chosen leaders.

I am not differentiating the so-called aristocracy into a group, because that is entirely a class distinction, based largely on heredity and capital, and the modern adjustments in nations are rapidly fusing them into the large middle class. We are dealing with basic matters, with the groupings which are founded on major attitudes, and not on divisions which emerge when *material* resources are under consideration. The bourgeois mind is today slowly and steadily permeating the masses, the proletariat, and it is also penetrating into that circle which has hitherto been called the upper classes. It is found existing as a state of consciousness in the aristocracy of any nation and absorbing them under the great present levelling process. Because of this levelling which is everywhere going on, the spiritual aristocracy can now emerge,—an aristocracy based on a realisation of divine origin and goal, which knows no class distinction, no barriers in religion, and no separating differences. We are therefore dealing with *human divisions* and not *class distinctions*.

This second group is the most fruitful field from which the new leaders and organisers are being drawn. They constitute an intermediate group between the world thinkers, the intelligentsia, and the masses of men. In the last analysis, they are the determining factor in world affairs. The masses suffer from world conditions and from the situations brought about through the activity of this second group as it responds in some way or another to the new influences, the new ideals, and the new controlling factors in the modern world. This great second group itself suffers at the hands of those who seek to impose the new rhythms upon the peoples, —the political groups, the religious idealists and fanatics, and the protagonists of the new social order and economic regimes (as interpreted to them rightly or wrongly by their leaders).

Because of their intelligence, due to the improving educational facilities, the ability to read, and the impact of the new methods of propaganda, the press and the radio, they provide the most powerful group in the world in each nation, and it is to them that the leaders make their appeal, and it is their backing and their partisanship which is demanded, and which means success to any leader. They are the ones who have the controlling vote in national affairs. They are today swept by uncertainty, by questioning, by deep-seated fears, and by the desire to see justice done and the new order of things established. Above everything else they desire peace, stable economic conditions, and an orderly world. For this they are ready to fight, and are today fighting in every party, every group, and for every kind of political, nationalistic, religious, economic and social ideals. If they are not literally fighting, in the physical sense, they are fighting with words, speeches and books.

Thirdly, *the thinkers of the world:* These are the intelligent and highly educated men and women, who sense ideas and formulate them into ideals. These people speak the words, write the articles and books, and utilise all the known methods to reach and educate the general public, and thus stir up the bourgeoisie to activity, and arouse, through them, the masses. Their function and the part they play is of supreme importance. From their ranks come those who are steadily influencing the trend of world affairs, sometimes for good and sometimes for selfish ends. They play upon the human mind as a musician plays upon his instrument, and the power of the press, of the radio, and of the public platforms is in their hands. Their responsibility is enormous. Some few, more perhaps than might appear, are working selflessly under the inspiration of the new era. They are dedicated to the amelioration of human conditions, and the betterment of world affairs along certain lines which seem to them (rightly or wrongly) to have in them the hope of the future, and the uplift of humanity. They are found in every government, party, society, and organisation, and in every Church and religious grouping. They constitute the most influential unit today, because it is through them that the large middle class is reached, swayed and organised for political, religious and social ends. Their ideas and utterances percolate down through the upper and middle classes and finally reach the ears of the more advanced of the undeveloped masses.

Fourth, *the New Group of World Servers:* These are the people who are beginning to form a new social order in the world. They belong to no party or government, in the partisan sense. They recognise all parties, all creeds, and all social and economic organisations; they recognise all governments.

They are found in all nations and all religious organisations, and are occupied with the formulation of the new social order. From the purely physical angle, they are not fighting either for the best in the old order or for the betterment of world conditions. They consider that the old methods of fighting and partisanship and attack, and the ancient techniques of party battle have utterly failed, and that the means hitherto employed on all sides and by all parties and groups (fighting, violent partisanship of a leader or a cause, attacks on individuals whose ideas or manner of living is deemed detrimental to mankind), are out of date, having proved futile and unsuitable to bring in the desired condition of peace, economic plenty, and understanding. They are occupied with the task of inaugurating the new world order by forming throughout the world—in every nation, city and town,—a grouping of people who belong to no party, take no sides either for or against, but who have as clear and definite a platform and as practical a programme as any other single party in the world today. They take their stand upon the essential divinity of man; their programme is founded upon good will, because it is a basic human characteristic. They are therefore organising the men of good will throughout the world at this time, outlining to them a definite programme, and laying down a platform upon which all men of good will can meet.

They state and believe that their initial appeal has been of such a nature that, given the assistance of the trained minds to be found in the third group outlined above, and given the needed financial assistance to do the required educational work and goodwill propaganda, they can so change the world (through the sole agency of the men of good will) that—without war, without arousing hatred between men, and without attacking any cause or giving partisanship to any cause—the new order can be firmly established upon earth.

Their programme and their technique is outlined a little later in this discussion.

Behind this fourfold panorama of humanity stand Those Whose privilege and right it is to watch over human evolution and to guide the destinies of men. This They carry forward, not through an enforced control which infringes upon the free will of the human spirit, but through the implanting of ideas in the minds of the world thinkers, and the evocation of the human consciousness, so that these ideas receive due recognition and become in time the controlling factors in human life. They train the members of the New Group of World Servers in the task of changing ideas into ideals. These become in time the desired objectives of the thinkers, and are by them taught to the great middle class, and thus worked up into world forms of government and religion, forming the basis of the new social order, into which the masses are patiently incorporated.

It should be remembered at this point that the men and women of good will belong to all the groups outlined above, and that herein lies their strength and herein lies their usefulness to the New Group of World Servers.

The strength of the New Group of World Servers lies in three factors:—

1. They occupy a midway position between the masses of men and the inner subjective world government.
2. They draw their membership (if such an inadequate word can be used) from all classes,—the aristocracy, the intelligentsia, the bourgeoisie, higher and lower, and the upper layer of the proletariat. They are therefore truly representative.
3. They are closely inter-related, and in constant contact and rapport with each other, through unity of objective,

definiteness of method, and uniformity in technique and good will.

Let us look for a moment at the world picture as we find it at this time, and as it is coming to be recognised by the intelligent observer of world affairs. Nothing that is here said must be regarded in the nature of criticism, for that would be infringing one of the basic rules of the New Group, and such is most definitely not contemplated. Therefore we mention no specific groups, nations or parties, nor do we refer to any particular personalities. We are concerned with only one subject, the ushering in of the new world order. To do this, we must recognise the situation as it exists. We are occupied with the formation of that new party which will gather into its ranks all men of peace and good will, without interfering with their specific loyalties and endeavours, though probably modifying their methods considerably, where based on the old order. This new party can be regarded as the embodiment of the emerging Kingdom of God on earth, but it should be remembered that this kingdom is not a Christian kingdom or an earthly government. It is a grouping of all those who—belonging as they do to every world religion and every nation and type of political party—are free from the spirit of hatred and separativeness, and who seek to see right conditions established on earth through mutual good will.

The ferment in the world today has permeated the very lowest depths of humanity. All fields of human thought are involved in the divisions and the confusions. In the past, time and time again, the nations were swept into wars of aggression. Such wars are rapidly becoming rarer, and our strifes today are based primarily upon our economic needs. For this there are obvious objective reasons. Over-population, trade barriers, the inequalities of supply and demand, plus the ambitions and well-intentioned experiments of individuals in all departments of human thought and life are responsible for the upheaval. More need not be said, for the causes are generally recognised, and we are outlining a solution of a practical nature. But the true reason is deep-seated and not easily recognised, though the world thinkers are beginning to deal with it and to see its outlines clearly. This reason is the conflict between certain great ideals, all of them based on spiritual ideas, but all of them prostituted to ends which lead to separativeness, to hatred, party strife, civil war, widespread economic distress, terror of a general conflagration, and fear on every hand. We are surrounded by fear and uncertainty, grinding poverty, suspicion, plus the general collapse of the bulwarks of religion and government which hitherto seemed to offer a refuge.

Leaders—both national and religious—are everywhere attempting to deal with these problems, prompted sometimes by a true love for humanity, sometimes swayed by ambition, or galvanised into violent activity by some ideal for human, racial and national betterment. Sincerity and insincerity, hatred and love, service and exploitation, divisions and unifications are found on every hand. Catch words are everywhere—religious unity, standardisation of mankind, human freedom, the problem of the left and the right party, communism, fascism, nazism, the New Deal, liberalism and conservatism, creative living, population problems, sterilisation, utopias, the rights of the people, dictatorships, re-armament defence tactics, public education, secret diplomacy, isolationism,—such are a few of the words which are today on everybody's lips, and which indicate the aliveness of humanity to its problems, to the difficulties with which it is confronted, and to the impasse which we seem to have reached. On every hand, people are coming to the front with some solution, gathering a party to put it over, and fighting for their ideal.

Every day sees money spent like water in order to offset the propaganda of some leader, or to support the ideas of another. Campaigns are held all over the world to raise the needed funds to overthrow some ancient entrenched ideal, or for the substitution of some new idea. Men and women in both hemispheres are swept today by the desire to change the old order and bring in the new era of economic comfort and peaceful living, and are dedicating their lives to the defence of some principle which seems to them of paramount importance, or to the overthrow of another principle of importance to their brothers. Attack of personalities, defamation of character, the imputing of motives, and the stirring up of hatred are a recognised part of the technique of those who—with good intention—are attempting to salvage the world, to bring order out of chaos, and to defend the right as they see it. Love of humanity and desire to aid is unquestionably present. Yet the chaos grows; the hatreds increase; the warfare spreads; past efforts seem futile to stem the tide which seems about to sweep humanity over the brink of disaster.

This factor of futility, and the fatigue incident to the long struggle, are today recognised by the leaders everywhere. There is a demand for a new way, a desire to know what is basically at fault, and to discover why the strenuous self-sacrificing and divinely motivated efforts of many hundreds of men and women have failed to stop war, solve the economic problem and release humanity.

It might be stated that the failure is due primarily to two things:

1. The effort has been expended in dealing with effects, and the underlying causes have not been touched, even when realised by a few. The attempt has been made to right wrongs, to expose evils and evil personalities, and to at-

tack organisations, groups, parties, religions and national experiments. This has led to what appears to be a futile expenditure of time, strength, energy and money.

2. No effort has been made to find and blend into one organised whole the men of good will, of peaceful loving intention, and intelligent kindliness and goodness in the world, so that they can cooperate together in their vast masses. Those constitute an incredibly large number of people who hate war because they regard all men as brothers, but who see no way to end it, as all the organisations to that end seem powerless in the last analysis. They grieve over the economic distress but do not know what to do, as all the various groups dealing with the problem are occupied with laying the blame on others and seeking scapegoats; they are conscious of the breakdown of the many efforts towards good.

This spirit of good will is present in millions, and it evokes a sense of responsibility. This is the first indication in the race that man is divine. It is upon this steadily growing good will that the New Group of World Servers is counting, and which it is their intention to utilise. It is found in the membership of every group which exists for world betterment, and constitutes an unused power which has never yet been organised into a whole, as the loyalty and effort of the individual man of good will has hitherto been given to his organisation or endeavour. It is the intention of the New Group of World Servers not to interfere with this loyalty or to arrest any activity, but to gather into one organised whole all these people, without creating a new organisation or sidetracking any of them from the work they have already undertaken.

The New Group of World Servers is already a functioning active group. Every man and woman in every country in both hemispheres, who is working to heal the breaches between people, to evoke the sense of brotherhood, to foster the sense of mutual inter-relation, and who sees no racial, national or religious barriers, is a member of the New Group of World Servers, even if he has never heard of it in these terms.

The members of the New Group of World Servers belong to no party or religion and yet belong to all parties and religions; they assume no attitude or position either for or against any existing government, religion or social order. They engage in no political activity of any kind, and attack no existing order. They are neither for nor against a government or a Church, and spend no money, organise no campaign, and send out no literature which could be interpreted as attacking or defending any organisation of a political, religious, social or economic nature. They say nothing and write no word which could feed the fires of hatred, or tend to separate man from man, or nation from nation. Yet these members will be found in every political party and every world religion. They represent an attitude of mind.

The members of the New Group of World Servers are not, however, a band of impractical mystics. They know exactly what they seek to do, and their plans are laid in such a manner that—without upsetting any existing situation—they are discovering and bringing together the men of good will all over the world. Their united demand is that these men of good will should stand together in complete understanding and thus constitute a slowly growing body of people whose interest is shown on behalf of humanity and not primarily on behalf of their own immediate environment. The larger interest will not, however, prevent them from being good citizens of the country where their destiny has cast them. They will conform to and accept the situation in which they find themselves, but will (in that situation and under that government

or religious order) work for good will, for the breaking down
of barriers, and for world peace. They will avoid all attack of
existing regimes and personalities; they will keep the laws of
the land in which they have to live, but they will cultivate the
spirit of non-hatred, utilising every opportunity to emphasise
the brotherhood of nations, the unity of faith, and our economic inter-dependence. They will endeavour to speak no
word and do no act which can separate and breed dislike.

These are broad generalities, governing the conduct of the
men of good will who seek to cooperate with the work being
done by the New Group of World Servers. As they learn
effective cooperation and achieve steadiness in the right attitudes to their fellow men, they are gradually absorbed into
the ranks of the New Group, not through a process of formal
affiliation, for no such process exists (there being no formal organisation) but through the development of the necessary
qualities and characteristics. It is of value to reiterate at this
point that *the New Group of World Servers is not an organisation.* It has no headquarters, but only units of service
throughout the world; it has no president or lists of officers; it
has only servers in every country, who are occupied simply
with the task of discovering the men of good will. This is the
immediate task. These men of good will must be found and
trained in the doctrine of non-separateness, and educated in
the principles of cooperation and the characteristics of the
new social order, which is essentially a subjective re-align-
ment, resulting in pronounced changes brought about through
the weight of a world opinion, based on a good will which
knows no national or racial barriers or religious differences.
Year by year there should develop much active work and
much dissemination of the teachings upon universal good will,
so that it changes from a beautiful sentiment and becomes the

practical application of good will by action in the affairs of every day life, in every country throughout the world.

In terms of Christian teaching, the citizens of the kingdom which Christ came to found must be discovered, and will be recognised by their spirit of synthesis, their inclusive point of view and their emphasis upon a world unity which is based upon our international synthesis (the recognition really of our human relations), our religious unity as children of the one Father, and our well known, though largely ignored, economic inter-dependence. The education of the men and women of good will will be in relation to the *expression of a practical loving understanding*. The New Group of World Servers will know who these citizens of the kingdom are and where they are to be found.

The next task to which the New Group of World Servers will consecrate their efforts will be to eliminate the fear in the world. This can be done and will take place when the men and women of good will awake to the fact of the wealth of good will there is in every land. There are millions of these men of good will in the world; they have been increasing steadily in numbers as a result of the agony of the world war, but, feeling isolated and alone, they have been impotent and futile. They have felt separated, useless and unimportant. As individuals, they are. As part of a great world movement, with a spiritual basis and expressive of the essential divinity in man, they are not. The massed power of good will, a thing which has remained hitherto unorganised, will be found to be irresistible. The work of the New Group of World Servers until May 1942 is to organise this latent power and bring it forth into expression by fostering it, by educational methods, and by indicating steadily the lines along which this potent spirit can manifest.

The New Group of World Servers should therefore organise for itself a programme covering this period, under the direction of Those who watch, on the inner, spiritual side of life. This programme must have three objectives:—

1. To discover, educate and blend together the men of good will, demonstrating to them the fact that in every country in the world, without exception, much is being done along the lines of

   a. International understanding and the brotherhood of nations.
   b. The betterment of human conditions by groups, churches and organisations, working along the new lines, without hatred, eliminating attack on groups or persons and the expressing of a partisan spirit,
   c. Religious unity and spiritual unfoldment within and without the churches,
   d. Educational activity, carried forward along lines of non-separativeness and broad inclusiveness.

   This can be done through the instrumentality of a new magazine which will be the organ of the men of good will.

2. To prepare the men of good will for a repetition upon a far larger scale of the "act of appeal" which took place on May 6th, 1936. Then the Great Invocation was used by millions, and of its effectiveness there can be no doubt. It greatly strengthened the hands of the Hierarchy and established a "channel of contact" which can never again be broken. Greater similar efforts can be launched during the next few years and they will embody the next great spiritual effort and expression of the men of good will for which the intermediate period is a preparation. It is desirable that there should be, if possible, a far

wider use of the radio, so that sequentially and following the journey of the sun, there may go forth over the air this appeal to God at the time of the full moon. The day of appeal will be the expression of the spiritual attitude of humanity and will lead to a subjective spiritual synthesis between the men of good will and the New Group of World Servers and the inner spiritual Hierarchy which is working to bring about the manifestation of the new order on earth, to inaugurate the New Age, and to materialise the kingdom of God on the physical plane.

To this future day of appeal or world prayer much thought and preparation should be given, so that the results achieved can be even more definite and potent than in the first quite successful attempt. Prayer or appeal is either a potent way of setting certain great forces in motion or it is not. The testimony of the ages is in favour of its efficacy along these lines.

3. To hold before humanity, as part of the living instruction which the men of good will will teach and live out in their daily lives, the necessity of a great group participation in a Day of Forgiveness and of Forgetting. This may be possible in a few years' time, but could be effectively tried in 1942. This is a forgiveness which is based upon a recognition of the universality of human error in the past, and the fact that there is no blame to be apportioned to this or that group, nation or church, but that we have all made mistakes, have all failed to understand, and have all been guilty of lack of love and of tolerance. It is not, therefore, a forgiveness which is based on a spirit of magnanimity or a sense of expediency or superiority, but upon a desire to forget the past, and to push

forward into the New Age and participate in the new social order, free from the ancient hatreds, relinquishing the memory of the old mistakes in policy, judgment and method, and ignoring the habitual barriers and our normal separative instincts.

This is the triple programme to which the New Group of World Servers is pledged and in which we are urged to participate. To this endeavour they will in their turn call the men of good will. They have no other programme or intention.

Loosely knit together by mutual understanding and similarity of objective, the members of the New Group of World Servers stand, whether they are conscious or unconscious of each other or the group, as it is here described. In every country they are found and actively are working. Through them the men of good will are being discovered. Their names and addresses are being noted and collected into mailing lists. Their capacity, whatever it may be, to serve their fellow men, will be also noted when possible and utilised, if desired. Thus through the men of good will everywhere, the principle of good will can be nurtured and developed in every country, and eventually turned to practical use. These people will constitute a new body of practical thinkers in every nation, who will be no menace to any government, nor will they work against the established order. They will throw themselves into those movements and undertake those activities which can in no way foster hatred, spread enmity, or cause division among their fellow men. To this group, no government or church can object.

Danger lies in laying down rules and in making forecasts. These will only lead to premature activity and hasty procedure. If the work which is outlined here proceeds along the desired lines; if, through daily use of the Great Invocation:

Let the Forces of Light bring illumination to mankind
Let the Spirit of Peace be spread abroad
May men of good will everywhere meet in a spirit of cooperation
May forgiveness on the part of all men be the keynote at this time
Let power attend the efforts of the Great Ones
So let it be, and help us to do our part

the channel is widened and firmly established, and a day of prayer is duly organised; if the daily recognition of forgiveness in the sense in which St. Paul wrote when he said "Forgetting the things which are behind, press forward," becomes the rule among the men of good will, leading eventually to a world-wide day of forgiveness, then the task of the New Group of World Servers will go forward along constructive and fruitful lines, and will lead to success. Those Who seek to lead and guide on the inner side will also have reason to go forward with increased confidence, and the Christ will see the fruits "of the travail of His soul and be satisfied."

Having thus the programme for this immediate period outlined before us, what are we going to do about it? This programme cannot succeed nor can this middle party in the world—intermediate between the partisans and the groups *pro* and *con* in world affairs—come to fruition and constructive activity without each one realising the need, and bending anew every effort—individual, financial and spiritual—to the helping of the Plan.

2. *The New Group of World Servers*

The first thing to be grasped is that there is a Plan for humanity and that this Plan has always existed. It has worked out through the evolutionary developments of the past ages and also through that special impetus which has been given it from time to time by the great intuitives and teachers of the races. Today there are a sufficient number of men and women in the world, adequately developed, so that they can contact it and work in connection with it. It is becoming more a matter of group recognition than of intuitive revelation. Secondly, it is to be noted that there is upon our planet a group of men and women belonging to every nation, who are definitely upon the Path of Discipleship and because of their status, they are all of them as definitely serving the race. They are subjectively welded together into a body, which we have called the New Group of World Servers, for lack of a better name. Their characteristics are well known, for many have made a careful study of this group for two or three years and many also form a part of it.

Prominent members of this group are to be found in every country in Europe, in China and Japan, in North and South America, and in South Africa. In Australia, New Zealand and other countries not enumerated above, members and servers of this group are to be found.

Many of these group members know or recognise each other from the similarity of objectives, ideals and methods, to be seen in their work, but in many cases they remain unknown to each other. Group members are to be found working in all fields of human enterprise,—economic, political, social and religious. These four groups are named in the order of their importance in the present world situation. Religious difficulties and problems are perhaps the most easily handled and realised, because they are the most easily recognised. Religious antagonisms are rampant today but they are known for what they are, hence the religious field is mentioned last.

It is encouraging for us to observe, however, that the New Group of World Servers working in connection with the rapidly emerging plan of the Great Ones, has been vitally increased in numbers during the past few years and there is a much closer inner welding than heretofore. The group will be found divided into two parts:—

1. An inner nucleus, composed of those active servers who know themselves to be disciples, is consciously in touch with the Plan, and is strenuously working at its development.

2. Those who have responded to the vision as it has been presented to them by that inner nucleus, and have ranged themselves definitely on the side of the Plan. They are, therefore, men and women of good will.

Connected with these two groups, there is a steadily growing public which is becoming increasingly responsive to the new ideas. They have expressed their interest and are eager to see the Plan materialise in proper form on earth. The diverse needs of all these groups must be met and this is the definite problem of all who are working in conscious collaboration with the Hierarchy.

It is not easy for all of us who are working and struggling in the battlefield of life to see the world picture as it really is. It is difficult to appreciate the urgency of the present time, and to evaluate correctly the opportunity that is offered for the bringing of sorely needed changes. It is hard too to gauge the extent and the power of the forces working in opposition. It would be useless to refer thus to these forces, if there were no chance of success and the victory were not possible. Both success and victory are possible, if there is a unity of ideal and method amongst us.

A picture of the immediate problem to indicate possible dangers and suggest at the same time what should be done in the period immediately ahead, has practical value. Some of what is here said is already well known, but a re-statement of the situation is in order, for it will enable us to lay our plans with clarity and precision.

a. Objectives and Ideals

The statement has been made that Those who constitute the inner government of the world, or the so-called planetary Hierarchy, are working to facilitate the entry of the new ideals and aims into the consciousness of the race. These new ideals and aims are characteristics of the New Age. This statement is of importance, because it indicates that the effort now on foot is in line with the evolutionary development going on upon our planet. It is therefore assured of ultimate success. The work that the New Group of World Servers is endeavouring to do is intended to hasten that process, and so avert a long period of distress and disorder. Whether this effort succeeds or not, the final aim is assured, but it can be hastened if men will only appreciate fairly the situation with which they are immediately faced and take the necessary steps to change the present condition.

The new Plan of the Great Ones is, therefore, in the last analysis, simply an extension of the Plan as it has always existed. No changes in the basic idea are involved. The success of the present endeavour is contingent upon the availability of the forces which stand for progressive righteousness and the ability of the disciples of the world to act in unison, and so to influence public opinion that there can be a world wide change in human attitudes, but the members of the New Group of World Servers must refrain from dissipating their efforts in secondary activities. For these latter, there will be time, once the main objective has been reached. The immediate objectives of the Plan might be stated as follows:

1. *To raise the level of the human consciousness* so that in-

telligent thinking men and women will be consciously in touch with the world of ideas and the realm of intuitive perception. This means that they will be oriented towards reality.

Average men and women will then be led definitely to shift their attention from the world of the emotions in which they have hitherto lived, and will begin to live more in their mental natures, and to think clearly and wisely. As a direct result of a growing awareness of the two above mentioned groups, the masses, as a whole, will be definitely benefited. They will find their living conditions so ameliorated and wisely ordered that the present state of fear and of intense competitive struggle for existence will be superseded by a real measure of stability and security. A more leisured life will consequently be possible and this will enable men to unfold their powers —mental and spiritual—normally.

This is no picture of an immediate Utopia. The modification of the present situation, even in a small measure, is a Herculean task, and will strain the resources of the New Group of World Servers to the utmost.

2. The second objective of Those who are working out the Plan is the *clarifying of the international situation*. It is necessary that each nation should realise two things:— First, the importance of attending to its own business and its own internal problems which are those of beautifying the national life, by the production of order, stabilisation, and above all, freedom. Each nation must internally adjust itself to peace. This must be done, not by the armed force of some powerful group, but by the wise consideration of the needs of the entire people, excepting no part of the national life.

Second, the prime importance of each nation realising

its responsibility to all other nations, and the inter-relation of all parts of the life of our world. This realisation will bring about a reciprocal interplay in the field of economics, for this is the most important field at this time. Practically all world problems and differences are based upon an economic situation. It is, therefore, more important in the solution of the present world problem than are the political rivalries and the selfish, individual, national ambitions.

The providing of adequate food, raiment and housing facilities to the unthinking masses everywhere will bring about a changed world psychology, which will be constructive and sound, and which will usher in the deeply desired era of peace and plenty. That the problem involved is difficult no one denies, and for this, man's selfishness and greed is responsible. It is, in reality, relatively simple, if not complicated by too much statistical deduction and the opposed selfishness of national and monied interests. The term "monied interests" is here used to designate no one class in particular for the transition of money out of one set of hands into another provides no real solution. Whoever possesses the money at any particular time wields power, and this is true, whether it is the present capitalistic class or an enriched proletariat or a grasping government.

3. The third objective is the *growth of the group idea* with a consequent general emphasis upon group good, group understanding, group inter-relation, and group good will. These four are the ideals of that subjective group, working on the physical plane, which we call the New Group of World Servers.

If these ideals can be materialised, this new group provides a nucleus for that future world group which will gradually knit together all men in the cause of true brotherhood. This group will not be occupied with experiments in the various fields of human life or in connection with world problems. Its members will not work for political prominence or for the success of any particular experiment in the field of economics, politics or religion. Their work is the emphasis of the underlying principles and the education of public opinion along the new lines. They will seek to reveal to humanity the true and underlying inner synthesis, which is based on uniform objectives and which leads to that universal good will which will enable a man in any country to identify himself with his brothers in other parts of the world.

This group will provide an international unit, made up of intelligent men of good will, which must inevitably control world destiny and bring about world peace and thus organise the new world order. They will do this without the use of the old political machines, the violent propaganda, and the organised force which are characteristic of the old order. Their method is the method of education; they will mould public opinion and foster mutual good will and national, religious and economic inter-dependence. What they are really attempting to do is to awaken into fuller activity an aspect of human nature which is always present but which has hitherto been subordinated to selfish or ambitious ends. Human beings are innately kind when their minds are not distorted and their vision impaired by the false teaching of any selfish interest, political propaganda and racial or religious difficulties.

Upon this fact we take our stand and, given right opportunity and adequate aid, the work of the New Group of World Servers will demonstrate this fact. This new group provides a field of effort and a centre of energy towards which all men of good will everywhere throughout the world can turn, thus pooling their resources, strengthening each other's hands and sounding forth in unison the note of mutual cooperation for the good and well being of all, irrespective of creed or race. This is not a vague and mystical generalisation, carrying with it no practical purpose or plan. It is a statement of the ideals of a very large group of intelligent men and women, found today throughout the world and working in cooperation with Those upon the inner side of life Who *know*. These aims will be achieved, not by propaganda backed by force, but by example, backed by sacrifice and love. Another important objective of the Plan, which will materialise later when world conditions are bettered, is the emergence into physical plane activity of that group of souls of Whom the New Group of World Servers are the outer representatives. This appearance can be called (in Christian phraseology) the second coming of Christ with His Disciples, or it can be called the manifestation of the planetary Hierarchy or the appearance of the Masters of the Wisdom, Who will restore upon earth the ancient mysteries and institute again the order of Initiation.

Such is a broad and general idea of the objectives of the Plan and the aim of its Custodians. Each phase of it constitutes a field of active service, and all men of good will everywhere and the members of the New Group of World Servers find their place in one or another of its departments. The members of this group are, in reality, an intermediate group, between the Custodians of the Plan, as They express the mind and purpose of God, and the intelligent public. They constitute the "brain trust" of the planet, for they are definitely wrestling with the problem of unrest and distress in the economic, political and religious fields. Through them the Plan must work out, and if they work with the desired selflessness and wisdom, and if they demonstrate adequate skill in action, they will eventually achieve much power. It will, however, be power based upon an intelligent good will, upon a right understanding of brotherhood and upon a determination to bring about the good of the whole body and not the good of certain sections of the national life or of certain nations at the expense of other sections and other nations. Hence, my constant emphasis upon the necessity of thinking in *terms of good will to the whole*. The very effort so to think is part of the technique required to expand the present human consciousness, and in these words I have stated the basic principle underlying the new technique of world unfoldment and integration. The development of self consciousness and of the uniquely separative individual has been the right and desired technique in the past. The development of group consciousness, through the activity of the New Group of World Servers, is intended to be the right and desired technique of the future.

Speaking generally, we have, therefore, in the world today the unintelligent masses who are rapidly becoming self-conscious under the pressure of modern life and our modern educational systems. We have secondly, the truly self-conscious thinkers or individuals who have assumed world control and prominent place in world affairs, through the power of their thoughts and the emphasis and magnetism of their personality. By the clarity of their thinking in their chosen field, they dominate the masses, but they are dominant in a separative sense. These masses whom they control can be divided into two divisions:—A restless, alert, discontented and intelligent minority (a minority of about forty per cent of the whole). The remaining sixty per cent is formed by the unthinking masses, who are little more than emotional animals. They live, work, suffer and fight, but have no real idea of what it means, or of where they, as a race, are going.

With these latter there is little yet to be done. With the forty per cent, however, much can be achieved when the New Group of World Servers is sufficiently coherent. Notice should be taken also of the world idealists and workers, who are pledged to the working out of some ideal which seems to them to embody all that is desirable and to solve the problem as they see it around them. Under this group could be placed the leaders and dictators of the world at this time, no matter by what name they call themselves. That their methods may not be desirable, is of course often true but is relatively immaterial. Rightly or wrongly, they are working under the inspiration of an idea; they are bringing about definite changes in the minds of their fellow men and in world conditions; they are evoking a mental response from the public and the world. They are, therefore, placing the world in their debt, by inaugurating those changes which are altering the world rhythm and speeding up its tempo. They are thus preparing us for the still more revolutionary changes of the new age. Some of them are to be found included in the New Group of World Servers.

Members of the New Group of World Servers stand for the following ideals:

1. They believe in an inner world government and in an emerging evolutionary plan. They can see its signs down the ages. That they may express the significance of this inner world government and of the planetary Hierarchy in varying terms, is inevitable. That they may regard it from the peculiar angle of their own tradition and schooling is also inevitable but unimportant. That which is of importance is that they are in touch with the centre of energy which is attempting to guide human affairs; they know something of the detail of the immediate

plan, and to the furtherance of this they are bending all their energies.

2. They are steadily cultivating an international spirit of good will and to this they consecrate every effort. They avoid all points of dissension, regarding them as incidental to the point in evolution which the race has reached and they are convinced of the inevitable change for the better which is on its way. They emphasise the point of common endeavour and seek to interpret to the public the trend of the present world efforts as these begin the work of swinging the world on to new paths and producing in the minds of the people new and better ideals.

3. They seek to teach also the fact that the many national, religious and social experiments are only modes of expansion, ways of growth and needed lessons. They seek to point out that the effects of these will be twofold. First, they will demonstrate the usefulness of those lines of thought and consequent methods which will eventually bring about the release of mankind from its present limitations and distress. These experiments are not lost effort. They have a definite place and purpose. Second, they will demonstrate the recognition of those methods and techniques in government and religion which are undesirable, because they spread the virus of hatred, breed class and racial distinctions and are consequently detrimental to world understanding, international good will and spiritual amity.

There is no thinking man today in prominent position who does not in his highest moments appreciate the necessity for world peace, international order and religious understanding —all leading in the last analysis to economic stability. The right order by which men will find that stability is the ancient one that certain fraternities have ever emphasised:—Unity, Peace and Plenty. They lead sequentially and automatically from one to the other. The major instrument today for the achievement of world unity is the New Group of World Servers. It is as yet only potential but, given opportunity, and the necessary means to go forward with its work, it can make real changes in the public consciousness during the next few years and eventually can swing the mass of public opinion behind it. It can go forward to a large usefulness and can constitute eventually a most potent instrument to bring about the needed unity, peace and plenty. Their usefulness, however, can only be brought about by a strenuous effort and by constant self-sacrifice on the part of all who know something of the aims of the group and what the Plan seeks to bring about.

b. Immediate Lines of Activity and Techniques

Two immediate lines of activity are imperative. The members of the New Group of World Servers must have the above outlined ideals and objectives held constantly before them and they must also, as far as is possible, be brought in touch with each other. This work calls for immediate attention. The aims and ideals of the New Group of World Servers must also be presented constantly and clearly to the thinking public. The form in which this must be done and the medium used is for the associated servers to decide. Attention should be called to those activities which are obviously in line with the Plan, and the work and the programmes of the World Servers wherever they are found and located must be made known and aided. To do this, we need to combine wise and deliberate action with speed, owing to the urgency of the crisis. Those whose function it is to cooperate and help will appear, but our spiritual perception must be alert to recognise them. They must evoke recognition, first of all, through their spiritual idealism and secondly, in the field of work, through efficiency and capability. It is essential that they possess, as far as possible, the qualities of intuitive spiritual perception, but it is also imperative that they possess practical experience and training in efficiency in the work of moulding public opinion, in the circulation of ideas and in the understanding of human relations in the various fields of human expression.

By means of right inner activity and wise leadership, the New Group of World Servers will respond increasingly to the presented new ideas and will grow in strength, optimism, inner relation and interplay. They will and should become a strong united body in the outer world. The test will then be to hold the inner clarity of vision and the inner subjective relationships and, at the same time, pursue the work in the world with united, intelligent effort and with success. The true values, based on good will and brotherhood and founded in man's innate divinity, must be skillfully preserved; the right use of opportunity, plus the consecrated utilisation of world power, will call forth that skill in action which comes from true dedication and right meditation.

The New Group of World Servers has the immediate task of achieving power in moulding men's ideas to the needed changes of thought and the new technique of work all over the world. To do this, there must be the explanation of the ideas which lie behind the group and a clear statement of those parts of the Plan which are of immediate application. There must be a steady emphasis upon the reality of that which is inner and subjective (the world of real values) and upon the dynamic power of ideas as they control, and can be shown to control, all that is happening in every disturbed nation today. *What is going on in the world today is the working out of ideas.* As to the technique to be employed certain contrasts might be touched upon.

All nations at this time are engrossed with the imposition of some idea, or group of ideas, upon their peoples. This seems to the leaders, no matter how enlightened they may be, to necessitate force in some form or another and to call for drastic coercion. This must necessarily be the case where the time factor is misinterpreted. The immediate good of the people as a whole is felt by the leaders far to outweigh any temporary happenings to individuals and smaller groups. In the work of the New Group of World Servers, this time element will be better understood and the work must be carried forward with as much rapidity as possible, yet without any coercion, mental or physical. The laying of right foundations and the promulgation of right principles is of tremendous importance and must be ensured, but there must be no undue emphasis laid upon the regimenting of men's thoughts within a given time. With care, with prevision, with forethought and with skill must the ground be laid and the arguments given for the fostering of good will and the growth and spread of brotherhood on an international scale.

Theoretically, the ideal of brotherhood has been presented by many organisations, by many fraternities and many theosophical bodies; but those who have promulgated the idea of brotherhood in these various organisations are themselves too separative and sectarian to carry forward the work constructively. Theirs is not now the function to organise the men of good will in the world for they insist on labels, on certain exclusions, on working for their organisation more than for humanity, and on the necessity of people to affiliate with them. They emphasise the need to adhere to certain formulated beliefs, such as the doctrine of reincarnation as the basis of brotherhood, or the fact of the Masters as the background of the Plan; but men of good will can believe all or none of this. Such doctrines do not affect their recognition of certain great evolutionary trends, nor the necessity to recognise man's essential relationships. That the service rendered by the groups who have promulgated these ideas is immeasurable and that humanity is deeply in their debt is undoubtedly true. That hundreds of the members of the various organisations are affiliated with the New Group of World Servers is also entirely correct; but the materialising of these ideas, which have hitherto remained theoretical, is the prime function of the New Group of World Servers. They have to remove the whole theory from the realm of sentiment, of idealism, and of mystical aspiration and must bring the question, as a concrete demonstrated factor, before the public.

They must place the emphasis upon the expression of good will and the fulfilment of the law of love and not upon affiliation with organisations, with their labels and their doctrines. The New Group of World Servers must keep itself free of all of these, for otherwise the work will crash upon the ancient rocks of doctrine and of organisation. The members of the New Group must remain loosely linked together by their mutual good will and the unanimity of their objectives, expressed irrespective of national boundaries, racial distinctions and religious prejudices. It must throw the weight of its influence behind all movements, which are struggling to overcome differences and which express similar aims. Its members will sponsor, aid and foster many endeavours which work toward international understanding and synthesis, and express those religious interpretations which teach the spirit of unity.

The power which the New Group of World Servers will eventually wield, will be drawn from two sources:—first, from that inner centre or subjective world government, whose members are responsible for the spread of those ideals and ideas which have led humanity onwards from age to age. This inner centre has always existed and the great leaders of the race, in every field, have been connected with it. The great idealists and world workers, (such as the Christ and His great brother, the Buddha, and those lesser workers, such as Plato, Spinoza, Abraham Lincoln, or Florence Nightingale) have all been associated with this centre. The range of these associates is tremendous and the grades of these workers are many, but self sacrificing work for the betterment of human living and love of their fellow men have distinguished them all. Yet all drew their light and inspiration from this central focal point. The members of this government may be alive in physical bodies or discarnate. It is assumed that there is belief in immortality among those who read these pages—a belief in the perpetuation of the conscious soul in some dimension. These great souls are primarily distinguished by the fact that they know no mental limitation, and their inclusiveness is such that for them there are no racial distinctions nor any religious differences.

The second source from which the New Group of World Servers will draw its power will be from the men of good will in the world at any given time. They will be able to swing into activity at any moment such a weight of thought and such a momentous public opinion that they will eventually be in a position definitely to affect world affairs. One of their functions will be to bring into touch with each other, men of similar ideals and also to direct and further their efforts.

Knowledge of these ideals will be spread everywhere in the face of opposition and distrust; these truths must be expressed in every possible language and by every available means, and every available person must be utilised to circulate them. No effort should be spared at the present time and for the next few years. This work must first of all, be undertaken through the medium of the printed page and later, when trained people are available, through the medium of the spoken word. There must be synthesis of effort and the elimination of unnecessary and personal aspects of the work.

Members of the New Group of World Servers learn mostly through the ear and through that careful attention which comes from an inner attitude of constant *listening*. They are unfolding that spiritual perception which is latent but unused in the average man. They have to catch the new Words of Power as they come forth from the centre of spiritual light and force in the world and, at the same time, they must be attentive to the cry of humanity as it voices its highest hopes, longings and desires. This attitude of listening and of a subsequent prompt readjustment of the inner, received commands, is characteristic of the New Group of World Servers. The mass of people whom they will eventually gather around them must be taught, and learn through the eye, through the printed page, and later through a sensing of the vision. These two points must be remembered in planning the work and in finding the workers.

A word should be spoken here about the dangers the New Group of World Servers should seek to avoid. It must not be forgotten, first of all, that many people of many races and religious views, form a part, consciously or unconsciously, of this group. Some of them are so close to the Plan that their clarity of vision and their understanding is very real. They know. They need to be very sure, however, as to their right action from the angle of time. Skill in action is their main problem and not accuracy of perception. Others are not so close to the Plan and only know it in a vague and general way. They are consecrated and dedicated souls, but personal ambition and national and religious prejudices, still govern their minds, their reactions and their habits of speech. They sometimes resent the fact that others of different race, tradition and religious sentiment may be as close to the Plan and the Custodians of the Plan as they are. They question the authority of individuals in the New Group of World Servers and sometimes work towards the undoing of disciples in the same field as their own. This must not be. There is no time today for such trifling things as personal prestige, or for the emphasising of one organisation at the expense of another, or for the assumed priority of this or the other teaching. These are the things that do not matter, but which do hinder. What is of importance at this time is the unified stand which can be made by the men of good will in the world during the next few years in order to turn the tide in human affairs, avert possible catastrophe and bring in the era of unity, peace and plenty. Personal ambitions have to go. Personal desire, self defence, or self assertiveness have no place in the ranks of the New Group of World Servers. How can good will be fostered in the world, if those who profess it are fighting amongst themselves? How can the Plan of the Great Ones make progress and the leadership of the world pass into the hands of those who have a definitely spiritual objective if they are quarreling over place, position, and precedence? Personalities do not count and only souls have power.

Let all of us, therefore, who belong to the New Group of World Servers or who respond to their message of good will, sacrifice our personal differences, our petty interpretations, and our selfish ambitions upon the altar of world service and friendships. Thus we can offer to the Custodians of the Plan an instrument which They can freely use.

Another danger may arise if undue emphasis is laid upon the organisation aspect of the New Group of World Servers. It must never be forgotten that there is here no ordinary organisation, such as is usually found in the world. The group is an organism, not an organisation. It is not a propaganda group, as that term is usually understood. It is not interested in politics, religion or place. Its work is the educating of the human being and the expanding of the human consciousness, so that the newer and truer ideas may be grasped. Its function is the spreading of the message of international good will and religious unity. The members of the New Group of World Servers are primarily interpreters. That they may have high place and position, that they may be powerful and influential people, that they may work through the spoken and the printed word, that they may employ every possible means which brains and money can use in their endeavour, and that they may evidence the highest skill in action will be true if things progress as desired; but all these things are to be regarded as simply a means to an end—the production of world-wide good will, of intelligent and loving understanding and unity, peace and plenty.

The outer organisation is of importance in so far as it leads to the skillful use of opportunity and money, but the organisation is again only a means to an end. The organisation of the New Group of World Servers is not possible. They must ever remain unorganised and unlabelled, free to work as they individually see fit. It is the organisation of the available resources to which we refer, so that the Plan may be promoted, the ideals become practical and the work be carried intelligently forward.

The various plans under consideration for the furthering and growth of the New Group of World Servers, should and will go steadily forward. The ideas briefly outlined above should be worked out in detail. People must be trained to work for the expansion of these ideas. The general public must be educated as to the aims and objectives of the new group. Meditation groups should be formed, dedicated to the work of contacting the vision and of drawing in the needed wisdom and power. The Great Invocation should be increasingly used, and daily and hourly must the Invocation be sent forth. The gist of that which is here set forth should be rearranged and readapted for the use of the general public for it is only through constant reiteration that men learn, and these things must be said again and again before the real work of the New Group of World Servers can make itself felt.

The function of the New Group is to balance the forces leading to disintegration and destruction by embodying in itself the forces of integration and construction. The New Group will eventually offset the tendency (so prevalent at this time) towards racial hatreds, and the teaching given out will tend to negate the present ideas which are powerful in producing the current cleavages and barriers among men, thus causing separation and war. Where there is an appearance of a group or groups, expressing ideas which potently emphasise one angle of public opinion and one aspect of life, there must inevitably appear, under the law of balance, that which will offset it. At the present point in the history of the race, the groups which foster the spirit of cleavage and which build up barriers to impede the free spirit of man, have appeared first. They do their needed work, for they too are included in the Plan. Then, under the law, there must appear the group or groups which embody those ideas which lead to integration and constructive building. They will swing the world on to a higher turn of the spiral; they will heal the breaches, break down the barriers, and end the cleavages.

c. FUNCTIONS OF THE NEW GROUP OF WORLD SERVERS

It would be of value at this time to indicate three of the functions of this New Group so that there may be a clear picture of the work that must be accomplished during the next few years. This work is intended:

1. To produce a balancing of the forces present in the world today and responsible for the widespread unrest and chaos, so that it will be possible for the race to swing back to a point of equilibrium.

2. To act as the interpreters of the new attitudes and the new activities which must eventually govern men in the coming New Age.

3. To bring about the eventual synthesis and unification of the men of good will and of understanding into one coherent body. The many who are working in isolated fashion in the various fields of human endeavour (political, religious, scientific and economic), must be brought into touch with each other, and thus made to realise their essential unity.

The major objective and aim of all who are associated with the New Group of World Servers is to bring order out of chaos, and to resolve the widely separative issues of modern life into some kind of stability. Men would then have time to make the needed readjustments, to think through to a few vital conclusions, and to bring about a period of relative quiet in which to order the newer ways of living, so that the wider issues may be perceived and developed.

At present, such is the distress of mind, so great is the economic suffering, and so deep seated is the widespread illusion, that there is no opportunity to precipitate that which is imminent. It is not possible for the new ideas, which constitute the coming ideals of the race, to make any real headway. As yet, these ideas are only sensed and appreciated by a few intuitives and thinkers; the masses remain unaware of the implications of the new order. These thinkers may be oriented towards unity and good will, but the majority seize upon the ideals presented to them, bend them to their own ambitions, and distort and misapply them to their own selfish ends. They enforce drastic measures upon the people in order to bring about the acceptance of these ideas by an ignorant and dissatisfied public opinion.

We live in an era of extremes,—of extreme riches and extreme poverty; of extreme ignorance and extreme learning; of extreme discontent and the extreme satisfaction of personal ambitions; of extreme selfishness and extreme self-sacrifice. On every hand can be seen the wrecking of the institutions of the past, with consequent chaos and disaster, despair and suffering. At the same time we have the loud shouting and the active work of certain idealists, who seize upon the presented opportunity to swing the masses and the nations into certain activities in the spheres of government and religion. Their measures seem right and good to the self-imposed leaders, but they are often, in the last analysis, only misinterpreted ideals, growing out of a dimly sensed idea, and are usually unjustly enforced and wrongly applied. Between these extremes the masses swing,—inert, helpless, unthinking, easily swayed, regimented and standardised.

In every country in the world today, men of good will and of true understanding are to be found. Many thousands of them are known. They are however, either ridden by fear or by a feeling of futility, and by the realisation that the work to be done is so stupendous that their little isolated efforts are utterly useless to break down the barriers of hate and separation everywhere to be found. They realise that there is apparently no systematised spread of the principles which seem to hold the solution of the world problem; they have no conception of the numerical strength of those who may be thinking as they do, and they are consequently rendered impotent through their loneliness, their lack of unity, and the dead weight of the surrounding inertia. The powerful thinker or the ambitious demagogue, and the man with a true love of his country (but with his own selected ideas as to the right solution of that country's problem) are today availing themselves of the general inertia and of the world crisis and depression in order to impose (if need be, by force) those systems of governments and of control which will materialise their interpretations of the ideal. These the masses have to accept, and because they normally take the line of least resistance without thinking, they are easily regimented into compliance.

The argument of the leaders is that the masses have not the long vision, and do not, and cannot, know what is good for them. This is undoubtedly true. They must, therefore, be told what to do, and be led blindly or by force to that state and form of civilisation which the leaders and their associates believe (often quite sincerely) to be the best. In the process, those who disagree or who are thinking for themselves must necessarily go to the wall and be silenced, for the good of the whole. Such is the general situation, with certain national differences of no major importance in the light of the basic problem. The well-being of the national life may be sensed and desired, but the integration of that national life into the greater whole of humanity—of this the leaders seem, as yet, to have but little vision.

Attack by one party upon another party in public, national or political life, or of one group of thinkers (advocating their peculiar ideas) upon another group of thinkers with differing ideas, has long been the custom. In this process the more powerful obliterate the weaker, and the masses are exploited and told what to do and to think, with no real effort to bring them into a condition of right understanding. It is the same in the religious field, but the religious differences of the race are of such old standing that there is no need to enumerate them here. Militarists and pacifists in their many groups, Communists and conservatives, socialists and Nazis, republicans and Fascists, democrats and progressives, labour and capital, Catholics and Protestants, agnostics and fanatics, politicians and idealists, criminals and the enforcers of the misinterpreted law, ignorant masses and the intelligent few, plus the class distinctions, the racial differences, and the religious feuds in both hemispheres, have reduced the world to turmoil and complete disunion and feebleness.

Out of this condition, how shall order be restored? How can the economic situation be stabilised, and the world be brought to a condition where there is a just and right sufficiency for all? How can national differences be healed and racial hatreds be ended? How can the many religious groups pursue their work of leading men to an expression of their divinity along the lines of individual heritage, and yet at the same time exist in harmony and present a united front to the world? How can wars be ended and peace be brought about on earth? How can a true prosperity be established, which shall be the result of unity, peace and plenty?

Only in one way. *By the united action of the men and women of good will and understanding in every country and in every nation.* Steadily and quietly, with no sense of hurry, must they do three things:—

First, they must discover each other and be in touch with each other. Thus the sense of weakness and of futility will be offset. This is the first duty and task of the New Group of World Servers.

Secondly, they must clarify and elucidate those basic principles of right living, good will and harmony, which are recognised, but not applied, by all right thinking people today. These principles must be formulated in the simplest terms and made practical in action.

Thirdly, the general public must be educated in these principles. Steadily, regularly and systematically, they must be taught the principles of brotherhood, of an internationalism which is based on good will and love of all men, of religious unity, and of cooperative interdependence. The individual in every nation and group must be taught to play his important part with good will and understanding; the group must shoulder its responsibility to other groups; and the responsibility of nation to nation and of all nations to the world of nations must be explained and emphasised.

This is no idle or mystical, impractical program. *It undermines and attacks no authority or government. It is not interested in the overthrow of rulers or the downfall of any political or national party.* It calls for intelligent and practical effort. It will call for the cooperation of many types of mind and many trained executives. The men of good will in every country must be discovered, and all who respond to these ideals must be gathered together through mailing lists. Their cooperation must be sought and systematised. This program will call, eventually, for the assistance of many lecturers and writers, who will work along the same idealistic lines but with differing methods. Through their knowledge of their own country, and of the best way to bring these basic truths home to their own nationals, they must be left free to work as they see best for their particular nation. They, and all men and women of good will constitute the New Group of World Servers. A central group, chosen from among them, should synthesise this work and coordinate it, whilst giving the widest latitude to individual servers and workers.

This program will require patience and much cooperative work. The members of the New Group of World Servers must be discovered through their reaction to these ideals; they must be trained in the new policies, and educated in the technique of right thought, non-aggressive action, and the elimination of antagonisms of every kind; they must be taught the manner by which these basic ideals of world unity, economic synthesis and religious cooperation are to be expressed and attained. The law of *Love*, expressed *intelligently*, must be applied to all human relationships.

This work of educating the men and women of good will in the world must be proceeded with as rapidly as possible. The work must, however, be carried on with no infringement of harmony. There must be no interference with national preferences and programs, and no belittling of national governments, no matter what they may be. No political activity should be carried on in the name of the New Group of World Servers. Such action would continue the old methods and perpetuate the old hatreds. There must be no attack upon any party or group, and no criticism of any leader or national activity. Such old methods have long been tried and have failed to bring peace on earth. The members of the New Group of World Servers, and those associated with them, stand for no party, neither for nor against any group or form of control. This is their imperative position. For attack or counter-attack they have not time, energy or money. Yet their attitude is not one of "passive non-resistance". They are at work balancing world forces, and fostering the growth of that group of men who stand for good will, understanding and brotherhood.

The world of men today can be divided into two major groups. They are those who are fighting *for* some political party, some form of national government, some religious, social or economic attitude. They are against all that is not of their inclination. There are those who are opposed to them, and who are ranged *against* them. Partisanship, fighting for or against, and party spirit distinguish the modern world of men. With these activities, which lead to separation and division and strife, the New Group of World Servers have no time or interest. They stand for those attitudes which will eventually produce a third party, free from political and religious hatreds. As yet they are unknown, unrealised, and relatively powerless to make a definite impression on world thought. If, however, there is skill in action and an adherence to the principles of harmonious cooperation, they can, in a very few years, demonstrate real power and influence.

The work can then swing into its second cycle of pronounced and definite influence. This will be possible only if those who have this vision will make every effort and every possible sacrifice of time and money to bring it about. Between the exploited and the exploiting, the warlike and the pacifist, the masses and the rulers, this group will stand, taking no sides, demonstrating no partisan spirit, fomenting no political or religious disturbance, and feeding no hatreds, either of individuals, nations or races. They will stand as the interpreters of right human relations, for the basic oneness of humanity, for *practical* brotherhood, for positive harmlessness in speech and writing, and for that inner synthesis of objectives which recognises the value of the individual and at the same time the significance of group work. The propagation of these ideas and the spread of the principles of good will will produce this third group in world affairs.

In a few years' time, if the work is carried forward along these lines, public opinion will be forced to recognise the potency of this movement towards peace, international understanding, and mutual good will. Eventually, the numerical strength of the men and women of good will in the world will be so great that they will be able to influence world events. There will then be enough people enlisted in the cause of good will to affect definitely the trend of world affairs.

No idle pacifism will be taught. It is no mystical dream which waits for God to take action and which relies on the future to straighten things out. It is no impractical idea, incapable of application. It is the plan for the development of a group of people, gathered out of every nation, who are trained in the spirit of good will, and who possess such a clear insight into the principles that should govern human relations in world affairs, that they can work with power in the field of human peace and understanding. It is a systematised process of education. By its means, men and women everywhere are to be trained to live as exponents of good will in every department of life, and the power of intelligent good will to adjust difficulties in every department of human affairs is unbelievably potent. But as yet, that growing spirit of good will has not been intelligently developed, applied, and systematised. Thousands of men and women are ready today throughout the world to be so trained, and to be brought into cooperation with each other, so that there can eventually be unity of effort in the cause of peace and harmonious relations. The New Group of World Servers seeks to discover these people, and unify them into a coherent group.

In conclusion, it might be said, therefore, that the New Group of World Servers seeks to help in the restoration of world balance and peace through the activity—coordinated, definite, and applied—of this emerging group of people, who can constitute a third group or "middle party" (to borrow a phrase from the field of politics) between those who are fighting for, and those who are fighting against, any group, religious organisation, political affiliation or form of government.

Through their work, the consciousness of humanity will be steadily evoked on the side of righteousness and peace. Righteousness will be regarded as the conscious establishing of right relations with one's fellow men. When the mass conscience is evoked and functioning, a stabilized opinion will be possible, and will be so strong that, in every country, acts of cruelty, of oppression, of enforced obedience through penalising, of selfish aggrandisement at the expense of the helpless, of personal ambition, and of war will no longer be tolerated.

The time must come in the history of humanity when so large a number of people have been awakened to the finer spiritual issues and values that the old attitudes and activities will be rendered eternally impossible on a large scale. This coming period will be the correspondence in the life of humanity to that stage in the life of the disciple and Christian wherein he is no longer a victim of his wrong tendencies and habits, but begins to dominate them by imposing his enlightened spiritual will upon his lower nature. This stage can now be developed in our present day humanity for the first time in its history. One of the main functions of the New Group of World Servers is to bring about these changed attitudes, to foster the growth of a true public opinion through the education of the thinking people in the principles of good will and right relations. They in their turn will educate the masses. Thus it will be possible to profit by the emerging tendency towards righteousness and good will which is today most definitely present, even if weak and as yet but little realised.

The second function of the New Group of World Servers is to interpret the ideals and objectives which should govern the race and to familiarise the public with the immediate possibilities. By these means, they will eventually awaken in the masses an intelligent response, an ardent desire and a right activity. In this way the idea of the few will become the ideal of the many, and will finally make its appearance as a working fact in human consciousness. The new, compelling, inner impulses must stand revealed to the human intellect. The growing tendency towards brotherhood (of which our modern philanthropic enterprises are an illustration), the ideal of group welfare in contradistinction to individual aims of a selfish and ambitious kind, and the enunciation of those principles which must and will govern the next world cycle,—these interpretations and their right and intelligent application must be carried forward. Through this form of mass education the new age will begin to make its potencies felt. The activities of the New Group of World Servers will lead to the establishment of two momentous facts. These are as yet only theories to the mass, though established knowledge to the few. They are:—

1. The fact of an intelligent, unfolding *Plan* which underlies the entire evolutionary process of the world, and which history and the growth of human consciousness demonstrate infallibly.
2. The fact of immortality, or of life which persists when divorced from the body.

The recognition of these two facts will bring about great changes in world attitudes and governments, when the underlying purpose of world events is grasped and when the hope of immortality becomes a known accepted fact. World affairs and modern life conditions will then be seen in true perspective. Upon this we need not here enlarge, but when it is seen that the growth of good will in the world is the normal emergence of that which is inevitable, and when all that is occurring is seen in its relation to an eternal future, there are carried to our minds implications of profound magnitude to the race.

The third function of the New Group of World Servers, and one that is of immediate import today, is to gather together into one loosely knit group, the men and women of good will throughout the world. Those who respond to these ideas and who show no antagonistic reactions to these truths must be brought into relation with each other. This group is today in existence. The nucleus for the work is already there. Their numbers must be steadily increased and their usefulness developed by a steady education in the basic principles of good will, during the next five years. Sufficient momentum will then have been developed so as to make it possible to initiate right activity. The New Group of World Servers should then be in a position to mould public opinion.

d. Rules of Procedure

Such is the task with which the New Group of World Servers is faced. What should be the immediate procedure?

The following procedure is suggested. The details of its application will vary from time to time in the different countries.

The men and women of good will who are willing to listen, to consider and to work, must be found and contacted in every country.

Secondly, these men and women of good will should be subjected to an intensive training. This should be carried forward through printed pamphlets, personal contact, and correspondence; through lectures and discussions and eventually, if possible, through the medium of some periodical which will literally be the organ of the New Group of World Servers. It will carry information as to the activities which foster good will, international understanding, world education and scientific achievement.

At the end of that period there should be enough people in the world who are alive to these principles and to the opportunity, so that they can begin to make a definite impact upon the public consciousness. In this way the contacting of the true intelligentsia of the world will proceed with increased rapidity. The education of these thinkers should be carried on by the World Servers in conformity with the following rules:—

1. No word must be spoken or written which could be construed as evidencing partisanship, or as an attack upon any ruler, any form of government, or any national activity. "Hatred ceaseth not by hatred; hatred ceaseth by love."

2. Nothing must be published in any pamphlet, newspaper, circular or letter which could evoke antagonism from any government, any political party, any economic strategist, or any religious organisation. Only principles of universal application must be expressed, and no partisanship is permitted.

3. No race or nation must be regarded (either in the spoken or written word) as of greater importance essentially than any other race or nation. Humanity as a whole must be emphasised. Yet those who think otherwise than this must not be subjected to attack. Racial hatreds, religious differences, and national ambitions are to be ignored by this balancing third group, the New Group of World Servers.

4. Members of the New Group of World Servers are never to identify themselves with any political, religious or social propaganda. Such propaganda is separative in its effects,

and breeds divisions and hatreds. Some of the World Servers and men of good will may themselves be members of political, religious or other organisations committed to activity of the kind which causes divisions. This may happen through their past inclination, by enforced national discipline, by heredity, or by force of circumstances. When men of good will find themselves in such a situation, they can refrain from breeding hatred and from active antagonistic propaganda, and can regard their position as one which will enable them—in a very difficult setting—to interject the theme of brotherhood by living in a brotherly spirit, and by expressing understanding and love.

5. Units of Service in all nations must be built up steadily. A number of such units already exists. Their objectives are as follows:—

a. To educate the people in their nation in service, in kindly effort, and in non-aggressive action. A *positive harmlessness* will be inculcated, which in no way negates intense, intelligent activity, and the propagation of those ideals which lead to mutual understanding, and eventually to unity, peace and plenty.

b. To provide in every country and eventually in every city, a central bureau where information will be available concerning the activities of men and women of good will all over the world, and of those organisations and groups and parties who are working along the lines of international understanding, mutual cooperation, religious unity, and economic interdependence. Thus, many will find those who will cooperate with them in their particular endeavour to promote world peace. What is being accomplished along these lines in the world today can thus be synthesised and studied.

c. To bring together the members of the New Group of World Servers and those associated with them through similarity of ideas and vision, so that in every country and major city the World Servers can find those whose aims are the same as theirs and who are pledged to the same service and activity. The same language of brotherhood and kindness will be taught, and thus mutual confidence and a spirit of optimism will be promoted.

d. To list and investigate the work and the ideals of all groups which purport to have an international program which tends to heal world differences and national quarrels, to work for a better understanding between the races, and to harmonise religious distinctions and class wars. A study will be made of their techniques and modes of work. When such groups are found to be coloured with aims that are truly spiritual and harmonising, when they are true healers of differences and under the guidance of men of good will, cooperation will be offered. Such groups now exist.

6. No secrecy must ever be permitted in the work of the New Group of World Servers. Secret societies are organisations ever open to attack and suspicion. The New Group has nothing to hide, and their files and methods of work must ever be open to investigation. The Secret Services and Intelligences of any country must find all literature and information easily available. No secret lists must be kept. Members of the New Group of World Servers must be encouraged to seek out those in high places in government circles and church, and enlighten them as to the objectives of the Group.

It takes no great effort of imagination to see that, if this work of educating public opinion is pursued, and the finding of the men of good will is carried forward, much can be accomplished. Thousands can be gathered into the New Group of World Servers and can work in the Units of Service. This is the initial task. How to use the weight of that good will and how to employ that intelligent understanding will gradually appear out of the work accomplished and the world situation. The needed right activity will be apparent when the time comes. The trained use of power on the side of good will and international understanding will be possible, and the complexion of world affairs can then be changed.

This can be done; not by the usual warlike measures of the past or the enforced will of some group, but through the educated opinion of the intelligent masses,—an opinion which will be based on a trained good will, the intelligent understanding of the needs of humanity, and with no antagonism to any living being. The initial concepts must be carried forward in their essential purity; the process of thus educating the public must go forward with diligence and tact, and wisdom must be cultivated in order to avoid all antagonism, all criticism and all hatred. The power of such a group, working in such a fashion, will be tremendous. They can accomplish phenomenal results. This is no idle promise, but it is contingent upon the preservation of the initial concepts and the steady practice of good will.

e. The World Servers and the May Full Moon

The Month of May is one of deepest significance to all who are affiliated with the Great White Lodge (as are all true esotericists) in that the Wesak Festival takes place and is of moment and deep import. The period is always one of prime interest and rare opportunity, but the Wesak Festival of 1936 was unique and the Lodge of Masters prepared for it for six months. May I add also that the Buddha Himself in His high place and the blessed Lord Maitreya (known to Christian disciples as The Christ) have since then been in close communication with each other and cooperating in order to bring about a receptivity on the part of the human family to a possible outflow of spiritual force which may serve to turn the tide of the present distress, depression and uncertainty and thus inaugurate an era of peace and of soul-culture. This item of information is of interest, is it not?

In connection with these Festivals every May, I am presenting you an opportunity to serve and to bring about the desired objective of peace. It is possible for us, each of us,—in our small measure to cooperate in the intended Plan, and therefore what I have to say takes on another aspect and lays the responsibility of materialising that Plan upon the Earth upon the shoulders of each and all of us. The work has been brought about through an intensive effort in two directions,—one the effort of the Hierarchy to impress that Plan upon the minds of men and to convey the needed power and understanding to effect the intended work, and secondly the effort of all disciples and aspirants to respond and bring through into manifestation that which is waiting on the subjective side of life. How, therefore, is that work at this time going forward?

This planet of ours, the Earth, is at this time the focal point of much attention on the part of the Administrators of the Plan Who today are working in conjunction with certain types of force and with certain Spiritual Entities other than those to be found at this time within the ring-pass-not of our planetary life. May I give here one hint without proceeding to elaboration? This hint can be accepted or rejected according to the intuition of the individual student.

The Buddha has a special function at this time as an interplanetary mediator, and in this capacity (at the coming May Festivals) He will attempt to bring certain Spiritual Beings into touch with our Earth Hierarchy. They have expressed Themselves as willing to aid in the present crisis. That aid, if the effort prove successful, will come in the form of a much increased spiritual inflow of energy of a kind more potent and of a quality somewhat different to any at this time pouring into and through our planetary life. Those aspirants and disciples who can train themselves to the realisation of an increased spiritual responsibility and can preserve an inner quietness and a focussed esoteric attentiveness can be swept into this tide of spiritual force and can then and thus serve humanity's need. As transmitters they meet that need; as interpreters they increase the capacity of the human being to respond and to understand.

In order to effect this transmission of force, a peculiar interchange of ideas and of cooperation is going on between the Lord Buddha and the Lord Maitreya, and They are subjecting Themselves to a most definite form of training in order to present to these interested Spiritual Beings Who are seeking to help the planet, more adequate channels of service. Three Masters from each of the seven ray groups of Masters are in Their turn attempting a closer cooperation with the Great Lords in preparation for the opportunity to be presented. These twenty-three spiritual forces are banded together to act as a group channel of service on the day of the Wesak Festival and particularly at the hour of the full moon.

A call has been sent out to the entire Hierarchy of Masters to prepare Themselves for an intensive "Holy Month" of accelerated service, and all of the Masters on the Seven Rays— no matter what Their departmental work may at this time be—are getting into immediate cooperation and close contact

with the three Masters on Their particular Ray who are acting as the ray intermediaries. The service is new and peculiar
and as to its particular nature there is no need for me to
explain as I should not be understood.

In Their turn, the Hierarchy of Masters is calling to all
working initiates and disciples and to all aspirants of mental
focus to cooperate as fully as they can in an intensive effort
to increase the receptivity of humanity to the new forces
which can be released to perform their benevolent synthesising work during the month of May.

To this intensive cooperation we are called. Should the
two Great Lords and the focussed and attentive Hierarchy
succeed in producing what might be regarded as a form of
planetary alignment and the needed open channel through
which these extra-planetary energies can pour, it still remains
for the disciples of the world and for the New Group of
World Servers to act as the medium of transmission and communication between the world thinkers and this inner spiritual group of workers. We have, therefore, the focussed
Hierarchy in deep attentiveness under the group composed
of the two Lords, the twenty-one chohans and the Masters of
the seven rays. We have the disciples of the world and the
New Group of World Servers given the opportunity to focus
in their turn and act as a channel of transmission. We have
also the unhappy and bewildered world of men, waiting in
eager expectancy for an event which can take place if the
aspirants of the world measure up to the opportunity.

One item of esoteric information is of interest here. The
period of the Wesak Festival on the inner planes in 1936 and
1937 was extended to cover five days,—two preceding the
Festival itself, and two succeeding the Festival. The Wesak
hour is of momentous import. The two days of preparation
are to be known as "days of renunciation and detachment".

The day of the Festival is to be known as the "day of safe guarding" whilst the two succeeding days are called the "days of distribution". These words mean something different to the Hierarchy of Masters than they do to us and it is fruitless (as well as forbidden) to elucidate them in their deepest meaning. They mean, however, five days of a most intensive effort in service, leading to the renunciation of all which could hinder our usefulness as channels of spiritual force. It means that after due preparation, dedication and upward striving for the first two days, on the day of the Festival itself we simply regard ourselves as the recipients of, or the custodians of, as much of that inflowing spiritual force as we can possibly hold. As channels, we must be prepared to forget ourselves in the service of touching, containing and holding force for the rest of humanity. We must regard the Festival itself as a day of silence (I refer to an inner peace and silent solemnity that can be preserved unbroken though the outer man may be serving with his speech and spoken interest), a day of service carried forward entirely on esoteric levels, and of complete self-forgetfulness in the remembrance of humanity and its need. During that period, two thoughts only will hold our constant attention,—the need of our fellow men and the necessity of providing a group channel whereby the spiritual forces can be poured through the body of humanity under the expert guidance of the chosen members of the Hierarchy.

Remember, no matter who we are or where we may be placed or what is the nature of our environment, no matter how isolated we may feel or apart from those who may share our spiritual vision, each of us can that day and for the period immediately following and preceding it, work and think and act in group formation, and function as a silent distributor of force.

For two days prior to the full moon, we will hold the attitude of dedication and service and seek to assume that attitude of receptivity to that which our soul will impart which will make us of use to the Hierarchy. The Hierarchy works through groups of souls, and the potency of this group work is to be tested out. These groups in their turn contact and feed the waiting dedicated attentive personalities. On the day of the full moon, we attempt to hold ourselves steadily in the light. We will not formulate to ourselves what will happen nor will we look for results or for tangible effects.

On the two succeeding days, the focus of our attention will be steadily turned away from ourselves but also from the inner subjective planes to the outer world, and our efforts will be to pass on, or to pass through, that measure of spiritual energy that may have been contacted. Our work then in this particular and peculiar field of cooperation will then be ended.

This effort of the Hierarchy is a five days effort, preceded by a most intensive period of preparation. The work of getting ready for the opportunity starts for the Hierarchy exactly at the hour when "the sun began to move northward." But They tire not as do human beings and it is not possible for the human aspirant to keep up so long a period of preparation, no matter how deep his devotion.

When the Great Lord was on Earth, He told His disciples that successful spiritual effort of a healing nature went not forth except by prayer and fasting. Will you ponder on these words? This is a group effort towards a vast group healing and by prayer (sanctified desire, illumined thought and intense aspirational longing) and by the discipline of the physical body for a short period and for a definite objective, the work can be done.

What is it that should be accomplished at each momentous full moon in May? I shall state the objectives sequentially and in the order of their importance, and with as much clarity and brevity as this abstruse subject permits.

1. The releasing of certain energies which can potently affect humanity, and which will, if released, stimulate the spirit of love, of brotherhood and of good will on the earth. These energies are as definite and as real as those energies with which science occupies itself and calls the "cosmic rays". I am speaking of real energies and not of emotionally desired abstractions.

2. The fusion of all the men of good will in the world into an integrated responsive whole.

3. The invocation and the response of certain great Beings, Whose work can and will be possible if the first of the objectives is achieved through the accomplishment of the second objective. Ponder on this synthesis of the three objectives. By what name these Living Forces are called is entirely immaterial. They can be regarded as the vice-regents of God, Who can and will cooperate with the Spirit of Life and of Love upon our planet, the One in Whom we live and move and have our being. They may be regarded by certain thinkers as the Archangels of the Most High, Whose work has been made possible through the activity of Christ and His body of disciples, the true and living Church. They may be regarded by others as the guiding heads of the planetary Hierarchy, Who stand behind our planetary evolution, and Who seldom take an active outer part in the world activity, leaving it to the Masters of the Wisdom except in the time of an emergency such as this. By whatever name we call Them, They stand ready to aid, if the call comes forth with sufficient strength and power from the aspirants and disciples at the time of the May full moon and the June full moon.

4. The evocation from the inner side of a strenuous and one-pointed activity on the part of the Hierarchy of Masters,

those illumined Minds to Whom has been confided the work of world direction. A responsiveness is desired and can be effective between the following three groups:

a. The waiting and (at this time) anxious Hierarchy—anxious because even They cannot tell how humanity will react and whether men will be wise enough to avail themselves of the proffered opportunity. They stand, organised under the direction of the Christ, the Master of all the Masters, and the Teacher alike of angels and of men. He has been constituted the direct intermediary between the earth and the Buddha, Who is, in His turn, the consecrated intermediary between the entire waiting Hierarchy and the attentive Forces.

b. The New Group of World Servers, composed at this time of all those sensitive and consecrated servers of the race whose objective is world peace, who aim at the establishing of good will on earth as the basis for future living and world expansion. Originally, this group was composed of a handful of accepted disciples and consecrated aspirants. Its ranks have been opened during the past ten months to all those men of good will who are working actively for real understanding, who are willing to sacrifice themselves for the helping of humanity, and who see no separating bar of any kind, but feel alike to the men of all races, nationalities and religions.

c. The masses of men and women who have responded to the ideas which have been set forth, and who react favourably to the objectives of international understanding, economic interdependence and religious unity.

When these three groups of thinkers and servers are brought en rapport with each other, and when the three groups can be *aligned*, *even momentarily*, much can be accomplished; the gates of the new life can be opened, and the inflow of the new spiritual forces can take place. Such is the Group objective and idea.

May I now make an inquiry? Of what importance is this full moon of May to you personally? Does it seem to you of sufficient importance to warrant your utmost effort? Do you really believe that on that day there can truly come a release of spiritual energy of sufficient potency to change world affairs, provided the sons of men play their part? Do you really believe, and can you stand practically by that belief, that the Buddha on that day, in cooperation with the Christ, and with the Hierarchy of Illumined Minds, plus the proffered aid of some of the Thrones, Principalities and Powers of Light, Who are the higher correspondence of the powers of darkness, stand waiting to carry out God's plans, when given the right and the permission of men? Your major job at this time is not to wrestle with the powers of evil and the forces of darkness, but to awaken an interest in and mobilise the forces of light and the resources of men of good will, and of right inclination in the world today. Resist not evil, but so organise and mobilise the good, and so strengthen the hands of the workers on the side of righteousness and love, that evil will find less opportunity.

If you have faith as a grain of mustard seed in what I have told you, if you have staunch belief in the work of the spirit of God and in the divinity of man, then forget yourselves and consecrate your every effort, from the time you receive this communication, to the task of cooperating in the organised effort to change the current of world affairs by an increase in the spirit of love and good will in the world during the month of May.

In your effort to help the world at this time there are three things of a practical nature that can be done. I touch not upon the task of preparation which each one of you, as an individual, will carry on within yourselves. Purification, sacrifice, clear thinking, and an increased sensitivity must be actively desired and worked for by each of you, alone in the secret place of your own heart. The arranging of your affairs so that the week of the full moon can yield to you the fullest opportunity to cooperate must be your effort, and the use of a sane judgment and the expression of a real skill in action must be your attempted demonstration, as you seek to awaken your immediate circle to the importance of the moment. This I take for granted. I speak here of the general effort that you can make. This falls into three categories:

1. The active instruction and mobilising of the known aspirants and disciples of the world, no matter in what group they work, so that they may make due preparation, working in their own groups as they see fit.

2. The call to participate of all who can be reached advising them of the day of opportunity, mobilising them for a vast world effort to arouse afresh a spirit of good will, and calling for a united use of the Great Invocation on the day of the Wesak full moon. Every possible effort must be made by the workers in every country to increase the numbers of those who use this Invocation, and to familiarise the public with the ideals for which the New Group of World Servers stands. All whom you can reach in the countries of the world must be instructed and helped to spread the use of the Invocation in their own language, and with the wording that

will make it acceptable, and a widespread effort must be made to organise its simultaneous use on the day of the May full moon. Those who use it must be instructed to say the words aloud, thus making a volume of sound of real potency, and they must say it with all the power of their wills behind it. It is the invocation of the "will to good" that is the objective of the Forces Who can aid at this time. This realisation is of paramount importance.

3. The arranging of public meetings on as large a scale as possible, to be held on the day of the full moon of May. I mean by this that meetings should be held for the public at some time during the eighteen hours which precede and include the time of the full moon. The exact hour is immaterial, provided as many people as possible participate at some time during the preceding eighteen hours, thus laying the foundation for and aiding in the work which will take place at the time of the full moon. Those aspirants who can arrange to do so must, however, arrange to be in meditation, in group formation if possible, at the exact time, and their work will then be to capitalise on the energy then available, and to take advantage of the vortex of force generated earlier at the public meetings, and so throw the weight of the public demand for peace and light on the side of the effort of the Hierarchy.

The way in which these three objectives must be brought about, and the world be swept into an organised effort for world peace and cooperation, is to be decided upon by the exigencies of the time, the necessities of the occasion, and the varying circumstances of place, country and environing conditions.

The representatives of the various Units of Service in the different countries must be called upon to cooperate, and may receive this instruction in the cases where you know them and their interests. It is the general, widespread and intelligent use of the Great Invocation which is desired. The general public must be urged, through all possible agencies, to employ it. The radio, the press, must all be utilised, and all men of good will must be contacted, even if unenlightened from the occult angle, and even if they do not realise the guiding presence of the Hierarchy and the opportunity now offered by the united effort of the Buddha and the Christ.

Let all who seek to help consider with care what they can do and what is the contribution which they can make. Let them weigh up, after due thought, what they can sacrifice, and in what manner they can submerge their normally selfish personalities in this great "push" on the part of the Hierarchy, of the New Group of World Servers, and of the men of good will throughout the world. The barriers which separate man from man and nation from nation can go down. The spirit of peace can become so potent that naturally and sweetly the necessary adjustments can be made. The illumination of men's minds and the renewed organisation of man's efforts to brotherhood can be stimulated into fresh and increased activity.

Out of this quite possible great effort at integration which can be focussed at the time of the Wesak Festival, and intensified during the twenty four hours preceding the full moon, there can grow the real germ of the new age group, and of the new world and the new ideals. This group will function under no name, and will remain perfectly fluid and a free organisation, directed by no committee, but governed through the means of the intelligent cooperation of a group, representing the New Group of World Servers. These will belong to all nations and religions.

The call for the help of the world disciples and aspirants, who constitute the New Group of World Servers, has gone forth from the side of the Hierarchy and it has been made abundantly clear that no one is too weak or too unimportant to have something to offer; all can do something to bring to an end this present impasse, and thus make it possible for us to inaugurate a new era of peace and of good will. I would like to make clear, however, that it is no millennium for which we are working, and that our prime objective at this time is twofold:

1. To break an ancient rhythm and to establish a new and better one. To do this, *Time* is a paramount factor. If we can delay the crystallisation of an evil necessity, and so prevent that which might occur of a calamitous nature, it will give time for the processes of transmutation, for the dissipation of that which must precipitate in some form or other, and for the applied activities of the New Group of World Servers, who constitute our instrument in the world today.

2. To fuse and blend the united aspiration of all peoples at each May full moon—so that a channel can be cleared, opened and established between the New Group of World Servers (composed of all true disciples, aspirants, and men of real good will, no matter what their nationality or faith) and the waiting Hierarchy. Once this channel is permanently established and a large enough number of thinking men and women realise its function and possibilities, it will be easier for the Guides of the race to impress the public consciousness, and so sway public opinion. Thus humanity can be more

definitely guided, for there will emerge some conscious cooperation. *The establishing of such a channel by the world aspirants is possible.*

This is a scientific programme of work with which I have presented you. It is more than organised aspirational longing on the part of a large group of people. It is a strenuous mental endeavour, and involves the working with certain laws of the spiritual realm which are only just in process of becoming known.

There is a law called the Law of Magnetic Impulse or Polar Union which plays an active part here. This law governs the relation of the soul of a group to the soul of other groups. It governs the interplay, vital but unrealised yet as a potency, between the soul of the fourth kingdom in nature, the human, and the soul of the three subhuman kingdoms, and likewise of the three superhuman kingdoms. It is, owing to the major part which humanity has to play in the great scheme or Plan of God, the law which will be the determining law of the race. This will not, however, be the case until the majority of human beings understand something of what it means to function as souls. Then, under obedience to this law, humanity will act as a transmitter of light, energy and spiritual potency to the subhuman kingdoms, and will constitute a channel of communication between "that which is above and that which is below." Such is the high destiny before the race.

It is just here that I can perhaps best illustrate this law and aid our work at the coming Wesak Festivals.

Just as certain human beings have, through meditation, discipline and service, most definitely made a contact with their own souls, and can therefore become channels for soul expression, and mediums for the distribution into the world of soul energy, so these same men and women, in their aggregate, *form a group of souls*, en rapport with the source of spiritual supply. They have, as a group, and from the angle of the Hierarchy, established a contact and are "in touch" with the world of spiritual realities. Just as the individual disciple stabilises this contact and learns to make a rapid alignment and then, only then, can come into touch with the Master of his group and intelligently respond to the Plan, so does this group of aligned souls come into contact with certain greater Lives and Forces of Light, such as the Christ and the Buddha. The aggregated aspiration, consecration and intelligent devotion of the group carries the individuals of which it is composed to greater heights than would be possible alone. The group stimulation and the united effort sweep the entire group to an intensity of realisation that would otherwise be impossible. Just as the Law of Attraction, working on the physical plane, brought them together as men and women into one group effort, so the Law of Magnetic Impulse can begin to control them when, again as a group and only as a group, they unitedly constitute themselves channels for service in pure self-forgetfulness.

This thought embodies the opportunity immediately before all groups of aspirants and allied men of good will in the world today. If at the time of the May full moon they work together as a group of souls, they can accomplish much. This thought illustrates also the significance of this law which *does produce polar union*. What is needed to be grasped is that in this work, there is no personal ambition implied (even of a spiritual nature) and no personal union sought. This is not the mystical union of the scriptures or of the mystical tradition. It is not alignment and union with a Master's group or fusion with one's inner band of pledged disciples, nor even with one's own Ray life. All these factors constitute preliminary implications and are of an individual application. Upon this sentence I beg you to ponder. This union is a greater and more vital thing *because it is a group union.*

What we are seeking to do is to carry forward a group endeavour which is of such moment that, at the right time, it will produce, in its growing momentum, such a potent magnetic impulse that it will reach those Lives Who brood over humanity and our civilisation, and Who work through the Masters of the Wisdom and the assembled Hierarchy. This group endeavour will call forth from Them a responsive magnetic impulse which will bring together, through the medium of the aspiring group, the overshadowing beneficent *Forces.* Through the concentrated effort of these groups in the world today (who constitute subjectively *One* group) light and inspiration and spiritual revelation can be released in such a flood of power that it will work definite changes in the human consciousness and ameliorate conditions in this needy world. It will open men's eyes to the basic realities, which are as yet only dimly sensed by the thinking public. Then humanity itself will apply the necessary correctives, believing it can do so in the strength of its own sensed wisdom and strength; yet all the time, behind the scenes, stand the grouped world aspirants, working silently, in unison with each other and the Hierarchy, and thus keeping the channel open through which the needed wisdom, strength and love can flow.

There are, therefore, to be found in this great task the following relations and groupings. These must be considered and are as follows:

1. The Forces of Light and the Spirit of Peace, embodied Lives of tremendous group potency.
2. The Planetary Hierarchy.
3. The Buddha.

4. The Christ.
5. The New Group of World Servers.
6. Humanity.

You will note that the Buddha focusses in Himself the down-pouring forces, whilst the Christ focusses in Himself the out-going demand and the spiritual aspiration of the entire planet. This makes a planetary alignment of great potency. Should the needed work be accomplished at the Wesak Festivals, the needed adjustments in the world can be made. The success or failure lies largely in the hands of the New Group of World Servers.

In this tabulation, I have portrayed for you a little of what is implied in the words "The Law of Polar Union". The whole process concerns consciousness, and the results are to work out in consciousness, with the subsequent physical plane happenings, dependent upon the conscious realisation of the men of good will in, or out of, the New Group of World Servers.

Carried forward successfully and intelligently, it should be possible to inaugurate a new relation between the Hierarchy and mankind. This effort could, and let us hope it will, mark the beginning of a new type of mediatory work,—a work carried forward this time by a salvaging group of Servers, who are in training for the establishing of that group which will eventually save the world. This mediatory work involves the recognition of the Law of Magnetic Impulse, and with a desire to understand it, and to cooperate with Those Who wield it. Through its medium and the right understanding of the Law, it should be possible to establish the needed union between souls, who are in themselves the symbol of the Soul in all forms, and souls in prison. Much of the success of this endeavour will depend upon the intellectual grasp of the members of the New Group of World Servers of the implied technique. It will depend also upon their willingness to accept the idea of the opportunity present each full moon period, and also upon their readiness to work along the indicated lines. As yet they have no guarantee as to the accuracy of the claims regarding the importance of the full moon period, nor have they any personal knowledge of the situation as outlined. Some do not even know that there is a watching Hierarchy, but they are consecrated and selfless souls, and as such, belong to the New Group of World Servers. If they can aspire, pray, meditate and serve, focussing in unison with all other servers at the time of the May full moon, the salvaging of humanity can go forward with much greater speed than heretofore, and the results will be appreciably apparent.

For the individual disciple, the significance of this Law of Magnetic Impulse and the corresponding relationships in his own life, might also be tabulated:—

1. The world of souls on the higher mental levels.
2. The Master of his group.
3. The solar angel.
4. The aspiring disciple on the lower mental levels.
5. The personality, integrated and often troublesome.
6. The aspirant's environing associates.

It is useful for students to have these analogies in mind, for they can often arrive at release from the limitations of their lives and true comprehension of the larger issues, when they see that their little unimportant lives are only the reflection of greater and more important factors.

It is wise always to remember that on the plane of soul existence there is no separation, no "my soul and thy soul". It is only in the three worlds of illusion and maya that we think in terms of souls and bodies. This is an occult platitude and well known to you, but the re-emphasis of the well known truth may eventually bring home to you its exactitude.

3. The Great Approaches (*The Coming New Religion*)

a. The Soul of Humanity

It can be seen, therefore, that a very difficult interlude is now taking place in the world today. It is one wherein a process is being undergone by humanity which is similar to that which takes place so frequently in the life of an individual. The soul of the world is taking cognizance of outer affairs, preparatory to taking hold of the world situation. In the life of an aspirant, such interludes frequently occur. The personality is aware of conditions of difficulty and of turmoil. It has, however, had in the past moments of high spiritual revelation and of divine impulsation. It has been sure of its goal temporarily and it has known that the soul is the directing factor; some dim idea of the goal and of the purposes underlying those impulses which have been granted to it by the soul have been vouchsafed. But, for the moment, all that lies in the past. It seems as if the soul has retreated; that the period of contact and of surety has ended; and that nothing remains except difficulty, a sense of futility, and an urge to be freed from conditions. This is frequently of such intensity that all other interests seem dwarfed.

But the soul has *not* retreated and the inner spiritual conditions remain essentially unchanged. The divine impulses are still there and the soul is but gathering itself for a fresh effort and for a stronger and more determined preoccupation with the affairs of its shadow, its dim reflection, the personality.

What is true of the individual aspirant is equally true of

humanity, the world aspirant. In May, 1936, a great forward moving effort of the world soul took place and definite and unchangeable progress was made. This had a three-fold effect:

1. The lives of all true aspirants and disciples were subjected to a stimulating process, with definite and specific results of the desired nature.

2. The stimulation of the masses of men also took place; so that they could be enabled to respond more easily and truly to the impact of ideas. This also was uniquely successful.

3. The Hierarchy of souls who have achieved freedom and whom you call the planetary Hierarchy were able to approach closer to humanity and to establish a more definite relationship and a closer contact than had been possible at any time since mid-Atlantean times. This result was more universal than had been anticipated. This was the third of the "Great Approaches" made by the Hierarchy towards humanity. The success of these approaches is largely based on the intensity of the desire found in the world aspirants and among those who have, on their side, established also a "way of approach" through meditation and service. Their numbers being phenomenally greater than at any previous time, the year 1936 saw the Hierarchy make a step forward that was unprecedented (I had almost said, unexpected) in its experience. This was due to the world-wide activity of the New Group of World Servers.

I would like here to call your attention to the phrase I used above: "the Hierarchy of souls who have achieved freedom." I am not using that phrase in the ordinary sense. The aspirants and the disciples of the world employ it to signify the achieving of that liberty and that freedom which will release them from the three worlds of human endeavour and make them free citizens of the Kingdom of God. With that point of view you are quite familiar, and you will recognise that in it there lies a large measure of selfish purpose—inevitable and some day to be eliminated, but at this stage definitely present and perhaps desirable because it provides the adequate incentive towards the needed effort. The freedom, however, to which I refer, is the achieved success of the soul to move and act and manifest with freedom in the three worlds, as well as on its own high plane. This is a point seldom if ever emphasised. The soul itself, the Ego, has its own task to do, which might be expressed as being the reverse of that with which the personality is familiar. It has to learn to be at home and to function effectively in the world of human living and there to carry forward the plan. Such is the task of the Hierarchy and I felt that a statement of their peculiar problem and the difficulty of free activity which it necessarily involves, would prove both of interest and of enlightenment to those who read these papers.

From this highest standpoint, the Hierarchy was enabled to make a definite step forward in 1936 as the result of the work done in the last fifty years; having made it, it became necessary to stabilise the position and from the point then reached to lay plans for the next move to be taken on behalf of humanity.

Thus we find the interlude with which we have been almost distressingly familiar. You may have been led to expect some great onward sweep, some clear time of reaping, or some spectacular climax of happenings. When all that occurred was an interim of relative silence and a period wherein nothing seemed to occur, it was natural for the majority to experience a sense of disappointment, a reaction which almost equivalent, in some cases, to loss of faith, and a feeling of emotional fatigue and mental futility which tried many to the utmost. It is wise to remember that these reactions do not affect the issue and in no way retard the event, though they may make the task of the approaching helpers more difficult and draw almost unnecessarily upon their spiritual resources.

These interludes of apparent silence, of inertia and of inactivity are part of the great preservative and constructive activity of the Hierarchy; they are both individual, group and planetary in nature. Aspirants must learn to work intelligently and understandingly with the law of cycles. They must not forget that they live in a world of seeming and have no real freedom in the world of reality.

In May, 1938, at the time of the full moon, the Council of the Hierarchy to which I have several times referred in the past, convened and the plans for the immediate future were laid down. I would remind you of something we are very apt to forget. The plans for humanity are not laid down, for humanity determines its own destiny. The plans to meet the immediate human emergency and the plans to make possible a closer relationship between humanity and the Hierarchy were established. The problem before the Hierarchy of Masters (speaking in a large and general sense) is to intensify the activity and the consequent potency of that hidden power. By thus bringing it to the fore in human lives, the needed changes in our civilisation can be produced. The average man works from the organisation angle and having visioned some illuminating idea, he begins to build the outer physical form which will house and express it. The planetary Hierarchy, working under the inspiration of the Divine vision as it is embodied in the Plan, seeks to evoke a response to that Plan in every human heart, and by fostering and fanning that response, to evoke not only a mental understanding but also an aspirational desire. These together will produce finally the emergence of the Plan upon the earth and thus express a conditioning factor in human affairs.

When there are a sufficient number of people who are in conscious touch with their souls, then the sheer weight of their numbers, plus the clarity of their intentions and their widespread distribution over the face of the earth, must necessarily become effective. These people will then bring about changes of such far-reaching importance that the culture of the future will be as far removed from ours today, as ours in its turn is removed from that of the red Indians who roamed for centuries over the American continent and of whose possessions the white race took charge.

This then is the task of the Workers in the field of human affairs: to awaken the soul ray to potency in the life of each human being, beginning with those whose mental equipment and achieved integration would warrant the belief that— once awakened—they would use the new forces at their disposal with a measure of wisdom and planned constructive intention.

The questions we shall first discuss are as follows:—What are the psychological advantages of somewhat understanding the nature of the egoic ray? What intelligent use can be made by psychologists of the fact, if the soul ray is determined and recognised?

Early in this treatise we dealt with the general proposition of the value to psychology of a knowledge of the rays. We have considered the possibility of there being a scientific acceptance of the hypothesis of their existence, even if this recognition is only tendered provisionally. We must not forget that aspirants are increasing all over the world. Perhaps the simplest way to proceed is to state some of the developments which will manifest when the ray of the soul is admitted and recognised and developed. These will be:

1. *The solution of the present world conflict.* This conflict now amounts in the material sense almost to an impasse. The results of soul contacts on human beings and the effect to be seen in the personality life might be stated to be as follows:

   a. *Conflict*, turmoil, opposed loyalties, inner warfare and a collision of divergent views.

   b. *A sensitivity to ideas.* This amounts in the earlier stages to a flexibility of response, amounting almost to instability, and producing constant change of viewpoint. This leads eventually to a sensitivity to the intuition which will enable an individual to distinguish promptly between the unreal and the real.

   c. *A process of detachment.* This is the difficult and painful process of laying down the lines of demarcation between the soul and the personality. This inevitably produces at first separation and divided interests, leading later to a submergence of personality interests in those of the Plan, and the absorption of personal desire in the aspects of the soul.

   d. *A period of creativity*, due to the third aspect of the soul which is the creator aspect. This development will produce definite habit changes in the physical plane life of the aspirant. It will lead to the consecration of the disciple to certain types of endeavour summed up in the words "artistic career".

These four effects of soul activity, which are in reality only the pouring in of soul force, through the channel of contact which the man has opened, will give to psychology the four major causes of the present world difficulty. Each of these causes holds latent within itself its own solution. The present conflict, the widespread response to widely different ideologies, the economic pressure leading to material depredation, a most certain creativity of all the arts in the world today, and a new standard of values, are all problems confronting the trained thinker and psychologist. These conditioning effects are all of them to be seen among men today.

2. *The emergence of world government.* This emergence will be the result of these "five areas of difficulty", and the consequence of a more general understanding of:

a. The causes of unrest.

b. The point in evolution reached by humanity.

c. The crises which must inevitably occur when man, the integrated human being, meets man, the spiritual reality.

d. The moment of opportunity which is upon us. This is the result of certain astronomical happenings, such as the pouring in of energy from a new sign in the zodiac, and the shift of the earth's pole.

3. *The development of the new art.* This will be expressive of a sensitive response to ideas. The art of the past expressed largely man's understanding of the beauty of God's created world, whether it was the phenomenal wonder of nature or the beauty of the human form. The art of today is as yet almost a childish attempt to express the world of feeling and of inner moods and those emotionally psychological reactions which govern the bulk of the race. They are, however, to the world of feeling-expression what the drawings of the cave man are to the art of Leonardo da Vinci. It is in the realm of words

today that this new art is most adequately expressing itself. The art of music will be the next approach nearer to the truth, and to the revelation of the emerging beauty; the art of the painter and of the sculptor will follow later. None of this is the art of expressing ideas creatively, which will be the glory of the Aquarian Age.

4. *The understanding of the diseases of mystics,* or the physical ills of the highly developed people of the world. These are predominantly psychological in character and may remain submerged in the realm of the mind and of sensitivity or they may work out as physiological effect with a definite psychological basis. These forms of physical disease are the most difficult to handle and are at present little understood. What do modern scientific investigators know of the distinction between those neurotic and psychological troubles which are based on personality integration, or on excessive soul stimulation, and those which are the result of wrong polarisation? On these matters we may not here enlarge as the theme is too vast. It can, however, be noted that a recognition of the soul ray (as it makes its presence felt in the personality), will very frequently lead to definite psychological trouble. It might be well to add here a word of warning. We must be careful not to let our desire for soul contact fool us at this time into believing that our present physical difficulties (if there are any) are the result of this soul contact. It would be quite surprising if this were so. They are far more apt to be the result of astral polarisation, of physical unwisdom and experimentation, and perhaps of the too rapid integration of the three aspects of the personality.

In these four points there is probably indicated enough to

make clear, or at least to suggest two important things. First, that much, if not all that can be seen going on in the world today, is caused by a greatly increased soul stimulation, to which the entire human family is reacting, even though, as individuals, they have not made a soul contact. This increased stimulation is due to two things—

1. A great many men, and the number is rapidly increasing, are making contact with their souls through an intense aspiration and—in many cases—very real desperation.
2. The Hierarchy of Masters is exceedingly active today, and this is due to two things:—

    a. The demand on the part of humanity which has reached Their attention continuously for the past few decades, and which is calling out an inevitable response.
    b. A stimulation of the planetary Hierarchy itself. This leads many in the ranks of the Hierarchy to pass through one of the higher initiations. They therefore become much more potent and their influence is much more magnetic and radiating.

If we take the four points above enumerated and apply them both to the individual and to the race, we will find the answers to many questions, and the potency of the effects can be noted.

A study of the egoic ray, when rightly understood, will give the clue to all that is happening today. It might be stated that, in the initial stage of this study, the theme should be approached as follows: A close analysis of the life, quality and characteristics of the aspirants in the world should be made from the standpoint of modern, academic, psychological research, but the fact of the soul should be accepted as a hypothetical possibility. From that premise, the investigator can seek to understand the complexity of the nature of the men and the women under observation.

Some study of the psychology of the mystics (mostly those of the Middle Ages and therefore of the past), and some understanding of the phenomena which they experienced, has been carried forward. Little, however, has been done in connection with the mystics of modern times, with their higher mental equipment and their wider knowledge of the world. Nothing has been done really as yet in relation to the psychology of the occultist, who is only the mystic functioning on a higher plane—that of the mind. These are the brilliant people, normal in most of their expressions of life but possessing that something plus which differentiates them from the rank and file of their fellow men. They rise to the top of their profession, whatever it may be; they have outstanding creative ability in some department of the creative arts; they are phenomenally magnetic and influential in their effect on others; they unify and blend and gather around them groups of people.

This group of advanced people is coming increasingly under the influence of, and responding to, the energy of their souls. They do this either consciously through aspiration, meditation and service, or unconsciously, simply expressing their point in evolution and demonstrating the work done in other lives. This group might be regarded in many ways as supernormal. Its members are frequently misunderstood and it is difficult to account for all that they are and do. They dominate in world affairs, in the realm of art or in the world of business and are the guiding group in the world today. They are found active in government and in churches. They express predominantly a sense of responsibility, or a sense of synthesis, or a sense of God, or a sense of beauty, and modern psychology must answer the question: What is it that differentiates these people from their fellowmen? Heredity, opportunity, environment and the state of the glandular equipment, are some of the reasons brought forth today, but the question really remains unanswered, and will so remain until some understanding is gained of egoic unfoldment, and of soul contact, with its consequences:—stimulation, integration, the inflow of energy, and the use of that energy, according to the predisposition of the man and his group response.

Much has been given in this *Treatise on the Seven Rays* which should serve to clarify the problem. The soul ray of an individual, the soul ray of a nation, the potency in time and space of an incoming or an outgoing ray—all these give hints and clues to the understanding of the problem and should eventually lead to a better handling of the human being and his equipment, both by himself and by those who are endeavouring to handle him.

Sometimes I ask myself what real use can be made of this teaching and whether the wealth of information is of real service. Knowledge when given must be used; it must be made of practical application in the daily life. Upon all of you who read these words, as they come fresh from my heart, my mind and lips, rests a duty of doing three things, which *I give to you in the order of their importance:*

1. The moulding of your daily lives upon the basis of the imparted truth, if it is to you indeed a truth. It is perhaps to you simply interesting, a fascinating side line of study; perhaps it is something which it pleases you to get because of its novelty and because it is a little different from the general run of teaching; perhaps it pleases you to get these instructions a little ahead of the rest of humanity. All these reactions are of small importance,

being those of the personality. They are perhaps the most probable reactions for the majority. If there is nothing deeper in your reaction than those I have mentioned, then these teachings are not for you, for the responsibility upon your shoulders is thereby very great; but if you are attempting, no matter in how small a way, to apply the truth as you see it to your own life, then they are for you.

2. The building of that structure of thought which will embody this newer teaching. You can—if you so desire—help construct the thought form of the New Age teaching. You do this, above all, by your thought; by your practical application of any truth, which you may have understood, to your personal life at any cost; by your sacrifice and your service to your fellow men and by the constant dissemination of any knowledge which you may possess.

3. Distribution of the teaching over a long period of time. Have you done anything along this line, thus shouldering your responsibility?

b. The Precipitation of the Crisis

The plans as established by the Hierarchy concern primarily two things: first, the plans for bringing about world stabilisation. This is essential if the human being is to find adequate time for the unfoldment of his consciousness, and for the recognition of his soul. In these two latter requirements all successful hierarchical work is covered, as far as humanity is concerned. Secondly, the programme for the immediate future, with its definite physical plane adjustments and its tentative suggestion for world cooperation. Why do we use the word "tentative"? We use it because (as has oft been stated) even the advanced members of the Hierarchy do not know finally the manner in which humanity will react, or the quality or the capacity of its ultimate achievement.

I have endeavoured above, carefully and simply, to express the immediate purpose of the hierarchical effort, as the Council met to prepare for the future. Is it possible for us to conceive the import of that phrase "for the future"? The past is gone, beyond recall; that fleeting moment which we call the present time is determined by that past of which it becomes a part in the flash of a second. It was the preparation for the future and the laying of those plans which will cover the coming destiny of humanity during the immediate decade which was of significant and engrossing importance to the assembled Masters, and also of basic interest to any student of the Ageless Wisdom and to the disciples of the Great Ones.

Only that is of importance to us which provides a needed momentum for action, and which will also give to the working disciple of the world a vision of sufficient clarity and an adequate incentive to enable him to work with sincerity and understanding. This is often forgotten. So much is said and written these days which purports to come from the Great Ones and which is stated to embody Their will and Their intention. It is based on astral sensitivity and astral reaction to the many thought forms found upon the astral plane; these include among their number many thought forms of the Great Ones. These thought forms necessarily exist, and are built by the devotion of the aspirants of the world, and by the selfish spiritual ambition of those aspirants. They are not constructed by the disciples of the world, for no man is admitted to the status of accepted discipleship until he has at least overcome the worst aspects of personal ambition. This freedom from ambition is proved or expressed by personal reticence and by freedom from the publicity-making activities of the aspirants of the world, and also by freedom from the making of statements as to relationship or status. It might be well for us to ponder on these words.

The preliminary plans which the members of the hierarchical Council considered might be stated to be as follows, regarding those plans as spheres of cooperation for the Masters implicated and for those among men who are minded to serve in cooperative activity:

1. The reduction of the pressure upon humanity by the means of a steady stabilising of world thought. Today it is the fears of man—expressed in thought, and therefore frequently backed by action—which lead them into the impasse of war and into any form of destructive activity. The pressure is created by man's desire for betterment as well as by the spiritual downpouring of the soul. It is this dual activity of the higher and of the lower which produces the crisis. When these two meet there is, of course, no conflict; but there is, however, a sense of strain, a pressure which seems past endurance, and an impasse from which there appears no exit. This may be a difficult truth to grasp, but the present world crisis is largely brought about by the bringing together of these two types of energy. It is with this problem that the Masters are today grappling. A human aspiration and a condition of struggle towards improvement brings about a period in which the spiritual urge on the part of masses of men shows itself in three ways:

   a. The urge to betterment already noted.
   b. The organisation of the minds of men, so that new ideas can be gripped and understood.
   c. The recognition by the spiritually minded that *today is the day of opportunity*.

Will it be of any assistance and any incentive towards renewed effort if we observe the words "*the* day", and not "*a* day?" This is a period of immense cyclic importance.

2. The renewed organisation of the New Group of World Servers. How far have we really yet grasped the task of this group, or the significance of its membership? It is a group of men and women who are upon the Path of Discipleship or upon the Path of Probation, and it is divided into two major divisions:

a. A group composed of disciples who are consciously working with the Plan and of those who, instructed by them, are consciously and voluntarily cooperating. In this latter category we can find ourselves if we so desire and if we are willing to make the necessary sacrifices.

b. A group composed of aspirants and world-conscious men and women, who are working unconsciously under the guidance of the planetary Hierarchy. There are many such, particularly in high places today, who are fulfilling the part of destroyers of the old form or of builders of the new. They are not conscious of any inner synthetic plan, but are selflessly occupied in meeting world need as best they may, with playing parts in the national dramas, or with persistently working in the field of education. The first group is in touch with the planetary Hierarchy and it works, if we might so express it, under hierarchical inspiration. The second is in closer touch with the masses of men and works more definitely under the inspiration of ideas.

The first group is occupied with *the Plan* as its

members can vision and grasp its essentiality, whilst the second works more definitely with *the ideas* which are today slowly emerging in the consciousness of the more sensitive members of the human family. These ideas are gradually instilled into humanity by the Hierarchy and by the senior workers in the first group. This first group is relatively small, and when first the information was communicated about the New Group of World Servers, (which was later embodied in the pamphlet, "The Next Three Years"), the number of conscious disciples was given as being under two hundred. Since then this number has materially increased owing to two causes: First: certain men and women are arriving at maturity. This has developed in them a recognition of their hierarchical status as disciples. Secondly: the unfolding of other human beings and their spiritual development as a result of the stimulation and the relatively successful work of the previous three years. The number of conscious disciples in the world today (1939), is nearly one thousand. We are here considering those disciples who are definitely working in the groups of those Masters Who are pledged to the present experiment.

It should perhaps be pointed out here that the entire planetary Hierarchy, though cognisant of the present endeavour and therefore participating in the plans of the Council, are not all occupied with the problem of humanity in this present moment of crisis. There are many other lines of activity and of evolutionary expediency and undertaking which must parallel the present endeavour. Work in relation to other kingdoms in nature (both subhuman and superhuman), and work in preparation for the period which must succeed this present time of crisis must be continued as usual. In the higher levels of the New Group of World Servers, the many divisions of hierarchical effort are represented, but there are, nevertheless, a large number of disciples in the world today who are in no way associated with the present plans. This is a point to be remembered.

3. The awakening of the intelligentsia in all countries to the recognition of *humanity* as a prelude to the establishment of brotherhood. The unity of the human family is recognised by many, but before that unity can take form in constructive measures, it is essential that more and more of the thinking men and women throughout the world should break down the mental barriers existing between races, nations and types, and that the New Group of World Servers should itself repeat in the outer world that type of activity which the Hierarchy expressed when it developed and materialised the Group. Through the expression and impression of certain great ideas, men everywhere must be brought to the understanding of the fundamental ideals which will govern the New Age. This is the major task of the New Group of World Servers.

One of the objectives considered by the Council in May, 1937, was the method of deepening the hold these new ideas must have on members of the New Group of World Servers. Thus the stimulation of the spiritual life of the group members, and consequently their sensitivity to the Plan will be carried forward. They will then be not only consciously in touch with the plans, but they will be occultly imbued by them, and in this way the radiating influence of the Group will be greatly enhanced. This will bring about an outer expression of real group importance and of such vital necessity that, during the next few years, the new ideas must become the ideals of the thinking level of the race. If this does not take place, the immediate salvaging of humanity will have to be postponed and a further period of distress and of widespread disciplining must then inevitably result. It is this urgency that is discussed in these pages, and it is this immediate need, and this momentous crisis with which the Hierarchy had to deal in its May Council of 1937.

4. The final aspect of the situation with which the Masters concerned dealt, is in fact, the precipitation of an imminent crisis. This precipitation is inevitable and its effects must be foreseen and dealt with in such a manner that its catastrophic results will be offset, and its subjective significances utilised to the full.

Having stated the four major points of consideration (which came before the Council in May, 1937, and which are all related to the impending world crisis), it is needful that we should point out two things:—

1. That this crisis is imminent and of epoch-making effects for two reasons.

    a. The work carried forward during the previous five years along spiritual lines had been definitely successful. This has caused a vital spiritual awakening in every land, and was the result of the activity and work of the first division of the New Group of World Servers.

    b. The strenuous efforts of the second division in the New Group of World Servers have also been successful. These people are far more the instruments of divine activity rather than conscious cooperators with the Plan.

2. That the Masters are not primarily concerned with the prevention of disaster to the *form aspect* of humanity, desirable as human beings might consider that objective. The salvaging of the form is but incidental to the Plan. The work of the Hierarchy is concerned with the expansion and awakening of the human consciousness, and that, in its turn, has an effect upon the form. It is possible (and so the Masters regard it) to lay such an emotional strain and mental stress upon the mechanism of human expression on the physical plane that the lessons cannot be adequately learned because the immediate physical stress is too great to permit the recognition and the assimilation of the significance of the event. Therefore the Masters, when meeting at the Council of May, 1937, had to consider the offsetting of the strain. Humanity can get too tired to react, and this fact constituted a definite problem with which the Hierarchy had to deal.

It will be apparent, therefore, if we have read the above intelligently and have endeavoured to synthesise it with the state of world affairs as far as we know it, that the problems before the assembled Council were three in number. More than these three, humanity cannot grasp nor do the facts concern them. There were necessarily many other problems, but they are of such a nature that we could not comprehend them, and it would not be possible to express these problems in words which would convey intelligible meaning to us. The three problems which came under consideration were:

1. The right resolution of the present crisis, so that equilibrium could be restored.
2. The stimulation of the New Group of World Servers so that they could—
   a. Recognise the emergency,

    b. Define the plan more clearly,

    c. Become more sensitive to inner, subjective, spiritual impression,

    d. Make the necessary sacrifices demanded for the success of the plan,

    e. Radiate more effectively out into the world of humanity.

3. How to keep the forces which had been set in motion since 1914 within certain definite limits.

These forces are many in number and it is possible to indicate the nature of some of them. This is done, however, more for the sake of future understanding and future rational comprehension than because we can specifically do anything in particular in relation to them. Let me simply list them, and if we read with the eye of the inner vision open, and with our intuition alert and awake, perhaps some apprehension of the problems before the Council may dawn upon our minds. It is not possible to enlarge upon these forces, nor may we interpret them. We can simply state what are facts to the Hierarchy but which may only be an interesting supposition, hypothesis or chimera to us:

1. *The cumulative forces of the great Piscean Age*—powerful, fundamental and, at this time, destructive. To these forces the unenlightened masses react; for them they are the line of least resistance. When we say masses, we refer to all who do not truly think, but who believe and who accept on the lower or ordinary levels of consciousness.

2. *The incoming forces of the Aquarian Age.* These are having a wide and general effect upon the ethers around the earth, upon the vegetation everywhere, upon the waters of the planet, and upon all human beings in the world today who are learning to think. The Aquarian inspiration is being registered by all who come under the in-

fluence of the new "schools of thought", so-called. The interpretation of the sensed ideals may be in error, but the power to respond to the new forces is there, and the effect upon the mind and brain is real and lasting. One of the first effects is the stabilising of emotional reaction.

3. *Influential and potent forces* pouring in at this time from the great stars Betelgeuse and Sirius. To these two influences, the disciples of the world in the senior ranks of the New Group of World Servers definitely react, and they produce a stimulation of the heart centre (Betelgeuse) and the head centre (Sirius). The secondary effect of these energies is upon the mineral kingdom, particularly upon that peculiar product, gold, and that enigma, money.

4. *Venusian forces of great potency* are also playing upon our planet. In this connection, I would suggest that astrologers would be well advised to pay more attention to the activity and the influence of Venus. Much emphasis has been laid upon Saturn and Mars in the charts now considered. In the future, equal emphasis will have to be paid to the planet Venus, which in the Aquarian age will supersede Mars as a basic influence.

5. *The forces of the planetary entity* who is beginning to stir in his long sleep, and is therefore causing much of the physical, cataclysmic phenomena of the present time. With this we have naught to do except to register the fact.

6. *The energy of the united Hierarchy of the planet* which has lately made one of its "Great Approaches" to the physical plane. This necessarily entails a more potent and significant and rapid pouring forth of the force of the Hierarchy with the subsequent stimulation of the higher centres in those sons of men who have reached the

point of their evolution where they are close enough to their own souls to be affected. They are then mentally polarised, and consequently react potently to this influence.

7. *The energy of the New Group of World Servers*, which (up to ten years ago) was a relatively negligible factor even though present, but which is now increasingly a force with which to reckon. From certain angles, the energy of this group constitutes the hope of the world, and the task of increasing that potency is the task which is being laid before us today.

8. There is also *the powerful vibratory influence of those important men and women* in the world who are today active in world affairs. From the side of the Hierarchy and the use of spiritual energy, these men and women are regarded as doors into human life, because through them the energy of certain great world souls, world potencies and Masters can be expressed. There are many such, and one of the tasks before the Council is to balance these forces in such a manner that they do not upset world equilibrium beyond the point of the re-establishment of balance. Students need to remember that a Master inevitably takes certain risks and chances when He "occultly inspires" a soul and drives a man to *unconscious cooperation* with the Plan. We must remember, however, that there is no infringing of human freedom, even by a Master. Sometimes a disciple or a member of the New Group of World Servers will (metaphorically speaking) take the bit between his teeth, and this will produce disaster and frequently a temporary destruction of that part of the Plan with which he has been entrusted.

9. *Certain forces which we* (in our ignorance and lack of perspective), *may call evil or black forces.* In worldly parlance, these forces are connected with what is regarded as the black side of nature and of energy. They are wielded by great and powerful human beings, the majority of whom are out of physical incarnation. They work from the astral plane and primarily through the agency of groups. These groups—being composed of ignorant, unstable, selfish and ambitious men—provide an easy field for their efforts. For this so-called evil work, the average individual in the group is not responsible, though there is usually to be found in the group those who are wilfully ambitious and selfish. Though the individual penalty is light, and the individual responsibility is small, yet the effectiveness of this method is very great. The result is in the nature of group obsession, which is a relatively new thing, but also is today becoming increasingly frequent.

These are some of the forces which are bringing about and constituting the world problem, and with these the Council has had to deal. All these forces are today playing upon humanity, and this whirlpool of energies is sweeping humanity into a period of definitely chaotic destruction, unless the Masters of the Wisdom, working through the New Group of World Servers in both its divisions, can arrest the process and bring order into a distressed and agonising world.

Therefore, the May full moon Council of 1937 was one of real import and of vital significance. Just as the full moon of May, 1936, saw an effort of the Masters and of the world of disciples to approach nearer to each other and thus establish a closer rapport, so the full moon of May, 1937, witnessed the laying down of certain lines of activity which, if rightly apprehended, and worked out into physical manifestation, could definitely change the present exoteric world situation. It also saw the re-stimulation of the New Group of World Servers, so that their group integration might constantly become more effective, and the personal lives of the group members become definitely more consecrated, more dedicated to humanity, and more influential in service. At the full moon of May, 1936, there was in evidence an inner, subjective, spiritual effort. This was definitely successful. The full moon of May, 1937, saw the establishing and the stabilising of the exoteric outer effect, of which the earlier effort was naturally and automatically the cause. Yet the problem remains ever the same:—can the inner condition, spiritual, potential, idealistic, subjective and *sensed*, be so clearly formulated and considered that nothing whatever can stop its materialising through the medium of some constructive and living form upon the physical plane? Can the inner integration of the New Group of World Servers find exoteric expression?

A prolonged period of such moments and points of danger can, nevertheless, in itself constitute a momentous crisis. The fanning of the hot embers (if persisted in long enough) must eventually bring about a conflagration. What then can be done to institute those arrangements and outer understandings (based on the inner inspiration) which will end this cycle of danger points, and permit the racial consciousness to subside into a period of quiet and of freedom?

The Hierarchy is doing all that is possible, but under the plan of unfoldment for the Aryan Race, the activity needed for the creative work must be inaugurated and carried forward by disciples, working in the outer world and by aspirants to the path of discipleship, who register the world need and earnestly seek to cooperate. This is, therefore, a matter for our consideration and for clear and skillful action in the immediate future.

As one contemplates the New Group of World Servers in its many departments—scattered all over the world and embracing the true and earnest seekers in every nation—there can be seen a body of men and women whose numbers and spheres of influence are entirely adequate to bring about the desired changes, *if they care enough, are ready enough to make the needed sacrifices*, and are willing to sink their organisation differences in the needed activity which would salvage the world, educate the race in a few simple and basic essentials, and so cooperate with each other that there would emerge a united inner movement—working out through the separated outer groups.

The Hierarchy held its Council during the week of the full moon of May, 1937. It could and did lay its plans for the helping of humanity. It could, and did mobilise and bring together every possible subjective agency and form of available energy for the stimulating of the human consciousness along right lines. It could, and did impress upon the disciples and aspirants everywhere the necessity of renewed and fresh efforts. But the development and actual functioning of the plans laid down and the actual working out into detailed expression of the intended ameliorative measures must be carried out by the New Group of World Servers, and by the men of good will throughout the world. Only by the united effort of the people of peaceful intention and of innate freedom from hatred can the forces of destruction be offset. These forces have been needed and useful, but the task they were intended to carry out has been accomplished, and that which is no longer required becomes, in its turn, a menace and a source of trouble.

c. STEPPING DOWN OF HIERARCHICAL METHODS

One of the first things which should be accomplished is the working out upon the physical plane of some of the achievements of the Hierarchy upon the inner side of life. For instance, each department and section of the Hierarchy is working together today as one unit. Though not all of the Masters and Their groups are occupied—as was earlier said—with the immediate problem of the human crisis, yet subjectively, all are engaged with the task of bringing order out of chaos and are working *together* (each in His own sphere and in the closest mental understanding), so that there are really no divided interests, no separate groups and no difference of opinion—no matter what Their diverse activities may be or Their specific undertakings. This condition *must* be duplicated, if possible, on the outer plane of physical life also.

Complete unanimity cannot be possible; complete subordination of individual and group interest to the general movement towards world understanding and stabilisation cannot as yet be achieved, owing to the selfish ambitions of group leaders, and the separative instincts of the senior workers in any group, who unduly influence the rank and the file of the membership. Yet a definitely closer rapprochement is far more possible today than at any previous time, and some real progress could be made towards mutual understanding if a sufficiently large number of the world aspirants and disciples desired it, if they were willing to participate in such an effort, and made the attempt to organise such a closer coming together and movement towards spiritual understanding. This would entail a restatement of the ideal on the part of each individual aspirant and disciple. It would involve a re-dedication of each of them to the immediate urgency of the Plan and to the demand coming to their ears of the world distress.

It would require the individual formulation of the ideals—sensed dimly or clearly—in terms of sacrifice and the resultant activity. These last few words indicate the attitude requisite and its needed consequences.

Therefore, one of the first things which would be of the next immediate assistance to be rendered to the Hierarchy of Masters (and this is only another way of saying, to humanity), is a widespread effort to get in touch with every group leader in the various towns, cities, and countries and continents. This refers to all those group leaders who are sensitive to what we might call the "doctrine of good will", and who can vision an ideal of group unity, carried forward without any attempt to disturb the normal outer group activity. This will entail the recognition of a common ideal; and the willingness to submerge (even if only temporarily) the points of difference and to emphasise the points of contact. Many might be willing to do this for the period of the emergency and as an interesting experiment, and thus endeavour to carry forward over a limited and stated time a united endeavour to spread good will and understanding in an effort to bring the hatreds of the world to an end. This will also entail the willingness to cooperate with all groups within a given radius of contact and the temporary relinquishing of personal ambitions and methods in order to meet the serious emergency by which humanity is faced. The basis of the possible success of such an effort consists in the fact that within each group are always to be found members of the New Group of World Servers. Upon this fact we can count, and we can depend upon the strength of the inner integration, produced by these synthesising "points of contact".

Another reason for the presumption of success lies in the fact that such an effort will only be the normal working out into physical expression of that which the Masters of the

Wisdom—distinctive as to Their fields of service, specific as to Their methods, and widely different as to Their ray and background of evolutionary development—have already established. This attempt on the part of all of us will, therefore, be a duplicating or a paralleling expression of an inner subjective fact. One of the facts upon the agenda of the Council was as to how They could more effectively stimulate the New Group of World Servers so that they could in turn see this vision with clarity, work with renewed optimism, and thus produce on earth the counterpart of the inner spiritual organisation.

The problem to be met by the disciples and aspirants in the world today is the possibility and right procedure, by means of a more specific and definite "push" or organised activity, to reach the leaders of groups everywhere. It would be well to discuss the ways and means to swing these leaders into a joint activity without interfering with their individual group purposes, loyalties and obligations.

Careful work must be put behind this effort. By this is meant considered mental work, subjective reflection, organised visioning and significant sacrifice. A start in this direction has already been made and the same general idea can be extended elsewhere and carefully developed. Group integrity, loyalties and purpose must be preserved, but the cooperation of the groups must be invoked in the task of spreading the healing energy of good will, which, as has been well and truly remarked, is the active principle of peace. And peace—not inert pacifism—is what is needed today.

Secondly, a plan should also be drawn up of such a nature that the various peace societies could at least temporarily be swung into an allied and paralleling activity. The leaders of the peace organisations could be approached with a definite and temporary programme, and their cooperation asked.

This programme of unification of the efforts of the more advanced groups in the world will demand sacrifice and satisfactory compromise on both sides, ours and the leaders of such groups, but where there is sincerity of purpose (and there is much) where there is a willingness to recognise the need for change in technique and terminology, then some definite progress can be made and the ranks of the men of good will, as organised under hierarchical impulse, can be greatly increased. It is not necessary for us to discuss in detail the methods which will be needed. Those who respond to this appeal will know the methods they should pursue. It is for those of us who do recognise the validity of this appeal to cooperate and aid, or *to know clearly why we will not.*

The Hierarchy is working primarily during the next few years through three groups of Masters who are on the first, second and third rays. Those on the first ray are dealing with the important figures today in world government, for all of them are subject to impression from their souls and all are fulfilling their individual destiny, and influencing their respective nations along the lines of national destiny. The period of intensive and seemingly destructive readjustment has been drastic and needed. This must not be forgotten. Mistakes in techniques have necessarily been made, and oft the law of love has been infringed. Sometimes, however, the love of the form aspect of consciousness has been interpreted as synchronous and similar to the law of love by critics of the methods employed. This is understandable. But the time of the great national readjustments must soon end, and the necessary processes of realignment be completed. This should then inaugurate a period of renewed relationships on a wide scale throughout the world; it should see the beginning of the establishment of friendships and the commencement of a new era of right and constructive world contacts. Hitherto this has never been possible on a large scale, owing to the fact that humanity had not suffered enough and therefore was not adequately sensitive to others. It had no inner integration such as is now possible through our developed means of communication, and the growth of telepathic sensitivity. The abuses of the law of living had not been generally recognised and known for what they are by a sufficient number of people. The work of the great first ray influences is rapidly and materially changing all this, and out of the lessons learnt, the structure of the new civilisation can become possible.

The work of the second ray Masters is now intensifying, and the builders of the new civilisation—working, through the religious organisations, the educational systems of every country and the great army of thinking men and women everywhere—can definitely begin to make their presence felt. It is in this department primarily that the work of the New Group of World Servers can be noted and can be developed.

The question may be raised whether we are omitting to recognise the presence of the vast millions of the unenlightened masses who hang like a heavy millstone around the neck of the leaders of the race, and who are kept down either through fear, through applied poverty (yes, that is the proper term) or through regimentation. These constitute (as may be easily recognised) a harnessed menace, but that harness is rapidly becoming worn, and when the leash slips or breaks, it is difficult to forecast what the dire results may be. The caged wild beast of the unenlightened—and therefore innocent human beings—who work without the means for pleasure or leisure, who are underfed and exploited, cannot indefinitely be held back. The one hope of the world is that the enlightened and responsible people will readjust world relations, world conditions and the world economic situation, so that contentment through the removal of abuses may succeed, and there will be no necessity for the prevailing and seething misery, which is rapidly reaching boiling point. Let us not forget, if this seems to be unduly optimistic, that one light, even if small, can light up a whole area.

The second ray influences are therefore being poured through the agency of the educational institutions and groups, through the religious bodies and through all men and women who can vision the higher possibilities and the world of spiritual values and of meaning. This is being done in the hope that a united stand will be possible and will produce a synthesis of effort; that this will be productive, in its turn, of a real world stabilisation.

The third ray Masters are working strenuously in the world of business and of finance through the agency of those who are animated by a spirit of selfless service—and there are many such. It is a new field for spiritual endeavour. It is not possible to enlarge within a brief space upon the methods and the plans of the Hierarchy at this time of crisis and emergency in connection with the field of money and its significance and right use. The general method employed is one of inspiration and of *the presentation of moments of crisis*. These moments offer opportunity for the activity of some disciple, and thus the learning of a needed lesson by the groups or nations implicated becomes possible. The technique employed by these third ray Masters is to develop the minds of aspirants and thinkers in the specific field of business so that they can think in larger terms than those of their own selfish business interests. Moments of contact are also arranged between members of the New Group of World Servers and these prominent people, working in the field of economic enterprise, and thus opportunities are provided for certain recognitions and certain definite cooperation. These are the methods which concern us. There are other subjective and spiritual methods employed which concern us not. If they were out-lined in detail to us, they would only serve to bewilder.

Let it be emphatically stated here that the major method with which we can concern ourselves, and the most potent instrument in the hands of the spiritual Hierarchy, is the spreading of good will and its fusion into a united and work-ing potency. That expression is to be preferred to the words "the organization of good will". Good will is today a dream, a theory, a negative force. It should be developed into a fact, a functioning ideal, and a positive energy. That is our work and we are definitely called to cooperate in bringing it about.

The task before the New Group of World Servers is great but it is not an impossible task. It is engrossing but as it con-stitutes an imposed life pattern, it can be worked out in every aspect of a man or woman's daily life. We are now called to serve intensively *for a period of years*, to abnormal living, and to the shouldering of a responsibility about which we have known for several years, but which we have not shouldered. Our interest has been powerfully evoked, but not demon-strated as it might have been. The demand for cooperation has been clearly sounded from the inner side, and by the leaders and workers in the New Group of World Servers. We have responded with some aid but not with sacrifice; we have given some assistance but it has been the minimum and not the possible maximum (except in a few cases, whose as-sistance has been whole hearted and recognised). We have been told that the members of the New Group of World Servers are working in every land to spread good will, world understanding and religious unity. The idea has been reassur-ing and we have rested back upon their efforts — the efforts of a hard pressed few.

d. Urgency of the Need and How to Meet It

Again let us recognise it—the urgency is great. The emergency is upon us and a united spiritual effort, prayerfully carried forward, wisely adjusted to environing need, widely blended with all the similar efforts which may be working cooperatively in every land with the forces of construction—national, religious and economic—can change the aspect of world affairs in the space of a few years. If there is not an appreciable change in human relations, then there will be little immediate hope of bringing about that united effort which will lead to world stabilisation, interracial and international understanding, economic interdependence and universal good will. For it is the good will of the powerful groups for humanity and therefore for the masses, and the good will of the intelligentsia and of the influential middle classes which will bring about the needed intelligent changes, which can affect every human being. The hope of the world today lies in the development of good will—not peace as the word is usually interpreted, to mean merely an enforced freedom from war, and an expediently enforced pacifism, but the cultivation of a spirit of good will, intelligently applied, and worked out with purpose into the fabric of the individual and national life.

We have here presented to us two modes of approaching the problem. To the consideration of this all of us are called who now are present workers or leaders in the New Group of World Servers, or who desire to enlist ourselves among them. The next consideration is how can these ideas be intelligently understood? How can they evoke the cooperation of aspirants and disciples over the world?

Let us state what I see to be possible, and what can be done if we—each and all—face the issue, deal with the opportunity presented on the basis of responsibility, and come to regard our world service in this crisis as a necessary part of our spiritual life, demanding from us, nevertheless, all that we have to give, plus that supreme extra effort which spells success in every case. This extra effort and this response to the demand for full cooperation, very few of us have yet given. If what is here set forth is true, and if what we know of world affairs gives in any way a true picture of the present world condition (and it is understated, if anything) then any intelligent man or woman can surely see that it is going to take the united sacrificing effort of every unit in the whole body corporate to promote good will as a healing factor (perhaps the only healing factor) in humanity.

The following suggestions are offered to those who seek to join in this service:

Meditation groups could carry forward their meditations in such a manner that an inner fusion can take place, producing the awakening of the *heart* centres of the members, and the consequent urge to go forth into the world of daily living to love, to give and to stimulate.

Privately, and in group gatherings the Great Invocation could be said, including the final words:

"*So let it be and help us to do our part*".

There are those who have learned to say these words with intensity of feeling, raising the clasped hands above the head, and then—at the last word—bringing them down to the forehead and then to the heart. The raising of the hands above the head and their return in touching the forehead and the heart are simply symbolic of the lifting of heart and life and consciousness to divinity, and the subsequent and consequent downflow of spiritual life into the personality—the instrument through which the loving soul must work out the expression of good will.

The emphasis is laid upon the *heart centre* and upon the necessity to hold the forces there (symbolised by the clasped hands resting upon the heart) because the heart is the centre of loving, giving energy, and the distributor of life.

It should not be necessary to restate any further what should be done, how anyone should give of himself, or in what way he could contribute for the aiding of humanity. The case has been presented clearly and most definitely. The responsibility now rests upon those who have received the message. One can only observe that until those who know and who have the way out presented to them, consecrate themselves and all that they have without reservation to the helping of the world in its hour of need, the work will not be done and the plans of the Hierarchy cannot then materialise. Should that not eventuate within the near future, then new and perhaps more drastic ways will have to be found.

At a gathering of the Great Ones not so long ago, the question was asked: "What can we do? for this emergency must be met." A silence fell upon the assembled group. This lasted quite a long time and then they, one and all, simultaneously voiced the reply, speaking as if they were one person, such was the unanimity: "Let us touch the *hearts* of men anew with love, so that those who know will love and give. Let us give love ourselves." The above may be a statement of fact, or it may be simply a symbolic and allegorical way of helping us to grasp our need. That is for us to decide. However, there may be those who will wish to say each morning in their morning meditation or at the noon day recollection the following words:

"I know, Oh Lord of Life and Love, about the need. Touch my heart anew with love that I too may love and give."

Let us in full surrender of our personal desires and wishes join in the common task of leading humanity into the fields of peace!

I approach you therefore, the conscious aspirants to whom I can speak with freedom and with no attempt to choose my words with care, to ask you, first of all two questions:

1. Do you, in truth, accept the situation as I have outlined it?
2. Where, at this time, do you place your life emphasis?

The answering of these two questions in the light of your soul and your personal earnestness will greatly clarify your minds and your way of living and working. It will also indicate to Those who are serving the Plan of God upon the subjective side of life, or along the lines of spiritual understanding and meaning, who are the servers, the aspirants and disciples upon whom it is possible to count at this moment of world crisis, for a world crisis is upon us. If the urgency of the hour is as indicated, and if the next few years are decisive years which will determine and condition the world situation till 1975, then it is necessary for everybody to take stock of himself and turn his spiritual theories and his humanitarian longings into *Facts* demonstrated in the life of everyday.

The lines of world cleavage are becoming more clearly defined and humanity is slowly forming itself into three camps or groups, as seen from the subjective side of life. These are:

1. The group of those who violently and actively and sincerely are partisans of certain basic and well-known ideologies which we can roughly divide into the fascist-nazi group, the democratic group and the communistic group. Such are the major ideas to which the leading

nations of the world are pledged and for which they are
ready to fight if need arises.

2. The relatively acquiescent masses who, under the regimes
endorsing the three above ideologies, live, love and seek
to understand a little of what is happening to them and
who accept the familiar or the newly imposed rule with
acquiescence and oft quite unintelligently, provided they
can eat and sleep and reproduce and the ordinary affairs
of life can proceed along the usual lines.

3. A rapidly growing group of those who are aware of the
other groups, who appreciate the idealism and effort of
the first group and also recognise the helplessness of the
masses. They stand ready to do what is possible to help
restore world equilibrium and so bring understanding
and cooperation and unity into play on a world wide
scale. These are the men and women of good will
throughout the world about whom I have so often
written.

Behind these three groups, equally interested in them all,
stands another group. It is numerically smaller but spiritually
potent and is composed of those whose work it is to further
God's plans consciously on earth; they work in touch with
the Plan and have a deep knowledge of the general trend of
the evolutionary urge; they are directing world force into
the desired channels and are assisted in their efforts by the
New Group of World Servers. They are all pledged to establish the kingdom of God on earth, for which the world is
ripe and whose coming was foretold by all the great world
religions. Nothing can stop the emergence of that kingdom.

I have briefly re-stated this line-up of the forces, prevalent
in humanity today. A little thought will show how practically

every human being can be placed under one or other of these groupings or categories.

It might be of value here if we endeavoured for a few minutes to get the point of view of the spiritual leaders of the race, of the planetary Hierarchy, of Christ and His Church.

These Workers look out upon a world distressed and full of pain. The economic problem looms large and is a determining factor in many cases. In a world of plenty, men are starving on every hand, or subsisting on a deplorable insufficiency whilst others of their fellowmen, in the same country, have too much and hold on to it, and frequently commit crimes to keep it. In a world full of activity, men are forced into a hated inertia through unemployment, and millions of men and women have nothing to do, but exist upon relief, through the charity of the well-intentioned, or upon crime, yet eating their hearts out (consciously or unconsciously) because the right of every human being to live and work and be self-supporting is denied them. In a world where all men desire peace and the opportunity to live in happiness at home or abroad, the nations everywhere are arming or are fortifying their frontiers in an effort to achieve that security which will enable them to live safely within their borders, free from attack, or to impose their ideas upon their fellowmen or nations. In a world of organised religions, the same condition of chaos is to be seen. The Churches in all lands are endeavouring frantically to keep their hold—spiritual, mental or financial—over the people and are playing a losing game, because the days of control by the priestly caste is in reality over, just as is the control of an autocratic dynasty. The work of the great world religions has been eminently successful and has been carried through to the desired consummation and now the new world religion, which is that of the kingdom of God, is definitely upon the way.

Such is the dark side of the picture and it is dark indeed and men are troubled and feel that there is no sure ground to be found anywhere. The present world situation has in it the seeds of dire trouble and catastrophe faces the people, as it has three times before, though on a much lesser scale. This can all be averted, however, if those who know the goal and see the vision and the emerging possibilities rally their force and—by the strength of love and sacrifice—offset the forces of hate and of death. As those who guide and teach upon the inner side of life look out upon the world they see in every country, in every race and in every religious body, thus coloring every ideology or school of thought (economic, political and religious) those who are moved by love of their fellow-men and are actuated by an earnest desire for their true welfare. I would like at this time to emphasise the following point:

A man's political and religious affiliations can be strongly held and inspire his true loyalty, and yet need in no way prevent his being an active part of the New Group of World Servers. They need not deter him from being actively on the side of world good will or provide a barrier to that spiritual sensitivity which makes him susceptible to the higher inner spiritual impression.

The servants of the spiritual Hierarchy and the world disciples are found in every nation; they are loyal to that nation's ideology or political trend of thought or government; the members of the New Group of World Servers embrace every political creed and recognise the authority of every imaginable religion. Men and women of good will can be discovered functioning in every group, no matter what its ideology or creed or belief. The Hierarchy does not look for cooperators in any one school of thought, political creed, or national government. It finds them in all and cooperates with all. This I have frequently said, yet you find it difficult to believe, so convinced are many of you that your peculiar belief and your particular acceptance of truth is the best undoubtedly and the most true. It may be for you, but not for your brother of another persuasion, nation or religion.

Thus we find, as well you know, members of the New Group of World Servers scattered everywhere. They are the only agents which the Hierarchy chooses to employ at this time and to them is committed the task of doing the following things:

1. Restoring the world balance through understanding and good will.
2. Bringing harmony and unity among men and nations by the revelation of the widespread good will everywhere existent.
3. Precipitating, through spiritual perception and correct interpretation, the kingdom of God on earth.

This is a gigantic task but not an impossible one, provided that there is united aspiration, united sacrifice and the inter-relating of the three groups:

1. The planetary Hierarchy, which is the spiritual Hierarchy, called in the West, the kingdom of God.
2. The New Group of World Servers or the disciples and aspirants and the spiritual intelligentsia of the world.
3. The men and women of good will found everywhere.

The task, therefore, in the coming year of climax for which preparation must be made is, first of all, to bring about this inter-relation on a large scale through discovering those who respond to this message and idea; secondly, to educate such people in the laws of love and of right understanding, which are in truth the laws of the kingdom of God which Christ came to initiate; thirdly, to reach and awaken the men and women of good will through the wide use of the radio, using it with wisdom and discretion, and the use of correct words and phrases; next, to discover men of like ideas and so organise their minds that each will approach the problem in his own way but with the same world wide objective of spreading understanding and bringing about harmonious adjustments. This will be done through the agency of the awakened world aspirants, the intelligent statesmen who love humanity and work self-sacrificingly for the general good, the men and women of good will (working each in in his own place, city and nation) and the quiet work of the Units of Service cooperating with all the above.

This is a simple programme but of such a practical potency that, if you once worked it out and made the needed sustained effort, in 1942 there would be no question but that success had crowned your efforts. The coming of God is the coming or emerging fifth kingdom in nature whose citizens always bring beauty into the world, thus glorifying that Intelligence to Whom we give the name of "God" for want of a better term; whose citizens are distinguished by the quality of good will which must, in the long run, bring the right kind of peace, but not pacifism, on earth. It is a programme of such simplicity that the over-active minds of many will reject it on the ground that it is too simple, and yet the great and controlling factors in the world are always simple. Simple ideas work out when complex and complicated ones fail in their objective. The Hierarchy of Masters is governed by simplicity and this, which is one of Their plans, must be distinguished by it also. What are the plans today, and in what manner can you aid in the task of saving the world?

It can be greatly helped by the discovery, registering and education of the men and women of good will in the world.

This is the major line of activity. Their united good will (at present latent, unused and unorganised) can become a world force and through sheer weight of numbers, these people can make their presence effectively felt. It will be a force which can mould public opinion through the expression of intelligent love (with the emphasis upon the word *intelligent*) but which will employ no separative devices, no armed force, no coercion and no political scheming and manipulation. Is it not possible so to evoke the spirit of good will, present but oft inactive in the hearts of all men, that there will be such a vast number of men and women of good will in the world—consciously in touch with each other throughout the planet—that their voice will not be negligible, nor their expressed desires impotent? It is this particular method of straightening out the world which the spiritual hierarchy has, at this time, determined to use. It is a somewhat slower method from your point of view, but the effects will be more lasting and it has in it dynamic possibilities. This method is based upon two premises: First, the proven fact of the success of the work which Christ instituted. He came to demonstrate in His Own Person the love of God. Prior to His time, there was little expression of that love objective in the world and little philanthropy or sense of responsibility for one's brother extant. Secondly: it is a method which has in it a long range success, and yet which can have, at the same time, an immediate reaction. This success and this reaction are dependent upon all of you who are aware of these facts and *set in to do the desired work*.

The New Group of World Servers provides a channel through which the power of God, focussed in the Planetary Brotherhood, can flow and that power is *not* intended (as is sometimes necessary under the evolutionary plan) to be destructive. The destructive forces of the planet are doing their directed and needed work, but the effects must be balanced and offset by the work of the World Servers. The power to be released can and will heal humanity's wounds and will bind all men together in a planned synthesis.

As you know, the New Group of World Servers has its members in every land. A vast number are known. They are practical intelligent people, not visionary idealistic mystics, working towards an object which may appear inaccessible, but towards one which is capable of immediate and practical application. They are talking of understanding and co-operation in all fields of human thought and life, and are emphasising the future and unavoidable expression of such love—unavoidable under the evolutionary law. It is the next great human development.

Behind, in the distant past of the race, humanity faced such a crisis as is now upon us. The race was then fecundated with intellect, if I may use such a phrase, and the human or fourth kingdom came into being. The great latent power of self-consciousness was born, and men became individuals. Now the race faces another fecundation, this time with Love and the fifth kingdom in nature, the kingdom of God can be born and can function upon the outer world of manifestation. Group consciousness will be seen and the power to identify oneself with the group and not with one's own selfish interests. The New Group of World Servers, standing at a midway point between the spiritual Hierarchy and the world of men, are the agents of this process and can lead men out of the crisis which it has brought about. They are expressions of the intended good will and a leavening force in their environment. They do and say nothing which could increase the existing cleavages among people, races and religions. Let us leave it at that, for it is a simple statement of a simple way to lay the ground for needed changes.

e. IMMEDIATE PLAN OF THE HIERARCHY

What, therefore, is the Hierarchy seeking to do today? Let me briefly state the immediate plan.

1. To make the lines of cleavage, already existing, so apparent that the issue is clear. This you can see happening every day if you read the world news intelligently and separate the spectacular and untrue details from the broad and true issues. These lines of cleavage fall into three general lines.

    a. Between the three major ideologies: the Fascists, the Communistic and the Democratic.

    b. Between the reactionary and fundamentalist groups and the liberal minded people who react to the newer spiritual impression and the emerging ways of approach to God.

    c. Between the old cultures and civilisations and the new incoming ways of living and thinking; between the Piscean way of life and the Aquarian attitude of thought and life; between the laws of the kingdom of God, the fifth kingdom and those of humanity, the fourth; between the self-conscious individualistic way of life and the way of brotherhood, of love and of group consciousness.

2. To heal those divisions and bridge these cleavages through the agency of the world group, which we call the New Group of World Servers, and the men of good will. These Servers and men of good will belong to all the nations, groups, ideologies and religions on both sides of the different cleavages, and yet hold firmly to the principles of good will and understanding. They are, therefore, non-partisan and inactive in the present pro-

cess of differentiation and separative trends. They hold out the hands of love and understanding to each other across the gulf of differences. They meet in thought upon the subjective level of the true realities—which are synthetic and eternal—and ignore all outer barriers, and separative differences in mental ideas and material ways of living.

3. To approach nearer to humanity and become a known and forceful fact in the consciousness of Their disciples, of the world aspirants and the New Group of World Servers. Then these can work with greater confidence, knowing for themselves, past all controversy, that the kingdom of God is emerging upon earth, that the inner world of light, love and meaning is fusing in a realisable sense with the objective world, and that the world of spiritual realities is now recognised on such a large scale that the precipitation of that which is spiritual is discovered to be present in everything that can be known. This realisation and this *approach to life through God* is the herald of the new world religion. I have already given you much concerning it in these instructions and if you will re-read it you will be preparing yourself for right participation in the coming Wesak Festival.

4. To bring about the "Day of Crisis" to which I have referred before. Through this crisis, in which the aspiration of humanity for peace, understanding, good will and truth can be raised to its highest possible expression, there will be brought about, at a given moment of fusion, the downpouring desire of the spiritual forces of the Hierarchy, of the Christ and of all associated with Him (call Them by what name you please) and thus there will be precipitated upon earth that spiritual stim-

ulation and that healing force which will end the present period of strife and misery.

It is for this "Day of Crisis" that we are called to work. It can be brought about in 1942, if all of us put ourselves and all our resources—spiritual, mental and material—into the meeting of the present opportunity and emergency. It can be brought about if the New Group of World Servers and the massed men and women of good will in every land use intelligence, plus good business technique and methods (which are spiritual faculties, not dedicated, as yet, on a large scale to the things of the kingdom of God). Practical utilisation of every possible agency—the press, correspondence, personal contacts and above all the radio—the avoidance of all the old methods such as attack on persons, peoples, nations and ideologies of force and coercion and of separative techniques must be strenuously inculcated. The forces existent today, directed by the spiritual agencies of the incoming New Age, have made the field of service clear. It is the bridging of the separative cleavages, and the harmonising of the warring schools of thought.

The workers on the inner side and the disciples who are responsible for the working out of the Plan have made great efforts to reach and stimulate the New Group of World Servers. They have been successful. Such success is in no way dependent upon any recognition of the Hierarchy on the part of the Servers. Where that exists it is a help, but it is dependent upon receptivity to spiritual impression, which means responsiveness to the new ideas which are expressive of the spirit of fusion, of synthesis, of understanding, and of cooperative good will. Look out for such people and work with them. Do not hold the prevalent attitude that they must work with you. It is for us, who perhaps know a little bit more about the Plan than they do, to do the moving forward. It is for us to evidence intelligent understanding and to set the needed example by submerging our own ideas and personal desires in the good of the whole.

There must be on our part, if we react to all this, the re-orientation of our entire lives for the next few years, to the urgency of the things to be done. This will necessarily involve the readjustment of our lives to the new impulses; it will entail the elimination of the non-essentials so that we can find time for the task; it will mean the cultivation of that spiritual sensitivity which will render us aware of the impressions and impulses coming from the inner side of life, and will make us quick also to recognise our brothers who are pledged to the same life of good will and who are awake —as we are—to the urgency of human need, and the immediacy of the day of opportunity; it will require the development in all of the spirit of silence, for silence is the best method whereby spiritual force is both generated and stored for use, and it will bring about the training of ourselves to see clearly the issues involved in any situation (personal, national or international) and then enable us to bring to bear upon it the interpretative light of expressed good will.

For the members of the New Group of World Servers and for the men and women of good will, the Hierarchy of spiritual Leaders have laid down the following rules:

1. That they must aim at achieving peaceful relationships with, and harmonious acquiescence in, as well as cooperation with the government or state to which they owe allegiance or loyalty. This does not mean endorsing all policies and lines of activity undertaken by such governments but it does mean the refraining from all that could cause difficulty. There is always scope for much con-

structive activity within any governmental policy or regime and it is to these constructive and peaceful enterprises that the servers of the Great Ones and of humanity will direct their attention.

2. They must refrain from all interference in the affairs of any political or religious group.

3. They must endeavour to express *practical* good will in the environment where their lot may be cast.

4. They must strive after harmlessness in speech and in life in relation to their family, community, nation or group of nations. This means a consistent policy of non-attack. No leader or nation or race must be attacked or defamed.

This is a matter of practical import and is not at all an easy thing to attain. It lays the foundation for the rapid formation and definite emergences of the New Group of World Servers, and for the discovery and organising of the men of goodwill throughout the world, wherever they may be found. The spiritual Hierarchy cannot work through people whose tongues are critical, whose ideas and attitudes are separative and who are violently partisan in their beliefs and comments. This is a statement of fact. I seek to have you train yourselves in such right activity, beginning with your own lives and your personal expression in the world.

As regards the required united work, I can but indicate the following lines of activity, and it is for you to follow them, if you will, or make it possible for others to do so:

1. Discover the men and women of good will. These you will not recognise if you are full of racial, national or religious prejudice.

2. Put these people in touch with the Units of Service in the countries where they live.

3. Educate them in the following ideas:

    a. The principles of good will and the medium and methods of their true expression in the daily life.

    b. The necessity of their being active and practical and consistent workers in the spread of good will in the world.

    c. The usefulness of building up live mailing lists (I think you call it) of those who see life from the angle of the spiritual values and who seek to build for the future.

4. The authorities of any and every nation should be kept in touch with your activities, so that they are aware of all that you are seeking to do and can, therefore, realise that there is nothing subversive in the planned activities, and nothing that has in it the seeds of trouble for any ruler or national government.

5. Keep constantly in touch with the Units of Service and use care in choosing those who represent the work you have all undertaken.

6. Let the meditation groups be carefully handled and have about them nothing that could be regarded as secret or might bring them under suspicion of being secret organisations. This they are not. This non-secrecy must be emphasised in connection with all the work.

7. As far as the use of the press and the radio is concerned, go forward as actively and earnestly as possible in preparation for the work planned in 1942 and its great united effort. Upon these two lay the emphasis, for by them the majority of human beings are reached.

8. Let each Wesak Full Moon be a period of intensive effort, preceded by personal preparation and purification and lay the force of the emphasis upon:

a. The producing of sensitivity to the inner spiritual impression, emanating from the Hierarchy and the Group.

b. The achieving of an intelligent appreciation of the steps to be taken during the coming twelve months, and the laying of careful plans so that they may indeed materialise.

c. The correct distribution of your time and resources so that you do become an active worker in the cause of good will.

d. The effort to cooperate with all that is being done along these lines, which entails the discovery of all groups and persons working with similar objectives.

e. The submergence of your temporary interests in the good of the whole and through love of humanity.

I will say no more at this time. I have sought to indicate that which should be possible. If my suggestions are followed, and if the work is carried forward diligently, there is every indication that the work of the Hierarchy and of the Christ will be tremendously expedited. The need and the opportunity call for right understanding, and they demand also a joyful cooperation and the sacrifice of yourselves and of your time and money, in the attempt to make our work possible.

I make no further appeal for your help. I have been endeavoring to educate you in the new ideals and in the work of the New Group of World Servers. The responsibility for right action and for the effort to reach the public rests upon the aspirants and disciples of the world who read my words. There is nothing that I, personally, can do. It is your *time* (and all of you, without exception, can give some) for which Christ and humanity are today calling. It is your activity and skill in reaching those you can reach for which we make demand. It is your money that is needed to enable us to reach the interested public. It is your meditation and intense inner cooperation which will construct that channel through which the spirit of peace can work and the forces of Light enter. *The Hierarchy waits.* It has done all that is possible from the angle of Its opportunity. The Christ stands in patient silence, attentive to the effort that will make His work materialise on earth and enable Him to consummate the effort He made 2000 years ago in Palestine. The Buddha hovers over the planet, ready to play His part if the opportunity is offered to Him by mankind. I beg you to note what I here have said. Everything now depends upon the right action of the men of good will.

Training for new age
discipleship is provided
by the *Arcane School.*
The principles of the
Ageless Wisdom are
presented through esoteric
meditation, study and
service as a *way of life.*

*Write to the publishers
for information.*

INDEX

753

knowledge, 30
man in, full-grown, 14
participation in —
    "Day of crises", 745
    initiations, 282
    Wesak, 684, 690, 691, 699
    presentation of significance of
    love, 398
quotations, 231-232, 688
seeing in dream, 501
service, 119, 123
spiritual forces, downpouring,
    745-746
symbolic activity, 89, 306
teaching, 155, 160, 165-166
thoughtforms of, 565, 570
unfoldment, 210
work as Avatar, 378, 398, 399
work with minds, 185
Christian Science —
    beliefs, 471-472, 483
    illusion of guidance, 483-484
    metaphysical thought, 100
Christianity, emphasis upon
    at-one-ment, 100
Churches —
    misrepresentation of will of
    God, 482-483
    situation today, 738
Civilisation, new —
    preparation for, 729-730
    production, 194, 233-234, 730-731
Clairaudience —
    correspondences, 559, 560-562, 584
    evocation, 476
    exhibition in trance of medium,
    568-570
    misinterpretation, 513-514
    reaction to, 558
    unfoldment, 579
    use in telepathic recording, 566-567
Clairvoyance —
    correspondences, 559, 560-562, 584
    evocation, 476
    example, 566
    misinterpretation today, 513-514
    reaction to, 558
    unfoldment, 579
    use in telepathic recording, 566-567
Clairvoyant —
    experience, misunderstanding, 565

sight of adept, 593-594
sight of Master, 595
trance of medium, 568-570
Clearing-house —
    for divine energy, 363
    centres, 359, 540, 553
    ray, 359
Cleavages —
    between —
        man and environment, 426,
        436-437
        man and his life task, 437
        mind and astral nature, 426, 437,
        441-442, 448
        mind and lower nature, 426
        personality and soul, 427,
        437, 448
    cessation, 668
    cure, means, 423-424, 430, 436,
    744-745
    cure, results, 437-439
    effect of seventh ray, 622
    etheric, types and remedies,
    418-419
    in man, most important, 426-427
    inherent relations, 435-437
    lines, clarification by
    Hierarchy, 744
    major, bridging, 448
    problems, 404, 409, 415-437
    realised, bridging by patient
    himself, 427-428
    recognition, results, 436, 441-442
    sense of, causes, 421-423
    spirit, groups fostering, 668
    tendency offsetting, 517, 668
    unrecognised, 436
    within astral body, 437
    within man himself, 436
Coherence, principle, 234, 240
Cohesion, Law, 152
Colour —
    seen clairvoyantly, significance, 568
    yellow, therapeutic value, 590
Combat, confused, ray, 41
Commandments, five, ray and
    law, 164
Complexes due to integration, 410
Compromise, righteous, producers,
    143

of abdominal area, diseases,
cause, 551
of patient, study by healer, 479
parathyroid, centre governing, 536
parathyroid, difficulties, 553
seven major, relation to
centres, 412
treatment, 423
Glandular —
equipment, relation to centres, 336
system —
defective, 315
factors conditioning, 64, 323
nature of, 434
problem, 611
See also Endocrine system.
Goal of humanity, 34
Goat and mountain, symbolism, 174
God —
attributes. *See* Attributes.
brain reaction, 5-6
consciousness, outpost,
establishment, 217
energy, 286-287
human approach, stultifying, 404
immanence, 96
instincts, nature of, 234
isolation in, 393
kingdom. *See* Kingdom of God.
life, conscious response to, 54
love, 398
mind, 4, 5
motivating urge, 231
nature of, 158, 227, 229-231,
397-398
purpose —
and plan, cognisance, 6
and will, embodiment, 4
demonstration, 4
expression, 8
vision of, 237-238
quality, 227
seeing, attainment, 612
self-limitation, 133-134, 245
vice-regents, 689
voice, illusionary, 484-492
walking on earth, 10
will. *See* Will of God.
See also Deity.
Goitre, cause, 537
Gold, extra-planetary influences, 721

Goodwill —
expression, 663
international, cultivation, 659
men and women of —
attitude, 642, 737
information regarding, 681-682
opportunity, 113
power, 664
synthesis, 669, 689
task, 672-679, 725
training, 644-645, 674, 679-680
spread, importance, 732
spread, recommendations, 664-665,
672-673, 675-676, 689, 747-750
universal attainment, 733-743
zodiacal aid, 196
Government —
methods and techniques
undesirable, 659
spiritual emergence, 451
world. *See* World government.
Great Illusion —
emergence from, 238
freedom from, 157
subjection to, 473-474
thoughtforms, 505
Great Invocation. *See* Invocation.
Great White Lodge —
affiliates, participation in
Wesak, 683
work with humanity, 259-260, 389
Group —
activity, factors affecting, 86-87, 579
activity, project, 182
antahkarana, establishment, 190
approaches, relation, 330
awareness, 122-123
channel of service at Wesak, 685,
687-688
cohesion, importance, 182-183
conditions, diseases connected,
615-622
conditions, emotionalism evoked,
cause, 595
conduct, relation to Law of
Sacrifice, 87
consciousness —
development, 215, 409, 415, 657
differentiation from self-
conscious individualism, 744
evocation, 103
intuition, 233

centre in universe,
establishment, 217
control, law, 152
field —
  below diaphragm, 524-525
  between soul and personality, 69
  dual, of centres, 117
  unified, in head, 608, 609
impulse, law. *See* Law of
Magnetic Impulse.

Magnetism, divine, reflection, 226

Mahachohan, work, 185

Maitreya, Lord —
  participation in Wesak, 684, 685
  See also Christ.

Man —
  activation, means, 521
  activity, 330-331
  all-embracing spirit, 219
  ambition, two final stages, 330-331
  as thinker, ascent out of matter,
  331-333
  as thinker, descent into matter,
  328-331
  at-one-ment with God, 234
  career, controlling factors, 581
  cognisance of Plan of Deity, 5
  consciousness, expression, charts of
  Master, 298-299
  consciousness, unfolding, symbols,
  505-506
  duality, nature of, 405
  evolutionary stages, 304-310
  five aspects, relation to larger
  whole, 519-520
  force expression, 340
  fusion with Hierarchy, 448
  goal, 484
  group activity, factors affecting, 579
  hypothetical, ray set-up, study,
  295-298
  initiated, law governing, 151
  instinctual nature, law
  governing, 151
  integrated, two types, comparison,
  349-350
  living below diaphragm, 524-525
  nature of, 340
  objective, explanation, 9
  of God, definition and becoming,
  17-18

penetration into revelation, factors
  enabling, 246-248
perfect, production, 8-9
problem, explanation, 9
rejection by world, 332
release, failure today, causes and
  remedy, 641-642
repulse of applied energies, 54
response to applied energies, 54
soul aspect, law governing, 151
subplanes, eighteen, parallels, 153
undeveloped, progress, 156-157
unfoldment, 406
See also Humanity.

Manas, influence, means, 151

Maniac, ray, 462

Maniacs, astral, cause and care, 459

Manifestation period viewed as
  whole, 324

Manipulation, selective, ray and
  method, 81-82

Mantram inaugurating seventh
  ray, 145

Manu —
  department, group work, 190-191
  work, 185

Marriage —
  in the heavens, 48
  symbolism, 448

Mars —
  conditions, 98
  evolution, 585
  influence, cessation, 103
  influence, displacement by
  Venus, 721
  Law of Sacrifice, 102
  ray life, 99

Mask of soul, 267

Masonry —
  degrees, parallelism, 153
  dramas, efficiency, increase, 48
  symbolic work, 77
  teaching, 152-153

Mass psychology, correction, 11

Masses —
  dominance of astral body, 22
  emotional solar plexus contact, 554
  guidance, 26
  ignorant, condition today, 633-634,
  657-658
  law, effects, reaction, 198